GOVERNING AUS

Studies in Contemporary
of Governmen

Inspired by Foucault's discussion of ⌄ ...., ...
book makes a major contribution to our understanding of
government. The book is interdisciplinary in approach, and
combines theoretical discussion with empirical focus. It
includes a substantial introduction by the editors, and contains work critiquing the central notion of governmentality. A
range of topics is discussed, including regulation of the
unemployed and people with HIV/AIDS, sexual harassment
in the military, the corporatisation of education, new contractualism and governing personality. While their topics are
varied, the contributors explore a range of shared concerns,
including notions of problematisation, expert knowledge,
rationality, freedom and autonomy, giving the volume focus
and rigour. This book will be essential reading in political
science, sociology, law, philosophy, education and economics.

Mitchell Dean is Senior Lecturer in Sociology at Macquarie
University. He is the author of *The Constitution of Poverty:
Toward a Geneaology of Liberal Governance* (1991) and *Critical
and Effective Histories: Foucault's Methods and Historical Sociology*
(1994). Barry Hindess is Professor of Political Science in the
Research School of Social Sciences at the Australian National
University. His most recent book is *Discourses of Power: From
Hobbes to Foucault* (1996).

RESHAPING AUSTRALIAN INSTITUTIONS

Series editors: Geoffrey Brennan and Francis G. Castles, Australian National University.

Published in association with the Research School of Social Sciences, Australian National University.

This program of publications arises from the School's initiative in sponsoring a fundamental rethinking of Australia's key institutions before the centenary of Federation in 2001.

Published in this program will be the work of scholars from the Australian National University and elsewhere who are researching and writing on the institutions of the nation. The scope of the program includes the institutions of public governance, intergovernmental relations, Aboriginal Australia, gender, population, the environment, the economy, business, the labour market, the welfare state, the city, education, the media, criminal justice and the Constitution.

Brian Galligan   *A Federal Republic*
    0 521 37354 9 hardback   0 521 37746 3 paperback
Patrick Troy (ed.)   *Australian Cities*
    0 521 48197 X hardback   0 521 48437 5 paperback
Ian Marsh   *Beyond the Two Party System*
    0 521 46223 1 hardback   0 521 46779 9 paperback
Elim Papadakis   *Environmental Politics and Institutional Change*
    0 521 55407 1 hardback   0 521 55631 7 paperback
Chilla Bulbeck   *Living Feminism*
    0 521 46042 5 hardback   0 521 46596 6 paperback
John Uhr *Deliberative Democracy in Australia*
    0 521 62458 4 hardback   0 521 62465 7 paperback

GOVERNING AUSTRALIA

Studies in Contemporary Rationalities
of Government

EDITED BY
MITCHELL DEAN
and
BARRY HINDESS

CAMBRIDGE
UNIVERSITY PRESS

PUBLISHED BY THE PRESS SYNDICATE OF THE UNIVERSITY OF CAMBRIDGE
The Pitt Building, Trumpington Street, Cambridge CB2 1RP, United Kingdom

CAMBRIDGE UNIVERSITY PRESS
The Edinburgh Building, Cambridge CB2 2RU, UK   http://www.cup.cam.ac.uk
40 West 20th Street, New York, NY 10011–4211, USA   http://www.cup.org
10 Stamford Road, Oakleigh, Melbourne 3166, Australia

First published 1998

Printed in Australia by Brown Prior Anderson

Typeset in New Baskerville 10/12 pt

A catalogue record for this book is available from the British Library

Library of Congress Cataloguing in Publication data

Governing Australia: studies in contemporary rationalities of
government/edited by Mitchell Dean and Barry Hindess.
       p.   cm. – (Reshaping Australian institutions)
Includes bibliographical references and index.
ISBN 0-521-58357-8 (hb: alk. paper). – ISBN 0-521-58671-2 (pb:
alk. paper)
1. Australia – Politics and government. I. Dean, Mitchell, 1955– .
II. Hindess, Barry, 1939– . III. Series.
JQ4031.G66 1998
320.994–dc21   97–49566

Contents

Contributors

JOHN BALLARD, a political scientist, is currently a visiting fellow in the Graduate School of the Australian National University. He has followed the development of AIDS policy in Australia since 1985 and been a member of various AIDS advisory bodies.

DAVID BURCHELL teaches in the Faculty of Humanities and Social Sciences at the University of Western Sydney, Nepean.

GARY CAMPBELL is in the Department of Sociology, University of Lancaster, UK.

MITCHELL DEAN is senior lecturer in Sociology at Macquarie University, New South Wales.

GARY DOWSETT is deputy director of the Centre for Sexually Transmissible Diseases at La Trobe University, Victoria.

BARRY HINDESS is professor of Political Science in the Research School of Social Sciences, Australian National University, Canberra.

IAN HUNTER is Queen Elizabeth II research fellow attached to the Faculty of Humanities, Griffith University, Brisbane.

DAVID MCCALLUM teaches Sociology and Social Policy at the Victoria University of Technology.

DENISE MEREDYTH is an Australian Research Council research fellow attached to the Faculty of Humanities, Griffith University, Brisbane.

JEFFREY MINSON teaches Ethics, Legal Studies and Cultural History in the Faculty of Humanities, Griffith University, Brisbane.

ALISON SMITH has completed a PhD in Political Science at the Australian National University, Canberra.

LAURAJANE SMITH is lecturer in Aboriginal Studies and Cultural Heritage, Aboriginal Research and Resource Centre, and School of History, University of New South Wales.

ANNA YEATMAN is foundation professor of Social Policy at the University of South Australia.

CHAPTER 1

Introduction
Government, Liberalism, Society

Mitchell Dean and Barry Hindess

if you would implant public virtue in the breast of him who seems heedless of the interest of his country, it will often be to no purpose to tell him, what superior advantages the subjects of a well-governed state enjoy . . . You will be more likely to persuade if you describe the great system of public police which procures these advantages, if you explain the connexions and dependencies of its several parts, their mutual subordination to one another, and their general subserviency to the happiness of society; if you show how this system might be introduced into his own country, what it is that hinders it from taking place there, how those obstructions might be removed, and all the several wheels of the machine of government be made to move with more harmony and smoothness, without grating upon one another, or mutually retarding one another's motions. (Smith 1976a: 186)

This book is concerned with governing Australia. The sense in which we use the term 'government' can be illustrated by this passage from *The Theory of the Moral Sentiments*. There, Adam Smith outlines a view, far removed from his own, of 'a well-governed state' and of the role of police in securing 'the happiness of society'. He uses it to illustrate his discussion of another issue and so, in passing, invokes an understanding of government as a pervasive, complex and heterogeneous enterprise with which most of his contemporary readers would have been familiar.

Smith's own view of a well-governed state and of the role of the system of public police in its government is set out most clearly in *An Inquiry into the Nature and Causes of the Wealth of Nations*, which follows the positive advice set out in this passage and in some respects inverts it. *The Wealth of Nations* follows that advice in showing how the free interaction of economic agents contributes to the overall 'happiness of society', what arrangements obstruct that free interaction and how they might be removed, and so on. It inverts that advice by presenting 'the policy [that is, police] of Europe' (in Book I, chapter X) and the mercantile system

1

(in Book IV) as things to be avoided because they detract from the good
of society. What Smith suggests here is that the advantages of a well-
governed state are not to be brought about by a 'great system of public
police' but rather by what seems to be its contrary, that is, by a system of
government which is limited not only in its objectives but also in its
subordination to what has since become known as 'the rule of law'.

The arguments set out so forcefully in *The Wealth of Nations* provide an
influential expression of the broadly liberal understanding of government which, with many variations, has since come to dominate public
and academic discourse in the societies of the modern West. As a result,
alternative conceptions of the nature and role of government, such as
that set out in our opening quotation, have been very largely super-
seded. We have not introduced it here in order to resurrect an earlier
conception of the nature and role of government, and even less to
advocate a return to any 'great system of public police'. Our aim rather
is to emphasise an element of the older view, which also informs the
contributions to this volume, but which is too often neglected in contemporary discussion of government. In insisting on the pervasive,
complex and heterogeneous character of modern government our contributors can be seen as engaging with, and for the most part as contri-
buting to, an expanding research program devoted to the study of
rationalities of government in the modern West and loosely based on
some of the later work of Michel Foucault.[1] Their primary concern is to
explore how the work of government in contemporary Australia has in
fact been conceived, to identify the manner in which state and society,
the Australian population and the individuals, groups and organisations
it comprises, and various internal and external conditions have been
represented both as posing problems for government and as resources
for dealing with them. The task, in other words, is to identify the concepts, arguments and procedures which are or have been involved both
in the formulation of governmental concerns and in the consideration
of ways in which those concerns could be addressed.

Since the understanding of government advocated here may be
unfamiliar to some of our readers we can best show what is at stake by
means of a contrast with the broadly liberal view of government which
we dispute. First, to say that government is heterogeneous and pervasive
is to suggest not only that it intrudes into all aspects of life but also that
it should not be seen as emanating from a single controlling centre –
such as that of the state. In its most general sense, government is the
conduct of conduct, where the latter refers to the manner in which
individuals, groups and organisations manage their own behaviour. The
conduct to be governed may be one's own or that of others: of the
members of a household or of larger collectivities such as the population

of a local community or a state. The last of these possibilities is particularly relevant to the arguments of this book. Our title, *Governing Australia*, identifies the population of a state and it refers to the diverse attempts to regulate the conduct of that population and of the collectivities, groups and organisations which it incorporates.

The government of a state may be conducted by agencies of the state itself and, in particular, by that group of agencies known collectively as *the* government – in the case of Australia by *the* governments of the Commonwealth and of its constituent States and Territories – but it may also involve agencies of other kinds. Thus, in the passage from *The Theory of the Moral Sentiments* quoted above, the point being made is that when you show someone how the great system of public police works towards the happiness of society you are inviting that person to join in as a virtuous (that is, public-spirited) citizen, not necessarily as an official of the state. It would be a mistake to confuse the police of seventeenth- and eighteenth-century Europe with the centralising tendencies of the absolutist state – as if the desire to regulate the detailed behaviour of a population could only emanate from a single controlling centre. While such centralising tendencies can certainly be identified in much of continental Europe, the enterprise of police was also understood more generally, and it was expected to be taken up locally and by a variety of non-state agencies. 'It had no unitary origin and no clear boundary as an instrument of government, but it permeated the state and gave it form' (Tribe 1995: 21–2; cf. Knemeyer 1980, Oestreich 1982, Raeff 1983). Indeed, while G. W. F. Hegel distinguishes in *The Philosophy of Right* between the state, considered as an overarching, unifying agency, and civil society, he is careful to locate police within the latter as an important part (along with guilds and corporations) of its own system of regulation. In England, where the term 'police' was also used in this governmental sense (although less commonly than on the Continent)[2] it was widely believed that a good national police could not be achieved by state officials alone.

The focus of police is on the production of good order in a civic or territorial community. The express object of the large police ordinance of the free imperial city of Strasbourg of 1628, for example, was to provide regulations for the 'common benefit' and to establish a 'well-ordered republic' (Oestreich 1982: 156). Like other police regulations, these laws are employed in the interests of the happiness of society, not primarily in the interests of justice. It is this aspect of police that Smith has in mind when, in the final paragraph of *The Theory of the Moral Sentiments*, he laments the fact (as he sees it) that 'In none of the ancient moralists, do we find any attempt towards a particular enumeration of the rules of justice . . . Their laws are laws of police, not of justice' (Smith

1976a: 341). What Smith understands by laws of justice here are laws appropriate to the government of free persons, and he insists that such laws should respect the natural liberty with which they are endowed. Laws of police, on the other hand, while not invariably opposed to individual liberty, do not have the maintenance of liberty as their primary objective.

On the liberal view, in contrast, government is seen from the top down – that is, primarily as the work of *the* government and of agencies which it authorises. The focus here is on the limits to government, understood in terms of a complex view of the importance of individual liberty. On the one hand, liberty is seen as desirable in itself, and therefore as setting limits to the character and objectives of governmental regulation. This view is commonly regarded as a central feature of liberal political thought, and it is clearly reflected in Smith's comment, noted above, that laws of police are not laws of justice.

On the other hand, individual liberty is seen as necessary to the well-being of the state itself. Smith's account of economic activity in *The Wealth of Nations* provides a particularly influential example of this latter perspective. In effect, Smith describes the realm of economic activity as a system whose laws and internal mechanisms of regulation are constituted in large part by the free decisions of a multitude of economic agents. Since the wealth of a nation depends on the productivity of its economy, this suggests that detailed governmental regulation of economic activity in the manner of police is likely to be counterproductive. On this view, a government which respects the limits to its direction of economic activity will be more effective than one which does not: limited government is a recipe for a powerful and effective state while unlimited government is a recipe for weakness.

This focus on individual liberty both as an end in itself and as necessary for the proper functioning of economic and other social processes leads liberalism into a persistent questioning of governmental regulation. One of the most interesting and least remarked points raised in Foucault's lectures on government is that liberalism can be approached as a *critique* of government which is animated by the suspicion that one is governing 'too much' (Foucault 1989b: 111). In this sense the early liberal preference for limited government can be understood as a counterpoint to its critique of a police style of government. The effect of this critique has been to displace a more general and, in our view, more useful understanding of the nature and role of government in modern states. It also has the perverse result of exaggerating the governmental capacities of the state itself. In arguing for a conception of limited government, the liberal critique identifies government itself with the work of a centralised, uniform body of formal political authority – that is, of *the* government.

This is not to say that the earlier governmental concern for 'the happiness of society' has been discounted in the liberal focus on limited government, but it has certainly been displaced. In Humboldt's *The Limits of State Action* (1969: 137–8), for example, the pervasive regulation and supervision of conduct is still regarded as an important part of social life, but it is now seen as the province of the national community or society itself rather than of *the* government or the state. The focus on liberty and the view that conduct is best regulated *in* society (rather than *by* government) are connected by a view of economic activity (and many other aspects of social life) as 'natural' processes of social interaction in which the freedom of participants (understood primarily as the absence of interference by agencies of the state) is seen as essential to their proper functioning.

The term 'natural', however, can be somewhat misleading in this context. Many contemporary liberals are careful to distinguish their view of social processes, such as markets, from the views of earlier liberals by arguing that these processes are neither natural in the sense of being biologically determined nor artificial in the sense of being an intended product of government and rational planning. For example, what Hayek calls 'spontaneous social orders' and the liberty they embody are unintended outcomes of the development of civilisation: 'Freedom was made possible by the gradual evolution of *the discipline of civilization which is at the same the discipline of freedom*' (Hayek 1978: 163, original emphasis).

A persistent feature of liberalism has been its not always successful struggle to elaborate a conception of society that avoids the twin dangers of a rationalism that reduces society to government and a naturalism that reduces society to biology. Indeed, it is tempting to suggest that the modern idea of 'society', as a reality independent of government, is itself a product of the liberal critique of police. For the German science of police, for example, society is co-extensive with the population and territory penetrated by the regulations of police. In part, this perception reflects a continuation of a view, inherited from the classics via medieval scholasticism, that there can be no proper society without government (Black 1992: 23–4). 'Police' was not simply a form of the 'regulation mania' of police, as Gerhard Oestreich puts it (1982: 157). Rather, 'police' 'was identical both with the government and with the object and nature of the community as a whole' (Oestreich 1982: 156). 'Police' thus refers both to the means of regulation and the condition to be achieved in a community governed by such means.

A liberal view of government, by contrast, entails not only the idea of limited government but the separation of the government from society, a separation instanced in such now familiar pairs as state and civil society or public and private. If government by state agencies is to be seen as limited, then something beyond the sphere of government regulation must be thought to exist within the governed population. There are several examples from which to choose in the late eighteenth century. In *The Wealth of Nations* it is the sphere of market exchanges. For Thomas Malthus, in his *Essay on the Principle of Population*, it takes the form of the relations between population and its resources. For Adam Ferguson, it is the sphere of customs and ranks found in civil society. What is emerging here in Anglo-Scottish thought is the idea of a self-regulating domain subject to its own laws, forces and tendencies which depend for their operation on the activities of free, rational and prudent persons. Where society once appeared as an artefact of the government of a state it now appears as a larger unity, encompassing government and the state on the one hand and various self-regulating spheres on the other.

> The family, the farm, the plant, the firm, the corporation and the various associations, and all the public institutions including government, are organizations which in turn are integrated into a more comprehensive spontaneous order. It is advisable to reserve the term 'society' for this spontaneous overall order so that we may distinguish it from all the organized smaller groups which will exist within it . . . (Hayek 1973: 46–7)

This liberal approach to government does more however than simply propose the existence of society in the sense of a reality independent of government. It makes the proper and efficient working of the processes of society, and the liberties they presuppose, necessary to security which, for Jeremy Bentham in *The Theory of Legislation*, remained the highest end of government. Thus, a liberal approach to government requires an abstract and theoretical knowledge of social processes that is not to be found, for example, in the comprehensive police manuals produced in the German states, which detailed the multiple and heterogeneous objects of rule. Instead we find the appearance of forms of political expertise which make use of the knowledge of social life provided by the social, behavioural, and human sciences. The notion of society as an artefact of the intricate labours of multiple agencies of rule is displaced by that of society as a network of spontaneous orders, as something to be known by specialised forms of theoretical knowledge.

Thus, the victory of liberalism over the earlier view of government involves a shift in the meaning of 'government' from a pervasive activity of regulation rooted in a multiplicity of agencies across the social body to a more focused, top-down activity of *the* government and its agents acting on and through relatively autonomous domains of social interaction. The earlier concern with 'the happiness of society' has not been abandoned here, but on both normative and prudential grounds it is no longer seen as best served by the activities of government (which is now identified with the work of *the* government). From our perspective, in terms of the broader view of government outlined above, liberalism should be seen as an influential rationality of government. It is a way of thinking about government (in the broader sense) which focuses especially on the place of the state in the overall government of society, and on the relation of law and more general forms of state regulation to other means of governing the conduct of the population.

So far we have contrasted a distinctively modern conception of government to an earlier and broader conception which it has displaced. We have suggested that this modern conception emerges from the critique initiated by what might broadly be thought of as a liberal rationality of government. This is not to say that the history of government in liberal-democratic polities can be identified with the history of liberal political philosophy. What is distinctive about the studies presented here, like much of the work influenced by Foucault's lectures on government, is that government is regarded as a complex activity that cannot be viewed as the expression or realisation of political or economic theories. These theories are only a small part of the history of government and there is no general or necessary form of the relation between political or economic theories on the one hand and the practices and rationalities associated with the exercise of various kinds of authority on the other. We should ask how, if at all, a particular philosophy or theory was taken up in the practices of government, what parts of it were selected, under what authority, how was it turned or incorporated into a definite program of reform, how was it connected to particular administrative techniques and rationalities and forms of calculation, and how, in such a process, this theory and its programmatic objectives were transformed.

The present volume provides two analyses of the limitations of attempts to derive governmental practices from philosophical or theoretic principles. In chapter 2 Denise Meredyth shows how educational policies, such as the Australian Labor Government's attempt in the early 1990s to establish a co-ordinated national education and training system bound by a common credential policy, cannot be reduced to a set of doctrinal and theoretical principles. In proposing to analyse governmental programs in such terms, she suggests, both conservative and progressive critics foreclose an understanding of liberal tactics of government and the instruments of educational policy. In a similar vein, David Burchell (chapter 11) notes that debates on economic rationalism in Australia have tended to regard economic policy and governance as an unproblematic application of marginalist economic theory. Such an approach, he argues, tends to regard the 'economic sphere' itself as a given empirical domain. It is more appropriate to treat it as the result of techniques of economic governance, procedures of public administration and modes of calculation.

For our purposes, government is approached neither as a definite and uniform group of institutions nor as the realisation of a certain set of political or constitutional principles. It is approached, rather, as an inventive, strategic, technical and artful set of 'assemblages' fashioned from diverse elements, put together in novel and specific ways, and rationalised in relation to specific governmental objectives and goals. These assemblages comprise a whole host of mundane and humble practices, techniques, and forms of practical knowledge which are often overlooked in analyses that concentrate on either political institutions or political thought. These might include: forms of practical know-how, from managerial doctrines of 'total quality management' to recipe books for 'entrepreneurial government'; intellectual tools, such as the flowchart, the map, and the architectural or engineering plan; calculative technologies, from the budget and the statistical table to sophisticated forms of the audit and cost accounting; modes of evaluating human, natural and financial resources, in terms of such entities as risk, profit, probability and danger; ways of knowing, training and regulating various agents, from those in positions of authority, such as politicians and bureaucrats, to those whose own self-government is thought to pose problems for the exercise of authority, such as the gay community, Aboriginal populations or even the long-term unemployed.

The study of these governmental assemblages can be loosely divided into several independent but inter-related domains. One is the study of problematisations. Rather than deriving its view of government from the normative principles of political thought, such a study would start from particular occasions on which authorities (both within and without the shifting boundaries of the national state) call into question the activity of governing and the attributes of those who govern and are governed. Problematisations in this sense concern both the conduct of government and the government of conduct. A national treasurer dealing with a large budget deficit or foreign debt might use this as an occasion for calling the conduct of national government into question. A schoolteacher faced with 'unruly' pupils might raise questions about her own and the pupils' conduct in and outside the classroom. Events such as the 1996 shootings at Port Arthur, Tasmania, can raise multiple problematisations. As David McCallum notes at the beginning of his chapter (chapter 6), such events led to a questioning of the conduct of governments (for example, in regard to gun ownership laws) and the government of conduct (raising, for example, the question of the personality or mental state of a mass killer).

Problematisations appear in definite social, institutional or professional locales and can be assigned a time and place. They reflect the

difficulties facing an authority given a set of tasks rather than the
application of a set of general principles. Nevertheless, it is possible to
identify distinctive styles of problematisation, of rendering diverse
situations problematic. Instead of regarding liberalism, welfarism or neo-
liberalism as principled theoretical endeavours, they might also be
approached as styles of problematisation. The term 'neo-liberalism', for
example, could be used to identify a characteristic set of formulas (the
introduction of contrived or quasi markets, the increase of competition,
the rendering of agents self-responsible) to problematise forms of conduct undertaken in diverse arenas (cf. Rose 1996). So too the postwar
Welfare State might be approached less as a coherent set of principles or
uniform set of institutions and more as a manner of reviewing governmental practices in terms of a distinctive conception of the welfare of
national populations.

As is evident from each of the above examples, problems do not exist
in themselves. They become known through grids of evaluation and
judgment about objects that are far from self-evident. The study of
government thus entails the study of modes of reasoning. This is to
emphasise the 'rational' dimension of government in which various
forms of knowledge are made to function in a multiplicity of ways. Thus,
certain knowledgeable discourses (from psychiatry to social policy,
economics to public health) represent and, in that sense, constitute
objects of knowledge (AIDS, unemployment, youth, the national economy), confer particular identities and agencies on political and social
actors (the dangerous individual, the delinquent, the active jobseeker,
the community), and make identifiable problems to be solved (youth
unemployment, the spread of disease, the prevention of crime, low
national efficiency or international competitiveness). We have already
noted that the forms of knowledge involved in governing are themselves
heterogeneous. For this reason, the study of government involves the
examination not only of normative principles derived from political
philosophy but also of the expertise and know-how of policymakers and
specialists of various sorts, including academics, economists, account-
ants, psychologists, bureaucrats, social workers, law enforcement officers
and so on. The study of government is never reducible to a kind of
sociology-of-rule content with a merely descriptive approach to how rule
operates. Government exists in the medium of thought, of mentalities
or rationalities of government. It is shot through with the multiple and
heterogeneous ways of making the world thinkable and calculable. It is
perhaps this feature of government Foucault had in mind when he
coined the neologism 'governmentality'.

In the present volume there are a number of examples of work
concerned to examine certain mentalities of government or the forms
of reasoning related to the exercise of authority. Thus, Laurajane Smith

and Gary Campbell (chapter 10) examine the way archaeology as an expert practice is involved in the management of conflicts involving Aboriginal populations. David McCallum (chapter 6) moves from the problematisations of various forms of conduct of 'dangerous individuals' to an examination of the conditions of possibility for the development of a knowledge of personality. Barry Hindess (chapter 12) traces the transformations of a notion of the national economy and its implications for forms of national government. However, none of these mentalities are purely theoretical. Hindess notes, for example, that Keynesian economic management was made possible by the superimposition of an abstract theory of the national economy as a functional system upon a technology of national economic accounting. The study of government, especially of its modern forms, must also encompass its technical aspects, the means by which objectives are to be realised, programs are to be implemented, and the interventions and withdrawals of a multiplicity of agencies are to be made.

Today we might note several broad types of technologies concerned in the first instance with deploying the agency and capacities of individuals and populations. As charted by Anna Yeatman in chapter 13, the extra-juridical and quasi-juridical use of 'contract' can be regarded as a pervasive technology of government employed today in the 'contracting out' of formerly public services to private and community agencies, the agreements made by the unemployed, the 'learning contracts' of the schoolroom, enterprise agreements and so forth. We might also consider in this context the use of what Barbara Cruikshank (1994, 1996) has called 'technologies of citizenship'. These are the multiple techniques of self-esteem, empowerment, consultation and negotiation used in community action and development programs, social and environmental impact studies, health promotion, community policing and the combating of various kinds of dependency. The technique of the contract and the technologies of citizenship are concerned to foster the agency of individuals and groups. They are complemented, however, by other technologies concerned to monitor, compare and evaluate the performance of those whose agency is thereby activated. Thus, we could talk about 'technologies of performance', such as the setting of performance indicators, the establishment of benchmarks, the devolution of financial responsibility to 'budget units' or 'cost centres', the operation of 'quality audits', and other indirect means for linking the moral and political requirements of the shaping of conduct into the optimisation of performance (Miller 1992; Power 1994).

Another component of the art of government in modern societies concerns the formation and shaping of the identities, capacities, and statuses of members of populations. As we have already suggested,

Foucault's injunction to study government as the 'conduct of conduct' entails a concern for the government of conduct as much as the conduct of government. To be concerned with the former is to be concerned with the ways in which authorities and agencies attempt to shape, mould and direct the conduct of individuals and groups. This applies as much to the government of those in positions of formal authority as to those without such position. To draw upon examples from the present volume, bureaucrats (Jeffrey Minson in chapter 3) and military officers (Alison Smith in chapter 4) as much as the unemployed (Mitchell Dean in chapter 5) are subject to practices concerned to shape their desires and aspirations and to attribute to them capacities, statuses, rights and obligations. Indeed, as Pat O'Malley insists in chapter 9, there can be a complex intermingling of formal government with indigenous self-government. In contemporary forms of rule, the division between governors and governed is rarely clear-cut. Even the self-government of the 'unemployed', as Dean observes, has become a component in labour-market programs.

Furthermore, rule in advanced liberal societies often entails the shaping or reshaping of the identities of those whose conduct is to be governed. There are striking differences between the arguments of John Ballard (chapter 7) and Gary Dowsett (chapter 8) but one point on which they agree is that the contemporary identity of the gay community should be regarded as an outcome not only of the struggles against oppressive police power and criminalising legislation but also of the public health mobilisation against HIV-AIDS. Practices of government, as much as practices of self-government, or modes of resistance, attempt to specify and fix our identities in definite ways in the service of particular ends. The 'dangerous individual' or the 'long-term unemployed' as much as 'active citizen' or the 'enterprising person' are personal and collective identities 'made-up', to use Ian Hacking's expression (1986), through particular forms of reasoning and technologies so that they might be worked with and upon to different ends.

Finally, one might want to consider the ethos of governmental practices. We have suggested that particular problematisations might be linked to different styles of thinking about government and its ends. 'Welfarism' and 'neo-liberalism', for example, might be considered in relation to the divergent ethical ideals with which they seek to invest the task of government, particularly that of national government. Again, there may be competing ethical investments in more limited domains of government. Both Jeffrey Minson and Alison Smith examine, in chapters 3 and 4, conflicts between different ethical regimes in the spheres of the bureaucracy and the military. Thus, Minson shows how a more conventional bureaucratic 'ethos of office' is under threat from the entrepreneurial ethos of the new managerialism. Through an examination of issues of sexual harassment in the Australian military, Alison Smith explores the manner in which therapeutic expertise has come to displace the conventional ethos of the military in official discourse and inquiry. In chapter 5, Mitchell Dean shows how advanced liberal practices concerning the unemployed can be subject to quite different ethical investments. These examples show how the components of contemporary rule can be invested and operationalised according to rationales derived from quite different ethical regimes.

Government can thus be studied as a pervasive and heterogeneous activity undertaken at a multiplicity of sites within liberal-democratic societies. Practices of government can be regarded as complex assemblages of forms of problematisations, modes of reasoning, techniques and technologies, the formation of identities and agencies and the investment of such practices with different kinds of ethos that gives them definite orientation. Such an approach differs from the more conventional study of political and social institutions. First it regards institutions and the powers they 'possess' as the temporary and changing outcome of these assemblages of governmental practices rather than as their condition or cause. Secondly, it regards these institutions as the locus of multiple kinds of political thought – not only the endeavours of political philosophers or economic theorists but also the multifarious, practical and pragmatic forms of programmatic thought and know-how produced by professionals, experts and specialists.

We noted earlier that our title, *Governing Australia*, refers to diverse attempts to regulate the conduct of the Australian population and of the collectivities, groups and organisations which it incorporates. However, while the governing of Australia is the principal empirical focus of this book our contributors are also concerned to engage with, and in most cases to develop, a distinctive theoretical approach to the analysis of modern government, elements of which have been sketched in the preceding pages. In several chapters this engagement leads them to take issue with important elements of Foucault's governmentality framework.

The most sustained criticisms of this kind are those by Gary Dowsett in chapter 8 (to which we return below) and Ian Hunter in chapter 14. Hunter disputes the account of the emergence and development of modern forms of government set out in Foucault's lecture 'Governmentality'. Hunter's work reminds us that we cannot be content merely to 'apply' Foucauldian schema on government to a national territory such as Australia. It is necessary to do basic historical and theoretical work that reconsiders the historical-philosophical schema of the emergence of modern forms of government that forms part of Foucault's legacy. Hunter thus criticises Foucault's account on empirical historical grounds using early modern German material and as a philosophical schema. In regard to the former, he emphasises the importance of what German historians now view as the 'confessionalisation of politics' in the sixteenth century, that is, the process by which a 'governmental state' could link a theological politics to administrative concerns. He then follows the process of the separation of governmental from religious doctrines and institutional power in the context of religious civil war. Finally, he notes the emergence out of this process of forms of reasoning that sought to transform religion into a private, non-political matter of conscience while making the maintenance of political order the ultimate end of legal regulation. Hunter's discussion here places the problem of religious toleration and the question of sovereignty at the heart of any account of the emergence of liberal government and a detheologized politics.

Foucault's own discussion of this period suggests that the sixteenth and seventeenth century's focus on issues of sovereignty was an obstacle to the development of the art of government. In this respect, Hunter's examination of the German material provides a useful corrective to Foucault's account of the historical record. Perhaps more fundamentally, Hunter also challenges what he sees as Foucault's philosophical schema. He suggests that, for Foucault, modern forms of government emerge as the mediation and dialectical interplay of two opposed forces: a police project which seeks to render the social body transparent to sovereign power, and a liberal project which aims to defend the freedom of the autonomous spheres of society. On this reading of Foucault's analysis the emergence of government, conceived of as a system of economic and societal management, is linked to the emergence of 'population' as both an object of government and a subject of interests and needs. The notion of population in this sense, for Hunter, is an objectification of the dialectical relation between the will to govern and the assertion of limits to government that will constitute liberalism.

As a result, Hunter suggests, Foucault's account downplays the problem of sovereignty as the state's self-preservation in favour of the liberal problematic of security concerned with the proper functioning of the autonomous spheres. This account of Foucault's dense and sometimes obscure 'Governmentality' lecture may be open to question,[3] but there can be no doubt that the problem of sovereignty has been relatively neglected by Foucauldian studies of government. A key virtue of Hunter's critique is that he reopens the problem of sovereignty as a local and particular end of government. In this way, the tendency to oppose government as a multiple, pervasive and heterogeneous activity to sovereignty as a unitary, uniform and centralised apparatus of ultimate power, is misleading. The objective of the maintenance of political order, as Hunter reminds us, can become a problem for particular rationalities of government.

Reference to the period of confessional states and religious wars in Germany allows us to raise an aspect of the problem of sovereignty which is not directly addressed in Hunter's discussion. This is that the maintenance of order within the territory of a state requires that there be no significant interference by powerful outside agencies. Thus, one of the conditions required for the development of effective sovereign states in Germany was only finally secured by the agreements which brought the Thirty Years War to an end in 1648. These agreements restricted the rights of participating states to intervene in each other's affairs in matters of religion, thereby assigning to each state the government of the population within its own territory – a condition which even today can hardly be taken for granted in much of the world. What this example shows is that prospects for the maintenance of order and thus for the development of the modern art of government depend in part on political conditions which operate above the level of the territorial state in question. More seriously, it poses problems for the focus on *society* which plays such an important part in the broadly Foucauldian account of liberalism that we have presented here. On this account the liberal rationality of government is predicated on the view that the life of the population is constituted in large part by a variety of self-regulating domains of social interaction. We have also suggested, if only by implication, that the most important of these domains from the point of view of government can be seen as coming together in the broader unity of a *society*. It is in these terms that Foucault describes the idea of society as 'one of the great discoveries of political thought at the end of the eighteenth century. That is to say, that government . . . has to deal with a complex and independent reality that has its own laws and mechanisms of disturbance' (Foucault 1989a: 261).

It is worth pausing here to ask how far such a view of society is necessary to the liberal rationality of government. The dependence of government within the state on political conditions without suggests one respect in which this societal focus may be misleading. Another is suggested by Barry Hindess' argument that governmental concerns for economic security will differ radically according to whether the national economy is seen as a relatively self-contained system or simply as part of a larger, supra-national unity. Hindess goes on to claim that much of the contemporary neo-liberal agenda can be understood as a liberal response to the difficulty of viewing economic interaction as constituting a self-regulating system at the level of the national society. Nikolas Rose has made a related point in his account of 'advanced' liberal strategies of rule as aiming to govern 'without governing *society*, that is to say, to govern through the regulated and accountable choices of autonomous agents . . . and to govern through intensifying and acting upon their allegiances to particular "communities"' (1996: 61). These examples suggest that the liberal project of governing populations through the workings of various self-regulating domains need not require that society itself be seen as an overarching domain of that kind.

A general concern with the concept of freedom, and related notions of autonomy and resistance, are raised in other chapters, but in quite different terms from those of Hunter's critique. Anna Yeatman (chapter 13) argues, for example, that Foucauldian work on government is unable to deal adequately with the 'new contractualism' because of its commitment to the notion that the capacity for autonomy is socially determined. Most of our contributors would place the emphasis rather differently, suggesting that investigation of the governmental contrivance of freedom and the capacity for autonomous action is at the heart of the Foucauldian account of liberal rationalities and practices of government. This account does not assume a general notion of the subject and its capacities, either as a being replete with essential attributes or as the terminal or end-point of practices exerting a social determination. Rather, studies of government analyse how specific kinds of agency are represented in particular rationalities of government as instruments for the achievement of governmental objectives. Liberal rationalities are interesting in this regard, not because they mask the social determination of individual agency but because they attempt to instrumentalise certain versions of autonomy in the service of governmental objectives.

Pat O'Malley (chapter 9) raises a similar point in regard to what he views as the failure of the Foucauldian literature on government to address the question of resistance – a failure that seems particularly ironic given the emphasis on resistance in some of Foucault's own discussions of power. O'Malley argues that resistance is actively thematised in liberal programs of government and that such resistance has the potential for destabilising those programs and reshaping their final arrangement. What is interesting here is that O'Malley construes as resistance 'indigenous governance' itself, that is, the forms of self-government practised by those who are subject to the governmental programs of external authorities. Rather than marking a break with recent studies of government, we would suggest that O'Malley's argument serves to clarify two fundamental points. The first is that liberal governmental rationalities depend on forms of agency and autonomy that are represented in, and in this sense 'constituted' by, specific forms of knowledge of the governed and mobilised through particular techniques and technologies of rule. It follows that such agency is in no way reducible to any of its particular governmental representations. The second point is that this reliance on the agency of the governed, and a knowledge of the self-government of those to be governed, is an uncertain and complex task that is open to transformation as a result of the way that agency is deployed. This, as O'Malley suggests, has consequences for the shape of liberal regimes of government themselves.

Finally, while several of our contributors are critical of elements of the governmentality approach, Gary Dowsett (chapter 8) remains sceptical of its utility. Dowsett maintains that sexuality is central to all social relations, not only to those involving acts of sex, and further, that gay sex can be seen as radically subversive of a fundamentally repressive social order. For this reason, he insists, the governmental regulation of homosexual men and women provides 'the best example of the deployment of modern forms of governance'. Since his chapter deals at length with the politics of HIV-AIDS the contrast with John Ballard's (chapter 7) is striking, and particularly revealing of what is at stake in Dowsett's critique. Ballard presents the governmentality framework as being especially useful in the analysis of governmental responses to HIV-AIDS. For Dowsett, in contrast, this framework is yet another example of the posthumous 'straightening of Foucault', a move which renders his work acceptable only by refusing his most fundamental insights.

A number of chapters have thus highlighted the importance of questions of freedom and autonomy in relation to the Foucauldian account of the emergence of a liberal rationality of government. These questions can be clarified if we take up Foucault's suggestion, noted earlier, that liberalism can be understood as a critique of government which is particularly concerned with the limits to our knowledge of the reality to be governed and their consequences for our capacity to act. This suggests a view of society, not as an extension and artefact of the multiple and pervasive forms of government located across a definite territory, but rather as a quasi-natural domain or set of domains of which the institutions of government are simply a part.

This conception of society entails two different but interconnected understandings of autonomy. One concerns the autonomy of society itself and its constituent spheres: 'civil society', 'the economy', 'the population', 'the community' and even 'culture'. These spheres are construed as being outside the domain of formal political authority and structured by forces and relations which must be respected in the exercise of that authority. Government thus becomes a question of making adjustments between the regulatory activity of political authorities and the self-regulatory processes of the different spheres of society. What is at issue in *laissez-faire*, Foucault suggests, is not the rejection of regulation but the making of 'regulations that ensure the play of necessary and natural modes of regulation' (Gordon 1991: 17). A liberal rationality of government that seeks to utilise a knowledge of forms of indigenous government of, say, Aboriginal kinship networks or the gay community would appear to work in a similar way. Here knowledge of a community or a culture is used to arrive at modes of regulation that work through, and are themselves adjusted to, the internal modes of regulation of that community or cultural group.

The second understanding of autonomy concerns the attributes of members of the governed populations. Liberalism requires a conception of political subjects, not so much as fully self-determining individuals but rather as having capacities for action that are not determined by the governmental programs in which they are implicated. Within particular governmental programs, then, certain agents will be regarded as legal subjects with rights and duties, economic subjects with interests and capacities for choice, social subjects with needs and aspirations, or prudential subjects with desires and capacities for the responsible management of them. Liberal conceptions of individual autonomy are not necessarily based on a normative commitment to the idea of a self-determining subject. Our point, rather, is that liberal rationalities and practices of government must treat definite attributes and capacities on the part of particular agents as necessary to the operation of the self-regulatory processes on which effective government depends. Considered as a political philosophy, liberalism is usually held to favour limited government because of its prior commitment to individual liberty; considered as a rationality of government, it views the operation of individual liberty as necessary to the practical ends of government. To make this point, to say that the liberal rationality of government must aim to work with and work through the autonomous conduct of individuals, is to say that it cannot be concerned only with what *the* government does. It must also seek to advance a more general understanding of comprehensive societal management in which the governmental role of the state is to be located.

Notes

1 See, especially, Foucault (1981, 1989b, 1991) and the contributions to Barry et al. (1996) and Burchell et al. (1991).

2 Blackstone's *Commentaries on the Laws of England* defines 'public police and oeconomy' as 'the due regulation and domestic order of the kingdom: whereby the individuals of the state, like members of a well-governed family, are bound to conform their general behaviour to the rules of propriety, good neighbourhood, and good manners; and to be decent, industrious, and inoffensive in their respective stations' (1978 [1783]: 162). For the history of the English use of the term see Radzinowicz (1956).

3 See the very different account and criticisms of the role of 'population' in Foucault's argument in Dean (1991).

References

Barry, Andrew, Osborne, Thomas and Rose, Nikolas, (eds), 1996. *Foucault and Political Reason: Liberalism, Neo-liberalism and Rationalities of Government*, London: University College London Press.

Bentham, Jeremy, 1871. *The Theory of Legislation*, London: Treubner.

Black, Anthony, 1992. *Political Thought in Europe, 1250–1450*, Cambridge: Cambridge University Press.

Blackstone, Sir William, 1978 [1783]. *Commentaries on the Laws of England*, New York and London: Garland Publishing.

Burchell, Graham, Gordon, Colin and Miller, Peter, (eds), 1991. *The Foucault Effect: Studies in Governmentality*, London: Harvester/Wheatsheaf.

Cruikshank, Barbara, 1994. 'The will to empower: technologies of citizenship and the war on poverty', *Socialist Review* 23, 4: 29–55.

Cruikshank, Barbara, 1996. 'Revolutions within: self-government and self-esteem' in Barry, Osborne and Rose (1996), pp. 231–51.

Dean, Mitchell, 1991. *The Constitution of Poverty. Toward a Genealogy of Liberal Governance*, London: Routledge.

Foucault, Michel, 1981. 'Omnes et singulatim: towards a criticism of "political reason"', in S. McMurrin (ed.), *The Tanner Lectures on Human Values, II*, Salt Lake City: University of Utah Press, pp. 223–54.

Foucault, Michel, 1989a. *Foucault Live*, ed. S. Lotringer, New York: Semiotext(e).

Foucault, Michel, 1989b. *Résumé des cours 1970–1982*, Paris: Juilliard.

Foucault, Michel, 1991. 'Governmentality' in Burchell, Gordon and Miller (eds), pp. 87–104.

Gordon, Colin, 1991. 'Introduction' to Burchell, Gordon and Miller (eds), pp. 1–51.

Hacking, Ian, 1986. 'Making up people' in T. C. Heller et al. (eds), *Reconstructing Individualism*, Stanford: Stanford University Press, pp. 222–36.

Hayek, Friedrich A., 1973. *Law, Legislation and Liberty, vol. 1: Rules and Order*, London: Routledge & Kegan Paul.

Hayek, Friedrich A., 1978. *Law, Legislation and Liberty, vol. 3: The Political Order of a Free People*, London: Routledge & Kegan Paul.

Hegel, G. W. F., 1952. *The Philosophy of Right*, ed. T. M. Knox, Oxford: Clarendon Press.

Humbolt, Wilhelm von, 1969. *The Limits of State Action*, Cambridge: Cambridge University Press.

Knemeyer, F.-L., 1980. 'Polizei', *Economy and Society* 9, 2: 172–96.

Malthus, T. R., 1970. *An Essay on the Principle of Population*, ed. A. Flew, Harmondsworth: Penguin.

Miller, Peter, 1992. 'Accounting and objectivity: the invention of calculating selves and calculable spaces', *Annals of Scholarship* 9, 1/2: 61–86.

Oestreich, Gerhard, 1982. *Neostoicism and the Early Modern State*, Cambridge: Cambridge University Press.

Power, Michael, 1994. 'The audit society' in A. Hopwood and P. Miller (eds), *Accounting as Social and Institutional Practice*, Cambridge: Cambridge University Press, pp. 299–316.

Radzinowicz, Sir Leon, 1956. *A History of English Criminal Law, vol. 3: Cross-Currents in the Movement for Reform of the Police*, London: Stevens & Sons.

Raeff, Mark, 1983. *The Well-Ordered Police State. Social and Institutional Change through Law in the Germanies and Russia, 1699–1800*, New Haven and London: Yale University Press.

Rose, Nikolas, 1996. 'Governing "advanced" liberal democracies' in Barry, Osborne and Rose, pp. 37–64.

Smith, Adam, 1976a. *The Theory of the Moral Sentiments*, ed. D. D. Raphael and A. L. Macfie, Oxford: Clarendon Press.

Smith, Adam, 1976b. *An Inquiry into the Nature and Causes of the Wealth of Nations*, ed. R. H. Campbell and A. S. Skinner, Oxford: Clarendon Press.

Tribe, Keith, 1995. *Strategies of Economic Order: German Economic Discourse 1750–1950*, Cambridge: Cambridge University Press.

CHAPTER 2

Corporatising Education

Denise Meredyth

Revising Critical Verdicts

Australian education is undergoing significant change. Over the period 1983–96, Labor governments built a national training system, geared to labour market reform and the government-organised promotion of national industrial competitiveness. Following extensive reforms of higher education in the late 1980s and early 1990s, the Commonwealth turned its attention to post-compulsory education, training and technical education. Australian economic competitiveness, policy emphasised, depended on the formation of a more flexible multi-skilled work-force, and this called for national planning, coordinating connections between schools, workplaces, training providers and higher education within a national training system.

These programs combined the 'advanced liberal' (Rose 1996) tactics of deregulation and deferred authority with a strong statist program of nation-building and institutional reform. Deploying expert advice, institutional liaison and consultation, the Commonwealth devolved the operational elements of an ambitious bureaucratic reform scheme to a constellation of institutions, stakeholders and agencies. Programmatic policy statements made persuasive appeals to individual choice, flexibility, enterprise and autonomy as answers to structural stalemates in the institutional relations between school, work, training and social welfare. However, they also emphasised the need for centralist national planning and resourcing, so as to maintain accountability and procedural consistency. In effect, these programs combined deregulation with re-regulation, creating government-organised institutional hybrids oriented both to immediate economic and industrial objectives and to longer-term governmental concerns with educational access, equity, commonality and accountability.

By contrast, the Liberal–National Party Coalition government in Australia which came to power in 1996 committed itself to providing a 'business-led' system of vocational education and training. Labor's national training programs were characterised as ineffective, 'government-dominated' and expensive. In their place, the Coalition promised 'non-bureaucratic, accessible and relevant' training that 'leads to real jobs'. The intrusiveness of big government would be replaced by informed rational choice, personal interest and responsiveness to the needs of the employment and training marketplace (Kemp 1996). This emphasis was borne out in Federal budget measures: public funding for social security and job search services was reduced; the role of private job search agencies was expanded; and training schemes were reorganised into 'user choice' arrangements based on individualised agreements between trainees and individual employers (Budget statement 1996).[1]

To some extent, these programs continued the initiatives under Labor. The previous government's Working Nation program of labour market reform (Keating 1994) set the pattern of privatisation and contractualisation, in which jobseekers and trainees were positioned as clients in a vocational marketplace ordered by the needs of industry. Like Labor, the Coalition emphasised the need to maintain a 'national skill pool' which would sustain 'Australia's industrial future in a global economy of increasing technical sophistication' (Kemp 1996). The difference lay, however, in the level of public funding dedicated to training programs and in the extent to which government was understood as responsible for maintaining the national resourcing and coordination of vocational education and training.

The shift of gear between the political directions of the two parties has presented a challenge to educational commentators. The temptation has been to treat the Coalition's electoral victory as evidence of the spread of economic rationalist principles within Australian political life, and as confirmation of the marginalisation of social democratic principles (see Pusey 1991). Such a response would be consistent with the terms in which the last decade of reform has been understood. Educationists were not slow to see that Labor's post-compulsory education reforms eroded the autonomy of State education systems and threatened the professional independence built into State and school-based curriculum design. The prospect that upper secondary education should have to orient itself to national industrial goals, to skills standards and to workplace training met with sustained criticism. The reforms were variously seen as an instance of the 'marketisation' of education (Marginson 1993), of 'corporate managerialism' (Lingard et al. 1993) and of the ascendancy of the class interests of industry (Sachs 1991).

This commentary displayed a characteristic ambivalence about the role of bureaucratic action – an ambivalence usually expressed in terms of abstract tensions between state, market and society. On the one hand, the reform programs were characterised as oppressively statist – as 'top-down' rather than 'bottom-up'. On the other, they were seen as market-driven and therefore as the product of a weak state, unable to intercede between the market and the community. In either case, they could be characterised as 'undemocratic', since both state interference and market expansion threatened the organic coherence of a potentially self-realising democratic community. It was in these terms – counterposing democratic will to bureaucratic instrumentalism and market calculation – that educationists defended Australian education from bureaucratic reform.

There are good reasons to revise these judgments. Not the least of them is their lack of purchase on current policy developments. With the change of government in Australia a sharp contrast has emerged between Labor's 'big government' tactics and the anti-bureaucratic emphasis of the conservative parties. The question is how much of the enthusiasm for radical reduction of bureaucratic activity will translate into workable programs, given that these goals will have to be translated into bureaucratically organised programs of devolution and deregulation. Understanding these issues may depend on drawing sharper distinctions between the doctrinal enthusiasms of professional politicians and the governmental reasoning practised by bureaucratic personnel (see Minson, chapter 3 of this volume). It also depends on understanding the institutional solidity of the education system itself, presenting as it does its own imperatives and governmental necessities. These are some of the issues explored here.

Taking Labor's reforms to post-compulsory education as a central case study, this chapter describes both the shape of these reforms and the terms of the academic commentary that accompanied them. In doing so, it attempts to develop a more nuanced understanding that avoids reducing governmental processes to an expression of political ideals, of interests or of economic doctrines. The competency reforms are described as an instance of 'advanced liberal' tactics of governance, enlisting semi-autonomous agencies in a consensual process of defining their own institutional needs and classifications, rewarded by financial incentives and guided by expertise. However, they also offer an example of the technical and political fragility of such accords and of the fallibility of the instruments on which these institutional exchanges pivot. Thus redescribed, the case study suggests both the capacities and the limitations of the dual processes of deregulation and re-regulation entailed in the forms of governance and self-governance that now operate in and between semi-autonomous institutions, agencies and professions.

The chapter begins by describing the programmatic ambitions that shaped the reform of Australian post-compulsory education and the procedures used to build the operational alliances on which the reforms depended. This concrete description of the complexity of these accords is contrasted with the more abstract explanatory formulations offered at the time by political commentary on education. This professional literature is characterised as a mixture of visionary pronouncement and empirical exposé, both 'other-worldly' in its invocation of democratic principle and sophisticated in its combination of expertise and advocacy. Observing that the past decade of reform must be understood in the context of the 'bureaucratic pastoral' settlements (Hunter 1994) negotiated over this century, the chapter argues that neither the educational present nor the past should be dramatised into the alternative tales of the strong state coercing the democratic community, or the weak state unable to contain the market. Instead, we begin to get a more mixed impression of the political, ethical and technical imperatives implanted within mass education: institutional imperatives which governing parties may not be able to dismiss as easily as educationists tend to imagine. This at least is the argument explored here: we turn now to our main case study.

Directing Vocational Traffic

Between 1991 and 1992 three reports (the Finn, Mayer and Carmichael Reports) set a template for an ambitious national reorganisation of Australian education, incorporating secondary schools, technical education, apprenticeship and training schemes. The main reform objective was to be the development of credentialling systems applicable across a number of educational and vocational sites, linking schools, technical and further education, private training institutions and workplaces within one national training system. These initiatives were later to be developed by the Working Nation program (Keating 1994) into the Australian Vocational Certificate Training System (NBEET 1992).

From the Commonwealth education bureaucracy's perspective, these reforms were designed to construct clear 'pathways' between a mess of unplanned, overlapping institutions. In contrast with some other countries in the Organization for Economic Co-operation and Development (OECD), Australia's systems of vocational education were felt to be scattered and ineffective. In contrast with Germany or Sweden's national systems of 'polytechnic' institutions with their close connections to secondary schools and industry, Australian technical and further education (TAFE) systems are neither nationally organised nor prestigious. TAFE incorporates an array of institutions offering both vocationally oriented certificates, adult education courses and education for leisure. Their funding and management has remained within the hands of the States, each of which has developed courses and certificates loosely linked to school curricula, to workplace training and to industry definitions of skill levels. These courses compete with an expanding array of private training providers and with vocational offerings developed in the higher education sector.

In place of a jumble of public and private training arrangements, the new system was supposed to provide a common system of certification portable across State barriers and sectoral differences (Carter 1993; Holland 1993). In answer to consistent complaints that schools and TAFE ignored the needs of employers and industry, it was to provide a common point of negotiation. The mechanism was the development of industry-specific registers of the basic 'competencies' required in particular fields of work. This was to be linked to a national system of certification based on on-site assessment of individuals' level of performance in a small number of generic Key Competencies, common to schools, workplaces and training sites.[2] The idea was to provide 'some common language, some common framework of description of outcomes that can operate in all education and training institutions and in the workplace' (Mayer 1992: 95).

Credentials were no longer to reflect the number or duration of courses that an individual had taken. Instead, profiles based on the 'Key Competencies' would assemble information on the skills or knowledge possessed by the individual, no matter where these capacities were learned. Students would gain a certificate by undertaking training across these different sites on either a full-time or part-time basis, developing both the Key Competencies and particular vocational competencies. Their performance would be evaluated within work-based assessment schemes certified by 'qualified assessors', on the basis of comparisons between work-based standards and individuals' performance in specific tasks.

The reforms depended on long-standing State–Commonwealth negotiations on educational provision, which had continued since the postwar period and throughout the Commonwealth School Commission's work during the 1970s and the Commonwealth's efforts in the 1980s to coordinate curriculum, assessment, certification and access and equity programs at a national level (Bartos 1993; Sedunary 1991; Ashenden 1990; Ramsay 1991), developments culminating in the programmatic 1988 statement 'Strengthening Australia's Schools'.[3]

The most obvious feature of the program was the prominent role given to industry in defining educational goals (Dawkins 1991). The definition of competencies also drew heavily on OECD benchmarks, and on German, Swedish, United Kingdom and New Zealand competency models.[4] But unlike equivalent systems in the United Kingdom, for instance, the Australian training reforms involved substantial negotiation with unions, with the Australian Council of Trade Unions and with reformatory industrial relations expertise. In the context of Labor's Accord arrangements with the unions, these reforms set out to address the problem of unskilled school-leavers, long-term youth unemployment and Australia's poor performance against OECD standards of national economic performance, training provision and the flexibility of the trained workforce (Dawkins and Holding 1987; Dawkins and Duncan 1989; Dawkins 1989).

The overall target of Labor's education and training reforms was to provide national planning for the 'multi-skilled' work-force required by rapid industrial and technological change, and to draw young school-leavers into this system. Then, as now, the Australian government faced substantial problems in finding a place for young people in the labour market. Youth unemployment is now an endemic problem for economic planning, due to the virtual disappearance of a sector of unskilled work once taken by young school-leavers (Freeland 1993; Senate Standing Committee on Employment, Education and Training 1992). School-leavers without qualifications face the prospect of either permanent dependence on social security or confinement within a limited labour market of intermittent, part-time or casual work (Sweet 1992b, 1992c, 1987, 1980; Carmichael 1992: 96). Since the beginning of the 1980s governments have reacted by attempting to raise school retention rates, by expanding university entrance and by encouraging families to invest in their children's education, in the hope of increased economic security and social mobility.

By the early 1990s retention rates to Year 12 in Australian schools had risen dramatically (Finn 1991, vol. 2: 11–46, DEET 1993b). However, this success posed further problems. The school system had to adjust to a larger and more diverse student population retained in courses originally oriented to forming a minority for university entrance. Furthermore, students' educational choices were disconnected from national training needs and employment opportunities. 15- to 24-year-olds were preferring to stay on at secondary school in the hope of gaining university entry, rather than choosing courses in TAFE.[5] Those who remained to the end of Year 12 in secondary school had no guarantee of either employment or a place at the crowded universities. Consequently, the Commonwealth was left with industry's complaints that education and training served few of its needs, as well as with the political problem of meeting the increased electoral pressure to provide more university places – a demand increasingly claimed as a right of all those who completed Year 12 (Williams et al. 1993; Baldwin et al. 1991).

Accordingly, the Federal education bureaucracy shifted its emphasis from the large-scale reform of higher education and concentrated on the national reorganisation of technical education – an area of low educational prestige and attention, especially in comparison with successful vocational training systems such as the 'polytechnic' institutions of Germany and Sweden (Sweet 1992a; Conyer 1993; Furth and Squires 1989). Traditionally, Australian TAFE systems were the province of State and Territory governments. In undertaking their reform, the government extended the tactics used to secure a national higher education system, using a now familiar dual strategy of centralising funding and planning and devolving decision-making (Kinsman 1993).[6]

These developments in State–Commonwealth coordination were cemented by the release of the Finn, Mayer and Carmichael Reports between 1991 and 1992. In 1991 the Australian Education Council Committee (chaired by Brian Finn of IBM) proposed an 'education and training guarantee', recommending the extension of compulsory school attendance to at least the end of Year 10, with all young people subsequently being guaranteed a place in school or TAFE for two years of full-time education and training or its equivalent (Finn 1991). It set a target that, by 2001, 95 per cent of 19-year-olds should have completed Year 12, have a post-school qualification, or be in training or education.

The rhetoric used in the Finn Report to persuade the public, parents, teachers and employers to adapt to the new system made heavy use of the term 'pathways'. The emphasis was on flexibility and choice: in moving more flexibly between school, workplace and post-school institutions on the basis of demonstrated 'competencies', young people would be able to 'participate effectively' in work and, by extension, in civic life.

Much depended on negotiation and persuasion. Developing the program involved aligning State and Federal education planning with the departmental objectives of diverse agencies concerned with areas as various as industrial relations, social security, job creation, youth affairs, higher education and national curriculum development. Implementing it entailed obtaining industry validation of the workplace-based competencies and State-based adaptation of the Key Competency framework within autonomous curriculum and assessment systems. The latter processes involved extensive negotiation between industry bodies, small business representatives, unions, industrial arbitration boards, TAFE, State secondary school systems, school communities, professional teachers' associations and universities.

It was a tough call. Competency standards had to be generic enough to be intelligible across a range of work and training contexts, but precise enough to be applicable in particular sites (DEET 1993a). They had to incorporate the expectations of employers and the classifications of the workplace, but fit within existing school assessment schemes. This meant finding points of translation between school-based assessment systems, apprenticeship standards, industrial awards, professional registration and international credentialling agreements, while persuading universities to make use of the generic Key Competencies and to adapt themselves, in accreditation for professional courses, to industry-based competencies standards (Lambert 1992).

The problems were both political and technical. The reforms encountered immediate objections during the first stages of public consultation and professional commentary. Predictably, these came as much from industry and employer groups as from educationists, TAFE and secondary teachers outraged by the Federal government's perceived intrusion and by industry's role in the reform program (Powles 1992). Teachers were not easily won over, despite the government's efforts to persuade them to 'take on the challenge' of enabling parents to understand what TAFE could offer and encouraging them to question 'the misplaced notion that university is the dream to which all young people must aspire' (Dawkins 1992: 8). Apart from arguing that the assessment of competencies would increase their workloads and would open the classroom to mass standardised testing, teachers objected to the proposition that learning outcomes could be treated as generic and abstracted from the context of the classroom or from the individual's personal development, learning experience and social context (Porter et al. 1992). For their part, employers objected to the importation of 'academic' and abstract educational goals as a substitute for demonstrable generic or vocational skills. These debates were especially heated during attempts to define cultural attitudes or ethical attributes.[7]

The insuperable obstacle to the development of the national Key Competencies scheme, however, proved to be the political struggle between the Federal Education Ministry and the 'vagaries and petty parochialism of State premiers' (Dawkins 1992: 8). Industry-specific skills frameworks and competency-based training arrangements continued to be negotiated in separate agreements coordinated nationally by the Australian National Training Authority. The Key Competencies program stalled, however, as soon as development was devolved to the State education systems, producing a deadlock in the bid for a consistent national framework. The process of 'benchmarking' Key Competencies within existing assessment systems continues in some States, but even without the change of government that occurred in 1996, it was already unclear whether the Commonwealth would be able to build a national system of certification and provide commonality in the competencies expected of all trainees and future citizens.

Even if the coordinated national training and certification system could be built, it was far from certain that it would solve the long-term demographic, industrial and economic problems it had been designed to address. There was no guarantee that reforms to credentialling would either provide more jobs or secure coordination between training, TAFE and universities. The education bureaucracies had limited success in persuading universities to alter their accreditation systems or to apply the competency vocabulary in their own courses, generalist or professional (Marginson and O'Hanlan 1993). Impact on workplace-based training also struck limits. As the example of equivalent British competency schemes had suggested (Cooper 1992: 18–22; Sobski 1992), it proved difficult to find competent assessors in the workplace or to persuade small employers to cooperate with the bureaucratic requirements of competency assessment, to promote the flexible retraining recommended by industrial relations expertise or to use the skills developed by training.

Under the subsequently developed Working Nation program (Keating 1994), the Labor government continued its efforts to make training and certification the answer to unemployment, while fighting off the charge that the extensive expenditure on job creation and training programs was doing little more than raising hopes without creating 'real jobs'. As youth welfare experts had warned, the danger was that the programs would serve to increase retention rates in schools and training courses (thereby hiding the scale of youth unemployment), but would be unable to address long-term training needs, youth unemployment or the consequent strain on family welfare.

These are some of the problems that the Liberal-National Party Coalition government inherited. As noted above, its response was to cut expenditure on job creation and training schemes, dismantling the national planning and provision of training, devolving remnants of the national certification system to the States and contracting out both training and job search arrangements. The rhetoric of consultation, choice and flexibility was amplified, but the emphasis on commonality and centralised planning reduced to a murmur.

Those who designed and developed the Commonwealth's training reform strategy under Labor began to adjust existing rationales and programs to new imperatives, cost-cutting among them. Educational commentary had to make its own adjustments. Gradually, academic commentators who saw themselves as defenders of progressive politics began to make some distinctions. At the level of description, they needed to discriminate between those elements of educational planning which were specific to party political rhetoric (and which could be countered on those terms), those that gave voice to sectors of political philosophical and economic research and consultancy with allegiances

to the political right, and those that stemmed from longer-term governmental problems and tactics, articulated in bureaucratic, industrial and
educational terms. A key part of this re-evaluation is to review the terms
in which educational commentators responded to Commonwealth
initiatives under Labor.

The Critics Respond

Initially, critical reaction to the Competencies program was mixed. The
1991 Finn Report received strong support from advocates of industrial
reform and supporters of earlier programs of democratic industrial
restructuring, such as those proposed in the ACTU's *Australia Reconstructed* (ACTU/TDC 1987). These campaigns for industrial democracy
were now, in the spirit of the Accord, to be extended to education,
building an alliance between labour market reformers and social democratic educationists (Bluer and Carmichael 1991; Freeland 1991). The
hope was that, in emphasising workers' 'prior learning' (evaluating what
they could actually do, as distinct from assessing their paper credentials),
the reforms would extend campaigns associated with the internationalisation of Australian industry, micro-economic reform, and award
restructuring. More visionary advocates urged that in linking generalist
and vocational education, the Competencies scheme also promised to
close the historical divide between the abstract and the practical,
between mental and manual training or vocational and academic education, thereby fulfilling the democratic potential in popular education
(Freeland 1992: 81; Kinsman 1992; Sweet 1992). Aligned against these
interests and possibilities, as some saw it, were 'the educational conservatives and radical free marketeers seeking to structure education, the
labour market and industry on models thrown up by theoretically
rugged neoclassical ideology' (Freeland 1992: 86).

   On the whole, educationists (both progressive and conservative) were
unconvinced. While agreeing that the changes afoot were in some way
epochal, progressive critics objected to the attempt to restructure
education provision within 'the language of skill training' and around 'a
set of principles which are fundamentally governed by an economic
discourse' (Porter et al. 1992: 53). The concept of 'competency' was
regarded as instrumentalist and reductive, listing only the 'measurable
and observable' and ignoring the real goals of education – 'social,
cultural, moral and spiritual purposes, which cannot be embraced by the
notion of competent performance' (Knight et al. 1991; cf. Porter et al.
1992, Sachs 1991).

   If competencies were anti-educational, the Competency program
was found to be anti-democratic. The national coordination of education and training provision was described as a 'statist' alternative to

privatisation (Porter et al. 1992: 51), in an overall strategy of 'corporate managerialism'. The ACTU, unions and teachers, it was argued, had been coopted by centralist bureaucratic manoeuvres ultimately serving the interests of industry. This alliance had been built through a persuasive liberal individualistic rhetoric of 'choice' and 'flexibility'. Along with 'multiskilling', enterprise bargaining and performance monitoring, the political rhetoric of those selling the Competencies program offered the illusion of consensus, choice and worker autonomy, distracting attention from structural disadvantage.

The federal education bureaucracy, it was held, had been infiltrated by 'neo-liberalism', a hybrid of classical liberal political theory and neoclassical economics. Mated with corporate managerialism, this had produced an 'economic rationalist' strategy combining interventionist state activity with the stripping back of state funding and services. The devolutionary tactics of 'corporate federalism' enabled the neocorporate State to centralise policy, while the burden of implementation fell on those at the State and local level (Sachs 1991, Lingard 1991, Lingard et al. 1993). 'Top-down' reform had replaced the 'bottom-up' processes of democratic participation and community decision-making. Instead of orienting itself to the will of the community and to the self-realisation of citizens, education had been transformed into a conduit for self-promotion, consumerism and entrepreneurialism. Autonomy had been traded for compliance with the corporate model of consensus.

'Competency-based reform has in its sights the modernised, universal, polyvalent worker whose desire for autonomy and control is restructured as the desire for an individual career, based on a history of compliance and programmed responses. Trade union leaders are the experts in practical industrial psychology best equipped to guide this transition' (Marginson 1992a: 37).

The Finn, Mayer and Carmichael strategy, it was argued, relied on ludicrously over-inflated expectations, particularly of education's capacity to reform the economy. 'Hanging all reform on a single organising concept through which all education and training in Australia is to transform itself into worker productivity and career advancement, as well as national economic development, is a rationalist's dream which is unlikely to come true' (Porter et al. 1992: 58). To debunk the rationalist's dream, these critics attacked the theoretical models and doctrinal assumptions that were held to underlie the reform rationales. Among these efforts was Simon Marginson's thorough and influential study of the deployment of human capital theories in education policy rationales (Marginson 1993). Recounting the history of the revival of this postwar doctrine in the policy-making of the 1980s, he exposed the failure of human capital theorists to find empirical grounding for their key proposition: that 'education determines productivity, productivity determines earnings, and therefore education determines earnings' (Marginson 1993: 51–2). There is little demonstrable connection between educational outcomes and economic productivity, given the extent to which existing skills are under-used in the workplace (Marginson 1993: 102–21). The theory also fails to explain or affect educational choice, since '[u]nlike machines or properties, human beings have conscious preferences and varying motivations. They seek non-pecuniary as well as pecuniary benefits and might acquire human capital in order to provide consumption goods for themselves, goods that would never be sold in a market' (Marginson 1993: 53). If human capital theory is a discredited doctrine and a failed strategy, he asked, how can governmental and industrial interventions into the education system justify themselves by calling on the rationale?

Marginson finds the answer in a longer historical perspective on Australian, British and United States education through the twentieth century, in the struggle between labour and organised capital and in the ideological battle between liberal democratic educational principles and classical economic liberal doctrine. Social democratic doctrines (both in 'mainstream' emphases on the common cultural heritage of citizens and in their more pluralistic emphasis on cultural 'diversity' and communal self-determination) struggled against the twinned 'master discourses' of liberal individualism and neoclassical economic theory, with their common philosophical emphasis on individualism (Marginson 1993: 233).[8] The effectiveness of human capital theory as economic and educational doctrine lies, then, in the liberal philosophical foundation of its emphasis on the choices of the educational consumer. What has been lost, in this view, is the democratic potential of liberal individualism, a potential that allows the rights of the citizens to become a counter to the rhetorical force of consumer choice. As a counter to 'consumer sovereignty', then, we are offered the ideal of democratic participation: both in education and (by extension) in the political process.

Participation – with its potential to transform choice and individual self-interest into collectivist ideals and action – is thus to be reclaimed from liberal political rhetoric. This common political romantic tendency (Minson 1993: 220) makes it possible for opponents of the competency programs to describe them in terms of a trade-off between citizenship and 'consumerism', just as it prompts others to herald them as precursors of true educational and industrial democracy. In both cases, the address to policy developments is made at the level of discursive effects and truth claims. Policy rhetoric is treated as political doctrine. In turn, political philosophical doctrine is treated as foundational to governmental planning, programmatic reasoning and institutional action.

This common preoccupation with the doctrinal and theoretical elements of educational rationales helps to pinpoint some effects of expert discourses on policy formulation, especially where the description is able to show the often arbitrary relationship between the truth claims of these discourses and their adaptation to governmental problematisations and programs. The problem comes with the abstraction of such exchanges into dialectical struggles on a higher historical plane, between the rational economic subject and the self-governing community (Hunter 1994). At such points, we leave behind the more plodding description of the ways in which expert vocabularies or political-philosophical doctrines actually inform party political rule, bureaucratic programs or educational practice.

No doubt some rationales deployed within bureaucratic public planning are indeed 'rationalist', in the sense that they over-theorise the individual, the market or the state, treating each as an inner principle that produces effects by virtue of its presence (Hindess 1987; cf. Marginson 1992b). But this tendency is hardly restricted to the philosophies of the political right: if classical economic doctrine is capable of idealising the market as 'an index of freedom', Marxian discussions of the modern welfare state tend to share this essentialism, treating the appearance of consumer choice or market considerations in public planning as 'a sign of exploitation'. In each instance the economic calculations and planning activities of the bureau are treated in rationalist and philosophical terms, as if they were the actualisation of political doctrines or economic theories (Hindess 1987: 8–9). Such models do little justice to the non-ideal circumstances in which governments set targets and decide between rival priorities.

We need a more precise vocabulary, then, when describing the elements of aspiration and calculation in national educational and training reform. Some help is provided by the recent interest in using the term 'liberal' to describe a technology of governmentality (as distinct from the activation of a political or economic theory by political agents). Others in this volume and elsewhere have put the case that the term 'liberal government' helps to describe the characteristic process by which modern states have simultaneously withdrawn from direct regulation of social welfare areas, while tightening their control through steering, accounting and information measures pursued at a distance (Burchell et al. 1991). Combining deregulation and re-regulation, centralised elements of government shape the activities of semi-autonomous sites, agents and institutions, coordinating their activities without resort to coercion. Expert knowledges provide the technical vocabularies deployed in managing these sectors, tying agents and institutions into governmental networks built through agreed common goals, vocabularies and constructions of problems (Miller and Rose 1990: 10).

This vocabulary can help to locate some of the elements at work in the Australian Commonwealth Government's reorganisation of post-compulsory education, under both political parties. In its relations with industry and employer groups, the federal education bureaucracy has enlisted private corporations in training and certification systems, providing both financial incentives and the attraction of consultation. While seeking to know the needs of business and while soliciting the 'educational attitudes and beliefs' of employers, it has sought to reshape the business environment, making employers responsible for their training needs (for example, Sinclair 1991). Instances include the development of workplace-based vocational education and the establishment of state-sponsored small business corporations and centres (Thompson 1992).

No doubt these efforts to encourage industry to express its needs and invest in training have made use of the vocabulary of human capital theory, among other considerations such as industrial flexibility and productivity. But at a directly applied level, the program deployed the identification of competency frameworks themselves as a point of reciprocal influence between corporate and bureaucratic operations. While the Australian competencies models were drawn from OECD equivalents and developed by independent consultancy bodies (Finn 1991), these were knitted to 'quality assurance' frameworks drawn from industry (Mayer 1992: 33). Other elements recall the Commonwealth public service systems of performance-based appraisal, with their emphasis on explicit criteria for judging performance, on transparent process and on transferable skills (Colwill 1992). The Key Competency framework, in particular, had the potential to act as a new relational technology in the workplace, requiring both employees and their assessors to adapt to new ethical routines. For instance, to be assessed as competent in 'Planning and Organising Activities', candidates must have developed 'responsiveness to factors affecting priorities', a capacity shown by 'accommodation of differing perspectives arising from cultural backgrounds' (Mayer 1992: 20). Identifying the ethical norms embedded in these criteria, the Mayer Report also noted that 'given the way in which they are embedded in context, their development is likely to support the development of the attitudes seen as desirable' (Mayer 1992: 9). These are features of the ethical environment of the bureau, with its systematic attention to the 'conduct of conduct'. Surely the strategy could just as easily be described as one of the 'governmentalisation' of the corporation, as well as the corporatisation of government?

Similar observations could be made about the 'private' sphere of domestic and familial choices. Here too, private ambitions were 'governmentalised', in the sense of being programmatically reshaped through the rhetoric of pathways and the technology of choice and vocational advice. The Labor government devoted considerable resources to changing the patterns of educational enrolments, persuading parents to alter their ambitions for their children, to choose TAFE rather then university, to avoid the blind alleys of part-time work or long-term unemployment. This meant lowering expectations of immediate access to universities as the mark of social mobility within the family, while persuading families to invest in education and training. Across the education and training sectors, public and private, government created educational marketplaces which provide students and parents with the means to conduct themselves in them as conscientious consumers – consumers with the capacity and the desire to choose (Smith 1993: 191). These processes took place not in a 'free market' but as part of governmental systems for allocating resources and for planning the provision of educational services – a process entailing considerable public regulation. The effect was the establishment of a 'government-made market', in the regulation of private schooling and the provision of privatised training.

This does not, of course, exhaust the problems that liberal governmental strategies meet in seeking to coordinate the self-regulatory operations of independent agencies. Indeed, the Competencies case study demonstrates the limits of these tactics of decentralised coordination. The sites and agents on which the education bureaucracy's national reform agenda depended (State education ministries and bureaucracies, industry bodies, small business, private training providers, TAFE teachers, secondary teachers, youth welfare bodies) had claims to autonomy built on long-standing institutional routines, rights claims and vocational commitments. Educationists successfully prompted State-based rejection of the federalist reform agenda, partly because they were able to withdraw from negotiations behind a bulwark of professional procedures, routines and commitments. When educationists invoked the classroom teacher's special knowledge of young people's learning development and learning context (an understanding irreducible to indices of skill or generic competence), they were able to call on a powerful professional persona, with the moral authority of a century of pastoral classroom governance (Hunter 1988).

Nor were teachers alone in this: welfare experts maintained a similar scepticism, on the basis of a professional and pastoral commitment to youth. Whereas the reform program was quite explicit in treating unemployed young people and early school-leavers as a 'problem population', such formulations were inimical to youth welfare advocates, who had been vocal opponents of 'victim-blaming' training schemes that perpetuate normative assumptions about 'unskilled' young people and rely on empty promises about the connections between education levels and economic recovery (Ashenden 1989; Blakers 1985; Dwyer and Stewart 1990).[9] Articulate opposition on these scores, added to the moral authority of the social rights advocate, is not easily dismissed by governments depending on consensus, consultation and the incorporation of reform agendas in existing education or social welfare programs.

Politics and Programs

With the advantage of hindsight, it is possible to note some striking anomalies in the educationists' critical response to Labor's education and training reforms. At the time, the competency program was treated as an instance of the governmental adoption of economic rationalism, of neoclassical economic theory, and of the doctrinal enthusiasm for small government. Nevertheless, this was a government extensively committed to centralist economic and social planning and resourcing. The Commonwealth made itself responsible for a process of settlement and accord-building that required the maintenance of bureaucratic statistical and advisory facilities, capable of monitoring patterns of educational choice and participation and able to register (if not remediate) the effects of unbalanced resources on particular populations, communities or types of person deemed to be 'at risk' (see chapter 5).

Under the Liberal–National Party Coalition government, there has been a significant shift of resources away from the national coordination of training and certification. Given the continuing cuts to public spending and to bureaucratic departments, and given the consistent emphasis on the contracting out of research, we have also seen some dismantling of the statistical and expert infrastructure previously used to monitor national patterns of educational participation and vocational outcomes. Certainly both governments emphasised the choices of education consumers within an expanding educational market. Students, families and employers were treated as customers and clients of education: choosing the product, taking the risk and hoping to gain comparative advantage in an inflating market for 'positional goods' (Marginson 1997). However, the Coalition policy documents lack the previous Labor government's stress on the capacities required to exercise the right of choice, on government's responsibility to build that capacity, and on government's duty to ensure that such choices do not undermine longer-term systemic objectives, whether those of national security and economic performance, or of social welfare and equity. In their place is an emphasis on choice, on competition and on freedom from bureaucracy.

Nevertheless, our survey of the Competencies case study indicates that it may not be so easy to translate the doctrinally-driven enthusiasm for individualised choice, consumer freedoms and market arrangements into practicable programs. Decentralising education planning, making training more flexible, listening to employers and 'creating real jobs' requires considerable resources and regulatory effort. Long-term youth unemployment remains an endemic governmental problem which presents significant problems for social stability and electoral good-will. The available alternatives ('work for the dole' schemes, traineeships, increased school retention and the expansion of further education) all require substantial public expenditure and planning. Even the contractualist alternative – making the unemployed into clients of job search brokers and independent training agents – depends on the creation and management of a training market and on the provision of consumer safeguards.

It may be possible to persuade the electorate that, as client and consumer, the individual is responsible for his or her own risks in choosing educational products and vocational directions. However, given that other consumerist relations are hardly unregulated (in administrative or legal terms), installing a choice-based system may entail the provision of consumer guidelines and protection, as well as the expansion of vocational advice. If the state encourages the privatisation of training and education, it becomes responsible (at least in electoral terms) for managing these consumer aspirations within the education market. As the Labor government found in its efforts to redirect students away from the universities and towards technical education, work on educational and vocational choice requires extensive liaison with families, employers and youth agencies. These negotiations, in turn, created their own pressures, giving rise to escalating rights claims and electoral expectations that may now have an institutional and demographic momentum of their own.

This momentum, and the strength of the social rights claims made on mass education, should be understood not as the expression of a social democratic spirit, but as one of the self-generating historical effects of the education system itself and of the governmental strategies that have constructed, maintained and expanded it. Since the growth of mass schooling at the start of the twentieth century Australian governments and educational bureaucrats have sought to use the school system as an instrument of nation-building and as the source of a skilled work-force equipped for international industrial competition (Bartos 1993). But they have also emphasised the importance of pastoral attention to the self-formation and self-determination of each individual, both as a soul and as a citizen. These 'pastoral bureaucratic' (Hunter 1994) obligations to care for the population stem from the state's own interest in maintaining a peaceful and governable citizenry, and in avoiding social or sectoral conflicts that undermine the security and prosperity of the state (Foucault 1991, 1988; Gordon 1991; Kosselleck 1988).

Recent scholarly work has established the core role of the school in the processes of state-building and secular settlement. Mass schooling has provided a central means to form warring populations into self-monitoring individuals and self-governing citizens. These government achievements, first made in the context of deconfessionalisation and state-building in the early absolutist states of seventeenth-century Germany, depended on a government-made hybrid of spiritual self-governance and social discipline (Hunter 1994). By the nineteenth century bureaucratically-organised mass schooling had built the secularised techniques of spiritual self-direction and pastoral care into its institutional routines and disciplinary ambitions (Hunter 1988). Enclosing child populations in a common environment, the school also transformed the surrounding moral environment, establishing a long-lived governmental strategy by which the classroom became a locus for transformative social programs, designed to build a healthier, moralised and literate population (Jones and Williamson 1979). Transported from Britain to Australia in the middle of the nineteenth century and adapted to local circumstance (Smith 1991), these models of non-coercive moralisation carried with them the pastoral bureaucratic imperatives to balance the imperatives of state-building and security against the pastoral care of each and all (Foucault 1991). These imperatives (uneasily co-existing with one another) have shaped both governmental rationales for mass education and public expectations of mass schooling.

Throughout the twentieth century the expansion of popular schooling (within both State and denominational systems) has produced some unpredictable historical effects on the developing domain of 'the social' (Donzelot 1979, 1991).[10] As a future citizen, each child was accorded a claim to common and minimum educational provision, sufficient to ensure access to an array of literate and ethical capacities required for the exercise of citizenship. The plausibility of this promise has depended on the extent to which the school system provides a common educational environment capable of offsetting social and familial differences. In turn, this common treatment has transformed social aspirations, making new rights claims possible and placing fresh demands on government. The administrative promise of the school system (constantly tested) has been that the unequal social rewards distributed by mass schooling will be allocated on the basis of educational performance within the common educational environment, as registered by caring but disinterested pastoral observation and by publicly accountable selection procedures. Acquitting these claims has depended on the extent to which educational institutions are able to defuse escalating familial and social expectations, convincing the educational community that they have been able to maintain intense attention to each individual, while differentiating between individuals within an education population. The intricate devices of assessment, certification, examinations and vocational guidance have thus been able to act as (faulty) valves that manage the pressure of social expectations, permitting the social expectations and vocational commitments to float against educational norms. But at the same time, these deflationary mechanisms are linked to a larger machinery that plots patterns of educational participation and social and vocational outcomes, mapping them against a normative conception of equity and regular distribution of life chances and social risk.

If the expanding systems of mass education have not been able to meet the high expectations of egalitarian social transformation applied to them, they have nevertheless been instruments of rapid social alteration within modern Western democracies. This is due not so much to the education system's historical mission to express a democratic political will, as to its capacity to give individuals intense pedagogic attention, while applying regular norms and providing common resources. It is hard to imagine these 'bureaucratic pastoral' capacities being replaced by private choice and independent agencies, because they are too heavily dependent on a centralised institutional capacity for close pedagogic attention, statistical normalisation, expert analysis and pastoral concern: a combined resource that so far, has been exclusive to bureaucratically-organised education systems (whether State or denominational).

Conclusion

Our case study of Labor's reforms to Australian post-compulsory education provides an instance both of the capacities of advanced liberal governance, and of the limitations which it meets. The program addressed the endemic social welfare problems of long-term youth unemployment, welfare dependency and the disconnection between secondary schooling, national industrial needs and international standards. Using the vocabulary of choice, flexibility and efficiency, it enlisted an array of institutions and agencies in large-scale institutional reform. This occurred through a process of negotiation, in which employers, unions, teachers and universities were required to find common ground between their respective institutional vocabularies, procedural norms and professional classifications. The instruments of performance appraisal and educational assessment became the fragile hinges on which these institutional exchanges swung.

These processes depended on the historical capacities of the 'pastoral bureaucratic' education system, with its ability to combine intensive individualisation and pastoral guidance with regular and systemic normalisation. It is these capacities that Labor sought to extend in bringing the broader field of vocational education and training within the compass of common national certification systems. Continuing the historical process of social settlement, the competency program was an effort to translate the 'bureaucratic pastoral' capacities of mass schooling into other environments, floating the norms of the school, the workplace and the training site against one another in a centrally monitored institutional exchange.

The new political circumstances in Australia highlight the degree of bureaucratic ambition entailed in these initiatives. At the same time, these circumstances expose the gaps between the ambitions of political reformers, the capacities and commitments of bureaucratic planning and the criteria applied to public policy provision by professional commentators. The terms in which the Commonwealth's reforms to postcompulsory education under Labor were understood by educationists shows a consistent distrust of bureaucracy. This distrust is partly directed at bureaucratic 'instrumentalism', a term sometimes understood in terms of social administrators' indifference to matters of political principle and their commitment to a disinterested application of purportedly neutral norms, measures and models (Pusey 1991).

Nevertheless, the advent of a new anti-bureaucratic political leadership presents an occasion to rethink this habitual dismissal of bureaucratic capacities. If the point of commentary is to find a political rhetoric in which to respond to the immoderate doctrinal enthusiasms of ruling parties, such as that for neo-liberal principles of choice and market freedoms, it will be necessary to explain and defend the historical achievements of mass education. These achievements include many of those which Labor's competency program extended, including the provision of common norms, the monitoring of uneven social and vocational outcomes and the protection of the population against social risk. The case to be put is that government must maintain a healthy level of resources and a central planning facility, in order to coordinate the movements of educational populations, to manage educational choices and to monitor educational outcomes. However swayed they may be by doctrines of market freedom, governments should be persuaded that social settlement and state security depends on ensuring that all citizens have access to a common plateau of competence and to reliable, accountable and regular forms of educational differentiation and vocational distribution.

To make these arguments, however, educationists will need to relinquish the standard distrust of the 'instrumental' character of educational governance. They will need to become more willing to appreciate the combination of state interest and pastoral concern built into mass education, to defend its historical achievements and to explain the settlements that it has made possible. As analysts, educationists will need to be more prepared to offer less partisan treatments of policy developments. As advocates, they may have to prepare a defence of publicly planned and funded education that is more prepared to speak of institutional capacities and is less insistent on absolute ideals. These adjustments may make it more possible to mount effective responses to political projects that undermine the long-term stability and achievements of social governance.

Notes

Thanks to Ian Hunter, Jeffrey Minson, Bruce Smith and Alison Smith for discussions that have contributed to this paper and to Barry Hindess and Mitchell Dean for editorial suggestions.

1 Trainees would enter into such agreements while obtaining a vocational qualification that was nationally recognised and portable, but that could be 'customised' to meet the needs of particular businesses. A 'Skills Passport' was proposed so as 'to record the competencies a person has attained in a form recognised by employers and training providers throughout Australia', fitting apprenticeship standards to a 'set of national quality assurance principles' (Kemp 1996).

2 The 1991 Finn Report identified seven Key Competencies required for performance in any workplace: those of language and communication, mathematics, scientific and technological understanding, problem-solving, cultural understanding and personal and interpersonal skills. These competency frameworks were elaborated by the Mayer committee, in consultation with educationists, industry groups and major employers. Various industry groups were asked to take each of the competencies and to devise a ladder of the performance standards particular to their field of work, identifying for each some appropriate means of assessment. Supplementing these preliminary industry validation studies with material on equivalent competency-based initiatives in other OECD countries, the Mayer committee revised the preliminary Key Competencies nominated by the Finn Report, elaborating them into a different set of common generic competencies divided into occupationally specific ladders of performance standards. The Key Competencies were defined as: 'Collecting, Analysing and Using Information'; 'Communicating Ideas and Information'; 'Planning and Organising Activities'; 'Working with Others and In Teams'; 'Using Mathematical Ideas and Techniques'; 'Solving Problems'; and 'Using Technology'.

3 This document set a number of goals, chief among them the increase of school retention rates (bringing Australia more in line with OECD levels), the building of closer links between schools and industry, the establishment of national curriculum and assessment frameworks, and the promotion of

particular equity and participation targets. It stressed that the need was not for increased funding to education, but for improved forms of national coordination. It also acknowledged, however, that since decisions on education funding and programs remained in the hands of the States, the Commonwealth did not possess either the means or the right to enforce a nationalised education system, as it had been able to do in the case of higher education. Instead, the rhetoric was that of 'inviting participation' from the States in a process of national planning. Similarly, the document also expressed the hope that the independent school sector would also take up the invitation to participate in centralised Commonwealth education planning.

4 As models for the Australian reforms the Mayer Report cites a number of programs carried out by the OECD, as well as work on the definition of competencies carried out in the United States by the Secretary of the Department of Labour's Commission on Achieving Necessary Skills (SCANS) and in the United Kingdom by the National Council for Vocational Qualifications, and work in New Zealand as part of the development of the national curriculum (Mayer 1992: 10). Marginson and O'Hanlan note that the competency approach was influential in the United States in the 1970s, and a small number of higher education institutions developed competency-based liberal education studies. The United States Department of Labour has defined five basic competencies and a three-part foundation of skills and personal qualities needed for job performance. The framework, known as 'SCANS', is to be adopted in all United States schools, and it is recommended that employers use it in their human resources programs (Marginson and O'Hanlan 1993: 2).

5 In 1992 the then Minister for Employment and Education, John Dawkins, noted that only about 40 per cent of young people were enrolled in any form of training (Dawkins 1992). Despite a proportional increase in university enrolments and in school retention since 1983, the proportion of enrolments in TAFE has stayed the same.

6 In 1991 the Commonwealth promised to undertake full financial responsibility for publicly funded vocational education beyond Year 12 or equivalent, making increased education funding for the States conditional on their cooperation in implementing new Commonwealth guidelines and in providing information on performance levels. These State-based agreements were facilitated by the establishment of new consultatory bodies, including the Australian National Training Board, which was supposed to provide a consistent framework of standards in industries regulated by industrial awards and to coordinate the definition of work-related competencies, developing an eight-level Australian Standards framework, stretching to senior professional skills.

7 This debate centred on efforts to include 'Cultural Understandings' or the 'Negotiation of Cultures' as the eighth Key Competency. This category, mentioned in the Finn Report, had been explicitly excluded from the array of Key Competencies specified in the Mayer Report. After extensive debate, and sustained advocacy from Queensland educationists, an attempt was made to reintroduce it and to develop a workable and assessable definition. The attempt failed.

8 The dialectical formulations built into Marginson's conception of liberalism at this point in the debate should be clear in the following formulation: 'if market liberalism has turned "the economy" and "the market" into

absolutes, in isolation from the historical and social conditions under which they are sustained, educational liberalism has made "the individual" into the absolute horizon of social policy, so that education policy has become reduced to the production of ideal individuals who are separated from the social relations that sustain them . . . the two forms of liberal individualism function as two sides of the same coin, arranging the education systems around the binary divide between academic elitism and economic rationalism: liberal studies and training . . .' (Marginson 1993: 235).

9 Even if the competency reforms did promote the portability of skills, youth welfare experts argued, the benefits were unlikely to be felt by the really disadvantaged (Cooper 1992). The bleakest scenarios associated the proposed reforms with British programs of competency-based training, in place since 1986. Rather than improving access to job opportunities, these schemes increased credentialling, causing an oversupply in skilled work and a depression of craft wages, doing little to alter patterns of long-term youth unemployment. Although conditions in Australia varied considerably – due, in part, to the greater involvement of unions and the ACTU – there were serious limits to the extent to which the program was likely to clear the jungle of social welfare problems surrounding the unemployed youth.

10 I have made this argument at greater length elsewhere: Meredyth 1997. This section, and the conclusion, draw occasionally on material in that article.

References

ACTU/Trade Development Council Mission to Western Europe, 1987. *Australia Reconstructed: A Report by the Mission Members to the ACTU and the TDC*, Canberra: Australian Government Publishing Service.

Ashenden, D., 1989. 'A universal system? Education and training for all 16 and 17-year-olds', *Bulletin of the National Clearinghouse for Youth Studies* 8, 2: 10–18.

Ashenden, D., 1990. *The Recognition of Vocational Training and Learning*, Canberra: National Board of Employment, Education and Training.

Baldwin, G., Ely, M., Hore, T., Doyle, J., Kermond, B., Pope, B., Cameron, B. and McClelland A., 1991. *Unmet Demand for Higher Education Places in Victoria and Queensland*, Canberra: Australian Government Publishing Service.

Bartos, M., 1993. 'The Schools Commission, citizenship and the national purposes of schooling' in D. Meredyth and D. Tyler (eds), *Child and Citizen: Genealogies of Schooling and Subjectivity*, Brisbane: Institute for Cultural Policy Studies, pp. 153–79.

Blakers, C., 1985. 'From transition to youth policy: an outline of developments and provisions', *Youth Studies Bulletin* 4, 4: 43–7.

Bluer, R. and Carmichael, L., 1991. 'Award restructuring in teaching', *Unicorn* 17, 1: 24–9.

Burchell, G., Gordon, C. and Miller, P., (eds), 1991. *The Foucault Effect: Studies in Governmentality*, London: Harvester/Wheatsheaf.

Carmichael, L. (chair), 1992. *The Australian Vocational Certificate Training System*, Canberra: Employment and Skills Formation Council, National Board of Employment, Education and Training.

Carter, D. G., 1993. 'Structural change and curriculum reform in an Australian education system', *International Journal of Educational Reform* 2, 1: 56–67.

Colwill, J., 1992. 'Competencies and competency-based training in the Australian public service' in Centre for Continuing Education, *Higher Education and the Competency Movement: Implications for Tertiary Education and the Professions*, Canberra: Australian National University.

Commonwealth Tertiary Education Commission, 1986. *Report*, Quality of Education Review Committee, Canberra: Australian Government Publishing Service.

Conyer, N., 1993. 'Post-compulsory vocational education and training: an overview of some developments in OECD countries', *Curriculum Perspectives* 13, 3: 66–9.

Cooper, T., 1992. 'Qualified for the job: The new vocationalism', *Education Links* 42: 18–22.

Dawkins, J. S., 1988. *Strengthening Australia's Schools: A Consideration of the Focus and Content of Schooling*, Canberra: Australian Government Publishing Service.

Dawkins, J. S., 1989. *Improving Australia's Training System*, Canberra: Australian Government Publishing Service.

Dawkins, J. S., 1991. 'The training guarantee scheme', *Management Update* 116: 7.

Dawkins, J. S., 1992. 'Postcompulsory education and training: the national challenge', *Unicorn* 18, 1: 6–12.

Dawkins, J. S., and Duncan, P., 1989. *Better and Fairer Achievements in Employment: Education and Training*, Canberra: Australian Government Publishing Service.

Dawkins, J. S., and Holding, A. C., 1987. *Skills for Australia*, Canberra: Australian Government Publishing Service.

(DEET) Department of Employment, Education and Training (Australia), 1993a. *Generic Competencies*, Canberra: DEET Higher Education Division.

(DEET) Department of Employment, Education and Training (Australia), 1993b. *The Transition from Elite to Mass Higher Education*, Canberra: DEET Higher Education Division, Occasional Paper Series.

Donzelot, J., 1979. *The Policing of Families*, New York: Random House.

Donzelot, J., 1991. 'The mobilisation of society' in G. Burchell, C. Gordon and P. Miller (eds), *The Foucault Effect: Studies in Governmentality*, London: Harvester/Wheatsheaf, pp. 169–80.

Dwyer, P. and Stewart, F., 1990. 'Transients or citizens: the economics of the transition to adulthood', *Youth Studies* 10, 3: 52–4.

Finn, B. (chair), 1991. *Young People's Participation in Post-compulsory Education and Training: Report of the Australian Education Council Review Committee*, Canberra: Australian Government Publishing Service.

Foucault, M., 1981. 'Omnes et singulatum: towards a critique of political reason' in S. McMurrin (ed.), *The Tanner Lectures on Human Values*, vol. 2, Utah: University of Utah Press.

Foucault, M., 1988. 'The political technology of individuals' in L. Martin, H. Gutman and P. Hutton (eds), *Technologies of the Self*, London: Tavistock.

Foucault, M., 1991. 'Governmentality' in G. Burchell, C. Gordon and P. Miller (eds), *The Foucault Effect: Studies in Governmentality*, London: Harvester/Wheatsheaf, pp. 87–104.

Freeland, J., 1991. 'Dislocated transitions: access and participation for disadvantaged young people', Appendix 3(C) in Finn (1992), pp. 161–224.

Freeland, J., 1992. 'Education and training for the school to work transition' in C. Deer and T. Seddon (eds), *A Curriculum for the Senior Secondary Years*, Hawthorn: Australian Council for Educational Research.

Freeland, J., 1993. 'Changing patterns of economic participation and full employment in Australia', *Impact* February (1993), pp. 14–20.

Furth, D. and Squires, G., 1989. *Pathways for Learning: Education and Training from 16 to 19*, Paris: OECD.

Gordon, C., 1991. 'Governmental rationality: an introduction' in G. Burchell, C. Gordon and P. Miller (eds), *The Foucault Effect: Studies in Governmentality*, London: Harvester/Wheatsheaf, pp. 1–51.

Hindess, B., 1987. *Freedom, Equality and the Market: Arguments on Social Policy*, London: Tavistock.

Holland, S., 1993. 'Schooling for the twenty-first century', *Curriculum Perspectives* 13, 3: 57–60.

Hunter, I., 1988. *Culture and Government: The Emergence of a Literary Education*, Basingstoke: Macmillan.

Hunter, I., 1993. 'The pastoral bureaucracy: towards a less principled understanding of state schooling' in D. Meredyth and D. Tyler (eds), *Child and Citizen: Genealogies of Schooling and Subjectivity*, Brisbane: Institute for Cultural Policy Studies, pp. 237–87.

Hunter, I., 1994. *Rethinking the School: Subjectivity, Bureaucracy, Criticism*, Sydney: Allen & Unwin.

Jones, K. and Williamson, K., 1979. 'The birth of the schoolroom', *Ideology and Consciousness* 6: 59–111.

Keating, P. J., 1994. *Working Nation: Policies and Programs*, Canberra: Australian Government Publishing Service.

Kemp, D., 1996. Training for Real Jobs. Ministerial statement, 20 August 1996, Canberra: Department of Employment, Education, Training and Youth Affairs.

Kinsman, M., 1992. 'Competency-based education in TAFE' in Centre for Continuing Education, *Higher Education and the Competency Movement: Implications for Tertiary Education and the Professions*, Canberra: Australian National University.

Kinsman, M., 1993. 'Stimulus and response in post-compulsory education', *Curriculum Perspectives* 13, 3: 55–6.

Knight, J., Lingard, R. and Porter, P., (1991). 'Re-forming the education industry through award restructuring and the new federalism?', *Unicorn* 17, 3: 133–8.

Kosselleck, R., 1988. *Critique and Crisis: Enlightenment and the Pathogenesis of Modern Society*, Oxford: Berg.

Lambert, J., 1992. 'Issues in the assessment and credentialling of the competencies identified in the Finn Review', *Unicorn* 18, 1: 80–3.

Lingard, B., 1991. 'Policy-making for Australian schooling: the new corporate federalism', *Journal of Educational Policy* 6, 1: 85–90.

Lingard, B., Knight, J. and Porter, P., 1993. 'Restructuring Australian schooling: changing conceptions of top-down and bottom-up reforms' in H. Nielsen and B. Limerick (eds), *Participative Practices and Policy in Schooling*, Sydney: Harcourt Brace Jovanovich.

Marginson, S., 1992a. 'Competent for what?', *Arena Magazine* 1: 35–7.

Marginson, S., 1992b. 'Economic rationalism in education', paper presented to the 'Rationalising Australia' conference, Flinders University of South Australia 12 February.

Marginson, S., 1993. *Education and Public Policy in Australia*, Cambridge: Cambridge University Press.

Marginson, S. 1997. *Markets in Australian Education*, Sydney: Allen & Unwin.

Marginson, S. and O'Hanlan, S., 1993. *Generic Competencies*, Occasional Paper 4, Higher Education Series, Canberra: DEET Higher Education Division.

Mayer, E. (chair), 1992. *Putting General Education to Work: the Key Competencies Report*, Canberra: Australian Education Council.

Meredyth, D., 1997. 'Invoking citizenship: education, competence and social rights', *Economy and Society* 26, 2: 273–95.

Miller, P. and Rose, N., 1990. 'Governing economic life', *Economy and Society* 19, 1: 1–29.

Minson, Jeffrey, 1993. *Questions of Conduct: Sexual Harassment, Citizenship, Government*, London: Macmillan.

Morrow, A., 1992. 'The Finn Review and the two cultures: but which two cultures?', *Unicorn* 18, 1: 17.

(NBEET) National Board for Employment, Education and Training (Australia), 1992. *The Australian Vocational Certificate Training Scheme*, Canberra: Australian Government Publishing Service.

Porter, P., Rizvi, F., Knight, J. and Lingard, R., 1992. 'Competencies for a clever country: building a house of cards?', *Unicorn* 18, 3: 50–8.

Powles, M., 1992. 'In like Finn: access to TAFE in the context of the Finn Review', *Unicorn* 18, 1: 56–61.

Pusey, M., 1991. *Economic Rationalism in Canberra*, Cambridge: Cambridge University Press.

Ramsay, G., 1991. 'The need for national policies in education', *Unicorn* 17, 1: 34–41.

Rose, N., 1996. 'Governing "advanced" liberal democracies' in A. Barry, T. Osborne and N. Rose (eds), *Foucault and Political Reason: Liberalism, Neo-Liberalism and Rationalities of Government*, London: University College London Press, pp. 37–64.

Sachs, J., 1991. 'In the national interest? Strategic coalitions between education and industry', *Australian Journal of Education* 35, 2: 125–30.

Sedunary, E., 1991. 'Constructing schooling, constructing nation' in D. Stockley (ed.), *Melbourne Studies in Education 1991*, Melbourne: La Trobe University Press, pp. 1–10.

Senate Standing Committee on Employment, Education and Training (Australia), 1992. *Wanted: Our Future. Report Into the Implications of Sustained High Levels of Unemployment Among Young People (15–24 Years Old)*, Canberra: Australian Government Publishing Service.

Sinclair, K. E., 1991. *Aiming Higher: Business/Higher Education Round Table 1991 Education Surveys: the Concerns and Attitudes of Leading Business Executives and University Heads to Education Priorities in Australia in the 1990s*, Camberwell, Vic.: Business/Higher Education Round Table.

Smith, B., 1991. 'Governing classrooms: privatisation and discipline in Australian schooling', PhD thesis, Griffith University, 1991.

Smith, B., 1993. 'Educational consumerism: family values or the meanest of motives?' in D. Meredyth and D. Tyler (eds), *Child and Citizen: Genealogies of Schooling and Subjectivity*, Brisbane: Institute for Cultural Policy Studies, pp. 181–206.

Sobski, J., 1992. 'Pathways to Finn', *Unicorn* 18, 1: 49–55.

Sweet, R., 1980. *A Labour Market Perspective on Transition Programs*, Sydney: NSW Department of Technical and Further Education.

Sweet, R., 1987. *The Youth Labour Market: A Twenty Year Perspective*, Canberra: Curriculum Development Centre.

Sweet, R., 1988. 'What do developments in the labour market imply for post-compulsory education in Australia?', *Australian Journal of Education* 32, 3: 356.

Sweet, R., 1992a. 'Can Finn deliver vocational competence?', *Unicorn* 18, 1: 31–43.

Sweet, R., 1992b. 'From school to work . . . we've lost the pathway', *Australian Higher Education Supplement* 8 January 1992, p. 12.

Sweet, R., 1992c. 'Recession takes its toll on the young', *Australian* 26 August, p. 36.

Thompson, M., 1992. *Key Competencies in Small Business: Focus on Communications and Maths*, Leabrook: National Centre for Vocational Education and Research.

Vanstone, A., 1996. Australia's Young People: Shaping the Future. Ministerial statement, 20 August, Canberra: Department of Employment, Education, Training and Youth Affairs.

Williams, T., Long, M., Carpenter P. and Haden, M., 1993. *Entering Higher Education in the 1990s*, Canberra: Australian Government Publishing Service.

CHAPTER 3

Ethics in the Service of the State

Jeffrey Minson

> Public servants have a professional interest in good government . . . This professionalism is difficult to state positively, but we sense its absence . . . when we use the term politicisation, which implies undue political interference with bureaucratic discretion. (Uhr 1988: 111)

The continuing restructuring of public service in Australia in the name of 'the new public management' or 'new managerialism' has lately been paralleled by official interest in revising codes of conduct and providing ethical training for public servants. This ethics agenda is, in part, a product of new managerialism's unsettling effects on what *counts* as good public service. In particular, the established ethos of bureaucratic office has been put in question. What follows is at once an investigation and a defence of that ethos.

In order to respond to the new managerialist challenge we first need to know what we are dealing with. This means 'economising' on moral-political generalisations about new managerialist programs in order to concentrate on specific differences between established and new criteria for good public service. It means placing these differences in a wider context of ethical and political culture.

The second step is to examine the possibility of restating the ethos of office in a way that makes it relevant to the restructured operating environments of the public service. Rather than dwelling on academic contributions, the argument is mainly built around an analysis of two contemporary Australian government documents which illustrate this possibility in a thoughtful but practical fashion. One is an official report which attempts to restate the ethos of office for Queensland state public officials. The other is an unofficial working paper on the professional qualities of a policy adviser to the Prime Minister.

The terms of the analysis derive from a way of thinking about ethical questions (and an ethical outlook) which is distinguished from most modern moral philosophy by its favouring the description of 'ethical cultures' – their history, distribution, moral psychology, effects, limits – over the theoretical reconstruction of moral foundations. From this angle, what is interesting is not supra-institutional forms of moral judgment and justification but rather the personal capacities and comportments (including styles of ethical reasoning) through which one subjects oneself to an 'order' of ethical life in a given, instituted milieu (Weber 1948: 123; Hunter 1993/94). 'Life orders' are ethically distinguishable from one another by special (or characteristically inflected) imperatives and points of honour; by their respective ideals of life in the form of model moral personalities and relationships; by typical ways of specifying and addressing ethical concerns (Foucault 1987: 25–32; Minson 1993: 3–40, 200–3). This plurality of obligation and comportment also occurs within as well as between particular institutional milieus where life orders intersect. In short, ethical existence is governed by an inescapable division of ethical labour: 'Is it true that any ethic of the world can establish commandment of identical content for erotic, business, familial, and official relations' (Weber 1948: 118)?

Accordingly, the questions to be addressed to our documentary sources on the ethics which govern 'official relations' are these: what, ethically speaking, are present-day bureaucrats variously required to be able to do? What kinds of personal manner does their status as unelected state officials and the contemporary administrative milieu require them to cultivate? These questions direct attention to the performance-related concomitants of both the formal and informal 'roles' occupied by public servants. Particular attention is paid to some rhetorical qualities of 'professional character', the ethical significance of which have become difficult to acknowledge. Behind this difficulty of articulating public service professionalism are the wider cultural threads running through the reforms. This context of ethical and political culture gives rise to misunderstandings about administrators' discretionary powers and to a tendency to magic away the ethical aspects of the relations of subordination which are constitutionally inseparable from the job.

In relation to the vexed question of 'the public interest', the final part of the argument touches on the shadowy connections between the ethos of office, 'good government', and the 'idea of a distinct administrative cadre' (Parker 1993: 177). The argument culminates in a 'modest proposal' that state service be seen as part of the ethical meaning of 'serving the public interest'.

Challenges to the Ethos of Office

Public service ethics for appointed officials in the misleadingly named 'Westminster systems' of representative government (Evans 1982; Finn 1990) is formally an ethos of office. Obligations are incumbent on officials, not as a consequence of their being 'moral agents' in a trans-institutional sense, but by virtue of their occupancy of an institutional role.

The traditional contents of the ethos are well known: professional bipartisan loyalty to the government of the day; confidentiality and anonymity; provision of 'frank and fearless' policy advice to ministers, and economic, efficient and beneficial services to the public; respect for merit and impartiality, for example, in allocative processes; and the obligation to set aside 'private' interests and commitments in the performance of public duties.

But how is the ethic known? In the past, as senior British civil servant Sir Edward Bridges' memoirs testify, it was more often shown than told (Chapman 1988). It would typically be passed on through 'the family and educational background and post-entry socialisation of officials' (Chapman 1993a: 105). Cadres of career public servants were formed through initiation into procedural routines and exposure to anecdotes of model career officials' professional flair. No mere 'automata of the paragraphs', in Weber's phrase, senior public servants possessed 'a kind of internal standard of political appropriateness which operates even in the absence of formal external standards' (Uhr in Parker 1993: xv).

Today 'formal external standards' have come to the fore. Around Australia, public sector ethics are undergoing codification. In general, these ethics reforms seem bent on renewing rather than displacing the traditional ethos of office (see, for example, Public Service Commission 1995). Why should this reaffirmation be necessary, at this time and on this scale, if new managerialism had not made many of the old safeguards against maladministration ambiguous, irrelevant or questionable? In order to set the scene for our discussion of one such attempt at renewing the ethos of office, two sorts of worries need to be reviewed, for some of these concerns seem quite legitimate: defence of the ethos of office cannot be premised on opposition to new managerialism *tout court.*

First, the new managerialist imperative to 'manage for results' lowered the premium traditionally attached to 'good process' in the delivery and regulation of services. Painstaking procedure and the cautious weighing of options came to be derided as 'doing things by the book' or 'snag-hunting' and associated with traditional bureaucratic inflexibility and depersonalisation (Dugay 1994; 1996). Even at 'street-bureaucrat' level, yesterday's strict regulation is often today's discretionary guideline. But which rules cannot be relaxed? How are public servants to master the discretionary components of all rules and regulations containing expressions like 'reasonable', 'fit and proper', 'fair', etc. (Chapman 1993b: 157)? Yet know these things they must – when they, rather than the 'responsible' minister, may have to answer for so-called 'operational' mistakes.

The reverse side of 'managing for results', devolution, risk-taking, etc., is the unstoppable 'audit explosion'. In the name of transparency, merit-protection, accountability, or, more commonly, expenditure-reduction (Ives 1996; Summers 1996), new managerialism has itself initiated new kinds and levels of bureaucratisation. It is not against procedure *per se*. Rather, procedural considerations now vie with other obligations in a more uncertain fashion: today's job-hopping public managers have less opportunity to build up process-oriented discretionary judgment.

This is due to a further worry about what once passed for professionalism in the public service. 'Out-sourcing', job rotation and employment of private sector 'change-agents' reflect a sense of the insufficiency of departmental 'line-experience' and its combination of specialised technical knowledge and generalist know-how, now derided as 'amateurism' (Fulton Committee 1968: paras 1, 3). Established criteria for public service professionalism are in competition with a professionalism defined in terms of generic organisational-managerial competences.

The shift seems to have occurred for various reasons. They include concerns about an allegedly disproportionate previous emphasis on policy advice at the expense of managing government services (seen by public choice theorists to have in-built tendencies to increase their expenditure); and political suspicion (hardly unprecedented, see Bagehot 1974: 177) of administrators' independent governing role (Zifcak 1994). A consequence of this shift has been that professional bipartisan loyalty to the government of the day can be deemed insufficient. Bipartisan loyalty and its component of political neutrality does not sit well with either conviction politicians (Chapman 1993a: 109) or the evangelical side of personnel management, committed to psychologising employees' ways of relating to their work (for example, Peters 1989; 1992; and for an incisive analysis, Dugay 1994; 1996). The call is out for enthusiastic personnel who will not withhold the proverbial 'last five per cent of commitment' to government objectives (Zifcak 1994: 11).

Yet the new public management is not all about casting public service and the personality of the public servant into a single entrepreneurial mould. We should not overstate its singleness of ideological purpose, its technical homogeneity, the extent of the changes involved in different countries or its destructive effects.[1] Healthy elements of ethical as well as economic competition have been introduced into public administration. In arguing for the retention of a professional administrative cadre, Robert Parker comes close to suggesting that new managerialists have succeeded in reinventing amateurism in government.[2] He may have a point, but it is a debating point. Different styles of professionalism (different combinations of generalist and specialised aptitudes) may have different things to offer public service in different contexts. Capacities for proceduralism and prudential judgment are not incompatible with the pragmatic sides of new managerialism's concerns about accountability and 'client-focused' service outcomes. The conflict between the ethos of office and the quasi-religious psychologisation trend in business-management training, on the other hand, seems less easy to negotiate.

In effect new managerialism throws down two different sorts of challenge to the ethos of office. Either competing criteria of good public service are introduced or an explicit *raison d'être* for a given practice is required in the light of government objectives. This demand for explicitness may be more troublesome than it seems. The trouble is rhetoric. It is possible that some of the 'virtues' of professional public service do not register in the dominant public languages of politics and ethics. These languages are a force to be reckoned with, not only within new managerialism but also in the field of administrative ethics itself. The challenge to the ethos of office rests on wider tendencies in ethical and political culture.

The first tendency which the ethos offends is the familiar assumption that to count as a moral agent it is necessary to be morally autonomous. People are only obliged to go along with rules, principles, or values, and will only in fact be wholeheartedly committed to them, if they (could) have rationally and consensually formulated them for themselves. The riders to the term 'rational' in this formulation (consensual, wholehearted) hints at the corollary of this assumption: namely that the locus of morally autonomous agency has to be 'the whole person', the relational, feeling individual, as distinct from a compartmentalised rational fragment of themselves – or from official ways of identifying moral agency with occupancy of institutional roles.

This assumption is at the centre of a widely distributed 'critical' ethos or life order (Hunter 1993/94). It is not surprising if it figures prominently in new managerialist critiques of bureaucracy and in those personnel management techniques which are psychology-based, participative and/or 'contractualist' (Yeatman 1997; Rose 1996: 348–9). Employees are contractually implicated (ethically as much as legally) as 'active elements in their own self-government' (Rose 1996: 347): people who reflect on and identify with their work; critics of the status quo, visionaries, troubleshooters, corporate community leaders, etc. But for our purposes a more appropriate place to see basically the same cultural ethos at work (albeit with more emphasis on its obligatory side) is in the critical suspicion displayed towards the ethos of office in some of the current Australian academic interventions in public sector ethics.

This suspicion is inevitable given the critical-philosophical impulse to ground the ethics of public service in values, virtues or principles which derive their salience from general moral and political theories. If there is no other basis for ethical decision-making then public officials must be encouraged in their work to cultivate 'authentic' independent reflection and commitment on the basis of moral considerations which transcend the givens of a particular organisational culture (Longstaff 1994). Conversely, if the only bona fide kind of moral agency is the morally autonomous 'whole' person, then 'the inadequacy of mere professionalism or role mentality' in public service follows as a matter of course (Coady 1993: 157).

Accordingly, obligations derived from official roles figure either as a foil to a 'critical morality', in the form of managerial, legal or political compliance (Sampford 1994); or as a preliminary – a topic of organisational 'training' leading into the work of moral education proper (Longstaff 1994: 145–56). Only in so far as role obligations are justifiable in terms of theoretically justifiable higher purposes, such as social justice and the 'fundamental renewal' of society, will public officials regard them as an altruistic 'personal' responsibility (Preston 1996: 3–4; Jackson 1987). Officials must therefore be prepared – that is to say, coached – to step out of role. They must become, in effect, their own critical philosophers (Longstaff 1994: 155); or, in other words, reflective 'citizens in lieu of the rest of us', specialists in the common good (Walzer 1970: 216).

A second, more worldly, cultural tendency informing the new managerialism which militates against the ethos of office is the democratic-political imperative underpinning the catchcry of 'responsive government'. By no means simply a logical generalisation of the ethos of moral autonomy, this imperative is connected to a less edifying historical 'metamorphosis' in representative government (Manin 1994). Factors such as the unpredictability of voting behaviour have forced public policy-making to be more oriented around calculations of 'community' opinion and ostensibly delivering on electoral promises. These opinions and promises tend to be unenthusiastic about fundamental social renewal.

Talk about 'breaking through bureaucracy' (Barzelay 1992) may be largely hyperbole. Nevertheless, the tendency of the reforms, and even some public sector ethics education, to put the proceduralism and professionalism of the traditional bureaucrat on notice should be recalled as we turn to a local attempt to meet this demand for explicit attention to the ethical expectations of public service.

Rehabilitating the Ethos of Office

Critical-philosophical reconstructions of administrative ethics do not have the field to themselves. Hailing from a hybrid 'realist' tradition of legal, public policy, administrative and political studies, there are those who see the administrative 'role mentality' as an adequate basis for a 'mundane ethos' of public service (Uhr 1990: 3). Far from being derivative of higher moral principles, the imperatives and form of conscience deriving from administrative office as such may legitimately act as a brake on the tendency to an unworldly 'administrative fundamentalism' (Uhr 1990: 18). A strategy for avoiding both narrowly self-interested malfeasance and altruistic 'overfeasance' in public service is to recraft the traditional ethic of office around a virtue ethic centred on professional agency and its associated political capacities (Uhr 1994b; Parker 1993).

In what sense are these capacities 'political'? A key argument is that the central problem of administrative ethics is to ensure the responsible use of 'the *governing* authority exercised by bureaucrats through their discretionary power' (Rohr 1978: 237, emphasis added; see also Parker 1993; Chapman 1993b). The dependence of the ethical dimensions of officials' responsibilities on their legal statuses and capacities has also been well canvassed (for example, Finn 1990; 1993). These approaches also link professionalism in government to concepts of professional accountability and merit which have a basis in continuing Australian liberal-constitutional traditions (Uhr 1993; 1996). The official report which we are about to examine is in some ways an attempt to operationalise such approaches.

An ethics regime for the Queensland Public Sector

The core of the recent Queensland public sector ethics reforms is a code, backed by legislation, setting out 'standards of conduct' for public officials. As set out in the legislation (Queensland Public Sector Ethics Act 1994), the code of conduct has two main constituents: an inventory of five primary 'ethics obligations' and a requirement upon agency chiefs to organise the development of a supplementary 'agency-specific' code. The primary obligations are: respect for the law and the system of government, respect for persons, integrity, diligence, and economy and efficiency. The supplementary 'agency-specific' standards must be

developed on the basis of consultation with agency employees and
employee associations. Agencies are required to provide ethics training
for employees. Existing disciplinary procedures may apply to infractions
of the code.

The rationale for the legislation is outlined in the canny and insightful
charter for the reforms, the Electoral and Administrative Review Committee's (1992) *Report on the Review of Codes of Conduct for Public Officials*
(hereafter, EARC).[3] For our purposes three aspects of the report are
especially worth noticing: the relations it establishes between principles
of conduct, concrete requirements of conduct, and the Australian
system of government; the way it conceives the 'sources' of public sector
ethics; and the overarching definition of the ethical public official as 'a
trustee of the public interest'.

A striking feature of the report is a three-columned diagram of the
proposed 'ethics regime' (EARC 1992: 16). The diagram locates the
equivalents of the legislative 'ethics obligations' in the middle of three
columns. To the right of these 'general principles of conduct' for
officials is an inventory of 'typical requirements', expressed as 'exhortations and prohibitions'. Here are found both traditional and more
recent staples of the ethos of office, such as not accepting gifts and
providing adequate information before parliamentary committees. In
the left-hand column sits the 'Westminster' system of government. The
standard chains of ministerial responsibility and final decision-taking
prerogatives are set out, but with an added emphasis upon the role
played by unelected officials in making as well as administering policy.

Reduced to its simplest terms, EARC's diagram of its proposed 'ethics
regime' (EARC 1992: 27, 163) is:

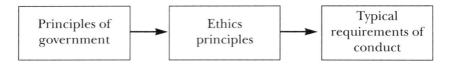

For my purposes, the value of this unusual diagrammatic representation of public sector ethics lies in its dramatisation of the distance
separating a role-based 'ethics regime' from the philosophical (and also
sociological) advice tendered to the Committee. 'Ethics' from these
latter points of view refers to fundamental values or principles from
which standards of right and wrong conduct are derived. The principles
of ethics are said to be grounded in rational deliberation or socially
constructed reflections of 'the community's theories' about how to get
to 'the good society' (EARC 1992: 7, 9). They are to be distinguished
from their 'formal' derivatives, 'principles of conduct' (EARC 1992: 9).

So defined, ethics would appear to possess a philosophical generality which transcends a specific role ethic.

By contrast, the ethics principles in the centre column could be said to differ in at least two ways from this picture of ethics in government. First, the EARC ethics principles do not theoretically underpin the specific prohibitions and exhortations. The need for the code to take the form of principles is said to be a function of the impracticality of a 'Justinian' code attempting to anticipate every possible eventuality (EARC 1992: 35).[4] The 'ethics principles' are, if anything, inductively derived from the typical requirements of bureaucratic office, and function as a memorable shorthand for them. On this 'mnemotechnical' construction, the principles are rhetorically honed rules-of-thumb[5] aimed at helping public servants recognise ethical problems and form professional judgments about what to do. With the aid of the principles, the problem situation can be located on an 'ethics road map'[6] of comparable cases.

Second, the EARC ethics principles do not provide a moral basis for the political system. Rather, they are derivative of that system. As a consequence (and following Uhr, Rohr, et al.) the principles possess an 'appropriately narrow focus' on 'the standards by which elected officials ought to use the power, influence and resources of their official positions' (EARC 1992: 7, 8) within the limits of their constitutionally subordinate place in the Australian revised version of a 'Westminster' system.

It is worth pausing to reconstruct the question to which this proposition is a possible answer. What is administrative ethics primarily about if the policy/administration dichotomy and the resulting instrumentalist view of the public servant's role is unsustainable as an operative premise for such an ethics? On that view, the public servant's role is to be a 'neutral' technician or conduit for implementing policies and associated values supposedly formed in the democratic-political sphere (Thompson 1992: 35). The literature on public administration is as one in regarding this postulate as largely a fairytale. Perhaps it is. But, having said that, what is the answer to the question about administrative ethics' 'core business' going to look like if the democratic-political imperative for governments to be 'responsive' gives a new twist to the official's traditional subordinate status?

The effect of the EARC/Rohr/Uhr emphasis on the governing role of bureaucrats, and hence on their professionally responsible use of discretionary powers, is therefore to drive a wedge between the bureaucrat's instrumental and subordinate statuses. While to treat someone as an instrument is to subordinate them, the converse does not necessarily follow. From the fact that official work is not purely instrumental and 'duty-free' in an ethical sense (as it would be if officials' duty was only to

mechanically comply with formal rules), it is commonly inferred that the
ethical dimensions of that work require officials to assume the moral
autonomy appropriate to 'a kind of professional citizen . . . fiduciaries
for the citizenry as a whole' (Cooper 1991: 141). Whereas the EARC
Report resiles from equating role-obligations with formal rules and
instrumentalisation it seizes on the idea of non-rule-book yet role-based
professional responsibilities. The allusion in the 'principles of government' column of EARC's diagram (figure 3.1) to the role of public
servants' discretionary ethical/policy-making judgments is a means of
clarifying the continuing place for a revised 'Westminster' ethic of role
in a milieu in which compliance with fixed rules has become less
relevant as a touchstone of good official conduct in all circumstances.

Flowing out of this endorsement of 'Westminster' government, the
second aspect of the rationale which concerns us is the hierarchy of
distinct 'sources' from which the ethical standards appropriate to
the regulation of official conduct are derived. The first of these sources
is 'the functional and legal limitations and obligations which constrain
the individual's role/official capacity' (EARC 1992: 14). A second source
of standards is located in the professional norms pertaining to how
they use their particular expertise. Finally, the report wishes to allocate
a limited place to what it calls an official's 'personal ethics' as long as
they do not conflict with government's constitutionally legitimate
policies.

Setting the professional and functional 'sources' aside for the
moment, there is a terminological point to be made about the report's
use of the term 'personal ethics'. An ethic of role itself may provide the
focus for a form of passionately dedicated, honourable and personable
comportment. 'Personal' dedication of that order need not be predicated on having a 'personal ethics' in the further sense of a moral outlook derived from an individual's own critical ethos or their group life.

Philosophical interventions in administrative ethics thrive on conflating these two senses in which administrative ethics has a 'personal'
component. We can see why. The price of failing to keep the two meanings distinct is to severely weaken the ethical case for according priority
to constitutional regime and role over philosophical and other supposedly supra-institutional foundations in determining public officials'
ethical obligations. Conflating the two senses of 'personal commitment'
makes it look as if officials will only be authentically committed to the
obligations if role obligations and personal ethics are brought into
alignment. (We are to assume that personal ethics is the natural home of
our moral personality *per se*.) Conversely, according priority to role
obligations over personal ethics looks like a result of a morally
questionable *Realpolitik*.

Consequently, if these implications are to be resisted, it might be more in keeping with giving priority to officials' public role obligations if what the report calls 'personal ethics' were to be reconceived in terms of individuals acting in their capacity as private citizens. The benefits of this terminological precision start to become apparent when we look at the difficulties of defining the 'public interest' dimension of the ethos of office.

The chimerical public interest

The EARC Report's approach to this question is built around a constitutional-legal notion of public office as 'a public trust' (EARC 1992: 25). The public servant is the trustee, as distinct from the bene-ficiary, of the public interest. What does this mean in the context of the Australian system of government?

There is no ready-made answer. 'For the most part', asserts the report, 'our working systems of government are not defined within any document, including the Constitution' (EARC 1992: 47). So what counts as the public interest must be determined by a combination of the requirement of particular 'circumstances' conjoined to an understand-ing of these 'working systems', that is, 'the traditions and values em-bodied in our system of government *and in particular the respective roles . . . of appointed officials*' (EARC 1992: vii, emphasis added).

The difficulty arising from this formulation is that, as the report recognises, public officials typically occupy a number of roles. In essence, the EARC Report conceives the plurality of public servants' obligations in terms of a 'fissure' between two different 'trusts': between serving the government in one role and serving the public in another. The first trust pertains to their obligations to serve their employer (EARC 1992: 19). It is a fiduciary relation, a relation of loyalty by a legal subordinate to a superior, who pays for the provision of professional services and skills 'on terms which the employer may determine' (EARC 1992: 51; see also Finn 1993). Serving the government *is* a public trust but, from the public servant's standpoint as an employee and as a functionary, it is only an indirect one: for it is for the elected government of the day to determine what is to count as the public interest. Or, in new managerialese, the 'client' of the public servant is not the public but the minister.

In their capacity as a government employee, the source of the administrator's role obligations are said to be the functions of the job as laid down by their employer. In consequence, it is assumed, the obliga-tions are voided of moral significance: '[T]he functional obligations of officials are primarily structural and legal rather than ethical in

character' (EARC 1992: 51). However, the official's functional obligations are complicated by their professional capacities (and, to a degree,
by their 'private' ethics). It is only in the responsible exercise of the
discretionary powers which they possess by virtue of their professional
skills and privileged access to information and resources that officials
assume moral agency as 'trustees of the public'.

Meaning what exactly? Little is added to the above-mentioned
formula for determining the public interest by reference to circumstances, traditions and values embodied in official roles, etc. The
report's studied reluctance to nail down the ethical side of officials'
'public interest' obligation is necessitated by the seeming impossibility
within a 'Westminster' regime of institutionalising an independent
definition of the public interest which might afford a charter for public
service agencies or individual officials to pursue policy directions
(reflecting their version of the public interest) which may differ from,
and override, the policies of the elected government (EARC 1992: 20,
45–9).

A few questions can be mooted at this point. Are there really only two
kinds of role obligations in public service and hence two ways of being a
public trustee? Equally questionable is the appropriateness of representing the two 'trusts' in question in terms of a morally asymmetrical opposition between serving the public and serving the government; the
former entailing independent moral judgment, the latter only a legal
relation of subordination.[7] The consequence of this bifurcated construction of the public official's multiple roles is to suggest that there is little
or no virtue in serving the government as such. That implication is
locked in by a further assumption which might also be profitably questioned. Is there no more to government service than a legal employer/
employee relation? Could there be any ethical mileage to be had from
the fact that to serve the government is also in some sense to serve
the state?

The roles of a policy adviser

In order to pursue these questions more concretely, let us first consider
a document pertaining to a specific type of Commonwealth government
service: a short paper developed for a training workshop entitled 'Policy
advising in the Department of Prime Minister and Cabinet: how the
Department adds value' (Sims 1993). The paper, authored by the then
Deputy Secretary to that Department, is worth quoting at length.

> *The role of the department.* More than any other Department this one exists to
> serve its Minister ... the Prime Minister chairs Cabinet and must weigh

competing views, resolve conflicts and maintain cohesion and strategic direction . . . the Department . . . takes a whole of Government view . . . is there to see the linkages across portfolios . . .

How to be an effective adviser in PM&C. [We] should understand the Government's objectives . . . [and] the views of the reader of our policy advice. A very difficult balance needs to be formed . . . it is up to the politicians to decide which options should not be pursued . . . there is little point in putting up options we know will be totally unacceptable. The policy adviser needs to consider the political environment in much the same way as might a benevolent dictator. A policy adviser is not party-political, but is aware of community attitudes and likely reactions.

A good policy adviser must probe carefully but diligently the apparent constraints to pursuing the desired policy outcome. We will often be confronted with an option we think is best, and an option we know is most politically acceptable. Within those two options, however, there will often be a range of other options. We must actively pursue the second best when the first is not available. Again, *judgement* is required . . . It is the continual balance between being responsive and advocating the hard issues.

We must know how hard to push, and we must accept the result. The trick to this is really understanding precisely the role of the policy adviser. That role is to put an array of options, by all means push one of them, make sure decision-makers know the views of all that will be affected, and be content if we are sure the politicians knew what they were doing even if we do not like the decision they make. If we are distraught over their decisions, we should not be a public servant, but a politician.

A good policy adviser in PM&C knows that good process is vital. It is a PM&C officer's role to ensure . . . decision-makers . . . have time to think through the issues, and to make sure the recommendations they are deciding on or between are clear and capable of implementation.

A good adviser must know the views of all relevant interest groups, relevant Ministers, and must know the wider environment . . . Your views can only be clear when they are tested against those who hold an opposing view. Those with different views to your own are usually not stupid or without integrity.
(Sims 1993)

No one would be more surprised than the author of this document to learn of its use as a repository of ethical wisdom. From subtitle to exhortations about 'responsiveness', the paper is redolent of Australian new public management concerns. Yet its tone is pragmatic. It does not attribute a single enterprise form to the work of policy advice. Nor, contrary to a widely voiced criticism of the emphasis on 'responsive government' (Preston 1995: 53–4), does the document encourage advisers to tell ministers only what they want to hear. It may then serve as a window on to the political ethics and the moral psychology of government service. But first we must drop the assumption that ethics and (all) relations of subordination are mutually exclusive.

This is not to question the importance of independent thinking to the ethical definition of professionalism. But 'the element of moral agency' in public service does not begin and end with 'discerning the public

interest and advising the politician about the wisest course of action'
(Campbell 1993: 126). To overemphasise independence from instructions is to ignore the moral psychology of professional service. In
Weber's classic formulation, it remains the policy adviser's duty and
point of honour, having made known their disagreement with a policy
direction, 'to carry it out as if it corresponded to his innermost
conviction' (Weber 1968: 1404). But how does a policy adviser do that,
or relate himself or herself with professional integrity to intellectually
complex yet subordinate requirements of 'responsiveness'? What kinds
of professional moral character does this require?

Seen through this interrogative grid, even a functional, legal or
subordinative requirement can take on ethical weight via the 'drama-
turgical' dimension of the role, that is, the ethical work of self-modifica-
tion involved in performing or acting out the function. And the roll-call
of ethical capacities and comportments which the Sims paper suggests is
involved in policy advice is quite impressive. One needs by turns to be an
expert, a bit of a politician, an assistant negotiator or broker of community differences, a stickler for procedure ('good process'), and a stoic
who can accept disappointments with equanimity (Minson 1997).

Let us concentrate on the comportments and capacities involved in
providing both expert and political advice. Far from being a neutral
instrument, the expert bureaucrat is hard-wired to ethics at several
points. Behind the policy adviser's 'unflappable' demeanour and the
'frank and fearless' qualities needed to get their advice across is a whole
stoic morality. In its current concern to furnish public service with a neo-
Aristotelian theoretical foundation the philosophical literature typically
passes over the 'virtue ethics' which was actually instrumental in forming
the ethos of public service psychology (Minson 1997). It is not to the
contemplative philosopher but the man of worldly rhetorical *paideia*,
not to Aristotle but the historian/rhetor Tacitus that we should turn for
guidance on the ethical capacities and comportments needed for
state service, as did so many European soldiers, jurists, diplomats, court
officials and others in the seventeenth-century neo-stoic revival
(Oestreich 1982; Luce and Woodman 1993).

There is also what might be termed the expert official's 'duty of care
for fact'. A function of technical competence and the departmental
memory, it also requires the cultivation of an ethical comportment
which in some ways resonates with the 'ethic of responsibility' for the
actual consequences of a given policy decision which, for Weber, was
critical to one of the essential comportments of a professional politician:
'the ability to let realities work upon him with inner concentration and
calmness' (Weber 1948: 115). However, the duty of care for fact is also a
reminder that criticism of the policy/administration distinction should

not be taken to the point of denying that *one* of the policy adviser's obligations is precisely to block out political questions in order to assist the minister to be clear about the technical concomitants of policy options (Finer 1966: 272–3).

Yet this is only so *pro tem*. Equally essential in an intensely political policy-making environment is appreciation of the limited pertinence of technical facts and administratively rational planning processes. In composing a 'ministerial' briefing paper, a policy adviser is obliged to imagine how the political issue and its environment might appear both to the electorate and to the Prime Minister, and to temper their expert advice accordingly. One reason that 'the hard issues' are so hard is because there is no necessary relationship between a competent decision from a standpoint of good government, and the question of what will attract democratic support. Looking at the policy landscape through the spectacles of an 'ethic of commitment' to democratic processes (Weber 1948; Finer 1966: 251), politicians are almost morally bound to squint at what experts (including expert citizen organisations) identify as real problems, but which can only be solved by policies that run contrary to persistent majority preferences. Something akin to this sense of the difference between the respective life orders of good government and democratic politics may be what lies behind the Sims paper's enigmatic remark about advisers needing, at times, to adopt the standpoint of a 'benevolent dictator'.

Let us put some 'How' questions to this array of 'internal standards of political appropriateness'. What kind of professional character does the ability to be equal to the demands of these multiple roles require?

As our discussion of both new managerialism and the tension between the governmental and democratic aspects of policy-making suggests, the milieu of central government is a point of intersection of several ethical life orders. So, in answer to our question, a good policy adviser on this argument needs to become the kind of person who can modularise their personal dispositions (Rorty 1988: 212–28) in accordance with the plurality of status-based capacities assumed by them in these different 'life orders', that is, those appropriate to an expert agency, a democratic-political milieu, a commercial society. How is it possible to do that 'in good faith'? In the process of making private and public judgments about the advice it is prudent to 'push', one must, so to speak, 'balkanise' one's various obligations by 'regionalising their respective dominance'; and then shift from one 'relatively autonomous personal sub-system' to another (Rorty 1988: 8, 213).

To do all that requires an ethical attitude of provisional indifference to the promptings of one kind of conscience for the sake of meeting no less ethically pressing professional obligations as an expert official (or any obligation pertaining to a different life order). During the Renaissance this disposition was called *adiaphorism*, or 'the indifferent mean'. It was applied to matters of great spiritual importance (doctrinal principles, ritual forms of worship) which provoked inter-communal strife. Finding an intellectual route to treating these matters as 'things indifferent' was one of the great contributions of ethical, theological and rhetorical reflection to the centuries-long task of curtailing internecine civil warfare (Minson 1993: 166–71; see also Ian Hunter's comments in chapter 14 of this book).

Adiaphorism is not simply an idea. It is a characteristic, a rhetorical ability, which requires casuistically reframing the contentious matter in terms of, say, professional conscience and maintaining a certain composure. In its contemporary, secular professional incarnations it is linked to the better known ability to wear several 'hats' (Solomon 1993: 45). It is also, recalling Weber's words, an 'ethic of the world' which is profoundly at odds with the consistency and interactive unity of heart and mind, citizenly and official commitments, which is expected of 'authentic' moral personality. An adiaphoristic comportment is thus a political-ethical bulwark against the 'unworldly' and ultimately uncivil wish to 'establish commandments of identical content' across different life orders.[8]

It was with a view to making this discrepancy between modular and holistic ways of assuming personhood intelligible that two senses in which ethics can be 'personal' were distinguished – as expression of an individual's moral and political stance *qua* private citizen or as focus of dedication and moral energy. Pluralising moral personhood allows us to appreciate the policy adviser's 'adiaphoristic' capacity for regionalising moral agency. If this argument on the plurality of personhood is valid, then the thesis about the 'fissure' in officials' public interest responsibilities between moral and amoral trusts cannot be sustained. There are more than two kinds of role and more than one of them is of ethical significance. Equally, the element of moral agency does not only come into play in the exercise of 'independent' discretionary judgment, if by 'independence' is always meant stepping out of a subordinate role *vis-à-vis* the government. The capacity to 'accept the result' when a well thought-out policy option you care about as a citizen or specialist is overruled – to be stoically resigned rather than resigning in protest – should perhaps be seen as an honourable part of an official's professional agency, not a negation of it.

The Ethos of Office, State Interest and the New Managerialism

One question remains to be canvassed. It was telegraphed as a query about representing the 'government service' component of public service solely through the employer/employee relation and as lacking a public interest dimension. The suggestion is that an inescapable part of the ethical role of the bureaucrat, as a bureaucrat, is to serve the interests of the state, as a state.

The absence in the EARC Report of an unambiguous definition of 'the public interest' by which the exercise of bureaucratic discretion can be guided is symptomatic of the antinomies produced for moral thought by the contemporary convergence of representative government and democratic culture in the electoral sphere. An antinomy is a contradiction to which one is led by pursuing two lines of argument, both of which are equally compelling. In this instance, ethically speaking, a definition of the public servant's 'public trustee' status which is independent of the will of the government of the day and its determination of the public interest seems to be both indispensable and impossible. Foreshortening the argument, I see no way of avoiding the conclusion that a truly independent definition would entail constitutionally redefining the bureaucracy as a semi-autonomous unelected branch of government, analogous to the judiciary. Irrespective of the merits of the case, it goes against the grain of Australia's democratic-political culture – now more than ever.

Yet one is equally driven to the conclusion that there ought to be some way for both elected and appointed officials to register the difference between government actions aimed at public well-being and those aimed at party-political advantage. Otherwise the only constraints on governments' and individual politicians' actions – or grounds for responsible whistle-blowing – are a few legal limits; a severely truncated convention of ministerial responsibility; and what electorates will not put up with. What else is there, then, that might urge politicians and officials to address, for instance, social responsibilities of government about which a majority of the electorate are possibly indifferent or resentful?

A way forward might be to ask whether there is any alternative to making the inference that if the 'public interest' is to be distinguished from the interests of the government, then the meaning of the former must be spelled out in terms of the democratic entitlements of 'the people' in whom constitutional sovereignty is theoretically vested. We saw that the multiplicity of roles through which the public service performed by policy advisers is effected is based in the fact that the expert tasks, powers and responsibilities of government in a sovereign state are irreducible to democratic terms. We might also recall the allusion to the government's responsibility as a minder of civil peace. These are pointers to the possibility that the 'public interest' which the government of the day is obliged to further includes a reason-of-state component.

The ignominious reputation of *raison d'état* thought has long concealed the leading role of early modern German reason-of-state jurists

and proto-political scientists in working through the political preconditions for religious toleration in an era of incessant religious-
communitarian civil war (Ian Hunter, chapter 14 of this book). These
preconditions include the assumption that no moral or spiritual value
overrides the security of the state itself, as an entity capable of securing
civil peace among its constituent moral communities and internally
strengthening itself against external (military, economic, cultural)
threats. The maintenance of state strength, even in emergencies, at the
cost of temporarily suspending constitutional norms (Rossiter 1948),
remains the responsibility of elected governments. Here the state service
obligations of the government may point to a partly ethical (civil peace)
rationale for the priority in public service ethics given to government
officials' constitutionally subordinate role obligations over their 'private'
citizenly or communal commitments. Let us also note that the ethical
qualifications needed by rulers and their staff for orienting the state
towards this limited but basic objective of civil order historically included
the adiaphoristic capacity for regionalising obligations and comportments (Ian Hunter, chapter 14 of this book).

Not surprisingly, these *étatiste* responsibilities of administration and
policy-making are rarely alluded to in polite democratic society, let alone
in administrative ethics (see, however, Chapman 1993a; and Rohr 1989;
1996). My proposal is not meant to give public officials a licence to think
in terms of reason-of-state but to define a component of the government's 'public interest' obligations. Still, something of ethical significance may have been lost when politicians and even senior public
servants ceased thinking explicitly in terms of the broader interests of
the state in good government.[9]

How could that be? Even at its most sophisticated, reason-of-state
thought, as such, is a deliberately non-ethical way of conceiving politics.
Its sole, and if necessary ruthless, concern is with laying the political
basis for the decisional sovereignty and security of the state itself (Ian
Hunter, chapter 14 of this book). Only to the extent that beneficial
consequences are taken to be a criterion of ethical value (a contentious
claim, of course) does the reason of state tradition perhaps have, as it
were, an inadvertent footing in the ethical by virtue of dedication to the
objective of civil peace.

But a government concerned to sustain a civil order may also impose
on itself duties of care in respect to the population which extend reason-
of-state calculation. Dwelling in the pragmatic shadows (and security) of
raison d'état is a state interest in a predictable legal environment and in a
free-standing, well-educated, healthy, prosperous and (even) democratic
people. Doubtless, the rationales for these 'reason of government'[10]
duties of the state to its population, as they might be called, may be
irredeemably utilitarian (for example, construing populations as

national resources; valuing democracy as a means of information-exchange between government and governed). But this restriction of reason of government interest in our persons to limited mundane purposes is its strength: it precludes hypostatising the state as a higher moral entity with which one and all must identify. For that reason, 'reason of government' might be a key constituent of a political ethics for senior public officials; a regional and prudential ethic of civil care. I am not implying that this 'ethic of the world' should replace officials' more idealistic citizenly commitments. It might, however, afford a more appropriate idiom for expressing official concern about the social price of some new managerialist reforms than polemics against the supposed general spirit of the reforms – economic rationalism, instrumentalism, etc. – which are almost invariably predicated on a general moral politics of social renewal.

Conclusion

This has been a case-study in what a professional 'role-mentality' tells us about the political and professional ethics of government service in the challenging context of new managerialism. By focusing on bureaucrats' capacities and character *as* bureaucrats, and locating their working environment at the intersection of distinct orders of governmental and political life, this 'essay in retrieval' has sought to represent the ethos of office as an extension of the repertoire of human moral possibilities rather than as a dehumanising subtraction. The argument has concentrated on 'the moral low ground', in this instance, the rhetorical, modularising forms of moral intelligence embodied in both the subordinate and discretionary aspects of the ethos of office. If the moral uncertainties of the present-day public service milieu are to be adequately addressed, organisations have to make provision for the cultivation of this kind of worldly professional conscience.

It has also been suggested that officials' ethical abilities might include a 'reason-of-government'-based sense of state interest. To develop this suggestion further we would have to investigate the conditions under which the ethos of office and its 'reason of government' presuppose state service. Historically, objects, agencies and techniques of government which have been conceived as answering to problems of 'state strength' have not always been minded by cadres of state officials. In this way, 'reason of government' might offer another way into the issue of limits to the new managerialist predilection for 'businessing' and privatising governance.

But no matter how it is nuanced, any bulletin on the 'state service' component of public service will do little to enhance the public legitimacy of the administrative vocation. Given the prevailing moral and political atmosphere, the more one appreciates what the ethos of office involves, the more difficult it is to give it official or constitutional status. It is not easy for children of freedom to 'own' a subordinate status. Administrative discretion will always have to be exercised discreetly.

Notes

I particularly thank Howard Whitton, the main architect of the Queensland public sector reforms discussed in this paper, for making himself available for extended discussion. A version of the paper was discussed at a 'History of the Present' discussion group in London; a discussion which led me to try for a more balanced attitude to new managerialism. Finally I am indebted to editorial and substantive comments on earlier drafts from Denise Meredyth, Janice Besch Minson, David Saunders, and the editors of this volume.

1 It matters, for instance, that in Australia, a leading figure behind the original Commonwealth new public management reform agenda in the 1970s was no Mrs Thatcher but an administrative intellectual, Nugget Coombs; and that the context for the changes included the provisions for review of bureaucratic decisions in Australia's 'new administrative law' (Uhr 1994a; 1996). In Britain, by contrast, a more ideologically driven 'businessing' of the public service has been officially linked in many areas to hitherto unheard-of levels of official misconduct, maladministration and shabby profiteering on the part of public servants (House of Commons Committee of Public Accounts 1994). For an informative but pessimistic look at the implications for even a 'thin' service-wide ethic of similarly drastic reforms in New Zealand see Martin (1994).

2 'Agency heads can be expected to resist a system which threatens to steal their most experienced staff, to offer them in return appointees ignorant of the agency's background, and to "borrow" precious staff for periods of generalist training that may be a prelude to losing them' (Parker 1993: 31).

3 By comparison with some interstate initiatives, such as the anti-corruption agenda in New South Wales, the typical requirements embody an aspirational dimension which goes beyond the mere avoidance of corruption (Uhr 1994a: 553–9). For instance, the principle of 'diligence' requires officials not merely to avoid fraud, maladministration and corruption, but also to actively disclose it where known.

4 On the advantages and disadvantages of a Justinian code, as distinct from an EARC-type 'Ten Commandments' model for a code of conduct, see Kernaghan and Langford (1990: 189–90). The former, for instance, may afford officials more protection.

5 On the mnemonic-rhetorical mode of moral character-formation, see Foucault (1993).

6 The expression is Howard Whitton's.

7 For an American parallel to this notion of a legal/ethical fissure in the public official's duties, see Cooper (1991).

8 'To many, what I hail as a civilising achievement will look like a rationalisation for compliance with totalitarian regimes' (Coady 1993). On the historical relationship between the ethos of office and Nazi authoritarianism,

see Caplan (1988) on the Nazis' relentless attack on the bureaucratic procedural 'role mentality' as detracting from the holistic nature of human personality . . . and as incompatible with the Führer principle.

9 For an early twentieth-century example of a senior Australian educational administrator's use of the idiom of the state's interest as a state, see Meredyth (1997) on the progressive educational thinking of Peter Board.

10 I am indebted to Ian Hunter for suggesting this formulation.

References

Bagehot, W., [1867] 1974. *The English Constitution*, London: Oxford University Press.

Barzelay, Michael, 1992. *Breaking Through Bureaucracy*, Berkeley: University of California Press.

Campbell, Colin S. J., 1993. 'Public service and democratic accountability' in Richard Chapman (ed.), *Ethics in Public Service*, Edinburgh: Edinburgh University Press.

Caplan, Jane, 1988. *Government without Administration: State and Civil Service in Weimar and Nazi Germany*, Oxford: Clarendon.

Chapman, Richard (ed.), 1988. *Ethics in the British Civil Service*, Edinburgh: Edinburgh University Press.

Chapman, Richard, 1993a. 'Reason of state and the public interest' in Richard Chapman (ed.), *Ethics in Public Service*, Edinburgh: Edinburgh University Press.

Chapman, Richard, 1993b. 'Ethics in public service' in Richard Chapman (ed.), *Ethics in Public Service*, Edinburgh: Edinburgh University Press.

Coady, Anthony, 1993. 'Ethos and ethics in business' in Anthony Coady and Charles Sampford (eds), *Business, Ethics and the Law*, Annandale, NSW: Federation Press.

Considine, Mark, 1994. *Public Policy: a Critical Approach*, Melbourne: Macmillan.

Cooper, Terry, 1991. *An Ethic of Citizenship for Public Administration*, Englewood Cliffs, N.J.: Prentice Hall.

Dugay, Paul, 1994. 'Making up managers: bureaucracy, enterprise and the liberal art of separations', *British Journal of Sociology* 45, 4: 655–74.

Dugay, Paul, 1996. 'Office as a vocation: bureaucracy but not as we know it', Australian Key Centre for Cultural and Media Policy, Cultural Policy Paper Series, Griffith University.

(EARC) Electoral and Administrative Review Committee, 1992. *Report on the Review of Codes of Conduct for Public Officials*, Brisbane, Goprint.

Evans, H., 1982. 'Australia and the "Westminster system"', *Table (Journal of the Society of Clerks-at-the-Table in Commonwealth Parliaments)* 50: 48–51.

Finer, Herman, 1966. 'Administrative responsibility in democratic government' in P. Woll (ed.), *Public Administration and Policy: Selected Essays*, New York: Harper.

Finn, Paul, 1990. 'Myths of Australian public administration' in J. Power (ed.), *Australian Public Administration*, Sydney: Hale & Iremonger.

Finn, Paul, 1993. 'The law and officials' in Richard Chapman (ed.), *Ethics in Public Service*, Edinburgh: Edinburgh University Press.

Foucault, Michel, 1993. 'About the beginning of the hermeneutics of the self: two lectures at Dartmouth', *Political Theory* 21, 2: 198–227.

Foucault, Michel, 1987. *The Use of Pleasure*, Harmondsworth: Penguin.

Fulton Committee, 1968. *The Civil Service, Vol. 1: Report of the Committee*, London: Her Majesty's Stationery Office.

House Of Commons Committee Of Public Accounts, 1994. *Eighth Report: The Proper Conduct of Public Business*, London: Her Majesty's Stationery Office.

Hunter, Ian, 1993/94. 'Bureaucrat, critic, citizen: on some styles of ethical life', *Arena* 2: 77–101.

Ives, Dennis, 1996. 'Ethics and accountability in the Australian Public Service: the new professionalism' in John Uhr (ed.), *Ethical Practice In Government: Improving Organisational Management*, Canberra: Australian National University, Federalism Research Centre.

Jackson, Michael, 1987. 'Official conduct or moral conduct?', *Canberra Bulletin of Public Administration*, October: 83–5.

Kernaghan, Kenneth and Langford, John, 1990. *The Responsible Civil Servant*, Halifax, Nova Scotia: L'Institute Recherches Politiques.

Longstaff, Simon, 1994. 'What is ethics education and training?' in Noel Preston (ed.), *Ethics For the Public Sector: Education and Training*, Annandale, NSW: Federation Press.

Luce, T. J. and Woodman, A. J., (eds), 1993. *Tacitus and the Tacitean Tradition*, Princeton: Princeton University Press.

Manin, Bernard, 1994. 'The metamorphoses of representative government', *Economy and Society* 23, 2: 133–71.

Martin, John, 1994. 'The New Zealand experience' in N. Preston (ed.), *Ethics For the Public Sector: Education and Training*, Annandale, NSW: Federation Press.

Meredyth, Denise, 1997. 'Invoking citizenship: education, competence and social rights', *Economy and Society* 26, 2: 273–95.

Minson, Jeffrey, 1993. *Questions of Conduct: Sexual Harassment, Citizenship, Government*, London: Macmillan.

Minson, Jeffrey, 1997. In Clare O'Farrell (ed.), *Michel Foucault: The Legacy*, Brisbane: QUT Press.

Oestreich, Gerhard, 1982. *Neostoicism and the Early Modern State*, Cambridge: Cambridge University Press.

Parker, R. S., 1993. *The Administrative Vocation: Selected Essays Of R. S. Parker*, ed. J. Uhr, Marrickville, NSW: Hale & Iremonger.

Peters, T., 1989. *Thriving On Chaos*. London: Macmillan.

Peters, T., 1992. *Liberation Management*. London: Macmillan.

Preston, Noel, 1995. 'What is the basis for public sector ethics?' in Seamas Miller (ed.), *Professional Ethics*, Riverina, Victoria: Charles Sturt University, School of Humanities and Social Sciences.

Preston, Noel, 1996. 'Presidential address to the Australian Association for Professional and Applied Ethics', *AAPAE Newsletter* 2, 3: 3–4.

Public Service Commission, 1995. *Guidelines on Official Conduct of Commonwealth Public Servants*, Canberra: AGPS.

Queensland Public Sector Ethics Act 1994, Act no. 67 of 1994.

Rohr, John, 1978. *Ethics For Bureaucrats*, New York: Dekker.

Rohr, John, 1986. *To Run a Constitution*, University Press of Kansas.

Rohr, John, 1989. 'Reason of state as political morality: a benign view' in N. Dale Wright (ed.), *Papers on the Ethics of Administration*, Provo, Utah: Brigham Young University.

Rohr, John, 1996. 'What a difference a state makes: reflections on governance in France' in Gary Walmsley and James Wolf (eds), *Refounding Democratic Public Administration: Modern Paradoxes, Postmodern Challenges*, London: Sage.

Rorty, Amelie, 1988. *Thought in Action*, Boston: Beacon Press.

Rose, Nikolas, 1992. 'Governing the enterprising self' in Paul Heelas and Paul Morris (eds), *The Values of the Enterprise Culture: the Moral Debate*, London: Routledge.

Rose, Nikolas, 1996. 'The death of the social? Re-figuring the territory of government', *Economy and Society* 25, 3: 327–56.

Rossiter, Clinton, 1948. *Constitutional Dictatorship: Crisis Government in the Modern Democracies*, Princeton: Princeton University Press.

Sampford, Charles, 1994. 'Institutionalising public sector ethics' in N. Preston (ed.), *Ethics For the Public Sector: Education and Training*, Annandale, NSW: Federation Press.

Sims, R., 1993. 'Policy advising in the Department of Prime Minister and Cabinet: how the Department adds value', unpublished manuscript.

Solomon, Robert, 1993. 'Corporate roles, personal virtues, moral mazes' in Anthony Coady and Charles Sampford (eds), *Business, Ethics and the Law*, Annandale, NSW: Federation Press.

Summers, Ian, 1996. 'The audit of empowerment' in John Uhr (ed.), *Ethical Practice In Government: Improving Organisational Management*, Canberra, Australian National University, Federalism Research Centre.

Thomas, R., 1989. *The British Philosophy Of Administration*, Cambridge: Centre For Business and Public Sector Ethics.

Thompson, Dennis, 1992. 'The possibility of administrative ethics' in Peter Madsen and Jay Shafitz (eds), *Essentials of Government Ethics*, New York: Meridian.

Uhr, John, 1988. 'Ethics and public service', *Australian Journal of Public Administration* 47, 2: 109–18.

Uhr, John, 1990. 'Ethics in government: public service issues', Discussion Paper No.19, Australian National University Graduate Program in Public Policy.

Uhr, John, 1993. 'Redesigning accountability: from muddles to maps', *Australian Quarterly* 65, 2: 1–16.

Uhr, John, 1994a. 'Public service ethics in Australia' in Terry Cooper (ed.), *Handbook of Administrative Ethics*, New York: M. Dekker.

Uhr, John, 1994b. 'Managing the process of ethics training' in N. Preston (ed.), *Ethics For the Public Sector: Education and Training.*, Annandale, NSW: Federation Press.

Uhr, John, 1996. 'From merit to multiculturalism' in J. Uhr (ed.), *Ethical Practice In Government: Improving Organisational Management*, Canberra, Australian National University, Federalism Research Centre.

Walzer, Michael, 1970. *Obligations: Essays on War, Disobedience and Citizenship*, Cambridge, Mass.: Harvard University Press.

Weber, Max, 1948. 'Politics as a vocation' in H. H. Gerth and C. W. Mills (eds), *From Max Weber: Essays in Sociology*, London: Routledge & Kegan Paul.

Weber, Max, 1968. *Economy and Society*, Berkeley: University of California Press.

Yeatman, Anna, 1997. 'Contract, status and personhood' in Glyn Davis, Barbara Sullivan and Anna Yeatman (eds), *Contractualism as an Organising Principle in Public Life*, London: Macmillan.

Zifcak, S., 1994. *New Managerialism: Administrative Reform In Whitehall And Canberra*, Buckingham: Open University Press.

CHAPTER 4

Bad Habits or Bad Conscience?
Sexual Harassment in the Australian Defence Force

Alison Smith

Since the Australian colonies took responsibility for their defence forces in 1870 there has been a steady industry of concern around the problems of recruiting, training and improving these forces. The years 1987 to 1997 have proved no exception, with the publication of five major reviews considering different facets of the management of the Australian Defence Force (ADF).[1] One of the most recent and most interesting of these governmental problems raised in relation to the Australian military has concerned the problem of sexual harassment and its elimination.

This chapter considers the way in which this problem of sexual harassment has been addressed as a governmental problem by looking at a report by the Senate Standing Committee on Foreign Affairs Defence and Trade entitled *Sexual Harassment in the Australian Defence Force: Facing the Future Together* (hereafter, 'Report') released in 1994. How the Report establishes and resolves issues around sexual harassment is considered in the light of earlier governmental problems posed by military forces, in order to sketch an outline of the military habitus, and to suggest the limitations of the contemporary approach to governing the military. The term 'habitus' is borrowed from Pierre Bourdieu, to direct our attention to both the environment and the attitudes and conducts that are generated by and supported by that environment (Bourdieu 1977). My argument is that the Senate committee fails to address conduct as a practical problem in its own right, because it dismisses the possibility that certain behaviours could be the outcome of a professional ethos which equips military personnel for service in a particular habitat. This leads the committee to misunderstand or ignore the ways in which people have learnt to conduct themselves in the specialised environment of the warship, and to propose the establishment of a new ethos in the Navy which may sit uncomfortably, and unsuccessfully, with the old.

The Problem of Sexual Harassment in the ADF

In September 1993 the Senate Standing Committee on Foreign Affairs, Defence and Trade was asked to examine the nature and incidence of sexual harassment generally in the ADF, and to inquire specifically into several allegations of sexual harassment of a female medical officer and two female leading seamen aboard the Destroyer Escort HMAS *Swan* during a deployment to South-East Asia in 1992. The committee heard evidence from a wide range of sources, including the Royal Australian Navy, Army and Air Force. It sought both to deliberate on the circumstances of the particular cases aboard HMAS *Swan*, and their subsequent handling by the Navy, and to set in train a broad strategy for eliminating sexual harassment throughout the ADF.

In its final report the committee endorsed the strategies that the Navy had put in place since the incidents occurring aboard HMAS *Swan*, particularly the 'Good Working Relationships' project, with its 'long-term aim . . . to bring about a cultural change in the [Navy], one aspect of which is a change from the norm of an all male workplace to a mixed gender workplace' (Report 1994: 279). The longer-term cultural change is the aim of a three-part strategy: an extensive awareness-raising program, elements of which should be included in all training courses; a better developed and resourced network of personnel to monitor and assist in cases of sexual harassment; and revision to sexual harassment legislation towards closer definition of sexual harassment and greater emphasis on the local resolution of problems as they arise.

While the Senate committee was supportive of the changes the Navy had already introduced to address sexual harassment, it was concerned to draw a sharp distinction between attitudinal change and behavioural change, arguing that:

> To bring about changes in behaviour it is not enough . . . to issue edicts, particularly when those edicts try to deal with an area as sensitive, complex and personal as sexual harassment, or harassment of any kind . . . A far more sophisticated approach, involving awareness raising and support mechanisms and a variety of conflict resolution mechanism[s] must be put in place if *genuine* attitudinal and behavioural change is to be achieved (Report 1994: 121, emphasis added).

Indeed, the Report goes on to say that 'Without a genuine change in attitude, an environment of constant policing and punishment of offenders is unlikely to produce a healthy and productive workplace' (Report 1994: p. 25).

The committee's concerns over an environment of constant policing are curious, given that the sum of its own recommendations is an extraordinarily extensive apparatus for monitoring and investigating sexual harassment. The 'monitorial' aspects of the reform package include the provision of a confidential toll-free telephone advisory service for complaints outside the immediate chain of command, better complaints procedures and disciplinary sanctions, reporting requirements both during and at the end of sea-postings for women, the creation of a confidential database to monitor trends and identify repeated perpetrators of sexual harassment, and the use of a private consultancy firm to monitor the success of the whole gender-integration program, of which the policy on sexual harassment forms only one part.

The reason that the committee does not see this monitorial apparatus as one of constant policing is the focus on attitude. The right sort of attitude, on the part of both women and men, will mean that, in time, such an apparatus will rarely be used, and then its proper use will be understood by both the person harassing and the person harassed. This is because any harassment will be dealt with early on, locally, and resolved to the satisfaction of both parties. The emphasis on attitude, on the personal capacities of the individuals working in the ADF, is drawn from, and reinforced by, the committee's assessment of the particular cases of sexual harassment it had to address, and especially from its detailed consideration of the experiences of the medical officer aboard HMAS *Swan*.

The medical officer had joined the ship at relatively short notice after the rest of the crew had completed a series of 'work-up' exercises in preparation for a two-month deployment to South-East Asia. Though a Naval Reserve officer for some time, the medical officer had never been to sea for any length of time prior to her posting to HMAS *Swan*. The committee describes her 'seasickness, her inadequate training and preparation for service at sea and what she describes as the hostility she felt in the wardroom' as evidence of her unfamiliarity with the physical, social and professional demands of 'ship-board life' (Report 1994: 196). The committee sought to set the medical officer's allegations of harassment in context by contrasting her experiences with those of others, particularly women officers and medical officers. After hearing that these officers had also experienced a degree of hostility when initially posted, which they had by various means sought to overcome, the committee concluded that the medical officer's experience of harassment was, in part, her responsibility: 'An important factor in the way the situation developed in the *Swan* wardroom was Dr Wheat's poor handling of behaviour she did not like' (Report 1994: 203).

In contrast to the negative view of the capacities of the medical officer, the committee constructed a composite picture of the ideal naval person with the right sort of attitudes, who will live within the new naval culture. In part, this composite is formed out of the qualities of those personnel the committee felt had learnt to fit in. The committee supported the approach taken by the Navy in carefully selecting those women who would be 'pioneers' in the early days of integrating female personnel aboard ships. In addition to awareness-raising and the setting of standards, 'it is also sensible, in the Committee's view, for the managers in the Navy to take special care in selecting appropriate people at this early stage of the integration process' (Report 1994: 58). Appropriate personnel are generally those with a capacity to tolerate a certain degree of 'initial resistance' when they are posted. They also have the capacity to quickly and unequivocally address any behaviour they find to be unacceptable, and to be alert to and concerned about the possibility that others might be being harassed.

Despite the committee's recommendations concerning the introduction of extensive awareness-raising seminars for all personnel, it is not clear whether the committee anticipates that the sort of people it feels will be well-suited to service in the military will be developed through the awareness training package or recruited. In drawing lessons about what constitutes appropriate and effective attitudes and behaviours the committee appeared to feel that 'successful' personnel had these qualities despite their previous training and any experiences of harassment. For example, the committee noted that the women officers-under-training at sea under the same circumstances as the medical officer who was harassed were not offended by the behaviour of their male colleagues on board, and in fact it comments that: '[One of these officers] had the "*advantage*" of having experienced the rigours of the Defence Force Academy, where, by all accounts the situations confronting women in the early years were more challenging and difficult than anything that happened in the *Swan* wardroom' (Report 1994: 206).

A male doctor gave evidence to the committee of joining HMAS *Swan* for an earlier deployment and being subject to continuous harassment, until he took someone aside and 'told him to pull his head in'. Another witness to the committee told of how she 'always met with a certain resistance initially' but overcame this. The committee goes on to conclude from these examples that 'the important point to make is that nipping sexual harassment in the bud by confronting it as early in the piece as possible and directly at the personal level if at all possible, is the most successful strategy in most cases' (Report 1994: 207). In its cataloguing of personnel who have been able to integrate themselves successfully in a potentially hostile work environment the committee glosses over the range of capacities necessary to achieve this integration, and it assumes too hurriedly that these capacities necessarily follow from having the right attitude. It also ignores the 'costs' that might be borne in developing such capacities. This includes investigating the 'challenging and difficult situations' experienced by men and women at training institutions such as the Australian Defence Force Academy.

Governmental Approaches to the Problem of Sexual Harassment in the ADF

The committee did not consider in any great detail the many references to a broader 'culture' of harassment raised in a number of submissions and, indeed, at a number of points noted that it found itself unable to consider in any detail whether there were particular aspects of military service which affected the issue of sexual harassment (Report 1994: 50, 304–7). The committee did emphatically disagree with a submission from the Returned Services League which said that:

> war is a brutalising experience, and it follows that training for war is also brutalising, to a degree . . . to recruit and train a military force on the one hand, and then recoil in horror when its members occasionally exhibit unseemly aggression or even brutality towards one another, is either deceitful or stupid. (Report 1994: 306)

and pointed to evidence taken from the ADF which insisted that the military actively discouraged recruitment of 'Rambo-types' (Report 1994: 307).

The committee's indifference to the role of training and the peculiarities of the military habitus is consistent with the way in which it privileges the importance of attitudinal change over changes to behaviour in its strategies for eliminating sexual harassment. The focus on attitudinal change is typical of what Nikolas Rose and others have described in their assessments of 'advanced liberal' modes of government, which vest authority in forms of expertise which configure governable relations in a psychological register; a therapeutic authority which 'visualises human encounters in terms of the psychological relations within and between individuals' (Rose and Miller 1994: 60). Within this register, the non-psychological means of governing characteristic of military forces are considered to be crude and ineffectual for achieving, in the committee's words, genuine change. Rather than considering the extent to which some of these traditional behaviourally-based techniques may have worked in addressing a problem like sexual harassment, the committee looks to having the ADF adopt a set of psychologically-based techniques for developing 'work-life quality' already tried and executed in a variety of settings, including large private sector organisations. The 'Good Working Relationships' project put together for the Navy was developed by a firm of consultants which has had considerable experience in both the public and private sector developing affirmative action, work-based childcare and anti-discrimination strategies for a number of large organisations.

The adoption of psychologically-based expertise to address military problems has been a frequent tactic of government throughout the twentieth century (Rose 1990). This has been the case in Australia also, though on a smaller scale than in either Britain or the United States. Psychologists were employed by the Navy, Army and Air Force during the Second World War to develop and carry out selection testing, and all three services continue to employ psychologists to assist not only with selection, but also with counselling military personnel and conducting a variety of questionnaires on matters affecting morale.[2] Since the First World War, when natural talent was seen to have been more crucial to success than the benefits of training, discipline and hierarchy, and limited expenditure on military forces has kept them to an 'expansion base', government has taken a somewhat modular approach to the formation and maintenance of military forces, assuming that individuals would quickly group together to form the larger units necessary only in wartime (Gammage 1988; Grey 1990). This economical approach to the maintenance of military forces was fertile ground for the ameliorative assistance provided by psychology in selecting personnel for specific jobs, and in providing a therapeutic environment in which to build a bridge back to civilian life. Psychology was able to construct a new way of approaching the governmental issues associated with managing military populations, through the concentration on group, 'social' or 'human' relations and the manner in which individuals resolved personal conflicts (Rose 1990: 48).

However, it should not be assumed that other, non-psychological means of addressing the 'conduct of conduct' did not continue within military forces. The role of psychologists has largely been a therapeutic one; such expertise does not appear to have had a marked influence on the formation and conduct of the military 'style of life'. The approach to the problem of sexual harassment within the ADF, for example, has been to address it within the register of acceptable behaviours, akin to the problems of fraternisation or insubordination. Moreover, while recruitment advertisements for the ADF, and particularly the Army Reserve, emphasise the extent to which service will make one a better person, this sits alongside an emphasis on what the Navy calls 'character training', conducted under the auspices of the chaplaincy. In this training, 'character is understood to be the whole of what one is as a person, as evidenced by consistent behaviour'; the training includes the inculcation of behaviours that are consistent with the 'specific needs of Navy society and convention', as well as the development of automatic responses that 'do not require the application of reason', training in skills, techniques and habits, and education to develop understanding (Royal Australian Navy 1993: 70).

As already noted, the committee gave considerably more weight to examining the attitudes of military personnel than it did to looking to the trained behaviours and forms of professional ethical comportment with which it was presented. In so doing, the committee was unable to grasp the extent to which certain behaviours or conduct might be the deliberate outcome of a professional ethos peculiar to military personnel that equips them for service in the conditions of a regiment or in the confines of a warship. Parts of such an ethos might easily be dismissed as sexism, and as anachronistic enthusiasm for hierarchy; but parts might also prove to have a certain salience that could act as a resource, or as a blockage, to the governmental aspirations for the elimination of sexual harassment. For these reasons, there might be governmental advantages in acknowledging and examining the contours of such an ethos.

Outlining a Military Ethos

The outlines of this professional ethos can be glimpsed in the struggles to challenge organisational and disciplinary practices in the military waged throughout the last three centuries. An early example of the central themes of this struggle is documented by Norbert Elias in his studies of the seventeenth-century British Navy, where 'one of the gravest practical problems confronting naval administration and naval officers' was that of overcoming the ethical difficulties associated with requiring gentlemen officers to acquire some mastery of the art of sailing and navigating ships (Elias 1950: 294). Gentlemen naval officers could not learn the technical aspects of sailing without risking their status as gentlemen, and seamen could not aspire to be gentlemen officers as they had, through their manual labour, excluded themselves from the ranks of gentlemen. This ethical dilemma exercised naval administrators for more than two centuries, and in both the Navy and the Army the 'technical' limitations imposed by respecting the ethos of the gentleman were regularly part of governmental calculation.

In the Navy, gentlemen officers gradually acquired some of the technical skills associated with sailing and navigation, but in ways which acknowledged the continuing status of the gentleman and maintained the distinction between gentlemen and masters (Elias 1950). By the early nineteenth century there remained a sharp distinction between the executive and the other officers and seamen aboard Her Majesty's ships, including in the maintenance of separate messes for the differing groups. In a series of inquiries spanning the nineteenth century, the British Admiralty sought to diminish the distinctions between the executive officers and the ships' masters and engineers, but was continually stymied by arguments against the integration of these officers which turned precisely on the ethical capacity of the masters and engineers to undertake the duties of the executive officer and to join the executive officers' wardroom. Similarly, a central question for Army administration in the nineteenth century concerned the optimisation of officer recruitment and training, and was always cast in terms of the best means of securing the governmental benefits of gentlemen officers while seeking to improve these gentlemen's technical capacity for waging war and managing regiments.[3] In the various Admiralty and parliamentary investigations into military administration in the nineteenth century the existence, utility and permanence of the gentleman officer ethos is a crucial part of any governmental calculation for improving the Navy and the Army, and operated as the standard up to which any other aspiring officer must eventually be brought.[4]

This ethos, at least as it operated during the eighteenth and nineteenth centuries, had at least two distinct components that are germane to the discussion of the contemporary ADF. The first of these was the maintenance of a social and physical detachment from one's subordinates in order to effect command. This is achieved by the physical distance of the officer from his men, in terms of the location and quality of accommodation, and by the maintenance of a social distinction in manner, and a training in detachment from the affairs of those under his command; as the Duke of Wellington explained, the British officer was *not* 'friend, companion and adviser' to his men (Wellington 1959). That pastoral function was performed by the non-commissioned officers. This detachment that characterised the officer from his men is the measure that the executive officers of the mid-nineteenth century Navy used against the engineer officers, and the gentlemen officers of prestigious regiments used against the recruitment of officers from the ranks, to great effect. Engineers worked below decks with their men and were thought to 'encourage informal connections' which would compromise their leadership ability.[5] Moreover, as the engineers entered the Navy through selection rather than nomination by the Admiralty Board, and were usually the sons of dockyard workers and seamen, it was felt that 'Their antecedents and their connections must to a certain extent lower their social bearing', thus diminishing their disciplinary capacity, for 'as they become officers, it is not fair to these boys, or to the Service, or to those with whom they will have to mess in after years as they rise in position' that they should be so closely connected to those they would command.[6]

In investigations into the discipline and training of the Army throughout the nineteenth century, the disciplinary advantages of the class distinctions between officers and men were always reiterated. In a characteristic statement in 1857 Sidney Herbert told the House of Commons that 'one of the main elements in the spirit of obedience in our army is, that the peasantry, from whom the private soldier is drawn, has a natural tendency to follow the lead of the gentleman from whose class the officer is drawn'.[7] Non-commissioned officers who sought to become officers were considered to have the disciplinary advantage of being familiar with the artifices of the men, but were generally held in contempt by the men for their 'unkind and harsh manner'.[8]

The second component of the ethos is that which fits the officer for the company of his fellow officers. While various governments sought for some twenty years in the mid-nineteenth century to introduce a system of officer recruitment and promotion to replace the practice of purchasing commissions, regimental officers themselves ensured that regiments did not recruit men they did not consider gentlemen. In certain prestigious regiments men needed to have considerable private incomes in order to afford the lifestyle expected of officers of the regiment; a private income also ensured that the officer was likely to have been educated at a public school and to be familiar with the manners and social pursuits enjoyed by the other officers of the regiment. Men whose incomes and social capacities were found wanting were bullied by their fellow officers until they resigned their commissions.[9]

An Admiralty committee inquiring into the best means of developing mechanical skill and scientific knowledge in the Navy in 1877 noted that:

> we are met, at the outset of the enquiry by a defect of much importance . . . [while] it is undoubtedly desirable that Officers should be highly educated to perform the duties of naval engineers, . . . it is equally desirable that they should be in all respects fitted to take their place with officers of corresponding rank in the . . . messes.[10]

If this seems a quaintly nineteenth-century concern, it was still present in the early twentieth century, when, after a fifty-year campaign to integrate the engineers and executive officers, the First Lord of the Admiralty noted, in the face of the paradox of executive officers who lacked technical knowledge and engineer officers who lacked 'character', that 'if I had to choose I would rather retain the [Navy as a] school for character, than run the risk of losing it by unwise attempts to improve the Navy as a machine for acquiring knowledge'.[11]

Ethics and Government

As we noted above, there has been a significant shift in the way in which military forces have come to be managed since the beginning of the twentieth century. One of the consequences of the employment of the mobile, economical and efficient therapeutic expertise of advanced liberalism is that it limits the interest shown by government in the subject-forming capacities of specific sites, particularly where part of that formation might inculcate deliberate subordination and role-playing. The governmental potential of psychology in the management of military forces during and after the Second World War lay in its ability to provide a therapeutic environment in which people 'returned to normal' precisely by leaving the confines of military subordination and status behind. As we can see from the Australian Senate's consideration of the problem of sexual harassment, governmental consideration no longer includes the kind of detailed assessment of the military ethos found in the nineteenth century.

No doubt there is much of that ethos that has undergone change – in part, because there has been a considerable change both in the composition of the military, and in the fortunes of a 'gentlemanly ethos' upon which the nineteenth-century military ethos drew. For example, in the Australian military there were explicit attempts in the early years of the twentieth century to 'democratise' officer cadet training by paying cadets a small salary in order to limit the extent to which the officer corps was a sort of club only for those with private means (Heydon 1965: 58); and there was much about the way in which the British gentleman officer led his men that Australian officers rejected (Chapman 1975: 116). However, while elements of that ethos may have been refashioned, there is no reason to suppose that an ethos of military office has disappeared entirely. Indeed, numerous examples of 'democratic' reform in the government of officer corps, in particular, can have the effect of heightening the demand for a distinctive ethos. Prefiguring reforms to the British Army by some seventy years, the Prussian military reformer Scharnhorst sought to remove the aristocratic monopoly on officer commissions, and to introduce standardisation of tenure, promotion and remuneration. In the course of these reforms the administration of the Prussian Army was decentralised, and the officers themselves were charged with self-regulation. As Hans Rosenberg notes, this 'process of internal democratisation' 'in fact resulted in a tightening up of aristocratic *esprit de corps* . . . by preserving the social structure and mentality of the professional military caste as an exclusive caste of cavaliers in uniform' (Rosenberg 1958: 216–17). Similar consequences accompanied the abolition of the practice of purchasing commissions in the British Army after 1870, when the governmental strategy of administrative decentralisation enhanced the importance of the regiment as the focus of an officer's career.[12] Individual regiments became very jealous of their reputations, and sought to develop distinctive styles and vigorous support from their officers and men, becoming a much less diffuse and thus more effective source of ethical training than the more generalised ethic of the gentleman could ever be (Keegan 1976).

There is much in the Australian Senate Report into sexual harassment in the ADF that suggests that aspects of the sexual harassment experienced by the medical officer could be recast as a kind of formulaic initiation test into the ethos of the naval wardroom. Further, the sort of 'personal competence' demonstrated by various other military witnesses might stand as good examples of the sort of detachment necessary to such a 'style of living'. In certain respects the committee's questioning of other witnesses to determine whether they had experienced similar harassment recalls that of the nineteenth-century inquiries into the integration of engineers in the British Navy: a picture of the 'habitus' begins to emerge. Only in the twentieth-century case is the governmental focus on the adaptability of the individual person, the human relations between members of a group (Rose 1990: 48; Rose and Miller 1994: 60); the salience of the ethos, the character of officers and the particular demands of the military habitus as a governmental concern has faded. Thus, the 'advanced liberal' focus of the Senate committee cannot grasp the extent to which there is a particular habitus, which acts on the individual bodily, habitually, and in which the criteria for successful integration might include cultivating a distinct lack of attitude.

There are at least two consequences of the committee's approach which are pertinent to the future government of the military. The first of these is that aspects of the way in which people conduct themselves, and have learned to conduct themselves in environments like wardrooms, are misunderstood or ignored. The second consequence is that the ideal person whom the committee hopes will come to populate the Navy and the Army and Air Force may be expected to operate in accordance with a new ethos which sits uncomfortably with the old. The combined effect of these problems has meant that the comprehensive 'work-life quality' program instituted by the Navy, for example, is seen by most as a specific set of measures introduced to help address the problem of sexual harassment – a problem that only occurs where women are employed, and where those women have not developed their own psychological capacities for addressing any 'challenges' in the work environment they may meet.[13] As the basis of a new ethos for the military, the committee's recommendations are yet to make their mark.

What the historical examples are intended to suggest, in part, is that there might (still) be governmental advantage in considering the habitus – the habit-forming environment in which military personnel live and work – as something more substantial, more engaging; as Elias puts it, as a *practical* problem for government to solve (Elias 1951: 294). For example, the committee had considerable evidence from witnesses and from the Navy's own Board of Inquiry investigation that the sort of harassing behaviour exhibited in the wardroom was not infrequently characteristic of officers of a certain age and seniority. The committee looked at the evidence of a number of witnesses which established a certain pattern to wardroom life, not in order to investigate that pattern but rather to use it to throw into relief the experience of the female medical officer. She stood out for her lack of competence in dealing with the apparently formulaic harassment experienced by newcomers joining the wardroom, while the habitus of which the harassment formed a part did not (Report 1994: 192–206). As a consequence, the equally habituated manner in which 'successful' Navy personnel dealt with harassment was taken as evidence of their 'attitude to life in the services which is both fostered and expected by the services' (Report 1994: 206), though it might equally be argued that the success lay in *not* having an attitude, but rather the sort of detachment and ability to mix with one's fellows that comes with suspending judgment and engaging in highly ritualised and non-personal conduct for the greater good of wardroom harmony. Success is the result of having certain social skills which can be exercised without necessarily having to address a 'deeper layer' of attitudes.

Similarly, not addressing the form and substance of an existing military ethos is likely to place limits on a key part of the committee's reform strategy, in which those with a raised awareness of the problem of sexual harassment will exercise a pastoral responsibility for others who might be at risk of harassment. For example, in mounting its case against the severity of the harassment experienced by the female medical officer, Dr Wheat, the committee was critical of her failure to take a greater interest in the other women sailors aboard HMAS *Swan* at the time:

> It is, in the Committee's view important to note that, despite her subsequent allegations about the unacceptable behaviour she herself was subjected to, Dr Wheat at no stage sought to inquire whether the female sailors may have been experiencing similar difficulties. It seems to the Committee reasonable for [the captain] to have expected that, following his request that Dr Wheat should make herself available to the female sailors, she would actively seek to establish if they, too, were experiencing any difficulties, and let him know if there were any difficulties not being resolved adequately at the Divisional level. (Report 1994: 161)

What should we make of this expectation and the committee's conclusion that perhaps the medical officer's experience of harassment was questionable since she did not use this experience to heighten her concern for other female personnel aboard? Given other evidence before the committee, it suggests the expectation that women will play an active role and make a 'personal commitment' in monitoring any possible harassment, using informal as well as formal channels. To stick to formal, and therefore to 'reactive', channels is to demonstrate a certain degree of defectiveness, as though there is a certain part of the personality that is underdeveloped. In this vein, 'well adjusted, aware' women bring a particular form of expertise that can flatten out the hierarchies established to deal with problems, casting their gaze around the ship and taking a personal interest in their fellow crew members. Over time, it is the expectation that men, with the benefit of the seminars on sexual harassment, will change their attitudes and develop similar capacities. Thus, the sort of reforms that the committee is advocating create a particular burden for women, who are charged, with their 'empathetic' skills, to be the principal vehicles in the monitoring and pastoral aspects of the reform strategy. In bearing this pastoral responsibility individuals are being asked to work against the disciplinary habitus of the ADF, which requires officers to learn to place limits on the interest they take in their personal circumstances and in the affairs of their peers and subordinates, and to use well-recognised systems of communication within the organisation. Many women officers may find it difficult to take on these new tasks, and the new ways of conducting themselves in relation to peers and subordinates, if these new ways will work to undermine aspects of the ethos they share with other officers and which guide them in the greater part of their everyday interactions with subordinates.

Conclusion

The package of reforms that the Senate committee seeks to put into place to address the problem of sexual harassment in the ADF is exemplary of the sort of therapeutic approach to governmental problems analysed by Nikolas Rose and Peter Miller and others. In the committee's enthusiasm for 'genuine attitudinal change' we can see the ways in which it expects that a therapeutic approach will 'make the new opportunities work for both men and women' (Report 1994: ix). As Rose and Miller put it, 'The relations that link one individual to another in the workplace . . . are thus perceived as if with new eyes. The very bonds that link individuals together undergo a metamorphosis' (Rose and Miller 1994: 59). At least, this is the governmental expectation.

I have suggested that this expectation may be met only partially, because the way in which the governmental problem is formulated gives insufficient attention to the possibilities that there is a distinctive ethos governing conduct in the military which may act as a practical limitation to the metamorphosis the Senate committee is seeking to engender. With the 'new eyes' with which the committee looks at the problem of sexual harassment, and the integration of women into the ADF more generally, the habitual behaviours which may equip women (and men) to negotiate their acceptance into a wardroom but which may leave aside addressing whether everyone really wants them there will be inadequate. What formerly counted as success may no longer be seen as such, and social relations in the workplace will need to be renegotiated with the assistance of a raised awareness. If the committee had been able to give some countenance to the form and substance of the military habitus it might have found that awareness-raising sat uncomfortably with an ethos of detachment, and that the adoption of better attitudes could be the kind of practical governmental problem of which eighteenth- and nineteenth-century administrators were all too aware.

Notes

I would like to thank Barry Hindess, Mitchell Dean and Denise Meredyth, and Jeffrey Minson in particular, for their help in thinking through many of the issues discussed in this paper.
 1 Joint Committee on Foreign Affairs, Defence and Trade (1987; 1988); Wrigley (1990); Senate Standing Committee on Foreign Affairs, Defence and Trade (1994); Personnel Policy Strategy Review Team (1995).
 2 See Rose (1958). A good example of the range of services that psychologists do and could provide the ADF is contained in Joint Committee on Foreign Affairs, Defence and Trade (1988).
 3 See the discussion of the effects of this ethos on the development of tactics in the British Army in the nineteenth century in Strachan (1985), especially chapter 3.
 4 See, for example, the discussions in: (1836) Report of Commissioners Inquiring into Military Punishments; (1857) Report of the Commissioners appointed to inquire into the purchase of Commissions in the Army; (1868–69) Report of the Royal Commission appointed to inquire into the constitution and practice of Courts-Martial in the Army, and the present system of punishment for military offences (Two Reports); (1876) Report of Royal Commission on Army Promotion and Retirement; (1866) Report of an Admiralty Committee on the Position of Masters in the Royal Navy; (1877) Report of an Admiralty Committee to consider the best means of securing the highest mechanical skill and scientific knowledge in the management of the various engines of Her Majesty's Ships of War; see also the (1854) Report on the Organisation of the Permanent Civil Service, for a

discussion of the manner in which the civil service sought to retain the services of the sons of the aristocracy while introducing competitive examinations.

5   Report of an Admiralty Committee to consider the best means of securing the highest mechanical skill and scientific knowledge in the management of the various engines of Her Majesty's Ships of War (hereafter Admiralty Report 1877).

6   Admiralty Report 1877, Minutes of Evidence pp. 23 and 76.

7   *Parliamentary Debates*, third series, vol. 147 (1857), col. 597.

8   (1836) Report of Commissioners Inquiring into Military Punishments, minutes of evidence Q5097.

9   The cases of Messrs Hodge and Bruce, reported to the British Parliament in 1896, are good examples of the narrow definition of suitability which persisted long after the abolition of purchasing commissions. See *Parliamentary Debates*, fourth series, vol. 41 (1896), cols 1481–98.

10 Admiralty Report 1877, p. 1.

11 Admiral Lord Selbourne, *Hansard*, vol. 110 (1902), col. 1063.

12 See the (1881) Report of the Committee on the Formation of Territorial Regiments; the 'territorial principle' was re-emphasised, with the intention of giving regimental officers greater responsibility, after the criticisms of the British Army during the Boer War, see (1904) Report of the War Office (Reconstitution) Committee.

13 The evidence for the view that the 'Good Working Relationships' project is principally about sexual harassment is anecdotal – but is consistent with the major focus of the project to date which has been on addressing sexual harassment and the integration of women. The view that the problem of sexual harassment will generally only occur when ill-equipped women are in the workplace is, in part, the view that the committee took of the originating case of the medical officer, viz.: 'It appears to the Committee that, in relation to the events surrounding Dr Wheat's tour of duty on the *Swan* . . . a different approach by Dr Wheat would also have made an important difference' (Report: 214–15).

References

Books and Monographs

Bourdieu, P., 1977. *Outline of a Theory of Practice*, Cambridge: Cambridge University Press.

Chapman, I. D., 1975. *Iven G. Mackay: Citizen and Soldier*, Melbourne: Melway Publishing.

Elias, N., 1950. 'Studies in the genesis of the Naval profession', *British Journal of Sociology* 1: 291–309.

Gammage, B., 1988. 'The crucible: the establishment of the Anzac tradition, 1899–1918' in M. McKernan and M. Browne (eds), *Australia: Two Centuries of War and Peace*, Canberra: Australian War Memorial in association with Allen & Unwin.

Grey, J., 1990. *A Military History of Australia*, Cambridge: Cambridge University Press.

Heydon, P., 1965. *Quiet Decision: A Study of George Foster Pearce*, Melbourne: Melbourne University Press.

Janowitz, M., 1971. *The Professional Soldier*, Glencoe, Ill.: Free Press.

Joint Committee on Foreign Affairs, Defence and Trade, 1987. *The Management of Australia's Defence*, Canberra: AGPS.

Joint Committee on Foreign Affairs, Defence and Trade, 1988. *Personnel Wastage in the Australian Defence Force*, Canberra: AGPS.

Keegan, J., 1976. 'Regimental ideology' in G. Best and A. Wheatcroft (eds), *War, Economy and the Military Mind*, London: Rowman & Littlefield.

Oestreich, G., 1982. *Neostoicism and the Early Modern State*, Cambridge: Cambridge University Press.

Personnel Policy Strategy Review Team, 1995. *Serving Australia: the Australian Defence Force in the Twenty-First Century*, Canberra: AGPS.

Rose, D. E., 1958. 'Psychology in the Armed Forces', *Australian Journal of Psychology* 10, 1: 42–8.

Rose, N., 1990. *Governing the Soul: The Shaping of the Private Self*, London: Routledge.

Rose, N. and Miller, P., 1994. 'On therapeutic authority: psychoanalytic expertise under advanced liberalism', *History of the Human Sciences* 7, 3: 29–64.

Rosenberg, H., 1958. *Bureaucracy, Aristocracy, and Autocracy: The Prussian Experience 1660–1815*, Cambridge, Mass.: Harvard University Press.

Royal Australian Navy, 1993. *Better Working Relationships in the Navy: A submission by the Royal Australian Navy to an Inquiry by the Senate Standing Committee on Foreign Affairs, Defence and Trade*, Canberra: AGPS.

Senate Standing Committee on Foreign Affairs, Defence and Trade, 1994. *Sexual Harassment in the Australian Defence Force: Facing the Future Together*, Canberra: AGPS.

Strachan, H., 1985. *From Waterloo to Balaclava: Tactics, Technology and the British Army, 1815–1854*, Cambridge: Cambridge University Press.

Wellington, Field Marshal Arthur, KG, 1959. 'Memorandum on the proposed Plan for altering the discipline of the Army, 22 April 1829', *English Historical Documents*, vol. XI, 1783–1832, London.

Wolseley, Field Marshal Sir Garnet, 1903. *The Story of a Soldier's Life*, Westminster.

Wrigley, A. K., 1990. *The Defence Force and the Community: A Partnership in Australia's Defence*, Report to the Minister for Defence, Canberra: AGPS.

Parliamentary Papers

1836, Report of Commissioners Inquiring into Military Punishments, *Parliamentary Papers*, vol. 22.

1854, Report on the Organisation of the Permanent Civil Service, *Parliamentary Papers*, vol. 27.

1857, Report of the Commissioners appointed to inquire into the purchase of Commissions in the Army, *Parliamentary Papers*, vol. 18.

1866, Report of an Admiralty Committee on the Position of Masters in the Royal Navy, *Parliamentary Papers*, vol. 47.

1868–69, Report of the Royal Commission appointed to inquire into the constitution and practice of Courts-Martial in the Army, and the present system of punishment for military offences (two reports), *Parliamentary Papers*, vol. 12.

1876, Report of Royal Commission on Army Promotion and Retirement, *Parliamentary Papers*, vol. 25.

1877, Report of an Admiralty Committee to consider the best means of securing the highest mechanical skill and scientific knowledge in the management of the various engines of Her Majesty's Ships of War, *Parliamentary Papers*, vol. 21.

1881, Report of the Committee on the Formation of Territorial Regiments, *Parliamentary Papers*, vol. 22.

1904, Report of the War Office (Reconstitution) Committee, *Parliamentary Papers*, vol. 8.

British Parliamentary Papers.

British Parliamentary Debates.

CHAPTER 5

Administering Asceticism
Reworking the Ethical Life of the Unemployed Citizen

Mitchell Dean

By March 1997 a certain shrillness had entered political debate and argument concerning the question of unemployment in Australia. The occasion for a renewed round of electoral politics over unemployment was the introduction of the Social Security Legislation Amendment (Work for the Dole) Bill 1997 into the Australian House of Representatives. The justification of the bill by the conservative Liberal–National Party Coalition government was to establish 'pilot' projects by which younger unemployed people, eighteen to twenty-four years, would be required to work on 'community projects' at award rates of pay up to the value of unemployment benefits. The terms of the justification of the bill by the Minister, Dr David Kemp, are interesting precisely because by 1997 they had become so commonplace:

> It will help break the cycle of despair experienced by thousands of young Australians who have been unemployed for many months or years. They will now be able to make a valuable contribution to the community through a worthwhile work experience. It will help build up their self-esteem and help establish a work ethic.[1]

Much to the consternation of opposition parties, however, the bill contained no delimitations by age or project, nor any 'sunset clause' envisaging an end to compulsory work programs. As one senior political journalist pointed out at the time, the only necessity for the bill was its establishment of compulsion and its implied rescinding of a right to assistance for the unemployed (Ramsey 1997). As the wrong-footed opposition Labor Party fumbled for a response that maintained the delicate balance between criticising the legislation and not the principle of working for benefits, it became clearer that the bill conformed to the 'local cynicism' of a certain kind of political logic rather than to an explicit governmental rationality. It is indeed tempting to agree with that journalist that its numerical concerns attended more to the opinion polls than the unemployment statistics. Nevertheless, the introduction of this bill is not without salience to governmental concerns as much as narrowly conceived electoral politics. For this rather astute political manoeuvre had its conditions in the recent history of the 'problematisation' of the government and, indeed, self-government of the unemployed in Australia.

The study of government can be approached as the study of 'problematisations'. This is to say that whatever the merits of our various theories of the state, of politics, or of power, a certain degree of intelligibility can be gained by examining the different and particular cases in which the practice of governing is called into question, in which actors and authorities of various kinds are forced to pose the question of how to govern. This is clear in the case of the recent history of the approaches by successive Australian Governments to the question of unemployment. The empirical material for this chapter is largely made up of these 'official' problematisations of how to govern the unemployed.

These problematisations have certain conditions, such as the existence of high and continuing unemployment in countries such as Australia, and its recalcitrance in the face of various policy initiatives. However, the investigation of these conditions is largely outside the scope of this chapter. Instead it examines what might be taken to be questions of the relation between governmental concerns and the ethical life of unemployed citizens. By this I mean that specific programs of government – in this case programs of the Australian Commonwealth Government – attempt to constitute a nexus between certain political objectives, social goals and economic requirements and the conduct of individuals and groups, and between how the unemployed are to be governed and how they are to govern themselves. Government becomes ethical in this sense to the extent that it is concerned with the conduct of individuals and groups and, most especially, with the way in which they conduct themselves. While this chapter analyses problematisations undertaken by Australian Governments, it is specifically concerned with their implications for the direction and self-direction of the conduct of the unemployed.

This chapter thus examines aspects of both *the* government and government in the broader sense outlined in the introduction to this book. It addresses how agencies of Australian Governments concern themselves with this broader sense of government in that they seek to assemble multiple and heterogeneous agencies and instruments in the direction of the actions, behaviours and orientations of certain classes of citizens. If other chapters in this book take up the question of the conduct of those who exercise authority over others, such as bureaucrats (Jeffrey Minson, chapter 3) and the military (Alison Smith, chapter 4), this chapter examines problematisations of the government of those whose exercise of authority extends largely only to their own lives and selves. An important point to note is that the eliciting of self-government in strategies of government extends to those who might be understood as 'disadvantaged' or, as I have put it elsewhere, *targeted populations* (Dean 1997), as well as those in positions of the exercise of formal and hierarchical authority over others. As we shall see, this is as true for a governmental program that regards the unemployed as clients of a public employment service as it is of one that views them as consumers of a market in employment placement services.

The work-for-the-dole legislation appears after a decade of recurrent problematisations of the role of national governments in regard to unemployment. One recent example is the ministerial statement of August 1996, Reforming Employment Assistance: Helping Australians into Real Jobs (Vanstone 1996). This statement is, in part, a response to the previous Labor Government's *Working Nation* White Paper (Keating 1994). Also relevant to our concerns is the extensive Social Security Review undertaken in the 1980s which dealt with unemployment in an 'issues paper', *Income Support for the Unemployed in Australia: Towards a More Active System* (Cass 1988). With *Working Nation*, the Commonwealth Government undertook to introduce case-management approaches to unemployment, deployed contractualist techniques, and coordinated access to job-search assistance, employment exchange services, training, job-creation schemes, and subsidised jobs. Perhaps the most radical feature of *Working Nation* was its 'Job Compact', under which the long-term unemployed were to be offered a job placement after eighteen months. The unemployed entered into a contract with the Government that promised access to benefits and services, and included a guarantee of a job, in return for their compliance and participation in activities that were to make them 'job ready'. In both the Social Security Review and under *Working Nation*, as in contemporary approaches of the Organization for Economic Co-operation and Development (OECD 1988, 1990; Gass 1988), the language of the 'jobseeker' displaced that of the unemployed, and an 'active' system of income support was held to displace the 'passive' system of welfare benefits that rendered recipients prone to the 'risk of dependency'.

The ministerial statement of the Liberal–National Party Coalition Government, elected in March 1996, retained the language of the 'jobseeker' and 'active' labour-market programs but inflected them with what had hitherto been a subsidiary term in Australia, 'enterprise', and appealed to the objective of placing the unemployed in 'real jobs'. It signalled the abolition of the Commonwealth Employment Service (CES), the public employment service created fifty years earlier, and the establishment of a new statutory authority for those seeking access to publicly provided benefits and services (the Commonwealth Service Delivery Agency – CSDA). Many of the functions of the CES were to be relocated within a 'corporatised' 'public employment placement enterprise' (PEPE) which would be in a position of 'competitive neutrality' in respect to a market in employment placement services. The statement rejected notions of a guarantee of a job and previewed the 'cashing out' of most publicly funded job-creation and wage-subsidy schemes in order to provide the financial resources to establish this competitive market in what it called 'employment placement services'. In other words, it announced plans to use funds committed for programs that were to be abolished, and their administration costs, to finance the provision of services through a competitive price-based tendering mechanism. The funding of 'employment placement enterprises' (EPEs) was to be in terms of performance measured in terms of outcome – outcomes being defined primarily as placement in 'real jobs'. In effect, the ministerial statement rescinded the notion of a contract between the Government and the unemployed and replaced it with the myriad of contracts that would constitute the market in employment placement services: between the department and private case-managers and service providers, and between the unemployed and the service provider.

There is a case for regarding the artificial employment services market as a fundamental change in policy direction. The decrease of public expenditure, the establishment of a market in services for the unemployed and the abolition of direct job-creation schemes, all mark a significant retraction of the Commonwealth's involvement in the government of the unemployed. However, the plans announced by the statement build on aspects of the development of labour-market programs and services under the Labor Government in a number of ways: the use of the language of the 'jobseeker' and 'active' labour-market policies; the emphasis on case-management; the employment of publicly funded private and community service providers; and the continued use of policy evaluation and advice from the OECD. It would be a mistake, above all, to think that these changes amount to a retraction of Commonwealth responsibility toward the unemployed. The new institutional arrangements, including the establishment of a market in services provided by competing EPEs, mark a shift in the instruments of the government. They are a clear example of what might be thought to be a recurrent refrain of 'liberal' government – the attempt to govern better by governing less. Nevertheless, I want to suggest, an intense concern for the ethical life of the unemployed remains.

Drawing on Foucault's work on ethics (for example, 1985, 1986a, 1986b), I have suggested elsewhere that we can ask several types of questions concerning practices of government to the extent that they seek to form selves in certain ways (Dean 1995, 1996). First, we can ask questions of *what* is to be governed, or of what I have called the *governed substance*. This is the part of ourselves and others we seek to know and act upon in a certain way. We are able to ask, secondly, questions of *how* we govern, of what I have called the *governing work*. This refers to all the means, techniques, rationalities, and forms of knowledge that are used to accomplish the enfolding of authority. Thirdly, we might ask questions of *why* we govern ourselves and others in a particular manner, with the position we take or are given in relation to rules and norms. This aspect concerns what I have called the *governable subject*, the mode of obligation of the subject in relation to rules and norms. Finally, we can pose questions of *who* it is hoped we might become when we are governed or govern ourselves in a particular way. This could be called the *telos of government* – that is, the systems of purposes that lead us to adopt certain practices, the plans and design of which they are a part, the mode of being we hope to create, and what we seek to produce in ourselves and others.

It is these questions I shall now pose to the successive official problematisations of the government of the unemployed.

Analysis

This chapter is concerned neither with the formation of unemployment as an object of knowledge and target of policy intervention, nor with the systematic examination of the practices and techniques of the government of the unemployed.[2] Rather it raises questions of the ethical character of the government of the unemployment. By this I do not mean to propose criteria by which these regimes of government might be regarded as right or wrong, but how to analyse them in so far as they concern the direction and self-direction of the conduct of those who exercise authority and those over whom authority is exercised. In this respect, I want to suggest that practices governing the unemployed can be regarded as governmental-ethical practices. By proposing this term I hope to indicate the hybrid nature of these practices, and that what we are investigating is a somewhat complex interchange between policies and practices sponsored by national Governments and practices concerned with the shaping and self-shaping of conduct. The government of the unemployed may be called upon, on the one hand, to meet various national goals such as increasing international competitiveness, decreasing national budget deficits, or securing social justice. On the other hand, however, it entails practices of self-formation, that is, practices concerned to shape and reshape the attributes, capacities, orientations and moral conduct of individuals, and to define the rights, obligations and statuses of such individuals.

While these dual aspects of the government of the unemployed are necessary to one another, there is a sense in which they remain an irreducible source of tension. Over the last twenty years in Australia, 'labour-market' and 'income support' policies and practices began to take a form that was relatively independent of goals such as the provision of income security or facilitating entry into the labour market. They came to be concerned with the formation and reformation of the capacities and attributes of the unemployed citizen. Moreover, especially under Labor, these policies marked an 'ethicalisation' of government in that they began to oblige the unemployed to participate in practices of self-shaping, self-cultivation and self-presentation. These practices were hence not simply governmental practices but ethical practices, and what emerged was a kind of national government organisation and resourcing of certain kinds of ethical practice or what might be thought of as forms of asceticism.

With the Liberal–National Party Coalition Government one might suspect a retraction of the ethical aspects of government of the unemployed in line with its retraction of publicly funded labour-market programs and its talk of 'helping Australians into real jobs'. Indeed, its plans exploit the tension between such 'commonsense' objectives and the proliferation of labour-market programs, with their 'ethical' designs, under Labor. However, under the Coalition, the retraction of public provision and the establishment of a market in services for the unemployed presages a continuation of the intensive scrutiny of the self-governing capacities of the unemployed. In relinquishing direct mechanisms, such policies are clearly hoping to rely on the ethical capacities of the unemployed – including and importantly, their capacities of rational choice as consumers within a market – as a means of placing them in such real jobs. The change of policies thus achieves a retraction of formal public authority by a reliance on the capacity for the self-direction of conduct of the unemployed. If it is possible to use a quantitative term, the government of the unemployed appears to have become *more* ethical.

I have detailed the recent history of policy during the Labor Government in a previous paper (Dean, 1995: 567–9). At the time of writing, the policies of the Liberal–National Party Coalition Government hardly amount to a history. In what follows, I draw upon the major official problematisations of unemployment, and mark where significant differences are emerging and where noteworthy continuities remain. It is too early to do a full comparison of the different forms of government of the unemployed under successive national Governments in Australia. Instead, I shall now address the four types of questions that we might pose to the question of unemployment as 'governmental-ethical' practice: those concerning the material or substance to be governed, the work of government, the governable subject, and the telos of government.

What do they seek to govern? There is a fundamental continuity along this dimension. Practices of assisting the unemployed have come to govern what they consider the social and personal effects of unemployment (Cass 1988: 129–38). These include the erosion of self-esteem, the effects on physical and mental health, the isolation of the unemployed from social networks, their marginalisation from the labour market, their poor morale and motivation, their attitude to the labour market, their boredom and their loss of social obligation. In other words, an 'active system' of income support for the unemployed not only acts on the financial plight of the unemployed and on their job prospects, but also on those attitudes, effects, conduct and conditions that form a disposition that prevents the unemployed returning to the labour market, and alienates them from social networks and obligations.

This disposition is conceived positively as the attribute of 'job readiness' or 'work readiness' of the unemployed (Committee on Employment Opportunities 1993: 97; OECD 1990). A 1993 Green Paper, Restoring Full Employment, argued that higher rates of economic growth will bring more jobs but it is necessary to increase the job-readiness of unemployed to ensure that the long-term unemployed attain a greater share of them and to prevent high unemployment coexisting with high levels of vacancies. In this it follows the OECD arguments (1990: 62–3) that social protection solely in the form of income support carries the risk of discouraging re-entry into the labour market and that maintaining job-readiness by active labour-market programs can actually lead to a reduction in the total cost of support.

The disposition of the unemployed is conceived, secondly, as the potential of a 'risk of dependence'. The suggestion here is that, by analysing the different subjective phases of unemployment, it is possible to identify the point at which the unemployed person risks falling into a cycle of long-term dependence on welfare benefits (Cass 1988: 132–3). What these systems seek to govern, then, are the attitudes, feelings and conduct decreasing the job-readiness of the unemployed and constituting the risk of dependence. Indeed, the very fact of addressing this risk distinguishes an active system of income support from a merely passive system of benefits (for example, Cass 1988: 4; OECD 1988: 7–8).

One innovation of Working Nation was that it used these two versions of the 'governed substance' to regulate the flow of clients through the

system of employment services. At registration, clients were distinguished between those already 'job ready' and those 'at a high risk of
long-term unemployment'. The assessment took into account factors
such as skill levels, English language ability, age and whether the client
belonged to a disadvantaged group such as Aborigines and Torres Strait
Islanders, sole parents, people with disability, and those absent from the
work-force for a long period (Keating 1994: 111). At particular points –
for instance, at a six-month assessment – those formerly designated 'job-
ready' could be judged to have become 'at risk' and their status changed
accordingly.

Once these ways of conceiving what is to be governed are constituted,
it is possible to construct quite different policies in relation to them.
Thus, one could argue that those at high risk require early intervention
to prevent long-term unemployment before it becomes manifest. Conversely, one could argue, as does the ministerial statement (Vanstone
1996: 40), that the long-term unemployed should receive the largest
share of intensive assistance, presumably because they manifest the
danger of which others are merely at risk. Furthermore, 'job-readiness'
becomes something that can be assessed through specific instruments.
There are a range of existing screening and classification instruments
for the job-readiness of the unemployed to identify those at 'high risk'
and classify the level of placement difficulty (DEETYA 1996: 109). The
ministerial statement announced the introduction of a new method of
screening and assessment of jobseekers, the Jobseeker Classification
Index, based on questions about factors that increase risk of long-term
unemployment, such as 'age, educational attainment, access to a viable
labour market, disability, country of birth, English-speaking ability,
reading and writing ability in preferred language, Aboriginal and Torres
Strait Islander status, duration of unemployment, recency of work
experience and stability of residence' (Vanstone 1996: 41). In regard to
the conception of what is to be governed, however, there is little difference between the Liberal–National Party Coalition Government's
policies and those of its predecessor.

How are the unemployed to be governed? By what means is this
complex of factors making up the 'risk of dependency' and 'job-
readiness' to be governed? As I showed previously (Dean 1995: 573–4),
the key here is the administrative practice known as the 'activity test' that
replaces the old 'work test' of the system of unemployment benefit (Cass
1988: 6, 141–7). The activity test marks a move to a more intensive supervision of the activities of the unemployed, by which the claimant must
demonstrate not only active job searching but also training and job-
preparation activities. In the case of the 'long-term unemployed',[3] by the
early 1990s this activity test took the form of an agreement between the

client and the CES on what constitutes appropriate job searching, employment and training activities. Included in the activity test, then, was not only active job searching but participation in a wide range of other activities deemed to be, or even agreed to be, useful in promoting job re-entry. These might include: English language courses, linguistic and numeracy competency courses, short courses on particular skills, participation in 'Job Clubs', on-the-job training and training courses, part-time or short-term work, courses and counselling to improve confidence, motivation and presentation, and participation in voluntary work (DEET 1992, chapters 6 and 7).

One might think of all these practices, then, as a kind of administratively governed 'inner-worldly asceticism', to borrow a term from Max Weber which describes the attempt to master what is creatural and wicked within oneself through worldly activities such as work in a vocation (Weber 1948: 325–6). An excellent example of this administrative asceticism is manifest in the various resume, application, interview and job-search techniques recommended in the Job Search Kit provided by the CES (Dean 1995: 574).[4] These forms of asceticism are, needless to say, backed up by sanctions, such as the cancellation of the allowance for varying periods for various groups of the unemployed. The intensification of an administratively directed asceticism is clearly related to the spectre of the punitive exercise of sovereignty.

New agents and forms of expertise are formed in relation to this governing work of the supervision of the various categories of the unemployed. Thus, one of the key initiatives of *Working Nation* concerned the resourcing, functions and training of a new agent, the case-manager. Under this plan, such case-managers were to operate both in public and private employment services and assist all those at risk of long-term unemployment or the long-term unemployed. The case-manager evinces a kind of 'pastoral' expertise, assessing the needs of clients, helping them prepare a plan to return to work, and directing them toward the activities that enhance their job-readiness (for example, vocational and remedial training, employment programs, counselling, voluntary work, placements under the Job Compact), and reporting breaches of agreements and conditions of allowances (Keating 1994: 110–18). The case-manager acts as a position of relay between the unemployed, local employers, and appropriate services and agencies. In order to foster 'healthy competition', private and voluntary case-managers were to compete with public ones, with their activities monitored and accredited by a new Employment Service Regulatory Agency (Keating 1994: 129–30).

It is noteworthy that case-management remains the mainstay of the Coalition Government's intended reforms. Here it is viewed as offering personalised relationships, fulfilling a deterrent role, and the means, after the removal of eligibility rules and restrictions on numbers of clients that use private case-management, of delivering flexible and appropriate service (Vanstone 1996: 8). The clear difference is that case-management is largely to be provided by the governmentally contrived market in employment placement enterprises – the EPEs – in which the public employment placement enterprise (the PEPE) is one player in a position of 'competitive neutrality'. The new Service Delivery Agency is largely concerned to provide self-help facilities and information – via Automatic Job Selection touch-screens – on locally available EPEs or jobs in a national labour-market database. The Commonwealth Government, then, still acts as a kind of 'obligatory point of passage' (Callon 1986: 196), for those who apply to it for income support, into the services and expertise that will assist the jobseeker. Now, however, rather than providing or brokering access to services, expertise, training or even direct job placement, it will principally provide access to information about markets – the national labour market or the market in employment placement services. The EPEs will be contracted to provide labour-exchange services (largely the matching of vacancies and jobseekers), job-search assistance (training in resume preparation, job-search techniques, etc.) or 'intensive employment assistance' (IEA) based on personalised assessment of the long-term unemployed and 'special groups' (for example, training, intensive job seeking, or employment subsidy assistance).

The major difference in how the unemployed are to be governed by the Liberal–National Party Coalition Government, then, lies not so much in the instruments and agencies that are employed as in their mode of coordination and regulation. Pastoral expertise and access to services is no longer guaranteed by a benevolent state which ensures their provision through a diversity of mechanisms and institutions; rather, they are to be provided, coordinated and regulated through the mechanisms of a governmentally contrived market. Under the Coalition, the individual is less a client of diverse agencies in a relation of obligation to the national Government than a consumer exercising choice within a services market contrived by the national Government. This observation allows us to move to the question of the 'governable subject'.

Why are the unemployed governed in such a way? What is the mode of obligation that they are placed under by these governmental practices? Here, I think, lies the clearest difference between the successive Governments. For Labor, the obligation was one that took place between the individual and the national Government. Fundamental to both the institution of the activity test and the agreements entered into by the long-term unemployed (the Newstart Agreements) was the principle of reciprocal obligation. This can be formulated thus: 'if the Government is providing income support, labour-market programs and other services, it is only fair that clients take up any reasonable offer of assistance and do whatever they can to improve their employment prospects' (DEET 1992: 21–2; cf. Cass 1988: 152–4). Benefits and services are not granted as a right of citizen or taxpayer but as a part of mutual exchange or contract between the individual and national Government, in which both parties accept a certain pattern of obligation. The peak of the practice of reciprocal obligation was the Job Compact of the *Working Nation* policies (Keating 1994: 115–16). Here the Government offered an employment placement to the long-term unemployed on the condition that they accept a reasonable job offer or lose entitlement to income support. The position of the unemployed in relation to national Government provision is evidenced in the shifts of the vocabulary of policy. Instead of granting a claimant her/his rightful benefit, the national Government provides an allowance and services on the condition that the client engages in job-search activities. Instead of a system of benefits for the unemployed we have a complex of services and allowances for the jobseeker.

The Coalition Government's ministerial statement explicitly rejects job guarantees and job compacts and, in so doing, significantly modifies, if not abandons, the idea of reciprocal obligation between client and state.[5] Certainly, there was a form of tutelage over the unemployed in *Working Nation*. In more than a residual sense the case-manager, as a pastoral agent and state functionary, decided what was best for the client, or at least guided the client to discover what was best for him or herself. Under the Newstart Agreement, the client must agree to perform the activities worked out with the case-manager. Reciprocal obligation – so far as the unemployed person is concerned – thus takes the form of placing oneself under the direction of a particular expert. In contrast, the primary obligation for the jobseeker under the Liberal–National assemblage is to make the right choice between EPEs based on the information made available through the Service Delivery Agency, that is, to act as an informed consumer. Those receiving intensive assistance will enter into contracts not with the national Government but with the employment placement enterprise (Vanstone 1996: 42). The mode of obligation for the jobseeker is less of a grateful beneficiary of the state's concerned tutelage and more an enterprising consumer of services exercising the best choices possible for him or herself. The jobseeker is an active subject not only in undertaking agreed activities but also in the very process of gaining access to the services they require. If the national Government has a form of obligation, it is to contrive a market in employment placement services and to ensure that the jobseeker can enter this market.

What is the type of 'relation to self' that these practices promote? Strangely enough, under Labor, the *Working Nation*-style practices were ones in which the market remained a kind of 'protected nature reserve' which the jobseeker could enter only after intensive preparation in establishing the proper competencies and capacities under the tutelage of the state.[6] The relation to self is one in which the individual is to become – under the pastoral state – the proprietor and marketer of his or her skills, qualifications, and even physical and psychological attributes. This is one version of what it might mean to be an active economic citizen or jobseeker. Here, the jobseeker is opposed to the individual rendered dependent by the old passive system of unemployment benefit. To be an active citizen is to take an active role in the management and presentation of the self, to undertake a systematic approach to the search for a job, and, ultimately, if possible, to participate in the labour force. If this last is not possible, the jobseeker as active citizen participates in activities that enhance his or her prospects of entering or returning to paid work, while at the same time remaining bound to social networks and engaging in practices that overcome those attributes (fatalism, boredom, loss of self-esteem) which constitute the 'risk of dependency'. Moreover, by installing the notion of contract in the Newstart agreements, the jobseeker is asked to become the active subject of his or her own destiny, at least as far as the labour market is concerned. Under the guidance of state-provided and regulated pastoral expertise, the unemployed citizen is to become an active entrepreneur of his or her own self, ready and able to take up such opportunities as the labour market, social provision, education and social networks may provide, and thus able to combat the risk of dependency.

This diagram of the active citizen as entrepreneur of the self, however, is still one largely of the producer. By contrast to Labor's tendency to provide policies which keep the 'market' as something safely maintained at a considerable distance, the Coalition Government's programs of reform take a constructivist view of markets. There is a conscious and active attempt to contrive markets where none had previously existed, or where they had been contrived previously in a very limited fashion. As a consequence, the jobseeker is no longer a client of the national Government being prepared for the entry into the labour market. He or she is already asked to exhibit the attributes necessary to effective participation in markets by gaining information on services available, making choices between different enterprises, and – this can only be inferred – taking or at least sharing responsibility for the effects of such choices.

Under Labor's policies there remained a lingering tension between the client–state tutelage and the somewhat deferred goal of forming active economic citizens. Under the Coalition, by contrast, this tension is resolved by making the relation of the jobseeker to required services and expertise itself a market relation. The market is no longer held at a distance from state sponsorship, provision and assistance, but is now a form that can be enfolded into the regime of government itself. The case-manager still exercises a pastoral authority, but this will now be regulated by the rationality of the market, the competition between service providers, and performance outcomes measured in terms of job placements. Expert and consumer gain a kind of formal market equality as agents exercising enterprise and regulated by its disciplines.

Who do we hope the unemployed will become through these practices of government? What sort of world do we hope they will participate in? What forms of existence do these practices seek to engender? What forms of life do they wish to avoid? This is to address the telos of such practices. To do this is to address the point where the administrative and utopian dimensions of these practices intersect. This is a more difficult and somewhat more speculative task than that undertaken so far. One influential way in which the telos of these practices has been thought of is through the notion of what the OECD has called an *active society*. To do this, I shall first summarise some points made in an earlier paper (Dean 1995: 577–9).[7]

The notion of activity binds the technical and calculative aspects of this political rationality to its more broadly programmatic statements. It allows, for example, the definition and measurement of unemployment, and 'active measures' of labour-market policies to be contrasted with passive social security systems of income maintenance. Thus, it is possible to measure the percentage of GDP spent on active measures and to assess the value of active measures relative to income support (OECD 1990: 52–3, table 14).

On the other hand, the notion of an active society displaces the expectation of full employment underwritten by a welfare state, and the assumption that work is full-time wage-labour for all adults up to retirement age, by invoking a society that guarantees access to a range of opportunities over the life-cycle of the individual (Gass 1988: 5). An active society includes not only participation in the labour market but also participation in education and training, in voluntary associations, in part-time work or periods of domestic work, in hobbies, travel and so on, or combinations of these, depending on individual preference and the point reached in the individual's life-cycle (Gass 1988: 5–7). Active societies are said to lead to 'a more ambitious and realistic form of full employment, which will require a variety of combinations of working time, education and other activities, in accordance with individual preference and family circumstance' (Gass 1988: 7).

In other formulations, particularly in the context of discussion of labour-market programs, the ideal of an active society downplays the degree of flexibility of lifestyles and places more emphasis on ensuring job-readiness and the promotion of active job-search (OECD 1990: 8, 61–3). However, the ideal does imply the existence of an institutional framework for augmenting job-readiness and facilitating entry into the labour force and for the exercise of choice of an active population. For example, the OECD envisages 'active equal employment opportunity policies' that facilitate the choices of workers with family responsibilities and childcare needs by an integration of training, labour-market, and childcare provision (OECD 1990: 8).

An active society is characterised by active income support policies rather than the passive form of benefits characteristic of the welfare state. On the other hand, it promotes an active population that is able to take up the opportunities presented by the labour market, education, social provision and, indeed, social existence more generally. Such a population is defined in opposition to a dependent population, that is, to the population rendered dependent on the welfare state by the merely passive system of benefits (OECD 1988: 21; Gass 1988: 6). The concept of an active society allows this form of political rationality to attach a critique of the welfare state as a merely passive system of hand-outs to the image of long-term dependency among the population.

This ideal of the active society is haunted by the spectre of the self-reproduction of a dependent group permanently living within the welfare system. This group is characterised by what the OECD calls a 'syndrome of deprivation' leading to a 'ghetto existence' (OECD 1988: 21) with no stake in official society and thus heavily dependent on welfare, and prone to illegalities and to exhibit a marked behavioural contrast with the mainstream. This document offers three terms to describe this group: 'persistent poverty', 'welfare dependency' and the 'underclass'. It may be the last that best exemplifies the displacement of 'social problems' for the proponents of the concept of an active society and active systems of income support.

The fear of the creation of this permanent underclass helps make intelligible the vigour with which these Governments have problematised the assistance of the unemployed and intensified its administrative asceticism. Moreover, it underlines a certain common ground between Labor and conservative approaches to unemployment in Australia. For both, the ethical capacities and orientations of the unemployed are central because it is only through these that it is possible to prevent long-term welfare dependency and its consequences. To prevent the formation of such an underclass our governmental-ethical practices oblige the unemployed to work upon themselves so that they may be ready and able to work when opportunities are available. During the period when we heard the clarion call for an 'enterprise culture' (Heelas and Morris 1994), contemporary public policy devised a range of different institutional conditions and governmental means by which the active subject could be formed, and could form him or herself, with an orientation toward such a culture.

There can be no question of taking an unequivocal position on the notion of an active society. For a start, there is more than one way of achieving the telos of governmental practices toward the unemployed. One way – indicated by Labor's *Working Nation* – is through extensive social provision that prepares individuals for participation in the market but which keeps the market as a quasi-natural domain that, if properly regulated, will provide for state and society but which remains at some distance from government itself. The strength of such an approach is that it ensures the provision of, and access to, such services as are needed by those understood as disadvantaged and the long-term unemployed. The cost of such an approach is that it remains caught in a kind of bind: the unemployed are asked to become active citizens exercising their freedom to participate yet they remain clients of the state. Another way – illustrated by the Coalition plans for an employment placement services market – is to reject the notion of the market as working at a distance, and to contrive a market in services to which national Government ensures entry. The beauty of such a plan is the consistency between the means and instruments of government and its goals, between the expectations of the unemployed today and the outcomes sought, between the practices and rationality of government and its telos. The downside is that, given the devolution of responsibility for ensuring the meeting of needs on to the employment placement enterprises and the unemployed as consumers of services, there can be no guarantee of any particular set of outcomes (for instance, that all the long-term unemployed will be provided with a job placement). In one case, freedom is to be exercised from a position of tutelage under a responsible and benevolent state; in the other, freedom is exercised within a governmentally contrived market in which the individual and service provider are made to accept responsibility for their choices.

Conclusion

In conclusion, I shall raise several issues that arise from a familiarity with the literature on contemporary liberal government of Foucault and others.

First, there is the question of the relation between this government of the unemployed and the portrayal of neo-liberalism in Foucault's lectures. Here we can note similarities between the jobseeker as active citizen and the version of *homo œconomicus* that Foucault identifies with the human capital theorists of the Chicago School of Economics, in which the individual seeks to use his or her own biologically endowed and socially acquired attributes as a form of capital presenting returns in the form of satisfactions (Gordon 1991: 41–4; Foucault 1989: 118–19). Indeed, the language of investing in human capital and human resource management is pervasive in the OECD policy literature (OECD 1990). In terms of one of our four sets of questions (those concerning the governable subject), it is difficult to distinguish the objectives of active policies from this kind of economic subject. The active citizen is obligated to act as an entrepreneur of his or her own capacities, skills, talents and so on. And, indeed, one of the alternatives for job-ready jobseekers may be to participate in new enterprise incentive schemes to create small businesses – a program that appears likely to prosper under the Coalition's plans (Keating 1994: 117; Vanstone 1996: 33).

Yet we must be careful here for several reasons. As we have already shown, the language of the active system of income support and of the active jobseeker can remain relatively stable while variations occur along other dimensions. In terms of the work of government, an 'active system' of income support can encompass a pattern of 'reciprocal obligation' envisaging a fundamental role for national government agencies in the provision and sponsoring of job-search and labour-exchange services, training, case-management and even direct job creation. It can also, however, be articulated as a conception of provision which limits the obligation of national government to providing jobseekers with entry into a governmentally contrived market in employment placement services. It may, for those who are deemed not yet to have the requisite capacities to exercise responsible choice in such a market, involve coercive work-for-dole schemes. Further, despite similarities with other diagrams of the economic subject, the language of the active citizen and jobseeker has its own specificity and its range of variations: in one version, as we have seen, the jobseeker remains a client of the state and will learn the capacities and competencies to become an entrepreneur of him/herself; in another, the practice of gaining access to services already obliges the unemployed to act as agents within a market. In the former, enterprise is a goal to be achieved under the pastoral state and to be exercised on a market still 'out there'; in the latter, it is a quality to be exercised immediately as a condition of entry to pastoral expertise and services.

In some respects, both versions of the active system would seem to replicate elements found in Foucault's account of postwar German neo-liberalism (the *Ordoliberalen*) with its institutionalist emphasis on the juridical and policy conditions under which citizens are required to play the 'game of competitive freedom' (Foucault 1989: 117–19). In the case of *Working Nation* and Labor's policy record more generally, we witnessed the attempt to establish a comprehensive set of policies and provisions through which those identified as 'disadvantaged', such as youth, the long-term unemployed, non-English speakers, Aborigines and Torres Strait Islanders, sole parents, and all those at risk of welfare dependency, could augment their human capital to take up the opportunities that markets and civil society provide. There was under Labor, as with the Ordoliberals, a protection of the market by vigilant social interventions in areas such as health and unemployment assistance and the establishment – particularly in departments such as the Department of Employment, Education and Training – of a bureaucratic officialdom charged with the activist creation of the conditions which allow citizens to exercise their freedom (Foucault 1989: 118–19).

There was, thus, a constructivist dimension to Labor's policies in respect of the market. However, this was limited to constructing the conditions of the labour market and to the establishment of a market segment of the provision of employment services. The Coalition policies, by contrast, attempt to construct markets themselves. In a more articulate version, the Coalition plans might evince what the Ordoliberal, Alexander von Rüstow, would have called a *Vitalpolitik* or 'vital policy' (Gordon 1991: 42). Here, the market as a game of competitive freedom is matched by a culture in which all aspects of life, not purely economic ones, would be restructured as the pursuit of a range of different enterprises. One can be just as enterprising in the consumption of employment placement services as one can in labour, property, stock or finance markets. In this regard, Coalition policies on employment services reject the statist and tutelary dimension of Labor's programs in favour of the confidence – perhaps closer to that of the Chicago School of Economics – that a market rationality can be extended to all spheres and provide policy guidelines for them (Foucault 1989: 118–19). Yet as the work-for-the-dole and cutting of immigration intake policies suggest, this confidence finds its limits in directly coercive measures. There is certainly confirmation in both Coalition's and Labor's policies of the view that neo-liberalism is concerned to bring market relations to bear on previously non-market spheres of allocation (see Barry Hindess, chapter 12 in this book). One implication of the present chapter, however, is that rather than regard such policies as an expression of a neo-liberal (or 'economically rational') dream trying to insert itself in reality, it is crucial to analyse and distinguish the different regulatory regimes through which such markets are to be constructed (Burchell 1994).

Secondly, it is worth considering the implications of the related notions of 'at risk' groups and indices of disadvantage. It does not seem to me to go too far to consider the whole panoply of active measures as constituting a specific kind of 'risk technology' and as sharing some of the other features of the most recent generation of risk technologies (O'Malley 1992). The grid of perception and evaluation shares with risk technologies analysed by O'Malley a division of the population into those who are capable of managing risk and those whose riskiness requires management under a tutelary relationship, a division that might be expressed as one between 'active citizens' and 'targeted populations' (Dean 1997). O'Malley's analysis of contemporary risk technologies suggests that we are witness to the privatisation of risk through the partial transformation of socialised actuarialism into privatised actuarialism and a down-scaling of earlier socialised risk techniques. Something quite different, however, is at work in the successive phases of the reform of unemployment assistance in Australia. First, the postwar Australian system of unemployment benefits did not take the form of social insurance with its related principles of 'social right' and the 'collectivisation of risk'. Rather, it took the form of means-tested benefits that were clearly subsidiary to the full-employment objective. Thus, the Australian reforms are not so much about the privatisation of risk and the abandonment of social right, as the grafting of a particular version of individualised risk assessment on to a system of public benefits. We might, therefore, talk of successive phases in the 'enterprisation of assistance' rather than – or at least, as well as – the privatisation of social insurance. In such a technology, indices of disadvantage become as much a way of isolating, dividing and targeting populations in terms of their risk factors as much as a manifestation of a concern for social justice. The Coalition's plan demonstrates how the identification of 'special groups' can be retained without reference to objectives of social justice or even a notion of disadvantage.

Finally, the active system challenges and forces us to refine our conceptions of 'advanced' or neo-liberal government (Rose 1993). Certainly, arguments for active measures contain a critique of the welfare state in which the circuit of social protection is viewed as interfering with economic circuits of wealth production and growth, decreasing the job-readiness of the population and increasing its dependency quotient. Moreover, there has been a pluralisation of the semi-autonomous powers brought to bear on the government of the unemployed, including quasi-autonomous non-government organisations (QUANGOS), communities, regions, associations and indeed, the choices of clients and service providers. Yet there remain different ways of displacing the welfarist ideal and coordinating and integrating these plural powers and agencies. The first is one in which the state is constituted as guaranteeing forms of provision through an exchange of reciprocal obligation with the needy citizen. The second is one in which the national Government ensures that the citizen can exercise choice by constructing a market in services. The 'enterprisation of assistance' can thus mean either the pastoral promotion by the state of capacities for enterprise or the enterprisation of the very process by which the citizen gains access to pastoral expertise. What has occurred is not simply the subordination of older forms of expertise to a new formal rationality, but the virtually simultaneous constitution of a pastoral expertise in risk management and its regulation by new calculative regimes. Moreover, we should note that both approaches in Australia maintain the position of the national Government as a kind of obligatory passage point into employment services for those who wish to receive public assistance, whether by ensuring provision through itself in conjunction with other agencies or by establishing the market in services.

Under both Labor and conservative rule in Australia, active policies toward the unemployed oblige the citizen to exercise choice and to undertake an intensive work on the self, as they undertake to ensure that the services and expertise exist to enable that work on self to be performed. What distinguishes the policies most clearly is how that provision is to be made and the kind of choices that are required of the unemployed citizen. The unemployed citizen, who might have become accustomed to a freedom exercised under the benevolent tutelage of the pastoral state, now, it appears, has to adapt to yet another kind of freedom: that of exercising the responsible and informed choice which absolves all collective obligation save that of providing the opportunity to exercise that choice.

If, however, we are to take seriously the work-for-the-dole scheme as a key component in the Coalition Government's strategy toward unemployment, we might say that the difference between the strategy of the two Governments is something like the following. Under one, power relations operate neither through pure coercion nor pure consent but under the careful cultivation of attributes by which choice can be exercised in relation to a labour-market. This strategy seeks to transform the targeted populations into active citizens. Under the other, choice and coercion are bifurcated so that while the active citizen is obliged to exercise choice, (at least some) targeted populations are simply forced to work.

Notes

This chapter draws on work presented in an earlier paper (Dean 1995) and contains several passages that are taken from that paper without substantial modification. The central analysis of the chapter also follows the structure of the earlier paper. It has benefited from the editorial suggestions of Barry Hindess.

1 Quoted in Media Release, 19 March 1997.
2 I have suggested what a focus on the practices and techniques of the government of the unemployed might entail in another paper (Dean 1995: 569–72). On the historical emergence of the concept of unemployment in Britain and its relation to ways of thinking about social questions and technologies for the government of poverty, see Walters (1994).
3 Those registered as unemployed for twelve months. From 1991 these people received Newstart Allowance and entered into Newstart Agreements.
4 Obtained by the author on a visit to the Chatswood, New South Wales, CES office in 1993.
5 In the Media Release of the new Minister, Dr Kemp, cited above, the notion of 'reciprocal obligation' between national state and the unemployed citizen seems to have been replaced by one of 'mutual obligation' between communities and those for whom they provide support.
6 I take this image from Graham Burchell's description of an early liberal version of the market as 'an existing quasi-natural reality situated in a kind of economic nature reserve space marked off, secured and supervised by the state' (Burchell 1996: 23). What is strange here is that an 'interventionist' approach to labour-market programs should maintain such a conception.
7 Unlike 'ideology critique', the study of governmentality does not reduce practices of government to the general forms of political rationality which seek to codify them in a certain way and to insert them in a system of purposes (see Dean 1998, Introduction). My analysis of the 'active society' is an analysis of one set of rationalisations of practices of income support and labour-market programs. The telos of government does not provide us with the ultimate end or meaning of a particular regime of practices but with one account of why such practices are necessary, why they should take a particular form, what ends they seek, and what kind of beings they hope to produce.

References

Barry, Andrew, Osborne, Thomas and Rose, Nikolas, (eds), 1996. *Foucault and Political Reason: Liberalism, Neo-liberalism and Rationalities of Government*, London: University College London Press.
Burchell, David, 1994. 'The curious career of economic rationalism: government and economy in the current policy debate', *Australian and New Zealand Journal of Sociology* 30, 3: 322–33.
Burchell, Graham, 1996. 'Liberal government and techniques of the self', in Barry, Osborne and Rose (eds), pp. 19–36.
Burchell, Graham, Gordon, Colin and Miller, Peter, (eds), 1991. *The Foucault Effect: Studies in Governmentality*, London: Harvester/Wheatsheaf.
Callon, Michel, 1986. 'Some elements of a sociology of translation' in J. Law (ed.), *Power, Action and Belief: A New Sociology of Knowledge?* Sociological Review Monograph 32, London: Routledge & Kegan Paul, pp. 196–233.
Cass, Bettina, 1988. *Income Support for the Unemployed in Australia: Towards a More Active System*, Canberra: Australian Government Publishing Service.
Committee on Employment Opportunities, 1993. *Restoring Full Employment: a Discussion Paper*, Canberra: Australian Government Publishing Service.

Dean, Mitchell, 1995. 'Governing the unemployed self in an active society', *Economy and Society* 24, 4: 559–83.

Dean, Mitchell, 1996. 'Foucault, government and the enfolding of authority' in Barry, Osborne and Rose (eds), pp. 209–29.

Dean, Mitchell, 1997. 'Sociology after society' in D. Owen (ed.), *Sociology After Postmodernism.*, London: Sage.

Dean, Mitchell, 1998. *Governmentality*, London: Sage.

(DEET) Department of Employment, Education and Training, 1992. *Department of Employment, Education and Training Annual Report 1991–92*, Canberra: Australian Government Publishing Service.

(DEETYA) Department of Employment, Education, Training and Youth Affairs, 1996. *Department of Employment, Education, Training and Youth Affairs Annual Report 1995–96*, Canberra: Australian Government Publishing Service.

(DSS) Department of Social Security, 1991. *Department of Social Security Annual Report 1990–91*, Canberra: Australian Government Publishing Service.

Foucault, Michel, 1985. *The Use of Pleasure*, trans. R. Hurley, New York: Pantheon.

Foucault, Michel, 1986a. *The Care of the Self*, trans. R. Hurley, New York: Pantheon.

Foucault, Michel, 1986b. 'On the genealogy of ethics: an overview of the work in progress' in P. Rabinow (ed.), *The Foucault Reader*, Harmondsworth: Penguin, pp. 340–72.

Foucault, Michel, 1989. *Résumé des cours 1970–1982*, Paris: Juilliard.

Gass, James, 1988. 'Towards the "active society"', *OECD Observer* 152: 4–8.

Gordon, Colin, 1991. 'Introduction' to Burchell, Gordon and Miller (eds), pp. 1–51.

Heelas, Peter and Morris, Peter, 1994 (eds). *The Values of the Enterprise Culture – the Moral Debate*, London: Routledge.

Keating, Paul J., 1994. *Working Nation: Policies and Programs*, Canberra: Australian Government Publishing Service.

(OECD) Organization for Economic Co-operation and Development, 1988. *The Future of Social Protection*, OECD Social Policy Studies No. 6, Paris.

(OECD) Organization for Economic Co-operation and Development, 1990. *Labour Market Policies for the 1990s*, Paris: Organization for Economic Co-operation and Development.

O'Malley, Pat, 1992. 'Risk, power and crime prevention', *Economy and Society* 21, 3: 252–75.

Ramsey, Alan, 1997. *Sydney Morning Herald*, 29 March.

Rose, Nikolas, 1993. 'Government, authority and expertise in advanced liberalism', *Economy and Society* 22, 3: 283–99.

Rose, Nikolas, 1994. 'Governing the enterprising self', in Heelas and Morris (eds).

Vanstone, Amanda, 1996. Reforming Employment Assistance: Helping Australians into Real Jobs. Canberra: Australian Government Publishing Service.

Walters, William, 1994. 'The discovery of "unemployment": new forms for the government of poverty', *Economy and Society* 23, 3: 265–90.

Weber, Max, 1948. 'Religious rejections of the world and their directions' in H. H. Gerth and C. W. Mills (eds), *From Max Weber*, London: Routledge & Kegan Paul, pp. 323–59.

1993 Your Job Search Kit, Commonwealth Employment Service.

CHAPTER 6

Dangerous Individuals
Government and the Concept of Personality

David McCallum

In the 1990s acts of extreme violence in Australia and other parts of the world have caused understandable shock and affront. After the Port Arthur shootings, for example, there was a demand to know how this could happen, what type of person commits this terrible act, to what extent are the links which bind a community being undermined by the effects of commercial culture, economic policy or a more general social malaise. A forensic psychologist gave a 'portrait' of the typical mass killer, but added 'what we don't know is why other lonely, isolated, angry men at the fringe of society don't become mass killers'. Another expert claimed it was possible to predict dangerousness by taking account of 'early warning signals in children', such as unhappiness, narcissism, self-centredness, uncertainty and an inability to form relationships. The signs are the antecedents, the classic symptoms of anti-social personality disorder in the making: 'prolonged bed-wetting, cruelty to animals, setting fires'. People who knew the perpetrator at Port Arthur described him to a journalist as 'a strange young boy', 'shy, sad, no friends', 'simple, not "retarded simple", but you know . . .', 'a loner' (*Four Corners*, ABC television, 1 July 1996).

What burden of explanation is carried by the psycho-medical term 'anti-social personality disorder'? The latest edition of the standard taxonomy of mental disorders, the *Diagnostic and Statistical Manual* (American Psychiatric Association 1952) published by the American Psychiatric Association, devotes almost fifty pages to personality disorders but its offering is limited (deliberately so) in terms of aetiology. A sensible person interested in community safety and good government might want to ask 'well, how do we prevent it'? 'What can we do to ensure the development of ordered personalities'? 'Is there a program we can implement'? On the Port Arthur killer, experts are divided on whether the causes are physiological or social. Dr Robert Hare in Canada testified that brain waves of psychopaths can be distinguished from the rest of the population in brain imaging experiments, which reveal almost no activity at all in the front parts of the brain; Dr Paul Mullen on the other hand, a forensic psychiatrist from Victoria, argued that it was 'cheaper to say they're ill than to provide every child in our community with a decent education . . . a chance of success'. The implication here seems to be that a program, an intervention or a remedy depends on the type of explanation for the existence of the problem, and that some explanations might even serve to close off possible (expensive) interventions.

Many of the relevant issues in the interrelations between law and psychiatry emerged in the case of *Attorney-General* v. *David* in Victoria during the early 1990s. In 1989 a parliamentary committee examining legal and medical opinion concluded that personality disorder could not be classified as a treatable mental illness (Parliament of Victoria 1990). The committee noted the limitations faced by both the criminal justice and mental health systems to effectively and legitimately manage persons considered to be dangerous. It reported at a time when the government, with uncertain authority and jurisdiction, could not resolve the problem of the need to confine a particular person considered to be dangerous. Gary David had completed a prison sentence and at the time of his release a Mental Health Review Board, made up of psychiatrists, lawyers and lay-persons, refused to rule that he was mentally ill. The board found instead that he suffered from an 'antisocial or borderline personality disorder'. Prior to this, the Victorian Law Reform Commission had recommended that the relevant mental health legislation should be amended so as not to prevent the involuntary confinement of persons who suffered from an antisocial personality disorder and who were dangerous. Eventually, the government enacted the Community Protection Act, described by an academic lawyer as an 'extraordinary and unprecedented piece of legislation' (Williams 1990: 162), which gave the Supreme Court power to detain one particular individual beyond the expiration of his sentence. The prisoner/patient was placed in specially constructed confinement and alternated between prison and hospital until his death in 1993 because of specific legislation enacted to secure him for what he might do. A psychiatrist who was also a member of the Mental Health Review Board commented later that 'society had failed' in the Gary David case, due to a 'fundamental inability to define conceptual boundaries' (Glaser 1994).

It is not the purpose here to set about clearing up these difficulties or to offer an alternative framework for more effective management of the problem of dangerousness, although I would not dispute the importance and timeliness of such an endeavour. It may be possible, however, to suggest some explanation for the difficulties encountered over 'conceptual boundaries' by giving some account of the emergence of the category of personality disorder itself. To allude to the title for a moment, I want to argue that the category of personality is the product of a governmental attempt to know and act upon the disordered and potentially dangerous individual. What becomes 'personality' is a particular rendering of aspects of past governmental activity and inquiry into the problem of managing disorder and inefficiency among certain groups in the population, which distilled as a kind of residue a location or space for techniques of personal formation (Hacking 1986) of which the individual becomes the entrepreneur. Under distinctively liberal forms of government, rational principles of population management have sought to deploy a machinery for calculating the strengths and weaknesses in the people, and on the basis of this knowledge, populations and individuals become the objects of government. Government is thus a type of 'action under a description'. The relations between personality and government become distinctive then, in the sense of the actions of government carving out a space in which individuals will come to deploy calculative techniques in the way they go about forming a discrete personhood. The space for these calculative techniques, I suggest, was 'invented' in the context of governmental attempts to know and act upon the disordered and potentially dangerous.

Historically, much of the interest of government in managing populations in the ways I have suggested can be demonstrated in the early twentieth-century inquiry in the biological and human sciences into the problem of mental defect. It became possible to think and act upon disordered and dangerous persons partly as a consequence of the development of specific techniques of calculating mental defectiveness.

Mental Defect, Disorder and Dangerousness

Observe the primary separation beginning in the latter half of the nineteenth century, of acute from chronic inmates, who previously shared space within the old lunatic asylum but who now found themselves in separate, rather more specialised accommodation. The acute patients occupied the newly named 'mental hospitals' while the chronic and hopeless cases were farmed out to peripheral institutions. The chronic and hopeless were described in 1915 as a loose aggregate of 'epileptics, congenital imbeciles, general paralytics, paranoiacs, and senile dements' (Victoria. *Annual Report of the Inspector-General of the Insane* 1915: 37). They attracted less interest from medicine, perhaps because little could be done in terms of treatment compared with the more interesting and prestigious acute patients. The chronics were also less 'valuable' in a strict economic sense too, because many could not perform work in the asylum. Further, their administrative separation from the mental hospital and from a strict medical gaze was underpinned by the increasing attention afforded them as suitable objects of education and training, as distinct from treatment. This separation occurs hand in hand with new tools which psychology and psychiatry either inherited, transformed or invented to bring persons into the field of the calculable.

One important historical moment was the formal status awarded to several new categories of person, as a result of specific legislation to improve the administration of mental defectives. In Britain, the classification of whole classes of what was previously called lunacy was carried out by a Royal Commission in 1908, which recommended that the term 'mentally defective' be used as a general term to cover the entire range of lunacy, and that making clear sub-divisions within the overall class of defective would enhance their administration (Britain 1908: 187ff.). The interest here was to classify in order to administer. Rather than 'high grade' and 'low grade' idiots and imbeciles, the Commission recommended a sequence of words already in use but needing clearer definition: idiot, imbecile, feeble-minded, moral imbecile, epileptic and inebriate. Better classification meant that institutions and homes could become more specialised and better suited. The old asylums could be transformed into proper hospitals, with the implication that people could be treated in them. The Commission also received advice from physicians seeking to clarify those classifications which did not display obvious defect or insanity. One such type which attracted attention was the moral imbecile.

The moral imbecile was distinguishable from the morally insane in that insanity was something acquired later in life: 'a person who, after many years of reputable life, all at once unaccountably exhibits vicious propensities, or takes to criminal courses'. In contrast, imbecility, including moral imbecility, by definition manifested at birth or in early years of life. The Commission recommended a remodelled statute which would deal with people who were 'not lunatics or idiots' and who would require very different administration from either. After the First World War a Mental Defectives Act was passed in Britain, providing for the segregation, training and education of defectives. The continuum of imbecility and moral imbecility as enshrined in the British Royal Commission was used for the next two decades or more in both Britain and Australia as an authoritative set of classifications which would separate them from the idiot, the insane and also the criminal. In Australia, these administrative and legislative moves were reproduced in the 1929 Report of Mental Deficiency in the Commonwealth of Australia (Jones 1929), placing 'moral defectives' into a fourth class of defectives much the same as in the 1908 British Report. The definition of moral defective was almost identical: 'persons in whose case there exists mental defectiveness coupled with vicious or criminal propensities and who require care, supervision, and control for their own protection and the protection of others' (Britain 1908: 21).

The point to emphasise here is that the development of specific tools of measurement, which would both form and be formed by psychology and its immediate predecessors, was premised on the prior set of administrative distinctions, a group of 'not lunatics or idiots', whose administrative separation from the asylum and from medical institutions was well underway. The administrative separation and relocation established the preconditions for developing knowledge of this group. As it became possible through the development of these tools of calculation to identify the higher grades of defective, it also became possible to know this group as distinct from the insane and to know them by means of techniques distinct from medicine. The bureaucratic physical separation of a group which comes to be known as the defective-deficient, their removal to special schools and institutions under the gaze of the psychologist/educator, goes hand in hand with the growth in the availability of tools by which to articulate their identity. There was no simple cause and effect relationship.

The Royal Commission distinguishes between the imbecile and the idiot on the criterion of 'danger', in this case to oneself rather than others. The imbecile was incapable of earning his own living but was 'capable of guarding himself against physical dangers', while the idiot was one so deeply defective in mind from birth or from an early age that he was 'unable to guard himself against common physical dangers'. The third group, the feeble-minded, was marked off according to another distinctive criterion: 'capable of earning a living under favourable circumstances, but is incapable . . . a) of competing on equal terms with his normal fellows b) of managing himself and his affairs with ordinary prudence' (Britain 1908: 188). In 1918, Dr Richard Berry and Stanley Porteus published a practical guide for recognising feeble-mindedness – 'having the intelligence of a normal boy of 12 or less and unable to manage himself or his affairs with ordinary prudence, for example, incapable of holding any responsible position where judgement and commonsense are requisites' (*MJA* 1918: 87ff.). In this they were reinforcing clause 1 of the British Mental Deficiency Act defining feeble-mindedness: 'Persons in whose case there exists from birth, or from an early age, mental defectiveness not amounting to imbecility, yet so pronounced that they require care, supervision, and control for their own protection or others' (cited in *MJA* 1918: 485). By 1921 Berry and Porteus claimed that diagnosis could be assisted in the form of the

Porteus Maze test, which could 'disclose capacities not tested by the Binet method, such as prudence, forethought, planning capacity, ability to improve with practice and adaptability to a new situation' (*MJA* 1921: 173). Was this a test of capacity for prudence?

So while the idiot and the imbecile are marked off from one another according to the criteria of safety and danger, especially to themselves, the feeble-minded – the group in closest proximity to the normal – is marked off according to a lack of prudence. And all these categories are defined according to degrees of ability to self-govern, the ability to manage oneself and one's own affairs. However, the point to notice here is that the closer the category approaches the norm in terms of ability to self-govern, the more dangerous the category becomes. Those belonging to this category are more difficult to detect, require finer and more sophisticated tools and more specialist expertise to read the stigmata, which become increasingly more subtle and more buried. The point was recognised quite early by the doctors. Dr R. Stawell, the physician at Melbourne's Children's Hospital, used the term 'mentally feeble' to pinpoint that group which were neither imbecile or normal:

> They are practically ignored by the education authorities, and allowed to drift downwards to the gutter and the gaol, for though they are intellectually feeble, their passions are often strong, and always uncontrolled. Indeed, the fact that they are a danger to society has formed the basis of classification, idiots and low grade imbeciles are classed by M. Sollier as 'extra-social', and the mentally feeble are classed as 'anti-social'. (*Intercolonial Medical Journal* 1900: 88)

One doctor complained to the *Medical Journal* that the definition of mental deficiency in the British law was 'so wide that it could be applied to the majority of the population' (*MJA* 1916: 501–2). Berry and Porteus quoted Lord Goddard on the hidden danger of the feeble-minded: 'the most dangerous group of mental defectives are those who are in no way different from the intelligent man; and not only in outward appearance but in conversation and bearing, these people often pass for normal' (MJA 1918: 87ff.); and finally Dr W. A. T. Lind, whose career was devoted to showing that insanity was caused by syphilis, showed how the great danger of the mentally deficient lay in their hidden role in spreading venereal disease (AMC 1924: 409). Certainly the language used was that of risk, elusiveness, the drifting and roaming in our midst, 'the danger hanging over our Commonwealth'. Indeed, the higher the grade of feeble-mindedness, the greater the person's indefinability and dangerousness.

What arrived to save the situation was the cell, the new unit of primary meaningfulness, and it is through the work of Richard Berry that the cell comes fully into its own in the study of defect. Berry wrote in his article 'The organic factor in mental disease' (*MJA* 1925: 180) that 'the neuron is really the one important item and it is very small and very elusive'. Berry's work indicated how a precise network must be put in place in order to catch the elusive signs of feeble-mindedness, and here Berry wanted to highlight not only the structure of neurons but also the structure of linking apparatuses – 'the physical, psychological and social diagnostic approaches' – which were to fix and arrest the defective. Under Berry, the association between teacher and medical practitioner, as personified in the working relationship between Berry and Porteus, had the semblance of an institutional structure all of its own. The *Medical Journal of Australia* described Berry's work on cranial capacity as leading the response: 'It co-ordinated the services of the neurologist and the psychologist, and showed how these two, with the assistance of the educationist and the medical man, might pick out from the abnormal types of school life the future inefficients of adult life' (*MJA*, 1917: 536).

Later, the number of neurons became secondary to questions of their structure. What physiology and the study of reflexology gave was a quantitative measure, a 'clinical thermometer or measuring rod' (*MJA*, 1917) with which to recognise defect – something severely lacking in a 1912 national survey of feeble-mindedness which had relied on a qualitative assessment of the defective by schoolteachers ill-equipped for the task. Berry anticipated the need for a science to guide the direction he knew would be hazardous, the outcome unknown.

A number of authors have suggested that the basis for conceptualising the reflex model of human behaviour after the mid-eighteenth century can be found in various technologies existing at the time; for example, the appearance of heavy industrial equipment, such as the steam engine, impressed physiologists and anatomists by what it showed about the capacities of 'mechanism' itself, but also how it could incorporate self-regulating mechanisms such as the planetary valve (Richards 1992; Herrnstein and Boring 1965). These authors make good points about the particular take-up of cell theory in biology, and that the theorising of the reflex arc allowed for a fresh problematising of action independently of will. Their work also underlines psychology's debt to physiology, a point often downplayed in the histories of psychology. The particularities of Berry's work on the reflex arc, however, were that a new 'space' was brought into existence by means of the inscription devices at hand – the pathology report, the microscopic slide, the tables and diagrams – rather than a representation of existing models. This new space, I would argue, becomes a surface of emergence for new ways of knowing individuals and managing them, but also new sites in which individuals can come to know and govern themselves.

Reflexology, the study of the reflex nervous system, provided the basic 'atom' or unit by which behaviour could begin to be counted. Just as the cell was the basic structural unit, so the functional coordination of sensory, central and motor neuronic cells into a simple arc was regarded as the 'unit of behaviour' (Allport 1937: 137). A new kind of non-voluntary behaviour came into focus which had nothing to do with being 'out of one's mind' or 'overcome by passions'. Leaving out the mind, as it were, allowed a concentration on the way certain kinds of behaviours could circumvent the brain entirely and become entirely independent of the will, yet still be measurable. Take the classic 'knee-jerk reaction'. In physiological terms, the arc from the stimulus (a blow to receptor cells in the knee) to the response (the motor cells cause the knee to jerk) does not have to reach the brain at all – it is a non-cerebral action, automatic and independent of will. Berry's work on the neuronic arc and his theory of the development of cerebral structure was first published in 1924 under the title 'The correlation of recent advances in cerebral structure and function with feeble-mindedness and its diag-nostic applicability' (*MJA* 1924: 393ff.). His work represents an import-ant transitional stage for the emergence of a psychological interest in feeble-mindedness and the subsequent category of psychopathic person-ality, and for this reason deserves a closer inspection.

Berry divided brain development into an evolutionary history of five epochs or types of 'neuronic arcs', so that as animals become more sophisticated (speaking in an evolutionary sense) the circuit becomes longer and more complex.

> In the higher animals such an immediate response to the stimulus would often be disadvantageous to the animal's welfare . . . [It becomes essential] to have a period of latency . . . as it were, for reflection and allows for a selection of the most advantageous motor reaction . . . The new element which so produces the period of latency by holding in check the effective response to the stimulus until the most favourable moment has arrived . . . the important factor of inhibition or delay in response. (*MJA* 1924: 393ff.)

At this stage of the development of neuronic machinery, behaviour cannot be any longer a matter of instantaneous impulse, but is made subject to a certain degree of supervisional review guided by a primitive form of judgment which may be taken to mark the beginning of psychic life. The fifth epoch, the addition of the psycho-associational neurone of the supra-granular cortex, was responsible for the receptive, the psychic and the voluntary psychic. Berry linked, or correlated, the achievement of epochs with brain functioning. So low-grade or 'more marked dements' showed a decrease in the depth of the infra-granular cortex ('the brain of the animal instincts') and hence idiots and imbeciles were 'unable to carry on the ordinary animal functions'. High-grade amentia (feeble-mindedness) had all the animal instincts intact but an insufficient neuronic development of the supra-granular layer – the site of reflection and control (prudence). Thus, the degrees of self-management as outlined in documents such as those of the Royal Commission were here given a grounding in biology. A kind of biological foundation to self-government – the ability to manage one's affairs – was able to be read from the epochal layering of brain cells.

For Berry, different grades of mental defectiveness could be constructed which corresponded to the network of neuronic arcs, and his hierarchical scale of idiot, imbecile and high-grade moron was directly proportional to the intricacy of the neuronic arcs or pathways involved from stimulus to response. Hence his belief that cranial capacity existed in direct proportion to mental capacity (*MJA* 1924: 393ff.). According to Berry's schema, the high-grade moron, or moral imbecile, was the outcome of a physiological defect – a truncated pattern of neuronic pathways, which, though less gross than other grades of defectiveness, narrowed the gap between stimulus and response, that gap in which the 'moral' qualities of prudence, forethought and judgment could take place. The model took in behaviour which might be seen to circumvent rational or prudent judgment. An example of reflexivity in the extreme was H. Cleckley's version of psychopathic personality in *The Mask of Sanity* (1941); the psychopath was not a 'complete' man at all, but something resembling 'a subtly constructed reflex machine which can mimic the human personality perfectly' (Cleckley 1941: 398; Bleechmore 1975: 37–8).

I have indicated how these transmutations allowed for the possibility of being deficient in capacity and how, through the development of such tools, the 'mentally deficient' became known. Psychological measurement's ties to physiological measurement also explain the virtual interchangeability during much of this early period of the terms 'mentally defective', an account of (physiological) structure, and 'mentally deficient', an account of (psychological) capacity. The category of moral imbecility was different, however. Although this group was initially calculable on a grid of the 'mentally deficient/defective' and was able to be known, through these tools of calculation, as a group distinct from the insane, the means for knowing the defective eventually proved to be inadequate to grasp the moral imbecile. This 'failure' was first observed in the recognition that the moral defective might score average or even above-average in intelligence. But the conditions of possibility for different means of calculation of moral defect lay once again in the administrative and spatial arrangements put in place for this group. There is perhaps no better place to document the setting out of these arrangements than Tasmania.

The Space for Personality

The Tasmanian Mental Deficiency Act was passed in 1920 and proclaimed in 1922, after which a Mental Deficiency Board and a State
Psychological Clinic were established. The head of psychology at Sydney
University, H. Tasman Lovell, congratulated the Tasmanians on recognising the necessity for an ongoing 'mental survey' of the people. Now
that the instrument had been delivered into the hands of scientific
psychology, the state could exercise its responsibilities towards those
found to be defective, especially the low-grade moron, the imbecile and
the idiot. The Act had recognised the problem as a scientific rather than
moral one, and Lovell commented at length about the social improvement it would bring, in terms of making mentally deficient people
healthier and happier and the likely reduction in antisocial acts (Lovell
1923: 285–89). Indeed, for the professional practitioners these latter
implications seemed to hold far more interest. The Mental Deficiency
Board reported in its first year that extensive surveys of the entire school
population had begun and several avenues of supervision, care and
training had been opened up. The Psychological Clinic had also begun
its diagnosis and classification of 'exceptional children . . . those who
deviate from the normal, positively or negatively':

> are retarded in schoolwork, mentally dull and backward; who manifest
> abnormal or aberrant trends, resent reasonable discipline, show undue signs
> of obduracy or stubbornness, misbehave as psychopaths, delinquents, truants
> or inferiors, reveal marked instability and want of control during puberty and
> adolescence; in fact, who are in any way maladjusted to the ordinary condi-
> tions of life whether in the home, school, or community. In short, the clinic
> is concerned with the mental hygiene of childhood. (Parliament of Tasmania
> 1922–23: paper no. 25)

The Act had given the Clinic certain duties regarding the legally enforceable placement of defective individuals but the major interest for the
emergent psychologists was not with classifying and batching the imbeciles and idiots, but rather with building a firmer knowledge-base of the
mental status and functioning of children who deviated from the norm,
but not too far: 'especially in cases where normality is latent or maturity
of mind is delayed; where aberrant or deviating trends are manifest; where
advice is desired concerning corrective pedagogics for special abilities;
where an analysis of the mental factors involved in delinquencies is
necessary' (Parliament of Tasmania, 1922–23: paper no. 25). So the Act
itself and the charter for Australia's first State psychological clinic showed,
at the very least, some degree of convergence of the problem of deficiency
on the one hand, and the problem of the delinquent and the dangerous,
the 'unstable and the psychopathic', on the other.

But there was by now clear evidence that the tool which had allowed the moral imbecile to share beds with the mental defective proved too narrow to obtain a reading of the dimension of the 'moral'. More 'space', or rather some other kind of space, was needed to incorporate a group previously but inadequately known as 'defective' or 'deficient' whose administration had early been recognised as a problem. That pioneer of educational measurement, Alfred Binet, observed in 1905 the limitations of the intellectual measure for knowing this group:

> in the definition of this state, we should make some restrictions. Most sub-normal children, especially those in schools, are habitually grouped in two categories, those of backward intelligence, and those who are unstable. This latter class, which certain alienists call moral imbeciles, do not necessarily manifest inferiority of intelligence: they are turbulent, vicious, rebellious to all discipline; they lack sequence of ideas, and probably power of attention . . . It would necessitate a long study, and probably a very difficult one, to establish the distinctive signs which separate the unstable from the undisciplined. For the present we shall not take up this study. (Binet 1905: 37–45)

So here, from the inception of the intelligence test, a group was recognised that although generally conceived as sitting atop the hierarchy of mental defectiveness-deficiency nevertheless sat in an uneasy relation to the overall category. Measurements of mental capacity, rather than leading to a thorough knowledge of this liminal group, tended to put a question-mark over its identifiability, progressively hewing it off from the main population of defectives-deficients. This group was unable to be known and governed, using the existing technology applied to the overall classification.

But how to capture this problem group whose identity was not fixed and arrested by intelligence tests? How to capture a group of 'defectives' who were not 'truly defective'? Kurt Danziger (1990) argues that through the proliferation of tools created to identify more knowledge of the useful components of 'normal' individuality, psychology forged that space it comes to know as personality. As he explains, performances on personality tests were taken to reflect inherent properties revealed in the task of doing the test: 'the fundamental psychological meanings and reference of the empirical data were constituted by an interpretive construction that was not derived from those data but preceded their collection' (Danziger 1990: 161). Danziger claims that personality tests transformed a set of language terms such as 'dependence' into unambiguous properties of the natural world which could be investigated as a physicist might investigate electrical resistance. What this amounted to, for him, was 'a masquerade in which categories generated by a very specific social order were held to represent an ahistorical natural order'

(Danziger 1990: 162). He then goes on to explore the cultural preconceptions and interests of groups who were responsible for the development of the tests.

I would argue a slightly different position to this, which has to do with
tracing some of the continuities of the historical argument outlined in
this chapter. It seems on the basis of the sort of historical evidence
reviewed above that the 'origins' of personality as a governable field can
be found not so much from the 'something more' needed to make up
the deficiencies of intelligence tests on the normal population (from the
demands, for example, that something other than intellect needs to be
known if we wanted to choose the right person to be a bank manager),
but rather from the 'something else' that was required to calculate that
space where dangerous moral defect resided but could no longer be
calculated. The 'content' of personality would seem, on this account, to
derive from an already existing space carved out by the physiology of
disorder, a space where morality seemed to reside but was no longer
calculable, rather than from the cultural preconceptions of an 'ordered'
personality derived from the inventors of personality tests. This space
developed as a response to a governmental problem of managing the
'problem' individual – the individual which needed to be governed.
Nikolas Rose (1990) argues this way in relation to the more general
application of the 'psy-disciplines' under liberal forms of government;
that is to say, that which was normal did not need to be governed.

A plea for that 'something' with which to know the 'not truly defective' defective began to appear from the late 1920s, accompanied by the
gradual abandonment of the term 'defective' and its replacement with
the term 'psychopath'. This signals the beginning of a splitting of a
group from the mentally deficient-defective category, and that the technology associated with the administration of this group can no longer
incorporate it. The invention of psychopathic personality allows a grid
of calculability over the entire population, whose chief defining characteristic is the government of defective morality.

There is a fundamental change in inscription processes as we move
from the measurement of performance capacities to that of personality.
With the multiplication of performance tests, the individual was able to
occupy a position on multiple grids or lines representing multiple
ratings for different abilities or characteristics, rather than merely on a
single line of intelligence. It was possible to expand the register of
human capacities (and, for that matter, the work of psychology) with
multiple lines gauging multiple performances. But if left this way, the
result is an unwieldy criss-cross of lines *ad hoc* and *ad infinitum*. In order
to serve the twin goals of turning this kind of work into a bounded
knowledge of psychology *and* transforming a loose aggregate of

inscribed gauges of performance capacities into a bounded space nameable by psychologists as personality, it was necessary to find some way of relating these lines to one another. Here, as I have argued, the problem requiring government (and knowledge of the population in order to govern) had to do with the disordered rather than the normal. What other inscription devices became important for this kind of shaping and binding? Let me mention just two which appear to be significant for subsequent studies of personality: Sir Francis Galton's normal distribution held the beginnings of a technology of charting the individual's relative position in space; and Sir Charles Spearman's work marked the earliest attempts at breaking up the single gauge into a multiplicity.

Spearman's work on the so-called 'general' or 'g' factor was concerned with finding relations between different gauges and thus trans-muting them into a bounded field by plotting their interconnectedness. The Australian psychologist, C. Jorgensen, makes the point that Spearman's ideas about specific and general abilities were certainly not new, but he did put the theory on a definite scientific basis: 'the obtaining of all the inter-correlations of all the abilities under consider-ation . . . for the purposes of ascertaining whether or not more than one factor, "g", has been in operation to cause the correlations' (Jorgensen 1932: 10). Once this transmutation from multiple dislocated knowledges into a space of interconnectedness has occurred a new 'whole' can emerge, amenable to measurement. Indeed, the very possibility of its emergence depended on the measurability of its constituent parts. This became clear in John Bowlby's subsequent reworking of Spearman's ideas on factor analysis in his chapter dealing with 'measuring person-ality' (Bowlby 1940). Bowlby noted that activities such as writing, dotting, tapping and so on are able to be measured and then correlated with 'salient features in the personality of the subject'. Motor tests could be used to isolate and measure certain general factors: 'These cannot be immediately correlated with superficial personal qualities but they probably do represent some fairly fundamental factor in the make-up of personality' (Bowlby 1940: 29).

This kind of work, and the proliferation of knowledge of this kind of work, is incremental in creating the possibility of speaking of personality as a whole entity or structure, whose components lend themselves to measurement. Bowlby manifested the psychiatrist's nervousness about psychology's failure to 'feel into' the person (as Hans Eysenck [1952] described it), that is, to really know the 'inside' of the person. But there is a strong argument to say that psychology was not born out of a set of practices concerned with knowing the person in this way. Rather, it was born out of a set of administrative problems to do with where individuals might be located in relation to other individuals – in institutions, in the company, the army, the school, and so on. Jorgensen's remarks on the usefulness of the Spearman factor outlined the problem of, and for, psychology as primarily one of predicting performance 'on the job'; psychology's own view of itself simply took for granted its status as a helpful tool of administration and management. While the concept of a countable unit of behaviour may be rooted in physiology, psychology's own primitive implement is the report card and the test result, not the microscope slide or the scalpel. In this sense then, psychology was born out of problems to do with charting 'the social' – the spaces between individuals – and thus about the synchronic coordination of knowledges across space rather than time. The space called personality, as produced out of a multiplicity of individual measurements and forged eventually into 'co-relations', was not the internal space of an individual psyche, but a synchronic mapping of the social – the spaces between individuals. With this emphasis on the synchronics of administration, psychology can be viewed as a kind of economics, bolstered by other discourses of efficiency of the day. Psychological processes became the means to achieve the desired success with the least expenditure of effort, such as increasing the efficiency of children in school.

Emerging from the separated group of defectives and deficients came the 'psychopathic personality', but it too comes to be understood with yet another set of tools, this time provided by the psychology of personality. I have argued that this category of person emerged out of the category of the defective, and this is also apparent from the administrative arrangements taking shape during this period. The word 'control' is used repeatedly, not 'care' or 'treatment', indicating the shift of this category of persons outside the medical framework of understanding. In Victoria, from 1937 until 1940 there were repetitions of earlier calls for adequate legislation and institutions to deal with the mental defective, but with a new emphasis on the 'control of higher grade mental defectives' who were beyond the ambit of education or child welfare. There was also now mention of the Mental Defectives (Convicted Persons) Act 1939, still under the Lunacy Act but with the unequivocal recognition that this group is 'not insane' (Victoria. *Annual Report of the Inspector-General* 1940). Hence, there was legislation in place to treat convicted persons who were mentally defective as a distinct group but no general Act. Mental defectives still fall under the Lunacy Act, even though they are recognised as 'mental defective but not insane'. The rhetoric slides between 'control' of the defective (the word 'control' being the pivotal signifier of the penal system) and 'care and treatment' (as the signifiers of the hospital system). Here we begin to see the congealing of a problem group. It is defined as beyond the parameters of education and child welfare and exists somewhere between 'control' and 'treatment', between the prison and the hospital. By 1946, however, there was an attempt at clarifying and delimiting a group which to that point still defied definite classification:

> The definition of a 'mentally defective person' laid down by the [Mental Defective (Convicted Persons)] Act is somewhat narrow, implying only the criterion of inherent intellectual defect. The Act should be amended so as to embrace individuals neither mentally defective nor insane, but who come within the category of psychopathic personalities. (Victoria. *Annual Report of the Inspector-General* 1946)

The move to personality as a grid for measuring dangerousness involved a shift of inquiry from the internal structure of individuals to a relative position of an individual to others in an external field. Diagnosis has then to rely on statistical correlation of actions, behaviours and conducts. What arrives in 1952 is 'sociopathic personality disturbance, antisocial type' presented under a listing of 'Personality Disorders – disorders of psychogenic origin or without clearly defined tangible cause or structural change', inscribed into the first edition of the *Diagnostic and Statistical Manual* of the American Psychiatric Association (American Psychiatric Association 1952). It was no longer possible to assess dangerousness on the basis of a calculation of the individual body.

Conclusion

This chapter argues that it becomes possible to think and act upon dangerous persons as a consequence of specific techniques of calculating mental defectiveness. Two aspects of this study are worth noting: firstly, the category of the moral imbecile produced by these techniques allows a carving out of a space or dimension which made individuals amenable to a kind of internal moral measurement. Here I want to argue, against some other accounts in the history of psychology, that certain inscription devices produced knowledge of persons and their internal dimensions as a means of seeking to manage and govern them – that certain types of person or conditions of personhood, such as the moral imbecile, came about as an artefact of government. Second, the failure to adequately grasp the measure of dangerousness through an internal gaze on the body provided the conditions for posing the problem using the conceptual machinery of 'personality' to permit the mapping of the spaces between people. I would suggest that one implication of the study is to disturb the understood nature of the modern categories of personality and personality disorder and, in particular, to unsettle the dichotomy of 'the biological' and 'the social' domains in which these categories are theorised.

Note

My thanks to Jennifer Laurence for her assistance with this work, and to the Australian Research Council for its support for the project.

References

Allport, G. W., 1937. *Personality. A Psychological Interpretation*, London: Constable.

American Psychiatric Association 1952, *Diagnostic and Statistical Manual. Mental Disorders*, Washington

(AMC) Australasian Medical Congress, Proceedings, 1900–25.

Binet, A., 1905. *The Development of Intelligence in Children*, New Jersey: Vineland Training School.

Bleechmore, J. F., 1975. 'Towards a rational theory of criminal responsibility: the psychopathic offender. Part Two: Psychopathy, logic and criminal responsibility: some conclusions', *Melbourne University Law Review* 10, 2: 207–24.

Bowlby, J., 1940. *Personality and Mental Illness: An Essay in Psychiatric Diagnosis*, London: Kegan Paul, Trench, Trubner.

Britain. Royal Commission on the Care and Control of the Feeble-Minded, London: Great Britain Parliamentary Papers, vol. VIII, 1908.

Cleckley, H., 1941. *The Mask of Sanity: An Attempt to Clarify Some Issues about the So-called Psychopathic Personality*, St Louis: C. V. Mosby.

Danziger, K., 1990. *Constructing the Subject. Historical Origins of Psychological Research*, Cambridge: Cambridge University Press.

Eysenck, H., 1952. *The Scientific Study of Personality*, London: Routledge & Kegan Paul.

Glaser, W., 1994. 'Commentary: Gary David, psychiatry, and the discourse of dangerousness', *Australian and New Zealand Journal of Criminology* 27: 46–9.

Hacking, I., 1986. 'Making up people' in T. Heller et al. (eds), *Reconstructing Individualism: Autonomy, Individuality and the Self in Western Thought*, Stanford: Stanford University Press.

Herrnstein, R. J. and Boring, E. E., 1965. *Sourcebook in the History of Psychology*, Cambridge, Mass.: Harvard University Press.

Historical Records of Australia (1914) Series: 1, *Governors' Despatches to and from England*, vol. I, 1788–96, Library Committee of the Commonwealth Parliament, pp. 2–8.

Intercolonial Medical Journal, 1900.

Jones, W. Ernest, 1929. *Report of Mental Deficiency in the Commonwealth of Australia*, Canberra: H. J. Green, Government Printer.

Jorgensen, C., 1932. *An Analysis of Certain Psychological Tests by the Spearman Factor Method*, London: E. A. Gold.

Lovell, H. Tasman, 1923. 'The Tasmanian Mental Deficiency Act', *Australasian Journal of Psychology and Philosophy* 1, 4.

(*MJA*) *Medical Journal of Australia*, 1900–24.

New South Wales. Mental Defectives Act 1938.

New South Wales. Mental Defectives (Convicted Persons) Act 1939.

Parliament of Tasmania. Paper No. 9, *Education Department Report for 1922*, Journals and Papers LXXXIX, 1923–24.

Parliament of Tasmania. Paper No. 25, *Mental Deficiency Board Report for 1922–23*. Journals and Papers LXXXIX, 1923–24.

Parliament of Victoria, 1990. Social Development Committee. *Interim Report: Strategies to Deal with Persons with Severe Personality Disorder who Pose a Threat to Public Safety*, Melbourne: Government Printer.

Richards, G., 1992. *Mental Machinery: The Origins and Consequences of Psychological Ideas. Part 1 1600–1850*, London: Athlone Press.

Rose, N., 1990. *Governing the Soul: The Shaping of the Private Self*, London: Routledge.

Treadgold, A. F. and Treadgold, R. F., 1953. *Manual of Psychological Medicine for Practitioners and Students*, London: Bailliere Tindall and Cox.

Victoria. *Annual Report of the Inspector-General of the Insane (Mental Health Authority)*, 1900–50.

Victoria. Department of Mental Hygiene. *Report of the Director of Mental Hygiene*, 1950.

Victoria. An Act to Make Provision for the Care of Mentally Defective Persons and Mentally Retarded Children and for other Purposes (Mental Deficiency Act) No. 4704, 18 December 1939, Victorian Acts of Parliament, 4 Geo VI, 1939.

Williams, C. R., 1990. 'Psychopathy, mental illness and preventative detention: issues arising from the *David* case', *Monash University Law Review* 16, 2: 161–83.

CHAPTER 7

The Constitution of AIDS in Australia
Taking 'Government at a Distance' Seriously

John Ballard

Australia's policy response to Acquired Immunodeficiency Syndrome (AIDS) has frequently been held up as a model of global best practice. The few comparative analyses of national AIDS policies (Kirp and Bayer 1992; Mann and Tarantola 1996) portray the Australian approach as enlightened and innovative, and a recent evaluation of Australia's National HIV/AIDS Strategy (Feachem 1995) has found such indices as its low rate of Human Immunodeficiency Virus (HIV) incidence exceptionally good.

A diagnosis of the conditions of possibility for government policy offers potential for a rich interpretation of this perceived success. Drawing on Michel Foucault's concept of governmentality, Nikolas Rose and Peter Miller argue that a liberal problematics of government is 'dependent upon technologies for "governing at a distance", seeking to create locales, entities and persons able to operate a regulated autonomy' (1992: 173). Government is a problematising activity, elaborating programs around perceived difficulties and failures and making 'the objects of government thinkable in such a way that their ills appear susceptible to diagnosis, prescription and cure by calculating and normalising intervention' (1992: 183). The strategies, techniques and procedures through which programs are rendered operable are designated 'technologies of government' (1992: 185), and elsewhere Rose (1995) examines the operation and effects of these technologies in the shaping of the human subject.

Rose and Miller raise questions not posed directly by more traditional literature on public policy. They provide a perspective for interpreting the ways in which government in Australia recognised AIDS as a problem for which it was responsible, and then applied a choice of available technologies to limit HIV transmission. In return, the Australian response to AIDS offers an exceptionally sensitive application of the Rose and Miller approach, since the novelty of AIDS makes it possible to discern precisely the processes of problematisation, choice of technology and subjectification.

Problematising AIDS

Early perceptions of AIDS have been recounted not only by journalists and historians picking through the evidence of individual and institutional records and memories (Shilts 1987; Grmek 1990; Garrett 1994), but also in several papers which examine more broadly the discourses which shaped AIDS as a new issue. Dennis Altman (1984) produced an early set of insights in a paper on the homosexualisation, medicalisation and Americanisation of AIDS, while Ken Plummer (1988), Paula Treichler (1988) and Cindy Patton (1990) have examined the structuring of scientific, social and political perceptions.

Epidemiology had a central role in the initial recognition and definition of AIDS. Concerned with the distribution of disease within populations, epidemiologists have come to see themselves as cartographers, drawing boundaries around risk. But while epidemiologists use highly sophisticated statistical techniques in the manipulation of data, their categories of identity for specifying risk are untheorised and drawn from everyday cultural classifications. This is perhaps inevitable in the preliminary identification of an epidemiological problem, when symptoms are the only evidence available and specific 'risk behaviours' and aetiological agents are unknown. But 'risk groups' are readily conflated with 'risk behaviours', particularly when the groups in question lie outside the pale of normality defined by the culture of the epidemiologists of a particular time and place.

Thus, epidemiologists of the United States Center for Disease Control (CDC) in Atlanta, when confronted in 1981 with evidence that exotic forms of cancer and pneumonia were appearing among young men whose only common feature was sexual activity with many male partners, adopted the category of 'homosexual' as its initial 'risk group'. In doing so they embraced a category with a century of psychological, medical and legal authority behind it, as well as a decade of social mobilisation by gay men in the United States in terms of their sexual identity. As AIDS was gradually recognised among people who did not fit the initial category, further ready-made risk groups were identified as 'heroin abusers', 'Haitians' and 'hemophiliacs'. Further research by CDC and others identified specific risk behaviours of body fluid exchange through sexual penetration, needle sharing and transfusion of blood and blood products, and these were confirmed once an aetiological agent (later named the Human Immunodeficiency Virus) was accorded recognition by scientific authority in the most respected peer-reviewed journals. Despite their lack of congruence with these risk behaviours, the designated 'risk groups' remained intact, enshrined in epidemiological statistics and adopted in the design of public policy, social research and educational programs.

As cartographers, epidemiologists are analogous to others who must identify, define, demarcate and label populations in the process of rendering them amenable to intervention. They provide 'the "representation" of that which is to be governed' (Rose and Miller 1992: 185). In comparable fashion early colonial administrators, when confronted with populations which needed to be differentiated for purposes of incorporation, segregation, control and 'development', defined 'tribal' and 'ethnic' groups within which to identify collaborative 'chiefs' and around which to draw administrative boundaries. These categories take on a life of their own as they become socially and politically useful for those who are ascribed or who assume an ethnic identity, and the same can be said of the evolution of a homosexual group identity over the past century in response to the activities of government (Ballard 1987, 1992b).

AIDS would not have been identified as early as it was but for the appearance of rare opportunistic infections among young gay men in Los Angeles and New York; its contemporary appearance in Africa and Europe was sufficiently buried among other symptoms to remain unrecognised and would have raised different categories of risk. It was perceived as a syndrome of rare diseases, with no clearly established methods of transmission and an assumption during the early years that it was fatal within months after transmission. Yet identifying AIDS as a disease primarily affecting socially stigmatised groups meant that stigma was central to the construction of AIDS as a medical, social and policy issue (Treichler 1988). It could be argued that without homophobia and the initial identification of AIDS as a fatal disease, it might have aroused little more public interest than another sexually transmitted disease, genital warts, which can produce cervical cancer. In addition, if AIDS had not been identified in Anglo-Saxon societies as a disease of gay men, a group already mobilised around a stigmatised identity, there is little likelihood that AIDS would have elicited a strong community response; it failed to do so in other societies.

The particularities of the time and place of recognition, together with the initial categorisation of risk of transmission, created conditions of possibility for the problematisation of AIDS. These did not in themselves require a governmental response, as is evident from the absence of response by the United States federal government and many others during the first years. The fact that the Australian Commonwealth government responded earlier than others (Ballard 1992a) suggests that there were further stages of problematisation.

Australia, like most of the English-speaking world, had gradually adopted the logic of the Wolfenden Report of 1956, reconstructing homosexuality and prostitution in terms of public proscription and private freedom (Hall 1980). Governments had withdrawn from the active policing of private consensual sex and were thus no longer responsible for its outcomes. As long as AIDS was seen as a problem arising primarily from homosexual activity, governments were not inclined to consider it their concern. However the possibility of transmission of AIDS through blood transfusion and blood products raised a particular concern for Australian governments. Geographical isolation had given rise to an exceptional measure of blood self-sufficiency, and the Commonwealth and State governments funded the collection and distribution of blood and blood products through the Australian Red Cross and the production of blood-clotting concentrates through the Commonwealth Serum Laboratories.

After an initial burst of activity in mid-1983, with the formation of AIDS Action Committees in the urban gay communities and the appointment of a working party of the National Health and Medical Research Council to plan AIDS surveillance and care, there was no serious concern focused on AIDS for a year. Despite a mounting number of AIDS cases and deaths among gay men, it was not until July 1984, with the announcement of the first Australian case of transmission by blood transfusion of the newly identified retrovirus, that media and government attention was seriously aroused. Until then, it was assumed that Australia's self-sufficient system of voluntary blood donation would be safe from contamination.

Close links between Australia's medical scientists and the United States centres which were developing the first tests for the virus made possible the detection of blood transmission and soon produced evidence of its wide spread among Sydney's gay men. In October 1984 it was discovered that the virus was present in the blood of one-third of those with haemophilia who had received Factor VIII concentrate, produced from the blood of large numbers of donors by the Commonwealth Serum Laboratories. Steps were quickly taken to exclude risk groups from blood donation and to apply heat treatment to kill the virus in Factor VIII (Ballard 1996).

What firmly established AIDS as a problem for government was an announcement by the Queensland Minister for Health on 16 November 1984, in the midst of a Commonwealth election campaign, that three babies had died after receiving contaminated blood from a gay donor.

This traumatised the media and galvanised the Commonwealth Minister of Health, Neal Blewett, into action. He called an emergency meeting of health ministers and advisers to standardise donor-exclusion procedures, fund the development of viral test kits and establish both a medical AIDS Task Force and a National Advisory Committee on AIDS. The latter, given responsibility for devising education programs, was broadly representative and included leaders of the Sydney and Melbourne AIDS Councils.

Elsewhere governments did not problematise AIDS in the same fashion since responsibility for blood safety was seldom clearly that of government, but more often diffused by commercial supply and importation. The nexus between Australian governments, the Australian Red Cross Blood Transfusion Services and the Commonwealth Serum Laboratories was unique. In addition, Australian virology laboratories were the only group outside the United States invited to participate in the evaluation of viral antibody test kits, enabling Australia by May 1985 to become the first country with a fully tested blood supply. In January 1985 its Factor VIII supply was the first to become fully heat-treated. Evidence of slower response by governments and suppliers of blood and Factor VIII raised major political scandals later in France, Canada and Japan.

While blood control was an issue in all Western countries by 1985, only in Australia did it serve to define AIDS as a problem both requiring and enabling political intervention. AIDS retained its identification with marginalised groups, but the political crisis created by blood contamination provided an opening in Australia for the incorporation of these groups into policy-making on AIDS. Other Western governments acknowledged responsibility for AIDS and began seriously funding education programs only after an international AIDS conference in July 1986 provided consensus among scientists on the actuality of vaginal transmission and, hence, risk to the 'general population'.

Technologies of Government

If Australia gained advantage from its early recognition of AIDS as a problem for government, it also benefited from its choice of technology for intervention in behaviour. While medical science and government funding could resolve the problem of blood transmission, there was no comparable solution in the form of a vaccine to prevent transmission of the virus through sexual intercourse and shared needles. There was, however, a choice of strategies for preventing transmission.

As in most countries, a battery of direct public health controls was enshrined in Australian legislation dating from early in the century, based on experience with tuberculosis and sexually transmitted diseases.

These involved surveillance, testing, notification, contact-tracing, treat-ment (when available) and quarantine. An alternative strategy of health promotion had been articulated since the 1960s, eventually promul-gated by the World Health Organisation in the Ottawa Charter of 1986. Emphasising community-based education and self-regulation, this strategy fitted with the ideas of the community health and women's health movements in Australia, and had gained substantial legitimacy within de-medicalised health departments through the perceived success of anti-tobacco programs in the late 1970s. Health promotion was insti-tutionalised in Blewett's restructuring of the Commonwealth Depart-ment of Health in late 1984, and the appointment of a leading exponent of the anti-tobacco campaigns as secretary of the department.

These two public health strategies neatly encapsulate the distinction drawn by Michael Mann (1986) between 'despotic' individualised direct control and the 'infrastructural', regular, continuing and indirect controls consistent with liberal principles. In coping with AIDS, Cuba has been the only country which attempted to establish a 'despotic' regime of systematic quarantine, although Vietnam's initial response to its first cases of AIDS in 1993–94 was to launch a campaign against the 'three social evils' of AIDS, drugs and prostitution through isolation in rehabilitation centres.

In Australia the allocation of AIDS to different branches within departments of health provides an index to initial differences in prob-lematisation and associated technologies. In the Commonwealth department, an AIDS Co-ordinating Unit was established within the new Division of Health Promotion, and there was an exceptional measure of political initiative from the minister's office for the first year. In Queens-land, Tasmania and South Australia AIDS was assigned to offices con-cerned with sexually transmitted diseases and tended to be dealt with through the containment strategies applied to these. By contrast, AIDS was allocated in Western Australia and Victoria to health promotion branches with quite different results in the early years. In Victoria the Director of Health Promotion considered that only gay men understood the possibilities of health education for gay men; over strong objections from medical specialists she hired two leaders of the Victorian AIDS Council to organise community education programs and she agreed to fund a Gay Men's Community Health Centre. This provided the Com-monwealth government with a model for treating AIDS as a problem for health promotion.

The two contending approaches of containment and education became institutionalised during 1985–87 at the Commonwealth level in the two advisory committees, the medical AIDS Task Force, headed by the forceful Dean of the University of Melbourne Faculty of Medicine,

David Penington, and the National Advisory Council (NACAIDS), with its strong community representation. Penington initially proposed the closure of gay bath-houses and argued for testing risk groups. NACAIDS, supported by Blewett's office and the Commonwealth department, consistently opted for community-based education in the absence of any available treatment. The challenge to community and health promotion posed by Penington's assertion of a medical rationality served to bind the AIDS Councils, NACAIDS and the Commonwealth department together; the States, with the exception of Queensland, were willing to follow the logic of Commonwealth financial support.

There ensued a veiled conflict over the ownership of AIDS, with Penington and later the Australian Medical Association accusing Blewett of following a 'gay agenda'. Blewett's success in persuading the opposition parties to participate in a parliamentary liaison group on AIDS, together with the absence in Australia of politically mobilised Christian fundamentalism, forestalled politicisation of the conflict. By 1989 the development of a broad range of technologies was articulated in the world's first National Strategy on HIV/AIDS, based on extensive community consultation, with an explicit commitment to the principles of the Ottawa Charter and formal support from the parliamentary opposition. Following on the comprehensive approach of the National Strategy, a legal working party examined all fields of State law impinging on AIDS issues and recommended model laws consistent with the principles of health promotion.

AIDS and Citizenship

Rose and Miller argue that, in the liberal welfare state, 'power is not so much a matter of imposing constraints upon citizens as of "making up" citizens capable of bearing a kind of regulated freedom' (1992: 174). In exercising power, 'political forces have sought to utilise, instrumentalise and mobilize techniques and agents other than those of the "state" in order to govern "at a distance"' (1992: 181). Health promotion through community education provided a technology for precisely this kind of government at a distance, but community education required as a site for action a community whose representatives had potential legitimacy for (re)defining responsible citizenship within the community.

In the 1970s the United States tradition of ethnic group mobilisation offered a model for the development of gay communities in the English-speaking world and beyond. In Sydney, echoing San Francisco, a gay ghetto developed, facilitating mobilisation and communication, and less concentrated communities appeared in the other capital cities. The gay media maintained detailed coverage of AIDS news from the United

States, providing education on risk well before government-funded health promotion began. Despite the marginalised status of homosexuality, no conceivable 'risk group' was better placed to raise a community response and contribute to policy-making (see Altman 1994). By contrast, gay men in France, without legal sanctions against which to develop a politics of identity, failed for several years to organise a community response to AIDS.

The Victorian AIDS Council, invited by the State health department to help shape AIDS education, was well integrated with the Melbourne gay community and had developed substantial expertise on AIDS. Drawing initially on programs developed by Gay Men's Health Crisis in New York, early in 1985 it articulated a concept of safe sex for gay men emphasising the use of condoms. In Sydney by contrast, despite several initiatives within a much larger gay community, both community and government responses were diffused among a number of organisations, with limited collaboration until 1988. Only then did the AIDS Council of New South Wales and the new State AIDS Bureau begin to set the pace in AIDS program innovation.

Gay sexuality since the 1960s had proved exceptionally plastic, and the notion of safe sex, unencumbered by the insistence in the United States on the narrower rationality of 'safer sex' (as on 'drug abuse'), was open to creative and inventive talents. Safe sex was a technique of the self, a form of ethical citizenship, which served several purposes. It was sex-positive at a time of maximum stigmatisation of gay men, whose self-image was vulnerable at the best of times. The Victorian AIDS Council produced the first educational poster, the erotic 'You'll Never Forget the Feeling of Safe Sex', while a program of 'Happy, Healthy and Gay' workshops was organised in Canberra; both were widely copied elsewhere. Safe sex reinforced the image of community, needed both for collective subjectivity and for legitimation of the Councils in the eyes of government. It also provided a credible alternative to Penington's proposal for testing those at risk, an approach which was individualist rather than community-based and which was seen as having the potential to divide the community between seropositive and seronegative men. As an effective strategy of prevention, safe sex was later validated by epidemiological cohort studies (Donovan and Tindall 1989; Feachem 1995).

Further education and research programs grew up around the model of community safe-sex education developed by the AIDS Councils, encouraged and funded by the Commonwealth's AIDS Unit and gradually also by the State health departments (Parnell 1992). The participation of the AIDS Council of New South Wales in the design and implementation of the Social Aspects of the Prevention of AIDS (SAPA) research project at Macquarie University helped establish an innovative approach to theorised surveys with continuous feedback into community programs (Kippax et al. 1993). The focus on the broad subjectivity and lived experience of gay men which typified safe-sex community education was maintained in SAPA and succeeding research programs. This contrasted with the dominant individual rationalist mode of AIDS social research, comprising untheorised, normalising surveys of knowledge, attitudes, behaviour and practice – a form of social epidemiology which could fuel only centralised, broadcast education programs.

Following the perceived success of the AIDS Councils, the logic of community health promotion began to be applied to other groups. Funding of the Australian Prostitutes Collective in Sydney for condom education in 1986 and the establishment of needle exchanges in drug-user-friendly settings in Sydney and Canberra in 1986–87 raised no publicity and none of the political protest that hindered such programs in the United States. The discourses of safe sex and clean needles then became a focus for the mobilisation of networks as communities of identity among sex workers and drug users. After a substantial increase in AIDS program funding in 1987, governments began actively to promote the formation of State and national organisations of sex workers, injecting drug users and people living with HIV/AIDS. The education and support programs elaborated through these groups involved the promulgation of new forms of responsible citizenship. They also implied a measure of recognition by governments that sex workers and drug users, in many cases still subject to legal sanctions for their community-defining practices, had a capacity for citizenship.

Perhaps the most difficult test for government at a distance, challenging the entrenchment of neo-liberal as against despotic rationality, arose in relation to cases of 'recalcitrant' individuals known to be HIV-infected and engaging in unsafe practices. The problematising of this issue arose in 1989 in the case of 'Charlene', a drug-using sex worker in Sydney who was persuaded by the *Australian* and television's '60 Minutes' to admit to 'unprotected sex' with clients. This raised a media and political furore and an expectation that public health law sanctions would be imposed, as they had been earlier in the isolation of a Queensland Aboriginal woman. Instead, the New South Wales government's AIDS Bureau and the Australian Prostitutes Collective negotiated a community-based response in the form of pastoral case management. A sequence of graded stages of community-based re-education and official warnings, culminating in a court hearing before the imposition of sanctions, was articulated and legislated, and variations on this scheme were adopted in other States (Gibson 1996).

Government at a distance served quite instrumental purposes in relation to AIDS education. It allowed governments to claim credit for all successes and to maintain a safe distance from any programs that aroused public or political dissent; on the rare occasions that explicit posters and pamphlets from AIDS Councils raised protest, governments could disclaim responsibility (see Bartos 1996). This fitted with a long-standing Australian tradition in the use of statutory authorities and royal commissions, autonomous from government, to undertake work which might create political risks. By contrast, in programs under direct government control, public AIDS education by television and publication provoked occasional political embarrassment, while AIDS education in schools moved slowly and the provision of condoms and needles in prisons not at all.

A further contrast is instructive about the extent to which programs for marginalised groups required a particular kind of government. A federation of State haemophilia organisations had been formed prior to the arrival of AIDS, similar to other groups organised for purposes of sharing information on treatment in close interaction with medical specialists. Once a large proportion of Australians who had received anti-haemophilia Factor VIII were found to have been infected, the Commonwealth government gave substantial funding to the federation for education and counselling and its national co-ordinator served as an active member of NACAIDS. The focus of government support here was not intervention in behaviour to prevent transmission, but an extension of existing practices and politics concerning the funding of care and treatment, and later concerning compensation for infection through medical treatment. Government at a distance in this case was not so much a matter of making up citizens with new kinds of responsibility, as incorporating claimants into structures with well established precedents. The same applied to people living with AIDS who, after mobilising a successful campaign for access to new drugs under the radical banner of ACT-UP (Ariss 1993), became absorbed in a politics of specific claims.

Normalising AIDS

The National HIV/AIDS Strategy of 1989, with its substantial increase in funding for a period of three years, proved to be the high point of government commitment to AIDS as a special problem. Shortly after its promulgation, Blewett, who had served as Minister of Health for a record seven years, moved to another portfolio and his key advisers, architects of the Strategy, departed. Their successors had other priorities.

The two years of extensive consultation preceding the National Strategy indicated that the creative phase of AIDS policy was being consolidated. There was further articulation of refinements in health promotion and community care, as well as their application to increasingly diversified and peripheral populations without community sites, for example, men who have sex with men at public 'beats' and casual weekend injecting drug users. But the establishment of conventional project funding schemes under the Strategy meant an increasing bureaucratisation of the burgeoning Commonwealth and State AIDS bureaux and of the well-funded Councils. Access to treatment of AIDS with new drugs was not even mentioned in the National Strategy, but quickly emerged as an issue requiring integration into conventional routines.

Two other considerations favoured a managerial approach to AIDS. First, the very limited increase in recognised instances of vaginal transmission created a sense that a heterosexual epidemic would not occur in the West. The continuity of statistics showing that over 80 per cent of Australians with HIV were gay or bisexual men was taken both as evidence that the epidemic had been 'contained' and that there had been complicity between governments and gay communities to dilute the image of AIDS and 'responsibility' for it.

Secondly, the managerial language of accountability and evaluation which pervaded Australian governments in the early 1990s implied a homogeneous approach to all programs. In the case of AIDS, while there was recognition of its wider impact on standards of health promotion, infection control and community care, there was also increased demand for 'mainstreaming' AIDS programs into broader strategies covering all infectious diseases or all 'public health'. One of the first actions of Blewett's successor as minister was to instigate an inquiry into the rationalisation of funding for all peak health and welfare organisations comparable to the Australian Federation of AIDS Organisations.

In the design of the Second National Strategy during 1992–93, perfunctory consultation led to competition for control between the Commonwealth department and the AIDS Councils, in conjunction with the advisory Australian National Council on AIDS, though all parties were ostensibly committed to 'partnership'. The negotiated result was essentially a continuation of the first Strategy, but it was accompanied by the Commonwealth department's determination to assert stronger control over future AIDS policy.

Planning towards a Third National Strategy during 1995–96 was conducted on more obviously managerial lines. A prominent international consultant was engaged and committed to evaluation in cost-benefit terms that would satisfy the guardians of the Commonwealth budget. Although his report (Feachem 1995) was fulsome in its praise of Australian achievement as measured by transmission rates, and advocated more precisely targeted programs, its narrow conception foreclosed consideration of the broader preconditions of that achievement and of continued innovation.

Conclusion

Although AIDS took up only a small percentage of the budget for health services, these services had in many cases been reshaped in terms of the experience with AIDS. This was most notable in the extent to which community participation had become the norm 'in all aspects of program delivery, from prevention and support through to treatment and research' (Hamilton 1988: 11). New health issues are problematised and dealt with through technologies reconceived in the context of the AIDS experience.

As primary bearers of the 'truth' of AIDS in Australia, the gay communities were also changed, refined and redefined by the experience of AIDS (Dowsett 1997). Safe-sex citizenship, a set of ethical norms shared with other communities, was only a part of the burden of AIDS, but it refocused the creative and assertive thrust of the gay social movement of the 1970s. The expertise of the AIDS Councils and other community-based groups, central to the perceived success of Australian management of AIDS, contributed to a new legitimacy for the communities themselves in Australian public discourse.

Government at a distance made good sense for a progressive government confronting a difficult new issue. It allowed the groups most concerned with the issue to deal with it, while constraining expenditure on medical solutions and avoiding public arguments conducted in moral terms. As a form of rationality, government at a distance had the advantage of flexibility, incorporating the rationalities of other groups and encouraging innovation. It reflected classic justifications of liberalism without adopting the limitations of individualism.

Note

Variants of this paper were presented to the Governing Australia conference, to the XIII International AIDS Conference in Vancouver, and to seminars at the Australian National University and the London School of Hygiene and Tropical Health. The author is grateful for comments on earlier drafts by Brigid Ballard, Michael Bartos, Glyn Davis, Norbert Gilmore and Bruce Parnell.

References

Altman, Dennis, 1984. 'AIDS: the politicization of an epidemic', *Socialist Review* 14: 93–109.
Altman, Dennis, 1994. *Power and community: organizational and cultural responses to AIDS*, London: Taylor & Francis.

Ariss, Robert, 1993. 'Performing anger: emotion in strategic responses to AIDS', *Australian Journal of Anthropology* 4: 18–30.

Ballard, J. A., 1987. 'Ethnicity as a mask of confrontation' in R. G. Stewart and C. Jennett (eds), *Three Worlds of Inequality: Race, Class and Gender*, South Melbourne: Macmillan, pp. 128–34.

Ballard, John, 1992a. 'Australia: participation and innovation in a federal system' in Kirp and Bayer (eds), pp. 134–67.

Ballard, J. A., 1992b. 'Sexuality and the state in time of epidemic' in R. W. Connell and G. W. Dowsett (eds), *Rethinking Sex: Social Theory and Sexuality Research*, Carlton: Melbourne University Press, pp. 102–16.

Ballard, J. A., 1996. 'HIV-contaminated blood and Australian policy', paper for international project on HIV-Contaminated Blood, Policy and Conflict, presented at the Fondation Merieux, Veyrier, December.

Bartos, Michael, 1996. 'The queer excess of public health policy', *Meanjin* 55: 122–31.

Donovan, B. and Tindall, B., 1989. 'Behaviour change in sexually transmitted disease patients' in R. Richmond and D. Saunders (eds), *AIDS and Other Sexually Transmitted Diseases*, Sydney: W. B. Saunders.

Dowsett, Gary W., 1997. 'Sexual conduct, sexual culture, sexual community: gay men's bodies and AIDS' in Jill Julius Matthews (ed.), *Sex in Public: Australian Sexual Cultures*, Sydney: Allen & Unwin, pp. 78–90.

Feachem, Richard G. A., 1995. *Valuing the Past . . . Investing in the Future: Evaluation of the National HIV/AIDS Strategy 1993–94 to 1995–96*, Canberra: Australian Government Publishing Service.

Garrett, Laurie, 1994. *The Coming Plague: Newly Emerging Diseases in a World Out of Balance*, New York: Penguin.

Gibson, Sally E., 1996. 'Knowingly and recklessly?: uncovering the meanings of the policy and practice of managing people who place others at risk of HIV infection', Master in Public Policy and Administration thesis, Flinders University.

Grmek, Mirko D., 1990. *History of AIDS: Emergence and Origin of a Modern Pandemic*, Princeton: Princeton University Press.

Hall, Stuart, 1980. 'Reformism and the legislation of consent' in National Deviancy Conference (ed.), *Permissiveness and Control: The Fate of the Sixties Legislation*, London: Macmillan.

Hamilton, Stuart, 1988. 'The role of government in health development' in *Health Development: Whose Baby?*, Canberra: National Centre for Epidemiology and Population Health.

Kippax, Susan et al., 1993. *Sustaining Safe Sex: Gay Communities Respond to AIDS*, London: Falmer Press.

Kirp, David L. and Bayer, Ronald (eds), 1992. *AIDS in the Industrialized Democracies: Passions, Politics, and Policies*, New Brunswick: Rutgers University Press.

Mann, Jonathan and Tarantola, Daniel, 1996. *AIDS in the World II*, New York: Oxford University Press.

Mann, Michael, 1986. *The Sources of Social Power: Volume I – A History of Power from the Beginning to A.D. 1760*, Cambridge: Cambridge University Press

Parnell, Bruce, 1992. 'AIDS prevention in the gay community' in Heather Gardner (ed.), *Health Policy: Development, Implementation and Evaluation in Australia*, Melbourne: Churchill Livingstone, pp. 307–35.

Patton, Cindy, 1990. *Inventing AIDS*, New York: Routledge.

Plummer, Ken, 1988. 'Organizing AIDS' in Peter Aggleton and Hilary Homans (eds), *Social Aspects of AIDS*, London: Falmer Press.

Rose, Nikolas, 1995. 'Identity, genealogy, history' in Stuart Hall and P. du Gay (eds), *Questions of Cultural Identity*, London: Sage, pp. 128–50.

Rose, Nikolas and Miller, Peter, 1992. 'Political power beyond the state: problematics of government', *British Journal of Sociology* 43: 173–205.

Shilts, Randy, 1987. *And the Band Played On: Politics, People and the AIDS Epidemic*, New York: St Martin's.

Treichler, Paula, 1988. 'AIDS, homophobia and biomedical discourse: an epidemic of signification' in Douglas Crimp (ed.), *AIDS: Cultural Analysis, Cultural Activism*, Cambridge: MIT Press, pp. 31–70.

CHAPTER 8

Governing Queens
Gay Communities and the State in Contemporary Australia

Gary W. Dowsett

In September 1994 the New South Wales State Parliament passed yet another law in relation to gay and lesbian communities. No, this was not a decriminalisation or legalisation of male homosexual acts, nor was it an amendment to include homosexuality in the Anti-Discrimination Act – these had already occurred. This new law removed the power of the Liquor Administration Board to rule on noise levels and impose other regulations on two nights of the year: the night of the Gay and Lesbian Mardi Gras parade and party, and for Sleaze Ball. For those unfamiliar with these events, let me briefly indicate that the first is the final event in a month-long festival held each February in Sydney that celebrates the gay and lesbian community and culture; the second is a bacchanalia held each October to celebrate homosexuality and the beginning of Summer.

Mardi Gras has its origins in over twenty-five years of political struggle worldwide for gay civil rights, initiated in a legendary moment in New York on 26 June 1969 – the evening of Judy Garland's funeral. This is no coincidence. On that night drag queens and gay men in a West Village bar called 'The Stonewall' for the first time fought back against yet another police raid, and then rioted in the streets for a week.

This international gay and lesbian community is a remarkable phenomenon. In just over twenty-five years it has constructed a global village of its own, complete with a range of common social and cultural manifestations, international associations, a network of cultural events, its own Internet connections, and a significant worldwide social and sexual economy. In 1994 New York City reaped the benefit of over US$400 million spent by gay men and lesbians at the 'silver jubilee' of international gay life – the Fourth International Gay Games. More modestly, in Australia in 1994 part of the reason for the then conservative New South Wales Government shunting the Liquor Administration Board

139

aside was the verification in an Economic Impact Study by an independent consultant from the Australian Graduate School of Management that the Sydney Gay and Lesbian Mardi Gras and its festival pumped A\$38 million into the Sydney and South Sydney local government areas and brought A\$15 million from international tourists into the Australian economy. The Mardi Gras continues to grow, and all this occurs without the sizeable government subsidies offered as a matter of course to other cultural events, most of which lose money.[1]

Mardi Gras in Sydney started in a 1978 street march held in response to a worldwide call for civil disobedience by the gay liberation movement. Fifty-eight gay men and lesbians were arrested in Sydney on that day, and by the end of the year 178 had been arrested in an ongoing struggle of civil disobedience. Further arrests were to happen over the next few years. The transformation of that struggle into a world-famous street parade and celebration took less than a decade. The Mardi Gras parade is now a remarkable tale of community development, for the global gay village is constituted by distinct local villages and Sydney's Oxford Street is regarded as one of the great gay quarters in the world.

The victory by the community-run Gay and Lesbian Mardi Gras Association over the Liquor Administration Board might appear less than world-shattering to non-gay people, but from the gay and lesbian communities' perspective it stands in line with earlier significant victories over the state, such as legalisation of male homosexual acts, and certainly is interpreted as being of a similar order.

But how are we to read the New South Wales Government's action? Was this simply a completely amoral application of economic rationalism? There is clearly big bucks in bent fucks! Was the then Chief Secretary Ann Cohen really a 'liberal' after all? Did prominent gay lawyer and civil libertarian John Marsden's lifelong friendship with the then Premier John Fahey prove that familiarity with gay people leads to a significant diminution in anti-gay sentiment? Whatever else might be in play here, it seems a paradoxical accommodation by government – any government really.

However, let us look again at that surprisingly liberal New South Wales Government. Not long after the liquor licensing decision, it announced that the discriminatory age-of-consent law in that State, which prohibits sex between men below the age of eighteen, would not be altered to bring it into line with the age of consent for sex between men and women and between women and women set at sixteen. The struggle over the age-of-consent laws will go on and be won, perhaps in the courts, as an indirect but not unintended consequence of the 1994 Commonwealth Government's human rights legislation on sexual privacy (discussed later). So there is a certain contingency in these political decisions that would seem to exemplify another moment in Michel Foucault's 'deployment of sexuality' (1976).

In this chapter I use one possible approach to this paradox, that is, to set up the question historically as yet another victory in the century-long struggle for equal civil rights by those who were newly classified as 'homosexual' only in 1869, with the invention of that word by Benkert (Weeks 1977). This struggle is emblematic of the development of modern governmentality and the centrality of sexuality to its achievements. This chapter seeks first to present a brief description of the terrain of struggle between gay communities and the state. Second, it tackles some issues thrown up by HIV/AIDS. Third, the age of consent in sexual relations is discussed and, lastly, some tentative comments on the relationship between gay communities and modernity are offered.

Before I go on I need to register that although I do see some significant benefits in the governmentality approach, I am not yet a fully accredited governmentalitarian. I feel a bit of a ring-in and must admit to have been attracted to the challenge of writing this chapter for two reasons: first, it forced me to start some new thinking and do so in an old area; and secondly, it offered an opportunity to mention again what I call the 'straightening' of Foucault. By this I mean the growing refusal of the centrality of the sexual (and specifically the homosexual), so prominent in Foucault's work, and a propensity in social theory to relegate sexuality to the margins of thought, pretending that it does not govern 'every move you make, every breath you take'.[2] To relegate sexuality to the bedroom, to the private, to the cultural, or to being derivative of, or subordinate to, other major concepts of social analysis is to neglect that vast literature now available on the centrality of sexuality to all social relations, particularly those not involving actual sex acts, and to neglect Foucault's insights on the intricate relation between power and sexuality.

Policing Poofters

In Tasmania in the mid-1990s a man called Rodney Croome fronted up to a police station and before two police staff, one man and one woman, signed a statutory declaration on committing the criminal offence of consenting sexual acts with another man, Nick Toonen. Here is part of the account of that event given by Croome in an interview with the national gay magazine *Outrage* (1994: 50):

> Even though the statutory declaration was quite explicit (the sexual encounter was written down shortly after it occurred) the police took Croome through his statement 'line by line'. If the statement referred to Croome and

Toonen being in certain positions, the police wanted to know how Croome got from position A to position B. They wanted to know what Croome was wearing, what he usually wore in bed, and whether similar behaviour had occurred before. 'Yes it has', Croome replied. 'How many times?' 'Over six years, about three or four times a week. That's about a thousand times'. Croome now recalls: 'They actually looked genuinely shocked that I was admitting to a thousand criminal offences'. He realised that what was to him the admission of 'fairly ordinary and unremarkable sexual activity' was to them an admission of a crime, and one with a maximum penalty of 21 years.

This voluntary admission of criminality from Croome and Toonen was one tactic in a carefully orchestrated and long campaign for equality before the law in Tasmania, the last State to reform its anti-gay laws (finally achieved in early 1997 and making Croome and Toonen national gay heroes). That makes it no less a brave act and one that might have brought them a long gaol sentence. As it was, it attracted considerable public vilification from right-wing moralist forces in Tasmania and the mainland on a number of occasions. The overall strategy targeted both the Tasmanian and Commonwealth governments as a response to the remarkable ruling in 1994 by the United Nations Human Rights Committee that Tasmania's anti-gay laws were a breach of the International Convention on Human Rights. The global ramifications of this ruling would appear yet to be fully understood.

Recast as the right to sexual privacy in an intention to implement its international treaty obligations, the Commonwealth legislation in response to the committee's ruling drew a wary response from the gay communities: privacy with respect to sexual activity was defined *in* law by the first British homosexual law reform, the so-called 'Wolfenden' Sexual Offences Act amendments of 1967, which also enshrined the word 'homosexual' in British law for the first time (Weeks 1977). As a result of this law reform, more British homosexual men were prosecuted than ever before, precisely because of this restrictive definition of what constituted 'private'. Croome, Toonen and colleagues quite rightly took the then still extant Tasmanian laws to the High Court, rather than await the vagaries of local court interpretation of individual cases to see exactly what 'privacy' was to mean. But this is not simply an issue that affects only gay men; this definition of sexual privacy reveals more clearly than usual how the policing of homosexuality lies at the very heart of the policing of sexuality, for the Tasmanian laws on sodomy were not sex-specific.

The then Labor Commonwealth Government's legislation was also geared deftly to producing maximum chaos within the ranks of the conservative federal Opposition at the time – yet another time when homosexuality itself is a political football with which heterosexuals play their own power games. That statement might appear a cheap shot, but it can be reframed within Eve Kosofsky Sedgwick's notion of homo-sociality (1985) in which, she argues, at the heart of the male bonding that glues patriarchy together lies homophobia, that is, a tremendous and irrational fear of homosexuals and homosexual desire, which forms the pedal point in the construction of relations between men.

Homophobia is distilled in sodomy and represents the ever-threatening possibility of the fragility of that conviction on the essential and arbitrary distinction between homosexual and heterosexual. Sodomy between men speaks of men's interiority and penetrability, and offers access to unique pleasures in the male body. In particular, in relation to the disintegration of the psyche that accompanies orgasm (Bataille's (1989) 'little death'), sodomy entails a denial and destruction of the self, a loss of power. It is by definition something masochistic, a violation. By being penetrated, as Leo Bersani argues (1988: 222), not only do gay men symbolically divest themselves of their power as men, but in their very avid pursuit of these mutual pleasures, in their multiple encounters, they refuse to enact power in sex by 're-presenting the internalized phallic male as an infinitely loved object of sacrifice'. This violation has two aspects. Gay men realise/embody men's capacity for anal eroticism, and they 'spread their legs with an unquenchable appetite for destruction' (Bersani 1988: 211–12). Bersani thereby also claims homosexuality as subversion; but subversion comes from the loss of manhood, the loss of self; it comes from being fucked.

The regulation of homosexuality involves more than the delineation of its circumstances. It relies on the governance of the body both at the level of its surface, that is, those parts of us that are allowed to be brought into intimate contact, and on the body's interiority, by driving a wedge into the indivisibility of the body and mind. For men, to engage in sodomy, to experience the pleasures of the prostate prodded into overdrive, to be contorted bodily to orgasm accompanied by ejaculations within and without is to experience not only double the personal pleasure and a unique reciprocal intimacy between men, but to deny the divide between mind and body, to dare to disbelieve the discursive manoeuvre that relegates the anus to a grease trap, and to disengage the phallus from the penis. It is to pursue, as Bersani summarises Foucault: '*jouissance* as a mode of ascesis' (1988: 222).

Sodomy in its very reciprocity speaks of the threatening possibility of non-patriarchal relations between men. Hence the importance of main-taining the boundaries between homosexuality and heterosexuality, of drawing a clean line around men's virgin anal sphincters. This is one of the most significant deployments of power for, as Foucault claims, its technique is desire, its ambit is the body, its object is the control of human pleasure – the least peripheral of all our needs. Something very vital is at stake here, something more than merely an Anglo-European anal phobia or Judeo-Christian procreative proclivities. Irrespective of reforms to the criminal code, ongoing efforts to police the sexual boundaries between homosexuality and heterosexuality represent an enormous deployment of social and political resources for far greater purposes than to get men to 'manage their sperm' (a phrase that gained currency at the 1994 Cairo World Population conference).

A Politics of Opposition

Robert Hughes (1987) offers a picture of endemic sodomy in all the colonies: the harsher they were, the more it seems the men sought solace in sodomy. A major issue for social order was the prevention of intimate relations between men. The Labouchère amendment of 1885 in Britain, which criminalised all homosexual acts beyond buggery, was in part fuelled by scandals in the Antipodes (Fogarty 1992). Hughes extends his argument about the prevalence of sodomy and its suppression to suggest that this dynamic provides the historical basis for the Australian characteristic valorisation of mateship as a tight form of male bonding. But there would appear to have been more actual mating in the mateship than we might like to acknowledge. That history now fuels a 'backs to the wall' trope in heterosexual male relations and one is reminded again of Sedgwick's configuration of homosociality.

Work undertaken by the Gay History Project at the University of Sydney unveils a picture of a country for which a constant theme has been the struggle between buggery and bureaucracy (Aldrich and Wotherspoon 1992; Aldrich 1993). Policing the 'poofters' (a word Australians invented by the way) reads like a modern analogue for Henry VIII's constant battle with the monasteries, which also occasioned the entry of 'buggery' into English law for the first time in 1533–34 (Moran 1993).

To come rapidly to the present, the Tasmanian example is the latest in a long struggle here to overturn laws criminalising consensual sexual activity between men, which began first in South Australia after the murder of Adelaide academic Dr George Duncan in 1972 by 'person or persons unknown'. Whoever committed that murder, they were certainly engaged in an act of policing some sexual boundaries of their own. In just over twenty years this struggle has led to all other Australian States and Territories reforming their laws, the last of which was Tasmania. Each State and Territory has a different law, partly related to differing and sometimes discriminatory ages of consent, and partly related to issues of what remains defined in law as offensive public behaviour.

Again, these kinds of laws remain causes for concern, for two men kissing in public in the United Kingdom step beyond not only the limits of privacy but also break the offensive behaviour laws. Although the legal position here is relatively better than in the United States and the United Kingdom, the overall Australian response remains lodged within a somewhat stiff Anglo-Saxon cultural framework, not deriving its detail from, for example, the Napoleonic Code that governs similar laws in much of continental Europe.

This struggle for law reform positioned, originally, the gay liberation movement and, latterly, the gay communities in direct and clear opposition to the state, which was defined as illegitimate in its regulation of sexual conduct: 'Get your laws off our bodies' was one loud demand. But this gay civil rights ascendancy, however, was always underpinned, at least among the gay intelligentsia, by a more insistent demand for something more – a sexual transformation of society.

Post-Jeffrey Weeks and Foucault et al., this analysis was reformulated in a complex stratagem that, *inter alia*, led to the multiplication of 'homosexualities' and even to the proposition of an end to homosexuality itself. This shift marks the major and significant difference between understanding the gay community as merely a minority civil rights movement, in the mould of the liberal pluralist tendency dominant in the West for the last two decades, and the formulation of homosexuality as a theoretical basis for the construction of a politics of sexuality that challenges the social order in the West. In this sense, the moralist Right, represented by Rev. Fred Nile and the like, were right all along: there is a 'gay agenda' larger than equal rights (although they project upon it their own brand of evangelism). After all, if homosexuality could bring down the Roman Empire, surely ending capitalism and patriarchy should be a breeze!

The oppositional politics implicated in a civil rights formulation and the internal dissension in the gay liberation movement over gender issues in the late 1970s led to a bifurcation in the trajectories of those until-then natural allies – feminism and gay liberation. The gay agenda, unlike the women's movement, did not move to a demand for specially earmarked government programs or service provision – there were no 'poofycrats' to parallel the femocrats. This is one reason why the Mardi Gras has always been almost entirely funded by the gay community itself.

One should be wary of too firm a distinction here. Gay men were very active in educational institutions, professional associations and trade unions during this period. Certainly, the demand for a State-funded refuge for gay and lesbian homeless young people in Sydney in the early 1980s marked an important exception. Demands for sex education, better sexually transmitted diseases (STD) services, and an end to discrimination on the basis of sexuality in the provision of services in the private and public sector were also pursued. The last of these led to an odd situation in New South Wales for a number of years: it was illegal to discriminate against homosexuals, but sex between men was still illegal! That said, it is important to highlight a politics of opposition and its difference from the specific uses of the state in the demand for services and programs that largely characterised the politics of feminism (and multiculturalism) at that time.

Gay men meanwhile (specifically not gay men and lesbians acting together) exercised their energies in developing their own gay communities and in exploring an emerging international gay men's culture. This period saw the first phase of declaredly gay commercial establishments in Sydney, a precursor to the so-called 'pink market', developed largely by gay men and gay-run small business, and the emergence of an international sexual economy for gay men. By the early 1980s gay men could travel to most parts of the developed world with guide books, gay hotels, resorts and precincts, and to some parts of the developing world. This globalisation of gay as an international subculture was almost entirely self-supporting and serves, by contrast, to illuminate the enormous changes in gay politics in relation to the state produced by the onset of the Human Immunodeficiency Virus (HIV) epidemic in Australia.

Responding to HIV/AIDS

In 1982 the first Australian case was diagnosed of Acquired Immune Deficiency Syndrome (AIDS), the usually fatal combination of illnesses that are facilitated by HIV infection. Since that time just over 4000 gay men have died, well over half of whom were gay men in the inner-Sydney gay community, and so far nearly eight times the number of Australian men who died in Vietnam.

From the start of the epidemic, the gay communities of Australia worked locally through their own institutions, but by the time of the national homosexual conferences in Canberra (1982) and Melbourne (1983), they had federated their locally based organisations into a national pressure group, recognising very early that even though the States were responsible for public health, their record on homosexuality at that time was very poor and the new Labor Commonwealth Government offered a much better prospect of a more appropriate response (see Ballard 1989).

Also, from the start, experienced gay activists recognised from a long history of dealing with the medical profession that biomedical control of HIV/AIDS would produce a disaster for gay men. This was not just a

paranoid activist position, but one clearly indicated by the early homophobic medical readings of HIV/AIDS as a disease of homosexuals, of
deviants requiring containment in the classic tradition of notifiable
diseases. There are many other accounts that exemplify HIV/AIDS as an
ongoing struggle to move government and the medical establishment
beyond a homophobic rendition of a viral epidemic to a keener awareness of what was actually at stake (for example, Altman 1986, 1992;
Watney 1987, 1988; Shilts 1988; Treichler 1988; Horton with Aggleton
1989; Patton 1990; Gott 1994).

The early feature of the epidemic in Australia was its incidence related
to male-to-male sexual activity, namely the powerfully symbolic act of
sodomy. Homophobia rendered this one of a number of vectors of HIV
transmission as: 'A man comes along and goes from anus to anus and in
a single night will act as a mosquito transferring infected cells on his
penis' (Professor Opendra Narayan, quoted in Bersani 1988: 197). 'Gay
and bisexual' men were identified as the 'risk group', as if they were the
same entity and all of a oneness. Even though the epidemiology of HIV
infection soon indicated that vaginal intercourse facilitated the transmission of HIV (now the major vector of transmission worldwide) and
that heterosexually active people also engage in anal intercourse, it took
an enormous effort on the part of gay men and their allies to transform
'gay and bisexual men' into 'men who have sex with men', that is, to
move from 'risk group' to 'risk practice'.

This semantic stroke achieved the recognition that non gay-
identifying, non gay-community-attached, homosexually active men
were also at risk themselves and, further, might pose a risk to others,
namely their female partners. This was the moment when the threat to
the general population was perceived as possible, and it is important to
remember that this assessment, based on the growing overseas evidence,
was seen as a very real threat at that time.

Those identified 'at risk', itself a problematic term, were identified
eventually as gay men, other homosexually active men, bisexually active
men, women, injecting drug users, haemophiliacs, youth and Aborigines. The general population needed to be protected from these 'at-
risk' persons (Waldby 1983). This mapping of risk and the techniques of
public health management failed initially to notice who this general
population was. For once these at-risk groupings are removed from the
general population, there are only white heterosexual adult males left!

The 'men who have sex with men' semantic stratagem achieved its
purpose in highlighting that danger lay in types of practices not types of
people, and in this it represented a significant reversal of Foucault's
theorem, but it also led to three unfortunate consequences for gay men.
The first was the accusation that gay men were trying to 'heterosexualise'

the disease (this accusation is regarded as deeply offensive by those fighting the epidemic in Africa) and at the same time of hijacking the HIV/AIDS debate. The second consequence was a belated recognition of the potential situation for women, and this led to the unfortunate collapse of 'men who have sex with men', 'men who have sex with men and women' and 'men who have sex with women' into one grouping, namely, 'men who have sex', that is, a singular masculine sexuality that obliterated the historical and structural subordination of homosexuality and revealed yet again the danger in collapsing gender and sexuality. The third consequence was that considerable public health money was diverted from gay men and their communities to the general population at a time when the epidemic was spiralling among gay men. It took another three years for the epidemiological evidence to indicate that gay men were at enhanced risk largely because of the prevalence of viral infection already within their communities. The semantic strategy then involved the reinsertion of gay men into the equation in phrases such as 'gay men and other homosexually active men', but not in such a way as to ghetto-ise the epidemic and thereby risk marginalisation and a reduction in public health efforts to stop the disease, as had happened in the United Kingdom.

The key issue here is that this was a disease involving highly developed gay communities with their own independent cultural bases, which had long and sophisticated political engagements with the state enabling them to engage with its shifts and manoeuvres. More importantly, the manoeuvres just described opened up the possibility that homosexuality might not be a single domain confidently contained on one side of the virgule in the homosexual/heterosexual binary opposition. What is now accepted, at least in public health, is the existence of a very blurred boundary between the two main categories of sexuality, a blurring warranting a new map. Although British research reveals an enormous disproportion between these two major categories and less blurring (Wellings et al. 1994), recent research in the United States would seem to indicate the contrary (Sell et al. 1995), and that Kinsey et al. (1948) may have been closer to the mark than we might like to think.

It might be useful to pause and revisit Alfred Kinsey et al., particularly their much-quoted figure of '10 per cent' of men being homosexual. They actually reported that: 37 per cent of all men have had some overt homosexual experience to the point of orgasm and 50 per cent of those who remain single until age thirty-five have had homosexual sex; 30 per cent of all males have had incidental homosexual experience and 25 per cent have had more than incidental experience over a three-year period; 18 per cent of all males have had as much homosexual as heterosexual experience and 13 per cent have had more homosexual than heterosexual experience over a three-year period; 10 per cent have been more or less exclusively homosexual and 8 per cent have been exclusively homosexual for at least a three-year period; 4 per cent remain exclusively homosexual throughout their lives.

Kinsey et al. were saying that at any given time there might be at least 10 per cent of the adult male population homosexually active, but not necessarily the same 10 per cent. Furthermore, and this is the real salience of Kinsey et al., patterns of homosexual experience change over time, that is, they are related to age and generation. They also change with level of education, marital status, and occupation. Kinsey et al. also noted the importance of institutional homosexual sex in the armed forces, educational institutions, prisons and the importance of opportunity in sexual exploration, particularly that offered by urban environments.

It is often said that Kinsey et al. were reporting a phenomenon related to the mammoth disruption to social (read sexual) relations caused by the Second World War. Yet that itself is significant, because it registers the possibility that sexual interests, rather than residing in some psychoanalytic destiny, resonate with more immediate social settings and potentials. The modern state, in particular its public health sector, has had to recognise finally that its cartography of concupiscence captured so comfortably in that binary opposition will not work any more, if it ever really did.

It was gay men who invented the term and content of what we know as 'safe sex', recognising through their sexual practice, quicker than the epidemiologists could, what would prevent the transmission of HIV. The unsurpassed taking-up of condoms by gay men (previously never in need of them) contrasts sharply to the slow rates of uptake by the heterosexually active at risk (Crawford et al. 1990; Kippax et al. 1990; Gifford et al. 1994) and could not be ignored by government. In order to reach others deemed at risk – now increasingly difficult to define simply as gay – the state had to include gay communities in its responses to the epidemic. If the state has managed to sustain its benignly configured desire to maintain public health, it has also had to share control – a sharing enshrined in Australia's national AIDS strategies (Commonwealth of Australia 1989, 1993, 1996). Through HIV/AIDS, the state in Australia has been forced to move toward the gay communities in particular, in a way it has never had to before. This, then, is the counterpoint to the earlier pre-HIV/AIDS tale of the attendance of gay communities on the state: that of the reliance of government on the very communities of those at risk: prostitutes, drug injectors and, most importantly, gay men.

Much social theorising in general and governmentalitarianism in particular has had little to offer as yet in the day-to-day struggle with this epidemic, its policy and programmatic exigencies, and in dealing with its social impact. Why is this? Part of the answer lies in its discursive confinement to public health, definitely not a sexy issue in either political or academic terms. Yet, beyond that discursive confinement, HIV/AIDS represents a major achievement of governance in Australia in that it has rarely become an issue of great controversy and contention outside its own small community of interest. This successful strategy of containment has perhaps precluded those interested in governmentality and in public administration from seeing clearly just what a transformation has occurred as a result of this epidemic.

Some might read this alliance between the state and gay communities as a none-too-subtle incorporation of the gay communities in the machinery of the power. Certainly, there is convergence of purpose: to stop HIV. But the gay communities have fought every step of the way for a sex-positive, non-repressive configuration of health promotion, achieving some loosening of sexual regulation and retaining an impressive autonomy in the representation of their sexual culture. HIV/AIDS has not destroyed the gay communities in Australia (or around the world, for that matter); they are stronger than they were in many ways. There is other more serious damage to these sexual communities (D'Emilio 1983) from the epidemic than is immediately obvious, and it will be a long time until these painful effects of such a tragedy have worked themselves through.

During the first decade of HIV/AIDS Australia witnessed not only the legalisation of sodomy between consenting men in three States but also the enactment of considerable anti-discrimination legislation at Commonwealth and State level. This response on the part of the state is not just the result of good strategy on the part of the gay communities; it represents an intelligent reading of the arguments made by those communities about human sexuality, especially since the early 1980s. The blurred sexual boundaries are now understood at different levels of sophistication by most HIV/AIDS public health officials and their political masters.

There is, however, something unique about this shift in Australian politics on sexuality compared with the United Kingdom, the United States and Canada: here, at different levels of government, arguments about gay culture and community have salience. HIV/AIDS, in particular, has opened up the debate about sex and sexuality in this country, and the gay communities are largely responsible for that. For example, as an HIV/AIDS researcher I gave evidence in 1992 on HIV/AIDS and the sexual culture of Sydney's gay community as an expert witness to the Land and Environment Court in a successful case that registered the first legal sex-on-premises gay bathhouse in Australia.

The Labor Party endorsed its first openly lesbian candidate in the 1995 New State Wales State election, although gay men have been nominated by that party in other seats before. The former Labor Prime Minister, Paul Keating, endorsed Australia's unsuccessful bid to host the 1998 International Gay Games – the only head of government to do so in that round of bids. Politics and sexuality are meeting in ways not envisaged easily even a few years ago.

The sticking points start to emerge when the difficult parts of the gay challenge to sexuality invades certain areas, namely pornography, public sexual activity and ages of consent. The raw edge of sexuality lies with young people. The discursive struggle over the sexuality of young people is as old in Western thought as civilisation (Symonds 1983; Foucault 1985; Halperin 1990). This is certainly the next battle ground, as homo-sexuality among adults becomes a quaint variation in the endless pro-duction of choice and pleasuring in post-industrial cultures. If you take, for the sake of argument, Foucault and his followers' work on Ancient Greece, the particular character of sexual activity between men and young men allows for a reading of such experience as pleasurable and healthy for the younger partners. This is a far cry from the discourse of paedophilia we often accept uncritically today.

The purity and innocence of childhood, taken for granted by the twentieth century, was always destabilised in the nineteenth century by its persistent masturbation. This sleight of hand was supplemented by the discovery/construction, in the perfection of Foucault's famous, almost Mozartian trio, of the homosexual and of the hysterical woman. This trio of deviants meld into one another throughout the period: the homosexual, offering 'the infinitely more seductive and intolerable image of a grown man, legs high in the air, unable to refuse the suicidal ecstasy of being a woman' (Bersani 1988: 212), is shadowed by the paedophile, *The Man They Called a Monster* (to use Paul Wilson's (1981) book title), who by implication facilitates the transformation of the wayward masturbating child into the hysteria and destruction of the homosexual.

This deployment of categories facilitates the othering of the 'proxi-mate' (Dollimore 1991): the paedophile in all of us is rendered quiet. Our desire only surfaces in foreign films like *Murmur of the Heart,* or in stories like 'Billy Budd' or operas like *Peter Grimes*; in the film *Rich and Famous* we can only watch Jacqueline Bisset pull down the pants of the teenage street hustler, revealing actor (ex-Mr Olivia Newton-John) Matt Latanzi's callipygian attractions, as she utters through glistening lips closing in on his exposed flat tummy the words 'young flesh'; teenagers Christopher Aitken and Brooke Shields can romp naked in the *Blue Lagoon.* Art replaces life.

We are, as a culture and as a society, immensely duplicitous with regard to this issue of young people's sexuality. It is a source of major division between some strands of feminism and gay and lesbian theory, and often an impossible subject to raise. Many refuse to hear the difference between 'intergenerational sex' and 'sexual abuse', or note the evidence in solid empirical research on consenting intergenerational sex in Australia and abroad (Wilson 1981; Sandfort et al. 1990; Li et al. 1990). The New South Wales Royal Commission into police corruption, in its brief to investigate paedophile–police relations, revealed magnificently throughout 1996 how the State's deployment of sexuality is a strenuous if disorderly act. The paedophile of the 1990s has replaced the homosexual of the 1890s, serving yet again to divert attention from the fact that policing of any desire is a policing of all.

Conclusion

The international gay community is a remarkable product of modernity. That statement should be without controversy in that sufficient consensus now exists on the part played by urbanisation in the expansion of sexual opportunity and in the possibility of clustering of sub-cultures in geographically safe places, in essence allowing the rise of the gay 'ghettos', as they are often inaccurately called, such as the West Village in New York and Oxford Street in Sydney. In the century between the invention of homosexuality and the Stonewall riots, homosexual men and women, as we now understand them, provide the best example of the deployment of modern forms of governance. In tracing that history, Foucault offered the template for understanding the development of 'sexuality' as central to power, and its operation in modern patriarchal industrial societies.

The pessimism engendered by Foucault's theorem still haunts gay life. The very success of the Sydney Gay and Lesbian Mardi Gras was accompanied by a disturbing claim from some gay men and lesbians during the 1994 International Year of the Family that 'We are family too',[3] disregarding the longstanding and trenchant critique of the heteronormative family in gay and lesbian theory. The 1995 electoral victory of New South Wales independent parliamentarian Clover More in the electorate of Bligh (which includes the Oxford Street precinct) declares the Pink vote real and positions gay and lesbian issues as marginal minority concerns rather than as challenges to social, because sexual, life. The publicisation of gay and, increasingly, lesbian sexuality is also leading to its commercialisation – not necessarily a bad thing. The reign of modernity would seem secure for the time being.

The internationalisation of gay and lesbian life proceeds with exciting speed, but its commercial edge (still) follows rather than leads desire enacted within that growing identity; it is global gay sex, not gay identity, that provides the pulse. Does this globalisation of gay identity and culture significantly challenge the nation state? On this question, the contribution of the international gay community to the global fight against HIV/AIDS indicates that this is a real possibility.

Is the globalisation of homoeroticism the only challenge left in gay, as gay business, gay culture, gay precincts, and gay and lesbian scholarship blossom increasingly comfortably within contemporary capitalist society? Or do gay men and lesbian communities gesture toward some sort of postmodern moment in the fracturing of normativity? Might it be that, post-Stonewall, gay communities, riding the resistance available within sexuality, have changed the terms for the deployment of power? The struggle around HIV/AIDS would seem to indicate that Foucault's lesson was well learnt. His own death from AIDS adds poignancy here, and there is no doubt that gay communities engage power differently as a result of his work. At the least, the ongoing struggles over the age of consent and other issues in sexuality not discussed here, such as pornography and public sex, keep alive a productive politics of opposition as well as a deep-seated suspicion and critique of the state. In these struggles, gay men represent a confrontation in which homosociality is now always openly faced with its foregone pleasurable possibilities – a notable subversion.

But there is more to it than that: gay communities constantly have to reinvent themselves. As the Moral Right argues, they cannot 'reproduce'. In their dialectics of desire, in their imaging of safe spaces for homoerotic expression, in the construction of visible sexual communities, in the globalisation of 'gay' as a site of primary loyalty in the struggle for human liberation: gay communities offer an endless possibility of pre-emptive strikes against modernity. For in the very act of gay sex itself, gay men insert themselves firmly in the historical transformation of relations between men.

Notes

1   To date, Mardi Gras has only received government funding for its activities on a few occasions: $50 000 per year from the South Sydney City Council from 1993 onwards (less in 1997), and a $6000 Australia Council grant once in the early 1980s. Other than that, this million (or more) dollar event is completely self-funding.

2 From a song by the band 'Police'.
3 Again, utilising the words of a very successful 1980s disco song.

References

Aldrich, Robert, 1993. *Gay Perspectives II*, Sydney: University of Sydney, Department of Economic History, Occasional Publications Series.

Aldrich, Robert and Wotherspoon, Garry, 1992. *Gay Perspectives: Essays in Australian Gay Culture*, Sydney: University of Sydney, Department of Economic History, Occasional Publications Series.

Altman, Dennis, 1986. *AIDS and the New Puritanism*, London: Pluto Press.

Altman, Dennis, 1992. 'The most political of diseases' in Eric Timewell, Victor Minichiello and David Plummer (eds), *AIDS in Australia*, Sydney: Prentice Hall, pp. 55–72.

Ballard, John, 1989. 'The politics of AIDS' in Helen Gardner (ed.), *The Politics of Health: The Australian Experience*, Melbourne: Churchill Livingstone.

Bataille, Georges, 1989. *The Tears of Eros*, trans. Peter Connor, San Francisco: City Light Books.

Bersani, Leo, 1988. 'Is the rectum a grave?' in Douglas Crimp (ed.), *AIDS: Cultural Analysis/Cultural Activism*, Cambridge, Mass.: MIT Press, pp. 197–222.

Commonwealth of Australia, 1989. *National HIV/AIDS Strategy. A Policy Information Paper*, Canberra: Australian Government Publishing Service.

Commonwealth of Australia, 1993. *The National HIV/AIDS Strategy, 1993–94 to 1995–96*, Canberra: Australian Government Publishing Service.

Commonwealth of Australia, 1996. *Partnerships in Practice: National HIV/AIDS Strategy 1996–97 to 1998–99*, Canberra: Australian Government Publishing Service.

Crawford, June, Turtle, Alison and Kippax, Susan, 1990. 'Student-favoured strategies for AIDS avoidance', *Australian Journal of Social Issues* 42, 2: 123–37.

D'Emilio, John, 1983. *Sexual Politics, Sexual Communities. The Making of a Homosexual Minority in the United States, 1940–70*, Chicago: University of Chicago Press.

Dollimore, Jonathan, 1991. *Sexual Dissidence: Augustine to Wilde, Freud to Foucault*, Oxford: Clarendon Press.

Fogarty, Walter J., 1992. ' "Certain habits": the development of a concept of the male homosexual in New South Wales law, 1788–1900' in Robert Aldrich and Garry Wotherspoon (eds), *Gay Perspectives: Essays in Australian Gay Culture*, Sydney: University of Sydney, Department of Economic History, Occasional Publications Series, pp. 59–76.

Foucault, Michel, 1976. *The History of Sexuality, Volume I: An Introduction*, trans. Robert Hurley, Harmondsworth: Penguin.

Foucault, Michel, 1985. *The Uses of Pleasure*, trans. Robert Hurley, Harmondsworth: Penguin.

Gifford, S. M., Mitchell A., Rosenthal, D. and Temple-Smith, M., 1994. *STD and HIV/AIDS Education for People of Non-English Speaking Backgrounds* [Report by the Centre for the Study of Sexually Transmissible Diseases, La Trobe University, to the Commonwealth Department of Human Services and Health], Canberra: Australian Government Publishing Service.

Gott, Ted, 1994. 'Where the streets have new aims: the poster in the age of AIDS' in Ted Gott (comp.), *Don't Leave Me This Way: Art in the Age of AIDS*, Canberra: National Gallery of Australia, pp. 187–212.

Halperin, David, 1990. *One Hundred Years of Homosexuality*, New York and London: Routledge.

Horton, Meyrick with Peter Aggleton, 1989. 'Perverts, inverts and experts: the cultural production of an AIDS research paradigm' in Peter Aggleton, Graham Hart and Peter Davies (eds), *AIDS: Social Representations, Social Practices*, London: Falmer Press, pp. 74–100.

Hughes, Robert, 1987. *The Fatal Shore*, London: Collins Harvill.

Kinsey, Alfred C., Pomeroy, Wardell B. and Martin, Clyde E., 1948. *Sexual Behavior in the Human Male*, Philadelphia: W. B. Saunders.

Kippax, Susan, Crawford, June and Waldby, Cathy, 1990. 'Women negotiating heterosex: implications for AIDS prevention', *Women's Studies International Forum* 13, 6: 533–42.

Li, C. K., West, D. J. and Woodhouse, T. P., 1990. *Children's Sexual Encounters with Adults*, London: Duckworth.

Moran, Leslie, 1993. 'Buggery and the tradition of law', *New Transformations*, 19, Spring: 109–22.

Outrage 1994, 138, November: 51–3.

Patton, Cindy, 1990. *Inventing AIDS*, New York: Routledge.

Sandfort, Theo, Brongersma, Edward and van Naersson, Alex, (eds), 1990. 'Male intergenerational intimacy: historical, socio-psychological, and legal perspectives', *Journal of Homosexuality* 20, 1/2 (special issue).

Sedgwick, Eve Kosofsky, 1985. *Between Men: English Literature and Male Homosocial Desire*, New York: Columbia University Press.

Sell, R. L., Wells, J. A. and Wypij, D., 1995. 'The prevalence of homosexual behavior and attraction in the United States, the United Kingdom and France: results of national population-based samples', *Archives of Sexual Behavior* 24, 3: 235–48.

Shilts, Randy, 1988. *And the Band Played On. Politics, People and the AIDS Epidemic*, Harmondsworth: Penguin.

Symonds, John Addington, 1983. *Male Love: A Problem in Greek Ethics, and Other Writings*, John Lauritsen (ed.), New York: Pagan Press.

Treichler, Paula, 1988. 'AIDS, homophobia and biomedical discourse: an epidemic of signification' in Douglas Crimp (ed.), *AIDS: Cultural Analysis/ Cultural Activism*, Cambridge, Mass.: MIT Press, pp. 31–70.

Waldby, Cathy, 1993. 'AIDS and the body politic', paper to the Regimes of Sexuality conference, Humanities Research Centre, Australian National University, Canberra, July.

Watney, Simon, 1987. *Policing Desire: Pornography, AIDS and the Media*, London: Methuen.

Watney, Simon, 1988. 'The spectacle of AIDS' in Douglas Crimp (ed.), *AIDS: Cultural Analysis/Cultural Activism*, Cambridge: Mass.: MIT Press, pp. 71–86.

Weeks, Jeffrey, 1977. *Coming Out: Homosexual Politics in Britain from the Nineteenth Century to the Present*, London: Quartet Books.

Wellings, Kaye, Field, Julia, Johnson, Anne E. and Wadsworth, Jane, 1994. *Sexual Behaviour in Britain: The National Survey of Sexual Attitudes and Lifestyles*, London: Penguin.

Wilson, Paul, 1981. *The Man They Called A Monster. Sexual Experiences between Men and Boys*, North Ryde: Cassell Australia.

CHAPTER 9

Indigenous Governance

Pat O'Malley

There is a difficulty, symptomatic of much work in the recent governmentality literature, which derives from its aim to understand government as a practical exercise – rather than mere reflection on the art
of rule – while at the same time avoiding historical sociology (Barry et al.
1993, Rose 1993). As Rose remarks, studies of governmentality are not
concerned to explain 'how it really was'. Rather:

> their concern is with the ways in which authorities have asked themselves
> practical questions which follow this sociological form: what is the condition
> of the people, the economy, the family; what accounts for the problems and
> what would lead to their improvement; what effects have our strategies
> produced in the past; what can and should be done and by whom, in order to
> do things better? (Rose 1993: 288)

This fundamental turn in analysis doubtlessly has produced one of the
most dynamic and fruitful lines of inquiry for understanding rule, in
part because it releases analysis from its ballast of explanatory duties. In
moving from 'why' questions, studies in governmentality have rendered
visible the array of liberal strategies and technologies of rule, and contributed much to a knowledge of how they achieve their effects. The main
questions this paper explores, however, concern ways in which this
approach privileges official discourses, with the result that it becomes
difficult for it to recognise the imbrication of resistance and rule, the
contradictions and tensions that this melding generates and the subterranean practices of government consequently required to stabilise rule.

The nexus between the two elements of the governmentality approach – the focus on government as practical problematics of rule, and
the eschewing of historical sociology – is formed through the identification of political discourse as an intellectual framework for rendering

reality thinkable as a site of practical activity. The obvious danger of discourse determinism is warded off by recognising collisions between government programs and a reality 'too unruly to be captured by any perfect knowledge'. Things external to official discourses and practices thus have a place in the literature, most notably because 'the real always insists in the form of resistance to programming; and the programmer's world is one of constant experiment, invention, failure, critique and adjustment' (Miller and Rose 1990: 14).

Reference to 'resistance' here is interesting, in part because it is so uncharacteristic of the governmentality literature to pay it sustained attention. Rather, collisions between government and reality are thought out primarily in terms of the 'failure' of programs (for example, Miller and Rose 1990; Hunt and Wickham 1994). While failure is understood to be a key dynamic of government, for it triggers the process of rethinking and reconstructing programs, failure is not an intrinsic property of an event so much as it is a property of a program. To think in terms of failure puts the emphasis on the status of the collision from the programmer's viewpoint, and consequently reduces resistance to a negative externality. No space is created for a productive and incorporative relationship with resistance – such as would exist where rule and resistance form each other reflexively. This feature of the governmentality approach remains true even of the one work which places resistance centre-stage. While Alan Hunt and Gary Wickham's (1994) *Foucault and Law* almost celebrates resistance for its contribution to the 'incompleteness/failure' of govern-ance, its role remains that of obstruction to rule. Its constitutive role in the governmentality approach is only indirect, that is, through the ways in which programmers seek to find solutions to the puzzles that resistance represents. One of the consequences is that what is missing from the literature is a sense of 'government from below' and, more generally, a rather pronounced silence about the ways in which resistance and rule relate to each other in positive and productive ways (for example, Osborne 1992; Rose 1993; Walters 1994; Greco 1993).[1]

This silence is at once both curious and intelligible once the Foucauldian origins of the governmentality approach are recalled, for Michel Foucault's (1980) emphasis on the idea that 'resistance is never in a position of exteriority in relation to power' was not translated into a prominent place in his own investigations. His suggestions envision resistance as potentially positive, appearing 'in the role of adversary, target, support or handle' for government. In this sense, resistance may be an integral part of and contributor to programs regarded as success-ful, and be incorporated into programs rather than merely acting as an external source of program failure. But, if resistance is positive and productive, if resistance and rule actively engage with each other, then rule is at least potentially destabilised and subjected to a transformational politics. This implies an approach in which politics is a far more open-ended process of contest and engagement than readily emerges from viewing it as 'a mentality of rule' (Miller and Rose 1990). This view of government as a political contest directs rather more attention to sociological forms of analysis – to investigate 'how it really was' – than has been characteristic of most governmentality work to date. In sum, by understanding politics from the vantage point of mentalities of rule which reduces the role of resistance to a source of program failure, and by the consequent elision of the constitutive role of resistance, the governmentality literature is unable fully to investigate major strategies of liberal governance, together with major sources of contradiction in, and transformation of, this form of rule.

Liberalism and 'Indigenous Governance'

Liberal governmentality is remarkable for its inventiveness, its eclecticism and the array of technologies that it enlists and develops for the practicalities of rule (Barry et al. 1993; Osborne 1992). In part, these characteristics may stem from the fact that in place of a sovereign exercising a totalising will across the entire span of nation or empire, the imagery of liberal government is of a regime which maximises the freedoms of the subject – so that rulers must rule through freedoms, or at least in ways that appear to delimit freedoms in minimal fashion. Accordingly, liberalism is attracted to the appropriation of 'indigenous governances' – the forms of government that arise in, and are endemic to, the everyday lives of subjects. Such forms are more likely to appear (to rulers and ruled) as the expression of individuals or groups rather than impositions from without. Thus, one of the particular attractions of the language of 'community' in advanced liberalism is precisely that it locates rule in the everyday, voluntary interactions or commonalities of interest of private individuals. Processes such as the stimulation of 'community crime prevention' or 'community enterprises' (in the form of charitable services, sports programs, etc.) may be thought of as the strategic enlistment or alignment of indigenous organisation into a governmental program, in order to govern a problem which cannot be left entirely to the management of individuals (O'Malley and Palmer 1996). At the same time, and of equal importance, this alignment permits the apparent retreat of formal, exogenous or imposed government, as rule is carried out by the community 'itself'.

This appropriation or alignment, of course, cannot be taken for granted – as if government simply selects ready-made options from a smorgasbord available to it. Rather, in each instance it must negotiate the appropriation, attempt to align it with the purposes of rule; and sustain the credibility of the resultant form. Often, as with the instance of community crime prevention and other examples of the enlistment of 'communities' in advanced liberalism, it is clear that governing manoeuvres aim to mobilise a *particular* sense of shared interests, train participants in *specific* skills, provide information about certain *selected* 'community' risks, enlist *targeted* local participation in 'community' efforts, and so on (O'Malley 1992). Yet even here, where the indigenous form is extensively an artefact of rule from without, government at a distance frequently becomes problematic as locals react by 'failing' to take their duties seriously, or grasp the reins of power and direct community activities in ways not intended by programmers (for example, Stenson 1993).

Where governing at a distance appropriates pre-existing indigenous forms, however, liberalism may incorporate alien and contradictory practices and assumptions. In such contexts, at least where the problems are recognised, subterranean work is likely to be carried out to neutralise, eliminate or transform these resistant elements. Such work is subterranean in the sense that, to be successfully effected, it must not violate the authenticity of the indigenous governance in the eyes of the programmers and the programmed. The resultant arrangements, incorporating or realigning indigenous governances, may contribute to liberalism's eclecticism and adaptability through the addition of new concepts, techniques and principles of governance. However, it will remain an open question, to be investigated sociologically in each instance, how far the resultant configuration of rule neutralises the resistance inherited within the appropriated governances. In their turn, these incorporated resistances may not leave intact either specific liberal regimes of rule, or indeed, liberalism *per se*. The transformational potential of appropriated indigenous forms of governance is difficult to know in advance, and it is always possible that resulting challenges to rule may be fatal. This suggests a rather different view of the relationship between resistance and government, a more open-ended view of the work of programmers, and of the fate of programs, than is implied by most existing governmentality studies.

A Genealogy of Self-Determination

Among the more translucent contexts in which to observe the alignment or appropriation of indigenous governances are those associated with policies of 'empowerment' in moves toward decolonisation. In part, this translucence stems from the greater formal distance between modern liberal forms and assumptions of government and those which are endemic to their colonised (as opposed to metropolitan and culturally familiar) subjects. Consider, as an example, the case of the federal Australian Department of Aboriginal Affairs' (DAA)[2] policy of 'self-determination'. This recognises 'the worth of Aboriginal culture and the right of Aborigines to pursue lifestyles which are in accordance with that culture. Self-determination also seeks to improve the social and economic circumstances of Aborigines by encouraging them to take charge of their own affairs' (DAA 1988: 233). Ignoring the characteristically (advanced) liberal reduction of Aboriginality to a 'lifestyle' variation, this policy appeared to mark a considerable advance in official discourses dealing with the practical meaning of Aboriginal self-determination (Rowse 1993; Tonkinson and Howard 1990). This first figuring of self-determination approximated to what Paul Havemann (1988) has referred to as the 'indigenisation of social control' – by providing colonised subjects with the forms of government associated with self-determination in the liberal state. In Havemann's work, this involved the transfer of British or European models of police to first-nation American peoples – in which the personnel are indigenous but the institutional arrangements are alien. In the Australian desert context, it involved the establishment of 'self-managing' corporate entities (especially in the form of Community Councils) together with an array of related discourses and practices of modern liberal rule, such as impersonal administration, impartial justice and meritocratic hierarchicalism.

It soon emerged, however, that many of these imposed corporate and impersonal governmental forms were almost unworkable in contexts of Aboriginal social relations. Indigenous Aboriginal governance – attuned to nomadic existence – reflects far more fissionable and temporary arrangements and non-corporate forms in which kinship, age, gender and sacred knowledge and status are central principles (Keen 1989). Consequently, Community Councils frequently 'broke down' into factions, primarily along kinship lines, and thus have come to be regarded in official discourses as 'failing' to govern Aboriginal settlements in an administratively satisfactory fashion (Wolfe 1989: 70). In addition, Aboriginal people have avoided or have not been appointed to many of the key administrative positions – for example, as community advisers, teachers and community store managers. The reason was not so much a lack of will to transfer authority to Aboriginal people, as it was the lack of fit between the role expectations of such positions and the situational demands placed on potential Aboriginal incumbents. Bureaucratic management, impartial principles of distributive justice, and a host of functions based on liberal models of abstract universal individuals, frequently came to grief when kin demanded and received the dues 'traditionally' accorded to their personal standing. Often, the experiment was not even tried as the result was thought to be so predictable.

There was a sense that government and administration were objective relations necessary to self-determination but were being 'impeded' by Aboriginality: 'failure to achieve a balance between the demands of cultural imperatives of Aboriginal society and the needs of good administration and proper accountability has been a major cause for the lack of success of self-determination' (DAA 1988: 255). However, the ironies of the policy – in which self-determination was obstructing good government – were beginning to be impressed on the administrators. The governmental version of self-determination was failing in its own terms because of the robust nature of Aboriginal forms of governance. These subjects of self-determination were not liberal subjects already primed with the taken-for-granted assumptions, knowledge and practices of the populace of urban, white Australia. Despite attempts to create such an Aboriginal citizenry, the strength of what David Trigger (1986) refers to as the Aboriginal 'Blackfella domain' frustrated white political programs. This resistance did not so much appear in hostile conflict as in more subtle processes which sustained indigenous governance. The resistance asserted itself through 'the exclusion of whites from physical space, styles of behaviour, modes of thought (and communication)', which often rendered white practices of rule unworkable (Trigger 1986: 116).

These resistant indigenous governances asserted themselves not through overt opposition, but rather by rendering white practices of rule unworkable in many contexts. In the face of this, profound observations crept into government discourse, the federal parliamentary Select Committee itself noting the irony in 'Aboriginal communities . . . being asked to accept non-Aboriginal structures in order to have greater control over their own affairs' (House of Representatives 1990: 19).

Such official recognition brings into question not simply the programs of self-determination but the applicability of basic concepts and forms of administration intrinsic to modern liberal government which were being problematised (impartiality, formal equality, individual responsibility and accountability). Further, they were being problematised not simply because they were rejected by Aboriginal people, but increasingly because these people *responded* to rule by sustaining and adapting their own practices and discourses, actively paralleling and even displacing those of white government (Lea and Wolfe 1993). In particular, extended family networks have been adapted to provide an enduring and effective framework for the delivery of support and guidance to those members in trouble with criminal justice or in need of welfare support. Aboriginal agencies have developed outside those of the state, along lines more consistent with indigenous forms and practices (for example, Palmer and Collard 1993; Minitjukur and Divakaran-Brown 1991). As a result, it is coming to be recognised officially that organisations 'that have emerged from within the Aboriginal community and which reflect Aboriginal aspirations and priorities are functioning better than other structures that are imposed by the government' (House of Representatives 1990: 45). In the wake of such realisations, a new phase of liberal government has been opened, in which indigenous forms of governance increasingly are appropriated to achieve ends sought by political programmers (Rowse 1993). In the process, however, it is evident that the subjects of rule have also brought the governors into alignment with *their* wills and *their* governances. Key liberal technologies of rule are reshaped or abandoned in pursuit of 'better' government. A new irony begins to emerge, in which (white) government has to accept Aboriginal structures in order to have greater control over *its* own affairs.

Translating Indigenous Governance

In some senses, this is an overly optimistic view of the processes of liberal governance, for while it highlights the processes whereby resistance may invest and transform government, it also begins to reveal a dark side to liberalism. The process of self-determination involves its constitution via the selective valorisation of those aspects of indigenous governance that produce administratively desired effects – that is, those which 'are functioning better' in achieving the goals of liberal government – and a neutralisation, suppression or eschewal of those aspects which are seen as counterproductive, hostile or incompatible with the project of rule. Such processes cannot be analysed readily by inspection of the discourses of liberal government for they rarely appear there, and their formal recognition would offend both liberal and Aboriginal sensibilities. Rather, they are likely to occur in ways which are subterranean to the discourse, rather than appearing overtly within it. This need not, of course, imply the operation of conspiracy, cynicism or covert interests. Rather, the processes involved appear more like those understood by Latour (1986) as translation. In the context of subterranean practices of rule, translation implies a process in which the programmers 'make sense' of the indigenous governances – ignoring aspects which are 'incomprehensible', thinking of practices as if they were situated within a familiar rather than an alien culture, 'correcting' obvious 'errors', assigning significance according to familiar rather than to alien priorities, and so on. This rather reverses the direction in which the process has been discussed by Latour (1986) and Miller and Rose (1990). In the context of governing at a distance, those writers focused on the significance of translation in producing unanticipated shifts in the operation of rule, between the intentions of the initiating programmers and the practices which are put into effect at relationally distant points.[3] The process of concern here, however, relates to the role of translation in forming government's understandings of that which it seeks to rule at a distance and of the indigenous governances that it appropriates for this purpose.

Commencing in 1990, an attempt was made to give the Ngaanyatjarra people of inland Western Australia 'ownership' of the enduring problem of petrol sniffing, and to provide appropriate training and support. The Marlba program was based on the idea that petrol sniffing was symptomatic of a broader malaise, brought on by learned helplessness of a shattered and demoralised people.[4] In this setting, the Western Australian Department of Community Services (DCS) sought to structure its petrol sniffing management program in terms of providing a moral technology which ultimately could be operated by the Ngaanyatjarra with minimal or no white intervention. Petrol sniffers were to be counselled about the dangers of sniffing, and a Ngaanyatjarra mentor assigned to ensure that in their day-to-day lives they gave up petrol sniffing. The program was given a 'traditional' name (*Marlba*, a term corresponding to an elder brother), and some emphasis placed on the idea that this program sought to restore traditional order rather than impose new and alien arrangements.

The scheme arose out of DCS' dissatisfaction with criminal justice interventions, which involved petrol sniffers being turned over to the police, removed from the community for hearings in the regional Children's Court, and then (usually) assigned to a distant institution for up to three months. DCS regarded this process as ineffectual, pointing to the frequency of recidivism, to the failure of criminal justice to reduce rates of offending and to the trauma suffered by children and kin. Moreover, reliance on the police was held to strengthen or reproduce the dependence of the Ngaanyatjarra people on white authority structures and agencies, thus further eroding their ability to manage the problem. In short, the existing colonial forms of liberal government were perceived to be failing, and (as Miller and Rose would suggest) the programmers set about seeking better models.

Accordingly, the alternative approach that was to be adopted stressed that 'community' (that is, Ngaanyatjarra) involvement and self-determination is essential to the proper and effective governance of Aboriginal people, and ultimately should displace external (state) involvement. In particular, it was hoped that the Marlba program eventually would train sufficient mentors so that the Aboriginal communities

would be able to manage the problem autonomously. In a very clear
sense, DCS officials perceived the program simultaneously as improving
the reach of government in an issue of state concern, while also extend-
ing the self-determination of the Ngaanyatjarra. Indigenous forms of
governance were being appropriated because these were seen to have
the potential to do the job better. Yet it is clear that the process was to be
far more than one of straightforward appropriation of indigenous governance, for the DCS and the Ngaanyatjarra entered prolonged (three-
to four-year) negotiations to shape the program for mutual satisfaction.
It was in this process that was effected the translation and selective
valorisation of Ngaanyatjarra culture which focused on three major
themes: violence, toleration and the power of traditional male elders.

Violence: Tradition Refused

Violent retribution is understood by all parties to have been, in the past,
an appropriate response to many categories of prohibited or intolerable
behaviour in Aboriginal societies. It is commonly stated by Ngaanyatjarra
people that many of the actions of petrol sniffers would have been dealt
with by spearing, clubbing, banishment or even death, and certainly
beatings of increasing severity would have been a minimal response to
persistent disruptive, disrespectful or sacrilegious behaviour. While it is
by no means universally the case that Ngaanyatjarra people now believe
that this response should be used against petrol sniffers, many comment
that 'in the old days' decisive interventions would have ensured that
there would have been no enduring problem with such behaviour. Such
reactions to all manner of offences in Ngaanyatjarra communities are
still frequent. Affronts to the dignity of senior men of powerful families
will generate spontaneous outrage, and if a spear is at hand it may well
be used. Beatings are still delivered to those who fail to act in accordance
with cultural prescriptions.

Physical violence as a response to petrol sniffing was often of concern
to the DCS and it is clear that officials were aware that it was sometimes
resorted to. The DCS was confronted with an acute dilemma, for the
claim of such violent responses, backed up by customary law, had to be
recognised. Yet, to the DCS such violence was morally unacceptable, and
without exception workers adopted the liberal view that violence solved
nothing. This was shored up by the observation that, in the eyes of some
DCS officers, the violent reactions were not 'traditional' responses of a
customary legal form, but rather were outbursts of irate men (and sometimes, women) sometimes under the influence of alcohol. Moreover, the
DCS has an institutionalised role to oppose and prevent violence to
young people because of its watching brief over child welfare – which

grants it a mandate to remove children on 'Care and Protection Orders'. The powers it holds in this latter respect help underpin its interventions in petrol sniffing cases.

However this situation is viewed, a struggle emerged over the issue of violence and its status as a traditional and effective response, in which the DCS consistently opposed violence as a means to controlling petrol sniffing. Tradition either was refused (that is, 'this is traditional, but it is not appropriate or relevant in this context'), or it is denied (that is, 'this is not really traditional'). Whichever way the DCS turned it confronted dilemmas. To accept violent solutions is abhorrent and probably would constitute a breach of its legal mandate in Western Australian state law. Yet to deny the relevance of the tradition is to pull the rug from under its claim that it seeks to uphold or restore traditional culture. Moreover, were it actively to prohibit violent responses it would appear to act as a colonial authority when it is claiming to empower. Its practical way out of this dilemma is to promote preferred and apparently more rational and beneficial alternatives among other facets of 'traditional' order, those options which make far more sense yet do not incontrovertibly contravene accepted traditions.

Toleration: Tradition Overtaken

Another 'traditional' Ngaanyatjarra response to petrol sniffing, frequently cited by DCS staff and often referred to in the literature (for example, Brady 1992; Menzies School of Health Research 1991) is that of toleration for others. It is argued that in Aboriginal society there is a profound respect for the autonomy of others, such that it is regarded as extremely rude to interfere in another's life. This interpretation of tradition is used to account for the apparent social tolerance toward petrol sniffing expressed by many Ngaanyatjarra. Despite periodic episodes of violence directed at petrol sniffers, it is far more frequently the case that sniffing may occur in sight of and in the full knowledge of adults, without this leading to any intervention. Needless to say the DCS found this perplexing and baffling, and accounts based on the 'tradition' of toleration were raised to explain the lack of intervention. The argument relating to the culture of personal autonomy here is usually backed up with a second account – that Ngaanyatjarra children are subject to a distinctive regime of upbringing. Whereas the modern culture exposes children to constant disciplinary surveillance and corrective training, Aboriginal children are given much greater freedom. The tolerance of sniffing is argued to reflect this *laissez-faire* approach to childhood (see, for example, Brady 1992). However, as is frequently argued both by Ngaanyatjarra people seeking intervention and by the

DCS, petrol sniffing is a new problem and 'therefore' is beyond the containing powers of traditional means of child-rearing. While Aboriginal tolerance of children's peculiarities and non-disciplinary child-rearing are conditionally admired, they are understood by many to be hopelessly inadequate to deal with petrol sniffing. Unlike violence, therefore, there is no prohibition or abhorrence of this particular 'traditional' pattern. However, it is regarded as relating to an ideal world passed, one overtaken by new problems for which people must take active responsibility. In short, while the 'traditional' status of this orientation toward children is neither denied nor rejected, it is passed over in favour of other 'more suitable' ways.

The Power of Men: Tradition Upheld

It was recognised that there was no possibility of introducing any such scheme in the Ngaanyatjarra lands without the approval of elders, and primarily, of the male elders. Partly for this reason, women were rarely consulted. This pattern was reinforced by the DCS' belief that as most of the (visible) petrol sniffing occurred among young men, and as Aboriginal societies are structured extensively around gender division, then it followed that controlling petrol sniffing was 'men's business'. This was all the more so because DCS staff argued that the young men concerned are physically too strong, and (under the influence of petrol) potentially too violent, to be controlled by women. Curiously, this overlooked the indisputable fact that it was very largely the women kin who cared for the petrol sniffers. In a sense, however, having constructed a vision of 'traditional' Ngaanyatjarra society, the DCS then acted upon it. The Marlba scheme was based on a vision of male kinship roles which, while no doubt appropriate in many respects, was not as immutable and pervasive as the DCS assumed.[5]

Of course, DCS officials were not alone in promoting the focus on the senior male elders in each community. Such men, it may be surmised, regarded this selective consultation as only right, for among other things the Marlba scheme would shore up their authority. It both confirmed their place at the pinnacle of Ngaanyatjarra politics, and provided support for their struggle against a recalcitrant and problematic set of young men (cf. Menzies School of Health Research 1991).

Despite this, there is no simple narrative in which male elders unanimously recognised a source of support to their collective status claims and thus threw their combined weight behind the scheme. Rather, there was considerable reserve about the scheme, and some direct opposition, especially from those who looked to the state criminal justice system for control of petrol sniffing. For many people, especially those in the older age groups, petrol sniffers were a source of tension and danger and they wanted nothing better than to be rid of them. The police should take these boys away, the magistrates would convict them, and they would be put away (in Kalgoorlie or Perth) for three months. Other Ngaanyatjarra, however, argued that the problems of petrol sniffing had been exaggerated, claiming that petrol sniffing only rarely has long-term effects, that it represents only an expression of youth resistance, and that most of the complaints stem from whites, who are far more concerned with damage to property than with the problems of the sniffers. From the DCS position these represented mistaken arguments which needed to be corrected. Such claims were seen as mistaken about the effects of imprisonment, factually underestimated the harmful effects of sniffing on the bodies of the young, and self-evidently reinforced dependency on whites. In turn, the effect of this interpretation of Ngaanyatjarra views was to narrow still further the practical definition of who and what is to be empowered – for the particular Ngaanyatjarra people asserting these types of claim are regarded as part of the problem, and thus to be neutralised by outflanking them politically, or educating them about the 'truth'. They join a whole range of Ngaanyatjarra people not credentialled to represent traditional values or regarded as outside the programmers' vision of relevant tradition.

Thus, by a considerable effort of cultural and political translation, a program of liberal governance was made palatable to the principal parties and more effective by locating it in (selected) forms of indigenous governance. One vital aspect of this process, already noted, is that as an essential condition for its program the DCS generated a particular view of what constituted the traditional Ngaanyatjarra order – or perhaps more precisely – a vision of traditional order that could be drawn upon to reconstitute a viable society capable of dealing with problems of order. This administrative anthropology was constituted out of a process which drew on many sources. Previous government reports and records, snatches of professional anthropology, discussions with Ngaanyatjarra elders and white officials, understandings formed inductively by DCS field-workers over many years: all rendered Ngaanyatjarra ways 'intelligible' and thus available for translation into government.

The Constitutive Role of Resistance

While this dark side of liberalism reconstitutes Aboriginal governance in ways that render it compatible with the program at hand, it cannot be overlooked that DCS officials have been involved in a reciprocal process of constituting their program in ways that are acceptable to Ngaanyatjarra people. An interpretation which sees *only* an appropriation of indigenous governances ignores the ways in which the program itself was shaped by nature of the Ngaanyatjarra domain. In particular, of

course, the entire program implies the importation of governance
through familism into the operations of a modern government agency,
and this in turn had many more specific effects which set up tensions with
principles of liberal, and indeed Keynesian, government. One example
serves to illustrate the point. Originally it was proposed that mentors
would be selected by the DCS on the basis of its own, liberal criteria of
suitability (sobriety, reliability, maturity, etc.). However, as negotiations
proceeded it became clear that this would create major problems. First,
no family would permit one of its young, male members to come under
the coercive authority of a member of another family. For such a person to
constrain or coerce a petrol sniffer would be to invite the instant
retaliation of the latter's male kin. No Ngaanyatjarra man would have
been induced to take up a mentoring role which failed to take this into
account. Second, it was clearly understood that, as the extended family is
at the core of everyday life in the communities, only a family member
would be able to be with the young man for very much of the time. The
essence of the Marlba program required that the mentor would play a
watchdog role over the day-to-day activities of the petrol sniffer. It was thus
unavoidable that the mentor be kin to the petrol sniffer. Third, because
of the continued strength of ceremonial life in Ngaanyatjarra communities the mentor had to be one who would have the *right* to be with the
young man on frequent ceremonial occasions, and the selection of this
person was a matter determined by the expectations of Ngaanyatjarra
kinship. DCS-appointed mentors would thus have faced major problems
were they not of the right kin relation. By passing appointment of mentors
to the relevant kin-group, the DCS gained in terms of the reach of rule, but
to a significant extent lost the ability to exercise control in terms of
bureaucratic criteria for appointment of mentors.

However the process is viewed – whether as the appropriation of tradition or as the concession to the power of the Aboriginal domain – the
process of government from below is crucial to the formation and the
final organisation of the program. In order to access the Aboriginal subjects and render them self-determining subjects of liberalism, it became
necessary to incorporate their forms of indigenous governance into the
organisation of the state. The entire character of the program reflects a
far more constitutive role for the resistant Aboriginal domain than is
compatible with its interpretation only as an obstacle to rule or a source
of failure.

Conclusion

One reading of the arguments reviewed in this chapter is that resistance
may be constitutive of rule, but only in ways allowed by governing
mentalities – so that the appropriation of 'indigenous' governances

involves their translation into the domain of the subjugators, weakening or severing their nexus with the indigenous domain. In this way, resistance is engulfed and neutralised, and its role in shaping rule is only formal, rather than politically consequential. To put it another way, in this reading resistance may shape rule but never be engaged in rule: its challenge to rule may never be fatal. This interpretation rather accepts an omnicompetence of rule which generally is not evidenced in history, nor takes up much room in the governmentality approach. On the one hand, it assumes that programmers are able to identify all of the unnecessary and potentially contradictory and disruptive elements. On the other, it would imply that they are able to strip away these extraneous and potentially problematic elements from that which has to be incorporated.

It takes comparatively little thought to identify ways in which the incorporation of indigenous governances can rarely be such an unproblematic exercise for liberal rule. For example, the incorporation of actual or potentially disruptive elements (for example, familial particularism in Aboriginal contexts) may be unavoidable because they are essential to the functioning of the 'sanitised' and appropriated governance in its liberal role. Likewise, because the indigenous governances must usually be negotiated into their new alignments, all manner of concessions may be necessary to achieve the desired result, compromising the project from the outset. Thus, the insistence of Ngaanyatjarra that they must choose mentors has been seen to bear risks for the program, but also to introduce into government principles antithetical to its own core precepts of meritocracy and impersonal universalism. Over and above these considerations, it remains the case that the incorporation and translation of elements of indigenous governances does not fix their nature for all time. As long as the indigenous domain still persists outside the particular engulfed practices, it is possible that its members will reappropriate them by means including the same subterranean translation processes which have been seen at work in this chapter.

Of course, programmers are not static either, and are likely to contest emerging retranslations, redefinitions, drifts in practice, etc. They are also likely to move against contradictory, incompatible or jarring elements as they emerge, in much the same ways that have been discussed with respect to the development of the Marlba project. But this indicates very clearly that the processes of resistance are carried into the subjugating program of rule along with the appropriated forms. Resistance inscribes its presence, then, not only by providing particular forms which are then unproblematically deployed to intensify government. The existence of indigenous forms within the subjugating regime provides sites within rule for the operation of counter-discourses and subordinated knowledges.

The process of governing at a distance is thus highly vulnerable to the 'Trojan horse' effect. If projects for Aboriginal self-determination (or any other process of incorporating indigenous governances) can result in the inscription of quite alien elements into liberal arrangements, the question that those concerned with the future of liberal governance may begin to ask is: how far can liberalism reach without becoming prone to internal fissions and substantial contradictions? This issue will be all the more significant to the extent that these imported elements of indigenous governance then become sites of resistance within rule. While governing at a distance may be a fundamental strategy of liberal rule, by accommodating the many and varied indigenous governances that this comes to involve, the pressure of internal contradictions and struggles may become a significant source of instability.

Notes

This paper was first published in *Economy Society*, vol. 25, no. 3, 1995. I would like to thank Nikolas Rose, Clifford Shearing, Patricia Moynihan, Tim Rowse, Mariana Valverde and Lorna Weir, among others, for comments and advice which have greatly improved and reshaped this paper.

1   I would stress here that this reference to relations of super and subordination ('bottom up' or 'top down') is not meant to imply that the governmentality literature focuses on supposedly 'peak' governing contexts, as represented by the central state or corporate management. The critique fully recognises the important advances made by such work in locating government in the host of everyday technologies and practices, major and minor institutions and agencies. The reference to 'bottom up' is made with respect to the normal direction ('top down') of the flow of governing – from the program to the programmed, from the rule to the target of rule – regardless of their location or scale.

2   Subsequently renamed and restructured as the Aboriginal and Torres Strait Islander Commission (ATSIC).

3   Thus, it was to the considerable frustration of the Australian Department of Aboriginal Affairs that land provided by the state for Aboriginal 'enterprise' was subjected to Aboriginal land management which was concerned more with its sacred status than its economic potential; that funds for enterprise development appeared to be applied for 'welfare' purposes; or again, that liberal efforts to 'raise' Aboriginal people out of their dependence on welfare increasingly have been refused because of Aboriginal interpretations that welfare payments represent compensation for the loss of their land and for two centuries of colonial degradation (see especially, Rowse 1993).

4   I would like to take this opportunity to thank the Ngaanyatjarra people for giving me access to their lands, the Western Australian Department of Community Services (DCS) for providing transportation and all manner of other assistance and support, and Garry Coventry who accompanied me on

the first of three field visits. An abbreviated version of this section of the paper appears in *International Journal of Drug Policy* 1994, 5: 136–41.

5   This attributed gender separation proved to be far from a matter of traditional consensus, as in October 1992 Ngaanyatjarra women formally protested over the lack of consultation by the DCS.

References

Barry, Andrew, Thomas Osborne and Nikolas Rose, 1993. 'Liberalism, neo-liberalism and governmentality: an introduction', *Economy and Society* 22: 265–6.

Brady, Maggie, 1992. *Heavy Metal: The Social Meaning of Petrol Sniffing in Australia*, Canberra: Aboriginal Studies Press.

Burchell, Graham, 1991. 'Peculiar interests: civil society and governing "the system of natural liberty"' in G. Burchell, C. Gordon and P. Miller (eds), *The Foucault Effect: Studies in Governmentality*, London: Harvester/Wheatsheaf.

Deleuze, Giles and Guattari, Felix, 1987. *A Thousand Plateaus*, Minneapolis: University of Minnesota Press.

(DAA) Department of Aboriginal Affairs (Australia), 1988. Submissions to House of Representatives Standing Committee on Aboriginal Affairs, *Official Hansard Report*, vol. 1.

Foucault, Michel, 1980. *Power/Knowledge*, ed. C. Gordon, New York: Pantheon.

Greco, M., 1993. 'Psychosomatic subjects and the "duty to be well". Personal agency within medical rationality', *Economy and Society* 22: 357–72.

Havemann, Paul, 1988. 'The indigenisation of social control in Canada' in W. Morse and G Woodman (eds), *Indigenous Law and the State.*, Dordrecht: Foris Publications.

Hindess, Barry, 1993. 'Liberalism, socialism and democracy. Variations on a government theme', *Economy and Society* 22: 300–13.

House of Representatives Standing Committee on Aboriginal Affairs, 1990. *Our Future: Our Selves*, Canberra: Australian Government Publishing Service.

Hunt, Alan and Wickham, Gary, 1994. *Foucault and Law: Toward a Sociology of Law as Governance*, London: Pluto Press.

Keen, Ian, 1989. 'Aboriginal governance' in J. Altman (ed.), *Emergent Inequalities in Aboriginal Australia*, Sydney: Oceania Monograph 38.

Latour, Bruno, 1986. 'The powers of association' in J. Law (ed.), *Power, Action and Belief*, London: Routledge & Kegan Paul.

Lea, David and Wolfe, Jackie, 1993. *Community Development and Community Control*, Canberra: ANU, North Australia Research Unit.

Menzies School of Health Research, 1991. *HALT: An Evaluation*, Darwin: Menzies School of Health Research.

Miller, Peter and Rose, Nikolas, 1990. 'Governing economic life', *Economy and Society* 19: 1–27.

Minitjukur, Alec and Divakaran-Brown, Celia, 1991. *Children of Dispossession. An Evaluation of Petrol Sniffing on Anangu Pitjantjatjara Lands*, South Australia: Nganampa Health Council.

O'Malley, Pat, 1992. 'Risk, power and crime prevention', *Economy and Society* 21, 3: 252–75.

O'Malley, Pat and Palmer, Darren, 1996. 'Post-Keynesian policing', *Economy and Society* 25: 137–55.

Osborne, Thomas, 1992. 'On moral regulation and practices of government', paper presented to the History of the Present seminar, University of London, April.

Palmer, Dave and Len Collard, 1993. 'Nyungar young people, youth policy and problems of theory', paper presented at Rethinking Youth Policies conference, Melbourne, April.

Rose, Nikolas, 1993. 'Government, authority and expertise in advanced liberalism', *Economy and Society* 22: 283–99.

Rowse, Tim, 1993. *Remote Possibilities*, Canberra: ANU, North Australia Research Unit.

Stenson, Kevin, 1993. 'Community policing as a governmental technology', *Economy and Society* 22: 372–98.

Tonkinson, Robert and Howard, Michael, 1990. 'Aboriginal autonomy in policy and practice' in R. Tonkinson and M. Howard (eds), *Going it Alone? Prospects for Aboriginal Autonomy*, Canberra: Aboriginal Studies Press.

Trigger, David, 1986. 'Blackfellas and whitefellas. The concepts of domain and social closure in the analysis of race relations', *Mankind* 16: 99–117.

Walters, William, 1994. 'The discovery of "Unemployment"', *Economy and Society* 23: 265–91.

Wolfe, Jackie, 1989. *That Community Government Mob*, Darwin: North Australia Research Unit.

CHAPTER 10

Governing Material Culture

Laurajane Smith and Gary Campbell

The pastoral care of things has been a long-term self-justification for archaeology, leading the practitioners of archaeology to view themselves as the stewards of the material remains of the past – irrespective of whose past it is. It appears, for example, in nineteenth-century obsession with the establishment of museums to help educate 'good citizens' (Pearce 1986; Merriman 1991; Bennett 1994), and later, in the stewardship role 'scientists' claim in the twentieth century for the conservation and management of material culture. This link between the disposition of things and the pastoral role given to those with authority by virtue of their expertise to negotiate disposition, takes on a crucial role in contexts where the interpretation of material culture has become tied up in re-creating cultural identities for indigenous people.

This chapter focuses on archaeology's origins in the nineteenth century, its contribution to liberal forms of governance and the governance of indigenous peoples in colonial empires and postcolonial Australia. We argue that archaeology, though less directly concerned with the conduct of conduct than other human sciences, is a part of the development of 'rational' liberal rule that drew on the authority of science in the nineteenth century (Rose 1993; Rose and Miller 1992). Archaeology, drawing on the new authority of evolutionary theory, distanced itself from its roots in antiquarianism and classicism, and became a 'science' of human cultural evolution in its own right (Trigger 1989, 1995; Gamble 1993; Silberman 1995). The new human sciences were as crucial in establishing colonial rule as force of arms and trade, rendering understandable, tractable and governable 'native' populations. Archaeology played its part, fitting 'native' peoples into the lower end of often fanciful evolutionary schema, which relegated them to the third division of conquered races. For the edification of the newly literate European populations, the material culture of these conquered peoples was displayed and interpreted alongside classical 'antiquities', as evidence of the inevitable and evolutionally-sanctioned superiority of Europeans. The result was the creation of a pastoral role for the emerging archaeological discipline – not over human subjects as such but over the domain of material culture.

We also consider the inclusion of modern scientific archaeology in processes of conflict mediation over competing claims to material culture, often referred to as cultural resource or heritage management. Here we argue that the discipline of archaeology, rendered a technically and methodologically exact science during the 1960s, became more directly a 'technology of government' (Rose and Miller 1992: 175). Archaeologists as experts on material culture were called upon to adjudicate on the disposition of material culture as indigenous people made increasingly forceful claims to control over sites, artefacts and human remains. These claims were often made in the context of contesting received notions of cultural identity. As such, the role of archaeologists as specific intellectuals, or in Norman Fairclough's (1993) terminology, 'discourse technologists', has a much more concrete role than its academic proponents are willing to recognise.

Before expanding on archaeology as a technology of government we would like to briefly mention the 'postmodern' turn in archaeology, referred to in the discipline as 'post-processualism'. Post-processual theory rounds up all the usual postmodern suspects in an ambitious attempt to theorise the role of archaeology in the modern world. Thus Tilley (1990) attempts to apply Michel Foucault's insights to archaeology, and in doing so to some extent recognises the importance of the concept of governmentality. However, his analysis uses concepts of discourse and text in a way which leads to a stress on the role of elite archaeological writings at the expense of asking: what are the consequences of archaeological practice and knowledge? A similar problem is faced by I. Hodder, whose influential textbook *Reading the Past* (1986) stresses narrative and interpretation as the key features of a critical approach to archaeology. We argue that a focus on archaeology as a technology of government allows a serious investigation of the relation between archaeology as an expert practice, archaeologists as specific intellectuals, and processes of the management of conflicts with indigenous people in colonial and postcolonial societies. Archaeology, despite the claim by many archaeologists that archaeology is a physical science, takes its place, alongside anthropology, as a human science concerned with the government of indigenous populations in colonial and postcolonial societies.

Liberalism and Archaeology in the Nineteenth Century

How then can archaeology, a self-avowed 'value free science' of the material remains of the past, be seen as a human science that played a constitutive role in the rise of liberalism? What, in particular, are the 'jurisdictions and interventions' (Watts 1994) that the emergent discipline of archaeology carved out for itself so that its right to authority over certain items and practices, and its technical capacity to both justify and enact the control of archaeologists, can be uncovered? The nascent discipline of archaeology mobilised knowledge claims to scientific expertise regarding material culture to place itself at the heart of the liberal problematic of rule. Central issues such as science and rationality, evolution, 'social improvement' of citizens and the proper disposition and government of the 'native' peoples of the colonies, were all brought together by archaeology's claims to act as interpreters of and stewards to 'material culture'.

Nor was this an innocent exercise – John Lubbock, author of the first popular work of prehistory, *Prehistoric Times, as Illustrated by Ancient Remains, and the Manners and Customs of Modern Savages* (1869), was a Liberal politician, zealous in adapting the claims of science over material culture to the creation of the virtuous citizen – 'Gladstonian liberalism with a time dimension added' as J. Carman (1993: 40) has characterised his work. Lubbock's most lasting monument was his championing of what was to became the Ancient Monuments Protection Act of 1882, the first such piece of legislation in the United Kingdom (Carman 1993). On the one hand, this Act could be seen as a typical piece of social improvement, but it also rested on the power of the new discipline to make authoritative statements on the disposition of the material remains of the past, and to have these statements taken up and recognised by state agencies.

An important factor here is the ability of archaeology to distinguish itself from antiquarianism – glorified grave-robbing and classicist curiosity about the past – and shoulder the mantle of science to become the 'steward' of the past. It has been widely argued in the archaeological literature that the collection of antiquities prior to the twentieth century was clearly linked to expressions of nationalism, formation of emerging middle-class identity, and struggles within the European aristocracy to maintain power and social status (for example, Murray 1989; Trigger 1989, 1995; Gamble 1993; Sherratt 1993; Khol and Fawcett 1995a). In this sense, antiquities and the past they represented were commonly used to construct or present the identity of the privileged groups who undertook the collection of material culture.

A significant shift in emphasis occurred as collection broadened to explicitly include studies of non-Europeans and of European society in general, rather than specific classes. In the late eighteenth and nineteenth centuries public collections of material culture began to be housed in museums (Pearce 1990; Hopper-Greenhill 1991, 1992). The nineteenth century saw museums establish themselves as 'stewards' of the past aiming to 'educate' the public and, as a consequence, promote national and cultural identity (Bennett 1988, 1994). Archaeologists, such as Julian Pitt-Rivers, were significant in this process arguing that the 'masses' must be 'educated', and 'must learn the links between the past and the present' (Pitt-Rivers 1898, quoted in Daniel 1978: 174).

What occurs with the development of public museums (as opposed to private antiquarian collections) is explicit commentary by antiquarians and museum curators on *other* cultural, class, social and historical identities. They can clearly be seen as governing ideas about nationalism through the institutions of public museums, reinforced by the brute presence of physical objects, which the archaeological discourse held to be objective repositories of knowledge, adding authoritative weight to pronouncements about the past and the nature of other cultures (Merriman 1991; Kohl and Fawcett 1995b). The physical nature of material objects lends tangibility and authenticity to interpretations of the past, and reinforces the authority of interpretations of intellectuals associated with their collection, curation and interpretation (McGuire 1992; Buchli 1995; Carman 1995). Museums became actively engaged with the collection of material culture from European colonies, defining and cataloguing the peoples encountered through colonial expansion.

Notions of cultural evolution that had developed with the discipline of archaeology in the early nineteenth century were, as Trigger (1989: 80ff.) argues, caught up in the intellectual revolution brought about by Darwinian evolutionary theory. Concepts of cultural evolution became inextricably tied to those of physical evolution, and cultural development and change were firmly linked with the pursuit of the origins of humanity. 'Cultural development' and 'national character' were conceived as having some form of physical basis in so far as they were reflected in artefacts and the archaeological record (Gamble 1993; Kohl and Fawcett 1995b). Further, 'cultural identity' was conceived both as having physical representations in material culture and being influenced by physical attributes defined by race and environment. This was to have disastrous results for indigenous people colonised by the British and other European nations. Not only could people be classified as 'primitive' on the basis of racial characteristics, but their 'primitiveness' could also be identified, defined and illustrated by their material culture.

Paleolithic archaeology gained immense scientific prestige during the latter parts of the nineteenth century (Trigger 1989; Gamble 1993) and was seen as part of the debate on the evolution of the species, through which the missing links in human evolution would be found (Gamble 1993). The important point here is that archaeology gained identity and authority as a discipline in this period through its alliance with evolutionary science; Darwin's evolutionary theory gave scientific legitimacy and lent credibility to ideas about the inequality of human races. Claims to scientific knowledge over material culture were crucial in helping establish modernity, and were mobilised to provide 'objective' expertise on cultural and social evolution. They became an important underlying colonial discourse influencing ideas of the proper government of native peoples.

Australian Archaeology and the Governance of Aboriginal Material Culture

The development of 'professional' interest in archaeology was hindered by views of Aboriginal people as 'unchanging' (Mulvaney 1989, 1990a). During the first half of the twentieth century research into the Aboriginal past remained the province of what the more recent archaeological literature refers to as 'amateurs' (Murray and White 1981; Moser 1995). Although many of these researchers were trained in other fields of research, such as anthropology or anatomy, they lacked formal qualifications in archaeology. The 'amateur' phase of archaeology in Australia has been characterised as a period largely concerned with the collection and description of Aboriginal artefacts, almost a 'remnant' form of antiquarianism (Mulvaney 1981a, 1989, 1990a; Murray 1992a, 1996).

The replacement of 'remnant antiquarianism' by a new, more explicitly scientific archaeology practised by a cohort of Cambridge-trained archaeologists who came to Australia in the 1960s, is a useful point of departure to consider archaeology as a technology of government relevant to late liberalism. This allows us to re-examine the relations between novel issues of citizenship and nationhood posed by indigenous political activism, a newly rigorous and abstract scientism that changed archaeological discourse and practice, and the network of relations between expert practitioners constituted by the creation of 'cultural resources management' (CRM) and heritage legislation. CRM is the process involved in the protection and preservation of material culture by archaeologists and other experts (see Pearson and Sullivan 1995). This process is embedded within and supported by legislation and government policy. Within Australian archaeology CRM has become the major employment area, providing work for professionally trained archaeologists within government heritage agencies, or as freelance consultants who provide expert advice and recommendations with respect to the management, interpretation and preservation of Aboriginal material culture (Truscott and Smith 1993).

The first point to make here is the way that 'sovereignty and rights of self-determination advanced by Aboriginal peoples call into question the stability of dominant conceptions of how and where politics is done in the contemporary world' (Purvis 1996: 55). The claims of native peoples to full citizenship rights, and even the questioning of the idea of the 'nation', posed a threat to the traditional modes of government of indigenous people in postcolonial societies.

Particularly in Australia, Aboriginal people used claims to land and material culture as crucial strategies to forge a new cultural and political identity (see Miller 1986; Keefe 1988; Dodson 1994; Goodall 1995). Increasingly assertive claims were made during the 1970s for ancestral lands via the land rights movement, and the ethics of the collection and research practices of museums and archaeologists were called into question (see Barunga 1975; Kelly 1975, 1979; Fesl 1983; Langford 1983). Land was redefined as both material and cultural by these claims, as were the Aboriginal 'artefacts' held in museums and studied by archaeologists. Perhaps the most pointed example is the conflict over skeletal material and the issue of reburial or cremation of skeletal collections, which one prominent archaeologist likened to Nazi book-burning (Mulvaney cited in Duncan 1984: 28; see also Mulvaney 1981b).

Responses to the threats posed by Aboriginal politics have become a part of modern exercises in nation building, and have substantively reposed the question of the links between certain forms of expertise, notably law and anthropology, as well as archaeology, and government departments. General public concern over the preservation of heritage, Aboriginal claims to cultural sovereignty, coupled with archaeological concerns to prevent the loss of what was judged as important archaeological 'resources', have all worked to establish the character of CRM in Australia (Smith 1993). The argument we develop here stresses more than the ability to make technical judgments about material culture. Archaeology, through the process of CRM, has, in response to Aboriginal cultural claims, reasserted its nineteenth-century role to interpret the 'meaning' of indigenous material culture, but in a more explicitly 'scientific' and value-free way.

The advent of what was referred to as the 'new archaeology'[1] in the 1960s and 1970s is the theoretical innovation that facilitated archaeology's 'technologising', and therefore its ability to play a part in 'governing' a new set of social and 'technical' problems. It embraced logical positivism, emphasised objective hypothesis testing, and argued that one of the principle aims of research should be the generation of general principles or 'laws' and predictive models (see Binford 1962, 1968, 1988; Watson et al. 1971; Bell 1994). Archaeology was aggressively redrawn as a modern scientific, rational and, above all, as a socially 'relevant' discipline. Archaeology's 'relevance' was argued to derive from its new ability to develop rational and objective law-like statements which could be used to educate the public about the past, and from which, it was proposed, 'lessons' for the present and future could be derived (for example, Fritz 1973; Fletcher 1981; see also Dark 1995: 34 who comments on this).

The new archaeology was perceived to have given the discipline intellectual prestige, authority and maturity (Yoffee 1993), and its adoption was enthusiastically hailed as marking the discipline's 'loss of innocence' (Clarke 1973). It was argued that the new identity of archaeology as a 'generalized science' would ensure that 'political constraints' would be removed (Ford 1973: 93; see also Watson et al. 1971; Binford 1988, 1990; Watson 1991). Ford, for instance, argued that adherence to scientific values would allow research to 'transcend national boundaries', and thereby leave behind attempts to claim the indigenous past as the specific province of indigenous and other political concerns (Ford 1973: 89). Further, by doing so, archaeology would be better able to 'serve humanity' by making the indigenous past accessible and meaningful to all of humanity (1973: 83ff.).

The new archaeology, or 'processual theory' as it is now called, was quickly incorporated into Australian archaeology in the late 1960s and early 1970s (Murray 1992b; Moser 1995). This allowed archaeologists to challenge the idea of the Australian past as a backwater and, with the discoveries such as those at Lake Mungo and Kow Swamp,[2] archaeologists were able to argue for the international scientific significance of the Aboriginal past and its ability to contribute to human history (see Mulvaney 1964, 1971, 1979; Megaw 1966; Jones 1968). By adopting a new, rigorous methodology the emerging discipline of professional archaeology in Australia could distinguish itself from racist and opportunistic antiquarianism. Australian archaeologists defined themselves as professionals and scientists, value-free and objective seekers after scientific truth, who pursued their vocation free of political taint or political interference in a disinterested academy.

Strangely enough these claims left Aboriginal people cold – they could distinguish little between the earlier racist history of 'scientific' study of Aborigines and the new claims to objectivity (see, for example, Langford 1983; TALC 1995). Nevertheless, Davison (1991: 11) notes that, despite the wide range of competing interests in, and the degree of public concern with, heritage, it is inevitably professionals, such as archaeologists, historians and architects, who have come to dominate the management of material culture. Treating archaeology as a technology of government illuminates this intersection of power, knowledge and state practices, and brings out the political character of its claims to expertise and the creation of the discourse and practices of CRM.

Secure in their scientifically validated role as stewards of the past, archaeologists in the 1960s and early 1970s agitated and lobbied for the protection of archaeological resources, and the development of government legislation to protect both Aboriginal and non-Aboriginal cultural heritage (Mulvaney 1989, 1990b; Flood 1993). However, they were concerned not only about protecting heritage, but also to ensure archaeological access to the database. Agitation for heritage legislation was often expressed in terms of the rights of archaeological science as 'universal knowledge' to unrestricted access to the 'archaeological resource' (see, for example, Mulvaney 1964, 1968, 1970; Megaw 1966; Jones 1968; Allen 1970; Coutts 1977, 1982, 1984; Wright 1986). Archaeological stewardship was stressed (see, for example, Mulvaney 1970, 1981b, 1989; Coutts 1977), and it was argued that an archaeologist had a 'moral' responsibility (Mulvaney 1968: 1), if not a 'duty to his [sic] sites' by ensuring that sites were excavated in a professional way and information conveyed to the public. Failure to adequately protect sites would be an act of 'scientific vandalism' (Mulvaney 1970: 115, also 1964).

Together with the discourse of 'stewardship' was a discourse which identified archaeological resources or archaeological sites. The constant use of terminology that identified an archaeological resource (as in cultural resource management) mapped out the intellectual rights of the archaeological discipline to access and control cultural heritage. This use of language firmly defines archaeology as 'scientific' interpreter of a universalised past, and firmly denotes the legislative intellectual authority of archaeology. For instance, Peter Coutts in a radio broadcast in response to increasing public interest in the Aboriginal past, depoliticises that past by claiming it as 'our' heritage and as under the professional guardianship of archaeologists: 'to take our legacy seriously an understanding of Aboriginal history can only be achieved through excavation of Aboriginal sites . . . An awareness of the importance of preserving and protecting archaeological sites for posterity is one response to an awakening interest in Australia's Aboriginal legacy' (1977: 76–7).

It is archaeological expertise that has the authority to arbitrate on conflicts over the disposition of material culture. Conflict often arises over the different values attributed to heritage by interest groups, over the use of heritage sites, over different conceptualisations and meanings attributed to heritage objects, sites and places; and, subsequently, over the various different expressions of cultural and historical identity symbolised by heritage items. The CRM process is directly concerned with the management, regulation and mitigation of conflict over the use of cultural heritage, and archaeology provides both the scientific discourse and professional practitioners to 'manage' conflict over material culture. In Zygmunt Bauman's (1987) terms, archaeology simultaneously exercises the authority of both 'legislator' and 'interpreter' by drawing on its intellectual authority to universal knowledge to authorise its interpretive role between competing claims to material culture.

The interaction of the various groups who have an interest in cultural heritage is controlled and regulated by the strategies and management processes embodied in CRM. CRM does not only manage physical objects, sites and places, it also regulates and structures conflicts between competing values and conceptualisations of the past. Heritage legislation establishes a hierarchy which tends to reinforce the authority of particular forms of expertise to arbitrate on procedure and knowledge. In Australia archaeologists are either explicitly recognised under heritage legislation as arbitrators over heritage conflicts, or employed by the government institutions responsible for the legislation to interpret and implement that legislation (see Byrne 1993; Smith 1993; Ellis 1994). In short, archaeological knowledge is ensured a distinctive role in heritage discourse and policy.

Archaeology as a Technology of Government

Heritage legislation

A closer look at Australian cultural heritage legislation, and the way that it recognises not only archaeological discourse but the practitioners of archaeology, shows the extent to which the discipline governmentalises the conflicts over material culture. It is through heritage legislation that archaeological knowledge and discourse becomes what Alan Hunt (1993) terms 'regulatory knowledge' – knowledge that is both incorporated within, and regulated and governed by, legislation. Heritage legislation subsequently works to govern the development and dissemination of knowledge within the discipline of archaeology, and knowledge about the nature and significance of Aboriginal material culture.

The prerequisites for the development of legislation identified by Hunt (1993) are the construction of an object of regulation, the 'discovery' of a social problem and the collection of information about the phenomenon. Scientific philosophies and the discourse of archaeology underlined the construction of material culture as the objects of regulation by defining it as both scientifically 'significant' and as 'archaeological data'. The transition from amateur to professional and the incorporation of modern emphasis on objectivity facilitated the development of regulatory knowledge and the incorporation of archaeological expertise into legislation.

The new social problem that was to be regulated through heritage legislation and the governance of material culture was posed by increasing Aboriginal political activism in the 1970s. The associated Aboriginal cultural revival used new claims about the Aboriginal past and present cultural identity to underscore Aboriginal demands for self-determination and political legitimacy (Keefe 1988). In the south-eastern States of New South Wales, Victoria and Tasmania this cultural revival was particularly poignant as it challenged the pervasive white settler discourse that Aboriginal people no longer existed. These States were among the first in Australia to effectively legislate to protect Aboriginal material culture and it is this legislation which is examined below.

Legislation in south-eastern States protects what the individual Acts define as 'relics' and/or 'archaeological' sites and resources.[3] Aboriginal people were not consulted in the development of legislation in south-eastern Australia (Sullivan 1975; NPWS 1989; Brown 1995), while archaeologists were actively consulted or employed in the drafting process. The term 'relic' has come under intense Aboriginal criticism: 'for us the strong connotation that items of Aboriginal cultural property so defined have no connection or significance to Aboriginal people today, that they belong to a dead past' (Fourmile 1989: 50; see also NPWS 1989; Geering and Roberts 1992).

The use of the term 'relic' works to deny the existence of concerns with the past to contemporary Aboriginal culture. Contemporary Aboriginal claims about the past become jeopardised by the institutionalisation of the idea that Aboriginal culture in the south-east had ceased to exist with colonisation. In distancing contemporary Aboriginal people from their past the term leaves open a space for archaeological claims to stewardship and interpretation of a past otherwise left without meaning or significance. In Tasmania the separation of contemporary Aboriginal people from their past is further reinforced with relics being specifically defined as those occurring prior to 1876 (Aboriginal Relics Act 1975, s.2(4)), that is, material made and used prior to the death of Truganini, popularly held to have been the 'last Tasmanian' (Ryan 1981). This definition of a 'relic' effectively denies the continuing culture of Aboriginal people in Tasmania (Brown 1995; TALC 1995), and relegates the politically active Tasmanian Aboriginal population to the status of 'Aboriginal descendants'[4] rather than Aboriginal people.

The materialist definition of relic and archaeological resources also renders the protection of what the CRM discourse refers to as 'mythological sites' somewhat ambiguous under the legislation. The absence of 'relics' or 'artefacts' at these sites can render these sites legally unprotected. Archaeological definitions of material culture or 'sites' define the objects, which in Hunt's terms, were to be 'regulated' by legislative intervention (1993: 318).

The incorporation of a vocabulary, language and concepts into heritage Acts works to privilege or exclude certain groups. It also sets the parameters of acceptable management practice and determines the scope of policy debate. Heritage legislation has been criticised by Aboriginal people for protecting 'archaeological' sites and values rather than Aboriginal concerns. They claim it excludes Aboriginal participation in management, yet privileges archaeological involvement, thus hindering the development and expression of contemporary culture by severing it from its past (see NPWS 1989; Fourmile 1989; Geering and Roberts 1992; Organ 1994; Brown 1995).

Aboriginal claims about the past and their identity become the subjects of regulation and regulatory knowledge and, as such, come into direct conflict with archaeological claims to expertise and stewardship over the past. Archaeologists as government employees administering heritage legislation, and as consultants working under the auspices of heritage Acts, must directly engage with Aboriginal resentment over the management of their material culture.

The contestation of archaeological expertise

Heritage legislation and the practices and policies embedded in the process of CRM work to mobilise archaeological expertise as a technology of government in the governance of Aboriginal cultural identity. However, legislation, policy and practices are explicitly and intensively scrutinised and criticised by Aboriginal people. The contesting of archaeological authority has arisen over specific cases of 'management', such as the reburial of skeletal material. But sustained criticism has also occurred regarding the research practices and methodology employed by the discipline, as well as attacks on archaeological claims to expertise and stewardship (Williams 1975; Fesl 1983; Langford 1983; Cook and Morris 1984; Ah Kit 1995; TALC 1995).

The relationship of archaeology, as a technology of government, with both Aboriginal interests and government agencies and policy-makers has become unstable in recent years. For instance, policy initiatives have been developed by the Tasmanian State government which have resulted in the forced return of Aboriginal artefacts held by archaeologists to Aboriginal communities (see Allen 1995; Auty 1995; Murray and Allen 1995; TALC 1995). In both New South Wales and Tasmania policies have been enacted which are neither explicitly or implicitly

supported by the legislation, and which require direct Aboriginal participation in CRM. Reviews of the legislation to amend Acts to give greater
participation to Aboriginal people have also been initiated. Whether or
not these reviews result in greater Aboriginal control over material
culture is yet to be seen; the point is that the position of archaeology,
Aboriginal people and policy-makers in the governance of Aboriginal
identity is not static. Relationships between these three groups are
continually renegotiated.

However, the embedding of archaeological scientific discourse and
philosophy in heritage legislation constrains the field of debate and
negotiation. This not only has implications for Aboriginal people but
also for archaeologists. It means that claims for access to and control
over the interpretation of material culture are debated within the confines of archaeological scientific discourse. Thus, the development of
heritage legislation, ostensibly in response to archaeological efforts to
halt the destruction of sites by amateurs and developers, has also worked
to regulate the scientific culture and profile of the discipline. Legislation
to regulate research through a system of permits reinforces the adherence by the discipline to scientific values of objectivity and systematic
and rigorous methodology. In short, the legislation works to govern and
regulate archaeological conduct.

In addition, by policing archaeological conduct the legislation also
helps to set the parameters of disciplinary debate about the value and
nature of 'science'. As R. V. S. Wright (1986) pointed out (albeit with a
different motivation) archaeologists employed by government agencies
can control research agendas via the permit process. This control is not
necessarily aimed at pushing individual agendas, but rather at a policing
of archaeological conduct in line with values and expectations recognised within the legislation, and in the archaeological disciplinary community. Archaeological power/knowledge is maintained by ensuring
certain standards and discourses that recreate and underpin archaeological claims to stewardship and expertise are also maintained and
regulated.

In regulating archaeological knowledge and maintaining its adherence to scientific principles, policy-makers and those (including archaeologists) who administer the legislation are ensuring that archaeology
remains a useful technical tool in governing material culture, and
arbitrating and regulating Aboriginal interests. The mobilisation of
archaeology as a technology of government hinges on its ability to make
legislative authoritative, technically value-free and neutral statements
about the past and, by inference, Aboriginal cultural identity. The
power/knowledge relation established by archaeological science is thus
transformed to the power/law/knowledge equation offered by Hunt

(1993: 314). Heritage law reinforces archaeological claims to scientific authority and underscores the 'interpretive' and 'legislative' role it plays over material culture and Aboriginal links to that material culture.

Aboriginal people have, however, continued to increase their contestation of the governance of their identity, and increasingly used control of Aboriginality as a political resource to underpin the legitimacy of their claims (see Dodson 1994). Further, the 1992 decision by the High Court in *Mabo* v. *State of Queensland*, which recognised prior Aboriginal ownership of Australia and challenged the concept of *terra nullius*, gave greater political legitimacy to Aboriginal claims to land and heritage. Both the *Mabo* decision and the use of Aboriginality to provide political cohesion and legitimacy to the land rights movement have explicitly challenged the governance of Aboriginal cultural identity. Subsequently, heritage legislation and other technologies used in the governance of identity have not been able to entirely contain Aboriginal resistance and contestation of the uses of material culture.

Changes in government policy, which has increasingly recognised Aboriginal claims to control the management and, by extension, the meaning of Aboriginal material culture, have led to attempts by archaeologists to renegotiate the position of archaeological expertise in CRM policy and practices. This has included the handing back of skeletal material to Aboriginal communities, such as the remains of the Mungo woman in 1992, and the development of codes of ethics that requires informed consultation with Aboriginal people during research (AAA 1994). However, the role of archaeology as a technology of government constrains the degree to which it has been able to make a disciplinary shift in its theoretical position and the discourse it utilises in debate with Aboriginal people and policy makers.

In situations where Aboriginal people directly contest archaeological stewardship and access to material culture, the archaeological response has been to invoke a discourse which rehearses the discipline's claims to objective science and the 'rights' this confers to the discipline (see, for example, Mulvaney 1991; Stone 1992; Allen 1995; Maslen 1995; Murray 1995; Murray and Allen 1995). The discipline is also constrained (or 'governed') by its attempts to retain power/knowledge relations through the authority derived from notions of positivistic science (Smith 1994, 1996). Further, the adherence to such an epistemology tends to undermine or contradict the practices of 'informed consultation' and the voluntary repatriation of ancestral remains and artefact collections (Smith 1995). This then presents confused and conflicting messages to both Aboriginal people and policy-makers, and allows for renegotiations of power/knowledge strategies within CRM in which archaeology can sometimes be marginalised. Thus, as Aboriginal people challenge the privileged position of archaeology in the implementation of heritage legislation and policy, archaeology's own position as a technology of government constrains the resources of power the discipline can bring to bear in these negotiations.

Conclusion

Our major contention is this paper is that it is possible to move from the dominant (self)perception in the discipline of archaeology – that it is in a major part a mature scientific discipline which closely resembles the physical sciences – to an understanding of archaeology as a human science, which plays its part in regulating the 'conduct of conduct'. Michel Foucault's writings on governmentality, and recent work developing this concept, have offered valuable insights into the history of the discipline and archaeology's role in the development of both nineteenth-century liberalism and colonialism. When applied to the discipline's practice in the period of late liberalism, where its technical expertise and experts have become so influential, the governmentality thesis has also shown its usefulness, by illustrating how links can be established between technical forms of expertise, and the explicitly political process of 'government'. This does not mean, however, that expertise cannot be questioned by those subject to its authority, and that a particular form of knowledge might not become more or less useful as its practitioners' claims to governmental authority are renegotiated.

Central to the political nature of archaeological stewardship of the past is that the acceptance of its claims to scientific rationality has allowed archaeology to play an important role in governing the meanings given to material culture. This has consequences for indigenous peoples and others, who use material culture as heritage items to symbolise and give material dimensions to otherwise intangible concepts of 'identity'.

The discourse of archaeology was drawn on in establishing the various Acts which regulate 'cultural heritage' – not anthropology but archaeology was the dominant intellectual influence in framing legislation. Claims to scientific knowledge over material culture were given precedence over the claims of culture. In the establishment of government agencies to oversee heritage legislation it was archaeologists who were employed to interpret and enact the new laws. Also, it is archaeologists who play a part as consultants in the heritage aspects of environmental impact assessments – and archaeologists who vet the reports and recommendations they submit. Archaeologists, originally trained as 'scientists' (note that they are not encouraged to study anthropology in Australia, and seldom do), are also responsible, in both bureaucratic and consulting roles, to determine not only 'scientific' significance of artefacts, sites and places, but also cultural significance, in order to assess their relative merits in impact assessments.

Though academics loudly proclaim that their discipline has nothing to do with 'politics', both the discursive function it plays and the practice of its experts suggest that archaeology as a technology of government has very concrete political consequences for indigenous peoples' claims to material culture. This is because the regulation of the meanings assigned to Aboriginal heritage and the Aboriginal past, and by extension aspects of Aboriginal cultural identity, will influence the way in which Aboriginal claims to land and their heritage are perceived and judged by governments.

As Aboriginal people question the privileging of archaeology in the management of Aboriginal heritage, and as they contest received perceptions of the Aboriginal past, the position of archaeology as a technology of government has itself been challenged. This has forced archaeologists to enter into renegotiations of established power/ knowledge relations. However, archaeology has itself become regulated by its position as a technology of government. This has meant that the resources archaeologists may bring to bear in any negotiations review previous positivist claims to authority based on the 'objectivity' and 'rationality' of archaeological knowledge. This has had further consequences for the discipline in Australia where post-positivist theoretical innovations, and theoretical debates which seek to examine the current positivist theoretical underpinnings of archaeology, are rare or tend to be treated with suspicion for attacking the 'robusticity' or authority of archaeology (see, for instance, Pardoe 1994: 13; Hiscock 1996: 162–3). The abandonment of prior claims to authority jeopardises the position of archaeology in CRM and thus access to the database gained through its stewardship over Aboriginal material culture.

Notes

1 The 'new archaeology' developed in the United States during the early 1960s and explicitly aimed to remake archaeology as a 'science' modelled on the natural sciences. It had proponents in the United Kingdom and was adopted into the teaching and practices of Australian archaeology in the late 1960s. It is the dominant (if not the 'default') theoretical position in Western, including Australian, archaeology. The new archaeology also played a significant role in the development and standardisation of cultural resource management practices.

2 The 1960s and early 1970s were characterised by a number of major archaeological discoveries that became recognised as internationally significant.

Lake Mungo, in western New South Wales, contains a rich assemblage of Pleistocene sites that became important evidence for claims that occupation of Australia dated to at least 30 000 if not 40 000 years ago. 'Mungo woman', excavated in 1969, is the remains of a young morphologically modern human dated to about 24'000 years ago, and is the first known human cremation. Due to its antiquity and high scientific value it is regarded as a high-status find within the archaeological community (see Bowler et al. 1970). About seventy skeletons dated to between 9000 and 15 000 years before present were found at Kow Swamp in north-west Victoria and were important evidence in debates about the origins of Aboriginal people.

3   See National Parks and Wildlife Act 1974 (NSW); Archaeological and Aboriginal Relics Act 1972 (Victoria); Aboriginal Relics Act 1975 (Tasmania).

4   This is a term used in Tasmanian popular discourse and is used by some non-Aboriginal people to describe someone recognised as being biologically descended from 'pre-1876' Aborigines. Embedded in this term is an explicit non-recognition of contemporary Aboriginal cultural identity.

References

(AAA) Australian Archaeological Association, 1994. 'Code of Ethics', *Australian Archaeology* 39: 129.

Ah Kit, J., 1995. 'Aboriginal aspirations for heritage conservation', *Historic Environment* 11, 2/3: 31–6.

Allen, J., 1970. 'Early colonial archaeology' in F. D. McCarthy (ed.), *Aboriginal Antiquities in Australia*, Canberra: Australian Institute of Aboriginal Studies.

Allen, J., 1995. 'A short history of the Tasmanian affair', *Australian Archaeology* 41: 43–8.

Auty, K., 1995. 'Aboriginal cultural heritage: Tasmania and LaTrobe University', *Aboriginal Law Bulletin* 3 (76): 20.

Barunga, A., 1975. 'Sacred sites and their protection' in R. Edwards (ed.), *The Preservation of Australia's Aboriginal Heritage*, Canberra: Australian Institute of Aboriginal Studies.

Bauman, Z., 1987. *Legislators and Interpreters*, Cambridge: Polity Press.

Bell, J., 1994. *Reconstructing Prehistory*, Philadelphia: Temple.

Bennett, T., 1988. *Out of Which Past: Critical Reflection on Australian Museums and Heritage*, Brisbane: Griffith University.

Bennett, T., 1994. 'Museums, liberal government and the historical sciences', unpublished paper, History of the Human Sciences conference, Melbourne.

Binford, L. R., 1962. 'Archaeology as anthropology', *American Antiquity* 28: 217–25.

Binford, L. R., 1968. 'Archaeological perspectives' in S. R. Binford and L. R. Binford (eds), *New Perspectives in Archaeology*, Chicago: Aldine.

Binford, L. R., 1988. *In Pursuit of the Past*, London: Thames & Hudson.

Binford, L. R., 1990. 'The "new archaeology", then and now' in C. C. Lamberg-Karlovsky (ed.), *Archaeological Thought in America*, Cambridge: Cambridge University Press.

Bowler, J., Jones, R., Allen, H. and Thorne, A., 1970. 'Pleistocene human remains from Australia: a living site and human cremation from Lake Mungo, western New South Wales', *World Archaeology* 2: 39–60.
Brown, K., 1995. 'Tasmania – Aboriginal Relics Act 1975', unpublished paper presented at the Australian Heritage Commission workshop on legislation, 15 February 1995.
Buchli, V., 1995. 'Interpreting material culture' in I. Hodder, M. Shanks, A. Alexandri, V. Buchli, J. Carman, J. Last and G. Lucas (eds), *Interpreting Archaeology*, London: Routledge.
Byrne, D., 1993. 'The past of others: archaeological heritage management in Thailand and Australia', PhD thesis, Australian National University, Canberra.
Carman, J., 1993. 'The p is silent . . . as in archaeology', *Archaeological Review From Cambridge* 12, 1: 37–53.
Carman, J., 1995. 'Interpretation, writing and presenting the past' in I. Hodder, M. Shanks, A. Alexandri, V. Buchli, J. Carman, J. Last and G. Lucas (eds), *Interpreting Archaeology*, London: Routledge.
Clarke, D. L., 1968. *Analytical Archaeology*, London: Methuen.
Clarke, D. L., 1973. 'Archaeology: the loss of innocence', *Antiquity* 47: 6–18.
Cook, W. and Morris, G., 1984. 'Aboriginal involvement in archaeology' in G. K. Ward (ed.), *Archaeology at ANZAAS Canberra*, Canberra: Canberra Archaeological Society.
Coutts, P. J. F., 1977. 'Australia: a new nation with an ancient legacy' text of an ABC broadcast, 29 May 1977.
Coutts, P. J. F., 1982. 'Management of the Aboriginal cultural heritage in Victoria' in P. Coutts (ed.), *Cultural Resource Management in Victoria 1979–1981*, Melbourne: Victoria Archaeological Survey.
Coutts, P., 1984. 'A public archaeologist's view of future direction in cultural resource management' in G. Ward (ed.), *Archaeology at ANZAAS Canberra*, Canberra: Canberra Archaeological Society.
Daniel, G., 1978. *150 Years of Archaeology*, London: Duckworth.
Dark, K. R., 1995. *Theoretical Archaeology*, London: Duckworth.
Davison, G., 1991. 'The meanings of "heritage"' in G. Davison and C. McConville (eds), *A Heritage Handbook*, Sydney: Allen & Unwin.
Dodson, M., 1994. 'The Wentworth Lecture – the end in the Beginning: re(de)fining Aboriginality', *Australian Aboriginal Studies* 1: 2–13.
Duncan, T., 1984. ' "Bone Rights" now an issue in Tasmania, too', *Bulletin* 4: 28.
Ellis, B., 1994. *Rethinking The Paradigm: Cultural Heritage Management in Queensland*, St Lucia: Ngulaig 10.
Fairclough, N., 1993. *Discourse and Social Change*, Cambridge: Polity Press.
Fesl, E., 1983. 'Communication and communication breakdown' in M. Smith (ed.), *Archaeology at ANZAAS 1983*, Perth: Western Australian Museum.
Fletcher, R. J., 1981. 'People and space: a case study on material behaviour' in I. Hodder, G. Isaac and N. Hammond (eds), *Pattern of the Past: Studies in Honour of David Clarke*, Cambridge: Cambridge University Press.
Flood, J., 1993. 'Cultural resource management: the last three decades' in M. Spriggs, D. E. Yen, W. Ambrose, R. Jones, A. Thorne and A. Andrews (eds), *A Community of Culture*, Canberra: Department of Prehistory, Research School of Pacific Studies, Australian National University.
Ford, R. I., 1973. 'Archaeology serving humanity' in C. L. Redman (ed.), *Research and Theory in Current Archaeology*, New York: John Wiley & Sons.

Fourmile, H., 1989. 'Aboriginal heritage legislation and self-determination', *Australian Canadian Studies* 7, 1/2: 45–61.

Fritz, J. M., 1973. 'Relevance, archaeology and subsistence theory' in C. L. Redman (ed.), *Research and Theory in Current Archaeology*, New York: John Wiley & Sons.

Gamble, C., 1993. 'Ancestors and agendas' in N. Yoffee and A. Sherratt (eds), *Archaeological Theory: Who Sets the Agenda?*, Cambridge: Cambridge University Press.

Geering, K. and Roberts, C., 1992. 'Current limitations on Aboriginal involvement in Aboriginal site management in centralwest and northwest New South Wales' in J. Birckhead, T. DeLacy and L. Smith (eds), *Aboriginal Involvement in Parks and Protected Areas*, Canberra: Aboriginal Studies Press.

Goodall, H., 1995. 'New South Wales' in A. McGrath (ed.), *Contested Ground*, Sydney: Allen & Unwin.

Hiscock, P., 1996. 'The New Age of alternative archaeology in Australia', *Archaeology in Oceania* 31, 3: 152–64.

Hodder, I., 1986. *Reading the Past*, Cambridge: Cambridge University Press.

Hooper-Greenhill, E., 1991. *Museums and Gallery Education*, Leicester: Leicester University Press.

Hooper-Greenhill, E., 1992. *Museums and the Shaping of Knowledge*, Leicester: Leicester University Press.

Hunt, A., 1993. *Explorations in Law and Society*, London: Routledge.

Jones, R., 1968. 'Editorial', *Mankind* 11, 6: 535–6.

Keefe, K., 1988. 'Aboriginality: resistance and persistence', *Australian Aboriginal Studies* 1: 67–81.

Kelly, R., 1975. 'From the "Keeparra" to the cultural bind', *Australian Archaeology* 2: 13–17.

Kelly, R., 1979. 'Why we bother: information gathered in Aboriginal site recording in NSW' in J. R. McKinlay and K. L. Jones (eds), *Archaeological Resource Management in Australia and Oceania*, Wellington: New Zealand Historic Houses Trust.

Khol, P. L. and Fawcett, C. (eds), 1995a. *Nationalism, Politics and the Practice of Archaeology*, Cambridge: Cambridge University Press.

Khol, P. L. and Fawcett, C., 1995b. 'Archaeology in the service of the state: theoretical considerations' in P. L. Khol and C. Fawcett (eds).

Langford, R., 1983. 'Our heritage – your playground', *Australian Archaeology* 16: 1–6.

Lubbock, J., 1869. *Prehistoric Times, as Illustrated by Ancient Remains, and the Manners and Customs of Modern Savages*, London: Williams & Norgate.

McCarthy, F. D., (ed.), 1970. *Aboriginal Antiquities in Australia*, Canberra: Australian Institute of Aboriginal Studies.

McGuire, R. H., 1992. 'Archaeology and the first Americans', *American Antiquity* 94, 4: 816–32.

Maslen, G., 1995. 'The death of archaeology', *Campus Review*, 31 August, pp. 7, 31.

Megaw, V. S., 1966. 'Australian archaeology – how far have we progressed?', *Mankind* 6, 7: 306–12.

Merriman, N., 1991. *Beyond the Glass Case*, Leicester: Leicester University Press.

Miller, J., 1986. *Koori: A Will to Win*, Sydney: Angus & Robertson.

Moser, S., 1995. 'Archaeology and its disciplinary culture: the professionalisation of Australian prehistoric archaeology', PhD thesis, University of Sydney.

Mulvaney, D. J., 1964. 'Australian archaeology 1929–1964: problems and policies', *Australian Journal of Science* 27, 2: 39–44.

Mulvaney, D. J., 1968. 'Field research in Australia' in D. J. Mulvaney (ed.), *Australian Archaeology: A Guide to Field and Laboratory Techniques*, Canberra: Australian Institute of Aboriginal Studies.

Mulvaney, D. J., 1970. 'Human factors in the deterioration and destruction of antiquities and their remedy' in F. D. McCarthy (ed.), *Aboriginal Antiquities in Australia*, Canberra: Australian Institute of Aboriginal Studies.

Mulvaney, D. J., 1971. 'Prehistory from Antipodean perspectives', *Prehistoric Society* 27: 228–52.

Mulvaney, D. J., 1979. 'Blood from stones and bones: Aboriginal Australians and Australian prehistory', *Search* 10, 6: 214–18.

Mulvaney, D. J., 1981a. 'Gum leaves on the golden bough: Australia's Paleolithic survivals discovered' in J. D. Evans, B. Cunliffe and C. Renfrew (eds), *Antiquity and Man: Essays in Honour of Glyn Daniel*, London: Thames & Hudson.

Mulvaney, D. J., 1981b. 'What future for our past? Archaeology and society in the eighties', *Australian Archaeology* 13: 16–27.

Mulvaney, D. J., 1989. 'Archaeological retrospective 9', *Antiquity* LX: 96–107.

Mulvaney, D. J., 1990a. 'The Australian Aborigines 1606–1929: opinion and fieldwork' in S. Janson and S. McIntyre (eds), *Through White Eyes*, Sydney: Allen & Unwin.

Mulvaney, D. J., 1990b. *Prehistory and Heritage*, Canberra: Department of Prehistory, Research School of Pacific Studies, Australian National University.

Mulvaney, D. J., 1991. 'Past regained, future lost: the Kow Swamp Pleistocene burials', *Antiquity* 65: 12–21.

Mulvaney, D. J., 1993. 'Australian anthropology: foundations and funding', *Aboriginal History* 17: 105–28.

Murray, T., 1989. 'The history, philosophy and sociology of archaeology: the case of the Ancient Monuments Protection Act (1882)' in V. Pinsky and A. Wylie (eds), *Critical Traditions in Contemporary Archaeology*, Cambridge: Cambridge University Press.

Murray, T., 1992a. 'An archaeological perspective on the history of Aboriginal Australia', *Working Papers in Australian Studies, No. 80*, London: Sir Robert Menzies Centre for Australian Studies, Institute of Commonwealth Studies, University of London.

Murray, T., 1992b. 'Aboriginal (pre)history and Australian archaeology: the discourse of Australian prehistoric archaeology' in B. Attwood and J. Arnold (eds), *Power, Knowledge and Aborigines*, Melbourne: La Trobe University Press.

Murray, T., 1995. 'Thoughts about the future of archaeology in Australia', *La Trobe University Bulletin*, August–September, pp. 12–13.

Murray, T., 1996. 'Creating a post-Mabo archaeology of Australia' in B. Attwood (ed.), *In the Age of Mabo: History, Aborigines and Australia*, Sydney: Allen & Unwin.

Murray, T. and Allen, J., 1995. 'The forced repatriation of cultural properties to Tasmania', *Antiquity* 69: 871–4.

Murray, T. and White, J. P., 1981. 'Cambridge in the bush? Archaeology in Australia and New Guinea', *World Archaeology* 13, 2: 255–63.

(NPWS) National Parks and Wildlife Service (New South Wales), 1989. *Report of New South Wales Ministerial Task Force on Aboriginal Heritage and Culture*, Sydney: National Parks and Wildlife Service.

Organ, M., 1994. 'A conspiracy of silence: the NSW National Parks and Wildlife Service and Aboriginal cultural heritage sites', *Aboriginal Law Bulletin* 67, 3: 4–7.

Pardoe, C., 1994. 'W(h)ither archaeology?', *Australian Archaeology* 38: 11–13.

Pearce, S., 1986. 'Objects, high and low', *Museums Journal* 86, 2: 79–82.

Pearce, S., 1990. *Archaeological Curatorship*, Leicester: Leicester University Press.

Pearson, M. and Sullivan, S., 1995. *Looking After Heritage Places*, Carlton: Melbourne University Press.

Purvis, T., 1996. 'Aboriginal peoples and the idea of the nation' in A. Clarke and L. Smith (eds), *Issues in Archaeological Management*, St Lucia: Tempus Publications, University of Queensland.

Rose, N., 1993. 'Government, authority and expertise in advanced liberalism', *Economy and Society* 22, 3: 283–99.

Rose, N. and Miller, P., 1992. 'Political power beyond the state: problematics of government', *British Journal of Sociology* 43: 173–205.

Ryan, L., 1981. *The Aboriginal Tasmanians*, St Lucia: University of Queensland Press.

Sherratt, A., 1993. 'The relativity of theory' in N. Yoffee and A. Sherratt (eds), *Archaeological Theory: Who Sets the Agenda?*, Cambridge: Cambridge: Cambridge University Press.

Silberman, N. A., 1995. 'Promised lands and chosen peoples: the politics and poetics of archaeological narrative' in P. L. Khol and C. Fawcett (eds), *Nationalism, Politics and the Practice of Archeology*, Cambridge University Press.

Smith, L., 1993. 'Towards a theoretical overview for heritage management', *Archaeological Review from Cambridge* 12: 55–75.

Smith, L., 1994. 'Heritage management as post-processual archaeology?', *Antiquity* 68: 300–9.

Smith, L., 1995. 'What is this thing called post-processual archaeology . . . and what is its relevance to Australian archaeology?', *Australian Archaeology* 40: 28–32.

Smith, L., 1996. 'Significance concepts in management archaeology' in L. Smith, and A. Clarke (eds), *Issues in Management Archaeology*, St Lucia: Tempus Publications, University of Queensland.

Stone, J., 1992. 'The ownership of culture: reconciling our common and separate heritages', *Archaeology in Oceania* 31, 3: 161–7.

Sullivan, S., 1975. 'Legislation and its implementation: New South Wales' in E. Edwards (ed.), *The Preservation of Australia's Aboriginal Heritage*, Canberra: Australian Institute of Aboriginal Studies.

(TALC) Tasmanian Aboriginal Land Council, 1995. 'Will you take the next step?', unpublished conference paper, Australian Archaeological Association annual conference.

Tilley, C., 1990. 'Michel Foucault: towards an archaeology of archaeology' in C. Tilley (ed.), *Reading Material Culture*, Oxford: Blackwell.

Trigger, B., 1989. *A History of Archaeological Thought*, Cambridge: Cambridge University Press.

Trigger, B., 1995. 'Romanticism, nationalism, and archaeology' in P. L. Khol and C. Fawcett (eds), *Nationalism, Politics and the Practice of Archaeology*, Cambridge: Cambridge University Press.

Truscott, M. and Smith, L., 1993. 'Some descriptive statistics of permanent employment in Australian archaeology' in H. du Cros and L. Smith (eds), *Women in Archaeology: A Feminist Critique*, Canberra: Department of Prehistory, Research School of Pacific Studies, Australian National University.

Watson, P. J., LeBlanc, S. A. and Redman, C. L., 1971. *Explanations in Archaeology*, New York: Columbia University Press.

Watson, R., 1991. 'What the new archaeology has accomplished', *Current Anthropology* 32, 2: 275–81.

Watts, R., 1994. 'Government and modernity: an essay in thinking governmentality', *Arena* 2: 103–57.

Williams, A., 1975. 'Letter to the editor', *Identity* October: p. 29.

Wright, R. V. S., 1986. 'Presidential address – changing faces of Australian archaeology: the need to get permission' in G. K. Ward (ed.), *Archaeology at ANZAAS Canberra*, Canberra: Canberra Archaeological Society.

Yoffee, N., 1993. 'Too many chiefs? (or "Safe texts for the '90s")' in N. Yoffee and A. Sherratt (eds), *Archaeological Theory: Who Sets the Agenda?*, Cambridge: Cambridge University Press.

CHAPTER 11

'The Mutable Minds of Particular Men'
The Emergence of 'Economic Science' and Contemporary Economic Policy

David Burchell

> The Method I take . . . is not yet very usual; for instead of using only comparative and superlative Words, and intellectual Arguments, I have taken the course . . . to express my self in terms of *Number, Weight* or *Measure*; to use only Arguments of Sense, and to consider only such causes, as have visible foundations in Nature; saving those that depend on the mutable Minds, Opinions, Appetites and Passions of particular Men, to the Consideration of others . . . (William Petty, quoted in Hull 1963: 244)

> When we dig into its discursive structure we see that economic rationalist discourse is given its anti-social valences not by anything intrinsic to economic reasoning *per se*, but rather, as Stretton puts it, by this 'deadly combination of positivism and specialisation'. (Pusey 1991: 172)

In the acrimonious and largely unhelpful debate over economic policy which dominated the last years of the 1983–96 Labor government, one point on which most protagonists were able to agree was that the core of economic rationalism lay in the realm of economic theory. Sometimes this was asserted at a fairly highly level of generalisation, and economic rationalism was attributed to a long and supposedly unbroken tradition of 'free market' or *laissez-faire* economics dating back to the original culprit, Adam Smith (cf. Wheelwright 1993). More often, as in Michael Pusey's *Economic Rationalism in Canberra*, economic rationalism was depicted as quite literally the offspring of neoclassical economics (Pusey 1991: 225). Many of Pusey's opponents shared this diagnosis. A common gambit in 'rationalist' polemic was the assumption of an identity between marginalist theory, 'serious' economic thought in general, and the exercise of reason in public affairs (cf. Warby 1993).

However, as so often when opposing views coincide, it is well to treat these claims with some caution. In fact, many of the features which so appalled critics of economic policy-making in the late 1980s and early

1990s are in no way specific to marginalist economic theory. Rather, an overview of the emergence of 'sciences' of policy-making in the early modern West suggests that the prominence of certain characteristically 'economic' features in our governmental thinking reflects features which are common to a range of different bodies of economic thought over a protracted period of time (cf. Burchell 1994a, 1994b).

Obviously I am not suggesting that 'economic' theory is all of a piece, or that changes within it have no bearing on economic policy. The specialised economic training received by particular cohorts of public sector and private sector economists clearly has an important influence on both their private beliefs and their professional conduct. And, of course, it is important to understand both the tenacity and power of marginalist economics as a body of thought and the formalistic and abstract frame of reference with which it is commonly associated. However, I *am* suggesting that to sheet home general criticisms of economic policy to the distinctive theoretical training of contemporary economists is to beg some important questions: why is a particular kind of theoretical training felt to be valuable intellectual equipment in the knapsacks of professional economists in the first place, and why do they use it as they do with such gusto? Why, in particular, does a certain sort of theoretical economic *habitus* retain its attractions for public servants who might otherwise seem to be immersed in the hurly-burly of their mundane tasks? This is a question which Pusey's book did not even begin to address, aside from a vague and implausible implication that neoclassical economics acts as a kind of caste ideology to a particular stratum of public sector bureaucrats.

This chapter addresses two distinct but related questions: how is it that economic policy has acquired its present centrality to public policy, and what specific characteristics have accompanied the emergence of 'the economic' as an object of contemporary policy-making? I outline some of the more prominent features of economic governance as these emerged in the governmental thinking and practice of the early modern world. Obviously these remarks can be little more than indicative, but they will serve to indicate an important part of what has been left out of the debates on 'economic rationalism' and its impact on economic policy.

Economy

My contention here is that contemporary economic policy-making is more usefully seen in the context of the long-run emergence of distinctive ways of governing and imposing policy which are characteristic of the modern West. In this assertion, of course, I am loosely glossing

Michel Foucault, who argued in his well-known lecture on 'govern-mentality' that economic reasoning was central to the emergence of modern rationalities of governing: 'the essential issue in the establish-ment of the art of government' in early modern Europe, he insists, was the 'introduction of economy into political practice' (Foucault 1991: 92). As was his wont, Foucault is using 'economy' here in a deliberately ambiguous sense which invokes distinct bodies of practical thought. One is the tradition of *oeconomia* derived from Aristotle, in which 'economy' refers to the adroit management and organisation of the household – a concept which became enlarged in the seventeenth century in Germany and elsewhere to the level of the state, following the time-honoured metaphor in which the ruler was father of his people. The other is not unrelated, but has followed a rather different trajectory: it is the geneal-ogy of what we refer to as the domain of 'the economic', or more simply 'the economy'. In this sense 'economy' is the product of a broad body of practical thought which helped to establish a sphere of action for policy which we would describe as 'economic'. The most well-known example of this process is the case outlined by Foucault, in which the 'art of government' in seventeenth-century Germany coalesces around a loose threefold distinction between cameralism (*Cameral-Wissenschaft*), seen as state administration, *Polizei*, seen as provision of good social order, and *Oeconomie*, seen as the direction of good policy to the wider objective of the happiness and well-being of the population (Tribe 1984: 266).

Of course, this 'science' of economics borrows from the earlier Aristotelian term, and it is clearly connected to the broader theme of policy-as-state-housekeeping. *Oeconomie*, after all, was in a sense the application of the techniques of police to the household-nation. But it also moved decisively beyond this, in defining as 'economic' not merely as a style of 'householding', but also in the application of a range of more specialised governmental techniques to define populations for specific purposes. In this sense, as Keith Tribe notes, it bore less resemblance to *oeconomia*, the art of patriarchal rule, than to Aristotle's conception of the 'low science' of 'chrematistics' as the practical technique of managing the household finances (Tribe 1987: 24). In this, both in Germany and elsewhere, the 'science' of *oeconomie* began for the first time to stake out a domain of certain kinds of governmental activity as 'economic' in something approaching the modern sense (Pasquino 1991).

The Economic

The importance of this legacy of economic technique in the emergence of public policy runs against the common tendency of historians of economic thought to depict a story of 'progress', in which early political economists are presented as heroic figures dimly intuiting the key tenets of modern economic theory in primitive guises (Tribe 1987: 1–18, 203–10). In this picture, the German 'state sciences' of cameralism and police habitually receive short shrift because of their obvious lack of affiliation to the classical economics of the French physiocrats and Adam Smith, let alone the marginalist world of the 1870s and since. Joseph Schumpeter's classic, *History of Economic Analysis*, for example, distinguishes between three groups of seventeenth-century political economists: the scientists in England, the cameralists in Germany and the merchants everywhere. Of these three groups, not surprisingly, it is only the first who are seen as carrying the torch of genuine economic knowledge (Schumpeter 1954: 153–5, 159–61, 170–3).

However, viewed from the perspective of the development of a sphere of the 'economic' in governance rather than economic theory for its own sake, these demarcations are less obviously helpful. Part of the problem lies in the different status of 'science' in the projections of twentieth-century historians of economic thought and seventeenth-century German writers on the 'sciences' of government. It is certainly true that the advocates of cameralism and police did not conceive of their 'economics' as a 'science' in the modern Anglophone sense of an enterprise analogous to those of the natural or physical sciences. For the cameralists, the association of their subjects of study with the suffix *wissenschaft* suggested, rather, that they were being considered for the first time as organised and relatively coherent bodies of thought – and in particular, bodies of thought capable of being taught within the German university system (Tribe 1987: 35–54). Nevertheless, by defining for the first time both the conception of policy and the grounds of policy upon which 'economic' reasoning might work, the German cameralists were instrumental in establishing an 'economic' realm in which advocates of 'economic science' might flourish (cf. Small 1909).

Still, it is among the 'scientific' economic writers of the seventeenth century that the origins of modern economic thinking have generally been sought. Thus, in William Letwin's history of seventeenth-century English economic thought, *The Origin of Scientific Economics* (Letwin 1963), the claim of modern economics to rigorous disciplinary status lies in its originary association with the 'new science' of Bacon in seventeenth-century England. In contrast to Letwin, the history of economic thought largely assumes that the reasons why seventeenth-century English economic argument became 'scientific', in the modern Anglophone sense of the word, are largely self-evident. Economics, in other words, became 'scientific' because that is what economics necessarily is – a scientific method of arguing, with standards of evidence and habits of method analogous with, though not strictly derived from, the natural and physical sciences. It is precisely this 'scientism' which Michael Pusey associates with marginalist theory, and which he blames for its weaknesses as a 'social' science.

That this link between economics and science is historically far from natural is clear enough from the German experience, where the chief methodological precepts of cameralist economic writing were drawn from within the emerging *wissenschaft* of public administration itself. Indeed, even when German economic thought became 'Anglicised' through the reception of Smith's *Wealth of Nations* and the later writings of Anglo-Scottish 'classical' economics, it seems clear that these works too were grafted on to policy and methodological assumptions derived from the 'sciences' of public administration, without the Baconian and Newtonian superstructure with which they were associated in Britain (Tribe 1987: 133–48).

Science

Letwin's account of the science/economics confluence is more subtle, suggesting that the early association of economics and science can be most usefully seen as an attempted solution to a crucial problem in political and policy argument in early modern England and elsewhere: the problem of credibility and persuasion. He notes that the subordination of the established church in the English Reformation destroyed its credibility as moral arbiter on questions of economic policy. By the mid-seventeenth century, he argues, writing on economic policy had become fractured into a plethora of competing arguments from merchants, aspiring courtiers and self-styled policy advisers, all of whom could be plausibly depicted as motivated by self-interest of one kind or another.

Biblical authority lost, the only credible means of persuasion was an appeal to the 'detached reason' of the natural sciences, with its premium on – in the words of the foremost 'economist' of the period, William Petty – arguments of 'sense', based on 'number, weight or measure' (Letwin 1963: 87; Hull 1963: I, 244). In Letwin's words: 'in the search for a way of dispelling the problem of special pleading, a scientific method was hit on. The needs of rhetoric brought forth the method of economic theory' (Letwin 1963: 97). If one can gloss over the excessive confidence of the use of 'science' and 'economic theory' here, it is clear that Letwin is pointing to an important association between economics, 'science' and the needs of policy which is rarely addressed in the stock histories of economic thought.

In the case of Petty the Baconian inspiration is readily evident: in the preface to his *Political Anatomy of Ireland* he insists on Bacon's 'judicious parallel' between 'the body natural and the body politick, and between the arts of preserving both in health and strength'. His political anatomy is strictly analogous with the medical variety, he stresses; and he even goes so far as to note that he has picked in Ireland a harmless subject for his dissection (Hull 1963: I, 129–30). Petty himself was a doctor and later professor of anatomy, as well as being a founding member of the Royal Society, and he clearly saw his 'economic' writings as operating on a level of verifiability analogous to that of the work of the natural scientists. However, in Petty's case at least, this Baconianism was filtered through the ideas of Thomas Hobbes, for whom the natural sciences posed the same problem of reliable knowledge on the altogether more abstract plane of post-sceptical philosophy.

For René Descartes the model of all reliable knowledge was mathematics; for Hobbes in his *De Homine* there is, as it were, a sliding scale from the purest forms of mathematical reasoning to the most applied, from the 'pure' mathematics of geometry and arithmetic to the 'mixed' mathematics of astronomy (Gert 1972: 41–2). This notion of 'mixed' mathematical arts, and the choice of geometry and algebra as examples, was borrowed from Francis Bacon's *Advancement of Learning*, which declares them to be a chief means of scientific advance 'as nature grows further disclosed' (Bacon n.d.: 165–6). For Hobbes, characteristically, the significance of the distinction between pure and mixed arts was a political one: pure mathematical arts are those 'that are learned not from use and experience, but from teachers and rules', while mixed arts rely upon *a posteriori* 'demonstrations' whose outcomes are necessarily a matter of contestation (Gert 1972: 42–3; cf. Shapin and Schaffer 1985).

Petty was deeply influenced by Hobbes and Bacon alike, but not always attentive to the intricacies of Hobbes' arguments. Petty's 'political arithmetic' made two claims to reliability: it was 'uncontaminated by "passion or interest, faction or party"' (and in *The Political Anatomy of Ireland* Petty insisted implausibly that he 'professed no politicks' – Hull 1963: I, 129); and it 'required the careful and controlled analysis peculiar to mathematics' (Buck 1977: 67). Thus, the ceaseless expansion of the 'mixt mathematical arts' seemed to provide an answer to the problem of how to create a science of policy 'free from the distorting effects of controversy and conflict' (Petty 1648: 157).

Both Hobbes' 'empiricist' appeal to sense-data and his 'rationalist' appeal to mathematical authority seemed reconcilable in a mathematical science of the social world, a science which could be expressed purely 'in terms of *Number, Weight* or *Measure*', and which would use 'only Arguments of Sense' rather than 'those that depend on the mutable Minds, Opinions, Appetites and Passions of particular Men . . .'. His program for a science of the state in a Hobbesian-Baconian sense was no quest for scientific knowledge for its own sake. Rather, it was the indispensable prerequisite of all effective policy.

Statistics

Why did 'economics' acquire this lasting 'scientific' association with natural philosophy in England and not in Germany? The answer is less to do with some innate affinity of the two domains of endeavour than with contingent circumstances of economic argument. The problem of credibility outlined by Letwin was a specific and contingent one, a product of the lack of a developed administrative machinery in English public life, and the necessity of constructing such a machinery in the context of the peculiar English political settlement in which the power of the sovereign was, in effect, unusually limited. In this respect, the generation or so after Petty's economic heyday marks in British political life a veritable renaissance of public administration, in which 'scientific economics' played a crucial role both as a key 'authoritative' voice, and as a source of practical policy technique.

The history of this nexus between 'scientific' political economy and the requirements of public administration in Britain in the two or three generations following the Restoration has largely been neglected by historians and economists alike, not least because of the received version of economic history which is essentially a retrospective creation of a particularly crude version of contemporary economic theory. On this account, the legacy of public administration in Germany simply 'interfered' with German economic progress, while the Industrial Revolution in Britain required precisely the absence of such a developed system of public administration (for example, Braun 1975; Schumpeter 1954; Dorn 1931). Likewise, albeit from the other side of the political divide, the Marxist historian Christopher Hill insisted that 'The destruction of the royal bureaucracy in 1640–41 can be regarded as the most decisive event in the whole of British history'. It is clear that Hill means this to be seen as an historically 'progressive' event, involving the 'triumph . . . of the economically dominant new forces' over the stifling governmental structure of 'Stuart paternalism' (Hill 1967: 97–8). This 'theory' has appeared so evident to its various practitioners that it has rarely been accompanied by a detailed consideration of the historical record.

In fact, as J. H. Plumb noted twenty-five years ago and John Brewer and others have outlined in more detail recently, the seeds of political and economic stability in Britain in the eighteenth century were sown, in large part, by the steady if idiosyncratic expansion of governmental capacity (Plumb 1967: ch. 1; Brewer 1989: xvii–xx). More particularly, they coincided with the emergence of a range of more ambitious administrative capabilities in the last decades of the seventeenth century – the period of 'the rise of a fiscal state' founded upon the central collection of taxation revenue at the exchequer in London (O'Brien and Hunt 1992). The political settlement after 1688, often depicted as the political foundations of economic *laissez-faire*, in fact introduced a new epoch of public finance and public administration, spurred on by the exorbitant expenses of the new Protestant monarch's Continental wars. The effect was to place increasing strain on older patterns of public office-holding, and to accord great prestige to those departments – most particularly the Excise Office – which were capable of adapting to the new circumstances (Aylmer 1980: 93; Brewer 1989: 100–14). At the same time, Britain almost alone in Europe possessed a sophisticated social welfare system funded out of centrally-collected taxation receipts but administered locally by the voluntary responsibility of local elites (Slack 1988). The result was a mechanism of 'police of the poor' which attained many of the ends of *polizeiwissenschaft* without the panoply of administrative regulations associated with German *polizei* – and, indeed, without the use of the term 'police' itself (Dean 1991: 55).

This distinctive blend of centralism and localism helped to fashion an apparatus of government which was at once much smaller than its counterparts in France and Germany and no less efficient in its effects: indeed, J. H. Plumb contends that 'by 1714 Britain probably enjoyed the most efficient government machine in Europe' (Plumb 1967: 13; cf. Barker 1966: 28–34). In the emergence of that apparatus a salient role was played by pre-Smithian political economy in general and the 'political arithmetic' of Petty in particular (Buck 1980: 28–9). And crucially, it was precisely the 'scientific' precepts employed by Petty in his political arithmetic which provided the statistical mechanisms in the development of key aspects of economic policy: taxation policy, the governance of poor relief, and the supervision of insurance and a national system of annuities.

Petty's own efforts in 'political arithmetic' had been inspired by John Graunt's ingenious employment of the most valuable source of vital statistics in seventeenth-century England, the 'bills of mortality' which registered deaths from the plague. Graunt's investigations had a chiefly speculative-scientific impulse – yet in order to generate useful data about life-spans he was forced to construct the first 'life table', the staple basis for calculation of life insurance companies. Ian Hacking has described how statistical methods took a leap forward with the development of systems of annuities in the part-public insurance technologies of the period. Here Graunt's 'life table' in his *Observations on the Bills of Mortality*, along with the exertions of the Dutch statesman John De Witt, was instrumental (Clark 1949: 135–6). But it was Petty who first argued for a statistical office devoted to 'furnishing the nation with an equitable system of annuities' (Hacking 1975: 110), and his efforts bore fruit in the developing governmental administration of annuities from the 1680s.

It was Petty, too, who first realised the significance of Graunt's 'discovery' as a principle of extrapolation for his own 'science' of political arithmetic (cf. Mykkänen 1994). Petty seized on the vast potential range of uses for official statistics as upon a new continent: he published an avalanche of booklets (designed with the frank but unfulfilled purpose of securing public employment) in which he proposed the statistical means of deducing the populations of major cities and regions, the extent of land, trade and commerce, and so on. And it was Petty who most forcefully and repeatedly argued for the establishment of a central statistical office to provide the hard mathematical data from which to construct plausible policy prescriptions. 'I have had only a common knife and a clout, instead of the many more helps which such a work requires', he complained (Hull 1963: 129).

His labours bore fruit posthumously: in 1696, at a time of financial crisis, parliament formed 'the first special statistical department successfully created by any Western European state', the office of Inspector-General of Imports and Exports (Clark 1949: 138; cf. 'Epinasse 1974: 351). There seems little doubt that 'the foundation of the new office was partly due to the popularity of political arithmetic' (Clark 1949: 139; Clark 1938: xiii is in error on this point): certainly there were no European models upon which to draw (Clark 1938: 4–5).

Arts of Calculation

It would be misleading, of course, to present these intellectual debates and practical governmental innovations in abstraction from their socio-cultural context. As recent historians have shown, the period exhibits a marked increase both in the range of applications for arithmetical calculation, and in the spread of the practical capacities to utilise these applications. The sixteenth and seventeenth centuries had seen the transference from Roman to Arabic numerals, and with it the explosion of a range of practical functions for written arithmetical methods as opposed to the simple outputs of abacuses and counting-boards. Double-entry bookkeeping – the practical prerequisite and intellectual rationale for political arithmetic (Cohen 1982: 16) – and commercial arithmetic flourished, and with it the kinds of commercial records and knowledge-bases by means of which balance of trade statistics were to be compiled. By the middle of the seventeenth century 'for tradesmen and private individuals alike, good book-keeping was a duty, both moral and prudential' (Thomas 1987: 107). This was clearly a decisive cultural shift.

However, this advance of quantification charted a decidedly uneven social course. Anything more than simple addition and subtraction was believed an ungentlemanly attainment in schools: when Samuel Pepys was training himself in the rudiments of the fledgling bureaucratic arts, he was forced to seek arithmetical instruction from a ship's mate (Thomas 1987: 111–12). In a scientific culture sharply divided by the distinction between virtuosi and 'mere empiricks', practical laboratory skills, including those of measuring and counting, were often only imperfectly acquired (Shapin 1994).

Of course, in one sense this only strengthened the mystique of calculation as a means of recourse to impartial authority for the likes of Hobbes and Petty. Since it stood apart from the curricula of the 'schools', and was chiefly acquired in the hurly-burly of shop-front commercial life, it could be portrayed as free from the interested attentions of scholar-theologians and large-scale merchant-princes alike. It was this perception, no doubt, that encouraged Petty to place arithmetic and geometry at the core of the curriculum of his proposed 'literary work-houses', or *ergastula literaria*, where all children were to learn the rudiments of at least one trade suited to their abilities, and where each 'may be taught as well to do something towards their living, as to read and write' (Petty 1648: 144). Petty's own mathematical skills were acquired in the technical employments of his youth and young adulthood: he learned arithmetic, in the form of navigation, at sea, and later expanded his understanding of geometry in his post as surveyor-general of the conquered lands in Ireland. It seems entirely plausible that his anti-intuitive association of mathematics with experimental science was derived from the practical understanding that both sets of knowledges were acquired while working with one's hands.

Administration

Petty's great administrative grandchild, the office of Inspector-General of Imports and Exports, was set up in 1696 at the request of William III for parliament to consider 'such laws as may be proper for the advancement of trade', particularly in the aftermath of an expensive and unsuccessful war against the French in 1695. As such, it might seem a product of the great body of 'balance of trade theory' which dominated the middle decades of the century, conventionally described under the rubric of 'mercantilism' (see Appleby 1978: 24–52). In fact, however, balance-of-trade theory had been in headlong retreat for several decades, and neither Petty nor Charles Davenant – the other major economic figure of his generation and the second of the inspectors-general – were balance-of-traders.

In reality the major impetus for the office was pragmatic – the need to bolster English industry by *ad hoc* protectionism at a time of international turmoil – and Davenant (at least, in principle, a Tory free-trader) in particular saw his role as inspector-general in at once a more 'scientific' and a more practical light. Davenant, like Petty, was an eager pursuer of both public office and the goals of public administration: he had been an excise commissioner in the 1680s, and was partly responsible for

introduction of the 'Method', the first exercise in specialist on-the-job
training for economic public servants, into excise assessment (Brewer
1989: 94, 225). His view of the science of statecraft would have delighted
Petty: the statesman required chiefly, he noted, 'a computing head'. 'The
abilities of any minister have always consisted chiefly in this computing
faculty . . . nor can the affairs of war and peace be well managed without
reasoning with figures upon things' (Brewer 1989: 224).

Petty's and Davenant's precepts and methods formed the basis on
which the pioneering civil servants of the period, William Blathwayt,
Samuel Pepys and others, built in order to develop the new system of
efficient public administration *ex nihilo*, as it were, after the disasters of the
Civil War period. Indeed, it is striking that almost every major figure in
English economic thought in the last two decades of the century – Petty in
his Irish land registry, Davenant as Inspector-General for Imports and
Exports, John Locke at the Board of Trade and Gregory King in what
would nowadays be called his 'consultancies' at the Treasury – played at
the least a bit-part in developing this new brand of statistically-based and
methodically-organised public administration (cf. Hutchinson 1988:
42–56; Clark 1949: 139–40). Many of the major public servants, like
Hobbes and Petty before them, secretly nourished a longing for the more
extended system of royal authority which marked public administration in
France and Germany; in the event, they had to operate within the confines
of the more complex British system of sovereignty. Their hallmark was 'a
rational approach to their needs as administrators' (Plumb 1967: 12).

Many of these leading public servants became members of the Royal
Society, convinced of the parallels between the methods of natural
philosophy and the types of knowledge required for reliable public
decision-making. Not surprisingly, the two leading individuals, Blathwayt
and Pepys, were both personal friends of Petty and professional admirers
of his methods. Contrary to those heroic histories which insist that the
course of British public administration is the outcome of a special and
unique constitutional heritage, Petty and Davenant 'were seeking the
foundations of good government not in the arrangements and limitations of political power but in the practical arts of administrative efficiency, rooted in practical knowledge' (Plumb 1967: 13). Indeed, they may
even have had an influence on the more celebrated public administration of the Germanic states.

Interlude

It may be helpful to pull together the scattered threads of this brief
historical argument at this point. In Germany, modern economic argument emerged out of the needs of developing 'sciences' (*Wissenschaften*)
of administration. Until at least the early nineteenth century it remained

largely subordinate to the 'higher' sciences of cameralism and police. And the latter posed a never-ending series of tasks for policy, all of which were potentially, if not actually, realisable.

At the same time, in England, economic argument emerged at a moment of crisis in public administration, where public life was dominated by the problem of establishing a credible and authoritative policy viewpoint among the welter of 'interest groups' confronting a relatively weak national authority. Here the methods of natural philosophy provided a claim to intellectual authority, while the practical technologies of political arithmetic, themselves derived from the precepts of the 'new science', provided the statistical know-how for new technologies of public administration.

It is not strictly necessary here to assign a greater or lesser role to either of these experiences, although the role of 'science' in the English case certainly marks it as having a particularly strong influence on the later self-image of economic policy-makers as well as professional economists. Rather, what is of interest here is the significance of the economic realm as one of calculative technologies and rationalities in the emergence of the modern domain of 'government' in the Foucauldian sense. The sphere of 'the economic' is important to governance of this type precisely because of its affiliations to the domain of 'the calculable', its capacity to inform specialised and purely practical arenas of policy, as well as its claim to a supposedly more reliable style of argument through its recourse to expression 'in terms of *Number, Weight* or *Measure*'. In other words, the attributes of contemporary economic policy which most irritate Pusey and others – and in particular the 'deadly combination of positivism and specialisation' of which Hugh Stretton complains – are more appropriately seen as reflecting the general character of economic governance as this has emerged in the modern West, rather than the more recent and specific economic theories. In turn, the extent to which these characteristics of economic governance seem novel or are attached to specific ideological formations at various times may be a consequence more of the kinds of tasks to which they are applied in particular contexts than of the technologies themselves.

Conclusion

By means of this potted historical account, I want to suggest that the forms of modern governance are, in a sense, 'rare'. By this I mean that only a few distinct types have emerged historically, that they have been common to governments of a wide range of different political casts, and that they have commonly persisted over long periods of time. Hence, there is often a sense in which modern governance is still strongly marked by its formative moments in the early modern world.

If we want to understand the continued centrality of economic reasoning as an 'art of the calculable' in modern policy-making, we have only to look at the travails of social policy-makers presiding over domains where the outcomes of policy are difficult to specify, where the relations between cause and effect are routinely unclear, where the 'happiness and well-being' of the citizens under their pastorate is difficult to measure, let alone attribute to their actions. An obvious example is health policy – at once a valuable and highly complex domain of modern welfare state practice, and one stubbornly resistant to many kinds of 'economical' thinking. I would hazard a guess that the occasions are very few in which health ministers in countries of the modern West have won decisive policy victories over economic ministers, and I would hypothesise that these stubbornly 'non-economic' characteristics of health policy may be important in this regard.

Finally, Letwin's problem of authority was clearly specific to the circumstances of seventeenth-century England in important respects. Still, it may or may not be coincidental that this same problem of authoritativeness in policy questions is often seen as characteristic of modern Western representative democracies, particularly by those theorists of governmental 'overload' who depict contemporary policy-making as weighed down by the demands of an open-ended list of competing 'interest groups'. In these circumstances, real or perceived, economic policy-makers have similar advantages to their counterparts three centuries ago. When policy-making can be only too easily depicted as a 'political' accommodation to interest groups rather than to the 'national interest' there is, at the very least, a decided rhetorical advantage to policy arguments couched in terms of *Number, Weight* and *Measure*', rather than 'on the mutable Minds, Opinions, Appetites and Passions of particular Men'.

In short, the salience of economic governance can not simply be argued away as a product of a narrow ideology. The forces of 'positivism' and 'specialisation' have an altogether more durable basis. This banal fact can be obscured in conditions of economic and social expansion, or of a seemingly benign social compromise over the ends and purposes of government. It is harder to ignore when governments see themselves as required increasingly 'to do more with less', as was the case in Australia in the 1980s and early 1990s. It is still harder to do so when governments are determined to set their policy compass explicitly against those 'special interests' of which they vehemently disapprove, and to call on economic authority for their support, as is the case currently in Australia.

In these circumstances the appeal of 'economic reason' as a purportedly impartial arbiter may be compelling. Indeed, more than this, it may be capable of 'speaking to' powerful assumptions in the field of popular commonsense, as did Margaret Thatcher's invocation of the household/national budget parallel in Britain in the 1980s, and as does the conservative polemic against social transfers to Aboriginal and migrant groups in Australia in the 1990s. There is a common refrain in contemporary neo-liberal argument which opposes the imperatives of 'sound' economic policy to the vagaries of electoral politics – much as Hobbes counterposed the political incoherence of the multitude to the coherence of the sovereign power (Tuck 1991: 114). Yet this patrician tone may be deceptive. 'Economic reason' of this sort has its own potential popular constituencies – and its capacity to speak politically, now as in the era of *polizei*, should not be underestimated by advocates of the vocabulary of 'nation building'.

Yet – to return to my initial point – the rubric of economic rationalism is ill-designed to offer a helpful analysis of these kinds of 'conjunctural' political phenomena. On the one hand, as we have seen, it grossly over-estimates the novelty of appeals to economic reason both as rhetorical strategy and as governmental repertoire. On the other it grossly under-estimates the room for substantive political difference within the field of 'economic government', subsuming quite distinct practical policy goals within an overarching framework of homogeneous 'free-market' ideology. The effect is at once to underplay the durability of certain kinds of economic reasoning (hence the invocation to 'overturn' economic rationalism) and to overplay the uniformity of their effects (hence the 'tweedledum-tweedledee' political analysis). There is little space in this kind of analytical field for the nuanced changes of strategy and tactics by which practical changes in economic policy-making are effected. It is a fair bet that when the last of the 'economic rationalists' in Treasury reaches for their pension packet, their heirs will still probably be irritating the social scientists.

References

Appleby, Joyce Oldham, 1978. *Economic Thought and Ideology in Seventeenth-Century England*, Princeton: Princeton University Press

Aspromourgos, Tony, 1985. 'Sir William Petty and the origins of classical political economy in England', PhD thesis, University of Sydney.

Aspromourgos, Tony, 1986. 'Political economy and the social division of labour: the economics of Sir William Petty', *Scottish Journal of Political Economy* 33, 1: 28–45.

Aylmer, G. E., 1980. 'From office-holding to civil service: the genesis of modern bureaucracy', *Transactions of the Royal Historical Society* 30: 91–108.

Bacon, Francis, n.d. *Essays Civil and Moral*, London: Ward, Lock & Co.

Barker, Ernest, 1966. *The Development of Public Services in Western Europe, 1660–1930*, Hamden, Connecticut: Archon Books.

Braun, Rudolph, 1975. 'Taxation, sociopolitical structure and state-building: Great Britain and Brandenburg-Prussia' in Charles Tilly (ed.), *The Formation of Nation States in Western Europe*, Princeton: Princeton University Press, pp. 243–327.

Brewer, John, 1989. *The Sinews of Power: War, Money and the English State, 1688–1783*, London: Unwin Hyman.

Buck, Peter, 1977. 'Seventeenth-century political arithmetic: civil strife and vital statistics', *Isis* 68, 241: 67–84.

Buck, Peter, 1980. 'People who counted: political arithmetic in the eighteenth century', *Isis* 73, 266: 28–45.

Burchell, David, 1994a. 'The curious career of economic rationalism: government and economy in the current policy debate', *Australian and New Zealand Journal of Sociology* 30, 3: 322–33.

Burchell, David, 1994b. *Economic Government and Social Science: The Economic Rationalism Debate*, Cultural Policy Paper no. 1, Brisbane: Institute for Cultural Policy Studies, Griffith University.

Clark, G. N., 1938. *Guide to English Commercial Statistics, 1696–1782*, London: Royal Historical Society.

Clark, G. N., 1949. *Science and Social Welfare in the Age of Newton*, Oxford: Clarendon Press, 2nd edn.

Cohen, Patricia Cline, 1982. *A Calculating People: The Spread of Numeracy in Early America*, Chicago: University of Chicago Press.

Dean, Mitchell, 1991. *The Constitution of Poverty: Towards a Genealogy of Liberal Governance*, London: Routledge.

Dorn, Walter L., 1931. 'The Prussian bureaucracy in the eighteenth century', *Political Science Quarterly*, vol. 36, 46–7.

'Epinasse, Margaret, 1974. 'The decline and fall of Restoration science' in Charles Webster (ed.), *The Intellectual Revolution of the Seventeenth Century*, London: Routledge.

Foucault, Michel, 1991. 'Governmentality' in G. Burchell, C. Gordon and P. Miller (eds), *The Foucault Effect: Studies in Governmentality*, London: Harvester/Wheatsheaf, pp. 87–104.

Gert, Bernard (ed.), 1972. *Thomas Hobbes: Man and Citizen (De Homine and De Cive)*, London: Harvester/Wheatsheaf.

Hacking, Ian, 1975. *The Emergence of Probability*, Cambridge: Cambridge University Press.

Hill, Christopher, 1967. *Reformation to Industrial Revolution: The Pelican Economic History of Britain*, vol. 2, Harmondsworth: Penguin.

Hull, Charles Henry (ed.), 1963 (1899). *The Economic Writings of Sir William Petty*, 2 vols, New York: Augustus M. Kelly.

Hutchinson, Terence, 1988. *Before Adam Smith: The Emergence of Political Economy, 1662–1776*, Oxford: Blackwell.

Landsdowne, Marquis of, 1967 (1927). *The Petty Papers: Some Unpublished Writings of Sir William Petty*, New York: Augustus M. Kelly.

Letwin, William, 1963. *The Origins of Scientific Economics: English Economic Thought, 1660–1776*, London: Methuen.

Mykkänen, Juri, 1994. '"To methodize and regulate them": William Petty's governmental science of statistics', *History of the Human Sciences* 7, 3: 65–86.

O'Brien, Patrick K. and Hunt, Philip A., 1992. 'The rise of a fiscal state in England, 1485–1815', *Historical Research: The Bulletin of the Institute of Historical Research* 65: 129–76.

Pasquino, Pasquale, 1991. 'Theatrum politicum: the genealogy of capital – police and the state of prosperity' in G. Burchell, C. Gordon and P. Miller (eds), *The Foucault Effect: Studies in Governmentality*, London: Harvester/ Wheatsheaf, pp. 105–18.

Petty, William, 1648. *The Advice of WP to Mr Samuel Hartlib, for the Advancement of Some Particular Parts of Learning*, reprinted in *The Harleian Miscellany*, 1810, vol. 6, London: Robert Dutton.

Plumb, J. H., 1967. *The Growth of Political Stability in England, 1675–1725*, London: Macmillan.

Pusey, Michael, 1991. *Economic Rationalism in Canberra: A Nation-Building State Changes its Mind*, Cambridge: Cambridge University Press.

Schumpeter, Joseph A., 1954. *History of Economic Analysis*, London: Allen & Unwin.

Shapin, Steven, 1994. *A Social History of Truth: Civility and Science in Seventeenth-Century England*, Chicago: University of Chicago Press.

Shapin, Steven and Schaffer, Simon, 1985. *Leviathan and the Air-Pump: Hobbes, Boyle and the Experimental Life*, Princeton: Princeton University Press.

Skinner, Quentin, 1966. 'Thomas Hobbes and his disciples in France and England', *Comparative Studies in Society and History* 8: 153–68.

Slack, Paul, 1988. *Poverty and Policy in Tudor and Stuart England*, London: Longman.

Small, A. W., 1909. *The Cameralists: The Pioneers of German Social Polity*, Chicago: University of Chicago Press.

Thomas, Keith, 1987. 'Numeracy in early modern England', *Transactions of the Royal Historical Society* 37: 103–32.

Tribe, Keith, 1984. 'Cameralism and the science of government', *Journal of Modern History* 56: 263–84.

Tribe, Keith, 1987. *Governing Economy: The Reformation of German Economic Discourse, 1750–1840*, Cambridge: Cambridge University Press.

Tuck, Richard (ed.), 1991. *Thomas Hobbes: Leviathan*, Cambridge: Cambridge University Press.

Tuck, Richard, 1993. *Philosophy and Government, 1572–1651*, Cambridge: Cambridge University Press.

Warby, Michael, 1993. 'Scapegoating and moral panic: political reality and public policy vs. anti-rationalism' in C. James, C. Jones and A. Martin (eds), *A Defence of Economic Rationalism*, Sydney: Allen & Unwin.

Wheelwright, Ted, 1993. 'Economic controls for social ends' in S. Rees, R. Gordon and F. Stilwell (eds), *Beyond the Market: Alternatives to Economic Rationalism*, Sydney: Pluto Press.

CHAPTER 12

Neo-Liberalism and the National Economy

Barry Hindess

The emergence of new ways of governing economic life in Western
societies, the extension of market and contractual relationships into
areas previously governed in other ways and the paradoxical appearance
in the wealthiest of all modern societies of persistent governmental
efforts to restrain public expenditure have all generated a substantial
academic literature. In Australia, for example, Michael Pusey (1991) and
other commentators have identified such developments in Australian
public life as effects of 'economic rationalism', a way of thinking about
the place of economic considerations in the overall life of society which
many would regard as dangerously misguided. In fact, while the term
'economic rationalism' has a distinctly Australian flavour, phenomena of
the kind that Pusey brings together under this heading have also been
placed under different labels: Thatcherism, Reaganomics, neo-liberalism, advanced liberalism, contractualism, managerialism and so on.[1] The
number and variety of such labels suggests that there is no general
agreement about the overall significance of these changes and, more
importantly perhaps, that they might profitably be regarded as the
outcome of several distinct lines of development.[2] Accordingly, the aim
of this chapter is not to provide yet another general characterisation of
the phenomena in question, but rather to suggest that they can usefully
be examined in the context of changing governmental perceptions of
the problem of national economic management. Briefly, I argue that a
move away from what might be called a 'Ricardian' view of relations
between distinct national economies has transformed the character of
Western governments' concerns with the management of their own
national economies, with consequential changes for governmental
perceptions of relations between economic activity and other aspects of
the life of the community.

Many commentators have argued that the problem of national economic management has been transformed by the impact of globalisation. What concerns me here, in contrast, is how the governmental
impact of changes in international economic activity will be mediated by
the prevailing rationality of government. I am therefore concerned with
the manner in which governments perceive their own national economies, both in relation to their international economic frame and as
objects of possible government regulation. Thus, whatever effects might
be ascribed to changes in the patterns of international economic activity,
I argue that the prosperous Western societies of the late twentieth
century are also experiencing a radical change in their broadly liberal
rationality of government. The liberal conception of the national economy as a distinctive field, both of economic activity and of possible
government intervention, involves a corresponding view of relations
between economic activity and other components in the life of the
national community. As a result, changing perceptions of the governmental problem of national economic management should be expected
to affect the character of government concerns in other policy areas.

Discussion of national economic management, at least in the more
prosperous Western societies, takes place against the background of
a ubiquitous modern view of 'economy', 'state' and 'society' as distinct
but largely coextensive systems of social organisation. Somewhat
schematically we can say that 'society' has been seen as providing the
cultural and normative framework in which economic and political
activities take place, while the 'state' has been seen as a relatively permanent set of institutions concerned with external defence on the one
hand and, on the other, with governing the population through the
making and enforcement of laws. Finally, 'economy' appears as a complementary system of production and exchange endowed with a natural
tendency to grow.

Liberals and most professional economists have tended to follow
Adam Smith in arguing that conditions provided by free markets are
likely to prove most propitious for the development of the economy, and
indeed for society as a whole. In contrast, conservatives, closely followed
by socialists and professional sociologists, have tended to take a more
sceptical view of relations between economy and society, regarding the
economy in general and markets in particular as sources of potentially
destructive social forces. Nevertheless, in spite of their belief that the
economy must be kept under careful control, many in the conservative
and socialist camps have shared the liberal belief that, if properly
managed by government, the economy can be expected to provide
resources for both state and society. With minor variations, then, the
image of the interdependence of 'economy', 'state' and 'society' and of

the national economy as a resource remained a commonplace of governmental thinking until the latter part of the twentieth century.

My central argument is that this image of the national economy is now being displaced by another, and that this has fundamental consequences for how we understand the relations between the economy and other aspects of the life of the national community. I locate this displacement as a component of the emergence of a novel governmental problem of economic security.

In the first section, I thus begin by discussing the implications of the relations between distinct national economies for governmental perceptions of the problem of economic security. I suggest that we are witnessing the displacement and transformation of a view of the national economy as a self-regulating system linked to a broadly Ricardian account of international exchange based on the concept of comparative advantage.

This does not mean, as the American Secretary for Labor once foolishly suggested,[3] that prudential governments will increasingly view their own and others' national economies as things of the past or that national governments are helpless in the face of supra-national economic developments. What it does involve, however, is a view of national economies as no longer being relatively self-contained unities. Indeed, as I argue in the second section, among the conditions of the displacement of this notion of the national economy are the developments in the technology of national economic accounting, which mean that governments are now much better informed about the performance of their own and others' national economies. As a result of this and other conditions, the question of the security of the national economic *system* has been transformed into a very different kind of problem, one dominated by the assumption 'that the only way to avoid becoming a loser – whether as a nation, firm or individual – is to be as competitive as possible' (Hirst and Thompson 1996: 6). In the final section, I examine the implications of this change for governmental perceptions of national economic management and of relations between economic activity and other aspects of the life of the community. Much of what passes for economic rationalism, in both its neo-liberal and social democratic guises, can be seen as responding to the emergence of this new governmental problem of economic security.

Perceptions of Economic Security

In the governmentality literature, security, and security of economic activity in particular, is commonly presented as one of the primary concerns of the liberal rationality of government. In fact, security is an important issue for any state, and the view that a powerful economy is a condition of the more general security of the state is one which liberalism shares with its cameralist and mercantilist predecessors and, indeed, with most of its more recent competitors. What is said to be distinctive about liberalism in this respect is not so much the importance it attaches to economic security but rather the connection it perceives between economic security and the liberty of individual members of the population. Not only is liberty seen, in Jeremy Bentham's words, as 'a branch of security' (Bentham 1843: 302), but it is also regarded as a necessary condition of security.

The connection here between the security of economic activity and the liberty of individuals is clearly presented in the work of Adam Smith, which Foucault regards as having a central place in the development of the liberal rationality of government. *The Wealth of Nations* contains a variety of policy recommendations, but the greater part of these are located within an account of the development of economic activity as a natural process constituted, in large part, by the free choices of a multitude of economic actors. In effect, Smith argues that in those areas of the world which have reached the stage of commercial society (that is, the more prosperous regions of Europe and North America), the field of economic activity can be seen as dependent on the free decisions of individuals. Since the ability of governments to pursue their objectives depends on the resources at their command, this view suggests that a prudential government will aim to secure conditions in which economic actors are free to pursue their own objectives. Thus, Smith tries to show that mercantilist regulation of economic activity and detailed intervention in the manner of police will often be counterproductive, and therefore detrimental to the goal of national economic improvement, precisely because of the manner in which it affects the conditions of individual choice.

The governmental character of Smith's argument is forcefully stated in the Introduction to Book IV:

> Political oeconomy, considered as a branch of the science of a statesman or legislator, proposes two distinct objects; first, to provide a plentiful revenue or subsistence for the people, or more properly to enable them to provide such a revenue or subsistence for themselves; and secondly, to supply the state or commonwealth with a revenue sufficient for the public services. It proposes to enrich both the people and the sovereign. (Smith 1976: 428)

The objectives which Smith ascribes to 'political oeconomy' can also be found in the science of police, but political oeconomy's methods are substantially different – largely as a result of 'political oeconomy's' discovery that the economic life of the population has many of the characteristics of a natural process operating according to its own laws and patterns of development. Smith's focus is on the national character of the population in question and therefore of the relevant economic processes (Smith 1976: 372). Accordingly, much of his discussion is concerned with outlining the natural development of economic activity within nations and with accounting for differences between them, and especially between commercial societies – that is, nations at the same stage of historical development, with roughly comparable levels of skill, technology, etc. These differences are said to result from a variety of causes, the most important of which are powerful landowners who (in the manner of their feudal predecessors) often treat their property as the basis for social and political activities rather than as an economic resource to be developed, and misguided 'policy' (police) interference with the natural processes of economic activity. Thus, while Smith's argument leads to a presumption against government interference in economic activity, it also suggests that such interference may sometimes be required in order to overcome feudal remnants, the consequences of earlier, misguided political interference, and other obstacles to the free flow of economic activity. Smith is clearly aware of the existence of international commerce but he treats it as a secondary development in the natural order of things, according to which 'the greater part of the capital of every growing society is, first, directed to agriculture, afterwards to manufactures, and last of all to foreign commerce' (Smith 1976: 380). In fact, as Smith goes on to observe, the development of trade in modern Europe appears to have followed what he can only regard as an 'unnatural and retrograde order'.

What is particularly interesting here is not so much Smith's explanation of this apparent anomaly (which he ascribes, in effect, to the emergence of feudal land-holding following the collapse of the Roman Empire) but two other features of his argument. These are: first, a conception of economic activity as developing naturally according to a variety of self-regulating processes; and secondly, the presumption that, notwithstanding the historical record, the greater part of these natural processes normally take place within boundaries which more or less coincide with those of a national state and society. Smith does not develop an explicit concept of a discrete 'national economy', but he is concerned with economic processes which take place within the 'national' population and with the consequences for those processes of 'foreign' commerce. Thus, while Smith clearly regards commerce as no respecter of national boundaries, the governmental focus of his argument nevertheless leads him to treat the economy of the nation both as relatively self-contained and, if left to its own devices, as a largely self-regulating system endowed with a benign tendency to generate increasing prosperity.

In effect, then, Smith's account of the national economy as a largely self-regulating system of interaction sets in place an important element of the modern view noted above of 'economy', 'state' and 'society' as coextensive systems of social organisation. Before turning to the demise of the seductive image of the national economy both as a system and as a resource for the national state and society, it is first necessary to consider the manner in which this image incorporates the impact of international trade.

Where Smith provides an account of national economies as self-regulating systems, David Ricardo's theory of comparative advantage is usually credited with the foundation of the modern theory of international trade. Ricardo takes the example of two countries, Portugal and England, and two commodities, wine and cloth. We are asked to suppose that Portugal is able to produce both wine and cloth cheaper than England, but that the cost advantage in wine is greater than it is in cloth. Under these conditions it seems that both countries would benefit if England were to specialise in cloth and Portugal in wine. In fact, Ricardo observes that it would benefit the capitalists of England and the consumers of both countries if wine and cloth were both made in Portugal 'and therefore that the capital and labour of England employed in making cloth, should be removed to Portugal for that purpose' (Ricardo 1971 [1817]: 154–5) – an outcome whose impact on the economy of England would be less obviously beneficial.

In practice, Ricardo maintains that such an outcome is unlikely because, while both capital and labour move relatively freely within nations, they do not move freely across national borders. Owners of capital, in particular, are constrained by the difficulty of controlling the use of capital invested in foreign parts, the difficulty of adapting to new laws and forms of government and 'the natural disinclination which every man has to quit the country of his birth and connexions' (Ricardo 1971 [1817]: 155).[4] In effect, then, Ricardo continues to treat England and Portugal as having relatively self-contained national economies, even while they are engaged in a mutually beneficial system of international exchange.

The Ricardoan theory of international trade deals with trading relations between a number of distinct and relatively self-contained national economies. It suggests that unrestricted international trade will be to the long-term benefit of each of the national economies concerned – although it may also expose them to short-term disturbances as the impact of free trade renders particular local industries unprofitable and as international commerce is affected by famines, wars, the outbreak of peace and other such disruptions. Or again, he notes that trade with a colony could well be managed to the advantage of the home country (and the corresponding disadvantage of the colony) but he also insists that such a system would be less beneficial overall than perfectly free trade.

However, while it clearly implies a presumption in favour of free trade, Ricardo's argument, like that of Smith before him, also allows that other things may not be equal in all cases – a point which suggests that there might sometimes be grounds for overturning that presumption. In a passage which opens the gates to all kinds of special pleading, for example, Smith (1976: 463ff.) suggests that import restrictions might be in order in the case of industries necessary for national defence. A reason of a different kind is that, while Ricardo's discussion takes as given the conditions which result in Portugal and England having comparative advantages in the production of wine and cloth respectively, it is clear that at least some of the national conditions of production of these and other commodities will themselves be open to change. A general argument to this effect is suggested by Smith's view, noted above, that there is a natural order to the development of a society's capital, beginning in agriculture and moving on to manufactures and then to foreign trade. Alexander Hamilton (1791) adopted this view in his case for the protection of industry in the United States, where the extensive development of foreign trade had preceded that of domestic industry. This nascent 'infant industry' argument was later taken up by Friedrich List in his polemic against the 'cosmopolitan' character of Smith's system.[5] For this reason, while not disputing the benefits to be obtained from a generalised system of free trade, List nevertheless insists that:

> In order to allow freedom of trade to operate naturally, the less advanced nations must first be raised by artificial measures to that stage of cultivation to which the English nation has been artificially elevated . . . those nations . . . must adopt the system of protection as the most effectual means for this purpose. (List 1966 [1841]: 131–2)

Thus a broadly Ricardoan account of international trade can also be made to accommodate particular cases for short or medium-term protection or for other governmental actions (such as investment in infrastructure or education) in order to improve the nation's competitive advantage.

A further adaptation which is important for our purposes concerns the regulation of currency exchange. Ricardo's tale of the beneficial workings of comparative advantage assumes a fixed exchange rate between the relevant national currencies. If, on the contrary, exchange rates were to be subject to substantial, unpredictable movements then the capitalists of England and Portugal would receive erratic and confusing messages from their comparisons of the relative costs of

producing wine and cloth in the two countries. The beneficial wor
of comparative advantage, in other words, require a reasonably :
regime of international exchange – which is also, of course, to sa
they require the participating national governments to exercise an
appropriate form of self-control. Thus, the effect of adapting the image
of a national economy, state and society considered above to incorporate
a broadly Ricardoan model of international trade, is to suggest that well-
behaved national economies require a suitably well-behaved international regime of relations between them – and to suggest also that
some national economies will be more vulnerable in this respect than
others. To the liberal concern for security at the level of the national
economy should be added a corresponding concern to secure a stable
regime of international trade.

In fact, the history of international economic relations throughout
the nineteenth and most of the twentieth centuries can be seen as a
series of attempts to manage exchange rate fluctuations, interrupted by
bouts of international disorder as old, reasonably stable patterns broke
down and new ones were negotiated. Hirst and Thompson (1996: 32)
identify at least seven international exchange-rate regimes in the last
hundred years. The most interesting of these for our purposes is their
'semi-fixed dollar standard', more commonly known as the Bretton
Woods system. I suggest that the postwar combination of Bretton Woods
management of exchange rates at the international level and 'Keynesian'[6] economic management at home (at least for the more advanced
capitalist economies) should be seen as the last gasp, and as the highest
development, of the Ricardian view of the place of national economies
within the larger international system.

I use the term 'highest development' here because, within the constraints of the Bretton Woods regime, what became known as Keynesian
economic management appeared to provide national governments with
a sophisticated array of instruments for managing the overall performance of their respective national economies. In effect, it brought
together two perspectives on the national economy. One is a version of
the classical view of the national economy as a system – a system which is
here defined by fundamental algebraic identities representing a series
of functional relationships between the economy's component parts and
processes. The other is the view of the national economy provided by an
increasingly sophisticated technology of national economic accounting.
The mapping of an abstract theory of the economy as a functional
system on to the output of national economic accounting suggested that
certain statistical aggregates could be treated as surrogates for variables
('investment', 'savings', 'money supply', etc.) in the equations which
defined the character of the economy as a system – the implication being

that if changes in some of these aggregates could be brought about by government action then corresponding changes in other aggregates could be expected to follow.

It seemed to many commentators in this period that governments had finally been provided with macro-economic levers for managing the overall performance of the national economy. Tony Crosland, for example, insisted that 'the government can exert any influence it likes on income distribution, and can also determine within broad limits the division of total output between consumption, investment, exports and social expenditure' (Crosland 1956: 27). Crosland argued that Keynesian techniques enabled socialists to pursue their economic objectives largely through government intervention at the macro-economic level. For all of its exaggerations, Crosland's understanding here illustrates an important political feature of the Keynesian promise of effective macro-economic management, namely, that it enabled many conservative and socialist political thinkers to finally make their peace with an essentially liberal rationality of government. It seemed, in other words, to offer a means of reconciling the conservative and socialist desire to keep the economy under control with a liberal view of the importance of individual liberty.[7]

Techniques of National Economic Accounting

Why should we see the Keynesian/Bretton Woods regime as the last gasp of the Ricardoan view of the place of national economies within the larger international system? Changing patterns of international economic activity are clearly important here. First, international trade has a much greater impact on most national economies than it did in Ricardo's time and even, in many respects, than it did in an earlier (pre-First World War) era of intense international economic activity.[8] Secondly, new managerial techniques and a range of sophisticated financial instruments have promoted direct foreign investment by overcoming the difficulty which Ricardo noted of controlling the use of capital invested in foreign parts – although they have also exposed foreign investors to risks of other kinds. Finally, the scale of financial movements in the period following the collapse of Bretton Woods has seriously affected the stability of international trading relations.

These developments have clearly affected the problems which governments face in dealing with their own national economies. However, as I noted in my introductory remarks, an important part of the impact of these developments has been on the perception of the national economy itself as an object of government. Even in the larger Western societies these developments have undermined the Ricardoan image of the national economy as a largely self-regulating system operating within a larger international frame.

In fact, it is tempting to suggest another factor at this point, which relates to a tension in the Keynesian synthesis itself. One such tension has been postulated by liberal critics who argue that Keynesian attempts to regulate the level of unemployment through macro-economic management (using incomes policies to contain inflation) have the perverse effect of gradually raising the non-inflationary level of unemployment (Brittan 1977). This argument shares with its Keynesian opponents the image of the national economy as a functional, largely self-regulating system. The tension which concerns me here, however, is a matter of relations between the abstract theory of the national economy as a functional system and the technology of national economic accounting.

My point is simply that the progressive refinement of national economic accounting should itself be expected to result in increasingly disaggregated econometric models of particular national economies – movement in this direction being limited only by the availability of computing power and the costs (for governments and for others) of data collection and surveillance. While versions of the Keynesian aggregate supply–aggregate demand model may still be used for various (largely rhetorical) purposes, governments (and other agencies) are also able to call on detailed information concerning interactions between different sectors of the channels, and particular effects of investments, borrowings and savings, and the exposure of particular sectors of national economic activity to international developments. None of this requires that the national economy as a whole should be conceptualised as a largely self-regulating system.

Among those who make use of economic models, then, the spreadsheet and the computational model has undermined the appeal of the older image of the national economy as an overarching self-regulating *system*. While econometric modelling makes use of standardised computational algorithms, the use of spreadsheet data allows national economic models themselves to be custom-built, and thereby to accommodate distinctive features of particular national communities. The change has been more complete in some cases than it has in others since, while the spreadsheet/computational model has been widely adopted, the image of the system nevertheless retains a certain pragmatic significance, at least within the larger, more prosperous national economies and trading blocs. At the same time, governments, business corporations and international agencies are now better informed than ever before about the workings of their own (and of others') national economies. Given these conditions it is more than a little disingenuous of Robert Reich and other exponents of the globalisation thesis to pretend that the more advanced Western societies are moving rapidly into a situation where there will 'no longer be national economies' (Reich 1992: 3).

In fact, Reich goes on to qualify this extravagant claim by adding 'at least as we have come to understand that concept' – which suggests that national economies may nevertheless be understood in other terms. My final section explores some of the repercussions of this changing conception of the national economy with regard both to the problem of national economic management and governmental perceptions of relations between economic and other aspects of the life of the national community.

Economic Management and the National Community

My earlier discussion suggested that the liberal problem of security involved a view of the national economy as a largely self-regulating system. I have now argued that this view is itself in the process of being displaced. Supposing that such a change can indeed be identified, what are its implications for governmental perceptions: first, of national economic management; and secondly, somewhat more generally, of relations between national economic activity and other aspects of the life of the national community?

I begin by recalling the governmental import of the image of the national economy as a largely self-regulating system operating according to its own laws and functional exigencies and endowed with a natural tendency to grow. This image suggests that a prudential government will be concerned with securing the individual liberty and other conditions in which economic activity can be expected to develop to beneficial effect (including, especially in the Keynesian era, setting in place an appropriate macro-economic framework) and with clearing away obstacles to economic growth. This image of the national economy also suggests that a prudential government will sometimes favour short- or medium-term protectionist measures, intended to allow infant industries time to develop, and a variety of educational and infrastructure programs designed to modify the ways in which the national economy has a comparative advantage over others.

The shift noted above towards the adoption of alternative views of the national economy involves a rejection not so much of the image of economic activity as a largely self-regulating system, but rather of the view that such an image can usefully be applied at the level of the national economy itself. The idea is retained that, if left to its own devices, the economy has a natural tendency to grow, but it now tends to be applied to the international economy as a whole (or to substantial trading blocs within it) rather than to particular national economies. It is in this respect that the new view of international economic relations differs most clearly from the earlier, 'Ricardoan' framework for incorporating international trade within a system image of national economies.

Thus, while the liberal presumption in favour of free trade (other things being equal) and of individual liberty (at least in the economic sphere) continues under the new dispensation, the Ricardoan argument that international trade can normally be expected to benefit the participating national economies now appears to be rather less compelling. There is nothing in the idea of a supra-national economic system, even one endowed with a benign tendency towards expansion, which requires that all geographical regions within that economy will benefit from its expansion. Nor, since national economies can no longer be seen as self-regulating systems of the appropriate kind, is it possible to rely on Keynesian or monetarist macro-economic techniques to secure their performance. Indeed, 'there is now no doctrinally grounded and technically effective regime of macro-economic management that can produce sustained expansionary effects' (Hirst and Thompson 1992: 371).

If macro-economic management cannot be relied upon in this regard then governments must engage in other measures to improve the condition of their particular portion of the larger international economy. In this respect, the larger national economies now find themselves in the situation which has long confronted some of the smaller Western economies: the situation, that is, of a politically independent region caught up in a larger, relatively open economic system but nevertheless aiming to defend its economic interests – and to do so as far as possible without resorting to protectionist measures of a character that might be expected to provoke more powerful nations to respond in kind. It has been argued (Katzenstein 1985) that the smaller nations of Western Europe dealt with this challenge through the adoption of corporatist arrangements in which governments worked to maintain both a coalition between representatives of capital and labour and a social consensus in support of that arrangement.

In effect, the move away from reliance on a system model of the national economy has brought about a corresponding change in governmental perceptions of economic competition between nations. Under the old regime it seemed that national governments could engage in a competition 'without losers' (Hirst and Thompson 1996: 6): nations which were more successful in the economic competition could expect to become more powerful in other respects as well, but the remainder could nevertheless expect to enjoy a gradual increase in prosperity. If the national economy can no longer be perceived as a system of the appropriate kind then even that consolation prize may no longer be available.

This perception underlies the widespread assumption that 'the only way to avoid becoming a loser – whether as a nation, firm or individual – is to be as competitive as possible' (Hirst and Thompson 1996: 6). Adopting this view, the pursuit of national economic security will involve working to improve the efficiency of the national economy: governments must aim to do better than their competitors, or at least to keep up with the pack. Hirst and Thompson recommend national-level corporatist arrangements as a way of coping with this challenge. However, they also acknowledge that national governments are 'trapped by the legacies of social cohesion that they inherit. Countries like the USA cannot just decide to adopt the more solidaristic and coordinative relations between industry, labour and the state that have hitherto prevailed in Germany and Japan' (Hirst and Thompson 1996: 148).

Whether or not such corporate arrangements appear to be feasible, the governmental pursuit of national economic efficiency will certainly involve programs of micro-economic reform. In the Australian context this point has been made forcefully in the 1989 Garnaut Report, *Australia and the Northeast Asian Ascendancy*. The Report insists on the 'complementarity' between the Australian economy and those of northeast Asia – which is a polite way of saying that Australia's economic security is fundamentally dependent on developments elsewhere. (The complementary dependence of the northeast Asian economies on the good health of the Australian economy is not so clear.) As a result, a major theme of the Report 'and one upon which all others depend, is that we must accelerate progress in domestic economic reform, to build a flexible, internationally-oriented economy that is capable of grasping the opportunities that will emerge in the decades ahead' (Garnaut 1989: 7). This theme is now a commonplace of Australian public life.

What are the implications of this new image of the national economy for governmental perceptions of relations between national economic activity and other aspects of the life of the national community? Under the old dispensation the national economy could be seen both as a largely self-regulating system and as a resource for other component parts or aspects of a larger national unity. Since prudential government would secure the conditions of economic growth its output, net of depreciation and replacement costs, would be available for investment on the one hand, and for such purposes as national defence, extravagant display and social welfare on the other. These latter expenditures would certainly be regarded as a cost to the economy but their net effect would only be to reduce the rate of growth to rather less than it might otherwise have been.

Under the new regime the pursuit of national economic efficiency appears as the indispensable condition not only of economic growth but also of all those other desiderata which must be financed out of the increment of growth. Furthermore, the distinction between the economy and other aspects of the life of the national community is less clear-cut than it was in the days when liberals could treat the national economy as if it were a relatively self-contained system. I noted earlier that the move away from reliance on a system model of the national economy has brought about a change in governmental perceptions of economic competition between nations, and a corresponding fear that the old consolation prize of modest economic growth may no longer be available to the less successful of the currently prosperous Western nations. In place of the image of a well-ordered national economy providing resources for the national state and society we now find the image of an extravagant state and society undermining efficient national economic performance. This change of focus accounts for the paradoxical circumstance that governmental discourse in the wealthiest of all societies now takes it for granted that we can no longer afford the welfare regimes of the postwar dispensation.

It is the emergence of a new problem of security and not, as Pusey suggests, the emergence of a new breed of economists which is the key to understanding the governmental importance of economic rationalism and the like. The pursuit of national economic security now seems to require that an overwhelming priority be placed on competitive economic efficiency. As a result, anything (welfare, health services, schooling and higher education) which might seem to have a bearing on economic life is assessed not only in terms of the availability of resources, but also in terms of their consequences for promoting or inhibiting the pursuit of national economic efficiency. Thus, in what is often seen as an 'economic rationalist' or 'neo-liberal' attack on the welfare state, the concern is not simply to save money but also to promote more efficient patterns of individual and organisational behaviour by bringing market relationships into what had once been regarded as non-market spheres of allocation.

After commenting on recent British attempts to require individual schools to operate according to an artificially constructed kind of market regime, Graham Burchell goes on to suggest that:

> the generalisation of an 'enterprise form' to *all* forms of conduct – to the conduct of organizations hitherto seen as being non-economic, to the conduct of government and to the conduct of individuals themselves – constitutes the essential characteristic of this style of government: the promotion of an enterprise culture. (Burchell, 1996: 29)

This desire to promote efficiency, not only in the narrowly economic sphere but in all areas of life, does seem to provide a standing incentive for governmental interference. In this respect it is tempting to suggest a parallel with the pre-liberal system of police, discussed in the Introduction to this book, in which the overall good of the governed population served to justify all kinds of particularistic regulations. The analogy is apt in some respects and seriously misleading in others. Neither police nor the emerging style of neo-liberal government are much restrained by the classical liberal understanding of the national economy as a system which should normally be left to regulate itself. From the standpoint of police all aspects of the life of the governed population were amenable to regulation, even if, in practice, the reach of such regulation was always considerably less than this ambition might seem to suggest. Similarly, Gary Becker and others have long argued that efficiency considerations can and should be brought to bear in all areas of human behaviour. Here too, however, the scope of governmental intervention in practice has been substantially less than the generalised concern to promote efficiency would suggest.

Nevertheless, while the similarities are undeniable there is at least one fundamental difference which concerns the underlying rationale of governmental intervention itself. The objective of police regulation was to promote the well-being of the governed population (and therefore of the state) by preventing behaviour which the authorities regarded as damaging and promoting behaviour which they saw as beneficial. The 'happiness' of the people was to be ensured by detailed regulation of their behaviour. In the context of the search for national economic efficiency on the other hand, the well-being of the people is to be brought about not by external control but by its contrary, by forcing the people to be free – although not at all in the sense that Rousseau had in mind. The aim is to remedy the effects of earlier, misguided policies which are thought to have promoted inefficient patterns of behaviour in the fields of education, health and welfare provision and in many other areas of government intervention. Rather than the reimposition of police regulation this represents a generalisation of Smith's liberal attack on the effects of police interference in economic activity, which is now brought to bear on areas of government intervention which had hitherto been protected because they had been seen as essentially non-economic in character.

Notes

This paper has had a number of revisions since its first public airing. I am particularly grateful to Stephen Bell, Ian Hunter, Nikolas Rose, Tim Rowse, Grahame Thompson and my co-editor, Mitchell Dean, for critical comments and suggestions.

1 There is a substantial and well-known literature devoted to most of these labels. The term 'advanced liberalism' has been used by Nikolas Rose to refer to the recent elaboration of governmental attempts to 'govern at a distance' (Rose 1996: 43).

2 As I have argued in Hindess 1996b, 1997.

3 'There will no longer be national economies, at least as we have come to understand that concept. All that will remain rooted within national borders are the people who comprise the nation' (Reich 1992: 3).

4 Here Ricardo protests too much. A memoir by one of his brothers (cited in Hartwell's Introduction to the Penguin edition of Ricardo's *Principles* . . . ,) notes that their father 'a native of Holland, and of very respectable connections, came over on a visit to this country [England], when young, *and preferring it to his own*, became naturalised and settled here' (p. 33 – emphasis added).

5 See 'Die Vernunft der List' (ch. 3 in Tribe 1995) on the American provenance of this aspect of List's argument.

6 Of course, as Leijonhufvud (1968) and others have insisted, this 'Keynesian' economics should not be confused with the economics of Keynes.

7 It goes without saying that not all liberals were convinced. Friedrich Hayek, in particular, has always been critical of the political implications of Keynesian theory.

8 Hirst and Thompson (1996: ch. 2) present a range of measures of internationalisation.

References

Barry, A., Osborne, T. and Rose, N., 1996. *Foucault and Political Reason: Liberalism, Neo-liberalism and Rationalities of Government*, London: University College London Press.

Bentham, J., 1843. Principles of the Civil Code in J. Bowing (ed.), *Jeremy Bentham: Works*, Edinburgh: William Tait.

Brittan, S., 1977. *The Economic Consequences of Democracy*, London: Temple Smith.

Burchell, G., 1996. 'Liberal government and techniques of the self' in A. Barry, T. Osborne, and N. Rose (eds), *Foucault and Political Reason: Liberalism, Neo-liberalism and Rationalities of Government*, London: University College London Press.

Burchell, G., Gordon, C. and Miller, P. (eds), 1991. *The Foucault Effect: Studies in Governmentality*, London: Harvester/Wheatsheaf.

Crosland, C. A. R., 1956. *The Future of Socialism*, London: Cape.

Garnaut, R., 1989. *Australia and the Northeast Asian ascendancy: Report to the Prime Minister and the Minister for Foreign Affairs and Trade*, Canberra: Australian Government Publishing Service.

Hamilton, A., 1966 (1791). *The Report on the Subject of Manufactures in Papers of Alexander Hamilton*, vol. 10, New York: Columbia University Press.

Hindess, B., 1993. 'Rehearsing a venerable debate: comments on Economic Rationalism in Canberra', *Australian and New Zealand Journal of Sociology* 29, 3: 374–8.

Hindess, B., 1996a. *Discourses of Power: from Hobbes to Foucault*, Oxford: Blackwell.

Hindess, B., 1996b. 'Liberalism, socialism and democracy: variations on a governmental theme' in A. Barry, T. Osborne and N. Rose (eds), *Foucault* and *Political Reason: Liberalism, Neo-liberalism and Rationalities of Government*, London: University College London Press.

Hindess, B., 1997. 'A society governed by contract' in G. Davis, B. Sullivan and A. Yeatman (eds), *The New Contractualism*, Melbourne: Macmillan.

Hirst, P. Q. and Thompson, G. F., 1992. 'The problem of "globalisation": international economic relations, national economic management and the formation of trading blocs', *Economy and Society* 21, 4: 357–96.

Hirst, P. Q. and Thompson, G., 1996. *Globalisation in Question: The Myths of the International Economy and the Possibilities of Governance*, Oxford: Polity.

Katzenstein, P. J., 1985. *Small States in World Markets: Industrial Policy in Europe*, Ithaca, N.Y.: Cornell University Press.

Leijonhufvud, A., 1968. *On Keynesian Economics and the Economics of Keynes*, Oxford: Oxford University Press.

List, F., 1966 (1841). *The National System of Political Economy*, New York: Augustus M. Kelly.

Pusey, M., 1991. *Economic Rationalism in Canberra. A Nation-Building State changes its Mind*, Cambridge: Cambridge University Press.

Reich, R., 1992. *The Work of Nations*, New York: Vintage.

Ricardo, D., 1971 (1817). *Principles of Political Economy and Taxation*, Harmondsworth: Penguin.

Rose, N., 1996. 'Governing "advanced" liberal democracies' in A. Barry, T. Osborne and N. Rose (eds), *Foucault and Political Reason. Liberalism, Neo-liberalism and Rationalities of Government*, London: University College London Press.

Smith, A., 1976. *An Inquiry into the Nature and Causes of the Wealth of Nations*, ed. R. H. Campbell and A. S. Skinner, Oxford: Clarendon Press.

Tribe, K., 1995. *Strategies of Economic Order: German Economic Discourse, 1750–1950*, Cambridge: Cambridge University Press.

CHAPTER 13

Interpreting Contemporary Contractualism

Anna Yeatman

Over the last twenty or so years the Anglophone liberal democracies have witnessed the revival of contractualist doctrines of governance. Interpreted narrowly, contractualist doctrines are those which locate the legitimacy of social obligation in the legally sanctioned and freely undertaken contractual choice of individuals. Interpreted more broadly, in a way which suggests the ethos of contractualism, contractualist doctrines are those which require social obligation to be mediated by some form of individualised consent. This means that social processes, outcomes and relationships have to be made accountable to individualised inquiry and judgment. Such accountability may or may not lead to individualised assent or dissent. Writ large as in the idea of the social contract, or writ small as in the idea of individual contractualist arrangements, contractualism appears to have a peculiar salience in the governance of self-regulated social life.

However, just exactly what this all means is currently highly debatable (for an indication of such debate, see the collection on contemporary contractualism edited by Davis, Sullivan and Yeatman, 1997). I will argue that it is the broad meaning, or ethos of contractualism, which is at issue: most instances of contemporary contractualism are not of legal standing and, it turns out, the legal doctrine of contractualism is itself highly dependent on this ethos.

When this ethos of contractualism comes into view, it becomes possible to see that contractualism is not to be equated with liberalism. Liberal versions of contractualism are not the only ones available. Where liberal contractualism emphasises freedom of choice for individuals assumed to be already given as individuals, and needing no further support for their existence as individuals, other and more contemporary contractualist ideas emphasise the conditions which permit persons to

227

be treated as individuals. For liberalism, individualisation is not at issue because individuals already exist. For social contractualism, as it might be called, individualisation is precisely what is at issue. What are the understandings, norms, procedures and institutions which foster and facilitate an individualisation of social life? By this term of 'individual-isation' is meant the mediation of social ties and connections by indivi-dualised consent. For individualised consent to occur, persons have to be valued and regarded as individuals. Persons become individuals cap-able of regarding others as also being individuals only as they become cognitively and morally oriented within an ethos of intersubjectivity.

Social contractualism is what I have termed the 'new contractualism'. It is a type of contractualism which depends on a postpatrimonial and anti-discriminatory ethos of personhood (for more elaboration of this see Yeatman 1997), that is, one which extends the status of individualised personhood to all, regardless of differences in marital status, race, ethnicity, sexuality, religion, ability and so on. While there are historical ties between social and liberal versions of contractualism, there are also serious tensions between them, not least with regard to the relative emphasis in social contractualism on the equality of individualised per-sons, as distinct from liberal contractualism's emphasis on the freedom of those who already have the capacities to forcefully present themselves as individuals.

What might one point to in evidence of this so-called new contract-ualism? A mix of examples indicates readily the different kinds of contractualism in view. Firstly, there is the increasingly influential idea that services should be designed around the needs of individuals, not the other way around. This was a principle adopted for the Australian Home and Community Care program in 1989, it is a core principle of the United Kingdom Citizen's Charter, and it influences the 1994 Australian White Paper on the needs of the long-term unemployed in its insistence that labour market assistance needs to be tailored to the needs of the individual jobseeker. Why or how is this idea contractualist? Contractualism is indicated in the requirement for the individual user of a service both to choose what it is they require of that service, and to make that choice explicit in such a manner that it can be determined whether or not the service has responded effectively to that choice.

Secondly, currently there is a plethora of contractualist instruments of public management. These include performance agreements between ministers and chief executives of public agencies, performance apprais-als as negotiated between the appraiser and the appraised, competitive tendering for publicly funded services and the contracting out of publicly funded services to external suppliers. Some of these contracts are of legal standing, others are not. What they have in common is a contractualist language that makes explicit the reciprocal expectations between the parties concerned. Such explicitness is arrived at through a mixed process of contract and negotiation, often, of course, in the context of established policies, guidelines or procedures. By situating these policies, guidelines and procedures in relation to a dialogical explicitness about tasks and processes, they themselves become subject to the principle of rational accountability. Explicitness and the kind of information sharing it presupposes fuel consent. Thus, contractualist explicitness and consent are linked principles. This does not mean that this consent is unconstrained, or that there are not different kinds of inequality operative in the relationship between the negotiating parties.

Thirdly, there are a number of relatively new statutes which work in terms of the norm of a self-regulated relationship. In this connection we can mention the 1991 New Zealand Employment Contracts Act, where the employment contract by statute is radically individualised in two senses: each party, employer or employee, can choose to negotiate on their own behalf or to be represented 'by another person, group, or organization'; and each has freedom to negotiate, whether the contract is an individual or collective employment contract.[1] This is not to argue that the 1991 Act is itself fully adequate to contractualist values – it is not, as I shall suggest below – but to suggest that it is symptomatic of the new contractualism, as is also the Australian government's dilution of a centralised wage fixing system in favour of enterprise bargaining. Whatever else may be said about these developments, one thing is clear: as much as they legitimise self-regulated modes of employment, in the same measure they contribute to the delegitimising of established legal and policy paternalistic discourses of worker protection.

The delegitimising of paternalistic principles of protection in the employment arena needs to be seen in the context of other important statutory developments, such as equal employment opportunity, anti-discrimination, and equal pay legislation. The directional force of such legislation is to constitute the parties to employment relations as equal persons in terms of their contractual capacities, rights and obligations. Contractual equality of this kind is an equal entitlement to individualised personhood. It requires the disestablishment of all state legislation and policy which 'protected' certain categories of person precisely because they were assumed to be incapable of protecting themselves from harm. Thus, for equal pay for women workers to be possible, protective legislation limiting the hours women could work had to be abolished.

Entitlement to status as an individualised person has been extended to those who belong to social categories that were, in some or all ways, excluded from the older discourses of contractualism. This extension has not occurred without the mobilisation of social movements which have both protested against these exclusions, and have unambiguously rejected the paternalistic principle of some speaking on behalf of others. In this way the so-called new social movements – feminism, the gay and lesbian movements, the various antiracist, multicultural and indigenous people's movements – have all contributed to the resurgence of contractualist principles.

In the following section, I want to say a little more about this broader ethos of the new contractualism, then to show how it is operative in current theoretical discourses of contractualism, and, finally, to address the critiques of the new contractualism. In conclusion, I will suggest that whatever else we do we cannot help taking the new contractualism seriously, and, paradoxically enough, one line of critique may lie in working to make the new contractualism more adequately contractual.

The Ethos of the New Contractualism

Nineteenth-century utilitarianism crystallised what we might call the classical doctrine of contract. Certainly this is the classical doctrine of contract as understood in law (see Atiyah 1986: especially chs 2 and 6). Contract refers to a legally enforceable exchange of promises. It is binding because the parties to it intended to be bound; 'it is their will or intention which creates the liability' (Atiyah 1986: 12). It is the promise itself which creates the liability, and contractual obligation resides in honouring the promise once made. The emphasis in this doctrine of contractualism is on the nature of the obligation that flows from freely-given choice. By the same token, if it turns out that the choice was not freely given, the courts may determine that the contract was not a fair or proper one.

Given contemporary democratic expectations, a contractualist emphasis on a legally consequentialist choice must inevitably lead into questions about the conditions under which a freely chosen obligation can be assumed to be given. If contract law is necessarily and inevitably oriented to the issue of whether or not choice has been freely exercised, then we are likely to see a range of developments in law which specify the conditions under which such choice may be assumed to be exercised. These can include what Atiyah (1986: 128) problematically regards as paternalistic protection 'for those who make rash and ill-considered promises', as in the provision of cooling-off periods and the like. They might come to include increasingly the requirement that, for example, banks explain the fine contractual print of different mortgage interest rate options and plastic surgeons explain the risks of silicon enlargement of bodily parts to their respective consumers.

The legal emphasis on a freely assumed or voluntary undertaking makes it appear that the origins of this relationship resides in choice. This may be an appropriate way of looking at a whole range of contractualist types of relationship, where the issue of entering the relationship in the first place is, or should be, a matter of choice. As we know, this is not true of many relationships: the chief executive of a government agency cannot choose whether to contract with the minister or not; the student taking a university topic cannot choose whether to be assessed or not; the person who lacks an independent income and who is ineligible for public income support cannot choose whether to be employed or not; the person who is medically advised to remove some skin cancers normally does not choose whether to have surgery or not. In all these cases it is not so much a question of choice as a question of whether the person concerned is effectively and appropriately participating in these relationships.

This is still, in many if not most contexts, a radical demand. Too few doctors involve their clients in an informed relationship to medically-oriented decision-making, far too few employers work with their employees in an explicitly negotiated coproducing relationship, and far too few academics engage students in the formation and negotiation of an assessment contract. At the same time, the direction of legislative and normative change appears to be clear: the expectation is that parties to a negotiated, contractualist type of relationship be adequately informed about the nature of this relationship, and that there be ways of making each accountable to the other.

At this point, it is useful to distinguish the principles of consent and choice. In many instances, even if a relationship is entered into by choice, once entered into it is not choice but consent that becomes the operative contractualist principle. Consent can be argued to be operating when the parties to a relationship are adequately informed about their relationship, and their respective entitlements within it, and they have the right to negotiate the substance, process and direction of this relationship. This right of negotiation involves the right to discussion, debate and contestation in respect of this relationship. Negotiation entails the additional principles of explicitness and accountability. A relationship can be adequately negotiated only if the parties concerned make explicit what they see as issues to be addressed, issues in relation to which they have distinct and separable, that is, individualised, interests. Explicitness will demand often that one party become accountable to the other – and possibly to third parties – for their actions.

Informed consent, negotiation by mutual adjustment (see Majone 1991) and accountability, then, are the central components of this looser, non-legal ethos of contractualism. In some cases, as we have seen, a statutory entitlement will underpin a right to information, and often there will be a legal contractual aspect of such relationships. In general, however, the ethos of contractualism works off a shared set of commitments to self-regulated relationships which do not have legal standing. This is not to say, however, that in order to be operative this ethos does not require resourcing. It does require to be resourced and institutionalised in a number of ways. These include: teaching persons how to act and orient as individuals who are capable of regarding others as also being individuals; capacitating persons in respect of the range of cognitive, social, ethical and technical skills required for negotiating their relationships; providing forms of independent facilitation and arbitration which uphold and secure individualised consent in relationships; and, not least, providing information and advocacy resources so that persons who are less socially advantaged than others can be effective as individuals in social exchange and relationships.

Theoretical Discourses of the New Contractualism

The new contractualism is evident in a number of theoretical discourses which model institutional design and governance. These are the discourses of public choice, rational choice, agency theory and the new institutional economics (for description of these see Boston et al. 1996: ch. 2; Trebilcock 1993; and Perrow 1986: ch. 7). These are liberal rather than social contractualist discourses, in that they assume the presence of individuals as already given. However, what makes them *new* contractualist discourses is the way in which they universalise the condition of being an individual, and thereby, participate in a non-discriminatory ethos of individualised personhood.[2] Additionally, these discourses imply that what have been historically intra-organisational relationships of hierarchical command can, or even should, be submitted to contract and, in this way, individualised. Liberalism thereby becomes entangled in contemporary organisational complexity in ways which fundamentally challenge its classical reduction of contract to market-based exchange.

Most of their critics have wrongly assumed that these discourses are essentially economistic in character. Or rather, in so doing, they have overlooked the political-economic conception of action which liberal economic theory offers. These discourses represent a wider intellectual movement in contemporary political and social science, where the nineteenth-century utilitarian calculus of individualised rational action has been turned into a sophisticated instrument of institutional design in all contexts, not just economic ones. If there is a master discourse among these, it is that of rational choice.

Rational choice is more sophisticated than most of its critics appreciate. It works in terms of a calculus of self-regulated, rational adaptation of individuals to what is taken to be a highly complex set of circumstances, including the complexities that attend extensive and intensive interdependencies between actors. Jon Elster's portrayal of rational action is helpful in understanding what is at stake here:

> An action, to be rational, must be the final result of three optimal decisions. First, it must be the best means of realizing a person's desire, given his beliefs. Next, these beliefs must themselves be optimal, given the evidence available to him. Finally, the person must collect an optimal amount of evidence – neither too much nor too little. That amount depends both on his desires – on the importance he attaches to the decision – and on his beliefs about the costs and benefits of gathering more information. (Elster 1989: 30)

It is to be emphasised that this concept of rational action does not preclude using the categories of culture, discourse, ideology or psychoanalysis to explain how the individual forms and ranks their desires. This is not at issue. What is at issue is the rational-choice theorist's normative insistence on the individualised nature of desire. This does not in itself make this desire self-regarding as distinct from other-regarding; individualised desire can be oriented in terms of all types and modes of social relationship, including those which we term egocentric.

The unit of desire is an individual actor not a collectivity. Or rather, desire functions to individualise an actor. On this approach, institutional design should work so that actors are enabled to pursue rationally their individualised desires in ways which make informed acknowledgment of the terms of their coexistence with other desiring individuals. These individualised actors can be either empirical individuals or corporate actors, such as firms. Agency theory and the new institutional economics can be seen as theorising rational choice on behalf of such corporate actors when they have become dependent on complex chains of transaction between the parts or wholes of a series of organisation.

Rational choice espouses a methodological individualism which is expressed in the proposition that 'there do not exist collective desires or collective beliefs' (Elster 1986: 3). It is arguable as to what this means. Taken literally, it is both empirically and normatively false. It neither explains how there is shared or intersubjectively maintained democratic values which enable such a theoretical orientation as that of rational choice, nor how these values provide a normative framework for individualised or self-regulated social relations. Yet if by this proposition is meant the idea that, in modern society, collective desires and beliefs exist only as they are mediated through individualised choice, consent, judgment and commitment, then this methodological individualism commands some purchase. It is, however, a purchase limited to modern democratic types of context and, this being the case, there is a circular relationship between the methodological premise and the types of explanation for which it is offered as a ground.

To date, liberal political economy and theories of government have offered the only elaborated theoretical specification of contractual sociality. For this reason they have to be reckoned with. They can be subject to two types of critique. One which criticises them for what, by the terms of their construction, they cannot accommodate: this type is an external critique of liberalism; the other which examines their internal conditions of coherence and discovers difficulties that require reconsideration of the principal theoretical assumptions of liberalism, especially those which concern the nature of the individual. Let us take the latter type of critique first.

Internal Critiques of Theoretical Contractualist Discourse

This is a large topic, and it will be enough to suggest the nature of the work that requires to be done here.[3] It is fair to say that both the theoretical expositors of the new contractualism and their external critics tend to take for granted the very category that should be problematised: namely, individualised agency. I have suggested above that rational choice requires desire to operate in such a way that it individualises the actor, that is, turns this actor – non-corporate or corporate – into: (a) an intentional unit of action, (b) one whose agency in relation to other such units is assumed to be bounded and, in this sense, (c) is independent. This is a self who understands selfhood as his or her separability from other selves in such a way as he or she can be treated and treat himself/herself as a distinct locus of judgment, volition and decision-making. This self's oppositional other is a tribal or patrimonial self, namely one whose selfhood is organically derived from the identity of some kind of communal self.

Because confusion is so rife in this area, it is important to emphasise that the individualised self exists only in terms of its relationship to other selves. Individualisation, in other words, is a type of social relationship. Thus, it is not the case that the tribal or patrimonial self is a self in relationship, where the individualised self is a self not in relationship. Rather, we have two different kinds of self in relationship. Tribal selves, for example, are communalised selves, while modern contractualist selves are individualised selves.

Liberals and their socialist critics, historically, have made just this mistake, namely to assume that the individualised self is an individual outside social relationships. For Marxists and socialists, this meant that an emphasis on the social nature of selfhood led to the assertion of collective identities which subsumed individuals at the expense of individualised social relationships. Either way, the individual has been left as a natural category.

Until we have an adequate theoretical account of how individualised social relationships work, and what makes them possible, we will not be able to check the individualistic and asocial excesses of liberal contractualist approaches. We need to ask questions like: how is the individualised capacity to choose developed? What does it mean to choose? Is choice necessarily an individualised capacity? What is the relationship of choice to informed consent and the intersubjective properties of dialogue, negotiation, and contestation? How does choice work in relation to accountability, and what is accountability in the context of individualised social relationships? How are the capacities to do all these things developed, and what kinds of knowledge and skill are required for these capacities to operate?

External Critiques of Contractualist Discourse

The external critiques tend to reject the assumptions of contractualism. Because they do so, they can be seen as critiques of theoretical and practical contractualist discourse. These critiques generally conflate contractualism with its liberal, not to say libertarian, versions. To this degree they overlook their indebtedness for the very terms of their critique to contractualism understood in its broader sense, that is, as referring to the ethos of self-regulated social relationships. At the same time, to a degree, it is reasonable for these critiques to mistake their object since the reduction of contractualism to its liberal versions is a widespread tendency.

The first critique rejects contractualism as a libertarian or free market doctrine of 'economic rationalism', where the value of equality is subordinated to the right of survival of the contractually fittest.[4] That there is a vulgar libertarian version of contemporary contractualism which deserves such critique in the name of equality cannot be doubted. The social welfare policies of the Reagan, Thatcher, Bolger and Howard governments, in part at least, appear to have been designed according to a libertarian-contractualist doctrine of the survival of the fittest, accompanied by a non-egalitarian defence of employer prerogative within the employment contractual relationship. It is this which explains the section in the New Zealand Employment Contracts Act which makes the rest of that Act incoherent by contemporary contractualist standards, namely section 57 which says that alleged 'harsh and oppressive' employment contracts can be determined by the Employment Court 'only on the application of a party to the contract and not of its own motion', nor, it would seem, of any third party. And the Act concludes with an extraordinarily arbitrary assertion of the non-contractualist and patrimonial principle of employer prerogative: 'Except as provided in this section, the Court shall have no jurisdiction to set aside or modify, or grant relief in respect of, any employment contract under the law relating to unfair or unconscionable bargains'.

Abandonment, however, of the value of equality is a minority position which cannot command legitimacy under contemporary conditions of liberal democracy. Contemporary contractualism can be made to serve, not to undermine, the value of equality: consider, for example, the principle of designing services around the needs of individuals rather than the other way around. Thus, the dismissal of contemporary contractualism as an inequalitarian economically-rationalist ethic is inadequate to the terms of the current debate.

The second position of critique is a feminist one. Liberal contractualism assumes that individuals are always already 'individuals', that is, independent persons who possess a mature, autonomous capacity for rational choice. As classical liberalism and utilitarianism argue, this rules out of the contractualist picture all those whose contractual capacity is neither sufficiently developed nor sufficiently autonomous. This obviously excludes children, and traditionally it has also excluded those whose cognitive or mental capacity is held to be so impaired or immature as to prevent them from making autonomous judgments in respect of their own interest.

The feminist theorists who talk in terms of a combined ethic of care and empowerment appear to address, and correct for, these exclusions. Theorists such as Virginia Held or Carol Gilligan counterpose to contractualist assumptions of an independent, even autarchic, individuality, an individuality that is relational. They use the mothering relationship as their ethical model, a relationship which is socially and morally adequate only if the mother is oriented to the well-being and development of her child as a particular other. Virginia Held counterposes contractualism and maternal morality in this way:

> Morality, for mothering persons, must guide us in our relations with actual, particular children, enabling them to develop their own lives and commitments. For mothering persons, morality can never seem adequate if it offers no more than ideal rules for hypothetical situations: morality must connect with the actual context of real, particular others in need. At the same time, morality, for mothering persons, cannot possibly be a mere bargain between rational contractors. That morality in this context could not be based on self-interest or mutual lack of interest is obvious; that a contractual escape is unavailable or inappropriate is clear enough. (Held 1993: 211)

Held's argument that mothering involves an ethic which cannot be accounted for by liberal contractualism is correct as far as it goes. By emphasising the inability of the child to contract in or out of this relationship, and the correlative inability of the ethical mother to contract in or out of allowing this child to be dependent on her, Held is effectively restating the classical liberal exclusion of children from contract. However, by her insistence on the effects of this exclusion for the adequacy of political and ethical theory, this is more than just its restatement.

Yet Held is involved in a difficulty which reflects her inability to develop an internal critique of contractualism:

> If we begin with the picture of rational contractor entering into agreements with others, the natural condition is seen as one of individuality and privacy, and the problem is the building of society and government. From the point of view of the relation between the mothering person and child, the problem is the reverse. The starting condition is an enveloping tie, and the problem is individuating oneself. The task is to carve out a gradually increasing measure of privacy in ways appropriate to a constantly shifting interdependency. For the child the problem is to become gradually more independent. For the mothering person, the problem is to free oneself from an all-consuming involvement. For both, the progression is from society to greater individuality rather than from self-sufficient individuality to contractual ties. (Held 1993: 208)

'The starting condition is an enveloping tie, and the problem is individuating oneself.' By this statement, Held turns the process of parenting into one of nurturing the progressive empowerment of individualised agency. Thus, mothering as care *cum* empowerment is a derived rather than an independent or complementary ethic in respect of contractualism, taken in its broader sense. This is precisely the reason why modern liberal-republican discourse distilled the idea of 're-publican motherhood' (see Landes 1988), and why, generally, liberalism has left mothering as a relatively unspecified, privatised relationship.

To argue that the individual *qua* unit of individualised action requires – in Talcott Parsons' (1955: 16) famous formulation, to be made not born – only goes so far to challenge liberal contractualism. Liberal contractualism is oriented to the fully formed contractual capacities of the individualised actor, not to how they were acquired. To show this to be a serious theoretical and practical problem requires something different from what Held is proposing. She concedes the territory of the fully formed contractual individual – even though she does not approve of its individualistic ethic – and thereby seems to suggest that liberalism is adequate, on its own turf at least. Logically, this forces those who have less than fully adequate contractual capacity to become residual categories.

Held could do something different. This would be to intervene on liberalism's own ground, to show that its contractualist understanding is less than adequately contractualist (an internal critique). Held (1993: 209) concedes that empirical mothering persons are not all that she (and we) would have them be: 'the relation may in a degenerate form be one of domination and submission'. At this point she needs to inquire into the grounds of her standard of adequacy for the mothering relationship. If they are the nurturing of an empowered, individualised agentic capacity in the one who has been child to this relationship, then she is using contractualist standards for the ethic of this relationship. This is a modern ethic for the parent–child relationship which social contract theorists like Locke and Rousseau had already conceived. Held does not inquire into how a mothering person contributes to, even constitutes, the individualised capacity of a newly emergent actor. This inquiry can proceed only as it is informed by inquiry into what it would mean to simultaneously deform this emergent individualised capacity by tying it to the needs of the mothering person's personality, that is, tying it to ongoing symbiosis. In this, Held, like the liberal contractualists she criticises, tends to take individualised agentic capacity for granted.

This brings us to the third external critique of contractualism, that which is offered by the neo-Foucaultian theorists of governmentality (see, for example, Rose and Miller 1992; Barry, Osborne and Rose 1996). Contract, for these theorists, is a technology of what they term 'neo-liberal government'. The virtue of this perspective is that it understands the relational character of individualised or, as it would have it, autonomised action. Thus, marketisation, privatisation, devolution and contractualisation are all technologies of government which fit the modern regime of regulation, namely one where government works by means of the self-regulating capacities of citizens as these are informed by the normalising effects of professional expertise, among other things.

The critical value of this perspective is its ability to see through the rhetorical fictions of liberalism, to show how it legitimises a particular regulative regime even when it is talking the language of deregulation. It can do this precisely because of its interest in the discursive practices by which individualised units of contractual capacity are formed. However, this interest turns out to be more formal than substantive in character.

Because this perspective is oriented to the sociological project of inverting liberalism's assumptions – to the proposition that the individual's capacity for autonomous action is socially determined – it does not inquire into the substance of what it means to be an individualised unit of agency. It does not provide a criterion whereby we can discriminate between different kinds of individualising governmental practices. Or if it can do this in principle, it cannot provide a criterion for discriminating when individualising governmental practices are adopted on behalf of non-contractualist principles, and thus suborned by principles contrary to them. I have in mind such examples as when a doctor or social worker uses contractualist protocols, but makes them over to paternalistic or maternalistic principles of speaking on behalf of another in the determination of their needs and interests. To be able to recognise when this is occurring requires a substantive criterion of individualising governmental practice which, in turn, cannot evade normatively oriented analysis.

Conclusion

I have argued that the new contractualism is a broader ethos of self-regulated social relationships than is adequately captured in liberal contractualist discourse. This ethos informs the terms of oppositional critique and contestation of contemporary social movements in the liberal democracies. It is not clear, however, that these traditions of critique, or the more established left traditions of critique of liberal contractualism, understand this, or that contemporary contractualism has broken out of its traditional liberal frameworks.

Instead of anti-contractualist discourse of the kinds represented by the external critiques I have identified, we would be better off asking questions which make a critical acceptance of the pervasiveness of the contemporary ethos of contractualism, and of our difficulty in escaping it. Questions like: how should we understand this contractualism? What are its many and different permutations? Can an orientation to a democratically oriented, individualised agency escape contractualist norms and assumptions? In what ways do contractualist protocols both reproduce and contest inequalities of power? What are the limits of contemporary contractualism, and how might we test them?

These are questions of considerable practical significance. For example, feminists currently have to decide their position in respect of the extension of enterprise bargaining, and its implications for women workers, especially those who are positioned in low-paid and often casualised jobs. Generally, in Australia at least, the feminist response has been the nostalgic gesture of holding on to a centralised wage-fixing system. This is a nostalgic gesture because, empirically, this is to lock the stable door after the horse has bolted, and, normatively, it means holding on to a patrimonial-paternalistic principle of wage-fixing. It is not clear that this is in the interests of women regarded as individualised agents. And, if we do not want to regard women as individualised agents, where does this leave them?

At the same time, we can grant the premise that in an enterprise-bargaining context most women workers are poorly positioned to be effective contractual agents. There is an alternative response to this difficulty, and that is to make an argument that the new contractualism should be more adequately contractual. Specifically, that women's (as all individuals') entitlement as effective contractual agents in enterprise bargaining be statutorily recognised, the presumption of employer prerogative in the employment relation be statutorily disestablished, and that employment contractual capacities of both employees and employers be socially developed and resourced.

I have suggested here also that our theoretical understanding of individualised or self-regulatory social relationships is not very well developed, because of our tendency to naturalise the freely contracting individual which liberalism celebrates. Where sociology intervenes to insist upon the social determination of individualised capacity, we have a good start on a more serious theoretical inquiry into the nature and conditions of individualised agency. However, this is the case only if we take this individualised agency seriously, that is, not cancel it because it is both socially determined and a particular type of social relationship.

Notes

This chapter is a clarified and slightly extended version of 'Interpreting contemporary contractualism' which appeared in J. Boston (1995). That version was a revised version of my inaugural lecture presented to Macquarie University, 25 October 1994.

1 The relevant sections of the 1991 New Zealand Employment Contracts Act are 5, 9, 10 and 18.
2 The universalisation of individualised personhood in these discourses is, in fact, limited to adult persons. This betrays a continuing patriarchalism with regard to the standing of children and young people.
3 The dominant critical reception of liberalism has been of the external critique type, that is, a rejection of 'individualism' in favour of some kind of communitarianism. Some important contributions to an internal critique include: Hegel's *Philosophy of Right* (1965); Durkheim's *The Division of Labor in Society* (1965), 'Individualism and the Intellectuals' (1969) and *Professional Ethics and Civic Morals* (1992); and the work of such feminist political-psychoanalytic theorists as Jessica Benjamin (1988).
4 Here I am synthesising the direction of critique from a large number of theorists who are deeply concerned about the subordination of public and collective values to what they see to be a relatively unconstrained and socially illiterate liberal individualism. These theorists include Jonathon Boston, Michael Pusey, Eva Cox, John Martin, Hugh Stretton and others.

References

Atiyah, P. S., 1986. *Essays on Contract*, Oxford: Clarendon Press.

Barry, Andrew, Osborne, Thomas and Rose, Nikolas, 1996 (eds). *Foucault and Political Reason: Liberalism, Neo-liberalism and Rationalities of Government*, London: University College London Press.

Benjamin, Jessica, 1988. *The Bonds of Love: Psychoanalysis, Feminism and the Problem of Domination*, New York: Pantheon Books.

Boston, Jonathon, 1995. *The State Under Contract*, Wellington: Bridget Williams.

Boston, Jonathon, Martin, John, Pallot, June and Walsh, Pat, 1996. *Public Management: the New Zealand Model*, Auckland: Oxford University Press.

Chodorow, Nancy, 1978. *The Reproduction of Mothering*, Berkeley: University of California Press.

Davis, Glyn, Sullivan, Barbara and Yeatman, Anna, 1997. *A New Contractualism?*, Melbourne: Macmillan.

Durkheim, Emile, 1965. *The Division of Labor in Society*, New York: Free Press.

Durkheim, Emile, 1969. 'Individualism and the intellectuals', *Political Studies* 17: 19–30.

Durkheim, Emile, 1992. *Professional Ethics and Civic Morals*, London and New York: Routledge.

Elster, Jon, 1986. 'Introduction' in J. Elster (ed.), *Rational Choice*, Oxford: Blackwell.

Elster, Jon, 1989. *Nuts and Bolts for the Social Sciences*, Cambridge: Cambridge University Press.

Hegel, G. W. F., 1965. *Philosophy of Right*, Oxford: Clarendon Press.

Held, Virginia, 1993. *Feminist Morality: Transforming Culture, Society and Politics*, Chicago: University of Chicago Press.

Landes, Joan, 1988. *Women and the Public Sphere in the Age of the French Revolution*, Ithaca: Cornell University Press.

Majone, Giadomenico, 1991. 'Professionalism and mutual adjustment' in F. X. Kaufmann (ed.), *The Public Sector: Challenge for Coordination and Learning*, Berlin: De Gruyter.

Parsons, Talcott, 1955. 'The American family: its relations to personality and social structure' in T. Parsons and R. F. Bales (eds), *Family, Socialization and Interaction Process*, New York: Free Press.

Perrow, Charles, 1986. *Complex Organizations: A Critical Essay*, New York: Random House.

Rose, Nikolas and Miller, Peter, 1992. 'Political power beyond the state: problematics of government', *British Journal of Sociology* 43: 2.

Trebilcock, Michael J., 1993. *The Limits of Freedom of Contract*, Cambridge, Mass.: Harvard University Press.

Yeatman, Anna, 1997. 'Contract, status and personhood' in G. Davis, B. Sullivan and A. Yeatman (eds.).

CHAPTER 14

Uncivil Society
Liberal Government and the Deconfessionalisation of Politics

Ian Hunter

In 1690 Christian Thomasius, one of Protestant Germany's leading jurists and civil philosophers, was forced to flee his home town of Leipzig in Saxony and take up residence over the border, in the city of Halle in Brandenburg. Thomasius thought it prudent to decamp because of a series of public disputations in which he had been involved with two orthodox Lutheran political theologians: J. B. Carpzovius, Leipzig's leading controversial theologian, and Hector Gottfried Masius, theology professor in Copenhagen and pastor to the Danish court (Lieberwirth 1953; Grunert 1997). While assigning church and state separate spheres of activity – in proclaiming the gospel and enforcing the law – orthodoxy none the less saw the 'two swords' of spiritual and civil discipline being wielded together in defence of the true faith and in the cause of the Christian state. Hence, Carpzovius advocated the use of civil force to compel attendance at the Lutheran eucharist, and Masius filled his role as court pastor by arguing that the sovereignty of (Lutheran) princes came directly from God. Thomasius' uncompromising rejection of this position is summarised in *Das Recht evangelischer Fürsten in theologischen Streitigkeiten* (The Right of Protestant Princes in Theological Controversies). Here it is argued that, while the prince's sovereignty is absolute, it flows not from God or community but from the secular end of the state, civil peace. Accordingly, the church should be stripped of its civil powers, expelled from the state apparatus, and turned into a 'college' or voluntary association of 'teachers' possessing no capacity to compel acceptance of its doctrines (Thomasius and Brenneysen 1696). These were the arguments underlying an earlier tract, written while Thomasius was still in Leipzig, in which – to the annoyance of the Saxon court and the professors of theology – he had justified the marriage of the Saxon prince's (Lutheran) brother to a Calvinist widow, who was in fact the sister of the prince of Brandenburg. It is not hard to see why his orthodox opponents secretly approached the Saxon court to secure Thomasius' arrest, and why Masius arranged to have some of Thomasius' tracts publicly burned by the Danish hangman.

No doubt this anecdote will seem an odd starting point for a set of comments on Michel Foucault's theme of 'governmentality' (particularly in a book titled *Governing Australia*) but I present it for two reasons. In relation to the highly schematic discussion that follows, it offers an historical snapshot of the intensity with which early modern intellectuals disputed the nature of sovereignty, mixing argument and threat, intellectual clarifications and political machinations. More importantly for our historical and methodological concerns, this story suggests that even at the beginning of the eighteenth century, the blows hammering out the doctrine of sovereignty were struck by intellectuals at war over the relation between political order and religious discipline, state and church. This is not the way things appear in Foucault's sketches of governmentality; for here disputes over sovereignty are put into the shade by the seventeenth-century emergence of an 'art of government', and religion has virtually no independent role in relation to political governance.

Government, for Foucault, is characterised by the multiple rationalities imposed by its various objects rather than by the single goal of sovereignty, which he understands in classical political-philosophical terms as the exercise of a sovereign will. In his comment that 'We need to cut off the king's head: in political theory that has still to be done', Foucault (1980: 121) gives characteristically vivid expression to his argument on the need to shift focus from the question of who holds paramount power to the issue of how power is exercised through multiple and specific means. Accordingly, Foucault is interested in religion not as a force contending for the general disposition of power but as the source of one of its particular forms: 'pastoral power', as a specific kind of governance combining individualising care and collective welfare in accordance with the 'shepherd-flock' model (Foucault 1981). Reinstating the significance of Thomasius' campaign for the secularisation of sovereignty thus provides an opportunity to reconsider Foucault's relegation of sovereignty in favour of government and with it the role of religion in early modern state-building. While this reconsideration does not bear directly on the theme of governing Australia it does concern the historical and theoretical instruments used to work that theme.

Governmentalities

For all its illuminating local insights Foucault's essay on 'Governmentality' – or the relation between rationality and governance – is organised around a single philosophico-historical opposition. This is between a mode in which governance is exercised in accordance with a commanding and exhaustive political instrumentalism, reason of state, and one in which it is shaped by the tensions between this instrumentalism and the local ends of the objects of governance. The former mode Foucault identifies with the themes of sovereignty and 'police', where the latter names an expansive attempt to govern all areas of life through regulatory *Polizei* or 'policy'. This represents a mode of political reflection that is 'transcendent' of the specific finalities of government, its end being the maintenance of the prince's 'external' control of the territory and its resources (Foucault 1991: 91, 95).

Foucault thus regards *Staatsräson* and sovereignty as impeding the development of the art of government during the seventeenth century, detouring politics into a concern with the sovereign's own wealth and power, hence distracting attention from the economy, territory and population as ends whose optimisation requires immanent knowledge and technical means. Conversely, the liberal art of government is seen as historically dynamic because of the tension it establishes between the mode and the object of political reflection. This tension and dynamic peak in Foucault's dialectical opposition between population as the inert object of governmental calculation and, in its proleptic democratic guise, as the subject who might make such calculations:

> The population now [from the middle of the eighteenth century] represents more the end of government than the power of the sovereign; the population is the subject of needs, of aspirations, but it is also the object in the hands of the government, aware *vis-à-vis* the government, of what it wants, but ignorant of what is being done to it. Interest at the level of the consciousness of each individual who goes to make up the population, and interest considered as the interest of the population regardless of what the particular interests and aspirations may be of the individuals who compose it, this is the new target and the fundamental instrument of the government of population: the birth of a new art, or at any rate of a range of absolutely new tactics and techniques. (Foucault 1991: 100)

In expounding and elaborating on Foucault's lectures on 'Security, territory and population', given at the Collège de France in 1978, Colin Gordon also mentions that doctrines of state-reason played a role in the 'detheologisation' of politics that occurred in response to the religious civil wars (Gordon 1991: 13). Yet, despite the resonances it has for an alternative account of the emergence of liberal civil society, this observation remains isolated, detached from the dialectical dynamic of rationality and governance driving Foucault's account of the shift from 'police' to liberal government.

Gordon's exposition of this account again stresses the relation of rationality and governance: 'What is distinctive, albeit not unique, about Foucault's perspective here is his concern to understand liberalism not simply as a doctrine, or set of doctrines, of political and economic theory, but as a style of thinking quintessentially concerned with the art of governing' (Gordon 1991: 14). Here, liberalism's way of thinking about governing is situated in direct opposition to that of the *Polizeiwissenschaften* and the theme of sovereignty, constituting in fact a 'critique of state reason'. For Gordon, liberalism is characterised by the manner in which it places the object of government beyond direct 'scientific' knowledge and control – as in the case of Adam Smith's account of the economy with its 'hidden hand' – thereby problematising the cameralist synthesis of knowledge and administration:

> Thus the immediate unity of knowledge and government which typifies *raison d'état* and police science now [that is, in the late eighteenth century] falls apart. The regularities of economic and commercial society display a rationality which is fundamentally different in kind from that of calculative state regulation. The new objectivity of political economy does not consist solely in its occupation of a politically detached scientific standpoint: more profoundly, it inaugurates a new mode of objectification of governed reality, whose effect is to resituate governmental reason within a newly complicated, open and unstable politico-epistemic configuration. The whole subsequent governmental history of our societies can be read in terms of the successive topological displacements and complications of this liberal problem-space. (Gordon 1991: 16)

The instability and openness of the liberal rationality of government result from its being organised around a fundamental tension: between the characterisation of economy and population as 'natural' hence ungovernable or self-governing phenomena, and the use of this characterisation as a means of subjecting them to a special kind of governance, one that is perpetually concerned with the limits of government itself. Liberalism is thus neither a technique of government like cameralism nor a purely intellectual critique of the *Polizeistaat* made in the name of abstract freedom; it is a problematisation of government from within government, which is the source of its openness and fertility.

Gordon's exposition of Foucault's lectures thus results in a more nuanced and substantive account of the relations between rationality and government than that found in Foucault's 'Governmentality' essay. It is not clear, however, that Gordon's exposition avoids the essay's basically dialectical treatment of the relation between cameralist and liberal rationalities. The problem is fundamental because it arises from the characterisation of cameralism and liberalism as signifying reciprocally opposed modes of integrating reason in government: cameralism signifying an improper transparency of the objects of government to state-reason; liberalism signifying an appropriate opacity that resists state-reason while none the less permitting access to immanent political reflection. The dialectical figuration of liberalism is clear enough in the concept of security, with Gordon himself commenting that 'here . . . a certain dialectical interleaving of the universe of police with that of political economy becomes crucial to Foucault's account' (Gordon 1991: 19). The repressive potential of the former is played-off against the fissiparous tendencies of the latter to produce the figure of the extra-juridical 'social' restraining of economic self-interest – the figure of civil society. Gordon thus treats the notion of civil society as constituting a model of social order that both criticises the regulatory science of police and offers a normative image for the socially regulatory role of commercial activity. With this, argues Gordon, the logic of state-reason and sovereignty fades from the governmental scene, which is henceforth concerned with the trade-off between order and liberty in a 'socially governed' civil society (Gordon 1991: 22–7).

Without denying the subtlety and fruitfulness of this account of liberalism, particularly its descriptions of liberal 'government through self-government', there are, I suggest, several problems attending its conception of the relation between cameralist and liberal modes of government. In fact, these problems arise from the basic characterisation of cameralism and liberalism in terms of their respective modes of integrating reason in government. Not only does this threaten to reduce complex historical relations to a battle between 'rationalities' – thereby breathing new life into the 'enlightenment' problematic of 'reason and politics' – it also risks positing a 'philosophical' relation between cameralism and liberalism, accepting the latter's view of itself as a 'critique' of state-reason, albeit in the highly qualified form of an alternative rationality for government. This schema seems to have much in common with post-Kantian philosophical history in that it portrays an inappropriately objectifying reason being replaced by one less inclined to impose its cognitive will on the immanent order of things.

In order to focus my questioning of this schema and the dialectical arrangement of governmental rationalities underpinning it, I offer the following three counter-propositions as topics for discussion. First, I suggest that the dominant rationality of government for (Protestant) German states during the first half of the seventeenth century was not the synthesis of state-reason and cameralism described by Foucault but a model of government that integrated cameralist administration and confessional Christianisation, with the prince being seen as both chief householder and spiritual father of a confessional state.[1] Secondly, when, in the wake of the Thirty Years War, the doctrines of sovereignty and *Staatsräson* that had been elaborated at the beginning of the century did re-emerge, they did so not as components of cameralist government but principally as part of a profound struggle for the deconfessionalisation of politics. Thirdly, setting aside the question of economic liberalism, the phenomena of social and political liberalism – pre-eminently religious toleration and freedom of worship – are best seen not as the outcome of a liberal 'critique of state reason' but as themselves products of the statist deconfessionalisation of politics and pacification of society.

The Confessional State

In recent years historians of early modern Germany have tended to replace the notions of Reformation and Counter-Reformation with the single concept of 'confessionalisation', a descriptor less indebted to Protestant historiography and better able to handle the fluid relations between religious discipline and political governance. In R. Po-Chia Hsia's definition, 'confessionalisation' refers to 'the interrelated processes by which the consolidation of the early modern state, the imposition of social discipline, and the formation of confessional churches transformed society' (Hsia 1989: 4–5). Seen historically, it refers not to a great awakening and reform of the medieval church but to the emergence of several churches each dedicated to transferring the spiritual disciplines of the faithful into the daily living of whole communities. During the sixteenth century the Lutheran, Calvinist and Catholic churches all undertook a mutually antagonistic tightening of their theological and liturgical systems, while simultaneously intensifying religious education and pastoral discipline with a view to forming closed confessional communities (Zeeden 1977: 15–82).

Confessional states emerged from the unplanned and uncontrolled convergence of this process with a second one, roughly coeval with it: the process of princely territorial state-building within the tottering framework of the German Empire (Schilling 1981). The princely state offered the emergent Protestant confessions political protection and the prospect of a spiritually homogenous territorial community modelled on the 'true church'. For its part, confessional disciplining offered emergent states an extraordinarily powerful instrument for governing the population, albeit one whose salvific end would outstrip and, soon enough, subvert the goal of political order (Heckel 1983). The run-away process of the second half of the sixteenth century, in which confessional communities withdrew behind the borders of territorial states and states allowed their domestic and foreign policy to be governed by the protection of their confessions, was thus driven by the unplanned convergence of religious and political interests in the spiritual-social disciplining of territorial populations (Schilling 1988b).

If then, as Foucault argues, population and territory emerged as prime objects of government in the early modern period this was not due solely to the arrival of the *Polizeistaat* with its program of social disciplining. It seems, in fact, that it was the confessional churches that were central to the creation of the first 'national' populations. They provided the disciplinary means for uniting the geographic enclosure of the population in a political territory with its moral enclosure in a confessional national culture (Reinhard 1983). This suggests a significant modification of Gerhard Oestreich's (1982) 'social disciplining' thesis, as the socialising goals of early modern state-building seem to have been less informed by the secularising disciplines of neostoicism and far more by the spiritualising disciplines of the confessionalising churches. It also fills a significant gap in Oestreich's account, explaining how the early modern states, lacking the means of intensive social governance, could have none the less created cohesive and disciplined national communities. In the case of the Calvinist city of Emden, for example, Heinz Schilling has shown that the central model for the urban community was the circle of communicants. Transgressions of urban-communal discipline – disputes, violence, sexual misdemeanours – were thus seen as impurities that threatened the integrity of holy communion and warranted suspension from it (Schilling 1989). Hence, if at this time population was emerging as an object of political governance and social disciplining, it was by no means distinct from religious community as the target of aggressive confessionalisation and spiritual disciplining.[2] Further, the political role of religion was not exhausted by the social deployment of 'pastoral power' as a specific disciplinary mode; for confessionalising religions were playing a role in defining the citizenship of confessional states (through processes of 'religious cleansing') and the political-military relations between states – both matters of sovereignty.

We can derive some insight into the mix of religious and governmental objectives in the confessional state from the political handbooks it spawned. Löhneyß' *Aulica-Politica* (Court Politics) published between 1622–24 and Veit Ludwig von Seckendorff's *Teutscher Fürstenstaat* (German Princely State) of 1687 were both written as manuals for the governance of Lutheran states. Löhneyß' work is particularly interesting for our purposes.[3] It consisted of three volumes, the first two being in the genre of moral advice to the prince ('mirror for princes'), written from a Christian-Stoic perspective and outlining the appropriate education and personal bearing of the prince. The third volume, though, contained a cameralist art of government in Foucault's sense, except that here detailed prescriptions on the economic development of the state were combined with an account of the prince as *Landesvater* – the paternal lord charged by God with the moral governance of his people.

Löhneyß had been appointed by Duke Heinrich-Julius of Brunswick-Wolfenbüttel (1552–1622) to provide expert advice on the economic and social development of the state, and this shows in Löhneyß' division of the domains of government into the following areas: schools, universities and churches; 'police', welfare, order and economic development; domains, forests and the prince's household; and finances, governmental administration and justice – each with its own *Kammer* or bureau. This work cannot be interpreted though as symptomatic of an art of government frozen at the mercantilist and 'disciplinary' level by the doctrines of *Staatsräson* and sovereignty. In fact, Löhneyß ignored the themes of reason of state and sovereignty as they had been (respectively) formulated by Machiavelli and Bodin, rejecting the idea that the prince could govern in the name of supra-legal and extra-communal political necessity. Instead, he argued on the one hand, that the prince should act only on the expert advice of his bureaus and, on the other, that the prince himself was God's official, charged with the responsibility for the spiritual well-being of his people. This Christian-cameralist viewpoint, in which it was assumed that economic development and religious observance coincided in the Christian state, is captured in Veit Ludwig von Seckendorff's comment that: 'Princely-territorial government consists in the achievement and maintenance of common goods and well-being in spiritual and worldly affairs'.[4]

These handbooks do not fit easily into Foucault's account of the pre-liberal *Polizeistaat*, for while they conceived government in terms of the *oikos* or princely *Haushaltungskunst*, the handbooks treat the prince as both the highest official of a cameralist government and as the spiritual father of a moral community, administering the worldly and spiritual weal of his subjects. In short, rather than signifying the freezing of economy and population in *oikos* by the transcendent rationality of sovereign power, the handbooks can be seen as indicative of the overlapping of political governance and religious discipline – territorial population and confessional community – in the confessional state. It would be anachronistic here to speak of population as a 'specific finality' of a (blocked) governmental rationality for, in the early modern confessional state, population was inseparable from confessional community. Bound together in the confessional state, population and congregation, political and moral community would remain two sides of the coin of government until they were smelted in the furnace of religious civil war and separated in an icier mode of political thought.

Staatsräson and the Deconfessionalisation of Politics

Historical description is not Foucault's central concern in the governmental essays, which are better seen as reconstructions of the relation between 'reason' and 'power' in the light of a series of observations regarding absolutist and liberal forms or rationalities of government. But this philosophical aspect of the governmentality schema actually turns out to be the more problematic, being itself responsible for the historical shortcomings of the account. We have already suggested that Foucault's historical differentiation between the *Polizeistaat* and the liberal art of government looks very like an improvisation on a post-Kantian philosophical distinction: namely, the distinction between a reason alienated from its object by its transcendent interests and an immanent reason, deriving from the local ends of its objects. That, at least, is the suspicion raised by the manner in which Foucault maps the duality of population – as the object of government and locus of self-government – on to the difference between a transcendent 'object-ifying' mode of political reflection (absolutist reason of state) and a mode of reflection immanent to the population itself (liberal arts of government).

Of course, Foucault does not argue that the population can ever become the self-governing subject of its own forms of liberal governance; but that is only because he treats liberal governance as (simultaneously and dialectically) the means by which sovereign power realises its own ends, by administering the forms of self-governance themselves. It is possible to suggest though that early modern doctrines of self-governing community derived neither from the immanent self-reflection of the population nor from the transcendent objectives of (secular) government, but from a quite different source. In fact, the most articulate and vociferous advocates of the natural law moral community in early modern Germany were the political theologians of the rival confessions: the Catholic Petrus Tolosanus, Luther's lieutenant Philip Melanchthon and the Calvinist Johannes Althusius. While attacking each other's theology, these early moral communitarians agreed in subordinating political science and the state to Christian social philosophy and the community, the latter conceived as the bearer of a (divine) natural-law sociality and hence as morally self-governing (Dreitzel 1970: 127–9).

Rather than emerging from a liberal 'critique of state reason', the prototypical image of the self-governing community was the community of the faithful constructed by the political theologians of the rival confessions. This enabled them to argue that the state should compel church attendance; that censorship was a religious office; that heretics should forfeit civil rights; and that the church should be exempt from taxation and other civil obligations. The moral communitarians were, in fact, the intellectual shock-troops of confessionalisation and by far the more potent spokesmen for the increasingly mutually hostile confessional states. If the prototype of the self-governing community was indeed the confessional community, then the tension that Foucault identifies in the concept of population – as administrative object and as self-governing community – may be symptomatic not of a 'philosophical' split between kinds of political reason, but of the historical relation between juristic-statist and religious-communitarian modes of government.

Somewhat ironically, it appears that the main sovereignty doctrine active in the heyday of the confessional states was the natural-law 'popular' sovereignty doctrine of the religious communitarians. Machiavellian texts did not begin to appear in Germany until the end of the sixteenth century, and we have observed that the Christian cameralists ignored the issue of sovereignty and were repelled by the notion of reason of state. When, in the early seventeenth century, the first doctrines of reason of state and 'absolute' sovereignty were elaborated, they were oriented not to defending the prince's 'transcendent' or personal interest in the state but to a quite different end: the deconfessionalisation of politics. We can use this phrase to refer to a protracted and incomplete process – beginning in the early seventeenth century, gaining strength in the wake of the Thirty Years War, and continuing today – in which the instruments of political governance were intellectually and constitutionally separated from the instruments of religious discipline, and the state was reconstrued as the political apparatus of a secular civil order.

Rather than signifying a period of stasis, in which the dynamic of government was blocked by a residual sovereignty doctrine, the seventeenth century saw the elaboration of several novel doctrines of sovereignty and state-reason whose objective was to separate politics and state from religion and community. Horst Dreitzel's reconstruction of the political science of Henning Arnisaeus provides an exemplary account of one of these lines of doctrinal development. Arnisaeus was a professor of politics at the University of Helmstedt in Brunswick-Wolfenbüttel in the early seventeenth century, and later political adviser and court physician to the Danish king. His path to an 'absolute' conception of the state and a realist conception of politics lay through his training in the 'medical empiricism' of Paduan Aristotelianism. Arnisaeus' conceptions of sovereignty and the state were thus symptomatic not of princely interest but of a profound intellectual objectification of the political domain. This was carried out, in part, using metaphors derived from Galen's medical empiricism: the state is subject to pathologies and in need of preventive care and therapeutic intervention; the politician or political scientist is a type of doctor whose relation to the state is characterised by his expert knowledge of its organisation and functions and by his capacity for technical therapeutic intervention (Dreitzel 1970: 116–29).

It was in this manner that Arnisaeus came to formulate the end of politics, not as general moral and economic well-being, but rather as political order – meaning both the prevention of disorder and the execution of the 'order' or form of rule characteristic of a society, regardless of what kind of rule or society. Arnisaeus separated *civitas* or civil society from politics by treating society as the pre-state 'matter' on which politics goes to work in elaborating its object. *Civitas* consists of an order or society of families and its science is oeconomy. Politics is distinct from oeconomy in that the different sciences each have their own perspective and object, rather than a shared object like social life. The state is of a qualitatively different order to the household and is not its aggregate form. *Homo politicus* is thus distinct from *homo oeconomicus* and also *homo religiosus*. This leads to Arnisaeus' fundamental distinction between the good man and the good citizen. The politician is concerned only with the citizen from the point of view of legality, not with the man and the perspective of morality.

Arnisaeus' doctrines of reason of state and sovereignty drew a little on Machiavelli and much on Bodin but reshaped them both according to the requirements of his political science. If the state was invested with an unchallengeable supreme power this was due to the empirical end of politics itself – political order – which required the existence of an ultimate power in order to be realised. In distinguishing government from sovereignty, by stressing the 'specific finalities' of the art of government, Foucault seems not to have considered that sovereignty too might be determined by a local end, and that the very specificity of its end might be the source of its paramount character. But this was precisely the case in Arnisaeus' political science. According to Arnisaeus, the political order of a society was distinct from its social form and economic organisation; as politics is concerned only with the maintenance of an empirically given form of rule or domination, whatever the moral and economic complexion of society. Yet it is just this specific goal of politics that gives rise to the concept of sovereignty as ultimate power; for the preservation of political order can only be achieved by the domination of contending estates and powers, which necessitates the deployment of a power superior to all others (Dreitzel 1970: 170–88).

It was on this basis that Arnisaeus advised the prince to acquire such appurtenances of sovereignty as absolute legislative power, a monopoly of armed forces and weapons, and sole power to raise public revenues and appoint magistrates. More importantly for our immediate concerns, it was also on this basis that he rejected the natural-law and moral-philosophical bases of sovereignty proposed by his communitarian opponents, Tolosanus and Althusius. The state was not born to combat human sinfulness; nor did it issue from a contract between men possessed of a natural desire for sociality or, alternatively, fearful of a war of all against all. Rather, it was the empirical form in which the order of domination in any society was maintained. The statesman's task was thus not to lead his people to salvation or to function as the executor of the natural law inscribed in the communal will; it was simply to preserve the empirical political order against the various political pathologies arising from estate society and international rivalry. This could be done by anyone possessing the necessary political expertise and will, whatever their religious persuasion, including heathens and atheists. Given that any kind of community requires the exercise of power to preserve its order, it is possible to arrive at a conception of politics that is neutral with regard to the moral physiognomy of community and also with regard to constitutional form. When critics charged that, on his model, even a society of pirates could throw up a legitimate political order, Arnisaeus simply agreed, adding that most European states had been founded on piratical expropriation in any case – that was just the nature of states (Dreitzel 1970: 183).

Sovereignty and reason of state were thus integral to the political-scientific discipline through which Arnisaeus objectified political order. They were also indicative of the broad historical strategy served by this discipline: the deconfessionalisation or moral neutralisation of politics, sought by many intellectuals and statesmen confronted by the staggering carnage of religious civil war (Zeeden 1985: 281–4; Koselleck 1988). The intellectual supremacy of political order in Arnisaeus' political science did allow political action a degree of independence from communal moral norms. It meant, for example, that the prince was free to commit supra-legal acts like political murder, to the degree that such acts were necessary to forestall *coups d'état*. This was less a case of the ends justifying the means, though, than of the means being adopted independently of the demand for justifying moral ends – as technical measures governed by the empirical end of politics. This end did not provide the prince with *carte blanche* to pursue his personal interests. On the contrary, the pursuit of personal satisfaction and aggrandisement meant the neglect of politics as the expert-technical preservation of order, giving rise to the only ground Arnisaeus accepted for deposing the prince: tyranny, which signified just this neglect and failure on the prince's part (Dreitzel 1970: 240ff.).

Needless to say, Arnisaeus' political science incorporated several other doctrines and disciplines which also existed as independent historical movements in the process of deconfessionalisation. Lipsius' neostoicism sought to equip a political elite with the detached fortitude necessary to act in the name of social peace and in the face of religious zealotry (Lipsius 1939; Oestreich 1982). Arnisaeus though drew on Lipsian neo-stoicism, not to define the object of politics but for two other reasons: to construe the domain of civil (social) actions as morally 'indifferent' (as *adiaphora*) hence open to detheologised political rule; and as a political psychology for the statesman – a source of inner discipline required to calm his personal interests and moral passions so that he might attend to the object of politics in a suitably detached manner.

Something similar occurred with jurisprudential thought, which offered another means of expelling religion from the civil domain, via the substitution of positive legal regulation for confessional spiritual discipline. Again, Arnisaeus rejected natural-law constructions of the state in order to allow the prince to legislate on the basis of *Staatsräson*. All enacted law was positive law. At the same time though, he used the notion of a natural legal order both within families (in the area of sexual relations) and between them (forming a kind of natural *Rechtsstaat*) to ensure that the prince's decisionistic law-making would steer clear of some areas and would itself have a procedural-juridical form (Dreitzel 1970: 195–200).

Finally, in the area of cameralistics and administration, Arnisaeus differed from the Christian economics of Löhneyß and Seckendorff in that he did not accept the economic and moral welfare of the popu-lation as the goal of political action. The end of politics remained political order, pure and simple. The prince was required to attend the economic and moral welfare of the population only to the degree necessary for the preservation of this order. Economics thus formed part of 'political hygiene', together with moral education and the forestalling of *coups d'état*. Again, this was not because Arnisaeus was blind to the 'specific finalities' of the art of government, but because the specific finality of politics – the preservation of the state – took precedence. Dreitzel comments that Arnisaeus' treatment of government (*qua* administration) was fairly minimal because he considered it a sub-branch of politics requiring independent technical elaboration (Dreitzel 1970: 400–6).

Sovereignty and reason of state in Arnisaeus were thus symptomatic not of a mode of political reflection cut off from government by its 'transcendent' objectivity, but of one that subordinated the ends of gov-ernment to those of politics, as part of a deliberate strategy of deconfess-ionalisation. We have already suggested that the apparent duality in the concept of population, as object and subject of government, should be treated as symptomatic of the manner in which civil rule and religious 'self'-governance were merged by the communitarian intellectuals of the confessional state. It was Arnisaeus' uncompromising separation of the problem of political order from that of moral redemption that allowed him to quarantine the state as the instrument of political order from society as the domain of fratricidal moral communities. One of the consequences of this divorce was that Arnisaeus recognised no general or absolute norm of freedom, accepting only an array of concrete freedoms and matching duties related to the capacities required to perform particular 'offices' (familial, parental, commercial, civil, administrative, etc). For him, moral self-determination ('free will') was a religious ideal that did not belong in the political sphere, its moral absolutism rendering it incompatible with the program for politically neutralising the confessional communities. This program meant that there was to be no direct path from doctrines of moral self-governance to the emergence of 'liberal' freedoms in the political domain. When such freedoms did begin to appear it was not due to a recovery of the principle of self-governance but as a result of the process of neutralisation itself.

Uncivil Society

The distinctive feature of Foucault's sketch of liberalism is his recognition that it involves the extension of government rather than its curtailment – or, perhaps, its extension and curtailment. Unlike liberal-democratic histories and philosophies, his account is not immediately embarrassed by the fact that the 'liberalisation' of early-modern German societies – pre-eminently religious toleration, followed by various economic and social freedoms – resulted from the policy initiatives of authoritarian governments. Foucault does not attempt to escape this fact by consigning such developments to the pre-history of 'true liberalism'. Nor, unlike Immanuel Kant (Kant 1970) and his followers, does he attempt to sublimate it by invoking the metaphysical distinction between the empirical and the noumenal, thereby allowing authoritarian liberalism to be treated as a temporary concession to the citizenry's actual political incompetence pending the emergence of an ideal self-governing community. Instead, Foucault transforms the fact of authoritarian liberalism via a dialectic that establishes an equilibrium between the extension of government and the growth of liberal freedoms – the oxymoron for this dialectic being liberal government, government through self-government, the conduct of conduct.

As it eventuates, Foucault's philosophical-historical sublimation of authoritarian liberalism is not as unlike Kant's as it first seems. For, by focusing his dialectic in the duality of population as, alternatively, transparent and opaque to government, Foucault allows liberalism to gravitate to its usual intellectual home: in the space between government and the limits imposed on it by self-government. In doing so, he explicates the mix of authoritarian and liberal elements in early modern government by establishing an equilibrium between the theme of government engineering spheres of self-government to achieve its ends, and the theme of self-determining spheres (economy, civil society) using government to achieve theirs. The problem with the formula that results from this equilibrium – liberal government as the exercise of government through self-government – is that it may have no content apart from that bestowed by the dialectical exercise itself. There is some confirmation of this diagnosis in the fact that the mix of authoritarian and liberal elements in early modern German politics seems to have emerged not from the dialectic of government and self-government, but from a quite different and far more concrete historical source: the disaggregation of political and religious governance aimed at the political neutralisation of civil society. That, at least, is the case we will now sketch.

In making this case I will focus on the emergence of religious toleration. While having lost the moral priority ascribed to it by Ernst Troeltsch – who regarded the religious freedoms demanded by the Protestant sects as the basis of all civil freedoms – religious toleration retains, none the less, a certain temporal priority. It is not the primacy of conscience that is important in this regard but the more basic fact that before populations can acquire the rights associated with commerce, sociality and political participation they must first cease slaughtering each other in the name of God and morality. The emergence of religious toleration is a far more complex phenomenon than can be dealt with in an essay of this kind, deriving as it did from a wide variety of interacting sources. These included the role of German imperial politics in establishing a purely secular religious peace on the basis of *cuius regio eius religio*, and the 'inverted' reflection of this reality in natural-law doctrines of the 'extra-state' character of religion (Link 1987); the juridical construction of churches as political entities within the context of the treaties of Augsburg (1555) and Westphalia (1648), with the consequent relativisation of theological truth and acceptance of the 'permanence of heresy' (Heckel 1992); the pragmatic policies of paternalist monarchs seeking to pacify warring confessional communities in order to facilitate commerce and society (Benad 1983); the appearance of religious movements like Pietism, seeking salvation in private rather than socially-enforced religiosity (Sparn 1989); and the refashioning of 'pagan' intellectual doctrines and disciplines ('neo'-Aristotelianism, -Stoicism, -Epicureanism) aimed at detoxifying Christian moral rigorism, typically through the expansion of the domain of morally 'indifferent' things or *adiaphora* (Schneiders 1979). We can, however, briefly indicate the interaction of such sources in the doctrines and activities of a single figure, Christian Thomasius, whom we last saw exercising the better part of valour, hurrying from Leipzig to Halle to escape the moral communitarians.

Once settled in the law faculty at the University of Halle, the protean and indefatigable Thomasius continued his campaigning on a number of fronts: launching a never-ending series of disputations against his orthodox opponents; attacking the educational value of university metaphysics and scholastic moral philosophy; arguing for their relegation in favour of a private discipline of the passions (*Affektenlehre*) and a secular juristic education (Thomasius 1696; Thomasius 1709; Thomasius 1994); lecturing and writing extensively on ecclesiastical law and polity as part of his program to expel the church from the state and reconstitute it as a civil association (Thomasius 1740); and, as part of the same program, leading the public campaign against witchcraft trials and heresy hunting (Thomasius 1712). Given our concern with authoritarian liberalism, Thomasius' campaign against the legal prosecution of witches and magicians provides a convenient entry point; for this is often appealed to in accounts of Thomasius as a harbinger of liberalism and enlightenment.

In the course of his campaigning Thomasius argued that witchcraft was not a species of action open to legal restraint but a moral error – a corruption of the will and understanding – hence beyond external coercion and open only to private moral correction. The state should, therefore, abandon witchcraft trials and treat witches and sorcerers either as ordinary criminals (to the extent that they engaged in fraud and civil mischief) or as misguided souls to be left to the mercies of God and conscience. This was also the way he treated heresy, with the added sting that here the misguided souls often turned out to be bearers of true religion. Given this separation of law and morality, and the limitation of state action to the former, it is not surprising that Thomasius' campaign against witch trials has been seen as a proto-liberal effort to set limits to government in the name of individual freedom and human reason (Wolff 1963; Herrmann 1971; Cattaneo 1975).

Closer examination, though, shows that Thomasius' campaign had a quite different objective, as we can see in his *Kurtze Lehr-Sätze von dem Laster der Zauberey* (Brief Propositions on the Iniquity of Magic) (1712). Significantly, the immediate object of this polemic was his old enemy Carpzovius, who defended the prosecution and burning of witches on biblical and theological grounds, treating the civil law as a direct extension of religious commandments. Carpzovius can thus be seen as a late representative of the religious communitarianism characteristic of the confessional state. It was against this position that Thomasius launched his assault, in a series of arguments designed to show that legal regulation and spiritual discipline belong to different domains and cannot be merged without mutual corruption. It is in this context that we must see Thomasius' argument that witchcraft, as a moral error, cannot be subject to legal coercion and must instead be pushed outside the law into the sphere of private religious and moral counselling. The object of this argument was not to set limits to state action in order to make room for individual freedom, or for civil society conceived of as a locale for the exercise of individual economic interests. Rather, the purpose of confining legal regulation to conduct that jeopardises civil order was to eject the church from the legal system as a state instrumentality – to detach the moral from the political community, the Christian from the citizen.

We can see this in the larger framing and direction of the argument. First, Thomasius treats the belief in witchcraft and magic as a superstition encouraged by the church itself, as a means of exerting illegitimate power over the religious and civil life of the people. Carpzovius' appeal to biblical accounts of diabolical magic should be seen in this light. They represent a disgraceful use of fables suited to an earlier phase of Christian history (Thomasius 1712: 25–8). Next we should observe that Thomasius' criticisms of witchcraft trials were not based on general claims as to their irrational, inhumane or repressive character, but on a mix of religious and technical-legal arguments. Thomasius accepted that the devil exists, but only in a spiritual form, working through the corrupt will of the person. It was for this very reason, though, that the central evidentiary requirements of the witchcraft statutes – either the existence of a written or spoken diabolical pact or sexual congress with the devil – were unreliable; because the devil lacked the corporeal form required to enter into such relations with human beings (Thomasius 1712: 28–30). Finally, and most importantly for our concerns, in deploying the criterion of civil peace as the threshold for criminality Thomasius was not attempting to limit state action by appealing to moral freedom or personal interests. Rather, he was attempting to extend the power of the state by excising that part of the legal apparatus which provided a foothold for the power of the church: the category of 'moral crimes' such as witchcraft, magic and heresy. In other words, Thomasius' strategy was for the state to make a tactical withdrawal from the policing of moral crimes as a means of politically neutralising the church, while simultaneously rendering itself absolute by making the maintenance of its own political order into the ultimate end of legal regulation. Hence, Thomasius and Enno Rudolph Brenneysen argued that just as this end does not require subjects to be morally virtuous – it being 'enough that they refrain from outward iniquities in so far as they disturb the peace' – so neither is the 'prince as prince' bound to act on the basis of moral law, his office requiring only the preservation of civil order (Thomasius and Brenneysen 1696: 28). Thomasius thus arrived at a concept of sovereignty and reason of state similar to Arnisaeus', albeit via a different doctrinal and methodological route.

Thomasius' arguments against the prosecution of witches and heretics and his moves towards religious toleration are a good instance of the co-presence of authoritarian and liberal elements in early modern law and government. This mix cannot be understood though via Foucault's antinomy between an all-governing sovereignty and a self-governing community, or between the political transparency and opacity of population. The object of Thomasius' tactical withdrawal of the state from the moral sphere was not to allow the development of a domain of self-government that might set moral limits to the state. That was the aim of Carpzovius and before him Althusius, Tolosanus, Melanchthon and all the other moral communitarians who saw the secular state as illegitimate unless the prince functioned as the executor of God's natural law. Rather, Thomasius' object was to segregate the spheres of moral and political governance: the former to become the domain of personal ethical self-restraint, the latter to be freed from the moral claims of the churches and confessional communities, who would themselves be subject to a political rule oriented to the secular end of civil peace (Schneiders 1971: 239–89).

The move towards religious toleration that accompanied the political neutralisation of the confessions was thus not a step towards providing the state with a moral basis, by uncovering its limits in the 'fundamental' freedoms and rights of individual and community. Neither was it achieved by liberal theorists of civil society enacting the dialectic between juridical regulation and economic self-interest. In fact, toleration and civil society can themselves be regarded as by-products and instruments of the process of deconfessionalisation, carried out by the state in pursuit of civil order. It is in this light that we should see Thomasius' own ambivalence regarding toleration. This finds him some-times arguing for the complete disestablishment of the church and freedom of worship, and at other times for the establishment of a terri-torial church, but purely as an instrument of civil government, wielded by a state with no concern for theological truth (Dreitzel 1997: fn 14). Both arguments are instances of reason of state, as the degree of religious toleration would vary with the degree of political pacification of the confessional communities.

Recently, some historians have begun to question whether Thomasius was 'truly liberal' and whether he might not have been a closet absolutist (Klippel 1976; Luig 1980). The problem with this argument over whether Thomasius belongs with the heroes or villains is its shared assumption: the definition of 'true liberalism' in terms of individual rights based on moral self-determination and functioning as a transcendental limit on state action. If our historical argument is tenable then this assumption is simply inappropriate for understanding Thomasius' doctrines and activities and, more generally, the character of early modern authoritarian liberalism. I have suggested that what looks like the 'dialectic' between government and self-government is actually a symptom of the unresolved conflict between a deconfessionalised politics of state interest and a political theology based on the figure of self-governing moral community. It was, in fact, the deconfessionalising of politics and the political neutralisation of moral community that created the first freedom of religious toleration, as a by-product of the dismantling of the confessional state.

How then should we regard all those accounts that treat the state's creation of pacified 'liberal' spheres as, at best, a crude stop-gap pending the emergence of a true liberalism based in moral self-governance? It is possible that such accounts represent both a systematic forgetting of the real origins of liberal society in the process of political pacification, and the resurgence of moral-communitarian doctrines in the modern form of democratic republicanism. It is worth noting that some commentators are renewing the theme of a continuity between the absolute *Polizeistaat* and the liberal *Rechtsstaat*, seeing the latter as heir to separation of politics and society achieved by the former (Schiera 1992). Others have tied the 'liberal-democratic' forgetting of this inheritance to the morally unpalatable character of *Staatsräson* and the emergence of a split between this doctrine and the rights-based discourses of moral self-determination that began to dominate public political discourse in the late eighteenth century (Weinacht 1975; Koselleck 1988). This would certainly help to explain why an intellectual like Kant could propose a notion of democratic self-determination, deriving from the model of the community of souls, while safely ensconced in the bosom of a recently state-pacified society.

Conclusion

One way to situate Foucault's governmentality theme is to compare it with two opposed research paradigms that one finds in German accounts of the emergence of civil society. These paradigms differ in treating civil society as the outcome, respectively, of a social delimitation of the state, and a political neutralisation of confessional society. This difference in paradigms is partly disciplinary and methodological, as the former account tends to be broadly sociological – in tying political and religious relations to evolutionary developments in economy and society – while the latter tends to be political-scientific and jurisprudential, in treating social relations as artefacts of political improvisation and juridical decision. But the difference is also theoretical and ethical, as the sociology of civil society tends to see it in terms of a progressive dialectic between social forces and moral imperatives, whereas the political-juridical account tends to have a more disenchanted and empirical view: civil society seen as the by-product of political pacification. Jürgen Habermas' (1974; 1983) communications-theoretic view of civil society is perhaps the best known contemporary German version of the ethical-sociological paradigm, although the use of this paradigm most relevant to our immediate concerns is to be found in a rewarding book by Jutta Brückner (1977). The political-juridical paradigm can be seen in works by Koselleck (1982; 1988) and Schmitt (1985a; 1985b), as well as in the works of Horst Dreitzel, some of which I have drawn on in this chapter.

Given this broad division of paradigms where should we locate Foucault's genealogy of liberalism? Somewhat surprisingly, it seems to fall largely within the sociology of civil society. The main reason for saying so is that, like Habermas and Brückner, Foucault places his emphasis on the 'social' delimitation of the state, effectively ignoring the political-juridical neutralisation of confessional society and the zones of regulated freedom arising from it. This is also the context in which to see Foucault's marginalisation of questions of sovereignty and the juridical domain more generally. Finally, I can suggest that Foucault's historical schema for governmentality is dialectical and evolutionary rather than empirical and 'decisionistic'. It treats liberalism as emerging in the wake of a 'splitting' of the *Polizeistaat*'s 'transcendent' unification of knowledge and government, and as ushering in an 'immanent' dialectical reflection on the limits of government from within government. This concept of liberal government in terms of an oscillation between opposed political rationalities is, of course, a long way from Thomasius' program for constructing authoritarian-liberal freedoms through the deconfessionalisation and juridification of confessional society.

Notes

This chapter originated in a series of energetic and enjoyable discussions with Graham Burchell and Nikolas Rose in 1993–94. Its final form has benefited from comments by Jeffrey Minson and David Saunders, further comments by Nikolas Rose and the suggestions of the editors.

1   For a general account of Christian cameralism, see Benad (1983).

2   One of the virtues of Schilling's social history is that it does not treat this convergence as uniform or inevitable, as tends to happen in those accounts that argue for a natural alliance between the 'repressive' theology of Lutheranism and the authoritarian politics of the absolute state. The confessionalisation of a community could also lead to its resisting the claims of the territorial prince, particularly if he belonged to another faith. This was the case in seventeenth-century Lippe, where a Lutheran urban community resisted the corporatist program of a Calvinist prince (Schilling 1988a). Where the convergence of confessionalisation and territorial state-building did take place – on the common ground of forming citizens and Christians – it did so with an intensity beyond the comprehension and control of the theologians and politicians involved.

3   This account of Löhneyß and Seckendorff is drawn from Dreitzel 1970; 160–9, with supplementary material from Schilling 1988b and Brückner 1977.

4   Veit Ludwig von Seckendorff, *Teutscher Fürstenstaat*, p. 57, quoted in Dreitzel 1970: 247.

References

Benad, M., 1983. *Toleranz als Gebot christlicher Obrigkeit. Das Büdinger Patent von 1712*, Hildesheim: Gerstenberg Verlag.

Brückner, J., 1977. *Staatswissenschaften, Kameralismus und Naturrecht: Ein Beitrag zur Geschichte der Politischen Wissenschaft im Deutschland des späten 17. und frühen 18. Jahrhunderts*, München: C. H. Beck.

Cattaneo, M. A., 1975. 'Staatsräsonlehre und Naturrecht im strafrechtlichen Denken des Samuel Pufendorf und des Christian Thomasius' in R. Schnur (ed.), *Staatsräson: Studien zur Geschichte eines politischen Begriffs*, Berlin: Duncker and Humblot, pp. 427–40.

Dreitzel, H., 1970. *Protestantischer Aristotelismus und absoluter Staat: Die 'Politica' des Henning Arnisaeus (ca.1575–1636)*, Wiesbaden: Franz Steiner.

Dreitzel, H., 1997. 'Christliche Aufklärung durch fürstlichen Absolutismus. Thomasius und die Destruktion des frühneuzeitlichen Konfessionsstaates' in F. Vollhardt (ed.), *Christian Thomasius*, Tübingen: Niemayer.

Foucault, M., 1980. *Power/Knowledge: Selected Interviews and Other Writings 1972–1977*, ed. C. Gordon, New York: Pantheon Books.

Foucault, M., 1981. 'Omnes et singulatim: towards a criticism of "Political Reason"' in S. McMurrin (ed.), *The Tanner Lectures on Human Values*, vol. II, Salt Lake City: University of Utah Press, pp. 225–54.

Foucault, M., 1991. 'Governmentality' in G. Burchell, C. Gordon and P. Miller (eds.) *The Foucault Effect: Studies in Governmentality*, London: Harvester/ Wheatsheaf, pp. 87–104.

Gordon, C., 1991. 'Governmental rationality: an introduction' in G. Burchell, C. Gordon and P. Miller (eds.), pp. 1–52.

Grunert, F., 1997. 'Zur aufgeklärten Kritik am theokratischen Absolutismus. Der Streit zwischen Hector Gottfried Masius und Christian Thomasius über Ursprung und Begründung der summa potestas' in F. Vollhardt (ed.), *Christian Thomasius*, Tübingen: Niemeyer.

Habermas, J., 1974. *Strukturwandel der Offentlichkeit*, Frankfurt: Suhrkamp.

Habermas, J., 1983. *Moralbewusstsein und kommunikatives Handeln*, Frankfurt: Suhrkamp.

Heckel, M., 1983. *Deutschland im konfessionellen Zeitalter*, Göttingen: Vandenhoeck & Ruprecht.

Heckel, M., 1992. 'Religionsbann und landesherrliches Kirchenregiment' in H.-C. Rublack (ed.), *Die lutherische Konfessionalisierung in Deutschland*, Gütersloh: Gerd Mohn, pp. 130–62.

Herrmann, H., 1971. 'Das Verhältnis von Recht und Pietistischer Theologie bei Christian Thomasius', PhD thesis, Christian-Albrechts-Universität zu Kiel.

Hsia, R. P.-C., 1989. *Social Discipline in the Reformation: Central Europe 1550–1750*, London: Routledge.

Kant, I., 1970. 'On the common saying: "This may be true in theory, but it does not apply in practice"', trans. H. B. Nisbet in *Kant: Political Writings*, ed. H. Reiss, Cambridge: Cambridge University Press, pp. 61–92.

Klippel, D., 1976. *Politische Freiheit und Freiheitsrechte im deutschen Naturrecht des 18. Jahrhunderts*, Paderborn.

Koselleck, R., 1982. 'Aufklärung und die Grenzen ihrer Toleranz' in T. Rendtorff (ed.), *Glaube und Toleranz: Das theologische Erbe der Aufklärung*, Gütersloh: Gütersloher Verlagshaus Mohn.

Koselleck, R., 1988. *Critique and Crisis: Enlightenment and the Pathogenesis of Modern Society*, Oxford: Berg.

Lieberwirth, R., 1953. 'Christian Thomasius' Leipziger Streitigkeiten', *Wissenschaftliche Zeitschrift der Martin-Luther-Universität Halle-Wittenberg (Gesellschafts- und sprachwissenschaftliche Reihe)* 3: 155–9.

Link, C., 1987. 'Naturrechtliche Grundlagen des Grundrechtsdenkens in der deutschen Staatsrechtslehre des 17. und 18. Jahrhunderts' in *Grund- und Freiheitsrechte von der ständischen zur spätburgerlichen Gesellschaft*, ed. G. Birtsch, Göttingen: Vandenhoeck and Ruprecht, pp. 215–33.

Lipsius, J., 1939. *Of Constancie*, trans. John Stradling, New Brunswick NJ: Rutgers University Press.

Luig, K., 1980. 'Zur Bewertung von Christian Thomasius' Strafrechtslehren als Ausdruck liberaler politischer Theorie', *Studia Leibnitiana* 12: 243–52.

Oestreich, G., 1982. *Neostoicism and the Early Modern State*, trans. David McLintock, Cambridge: Cambridge University Press.

Reinhard, W., 1983. 'Zwang zur Konfessionalisierung? Prolegomena zu einer Theorie des konfessionellen Zeitalters', *Zeitschrift für Historische Forschung* 10: 257–77.

Schiera, P., 1992. 'Polizeibegriff und Staatlichkeit im aufgeklärten Absolutismus. Der Wandel des Staatsschutzes und die Rolle der Wissenschaft', *Aufklärung. Interdisziplinäre Halbjahresschrift zur Erforschung des 18. Jahrhunderts und seiner Wirkungsgeschichte* 7: 85–100.

Schilling, H., 1981. *Konfessionskonflikt und Staatsbildung: Eine Fallstudie über das Verhältnis von religiösem und sozialem Wandel in der Frühneuzeit am Beispiel der Grafschaft Lippe*, Gütersloh: Gerd Mohn.

Schilling, H., 1988a. 'Between the territorial state and urban liberty: Lutheranism and Calvinism in the County of Lippe', in R. P.-C. Hsia (ed.), *The German People and the Reformation*, Ithaca: Cornell University Press, pp. 263–84.

Schilling, H., 1988b. 'Die Konfessionalisierung im Reich: Religiöser und gesellschaftlicher Wandel in Deutschland zwischen 1555 und 1620', *Historische Zeitschrift* 246: 1–45.

Schilling, H., 1989. 'Sündenzucht und frühneuzeitliche Sozialdisziplinierung: Die calvinistische, presbyteriale Kirchenzucht in Emden vom 16. bis 19. Jahrhundert' in G. Schmidt (ed.), *Stände und Gesellschaft im Alten Reich*, Stuttgart: Franz Steiner Verlag, pp. 265–302.

Schmitt, C., 1985a. *Political Theology: Four Concepts on the Concept of Sovereignty*, trans. George Schwab, Cambridge Mass.: MIT Press.

Schmitt, C., 1985b. *The Crisis of Parliamentary Democracy*, trans. Ellen Kennedy, Cambridge Mass.: MIT Press.

Schneiders, W., 1971. *Naturrecht und Liebesethik. Zur Geschichte der praktischen Philosophie im Hinblick auf Christian Thomasius*, Hildesheim: Olms Verlag.

Schneiders, W., 1979. 'Vernunft und Freiheit: Christian Thomasius als Aufklärer', *Studia Leibnitiana* 11: 3–21.

Sparn, W., 1989. 'Auf dem Wege zur theologischen Aufklärung in Halle: Von Johann Franz Budde zu Siegmund Jakob Baumgarten' in N. Hinske (ed.), *Zentren der Aufklärung I. Halle: Aufklärung und Pietismus*, Heidelberg: Verlag Lambert Schneider, pp. 71–89.

Thomasius, C., 1696. *Ausübung der Sittenlehre*, Hildesheim: Georg Olms.

Thomasius, C., 1709. *Grund-Lehren des Natur- und Völcker-Rechts, nach dem sinnlichen Begriff aller Menschen vorgestellet*, Halle.

Thomasius, C., 1712. *Kurtze Lehr-Sätze von dem Laster der Zauberey*, Frankfurt and Leipzig.

Thomasius, C., 1740. *Vollständige Erläuterung der Kirchenrechts-Gelahrtheit*, Frankfurt and Leipzig.

Thomasius, C., 1994. *Einleitung zur Hof-Philosophie*, Hildesheim: Olms.

Thomasius, C. and Brenneysen, E. R., 1696. *Das Recht evangelischer Fürsten in theologischen Streitigkeiten*, Halle: Christoph Salfeld Verlag.

Weinacht, P.-L., 1975. 'Fünf Thesen zum Begriff der Staatsräson: Die Entdeckung der Staatsräson für die deutsche politische Theorie (1604)' in R. Schnur (ed.), *Staatsräson: Studien zur Geschichte eines politischen Begriffs*, Berlin: Duncker and Humblot, pp. 65–72.

Wolff, H. M., 1963. *Die Weltanschauung der deutschen Aufklärung in geschichtlicher Entwicklung*, Bern: A. Francke.

Zeeden, E. W., 1977. *Hegemonialkriege und Glaubenskämpfe 1556–1648*, Frankfurt: Propyläen Verlag.

Zeeden, E. W., 1985. *Konfessionsbildung: Studien zur Reformation, Gegenreformation und katholischen Reform*, Stuttgart: Klett-Cotta.

Index

compiled by Robert Hyslop

Endurance Techniques

Endurance Techniques

Chris McNab

CHANCELLOR
PRESS

Copyright © 2001 Amber Books Ltd

ISBN 0-7537-0408-0

This edition published in 2001 by
Chancellor Press
An imprint of Bounty Books
A division of the Octopus Publishing Group Ltd,
2–4 Heron Quays,
London,
E14 4JP

Editorial and design by
Amber Books Ltd
Bradley's Close
74–77 White Lion Street
London N1 9PF

Project editor: Charles Catton
Editor: Siobhan O'Connor
Design: Hawes Design
Illustrations: Tony Randell and Patrick Mulrey

Printed in Portugal

Contents

CHAPTER ONE

The Will to Survive

In the martial arts, the mental state should remain the same as normal. In ordinary circumstances as well as when practising martial arts, let there be no change in the state of mind – with the mind open and direct, neither tense nor unfocused, centring the thoughts so that there is no imbalance, calmly relax your mind, and savour this moment of peace.

Miyamoto Musashi,
The Book of Five Rings *(1643)*

Despite this opening quotation's mystical ring, it is actually about the brutal art of killing. It was written in the 17th century by the samurai warrior Miyamoto Musashi. Musashi was no detached philosopher – he killed his first man at the age of 13 – and he was intimately acquainted with the mental ability required to take the life of another individual and to guard your own in a violent duel. His vision was a strange mix of peace and aggression. In combat, he said, the mind should be quiet rather than angry, responding to attacks naturally without predicting results, the state of calm allowing the samurai to see everything clearly and not become clouded by furious emotion.

Musashi's recommendations for developing mental endurance in combat – the theme of this book – were practised by few in history and mastered by even fewer. Yet what Musashi was exploring was the fact that, in the critical seconds of combat, the mental state of the fighter can have a more decisive effect on the outcome of the fight than the weapons he wields. This was a conclusion to which the great military leader Sun Tzu also came, some 1500 years before Musashi, in relation to the performance of officers:

If officers are not thoroughly drilled, they will be anxious and confused in battle; if generals are not competently trained, they will suffer mental anguish when they face the enemy.
Sun Tzu, **The Art of War**

Here, Sun Tzu comes at the issue of mental performance from a different angle to Musashi, that of training. Training, Sun Tzu implies, should accustom the soldier's mind to face combat with resolution and not buckle under the impact of violence and chaos. Only when the mind is disciplined can the body follow it into battle.

Both Sun Tzu and Musashi were writing during the days when steel held in the hand still decided the outcome of many battles. Yet, even though there is an immeasurable contrast between those battles of the ancient past and the ultra hi-tech conflicts of the present, the fact remains that the role of the combat soldier is one of the most psychologically demanding professions. Whatever the period of history, the soldier in action must not only cope psychologically with the traumatic visions of death and mutilation surrounding him, but he must also come to terms with the fact that he himself may die or have to kill. On top of this, he must retain focus on his mission, staying sharp and responsive in the midst of incredible chaos, noise and aggression.

For those who master this level of mental control in war, the rewards can be extraordinary. It has long been noted by military strategists that a small group of highly motivated, focused and resilient men can overwhelm or resist a much larger group

lacking such qualities. During Germany's early Blitzkrieg actions against the Low Countries in World War II, for example, it took only 85 highly trained and ruthless Fallschirmjäger paratroopers to capture the Belgian fortress Eben Emael, despite the fact that Eben Emael had a garrison of up to 2000 men, some 4.5km (2.7miles) of underground passages and a vast array of heavy gun, anti-aircraft and machine-gun emplacements. Similarly, when entire Iraqi companies encountered tiny SAS units during the Gulf War, so effective was the SAS response that panicked Iraqi soldiers reported that battalion-strength forces had attacked them.

The examples of mental force over physical strength are legion, yet our actual understanding of the relationship between mental capacity and combat ability is fairly recent, beginning in earnest during World War I. This book focuses on bringing out the lessons of nearly 100 years of research. Through concentrating on the fundamental aspects of military mental performance – resistance to combat stress, tactical intelligence, leadership and so on – we will look at the techniques derived to achieve the optimum state of mind for military efficiency. Some are fairly obvious; for instance, regular sleep must be observed to prevent deterioration in decision-making abilities and morale. Yet the research has also uncovered the unusual; for example, viewing an attacking aircraft through a hand formed like a telescope allows the viewer to make a more accurate judgement of its range. What is common to all the techniques included here is that they were born from the hard experience of the battlefield and thus are known to work in the most abject of circumstances.

THE CODES OF WAR

Prior to the 20th century, there was little explicit focus on mental development in the world's armed forces. The exception to this could well be the samurai tradition already noted. As well as practising Buddhist techniques of 'self-emptying' – living under the expectation of death and suffering until both of these influences held no fear – the samurai followed the code of bushido. One of the clearest descriptions of bushido came from Nitobe Inazo in 1905, who distilled centuries of samurai tradition into six virtues to which the samurai should aspire. These were duty (*giri*), humanity (*ninyo*), strength of spirit (*fudo*), magnanimity (*doryo*), resolution (*shiki*) and generosity (*ansha*). By ascribing to this set of values, the samurai, it was supposed, would not only attain moral virtue, but his mind would also attain the strength and power necessary for the warrior.

The code of bushido developed over centuries as a set of values which distinguished the warrior from those were not members of the elite. In varying ways, it is a form of 'mental training' through example that has accompanied elite soldiers from the most ancient of times until around the late-19th century. Casting our view back into the realms of Greek and Roman mythology, the Homeric and Virgilian heroes of Ajax, Achilles, Odysseus and Aeneas were archetypal warriors who acted in ancient society as models for what the warrior should be. This was, in effect, mental training through aspiring to be like these great figures. Uniting such elites as Xerxes' 'Immortals' of the fifth century BC, the Roman Praetorian guard, the Islamic warriors of the seventh century AD and Viking and Norman raiders is the principle that mental preparedness for combat is something learnt by emulating the warriors of old and striving to live up to the virtues of courage, determination and ruthless strength.

This trend is particularly visible in the standards of 'chivalry' which governed the field conduct of knights during the medieval period. Chivalry originated as a code around 1100 and acted like a form of bushido that was less death-centred. Values such as courage, loyalty, prudence and honour were

Samurai warrior

The Samurai saw combat as a natural extension of a strong and calm spirit, and they trained themselves to accept, and thus overcome, any fear of death.

Trooper 22 SAS

The SAS have gained their reputation not from ruthlessness in action, although this is present, but through the intelligence they bring to tactical manoeuvres.

mixed with stealth and intelligence in attack, and formed a set of expected behaviour which acted like a form of psychological training. How effective it was is difficult to tell, as much of the evidence comes from embellished myths and legends, rather than battlefield accounts. In a sense, however, this type of 'mental training' persisted until the end of World War I and perhaps even lingered into the next war.

The absurd image of the British Army officer leading his men at walking pace into the lethal spray of German heavy machine-guns carrying only a riding crop is a legacy of the supposed warrior virtues of the noble classes. Yet the hideous damage that the new weapons inflicted on the belief that spirit could triumph over technology was irreparable. The Western Front produced a massive increase in psychiatric casualties, with shell shock and personality disorders. This awoke Western medical authorities to the fact that the mind of a soldier could be damaged just like a physical organ.

MILITARY PSYCHOLOGY

The seeds of military psychology were sown when the nature of warfare itself changed in the early part of the 20th century. The sheer force of new military tactics and weapons, with huge

Typical equipment of the Spetsnaz soldier

Handling such a range of equipment requires excellent skills in organisation, technical knowledge and combat awareness, as well as a strong back.

Anti-tank Missile

Rucksack

Radio

Sniper Rifle

Grenades

Claymore Mine

Anti-personnel Mine

Radar Detector

Rations

Water Bottle

A range of SAS equipment

During the Gulf War, the SAS often carried 40kg (88lb) operational packs, which can lead to a lack of focus and concentration if the soldier is not fit enough to cope.

Bergen Rucksack

Anti-aircraft Missile

Silenced Sub-machine Gun

Claymore Mine

Radio

Maps and Compass

First Aid Kit

Knife

Survival Kit

Torch

Wire

Escape Belt

the qualities of the elite leader to focusing on the experience of the common soldier. As total war seemed to produce a disproportionate level of psychiatric casualties amongst these men, medical answers had to be found to prevent and cure the drain on manpower through combat fatigue and traumatic reactions. All of a sudden, the psychological collapse of a soldier during combat became an issue of mental health, rather than being about his lack of 'moral fibre' or 'manliness'.

One of the earliest nations to catch on to this message was Russia. During the Russo-Japanese War of 1904–05, Russian psychologists and mental health experts actually went to the front with the combatants to offer treatment. By World War I, psychologists were increasingly becoming part of regular army units, giving treatments to mentally injured soldiers which ranged from the considerate to the barbaric (soldiers struck dumb by trauma, for instance, were often given electric shocks of increasing severity until they spoke again).

destruction and mobility becoming the dominant conditions, meant that massed armies were required on a scale never before seen. This brought about a shift of emphasis from

Between 1915 and 1916, the Allied Medical Services recognised that most incidences of shell shock were actually cases of psychological collapse, and should be treated as such. When the United States entered the war in 1917, the American Psychological Association was already considering ways of applying psychological testing and treatment to shape battlefield performance. Mental tests such as the US Army's Alpha and Beta tests were instigated to screen recruits for mental characteristics and place them in the appropriate military jobs. Testing then proliferated into other areas of military life. Leadership, intelligence, tactical skills, emotional resilience – all aspects of the military personality came under the psychologist's gaze. It should be noted that there was no equivalent acceptance of psychological disorder from the German military. The idea that the German soldier should become mentally incapacitated was anathema to the German warrior culture and so psychological casualties were generally treated either as cowards or as physically damaged in some way. This outlook persisted throughout World War II; some 15,000 German soldiers were court-martialled and executed for what we now know as psychiatric disorders.

GROWING SUCCESS

As treatments advanced – by the end of the war, 60 per cent of Allied psychiatric casualties were successfully returned to the front – so did the understanding of how to design training and military organisation to prevent mental problems and produce more efficient fighters. The interwar period was marked by a reduction in investigation into military psychology in general, although the postwar problems of many soldiers returning to civilian life did provide a new vision of the longer term effects of combat trauma. Yet the defining moment of the development of military psychology was just around the corner.

World War II produced an explosion of psychological research on an unparalleled scale; indeed, military psychology became the largest sector of mental health studies in the United States. War was growing ever more complex in its weaponry, tactics and communications, and the mental demands this produced led to a major investment in improving the performance of the individual combat soldier. After some of the early battles in North Africa, the Allies were shocked at just what effects modern warfare could have on the common soldier. Aid stations started to receive men who had to be led around by the hand like children, or who would defecate uncontrollably at any sudden, loud noise. Others were rendered completely catatonic or would lose the ability to speak or to move one of their limbs.

New programmes of treatment were designed to cope with these terrible mental injuries. On the whole, these programmes saw a high percentage of casualties restored to health, but they were much needed. Of all Allied medical evacuations, 23 per cent were psychiatric (compared with only six per cent in the subsequent Korean War). Although in part owing to the hugely traumatic nature of total war, this was also because the massive level of conscription allowed a greater number of personality disorders to slip past screening into the military ranks. Greater questions were being raised over the whole screening process in recruitment and a truism was discovered that holds good to this day – it is impossible to predict from screening who will submit to combat trauma and who will not (although present-day analysis does give a higher degree of certainty).

The treatment of psychiatric casualties was naturally an urgent priority; however, now military psychology was not exclusively about preventing mental problems, but also focused on making the human machine perform at its best in a multitude of roles. Thus, the range of topics studied greatly expanded to include morale, environmental effects on fighting ability, the psychological effects of different weapons, the use of propaganda, selecting personnel for special missions and personality types. World War II gave the 20th century much of its understanding about how the human mind works in combat. It also introduced many common terms for psychological conditions related to soldiering. Perhaps the most significant of these was 'exhaustion', a term which referred to psychological and physical disintegration beyond the limits of individual's endurance. The great distances and varied terrain covered in World War II made this an acute problem; the attempt to solve it led to a better appreciation of how an unstable mind and an exhausted body feed off one another. Also, apart from the obvious strains of physical effort and combat shock, psychologists and psychiatrists noted many non–combat-related phenomena which contributed to mental disturbance in soldiers. These included factors such as the quality of leadership, the access to comrade support, separation from family and home, and also the problems that could arise from nervousness about future combat.

INTEGRAL MENTAL TRAINING AND TREATMENT

When World War II ended, psychological assessment, training and treatment were a fully-fledged and integral part of military life. Not only was there a much better comprehension of what was required to keep men sane and stable in the 'fog of war', but there was also a new understanding of how to foster the soldier's mind as part of his essential weaponry. Both these lessons went on to inform training in conflicts such as Korea and Vietnam, and with each new conflict fresh insights were gained into the art of war and soldiering. Work during World War II had laid the foundations for much of our understanding about phenomena such as combat stress, exhaustion (or 'combat fatigue', as it became known), leadership qualities and interpersonal influences on mental state; however, post–World War II military conflicts have presented demands of a type rarely encountered prior to 1945.

Vietnam was, perhaps, the watershed between the old and new style of wars. US combat soldiers in Vietnam faced many unusual and troubling pressures. First, they experienced a form of conflict in which an ambush would wrench them from extreme boredom to extreme violence in seconds, only to subside quickly and leave nothing but the horrors of the injured and the dead behind. Occasionally, full-scale Vietcong or NVA attacks would interrupt this pattern. In places such as the Central Highlands and areas around the DMZ, these attacks made battlefield landscapes akin to those of France and Belgium during World War I. As the war lost its popular support worldwide, the soldiers in the field came to feel that they did not have the backing of the people at home. Drugs and alcohol were freely available and the logistical might of the United States made the soldiers live in a curious no-man's land between third-world poverty and the painful nostalgia of the comforts of home. Weaponry became ever more brutal and the Vietnamese heat kept soldiers teetering on the brink of sunstroke and dehydration.

The much-publicised atrocities committed by US soldiers in Vietnam awoke many to the fact that wars and soldiering had changed utterly. Although actual numbers of psychiatric casualties in Vietnam were relatively small – about five per cent of the medical evacuations – the cohesion amongst units often seemed lost and this was taking a dramatic psychological toll on performance. 'Fragging' – the killing of one's officers using fragmentation grenades – reached almost epidemic proportions in some units. Also, standard military training did not prepare soldiers for the great cultural transformation of operating in Southeast Asia. By the end of the conflict, military psychologists realised that they would have to broaden the focus of their work. Cultural attitudes, feelings about race and gender, the relationship between

British Army Intelligence Test, 1940s

In the example given to the right, the total of each row is 12. This is the same whether the row is formed horizontally, vertically or diagonally.

Complete the boxes laid out below, following the same principles, but to the totals given underneath each of the boxes.

3	2	7
8	4	0
1	6	5

8		
6		2

Total: 15

	9	
3		7

Total: 27

16		4
		10

Total: 39

2		
	3	

Use 2,3,4,5,6,7,8,9,10 Total: 18

Use 4,5,6,7,8,9,10 Total: 24

Use 0,5,10,15,20,25,30,35,40 Total: 60

drugs and fighting ability, morale and political cause, the strain of handling advanced technology – many new factors fed into the understanding of how soldiers perform and how treatment and training techniques had to keep pace. Vietnam focused attention on the soldier in his broadest possible context, from his beliefs to his bravery, examining how the qualities he possesses fit into the operational situation.

The lessons of Vietnam were taken forwards into subsequent conflicts. Following wars such as those fought in the Falklands and the Gulf, in recent years the focus has shifted towards realistic training methods which partially 'battleproof' the soldier and make him less shocked by the actuality of combat. Most military mental training is now designed to produce soldiers who are intelligent and thoughtful individuals, with adaptability taking equal importance with courage and strength of mind. The modern soldier must have the mental capacity to switch from aggressive fighting patrols to food distribution in a matter of hours, even minutes, a phenomenon that the US Marines label the 'three-block war' – you can literally go from combat to non-combat duties in the space of three blocks. Today, peacekeeping and humanitarian actions are presenting the

psychological challenge of how to keep soldiers motivated in combat areas where they are not actually allowed to participate in the fighting, even if grave crimes against civilians are being committed within visual range. In light of the recent experiences in Yugoslavia and Somalia, this will no doubt be a theme of investigation for many years to come.

THE ELITE FIGHTING MIND

Somewhere along the line, all soldiers from most nations have benefited from the knowledge of military psychology. Yet where do the elite soldiers, those at the very top of military practice, fit into this equation? In one sense, it is difficult to know, as elite units such as the US Navy SEALs, the British SAS, the Israeli Sayeret Mat'kal and the Italian Combusin are among the most secretive organisations in the world. Most elite unit research into psychological techniques is highly classified, even work that was done back in the 1940s and 1950s. Yet details have started to filter down through autobiographies, independent research and, most importantly, those units which have an elite capability, but which do not have the same protective cloak of secrecy. Examples would include the US Marines, the US Rangers, the Royal Marines, the Israeli and British paratroopers, the Italian Alpini and many other infantry and specialist fighting squads around the world. Such units tend to have a strong intellectual interchange with other special forces and actively borrow techniques. Thus these techniques become more visible to the outside world.

In order to understand the nature of elite unit psychological training, it is worth reminding ourselves why such units were born in the first place. Special forces – units created to perform advanced duties beyond the capability of the average soldier – have been with us since the beginning of military history in one form or another. Yet, prior to the 20th century, elite units tended to take

Choosing semi/full-automatic fire

Psychologists found that at under 25m (82ft) soldiers achieved better kill ratios with automatic fire, and over 50m (164ft) with semi-automatic.

their place alongside the ranks of other units in conventional battles. Special forces as we know them today are another matter. In the immediate aftermath of World War II, many of the elite units that had been developed for covert operations were disbanded, including the SAS. However, the Cold War, and upheaval in the colonies of European nations quickly followed the war's end. Short of outright war in many instances, military establishments around the globe soon recognised the need for small groups of soldiers with supreme fighting ability to fight the new wars of counterterrorism, counterinsurgency, small-scale wars and espionage. Many units would be created in response to a specific international challenge, only achieving permanence once they had proved their ruthless worth.

Especially pertinent to our discussion of military psychology is the emergence of US Army Special Forces in the early 1950s. In 1952, the Psychological Warfare Centre was established, its base at Fort Bragg, North Carolina. The remit of psychological warfare extended into the realms of counterinsurgency and spying, and thus the centre gathered units of uniquely trained men to perform such missions. The growth in such units provided the context for the emergence of official special forces squads and,

on 20 June 1952, the 10th Special Forces Group (SFG) was established at Fort Bragg, the 77th SFG emerging just over a year later.

The link between psychological warfare and special forces suggests the distinct requirements of elite forces for men and women who exhibit exceptional intelligence, as well as almost superhuman endurance in the execution of their missions. The US Army Special Forces would go on to prove these qualities in Vietnam during their main operational programme, the setting up of Civilian Irregular Defense Groups (CIDG) in co-operation with South Vietnamese civilians, the ARVN and the Montagnard mountain dwellers. This programme not only required counterinsurgency skills in a jungle environment, but also necessitated formidable social skills in building understanding and trust with the Vietnamese. The enormous flexibility demanded of the Green Berets, the frequent political sensitivity of their missions and the self-reliance required to complete such missions meant that only the best could pass through training to become full-fledged Special Forces warriors.

The US Army Special Forces soldier is typical of the requirements for elite soldiers worldwide. An SAS soldier, for example, can be expected to possess one or two extra

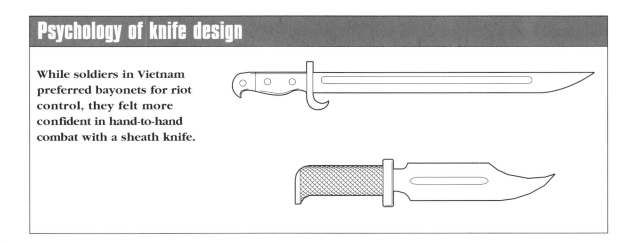

Psychology of knife design

While soldiers in Vietnam preferred bayonets for riot control, they felt more confident in hand-to-hand combat with a sheath knife.

Judging distance

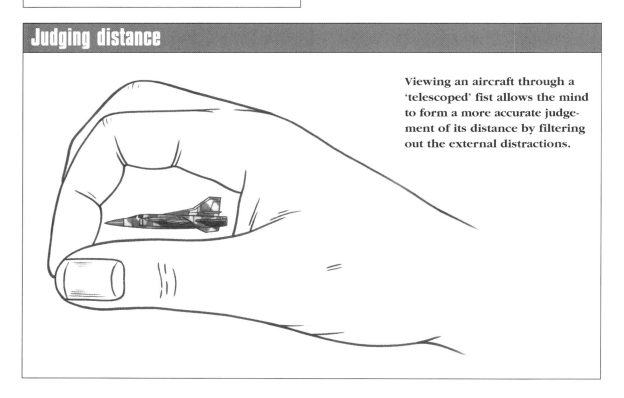

Viewing an aircraft through a 'telescoped' fist allows the mind to form a more accurate judgement of its distance by filtering out the external distractions.

languages and specialist understanding of military applications such as communications, demolitions, combat medicine, parachuting, diving or marksmanship. Naturally, recruiters for such units look for individuals with minds that can handle such a multitude of skills in a life-or-death setting.

The actual psychological testing procedures of elite units are highly confidential. What we do know is that there is a defined body of psychological qualities that are common to most elite squads. This is not to say that there is conformity amongst elite personnel – indeed, special forces soldiers are usually selected on the basis of their individuality – but all elite soldiers will be found to possess the following attributes.

Intelligence

All soldiers must display intelligence, but, in elite units, it must be to a heightened

degree. Even in large-scale elite units such as the US Marines, with 172,000 personnel on active duty, about 90 per cent of their entrants are high school graduates. This predisposes the Marine Corps towards excellent decision-making skills at every level of rank and operation. Also, studies conducted in the 1950s discovered that men who committed themselves to battle with greater motivation had a mean IQ of 91, whereas those that hung back from the fight or displayed indecision had a mean IQ of 78. Ironically, in most regular military units, those with lower IQs are usually sent into combat; however, a capable intelligence is a must for elite units.

Self-Control

Self-control is perhaps the primary virtue of a special forces soldier. Whereas regular military forces often operate in large-scale units or movements, elite units tend to work in small squads or even as individuals. This means that each soldier must be able to execute a demanding mission with little or no external pressure to perform. Instead, his or her self-discipline will be the impetus behind the mission's success. Elite forces can also spend a great deal of time in static observation and reconnaissance missions, so must be able to deal with the crushing boredom of long, solitary watches, while maintaining an alert attitude.

Ruthlessness

Special forces soldiers sometimes have to perform some of the most unpalatable operations of all military forces, operations which require great violence to be imposed upon the enemy without mercy or relief. During the Moluccan train incident – a Dutch train was hijacked in 1977 by terrorists demanding independence for the Molucca Islands – hand-picked Royal Dutch Marines stormed the train and slaughtered six of the nine terrorists. The killing took place in a matter of only seconds, the marines using their automatic weapons against the enemy with brutal efficiency. Two hostages were also killed in the interchange of fire. The successful action illustrates

US Navy SEALs 'drown-proofing'

Drown-proofing proves to the instructors that the SEAL recruit can manage stress and disorientation over long periods without panic or confusion.

that combat must be prosecuted with an absolute disdain for the lives of the enemy, yet each soldier must keep his aggression controlled to avoid lethal errors.

Knowledge

One of the defined duties for a US Marine is to become 'a lifelong student of the Art of War'. This stipulation is typical of elite forces worldwide, in which a high precedent is placed on their soldiers being acutely well informed about military history, tactics, international politics and foreign cultures, as well as having a heightened knowledge of combat craft. A typical test for this general awareness can be found in officer recruitment for units such as the Royal Marines. In this test, a member of the examining board points to an unlabelled country on a map of the world and the recruit must identify the country and talk for one or two minutes on the cultural and political situation within that country. Knowledge of foreign cultures and languages is also especially valuable, as this allows a soldier to function more easily on foreign operations and develop a more intelligent basis to his or her actions.

Resistance to Physical Discomfort

Because many special forces operations are conducted well away from the logistical support of main forces, powers of endurance must be formidable. Not only must special forces soldiers be able to withstand traversing long distances on foot and at speed, but they also must be prepared for the capture and violent interrogation which threaten all elite operatives. The skill of mentally dismissing physical pain is usually created and tested during exhausting training. An example of this is the US Navy SEALs' 'Hell Week', a period of seven days which recruits spend almost entirely without sleep and usually immersed in freezing water. One peculiar aspect of this training is 'drown proofing'. This is where the soldier is dropped into a

swimming pool with wrists and ankles bound, after which the recruit must keep afloat for 20 minutes and then perform underwater exercises (still with arms and legs tied) for another 10 minutes before swimming 100m (100 yards). Such training is not simply a form of torture (although many SEALs would disagree), but also actually allows the trainers to see if the soldier has the mental fortitude to keep pushing through what seems like interminable discomfort. Only when this is proved can unit members have the confidence that their personnel will never give in to adversity and will push themselves to the limit to achieve mission objectives.

These are just some of the mental qualities demanded of the special forces soldier; it is these and others which are the focus of this book. Psychological training aims to instil an exceptional degree of motivation and produce soldiers who are less susceptible to adverse combat reactions and more inclined to pursue their military goals despite any surrounding danger, no matter how hazardous. It also serves to debunk conventional wisdom. A good non-military example would be that some US police departments found that their officers were adopting TV tactics in a gunfight, frequently ending up killed or wounded as a result. Training had to be amended so that the officers were aware of this subconscious tactical predisposition and were also capable of overriding it with proper manoeuvres.

The same applies to military training, especially in the elite units. Special forces are trained to look beyond the conventional and that is why they are so feared – their patterns of behaviour are difficult for the enemy to predict. By understanding how their own minds work, they know how their enemies' minds work. Thus it is that psychological training is not simply a tool for mental resilience; it is, in essence, part of the elite soldier's arsenal.

Fighter or non-fighter

During World War II and the 1950s, several studies were commissioned to judge what distinguished fighters from non-fighters. S. L. A. Marshall produced a hotly contested study in the late 1940s which singled out fighters as men who actively threw themselves into the battle, engaging the enemy with their weapons from the start. This was opposed to non-fighters, who tended to take a passive role in action, often not firing their weapons at all. This was drawn from Marshall's conclusion that, in World War II, only around 15 per cent of an Allied company would actually fire their weapons in combat. Marshall's conclusions were expanded by further research from the Personnel Research Branch of the US Army's Adjutant General and the Human Resources Research Office. Their research was carried out in the context of the Korean War and consisted of an exhaustive series of interviews and testing procedures on actual combat units. From these studies, and from subsequent research which was carried out both in the United States and abroad, the following distinctions emerged:

FIGHTER

● Tends to engage in violent actions without requiring external pressure
● Instinctively pursues leadership roles either as a function of his rank or in the absence of the usual squad leader
● Maintains composure and clear thought processes even under fire
● Accepts responsibility for his actions
● Tends to be supportive of the group as a whole
● Usually possesses a higher rank than non-fighters
● Generally of higher intelligence than non-fighters. Mean IQ of 91
● A higher percentage of fighters are regular army, rather than draftees
● Displays an independent personality resistant to depression. Capable of being spontaneous and avoids introversion
● Has a strong sense of humour
● Family background tends to be financially and emotionally stable. Parents often engaged in running their own businesses
● Faster reaction times than the non-fighter
● Generally taller and heavier than non-fighters
● Tends to do well at physical sports

NON-FIGHTER

● Plays a minimal part in any combat, tending to withdraw away from action when it takes place
● Becomes psychologically reticent under fire and needs strong external motivation (for example, orders, immediate threat to life, etc.) to perform
● Overimaginative, seeing matters as he imagines them, rather than seeing them as they really are
● Avoids performing duties, idle
● Succumbs to mental terrors and is prone to psychological problems
● Generally less intelligent than fighters. Mean IQ of 78
● In some research, 40 per cent of non-fighters had lost their fathers before they reached the age of 18
● More financially constrained background. Often had to contribute to the family income from an earlier age
● Tends to be interested in the opposite sex from an earlier age than fighters
● Has more financial obligations to family than the fighter while in service
● More prone to periods of depression and despondency

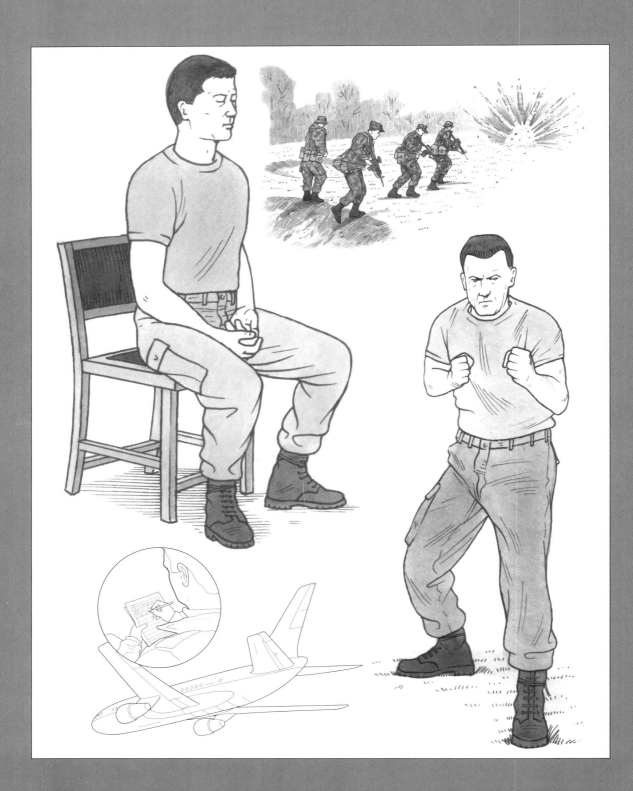

CHAPTER TWO

Handling Combat Stress

However hard the training, however tough the mind, few soldiers are totally immune to the trauma of combat. During battle, a soldier will experience sights, sounds and smells which are extreme and bewildering, and unlike anything encountered in civilian life. To function effectively, a soldier must quickly learn to cope with combat's mental pressures in the midst of battle.

Mutilation, the sudden death of friends and comrades, the almost animal noises of human beings in agony, the huge gas blast of artillery shells, personal injury – the range of sensations goes beyond almost anything encountered in civilian life.

Such experience takes its toll. Soldiers have likened combat to being in continual car accidents, or being part of the worst civil disaster imaginable, but actually participating in making it worse. For some, it is too much.

The shock of seeing death and chaos leaves them emotionally crippled. Unable to cope, their condition damages them as individuals and also detracts from the efficiency and morale of their unit. Detailed studies of 20th-century conflicts have shown that units experiencing sustained combat over several days suffer an average psychological casualty rate of one in every four soldiers. This rate climbs with every extra day of combat. Facing such a significant problem, military researchers have devoted huge amounts of time and money to finding ways of 'battleproofing' the soldier. This chapter will reveal their discoveries and also reflect on why elite special forces units have almost negligible levels of mental casualties as compared to regular units.

THE CHANGING FACE OF WAR

Although there is a modern label for adverse psychological reactions to combat – combat stress reaction (CSR) – combat has obviously always been traumatic. Yet the battlefield developed during the 20th century in such a way as to make mental damage a much greater likelihood.

The first development was mobility. The 20th century saw the true advent of mechanised warfare on land, on sea and in the air. Achievements in vehicular design during the 1930s led to the application of Blitzkrieg warfare by the Germans in 1939. Blitzkrieg placed a premium on violent and deep penetrations into enemy territory while maintaining effective communications between the various aircraft, armoured units and infantry squads involved. The effect was to create a highly fluid battlefield, constantly changing and uncertain. Rather than there being clear battle lines, opposing forces could be confusingly enmeshed to depths of hundreds of miles. A soldier involved in such combat therefore had to cope with the tremendous strain of not knowing his overall situation, frequently being surrounded by enemy forces and all the time trying to maintain efficient use of equipment, vehicles, communications and tactics. Facing or executing the Blitzkrieg warfare in World War II was thus psychologically exhausting. Some US divisions, for example, during the Tunisian battles of the Kasserine and Faid passes, actually had 35 per cent stress casualties out of their overall casualty figure, a figure no doubt heightened by the rawness of the US troops who were all experiencing their first battle. In other theatres, it was common for a division of men to lose 1600 soldiers to combat-related stress.

Since World War II, the trends of mobile warfare have continued expanding. Modern aircraft, vehicles and communications now have all-weather capabilities – capabilities which led to what is known as continuous warfare (CW). Continuous warfare was a doctrine that emerged during the Cold War. On both sides of the iron curtain, tacticians recognised that to be decisive, the tempo of warfare would have to be maintained night and day. For the soldier, this introduced some of the critical causes of CSR: sleep deprivation, low–light-level operations, increased fatigue through longer operational hours, operations in harsh weather, longer periods without rest or food, and isolation from one's colleagues because of the greater operating distances. The effect of CW can be seen in recent conflicts such as the Yom Kippur War in the Middle East in 1973, when some 30 per cent of Israeli casualties suffered during the war were psychiatric.

Another major change is technological. Modern weapons are perfect killing machines and the mutilation they inflict can be appalling to witness. A simple high-velocity bullet from an AKM assault rifle, for example, will tumble through the human body, tearing and shattering internal tissue, before exploding out the other side of the body and leaving a gaping, infected hole. Soldiers in the Vietnam War were often stunned when only two or three rounds from their M16 rifles would tear limbs off their opponents. Conversely, they had to handle the sickening experience of seeing friends physically annihilated by modern anti-personnel mines. For Iraqi soldiers in the Gulf War, artillery and air power had such enormous range, accuracy and destructive force that even rear areas became dangerous, and there was consequently no place in which the soldier felt safe or able to relax.

Defensive positions

Defensive positions provide confidence to face an attack, although studies show that soldiers tend to be less aggressive with their weapons when in dug outs and bunkers. The soldier needs to treat them as fighting positions and not as hiding positions.

The final change, also related to technology, is the intellectual demand of operations. Almost all soldiers in developed armies must now be accustomed to using highly advanced machinery. Tools such as satellite positioning systems, computerised artillery ranging devices, ground-to-air missile defences and coded communications require great concentration to use. In the heat of battle, this concentration is stretched to the absolute limit and the conflicting demands of preserving life while focusing on equipment operation prove a further drain on mental stamina.

All these factors of the modern battlefield create the perfect environment for breeding

CSR, and we will turn to its symptoms and treatments in a moment. What is enlightening is that, among elite units such as the SAS, Green Berets, US Marine Corps, Royal Marine Commandos and so on, CSR is much more of a rarity than in regular units. This fact stands despite the fact that elite troops will frequently be placed in situations of greater stress than almost any other fighting man or woman. A telling example of this comes from World War II. During the 38-day period between 6 June and 13 July 1944, two units were compared for their percentage of stress casualties amongst their wounded in action (WIA). The elite 82nd Airborne Division was involved in horrendous fighting around

Fighting stance

In unarmed combat, adopting a strong physical posture actually leads the brain to generate greater confidence – the body actually leads the mind, not the other way around.

Normandy at this time and suffered an appalling 4196 WIA, yet stress casualties never exceeded 6 in every 100 casualties. By contrast, an infantry division in Italy endured 1800 WIA, but its level of stress victims was 13 to every 100 casualties – twice as high as the airborne unit. The figures are not just restricted to particular battles; the percentages of stress casualties remained at those levels for the rest of the war. Another telling figure was that the 442nd Regimental Combat Team, which recruited troops mainly from a Japanese background, but who lived in Hawaii, suffered almost no stress-related casualties in the entire Italian campaign. This was despite their being very highly decorated; it seems that their desire to prove their national commitment to the United States, despite their ancestry, created extraordinary levels of motivation (source of figures: US Army Research Institute).

So what separates the elite soldier from the regular soldier, the strong mind from the vulnerable one?

COMBAT STRESS REACTION

Combat stress reaction (CSR) covers a multitude of psychological conditions. For the purposes of definition, we can say that it is a mental state induced by combat which impairs an individual's emotional, intellectual and physical ability to function as a soldier. CSR is different from mental injuries or instabilities which result from physical injuries. Constant exposure to artillery fire can disrupt the inner ear through a constant pounding from rapid changes in air pressure, the result being physical shakiness and a confused mental condition – what was in part termed 'shell shock' during the first half of the 20th century. Similarly, blood loss or oxygen deprivation during battle will profoundly alter the casualty's mental state, with symptoms including confusion, aggression and inability to concentrate.

By contrast, CSR is a purely mental condition, born out of the response to witnessing and participating in combat. The symptoms vary considerably between individuals, but the following list is typical:

- **Aggression/irritability** – The casualty experiences uncontrollable aggression which is not only directed at the enemy, but also at those around him and inanimate objects. This aggression can be hair trigger and need only minor incidents (such as loud noises) to activate it.
- **Alcohol/drugs** – The casualty's alcohol/drug intake may increase dramatically as he attempts to shut out traumatic memories. In actual fact, the taking of drugs in whatever form usually aggravates his depression and anxiety.
- **Anxiety** – Not just simple worry, anxiety is an abiding and obsessive tension which dramatically affects the person's ability to sleep, think and control his behaviour. Symptoms often include a physical jumpiness.
- **Apathy** – The combat-shocked soldier may mentally withdraw from the outside world and show little interest in the events or situations around him.
- **Body temperature variations** – Alternation between feeling hot and sweaty, and chilly is common and often bears no relation to the outside temperature or climate.
- **Bowel/bladder problems** – Particularly during the build-up and the battle itself, a soldier may lose the ability to control the bowel and bladder muscles. Urination may become involuntary and the soldier will have bouts of diarrhoea. The frequency of urination is also greatly increased.
- **Catatonia** – A CSR casualty can physically freeze and be unable to move his limbs, even under extreme coercion.
- **Concentration deficit** – The CSR casualty is unable to hold his attention on one subject or object for very long and thus is not capable of rational thought.
- **Depression** – Chronic depression often accompanies CSR and features a deep sense of self-criticism, an acute pessimism, fear of the future and fatigue.
- **Eating/drinking disorders** – The casualty becomes uninterested in food or drink, resulting in weight loss, fatigue and illness.
- **Fatigue** – Fatigue is normal after long hours spent in combat, but CSR victims can often exhibit chronic fatigue even after adequate rest.
- **Memory loss** – Even short-term memory is lost under acute stress; the combatant may have a general inability to remember orders even when given only moments ago.
- **Mood swings** – Mood alters constantly and ranges from deep depression to strange moments of elation.
- **Nausea/vomiting** – The soldier may experience attacks of nausea and vomiting, even when the danger has passed. Eating can often be difficult because involuntary 'heaves' accompany the swallowing of food.
- **Obsessive activities** – The casualty undertakes repetitious actions to no purpose, such as field stripping and assembling his weapon beyond normal maintenance requirements or obsessive talking about a single subject.
- **Recklessness** – The soldier may display a disregard for the safety of himself and others in his actions.
- **Self-loathing** – The soldier may feel a sense of deep personal unworthiness and constantly make unfavourable comparisons with others.
- **Speech disorder** – The casualty may suffer a breakdown in communication skills, with pronunciation becoming slurred and unintelligibility increasing.

Effects of altitude on marksmanship

At high altitudes, marksmanship deteriorates by nearly 50 per cent and takes up to two weeks of acclimatisation to regain its sea-level standards of performance.

Sea level

High altitude

- **Trembling** – The hands in particular may shake, but this can extend to whole-body trembling.
- **Withdrawal from reality** – Overwhelmed by the world around him, the soldier might suddenly withdraw into himself and either succumb to complete inertia or inhabit an imaginary or hallucinatory world.

A glance at all these symptoms makes it obvious that combat stress can destroy the soldier's capacity to function as part of a military unit. Furthermore, entire units can suffer from group symptoms as a whole. These can include: high rates of desertion and AWOL (absent without leave); disintegration of unit cohesion; lack of discipline; defiance of officers' orders; tasks left undone or completed slowly; general deterioration in appearance; infighting; open disrespect of unit routines and traditions; low morale; and complaints. Another common symptom is a high degree of sickness reported – usually minor illnesses such as headaches, stomach pains or flu – especially prior to combat. Indeed, medical officers are trained to expect a sudden rush of minor ailments to be treated prior to any action and also to expect the highest percentage of CSR patients to arrive for treatment during the first few days of combat breaking out.

We have already touched on the overall context of modern warfare in which CSR occurs. Yet there is also a more specific range of reasons for CSR and it is these which form the focus for the conditioning training of the elite forces.

THE LIMITS OF ENDURANCE

Although many things can trigger combat stress, there is a certain range of conditions which are more responsible for this than others. A central pillar of combat stress is sleep deprivation. Disruption of the body's natural sleep rhythms, particularly between the hours of 0200 and 0600 when sleep is usually at its deepest, significantly affects the soldier's ability to think and operate. Studies in both the United States and United Kingdom showed that, if sleeplessness is maintained for more than 48 hours, then a military unit will almost totally cease to function and the soldiers will start to display psychological disorders. Even auditory and visual hallucinations occurred. Particularly affected were the soldiers' decision-making skills and memory, and they became more susceptible to fear and anxiety (interestingly, weapons maintenance and map plotting were not affected). The problem with sleep deprivation is the disruption of the body's natural rhythms and it is compounded by travel, especially when a soldier crosses time zones during transport flights. Sleep-deprivation stress is often exacerbated by having to operate in low-light conditions. Working in the dark has the simple effect of making the soldier more susceptible to his imagination, as fears are projected into the blackness rather than being actually seen and understood. This type of problem is particularly acute for special forces soldiers, who undertake many of their operations during the cover of night.

Another major factor in CSR development is, unsurprisingly, the weapons that the soldier has arraigned against him. Investigation into the psychological impact of weaponry was begun in World War I, when whole new categories of weaponry entered the fray, with a deplorable increase in levels of mortality. World War II continued the research. Work conducted in North Africa threw up a fascinating spectrum of results, including which weapons men feared the most and how they adjusted to those weapons over a period of time. The weapons judged 'most frightening' by 97 per cent of 120 psychiatric casualties were those used in various types of shellfire and bombing. At the point of first contact, air attack was the most alarming according to 50 per cent of those involved; artillery fire was nominated by 20 per cent. Yet, only 11 days into battle, those priorities had switched entirely as the soldiers became more familiar with the actual results of the weapons deployed against them (artillery was accurate and destructive, whereas dive bombing was noisy, but generally ineffective). Further studies into the reasons why men feared weapons tended to show that

Stress testing

A controversial stress testing device used by US military research groups was to get soldiers to fill in complicated life-assurance forms while flying aboard a plane which they believed was about to crash land.

accuracy, rapidity of fire and volume of noise were the primary sources of anxiety.

Fear of weapons induces a central cause of CSR in soldiers – death anxiety. As the term suggests, this is quite simply the fear of death. An individual concerned about his mortality is under the constant stress of predicting the nature, time and experience of his demise. As we would expect, this problem increases with the duration in combat. During World War II, almost any soldier who was engaged in heavy fighting on a daily basis was rendered mentally unstable after about five to 10 days of action, depending on how effectively his basic needs (food, sleep etc.) had been catered for.

BATTLEPROOFING

Having looked at what combat can do to the mind, we now turn towards the techniques of avoiding, or at least mitigating, combat stress. The elite forces act as our guides in this.

Special forces, as already noted, have a much lower incidence of mental difficulties than regular troops. Yet elite-unit operations would, on the surface of things, seem to have some of the most stress-inducing conditions that combatants can face. The operations tend to have a disproportionately high risk of death and failure. Units are small and, once operational, tend to be isolated from the protective umbrella of the general might of the armed forces. Many special operations soldiers work entirely alone, coping with stress without a sympathetic ear and also handling the intense boredom of long vigils. The physical strains are likewise enormous, with pack weights reaching up to 54.5kg (120lb) in weight on some operations (such as those conducted by the SAS in the Gulf War which required the soldiers to be self-sufficient for a period of time) and sleep deprivation being a persistent drain on energy and motivation. And yet their resilience nonetheless is legendary.

Top reasons why men fear weapons – World War II study

Conventional bomber –
Accuracy

Dive bombers –
Noise

Mortars –
Accuracy

Machine guns –
Rapid fire

Artillery –
Accuracy

Adjusting to artillery

The soldier must have experience of close artillery fire in training, otherwise the sensations of blast and noise will leave him unsettled and confused in combat.

So, why do special operations soldiers endure where so many ordinary soldiers would succumb? Naturally, details are hard to come by, as the special forces are secretive about all aspects of their advanced training. Yet details of their methods are steadily becoming more available, if only for the fact that elite forces expertise tends to filter itself out towards other more regular units, such as the US and Royal Marines, which exercise elite capabilities, but are less concealed.

Of central significance to producing soldiers resilient to the traumas of combat is the process of 'battleproofing' or 'battle inoculation'. Battleproofing is based on making the mind 'familiar' with the experience of combat through realistic training. The human mind is effectively like an enormous filing system. When a person comes upon a new experience, that experience is tested against the files of memory to find an experience which was similar in the past which can guide future actions. Depending on the relevance of the match, the individual is able to make a judgement and respond to the situation. If there is little previous experience to guide in a particular situation, the brain finds the nearest equivalent and then makes a new 'file' based on what happens. The problem with combat is that, because it is so extreme by nature, unless you have actually experienced it, there is almost no way to prepare for it. This is where battleproofing comes in. The essence of battleproofing is to generate as much realism in the training scenarios as possible, thus taking away the shock factor of actual combat.

So how is this accomplished? A good example can be taken from SAS counter-terrorist training. During hostage-rescue exercises, SAS soldiers use a specially constructed sequence of rooms known as the 'killing house', in which a hostage, usually an SAS colleague, is positioned surrounded by

Coping with confinement

Armoured crews are especially vulnerable to combat stress because of the cramped, hot conditions in which they work. In battle these conditions often lead to fears of fire and being trapped, and communications with other units must be maintained to avoid feeling isolated.

life-size cut-out figures of his terrorist captors. With incredible speed, an SAS team then makes an explosive entry using stun grenades – grenades which impart a huge flash and bang, but which have almost no lethality. The noise and the smoke are intense and the room is plunged into darkness. In this confusion, the entry team target the terrorists with their laser sights and then take them out using live ammunition, often firing bullets only inches from the prisoner's head. With all the terrorists dead, the prisoner is snatched and dragged out of the room at lightning speed.

The training exercise must be exercised with real aggression and it is repeated over and over again until the demands of the action become almost second nature. It battleproofs the soldiers on several levels. First, the use of live ammunition helps the soldiers become accustomed to the actual sounds and sensation their firearms have when being fired in earnest in a certain physical space. Secondly, the fact that there is a live person within the firing range makes the soldier accept the responsibility of his actions. Thirdly, the person who is acting as the hostage is himself trained by becoming used to the noise of bullets hissing past him while remaining composed and alert. It is the final

stage, however, the constant repetition of the training, which is perhaps most important. Repeating the exercise over and over again allows the sensations of the shooting, smoke and impact of rounds and the mental processes of lightning-fast decision-making to enter the 'files' of the familiar. Thus, were the soldier actually to go into real combat, the brain would not be as traumatised by the sensations as that of someone not trained by these methods.

LIVE EXERCISES

Battleproofing exercises of this type are practised by elite forces around the world

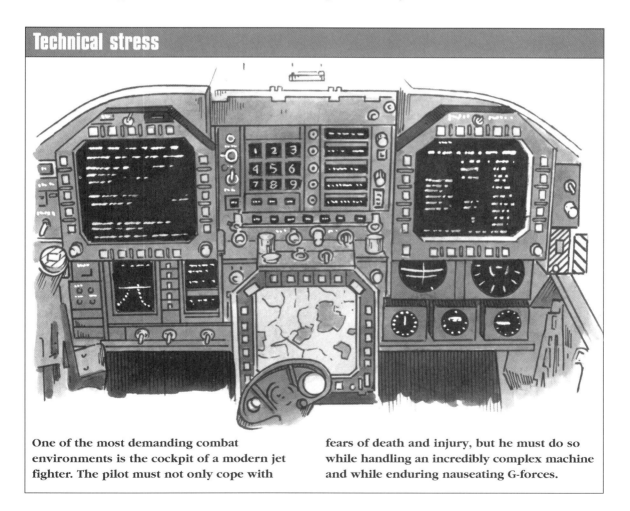

Technical stress

One of the most demanding combat environments is the cockpit of a modern jet fighter. The pilot must not only cope with fears of death and injury, but he must do so while handling an incredibly complex machine and while enduring nauseating G-forces.

and have become more of a presence in regular units. The US Marine Corps, for instance, has huge combined arms exercises in which live ordnance is fired from artillery and dropped from aircraft so that soldiers become accustomed to the huge percussions. Iraqi soldiers undergo training in which they crawl under barbed wire while instructors fire live rounds into the ground literally inches from their heads. Recently, more insidious training methods have come to light. US Special Forces soldiers, around the time of the Vietnam War, underwent special training in which they were sat in front of a TV monitor which reeled off horrific and distressing images for hour after hour. The viewing individual eventually became desensitised to watching human suffering and so, it was assumed, would be less susceptible to the trauma of actual violence. The effectiveness of this technique is actually questionable, for, although the subject becomes acclimatised to the two-dimensional violence of the screen, this actually has little sensory correspondence with the three-dimensional world. However, part of current US Marine officer training is to send the officer candidates to the trauma ward of a major hospital for several days. Here, they become used to the sight of serious injuries and sudden death in a way that battleproofs them for the sight, sound and smell of casualties in a war zone (they are usually sent to a hospital in a large city, such as Washington, where they can expect a high number of gunshot wounds). In a similar manner, special forces instructors in Ecuador use real corpses as training aids when teaching recruits about anatomy for combat purposes.

NEED FOR REALISM

The key to battleproofing training is to make it as close to the experience of real combat as possible, replicating its brutality, pressure and sensations with close attention to detail. Such training should also build the exceptional physical stamina required by modern soldiers, for physical durability tends to guard against mental fragility. Elite units tend to have the financial resources to invest very heavily in training and to be able to use copious amounts of live ammunition, thus their battleproofing has been seen to be especially effective. Furthermore, elite units tend to have each individual in possession of the full range of information about the nature of their mission. Unlike regular units, where there is sometimes an information deficit amongst the lower ranks, elite squads will usually have undergone full and complex rehearsals of what is operationally required. This in itself reduces the likelihood of CSR, as the soldier has a clear understanding of what is needed to survive in combat.

Military training should not only bring about a familiarity with fighting, but it

---

Stress testing exercise – US 1950s

Pick out the Cs from the Os. Keep the eye moving quickly; if your attention wanders, go back to the beginning and start again. Are you composed or increasingly frustrated?

COOOOOOCOOOCOOOCOOCOCOCOCOCOCOCOCOCOCOCOC
COCOCOCOCOCOCOCOCOCOCOCOCOCOCOOOCOCOOOCOCOCO
OOOCOOOCOOCOOOOOOCOCCOOOOOCOOOOOOOCOOOOOCO

should also impart confidence in self and unit. Instilling confidence is vital to the prevention of adverse stress because the confident soldier is far less likely to suffer from the sense of helplessness than can come from being separated from the unit or cut off from the flow of information from the rear. Confidence must be built around several themes. First, there is confidence in decision-making skills. Elite units are trained so that if the leader of a unit is killed or put out of action, all others are sufficiently trained in decision-making so as to be able to step into their shoes immediately. The US Marine Corps also uses this philosophy. Following extensive research into the vital leadership role of NCOs in World War II, all Marine recruits are now placed in intensive

decision-making environments from the moment they arrive at training camp.

Confidence should also exist in weapons handling. British SAS and US Navy SEALs training involves recruits becoming familiar in handling almost every significant firearm used by the world's armies. This enables them to have a complete command of the tools of their trade and thus there are no gaps in competence which might prey on the soldier's mind. The confidence in weapons handling, however, is a two-way street. Elite units tend to hand-pick their weapons for reliability and firepower, so that they have little fear of being let down by their weapons at crucial moments. This is why the SAS have rejected use of the problematic British Army SA80 – which tends to

Effects of altitude

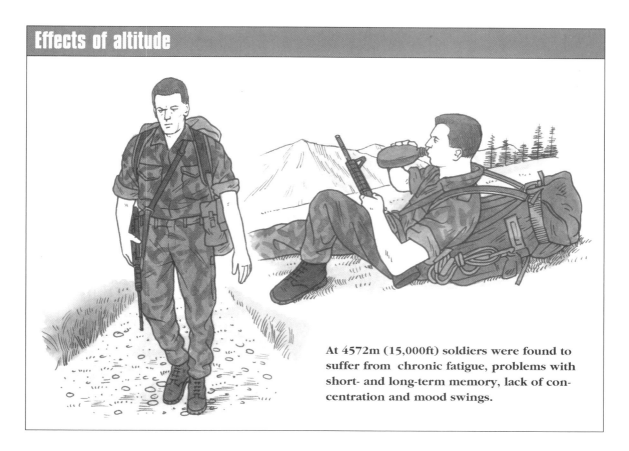

At 4572m (15,000ft) soldiers were found to suffer from chronic fatigue, problems with short- and long-term memory, lack of concentration and mood swings.

Hypnosis 1 – sitting position

Self-hypnosis begins by focusing on the slow rise and fall of the breath, while simultaneously relaxing the body, working from the toes to the top of the scalp.

suffer from alarming mechanical failures, such as the magazine suddenly dropping out – in preference of battle-tested weaponry such as the US M16A2 and the older L1A1 self-loading rifle.

Confidence also derives from unit support. Elite forces train in small, tightly knit groups, the members of which come to know one another intimately and which have an implicit trust in one another. In combat, this trust translates into motivation. Among soldiers motivation tends to come not from great ideals, though these are important, but from the desire not to fail one's comrades and not to let down the regimental name. Once soldiers have been through the shared exhaustions and demands of training, they tend to become highly motivated by their desire to protect and enhance the group. Once motivation is present to a high degree, CSR is less able to set in as the soldier keeps more of an outward-looking perspective towards his or her comrades-in-arms, rather than an introspection.

The role of the leaders also comes into play. They can be vital in motivating, or demotivating, the individual and the unit as a whole. Leadership qualities are explored in detail later. In terms of controlling combat stress by building up team and individual confidence, the leader's primary roles are, according to the US Army Research Institute, to:

- set realistic goals for the progressive development of individual, team and unit competence;
- systematically test the achievement of these goals;
- praise improvement and coach units towards achieving higher competence;
- single out individuals and teams for recognition and develop a spirit of accomplishment;
- point out reasons for confidence at every opportunity;
- present realistic and detailed expectations about future combat conditions;
- point out that the enemy faces the same conditions;
- develop in each soldier confidence in self, equipment, unit, training and leadership.

This list of confidence-building objectives is designed not only to give soldiers belief in their own abilities, but also to enable them to accept that they are being competently led

and that their lives are in the hands of someone who knows what he is doing.

It is also up to the leader to look after the welfare of his men. Sleep and food delivery should be high on his list of priorities, for reasons we have already noted. Sleep breaks should be scheduled by the leader for whenever possible, and this includes elite units who need to keep their decision-making abilities fresher than most. If regular and lengthy periods of sleep are not possible, sleep research for the US Army has shown that some of the wearing effects of sleep deprivation can be offset by a simple 20–30-minute nap with a similar period for wake-up before an action is to take place. If the soldier can train himself to sleep in these circumstances, his energy levels will temporarily restore themselves just as he is going into action and he will become less susceptible to fatigue-related CSR.

Through battleproofing, confidence building, group motivation and good leadership, a soldier is far less likely to become a psychiatric casualty of war than those who have not benefited from such training. Yet battle is still a shocking experience to even those who have been recipients of the most rigorous training.

Hypnosis 2 – prone position

The soldier visualises the situation he fears, seeing himself performing confidently and boldly. The 'waking' brain will use the scenario as a model for future conduct.

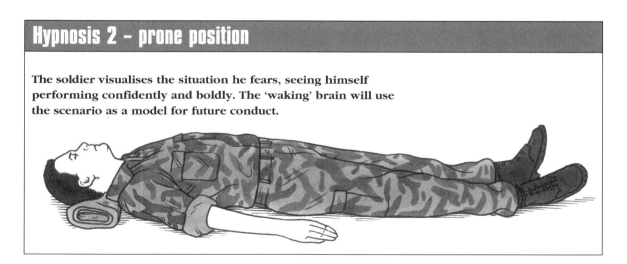

COPING WITH CHAOS

Even when CSR has set in, it is not irreversible. There is a body of recommended techniques which are designed to stop the progression of the condition and ultimately restore the casualty to some level of normality. The processes of professional psychiatric treatment of advanced CSR are scientifically and pharmaceutically complex, and are rather beyond the scope of this book. However, what has been deemed vital is that the casualty has the chance to air his anxiety to someone able to listen without judgement. In military terminology, this is known as 'ventilation'. The important factor of ventilation support is that the casualty is speaking to someone with genuine listening skills. This means that the listener does not interrupt the flow of speech unless there is a natural pause and then only to say something helpful. The listener should encourage the talker to pour out all his anxieties and must never indicate signs of boredom or lack of interest. By articulating most of his troubles, the traumatised soldier can share them in a wider context and thus see himself less as an isolated sufferer.

For more severe cases of CSR occurring suddenly on the battlefield, the 'crisis management' technique is the one advocated by the US Army Research Institute. The first stage of crisis management is to calm the distressed soldier as much as possible. This should be through a gentle but firm voice, clear commands and the enlistment of others who may be better placed to control the outburst. Secondly, the soldier should be protected from danger, either from himself or from putting himself in a vulnerable position. This, if necessary, can involve physical restraint. Thirdly, the officer or man who is dealing with the crisis must gather enough information to assess the cause of the CSR and judge what the best mode of action will be. If, for example, the soldier has just witnessed the violent death of a friend, he is talking incoherently and seems to have lost the ability to listen to even simple instructions, he is a danger to himself and others, and evacuation is the best course.

Human support is the frontline of CSR care. However, there is also a series of physical relaxation techniques which, during the phase of pre- or post-battle, can go some way towards helping a soldier cope with trauma. Central amongst these relaxation techniques are those of breathing and self-hypnosis. Although such techniques may have a somewhat New Age stigma attached to them, in some military units around the world they are nonetheless now slowly gaining a wider currency. The US Army Research Institute recommends using breathing and self-suggestion techniques as part of regular military stress-control measures. and units such as the SEALs also have been known to use relaxation techniques as a regular part of their aikido martial arts training.

BENEFITS OF MEDITATION

The actual techniques of breathing-based meditation and self-suggestion are described in the diagrams here in this chapter, but the benefits of the techniques are clear.

Meditation allows the heartbeat to slow down as well as the blood pressure to drop, and this reduces the physical symptoms of anxiety, which in turn leads the mind to feel more balanced and restored. Also, it allows the soldier to perform his own form of internal battleproofing. This is done by the soldier imagining himself coping with situations about which he is fearful during the process of meditation. The human mind is remarkable in that its 'filing system' cannot actually tell the difference between events that are vividly imagined and those that are actually experienced. Thus, a soldier who is particularly afraid of artillery fire can, to some measure, 'inoculate' himself against CSR by visualising himself in the midst of a

Environmental stress

The physical environment adds to the soldier's mental state. Four negative elements are cold, heat, altitude and wetness; all can lead to lack of concentration and change of mood.

barrage being calm, alert and focused on his objectives. Likewise, a special forces soldier can mentally rehearse a mission in order to give himself a clear sense of what he is doing when he does actually go into the arena of combat. Of course, the technique is not a substitute for the physical experience itself, but it can go some way to helping a soldier control and prevent CSR, without initially exposing himself to danger.

At the end of the day, however, perhaps the only surefire way of resisting adverse reactions to combat experience is to go through the experience itself and come out on the other side.

Battle can break or harden the soldier, but if the chaos of battle is managed with some degree of confidence, then that confidence will be taken forward into the next encounter.

Of course, underlying this chapter is the harsh fact that human beings do not have infinite tolerance for sights of horror and death. The realities of combat will forever leave their psychological mark on those who have to face them.

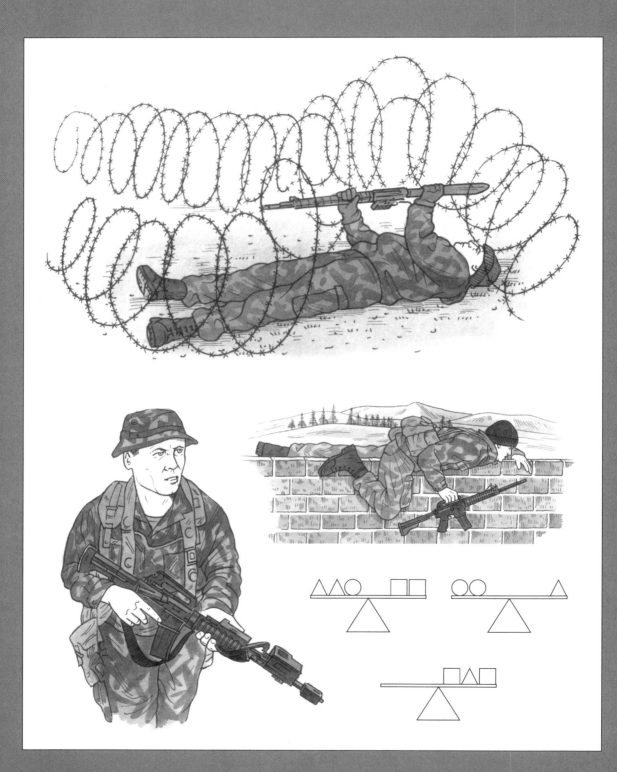

CHAPTER THREE

Recruitment and Training

The 20th century saw an increasing professionalisation of the world's military forces, particularly following the technological and tactical revelations of the German Blitzkrieg in 1939 and 1940. The success of the German Army against superior numbers proved that the more professional the soldier, the more chance he or she has of achieving success.

At the opening of World War II, the Allies expected a repetition of the defensive stalemate of World War I. Yet, when only seven German armoured and motorised divisions punched through the Low Countries and achieved the capitulation of France between 10 May and 19 June (little more than five weeks), the world awoke to a new military reality. The German forces had used excellence of training, a strong application of new technology, modern communications and disdain for old styles of warfare to produce a combat style which overwhelmed now-outdated defensive strategies.

The Allies did catch up, but a profound change had now occurred within the structure and function of armies. The lesson of World War I – that sheer manpower could be dominated by sheer firepower – reached its peak in World War II. What the military establishment of all nations now required was not only men and women of courage, but also individuals who could apply themselves with great intelligence to a mobile, technically governed battlefield.

Following the Vietnam War (1963–75), more of the world's armies realised that a non-professional, conscripted army was, in many cases, a political liability and also a military drain. Weapons technology and the need for quick, decisive military solutions has led to armies reducing the numbers of personnel, but investing more in their training and professionalism. Concurrently, the continuing rise of 'low-intensity' and 'guerrilla' warfare since 1945 means that armies must have specialists who can deal with situations alternating between high-impact combat and humanitarian care, a switch most ordinary soldiers are unable to handle.

As a result, recruitment and training in armed forces has become more specialised. Recruiters now look for individuals to make a definite contribution of character and skills, rather than just fill out quotas. Nowhere is this truer than in the elite forces. There can be no such thing as a 'weak link' in a special forces team. Each element of the whole must function with confidence and tactical aplomb. Standards must be rigorously applied to every elite soldier, making the recruitment and training processes for these squads the hardest in world, far beyond the capabilities of most individuals. This chapter is about choosing and creating an elite soldier. Our focus here is on what qualities of mind a recruiter looks for when selecting personnel for an elite unit, and also what mental abilities the soldier must develop and demonstrate during his harsh training.

SELECTING THE ELITE

The irony of selecting military personnel is that the higher you go up the ladder of expertise, the more subjective the selection process becomes. Many members of elite regiments come from existing military backgrounds – the SAS, for instance, tends to use the Royal Marines and the Parachute Regiment as its recruiting grounds – so the recruiters already know that the individual has good basic military skills. This is not always the case, however, and many elite units (especially those of a larger scale, such as marines) do take in raw recruits. Whatever their background, what the recruiters are looking for is that extra depth of personality and intelligence, which can only be judged by putting the would-be soldier through severe physical and mental challenges over a prolonged period.

We shall turn to that process shortly; however, before any soldier can enter an elite force, their mental profile is effectively screened through a battery of tests and questions. A would-be US Marine, for example, has to pay a visit to the US Marine Corps office recruiter before he or she gets anywhere near a training camp. The US Marine Corps distinguishes itself from the US Army by promising membership of a close brotherhood of elite troops more akin to a religious order than a military unit. Yet the reward for this acute sense of belonging – which will last the recruit's entire life – is nothing more than the promise of hardship, toil, adversity and pain. The recruiter's job is to see whether the young person before him is up to that challenge.

Naturally, a first level of screening consists of a physical assessment. This generally focuses on illnesses or problems such as unacceptably defective vision, epilepsy or asthma, or sexually transmitted diseases such as hepatitis or HIV. Physical problems are an easily identified source of rejection. More complex is the recruiter's assessment of the candidate's character and background. Marine recruiters will probe deeply into the applicant's background to find moments of courage, determination or leadership which may indicate performance as a future US Marine. If the individual struggled through poverty to gain qualifications or support a

Intelligence Tests

Intelligence Test 1

Three white and three black blocks are shown separated by spaces. Can you completely reverse their position by moving one block at a time to an adjacent position or by jumping over an adjacent block or space?

 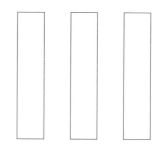

Intelligence Test 2

Which shape should be used to fill in the blank space?

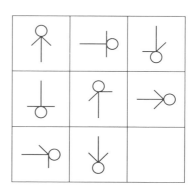

Intelligence Test 3

First, work out the numercial values of the triangle, circle and square shapes on the see-saw. Once you have this, which collection of shapes (A, B or C) should be used to balance the last see-saw?

 A

 B

 C

family, then such might indicate strength of mind. If the person has captained sports teams, this shows that he or she can take responsibility for his or her actions when these affect others. There are no hard and fast rules about what questions the recruiters should ask, but, as experienced selectors and long-standing US Marines, they become adept at picking out those with promise. They are equally adept at defining those whose characters are flawed or who will suffer from mental problems. Criminal records usually constitute a complete barrier to entering the US Marine Corps – a respect for society and people is a prerequisite – whereas those who have dependants are often rejected because of the problems which arise over supporting a family on a meagre military wage.

Gradually, the recruiter will build up a profile of the candidate and form a judgement as to whether he or she is suitable to

Training realism

Training for combat must be as realistic as possible. If carried out in this way, then the shock of actual fighting is reduced during the actual experience. Here a soldier is pictured undergoing an accurate simulation of minefield clearance.

be a US Marine. Although the person may have a strong character, he or she also has to display the another mental quality demanded by all military elites – intelligence. All entrants to any branch of the US military forces take the Armed Services Vocational Aptitude Battery (ASVAB) tests. These test all aspects of mental dexterity; however, whereas some US units take personnel with scores of as low as 21, the US Marine Corps will not accept candidates with a score of below 31 (actually, two-thirds of US Marines have scores of more than 50).

The exacting standards applied by the US Marine Corps are typical of the world's elite forces. The US Marines' British equivalent, the Royal Marines, generally require a good academic background and competence in both mathematics and English – both will be required in tactical manoeuvres and communications. The Royal Marines does not, however, confuse academic achievement with actual intelligence, and it looks for recruits who can demonstrate mental ability in situations of stress and difficulty. The selection criteria of more secretive units are less easily identified. Initial selection for units such as the SAS, Green Berets, US Marine Force Reconn and Russian Spetsnaz is often conducted by a trained psychologist, who will open up highly personal issues with the candidate and make very critical observations to see how the candidate reacts to stress. If the soldier is to go on to special duties – such as undercover work – his or her abilities with foreign languages will be tested and approved. During World War II, agents being recruited for the British Special Operations Executive (SOE) would find the recruiter slipping continually into French or German to see if the candidate hesitated or became lost. Any sign that the soldier lacked total comprehension of these vital undercover languages would lead to his being dropped.

A final measure for the special forces recruiter is to test the candidate's discretion.

Many elite units conduct work of the utmost secrecy, a situation often at odds with the unit's glamorous status in the public mind. Individuals who thrive on public recognition often make bad special forces soldiers and cannot be trusted to maintain official secrets. After the globally visible action by the SAS during the Iranian Embassy siege, the SAS training camp at Hereford was besieged by gangs of young men marching outside the camp gates in an attempt to join up. As the attempt to enlist was in most cases prompted by the desire to share in the 'hard man' public image of the SAS, almost all were entirely unsuitable (most were dispatched by making them run continuously around a track until they collapsed and were sent home). Units such as the SAS tend to look for individuals who are very mentally self-sufficient and have no need for public notoriety. Because the human drive for status is very strong, these individuals are quite rare. The maxim of organisations such as the Israeli Sayeret Mat'kal – that all is well as long as its operations do not make the headlines – is only true because of the exceptional levels of self-restraint shown by its officers and men.

Yet, while the elite forces require people who are emotionally stable, they do not want people who tend to be passive. Elite forces' missions tend to require unusual levels of aggressive commitment. Special forces soldiers have to have the flexibility to see all sides of a problem, but they also have to be able to pursue a military goal with a single-minded vigour. This is the quality known as 'mental endurance' and it is this which is tested during training.

TEACHING TO SURVIVE

Fighting is actually not one of the most natural human pursuits. A study conducted by Colonel S. L. A. Marshal during World War II found that, in battle, only about 15 per cent of combat troops actually found the presence of mind to fire their weapons at the enemy. The remainder were paralysed or confused about the events around them and simply clutched their weapons. This did not just apply to 'green' units of new recruits; even supposedly battle-hardened squads showed the same tendency. Marshall analysed a particular battle on Makin Island in the Pacific, in which a charge by Japanese troops against positions of the US 165th Infantry Regiment was resisted by only 36 men actually firing back. This accounts for the fact that all the US soldiers in the forward positions were killed, even though their weaponry was more than a match for the Japanese bayonets and swords.

The conclusion of Marshall's report was that, in general, men only actively fight in a battle if the sheer weight of circumstances compels them to do so or if their officers force them into action. This latter fact places an incredible burden on leadership – Lieutenant Colonel Robert G. Cole of the 502nd Parachute Regiment fighting at the Carentan Causeway in 1944 found that he had to walk up and down his lines bullying each man into using his weapon.

The reasons for this are complex and are well explored in Joanna Bourke's book *An Intimate History of Killing* (London: Granta; 1999). Central amongst these reasons is the effect that long-distance weaponry has on the mind of the soldier. If killing can be accomplished at a significant distance from the soldier – with some weapons, the enemy does not have to be even seen – the enemy can start to seem 'unreal', despite the presence of bullets and explosions. For the elite soldier, the situation is somewhat different. Special forces operations tend to achieve a violent intimacy with the enemy, closing on him in the claustrophobic confines of a building, jungle or hijacked aircraft. Chris Ryan, the former SAS soldier who served in the Gulf War, has recounted how he had to break the neck of an Iraqi soldier with his bare arms when his presence was detected.

Elite missions, by their covert nature, often bring the soldier into very close contact with the enemy and sometimes demand the silent or rapid killing of people at close quarters. So how is this violent instinct instilled and mixed with the ability to survive all manner of adversity and still prosecute a mission with intelligence and commitment?

The secret, as ever, lies in the intensity and realism of the training. Training serves either to instil skills or to refresh them. For those giving the training, it is the arena in which they judge whether someone is suitable for service in an elite regiment. Training tends to fall into two different types. First is the basic level of training which builds up the soldier's (or candidate's) levels of mental fitness and also tests their ability to reason under pressure. This stage is mainly a testing of character and personal endurance. The second is the training in specific military skills: firearms technique, demolitions, surveillance, communications etc. In this, the soldier is turned from a fit, stable individual into a military specialist. We shall look at each of these training levels in turn and see what mental characteristics are required to survive and excel in them, and which attitudes and behaviours are looked for.

BASIC TRAINING

For the elite soldier, there is no such thing as 'basic' training. Induction into an elite unit requires the soldier to undergo some of the most punishing physical exertion the human frame is capable of enduring. Basic training can last for anything up to 40 weeks and, during that time, the candidate is assessed on many different criteria. From a psychological point of view, the trainers are looking for:

● **Tenacity.** Can the soldier maintain his commitment to succeed even when he is physically and mentally at the limits of his endurance? This tendency is primarily tested through seeing how the character

The Killing House

The Killing House tests SAS soldiers for the ability to make quick-fire decisions in chaotic and unpredictable situations filled with noise, smoke and confusion. Instructors look for clarity in action and maintaining a ruthless combat tempo.

holds up to exhausting marches and physical tasks.
- **Innovation and intelligence.** Does the soldier demonstrate distinctive methods of problem-solving under pressure and are his thought processes clear even under times of acute stress? Clear thinking is hampered by exhaustion, so

the elite forces push the limits of each soldier's physical endurance and then see if he is still capable of making tactical and practical decisions.
- **Team spirit.** Although there is a place for isolationists in the elite forces, most special forces training looks for people who will actively look towards the

Target minimisation

Even in the simple act of crossing a wall, the soldier must be trained to make himself as small a target as possible, imagining himself from the enemy's point of view. Failure to do this should be penalised in training to give the exercise consequence.

welfare of the group and put their own interests second. Team players will also tend to make better tacticians because they accept that others have talents which they do not possess.

- **Self-control.** Soldiers should show a solid control over their emotions. Elite troops are often called upon to make split-second decisions, the consequence of which is that someone lives or dies. Any sign that an individual is predisposed towards psychotic violence brings almost immediate dismissal – studies have shown that excessively violent personalities cannot adapt to discipline, are egocentric and boastful, and also tend to crumple during times of real danger.
- **Sense of humour.** A sense of humour is not just welcome, but essential. Studies conducted during the Korean War found that soldiers with a sense of humour (particularly a dry, cynical type) tended to make better fighters.

Each individual trainer adds to this list his own set of criteria and his own tests to bring out the soldier's true character. The initial training period is designed to be as punishing and demanding as possible. Although people can hide their true character for a short time, in hard, prolonged training, an individual will not have enough stamina to maintain this. To give us an idea of the mental demands a soldier faces during basic training, we will look in detail at the initial training course for entry into the SAS.

SAS Basic Training
The SAS training regimen is justifiably claimed as amongst the very hardest, if not

the hardest, of all military training programmes. Those who want to join the SAS can usually gain a 'taster' of the actual training by attending the Special Forces Briefing Course (SFBC) held at SAS HQ at Hereford. This is a weekend course which forms an introductory test of the candidate's mental and physical stamina, and gives the candidate a chance to discover whether the SAS is for him. The course lasts three days (usually from Friday to Sunday). On Friday, the candidate undergoes a series of mental tests relating to military practice. These include tests in comprehending and handling maps, IQ and first aid tests, and assessment of levels of military knowledge. Almost all of the rest of the weekend is devoted to physical testing. Saturday usually consists of two runs: two miles (3.2km) in 18 minutes and eight miles (12.9km) in 1 hour 40 minutes. Sunday

involves runs of about 1.5 hours in length, but this time the students have to carry a colleague for most of the period.

The physical aspects of the SFBC are interspersed with briefings and seminars on the traditions and lifestyle of the SAS. Although this is only the very first step on the ladder to becoming an SAS soldier, the trainers are still watching the candidates extremely closely for their mental qualities. In particular, they look for someone who:

● responds quickly and without procrastination to commands;
● does not attempt to show off or catch attention;
● shows the ability not only to complete the physical tests, but also to prove the spirit of effort by trying to maintain a place in the lead group;

Adaptive thinking 1

A soldier should be able to adapt whatever he has to hand to a new purpose. This 'adaptive thinking' gives a good indicator of the soldier's tactical acumen.

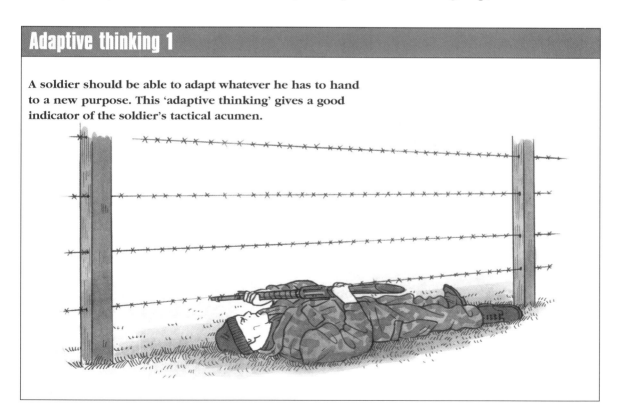

- demonstrates the self-awareness to make his own decisions and not merely follow the will of the group;
- shows that his physical skills are matched by his intelligence and judgement, something especially important in navigation exercises.

If the trainers are satisfied that the person meets these requirements, they can proceed to the selection phase of basic training. This is known as Route Selection and much of it takes place in the Brecon Beacons in Wales. Although the mountains in the Brecon Beacons are not particularly high, during winter they are very inhospitable, with high winds, fog and freezing sleet making hypothermia a real possibility. For around 18 days, the recruits are put through a series of increasingly harsh survival marches. The pace is relentless. Each day, the recruit finds himself either struggling up mountain sides with 22.6kg (50lb) of Bergen pack strapped to his back or doing special exercises such as swimming 20 circuits of a swimming pool wearing heavy clothing and items of kit. Typical distances to cover each day are around 29km (18 miles), with only hours to complete them, and periods of sleep are ever compressed. The 'highlight' of this period is the 'Long Drag'. The Long Drag takes place on the last day of Route Selection. It begins at midnight, with very little rest from the previous day's march of 15km (9 miles) carrying a 31.7kg (70lb) Bergen. The task ahead of the recruits is to march 64km (40 miles) over the Brecon Beacons in the middle of winter with 24.9kg (55lb) of pack and to complete the distance in 20 hours. As with all the marches of the past weeks, the soldier must also

Adaptive thinking 2

The soldier again faces the need for adaptive thinking, but the configuration of the barbed wire requires another approach using the same tools.

Assault mentality

Although clear thinking is essential for any assault, soldiers must also be able to summon a genuine aggression which has little pity for the enemy. The soldier must also be motivated by an overwhelming desire to see the given objectives achieved.

demonstrate first-class navigational skills using his map and compass, and prove that he can survive in truly inhospitable wilderness.

During this last stage of Route Selection, the trainers will meet the soldier at several points in the journey. At these stages, the trainers are looking for someone who is alert and confident, and someone who knows exactly where he is on the map. This is the quality known in military circles as being 'switched on', and signifies a state of mind that stays alert, focused and motivated despite the body being exhausted. If the candidate can survive the Long Drag physically and mentally, then he will be able to pass through to the 14-week Continuation

Rapid reactions

The rapid-reaction firing range tests the soldier's weapons handling, as well as seeing whether he can distinguish between targets, rather than just randomly firing.

immersion in freezing waters. One special test during this period is 'drown-proofing'. The recruit is thrown into a large, deep swimming pool with his ankles and wrists tied together. In this situation, he must first dive to the bottom of the pool and come back up again for five minutes. He then has to stay afloat for 20 minutes; do underwater back flips for five minutes; retrieve a face mask from the bottom of the pool using his teeth; and finally execute a quick 99m (100yd) swim. In South Africa, the South African Reconnaissance Commandos are left for two nights in the African bush with just a rifle and ammunition, and have to protect themselves from heat exhaustion and wild animals.

The purpose of these tortuous physical exercises is not only to weed out unsuitable candidates, but also to mark out those who are capable of summoning great mental strength when forces are arraigned against them. During SEALs training, recruits are at one point simply left standing in freezing sea water. As their body temperature drops, it is not uncommon for the instructor to make jokes and get all the recruits laughing, only then informing them that laughing increases the outflow of body heat. This treatment may seem exceptionally cruel, but the instructors need to know that the recruit's mind is durable enough to take all manner of knocks and still keep going.

Training in which he will learn the fundamental combat and operational skills of the SAS. This means that he still has a long way to go before the SAS beret can be worn, but the initiation is over and the soldier has demonstrated that he has grit and determination.

The Long Drag is typical of elite forces training, which tends to build up to a single defining moment of endurance and mental testing. Towards the end of a US Marine recruit's period at boot camp, he will have to undergo a final day-long march which takes him to the very brink of exhaustion – recruits in San Diego do a 16km (10 mile) run which includes a steeply inclined section known as the 'Grim Reaper'. US Navy SEALs experience the torments of 'Hell Week', an extraordinarily tough seven-day period of almost no sleep and constant

BECOMING THE ELITE

If the recruit passes the initial physical cauldron of basic training, it is at this point that

Training for endurance

Mud-walking is an exhausting exercise used by many armies to see how long the soldier can maintain his force of will and keep mounting frustration under control.

he will usually go on to learn the skills that will set him apart from other soldiers. The first phase of training will have demonstrated that the candidate has the toughness essential to endurance operations; the second phase will see if he has the mental acumen to perform some of the most complex military procedures in existence.

Much investment has been made into researching what type of military training gives the soldier the best form of mental preparation for combat. The conclusions have slowly emerged over the past 50 years, but can ultimately be boiled down to two main principles: motivation and realism.

Motivation is vital to military performance. Although the early phases of training tend to attack the recruit's ego and try to get him to fail, during the later skills training, soldiers tend to receive more encourage-

ment and help towards success. Research conducted in the United States and within European armies has emphatically proved that the greatest impetus to perform well during training is to receive the approbation of senior officers and one's peers, as well as access to more benefits such as extra pay or leave. Constant criticism tends to depress any person's level of motivation, so although training remains hard and critical, if the soldier does something right, the trainer will let him know. Praise has the valuable function of giving the soldier confidence and, with confidence, there is an increased self-belief which will be carried forwards into combat.

Perhaps the most vital ingredient to military training is its level of correspondence to the actual conditions of combat. There are two elements to developing realistic combat training that will support a soldier's mental performance in battle. The first of these is that the soldier should have the opportunity to experience as many of the munitions, stresses, decisions and scenarios as he will in a real firefight. This enables the soldier to enter battle without being overwhelmed by unfamiliar noises and sensations. The second is that the training exercises must be repeated again and again until the soldier is performing them without conscious thought. This is what soldiers mean when they speak after battle and say that their 'training took over'. Actions that are repeated constantly become second nature and, even if the soldier is consciously confused, his body will tend to follow familiar actions. The upshot of this is that, in action, the soldier's reflexes become lightning fast, as his subconscious mind tells him what to do well before he has consciously arranged his thoughts.

So, what are the practical methods of instilling the combat mentality in an elite soldier? Central to any elite programme of instruction is that training must both introduce a genuine element of danger and impose pressure upon the soldiers. Live firing exercises are therefore imperative. The Soviet Spetsnaz soldiers were particularly renowned for the brutality of their combat training. During exercises, the Spetsnaz trooper would not only have high-velocity rounds fired close past his head, but explosives and even chemical weapons would be detonated within his vicinity as well. The Spetsnaz training may have taken realism too far – fatalities during instruction were far higher than in most elite units – yet, by the time the soldier qualified for operations, he would to a certain extent know what it is like to have faced death. Such mental hardening would have been tested in campaigns like those which occurred in Afghanistan in the 1980s. More than 4000 Spetsnaz soldiers operated in Afghanistan, conducting raids against mujaheddin rebels holed up in the Afghan mountains. If captured, the Spetsnaz soldiers would face a gruesome and prolonged death at the hands of the

Laser-weapon training

Using laser-firing attachments on firearms enables soldiers to practise shooting at live targets, acclimatising them to putting a human being in their sights and pulling the trigger.

guerrillas, so an incredible level of nerve was required, which in part was derived from training. Similar effects are achieved in the SAS 'killing house' – the training building designed for urban combat and hostage-taking exercises. New officers used to undergo a violent initiation in which they were stood against a wall and told not to move, before an SAS team would burst into the room at speed and empty their H&K MP5s into the wall inches from the junior officer's head. After a fatality, this rite was stopped. Yet, in the killing house's more regular activities, mock assaults are conducted using live ammunition, tear gas and the disorientating G60 stun grenade (this produces an incredible blast of noise and light, and is used as a tactical device to overwhelm terrorists in hostage-taking situations without hurting hostages). These repeated assaults enable the soldiers to become mentally adjusted to the sensations of combat.

Elite soldiers must not only gain experience of being on the receiving end of fire; they must also become accustomed to delivering it. Range marksmanship is all well and good for competition shooting, but soldiers need to accustom themselves to using their weapons in rapid, confusing situations with limited time for either aiming or standard usage. The most typical exercise involves pop-up wooden targets which spring out at the soldier. The trainers will watch to see whether the soldier's reaction time is sharp and also whether he takes in target information before he fires – some of the targets will be civilian forms and there can be harsh penalties for shooting these.

New Technology

Technology, however, has taken fire training to a new level of dynamism. Laser firing systems can now be fitted to the muzzles of assault rifles and each soldier wears a laser receiver in his helmet. When the soldier fires his weapon, loaded with blanks, at his live enemy, the laser also fires. If the target is hit,

the receiver picks up the laser signal, the victim's identity is forwarded to a central computer and his own laser beam is cut off to signal a loss of ammunition and therefore a 'death'. This training device has proved invaluable in most of the world's developed armies. Not only does it enable the soldier to experience the fluidity of combat against a human opponent, but it also lets him actually place a human being in his sights and pull the trigger. Soldiers who perform such training sessions regularly develop much faster reaction skills and the ability to deal with the human factors of warfare.

Psychological training in firearms usage has yielded some interesting results. For instance, at ranges over 50m (164ft), semi-automatic fire produces more kills than automatic fire. Other revelations included the fact that, at night, the three-round burst seems to be the most effective configuration of fire at all ranges. A piece of white tape along the barrel improves night aiming, while men only trained in using tracers in night firing will shoot considerably worse without tracers than those men who have never received tracer training. Ingenious tests have also been devised to test firing abilities under stress. At HumRRO in the United States, an exercise was set up in which a soldier had to hit three bull's-eyes on a target to stop a sequence of dynamite explosions travelling closer and closer towards him. As expected, the closer the blasts came, the more the stress of the approaching blasts impaired the soldier's marksmanship. Elite training aims to overcome this tendency by acclimatising the soldier to the presence of explosions and bullets being discharged so that they no longer disrupt his mental balance. Thus he has an invaluable mental edge when he goes into combat against less-prepared individuals. By being more accustomed to noise and violence, he is therefore less impressed by it and more able to keep a perspective on the

Dark-room combat testing

A unusual test in the 1960s: US soldiers in a darkened room had to respond quickly to 'attacks' from dummies looming out of the darkness. The low light increased the levels of stress involved.

action and make the rapid tactical decisions for which the elite forces are renowned.

TOTAL SKILLS

Training to be an elite soldier means acquiring an enormous breadth and range of skills. Special forces troops require a high degree of intelligence, not just to make tactical predictions and actions on the spot, but also to apply the sheer diversity of their knowledge. The acquisition of any new skill goes through several phases. First, there is the stage of introduction. Here, the soldier encounters a new skill for the first time and must consciously learn its techniques. Second comes practice. Practising a skill over and over again reinforces the fluency with which the action can be performed. Finally, there is familiarity. At this stage, the practice pays off and the soldier can perform the skill almost without conscious thought: the physical and mental actions have become so familiar that they can be accomplished instinctively.

All elite soldiers must take every skill they are taught to that final stage of familiarity, an enormous task considering the amazing range of techniques and knowledge they must acquire. For example, a typical list of skills for an SAS soldier would include:

● **Weapons expertise.** Just the basic range of weapons which an SAS soldier must know how to strip, maintain and operate includes: M16 assault rifle; M203 grenade launcher; SA80 assault rifle; H&K MP5 submachine-gun; AKM assault rifle; SIG Sauer P226 and Browning Hi-Power pistols; the RPG7 rocket-propelled grenade and LAW rocket; FN MAG and FN Minimi machine-guns; conventional grenades and stun grenades; various sniper rifles; Arwen smoke- and gas-grenade launchers; and demolitions explosives.

● **Communications.** These are communications using radio- and satellite-based means, plus techniques of coding messages, deciphering coded messages and improvising communications in survival situations. Communications also includes how to direct air and artillery strikes.

● **Escape, evasion and survival.** Covered more deeply in Chapter Eight, these three skills involve knowing the means of staying alive in all the world's climates and environments – arctic, temperate, tropical, desert, sea – how to evade the tracking efforts of the enemy and how to resist interrogation if caught.

● **Combat first aid.** As almost all special forces operations are carried out a long way from easy medical evacuation, the soldier has to be conversant with all likely first-aid situations. This can cover everything from treating gunshot wounds and tropical disease to making natural remedies from plants and performing amputations.

● **Reconnaissance and surveillance.** As well as requiring the quality of patience, reconnaissance duties necessitate the knowledge of how to construct observation posts invisible to the enemy, how to identify the military hardware and installations correctly, and then how to decide on the most appropriate course of action in sympathy with the mission. This section of the soldier's skills also includes tracking techniques.

The list here refers to only the most fundamental areas of skills; these are added to depending on the type of unit. For example, members of Brazil's 1st Special Forces Counter-Terrorist detachment learn evasive and defensive driving techniques and spend time with Amazonian tribes to hone their jungle survival skills. Austria's GEK, Britain's Special Boat Service (SBS) and Greece's MYK are specially trained in ship boardings (during the Gulf War, MYK troops boarded some 217 freighters in the Red Sea, Persian Gulf and Indian Ocean as part of the enforcement of the UN's import embargo on Iraq). Yet, whatever the type of skill possessed, the soldier must show that he is not a slave to the learning, that he can adapt his skills with flexibility and tenacity when needed.

Ultimately, what instructors look for in elite soldiers is someone who is capable of free-thinking action, reinforced by undoubted combat skills. The time and the money invested in training a special forces soldier is exceptional. The return, however, is someone who has the confidence to accept missions that border on the impossible and execute them with unusual bravery, vigour and confidence.

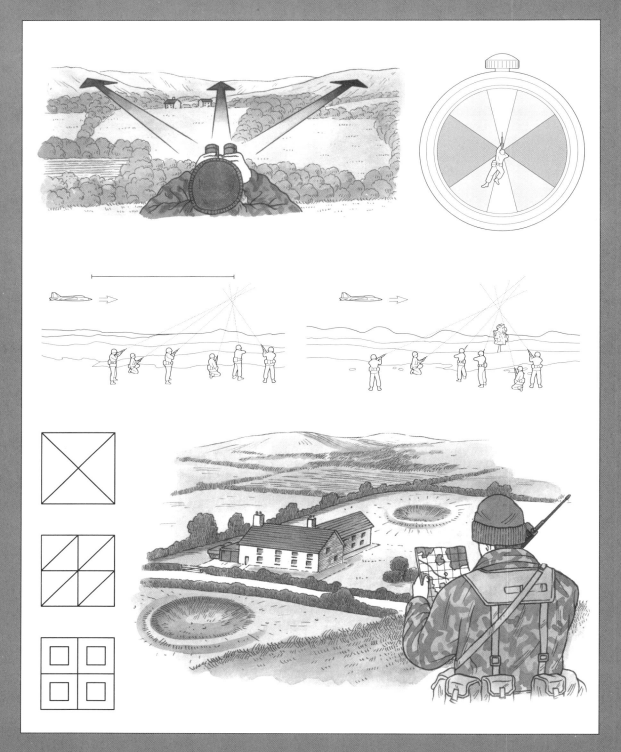

CHAPTER FOUR

Intelligence and Concentration

During World War II, military technology was proved to be one of the deciding factors in battle, culminating in the ultimate low-risk maximum-damage atomic bomb missions that destroyed Hiroshima and Nagasaki in 1945. Since then, weapon systems have continued to develop into demanding tools that require a number of skills to operate successfully.

After 1945, military technologists saw that huge investment in advanced weaponry – both conventional and nuclear – was a way forward in battlefield domination. Consequently, the tools of war rapidly became bigger, faster, more destructive. A Saratoga-class aircraft carrier which had weighed 30,000 tonnes in World War II had, by the 1950s, grown to 60,000 tonnes. World War II tank engines produced 350hp of power; today's equivalents are capable of 1500hp. Advanced munitions such as cluster bombs can now do the equivalent damage in a single aircraft pass to that of a whole flight of World War II fighter-bombers in the 1940s.

The list of technological improvements could go on and on. There is one crucial point here for our study of the military mind. Following World War II, the tools of war became increasingly complex to use and also there were simply more of them. An infantryman in, say, the Pacific campaign of 1944 would be trained to use his personal weapon (M1 Garand, Thompson M1A1, BAR or M30), basic explosive devices such as grenades, and some other tactical weapons such as the bazooka and the flame-thrower. Today's soldier, by contrast, will have a personal weapon (such as the M16A2, to take a US example), but he or she will also need to be able to use ground-to-air shoulder-launched rockets, guided anti-armour missiles, laser-targeting systems for guiding air-ordnance delivery and very sophisticated computer networks in tactical roles.

The intelligence required to handle these weapons is ever expanding, especially as many of the weapons systems require solid mathematical or computer skills. Nowhere is this truer than within the ranks of elite units. Special forces, because of the nature of their missions and the fact that they tend to attract a higher proportion of the military budget than other personnel, are expected to handle, deploy and understand the most complex weapons on the military market. Yet they must also be able to survive those weapons when used against them. For example, even before they reach their objective, an elite force making an incursion against an enemy coastline must use all their intelligence to negotiate surveillance technologies of incredible sophistication. Over-the-horizon (OTH) radar bounces off the ionosphere to scan the

Sniper's range card

The sniper's range card gives the sniper the ability to 'map' the world in front of him in a clear way. This method serves to support better tactical decisions when it comes to the problems of firing , as well as the challenges of escape and evasion.

airspace up to 6437km (4000 miles) away. Ship- and submarine-borne radar may be guarding against underwater intrusion. AWACS (airborne warning and control system) aircraft such as the Tu-126 Moss scan the ground and airspace up to a range of 482km (300 miles). An elite insertion team must use incredible tactical and mathematical judgement to work out how to penetrate these defences effectively without being discovered and compromised.

Following the increasing complexity of military weapons systems are a whole other range of difficulties which the elite soldier must negotiate. The advances in weaponry have led to more demanding tactics, where outmanoeuvring an advanced enemy becomes as much a battle of technical acumen as courage. Many elite operations will also be conducted in politically sensitive low-intensity wars where the enemy may well be mixed into the civilian population. In such situations, a single misplaced demolitions device can send diplomatic ripples around the world, so the special forces have the additional pressure of mixing military with political objectives. This has been especially true following the Vietnam War, when Vietnamese civilian casualties led to the collapse of domestic and international support for the US effort. Finally, both the speed and distances involved in fighting wars have accelerated and increased, respectively, since World War II. Battlefield data is now more readily available from sophisticated surveillance and

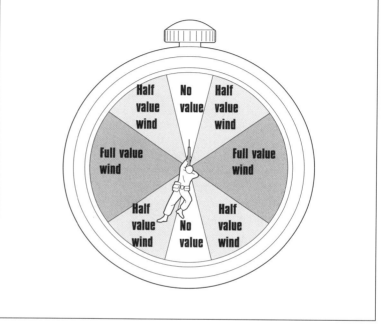

Wind-direction clock system

A sniper makes several complex calculations before he can be confident of a long-distance shot, including wind direction and speed. He can evaluate windage with the clock system.

Half value wind
No value
Half value wind
Full value wind
Full value wind
Half value wind
No value
Half value wind

satellites. The pace of decision-making for soldiers on the ground is relentless and intellectually challenging.

This chapter is about the above-average intelligence required to be a modern soldier in an elite regiment. Physical stamina and courage are prerequisites of a special forces operative. Yet without a keen mind, practically trained, the physical and moral efforts will be undone by poor judgement and inefficient thought-processes.

TESTING FOR INTELLIGENCE

The professionalisation of military forces since World War II and the related fall in manpower has meant, in many nations, that army, navy and air force recruiters can be much more selective in the personnel they take on board. Academic standards have become much more of a feature in selection processes, although, as we shall see, these are far from the main measure of intelligence. After all, most of the senior-ranking British officers of World War I were the beneficiaries of a public school and university education, but history now dwells upon their appalling tactical ineptitude which sent hundreds of thousands of young men to unnecessary deaths. Surprisingly, well into World War II, there was often an anti-intellectual attitude towards those units which professed themselves specialists. The Special Operations Executive (SOE), Britain's adaptable and courageous secret agent network, spent much of the war trying to convince mainstream military officers to support important and valuable operations. The intolerance for special operations and the secretive skills of its practitioners led to some labelling SOE as 'assassins', while people like Arthur 'Bomber' Harris (Commander in Chief of RAF Bomber Command, 1942–45) resisted using single bombers to aid SOE missions. The root cause of much of this resentment was mistrust for advanced intelligence, which so often seemed to threaten classic military tactics. Since the war, military leaders' decisions have become much more transparent to the world's media, so soldiers have to be seen to be acting intelligently. Also, as we have seen, studies have indicated that more intelligent individuals actually make better fighters in combat. Thus intelligence is now held to be a primary value in elite soldiers.

Most military units have minimum academic standards for entry. US Marines need to score 30-plus on the standard Armed Services Vocational Aptitude Battery (ASVAB) intelligence test, although as 90 per cent of US Marines are high school graduates, two-thirds of entrants have scores of 50-plus. The Royal Marines in the UK usually require officers to have two A levels (equivalent to a US high school diploma) and, commonly, a good honours degree. Opportunities are also usually available for pursuing education once inside the military. In the US Army, for example, most soldiers can access Army Continuing Education System (ACES) courses to study everything from literature and languages to computing and engineering, while pursuing their standard soldiering.

Yet while academic qualifications may indicate the ability to handle difficult concepts, military recruiters will usually be aware that the most adaptable intelligence may not be indicated by school or university performance. Proficiency in subjects such as mathematics and English is usually required to be a soldier, but education cannot indicate some of the other aspects of intelligence which are equally important – perhaps more important – in a good combat soldier:

- **Independent thinker**. Elite soldiers need to show absolute self-reliance and demonstrate that they can think for themselves even if their conclusions seem to fly in the face of conventional wisdom.
- **Creative thinking.** Combat is largely chaos. Soldiers that look beyond obvious solutions to tactical problems (of which the enemy is probably aware) can often control the chaos through creative and innovative thinking. General Gray of the US Marines, author of the influential *Warfighting* manual, states that war is both an art and a science, and the soldier must be able to think in both spheres if he is to be effective.
- **Able to concentrate.** Studies have shown that some very intelligent people show a marked lack of ability to focus on one project for a long time – their minds flit about through boredom and the need for stimulus. Such people would generally make poor elite soldiers, as special forces units require individuals who can lock their concentration onto

one objective and follow it through with total commitment.

● **Able to control emotions.** Although 'emotional intelligence' has become a buzzword in popular psychology, the same quality is required for elite soldiers. Unless the soldier has an essential maturity and the ability to control his own emotions, it is doubtful whether he will be able to give the consistent operational performance required by an elite unit.

● **Strength of mind.** Being able to think effectively is only part of a soldier's fighting capacity. More important is the nature of those thoughts. If a soldier constantly sees only the odds against him, he is likely to become demotivated and indecisive. If, however, his tenor of thinking is founded on the belief that he can take on any situation and dominate it utterly, he is more likely to succeed with his plans.

These qualities are just some of the elements of intelligence which recruiters look for in military personnel. The selection

Zones of fire range card

This shows a typical range card used by an artillery officer. Handling artillery fire requires a detached sense of control which is not swayed by the power of the detonations. Using the zone card helps develop such an attitude, as well as assisting accurate fire.

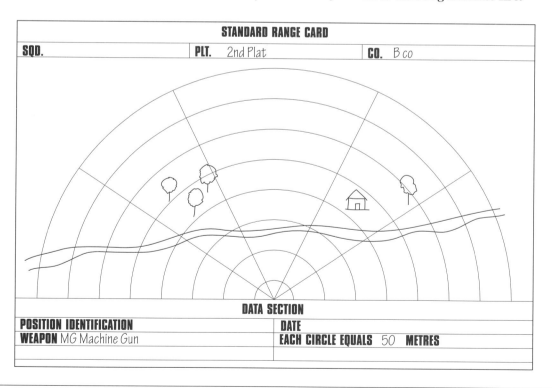

STANDARD RANGE CARD

| SQD. | PLT. 2nd Plat | CO. B co |

DATA SECTION

| POSITION IDENTIFICATION | DATE |
| WEAPON MG Machine Gun | EACH CIRCLE EQUALS 50 METRES |

Ground-to-air fire

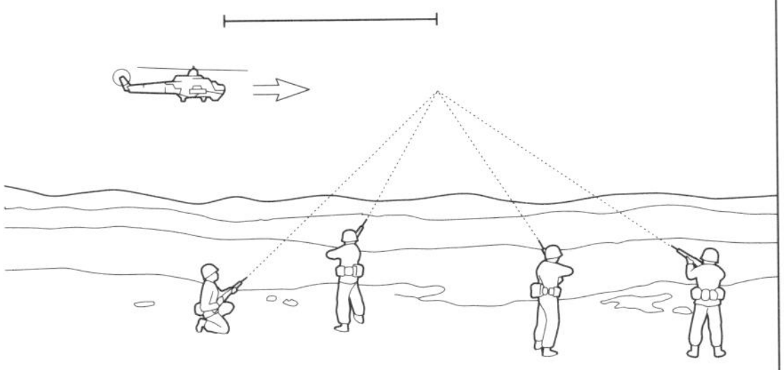

When shooting at helicopters or jets, a group of soldiers must be able to determine a point in time and space through which the aircraft must fly. With jets, that point is about 200m (219yds) from the nose; with helicopters it is a distance of about 50m (55yds).

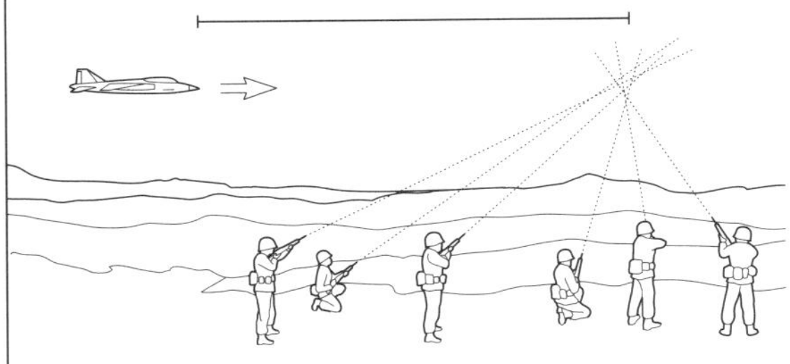

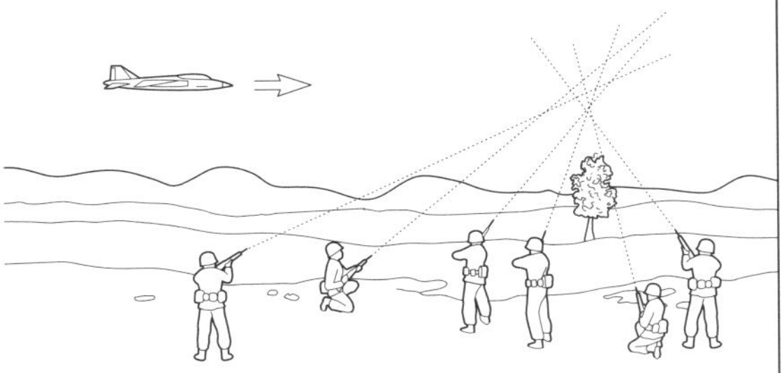

The small-arms fire aimed from the ground can be co-ordinated by using a visual reference point on the landscape as a line of fire. In the case illustrated here, the soldiers are using a tree as a marker, gathering a storm of bullets above it.

process for soldiers (especially elite soldiers) tends to examine both practical and abstract intelligence. Abstract intelligence – powers of reasoning, logic and deduction – can be tested through standard IQ tests. A range of these is used throughout the world and their contents are usually classified. However, they are known to consist of a straightforward run of tests and the results are a good indicator of the applicant's linguistic, mathematical, logical and observational skills. Yet paper tests are only one method of reaching an assessment.

In the Royal Marines, all officer candidates are subjected to the three-day Admiralty Interview Board (AIB) aboard HMS *Sultan* in Gosport, Hampshire. The board consists of a panel of highly critical (and unsmiling) RM officers, plus a psychologist, a civilian headmaster and an RM careers officer. Over three days, the candidate is put through an exhausting sequence of verbal interviews, mental tests and assessments of his general knowledge and his knowledge of RM history. Weakness in any area will be ruthlessly exploited and evaluated, mainly to see how the candidate's intelligence stands up to being placed under extremes of pressure. A typical exercise would include being asked how a group of survivors on a desert island might live through their ordeal and be rescued. Every twist and turn in the candidate's logic is queried and analysed by the board until the candidate twists himself into logical knots. That his logic is shaky is not necessarily a problem; how he handles himself emotionally in argument is what is important.

All candidates for elite forces have their practical intelligence and their theoretical intelligence tested. There is little difference between the two, for practical intelligence is generally a test of whether theoretical intelligence is actually working. The elements which make up practical training are explored more fully in the previous chapter. To summarise, recruits for the special forces are trained by simulating actual battlefield circumstances, with real stress and real danger being constantly present. In all special forces, mock battles of varying scales and sizes are played out to see whether the soldier's thought-processes stay clear under fire. In the US Marine Corps boot camp, groups of soldiers fight against one another in mock battles, realism provided by 0.11kg (0.25lb) blocks of explosive being detonated around them and live ammunition being fired over their heads. All the while, instructors observe the soldiers' ability to handle pressurised decision-making environments.

Defensive thinking

The diagram here shows an all-round defence procedure for use when disembarking from a helicopter. Combat intelligence often consists of predicting worst possible outcomes and adapting tactics to this prediction.

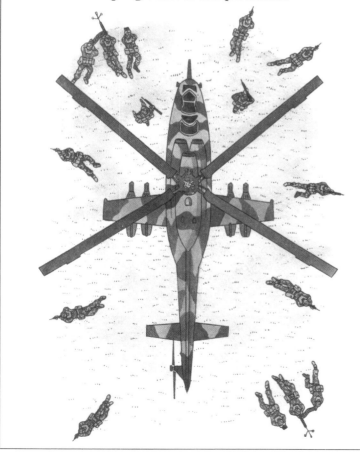

Through this mix of practical and theoretical testing, recruiters gain a good overall picture of the levels of intelligence and concentration which an individual will be able to muster in battle. But let us return to specifics. What are the individual intelligence skills that a soldier must possess to make him a part of the elite? Basically, an elite soldier must possess the following qualities of mind if he is to make it as a special forces operative:

- mathematical intelligence
- communication skills
- technical intelligence
- tactical intelligence
- focus

Now we will turn our attention to why each of these individual types of thinking or attitude is required on the modern battlefield. Once we have assessed each type of intelligence, then we will look at how all of them come together in one particular mode of special forces operation: sniping.

Mathematical Intelligence

The modern soldier almost invariably cannot escape the need to use mathematical skills. Even the act of navigation alone – a basic requirement for any soldier on land, sea or air – needs someone to calculate angles, distance and time. The list of activities for the elite soldier which require good mathematical intelligence is extensive and includes:

- navigation
- estimating logistical requirements
- artillery/airstrike control
- coding messages
- range finding
- estimating enemy troop strength during surveillance

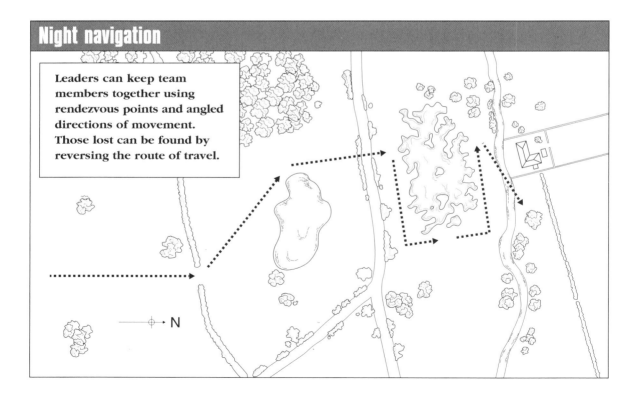

Night navigation

Leaders can keep team members together using rendezvous points and angled directions of movement. Those lost can be found by reversing the route of travel.

N

Visual intelligence

When viewing terrain through binoculars, the ground is scanned from right to left, increasing towards the horizon. Key features are memorised and reported.

This list is not exhaustive. It will be noticed that mathematical skills are as essential to actual combat performance as they are to barrack-based duties. Good illustrations of this are the activities of directing anti-aircraft fire using small arms and artillery control.

Shooting down modern jets using only personal weapons or machine guns is difficult in the extreme. A modern strike fighter can be moving at the speed of sound when it draws past in the attack, so to hit it from a standing position using only an assault rifle is fairly implausible. Yet it can be done, and elite soldiers are trained in aircraft-downing techniques which use processes of mathematical judgement. The speed of the aircraft

Mapping the terrain

Tactical decisions are made more simple by mapping the crucial environmental and tactical features. This cuts out surplus data and allows the clear sight of objectives.

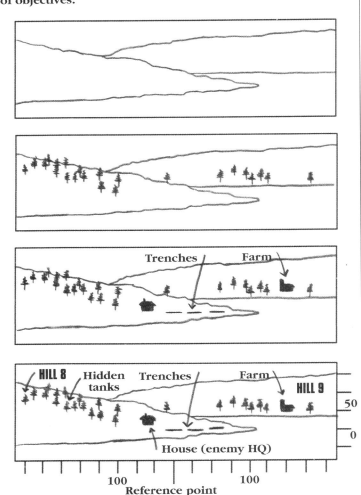

the ground. Thus, against jets, soldiers need to calculate a point approximately 200m (656ft) from the front of the aircraft at a particular moment of its flight, and then concentrate a shower of small arms rounds into that point so that the aircraft then flies through the hail.

To calculate that distance, the soldier can either do a visual multiplication of the length of the aircraft (which should ideally be known by the special forces soldier) or use techniques such as placing the index finger over the centre of the image of the flying aircraft (for a standard fighter, if only the nose and tail overlap the finger, the aircraft is about 350m (1148ft) away).

This example is a matter of basic distance calculation using techniques of visual estimation, rather than a distinct mathematical process. More advanced mathematical techniques are applied in field tactics, especially when the soldier needs to define his position in relation to a particular target (say, for the purposes of artillery control). If the soldier needs to calculate how far he is from a target object, he first takes a compass reading on the target. Then he moves parallel to the target until the compass reading to the target changes in either direction by 45 degrees. Using basic geometry, the soldier can now work out that the distance between the point of his original reading

cuts out the possibility of directly aiming at the aircraft; by the time the bullets get to the point of aim, the jet has already passed that point. What is needed is for the aircraft to fly into the stream of bullets coming up from

Controlling artillery

This requires mathematics, ballistics, communications and munitions skills. The controller must 'walk-in' the fire onto the target by giving instructions on range and bearing to the firebase.

and the point of his 45-degree angle reading is actually the same distance as that from his starting point to his target.

Similar techniques can be used to estimate the height of target features such as buildings and aerial masts. Once the distance between observer and object is known, the soldier holds up a pencil at arm's length and marks the visual height on the pencil. This height is then measured in centimetres. The distance between the pencil in the hand and the observer's eye is also measured. These two measurements actually form an angle between eye and pencil proportionately equal to the angle between observer and the top of the target. Again, turning to geometry, 'a' equals the height measured on the pencil, 'b' equals the distance between pencil and eye, 'A' equals the height of the target and 'B' equals the distance to the target. Thus the equation a/b x B = A will yield a good estimation of the target height.

These two examples show how acts of mathematical intelligence are written into the fighting ability of an elite soldier. Thus, numeracy is thoroughly tested before any individual can become a member of a special forces unit.

Angles in artillery control

A soldier can utilise his fingers to measure angles for artillery control if there are no technical aids. There are 6400 mils (a unit of measurement) in a circle, and one mil is an angular distance of one metre at 1000m. The diagram shows how the hand can be used to calculate mils and then transfer this into distance.

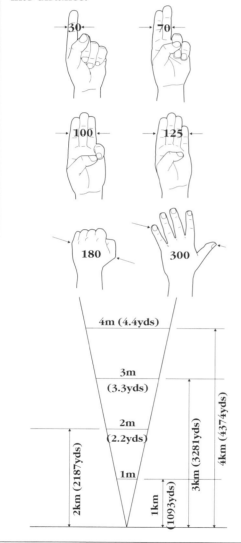

Communication Skills

Communication skills are invaluable in all walks of life, not just soldiering. Most intelligence tests for military units contain some element of linguistic or comprehension assessment. The would-be soldier needs to demonstrate that he has control over language and its meaning. The assessors will be aware that the ability to put together coherent, easily understood sentences and understand complex orders when received means that the soldier will be able to shape tactics with confidence, rather than add to battlefield confusion.

Intelligent use of language for the elite soldier often means that they acquire foreign languages to aid in international missions.

Calculations in range-finding

How to calculate range and height of a target (see main text): mathematical skills are an often forgotten part of the Special Forces portfolio, but they are vital.

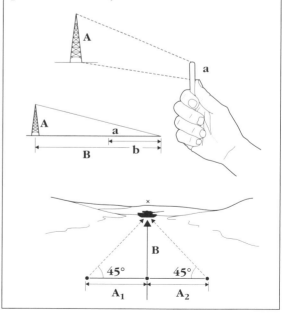

Memory exercise – British Army (1940s)

Observe a shape, one every few seconds. Cover them over. Try to draw as many from memory as possible. This is good training in both observation and recall.

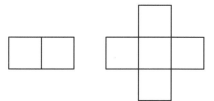
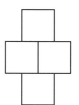
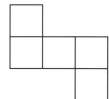

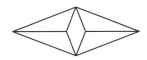

Linguistic test

An example of a language puzzle used by Special Forces recruitment papers. Try to crack the code of this puzzle to reveal a comprehensible sentence.

Vjg iriqc jt up vjg ohiw jpero.

Acquiring another language for military use need not be difficult, as, unless the soldier is working undercover or he is participating in advanced social programmes, then all he needs is a basic working vocabulary and grammar. During the Vietnam War, studies were conducted in the US Army into the minimum Vietnamese-language requirements for soldiers to be able to conduct basic interrogation and liaison. Knowledge of 450 words was found to be sufficient in most cases to sustain a basic conversation.

In terms of practical languages, English, French and Spanish are the most useful trio. These languages linger in the extensive former colonies of the three countries and English itself has been adopted as the international language of business and commerce. Many SAS soldiers attend the British Army School of Languages to acquire different languages suited to their operational destinations. Arabic, Malay and Norwegian are three of the most popular languages, and vocabulary of between 500 and 1000 words of each plus a knowledge of the essential grammar enable the soldiers to converse with some degree of confidence and versatility.

Technical Intelligence

The issue of technical intelligence in many ways links us back to our opening points concerning the advances in weapons technology. The simplest assault rifle may consist of hundreds of parts, including many delicate mechanisms such as gas-operation systems and cartridge extractors. Being able to maintain and use this weapon is the thin end of the technical wedge for the elite soldier. Special forces troops are called on to perform duties which encompass the roles of several soldiers in the regular army. Thus, while a regular army unit may have a field medic, driver and demolitions expert as separate individuals, in the special forces, these roles will often be performed by the same man. Furthermore, elite soldiers may have to engage in unusual technical pursuits as part of their operational portfolio. Members of the US Army's secretive Delta Force, for example, are not only obliged to understand the technicalities of modern weapons, but also have to pick up several specialist skills which rely on good manual dexterity and the ability to understand engineering principles. Examples include lockpicking – a skill essential for silent entry assault operations – and other more dramatic talents such as how to drive racing cars and even trains. Because Delta soldiers are also on hand for aircraft hostage situations, they are trained in how to supply an aircraft with aviation fuel and hydraulic

Number test – British Army (1940s)

Fill in the blanks in these sequences of numbers. Such tests are commonly used to evaluate general intelligence and numeracy amongst army recruits.							
3	5	6	10	9	15	…	…
1	2	6	12	36	72	…	…
1	4	10	22	46	94	…	…
1	2	6	21	88	445	…	…
4	7	15	31	63	127	…	…

fluid. When it comes to building assaults, they must know how to ascend or descend the face of the tallest skyscrapers.

The Delta Force example shows why the elite soldier needs to possess practical knowledge and a capacity to turn the mind to handling what are essentially engineering problems at any moment during an operation. Even skills such as demolitions – involving the actual destruction of buildings, bridges etc. – need to be based on comprehension of factors such as structural loading, points of tension and material properties in order to be conducted successfully.

Tactical Intelligence

Tactical intelligence is covered more fully in later chapters, but suffice to say that it is one of those aspects of military intelligence which is taught, rather than natural. Yet there are ingredients of being a good tactician that come from personality, rather than learning. One of the key ingredients is being able to make decisions. Most elite training programmes place the recruits into pressurised decision-making environments from the moment they step off the bus. At US Marine Corps boot camp, for instance, a recruit may well find himself between two instructors who are shouting apparently contradictory and impossible commands at him. The purpose

is not just to see if the recruit will break under the pressure, but also to see if he can make a decision and then stick to it. The Marines are taught the 'rule of three' when making decisions – come up with three possible solutions to every problem (no more, no less), look at the pros and cons of each, then choose one and stick with it. This technique has extraordinary success and, by the time the recruits become Marines, they are very comfortable with handling decision-making at every level.

Tactical intelligence is a massive subject and requires everything from a good eye for detail, a strong memory and the ability to visualise problems and solutions to a capacity to organise and also the tendency to be able to stick with one's choice. However, it is a common misperception that tactics should be complex and overtly daring. The acronym 'KISS' is prevalent in the US forces, standing for 'Keep it simple, Stupid'. The penalties of overcomplex tactical efforts can be seen at their most tragic in Delta Force's Operation Eagle Claw in 1980. American hostages were being held in the US Embassy in Tehran, Iran. Delta Force was charged with their rescue and produced a plan consisting of several stages. First, the soldiers were to be flown in a flight of seven MC-130E transport aircraft (three for Delta, three for fuel and one carrying

Calculating aircraft distance

A fighter aircraft's distance can be judged using the forefinger. With a MiG 21, if the finger covers from the start of the tailplane to the cockpit's front, it is 350m (1148ft) away.

a company of US Rangers) from Masirah Island off the coast of Oman to a base (Desert 1) about 320km (200 miles) from Tehran. Once there, eight RH-53D helicopters from USS *Nimitz* would arrive, refuel, then transport them to a secret location just outside Tehran where they would wait to effect a night attack against the enemy. During this time, the Rangers would have secured Manzariyeh airfield 48km (30 miles) south of Tehran. It was intended that, after the rescue of the hostages, the helicopters would airlift the soldiers and freed embassy officials to Manzariyeh, where a C-141 Starlifter transporter would fly everyone out.

The complexity of the plan made it open to many problems, although much of what subsequently happened was down to bad luck as much as bad judgement. Arrival at Desert 1 on 24 April found not an unused strip of desert road, but an active route. A passenger bus with 30 Iranian civilians had to be captured and held. A Ranger ended up firing an LAW anti-tank rocket into an fleeing petrol tanker, although the driver actually escaped in a smaller truck. Compounding

this loss of surprise, only six of the helicopters arrived, half an hour late. One of these then had mechanical problems and one, tragically, collided with a MC-130E; eight US servicemen died in the resulting blast. The mission was then called off and the hostages in the US embassy were later released after negotiations.

Eagle Claw was blighted by unfortunate accidents, but military observers have since commented that the mission was too complicated, relying on too many sequences of complex events to be successful. The lesson was a hard one, but elite missions today try to strip tactics down to the bare minimum, relying instead on tempo and hard-hitting combat skills. Those who are members of elite regiments need to show that they can think in clear tactical movements and develop plans that are workable from insertion to escape.

Focus and Concentration

Concentration is needed by all soldiers, but none more so than those belonging to elite units. Elite operations have a surgical quality to them, and frequently require the soldiers to operate on their own and face considerable periods of inactivity. Boredom and restlessness thus become genuine enemies to concentration, and only if the soldier can resign himself to these and keep his mind lively and alert will he be effective in his role. All elite soldiers are screened for the ability to concentrate. Particularly revealing exercises into the relationship between personality and concentration were conducted in Northern Ireland from the 1960s to the 1980s to do with the recruitment of bomb disposal personnel. People who were discovered to have feelings of resentment at some past incident in their lives, or those who had a fascination with elements such as fire, wind, or storms, were generally unsuitable for bomb disposal; the psychologists found that, under pressure, the disposal officer's

Using tracer fire

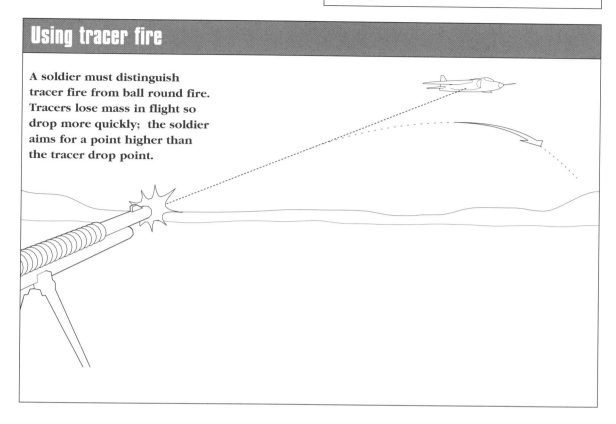

A soldier must distinguish tracer fire from ball round fire. Tracers lose mass in flight so drop more quickly; the soldier aims for a point higher than the tracer drop point.

attention could be pulled away from his task by either suicidal thoughts or a fascination with the potential explosion. These thoughts may well be in the back of the soldier's mind, but even this is enough to distract him. Psychologists also found that successful EOD (explosive ordnance officers) demonstrated an eye for detail, an enjoyment of manual dexterity and the ability to distinguish objects out of place against their background.

Similar principles apply to elite soldiers. To show the concentration needed for special operations, they must be balanced and composed, and able to direct their attention at will to their chosen task. Nonetheless, their minds should also remain flexible and not become fixated on one course of action.

So how do the above forms of intelligence actually come together in an operational role? To see them in action, we shall now turn to one of the most demanding of special forces roles: sniping. As we shall see, sniping requires that all aspects of the elite intelligence unit in one smooth-functioning operation. To see this clearly, we shall run through the list of intelligence qualities above once more, applying them this time specifically to the sniper's role.

SNIPING
Mathematical Skills

Mathematical calculations and deduction feature surprisingly highly in the sniping mission. First, the soldier must accurately calculate the distance between himself and his target. This he can do using the method above, using map coordinates or, if he is being fired upon, by a simple calculation. When being fired at, the crack of the bullet is heard before the blast of the rifle. The further the shooter is away, the longer the time between the two noises. Working on the basis of a high-velocity (3000fps+) rifle being fired, a sound gap of one second indicates that the shooter is about 630m (2060ft) away. Using this as a landmark, the sniper can calculate other distances and position himself correctly (snipers generally fire at ranges of more than 500m (1640ft) to avoid detection upon firing).

Once he has a target distance, the sniper must calibrate his sights to perform correctly at that distance, and he must also make an allowance for windage. Calculating windage (the influence of wind upon the flight of a bullet) begins with estimating wind speed and direction. This can be done by tying a piece of cloth to a tree or other mast, and then measuring the rough angle the cloth assumes from the tree and dividing this angle by four to get the wind velocity in miles per hour. With this measurement, he can calculate what windage adjustment in minutes (a unit of measurement) to make using the formula: range (R) multiplied by wind speed (V) divided by 15 (for distances up to 457m/1500ft), 14 (550m/1800ft), 13 (640–732m/2100–2400ft), 12 (823m/2700ft) or 11 (914m/3000ft). Once the soldier has made all of these calculations, he is able to confidently deliver an accurate shot.

Communication Skills

Communication skills are perhaps not the most obvious intelligence quality for the solitary profession of sniper, but one which makes more sense within urban counterterrorist and hostage-taking situations. When there are multiple targets, the many snipers employed need to relate their opportunities for fire to each of the other snipers and the communications centre. By doing so, each sniper can fire simultaneously and, in an ideal world, take out all the terrorists in one wave of fire. For example, during a hostage situation in Somalia when guerrillas took 28 French schoolchildren hostage on a bus, French GIGN snipers shot four terrorists in the head simultaneously with 7.62-mm FR-F1 rifles. Such coordination required clear expressions of intent from each sniper and an awareness of his position as part of a team.

Technical Intelligence

A sniper must be an absolute master of his rifle. He must know how it fires, how it is maintained, how the weather might affect its performance, what heat build-up in the barrel will do to its accuracy, and how to get the best out of the sights fitted (including telescopic, optical and thermal imaging sights). His technical awareness must also extend to such factors as the best clothes to wear for the sniping role (soft cloth to stop branches making a noise when rubbing against the material, and tightly fitted at wrists and ankles to avoid snagging), and how to construct a natural hide to best conceal his position.

Sometimes, a sniper will also be used in anti-materiel roles – especially if he is armed with one of the new breed of enormously powerful sniper rifles such as the .50 calibre Barrett M82A1 which can punch through an engine block at distances well in excess of 1.6km (1 mile). In this capacity, the soldier will have to possess enough technical knowledge to identify the most structurally vulnerable point on, for example, a satellite communications system and then be able to put a round into that point at extended distances.

Tactical Intelligence

The two main tactical considerations for a sniper are 1) how to get into position to be able to deliver the shot; and 2) how to get out of the area safely once the shot has been fired. Both considerations must organise the tactical intelligence of the soldier. For example, he must select a position in which he is obscured from view, with a clear line of fire to the target, but also position his gun so that the blast from firing will not raise dust and consequently reveal his whereabouts. Ideally, once the shot is taken, he should be able to fall back over the brow of a hill or disappear into dense woodland.

In a hostage-rescue setting, the tactical priorities shift towards preserving the safety of the hostages. This means assuming a sniping position high up on buildings, the theory being that, with a steep angle of fire, the bullet will pass through the terrorist and quickly bury itself in the floor a short distance from him and not go on to endanger the safety of those held captive. If shooting from behind a car, the sniper will position himself automatically behind the engine block to provide himself with the strongest protection should fire be returned. If shooting from a window, the sniper will not stand directly in the windowsill – where he would be fully visible and framed for a terrorist shot – but stand back in the room where his silhouette will be darkened and less prominent to observers outside the building.

As we can see, the final act of aiming and pulling the trigger is only part of a long tactical process in which the sniper must engage and he must use considerable judgement from the beginning of the operation to give himself the highest chances of surviving a mission.

Focus and concentration

Once the moment does finally arrive for the sniper to aim and take the shot at his intended target, his levels of concentration must be at their optimum. To assist his aiming, the sniper should control his breathing properly. This should be carried out in the following way:

- **1.** Draw in a deep breath and let it out calmly.
- **2.** Draw in another deep breath, but this time hold it for a second, then let it out naturally but slowly.
- **3.** At the bottom of the breath is a natural pause before breathing begins again and the body is very still and calm. In this moment, pull the trigger.

By assisting his concentration with breathing, the soldier should be in a perfect mental and physical state to take his shot. Of course, his concentration will have been exercised before this moment by activities such as targeting and even waiting for the target to appear. Remember, the target may be exercising all the fieldcraft skills of the elite soldier himself, so a sharp eye is required to stop the sniper becoming a victim of a sniping attack himself.

Despite the tension of sniping, boredom is possibly the greatest enemy to the sniper in the effective execution of his role. Once he is bored, concentration lapses and then mistakes can be made. Thus, the genuinely proficient sniper is a rare breed indeed and this role therefore requires men of exceptional mental stamina.

NEED TO BE ADAPTABLE

The example of the sniper is only one of many possible illustrations of mental intelligence in action that we could take from looking at the elite units. The soldiers from special forces necessarily have to be supremely adaptable and psychologically dextrous if they are to stand any chance of survival in the hostile environments which they have to frequent.

It is hard to think of any other 'job' in this world which equals the mental and physical demands of the elite soldier, and therefore they deserve our genuine respect for the very large capabilities that their minds must possess.

CHAPTER FIVE

Building a Team Mind

Teamwork is essential for success, particularly for small special forces teams operating in hostile or potentially hostile environments. On 9 April 1973, elite Israeli soldiers from the exceptional Sayeret Mat'kal special forces unit demonstrated the principles of teamwork in a bloody and ruthlesslessly efficient manner during a counterterrorist operation.

The operation they were involved in was motivated by revenge. The early 1970s were a period of virulent terrorism within Israeli borders and against Israeli-linked targets worldwide, with multiple Islamic, Arabic and Palestinian factions venting their anger against Israeli civilian and military targets. This culminated in the massacre of Israeli athletes at the Munich Olympics, an act which stunned the world and mobilised Israel to mount Operation Spring of Youth.

This was to be one of the largest counterterrorist operations the world had ever seen, and the first target was those who had masterminded the Munich massacre.

The leaders and members of the Palestinian 'Black September' terrorist organisation were living in an expensive district of West Beirut. Their flats were well protected by bodyguards both inside and out, these men being all too aware that Israel could be contemplating action against their forces.

Sayeret Mat'kal operatives knew that deception and fast, stunning violence was the only way to take out the Black September leaders. Dressed in civilian clothes, they waited outside the Black September apartments in three rented Opel cars, nothing on their person connecting them with Israel; the mission was a political minefield (even their Ingram Mac-10 and AK-47 weapons were traceable only to Palestinian or Syrian sources). When the time came to act, they did so with cunning and co-operation, two of the defining features of special forces operations.

A group of male and female agents, the men dressed like hippies and the women dressed seductively, walked casually up to the PLO guards who were sat in two black Mercedes in front of the apartments. The women had been selected for their physical allure, and the guards engaged in some flirtation. It was the last thing they would ever do.

Seconds later, one of the guards had been shot through the head by a .22 pistol round and two other guards mown down by fire from the agents in the cars. All the gunfire so far had been silenced, but one stray round had penetrated the bonnet of a Mercedes and triggered its horn; their cover was blown.

Sayeret Mat'kal operational planning is exhaustive, so allowances had been made for such a potential disaster. The agents scattered to positions around the streets to guard against reinforcements, while dedicated teams rushed into apartments on opposite sides of the street to find and eliminate their targets. One group of four men, led by Major Yoni Netanyahu, rushed straight to the sixth-floor apartment of creator of the Munich massacre, Abu Yusef, and blew the door off with specially prepared charges. Major Netanyahu machine-gunned Abu Yusef to death in front of his wife and children, while the other men

Team reconnaissance

A good example of team thinking. Each member acts in a supporting role to each other, with the flank men protecting the central advance with 360 degree coverage.

searched out important files and paperwork. Across the street, two other teams were killing Black September frontmen Kamal A'dwan and Kamal Nasser with a similar bloody efficiency. Down in the street, Israeli agents and Lebanese troops were by this time engaged in a ferocious street battle. Yet once the assault teams had completed their work, an incredible display of driving by men from Mossad (the Israeli secret service) took all the agents at speed out of the firefight and down to the Mediterranean coast. There, Israeli special forces frogmen had deposited dinghies which the agents then used to make their escape.

This stunning raid by Sayeret Mat'kal has many military virtues: good intelligence, effective use of weaponry, courage. Yet what stands out most is the impressive level of integration between the team members, even under incredible pressure and violence. If any one element of the attack force had been weak and failed in its objectives – if the guards on the street had not been successfully killed or the frogmen had not deposited the dinghies in the right place –the mission would have almost certainly spiralled into disaster.

THE 'TEAM MIND'

The co-operation and unity displayed by the Israeli soldiers in this mission illustrates one of the key factors in what makes an elite team more than just a collection of highly trained individuals. Special forces have to rely on each other implicitly in the field and, if the soldier does not develop the 'team mind', he will deprive the unit of confidence in one another. If this happens, the unit will have a gap in its defences that will render it vulnerable.

The US Navy SEALs have a saying that 'There is no "I" in team or SEAL'. This chapter is about how elite units develop or target that team-centred attitude which puts the welfare of others first and rejects egocentric

File formation

In this formation the line of advancing soldiers must place great trust in the reconnaissance troops on the flanks to warn and protect them from any emergent dangers.

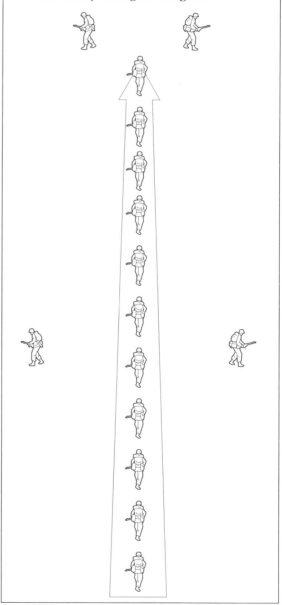

or attention-grabbing mentalities. This is not to say that a competitive nature has no place within elite forces; most elite soldiers strive to be the best of their units. Yet the history of elite operations has shown that, unless a special force units coheres as a team, its likelihood of being a military success and achieving its goals is almost nil.

SMALL IS BEAUTIFUL

As in so many other areas, psychological research into the nature of military units really achieved prominence in the period immediately after World War II. World War II had provided leaders and military thinkers with information about the performance of all manner of units, from two-man behind-the-lines teams to divisional-strength manoeuvres. It had become clear that many different factors fed into an effective combat squad; however, if a group of fighting-focused men truly united in a single grouping, their worth was tenfold that of less motivated units. So what is it that makes a group of different soldiers become a team? And how does the outlook of elite forces' teams differ from that of regular units?

The first thing to note about military units is that, when people are in groups, they behave in radically different ways to when people are on their own. From a military point of view – and studies at West Point in the United States have confirmed this – group behaviour tends to be less restrained than individual behaviour. Military atrocities, for instance, are very rarely committed by unobserved individuals, but usually by groups of people whose emotions start feeding off one another until they find themselves in the grip of violent emotions they had not previously known. In the civilian world, riots have been demonstrated to be caused by the same effect, as explained in a later chapter. The specific problem which was discovered by the various studies was that groups of people tend to become more

emotionally 'wound up' and, once they are aggravated, that emotion will remain for a longer period than if individuals were left to themselves. One US soldier from Vietnam recounts the grim tale of how he shot an old Vietnamese woman tending her crops just because he was dared to do so. Afterwards, he was stunned that he could have performed such a hideous act. The action only made sense amongst the group, a body of people typically having less self-control than people on their own.

In the past, particularly in the 1960s when elite forces were being formed to cope with the extremities of counterinsurgency in Vietnam, such excessive aggression was actively fostered in some units. During World War II, the British Home Guards' manual recommended that killing the enemy by bayonet or club was preferable to shooting them because of the effect on enemy morale produced by the mutilated corpse. Lieutenant William Calley – a participant in the infamous My Lai massacre – told the military court of the US Marine Corps unarmed combat training in which men would be significantly injured by high-power kicks and punches to vital areas. Apocryphal stories from Vietnam tell of training regimes in the special forces where groups of men had to torture and kill harmless domestic animals as a toughening exercise. Even today, legal action was recently taken against some US elite units for gruesome initiation rituals such as pinning badges directly into a soldier's chest.

Perhaps the most famously aggressive unit is the French Foreign Legion. Life for recruits is particularly hard. Some exercises have involved crawling through filth-filled ditches while the seasoned soldiers stand on the side and urinate onto the men below. Beatings from NCOs can be harsh punishments and it is reputed that no soldier who trains in the legion will finish his training without at some point soaking his

Spearhead formation

Holding a pattern such as the spearhead formation shown below requires discipline, as well as the ability to accept responsibility for each position. If one member of the group is weak, then the whole group is consequently vulnerable.

socks with his own blood. The French Foreign Legion is certainly one of the fiercest of the world's elite units, but many military observers have argued that it is at the expense of its military skills. Many legionnaires often feel degraded and abused, and the desertion rate currently runs at one in eight.

SELF-CONTROL

We can straight away see the problem of overly aggressive training for elite units. Elite operations require a maximum of self-control. If the group gets carried away with personal emotions or blind rage, it is likely that vital operational data or objectives will

be either overlooked or mishandled. Yet another conclusion of the research was that the more actual combat a group had seen, the more able they were to control their emotions and actions in battle. In this light, the harsh training of elite units makes even more sense. Putting soldiers through tough, realistic and punishing training not only makes the individual men harder, fitter and stronger, but it also makes the group more accustomed to meeting stress and violence as part of their natural behaviour. As the group adjusts to combat, wayward emotions become less acceptable and the soldiers start to achieve a self-control that bonds the group members together. This we saw in the opening illustration of the Israeli operation. The targets of the Sayeret Mat'kal agents were people who had committed appalling atrocities against the Israeli state and people. Yet, during the mission, each soldier did not let the desire for outright revenge cloud their team-mindedness. Although the assassinations were performed brutally, they were performed without any excesses of action or rage.

Much of the research into the psychology of military units was conducted in the Korean War and one particular conclusion that emerged was of special relevance to elite forces teams. Tests were conducted at the front line to find out what size squad was the most conducive to stability, uniformity and fighting spirit. When a group became too large, say, the size of a company (around 120 men), the cohesion was lessened because the unit was too big to develop personal bonds between all the individuals. The conclusion seemed to be that the best form of fighting group consisted of single-figure units, ideally groups of between three and eight men (five was actually decided as the optimum size). Within a smaller group, the attitudes, expectations and combat talents tended to show a greater degree of conformity. This meant that each member tended to pull his weight in equal measure with the others, and this in turn added up to a much more effective combat unit because there were no weak links.

The lesson was a valuable one for elite units, even though it was also a lesson they perhaps already knew. Many special forces units work in operational teams of rarely more than 10, unless on a particularly major operation. These men will have trained together, fought together and experienced the shared grief of lost friends. As such, they

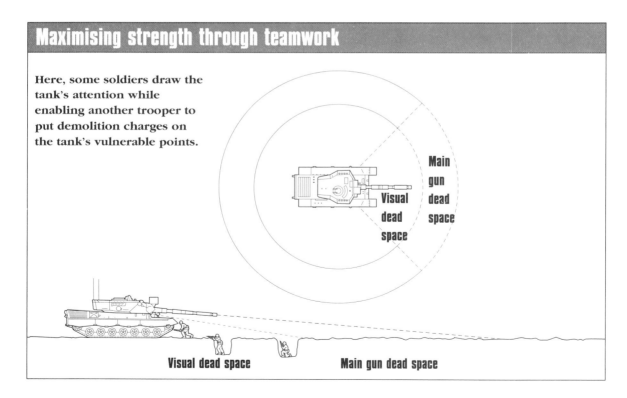

Maximising strength through teamwork

Here, some soldiers draw the tank's attention while enabling another trooper to put demolition charges on the tank's vulnerable points.

Main gun dead space

Visual dead space

Visual dead space   Main gun dead space

tend to show unique levels of trust in one another and also the tactical ability to let others take over a role if they are better qualified to do so. The lesson that 'small is beautiful' seems to have sunk through to even those elite forces which tend to operate on a more regular scale. The US Marine Corps, for instance, is capable of enormous multi-arm manoeuvres, but regardless of the size of force, it is still governed by what it calls the 'rule of three'.

The rule of three means that a Marine leader has basic responsibility for only three individuals or subunits. Thus, a Marine private belongs to a three-person fire team. A Marine corporal has responsibility for that fire team. A sergeant must exercise control over a squad of three fire teams. A staff sergeant or lieutenant leads a platoon made up of three squads. Although the number of people involved expands every time you go further up the ladder of rank, the system means that each person has a limited responsibility to an identifiable group of people. The effect of this is that the US Marines have a very close-knit relationship with one another and a dedication to their immediate network of three. Not only does this breed the esprit de corps for which the US Marines are so famed, but it also helps to make decision-making clear and efficient, which is obviously a vital factor in the performance of a military unit.

Not all elite units operate on similar principles, but generally there are codes of individual responsibility to each other which make real tactical sense once applied in combat. On the smallest scale possible, the SAS operates a 'buddy-buddy' system within all its operations, where two or more people are involved. Especially in arctic warfare or anti-guerrilla operations, the soldiers are teamed up in pairs, with each soldier having responsibility for protecting his partner and also for stepping in if the partner is killed or injured. Although the buddy-buddy system is actually a safeguard for the mission when personnel could be lost in action, it also has the psychological effect of reassurance in knowing that another set of eyes are looking out for you.

A SENSE OF BELONGING

Although there are many ways of organising a military unit to aid its efficiency, not all groups turn into effective combat squads. Sometimes the opposite is the case. We have already noted elsewhere the problem of 'fragging' in US units during the Vietnam War, whereby officers were being deliberately killed in firefights by their own men using fragmentation grenades. Fragging had many causes: low morale, high casualty rates in some units, the inexperience of junior officers, drug abuse and sheer malice. What these incidents taught was that groups did not automatically come together and that antagonisms would seriously impair the performance of the squad in combat.

By contrast, when psychologists in the Korean War set out to define the qualities of those squads who had proved themselves in combat, what they found was that each member had a sense of belonging to his unit and a sense of personal closeness to his comrades. In short, men tend to have to like each other as people before they can become a truly effective combat squad. The relationship between each man is not always the same. For instance, one person may be valued for his sense of humour, whereas another is liked because of his fighting ability. All the differences come together, however, to make a squad that has bonded and will go a long way to protect the welfare of each individual member.

Of course, soldiers cannot be made to like one another; who one likes is obviously a matter of personal preference. Yet, in elite regiments, there are several types of experiences, rituals and behaviours which tend to make the soldiers have some sort of empathy

Special Forces beach reconnaissance

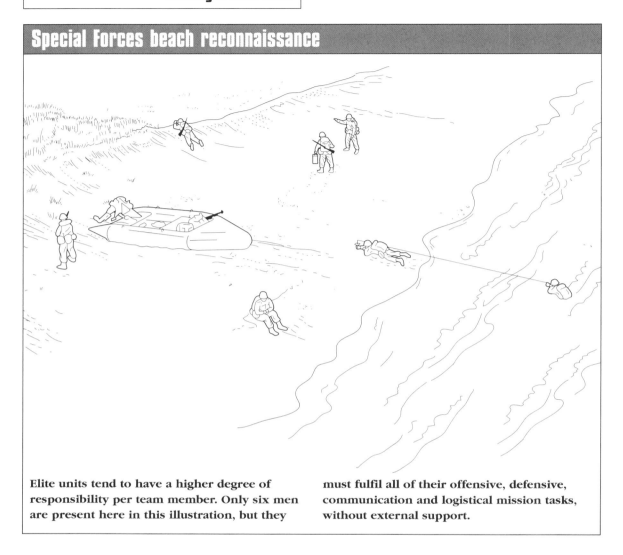

Elite units tend to have a higher degree of responsibility per team member. Only six men are present here in this illustration, but they must fulfil all of their offensive, defensive, communication and logistical mission tasks, without external support.

with one another, and this helps them to bond as a unit.

Belonging to an Elite

Just the fact that the soldiers are members of an elite force, distinct from the rest of the military world, tends to breed a greater respect for one another. The British Parachute Regiment, for instance, usually refers to all other non-elite regiments as 'crap hats'. This is no doubt offensive to those outside the regiment, but to those inside it signifies that they are special individuals who have a duty to protect the standards of the regiment and take pride in what they have achieved.

In both the British and US marines (and many other marine forces worldwide), once you have actually been a marine then you are 'a marine for life'. It is not uncommon for soldiers who left the marines decades previously and then who find themselves in trouble or facing hard times suddenly to receive support from the military fraternity who believes that being a marine means being accepted into a huge extended family for the rest of your life. Such a sense of belonging is one of the strongest forces for bonding men into a coherent team. This will express itself when entering combat.

Surviving Training

Elite training is an appallingly difficult business (attrition rates run at anywhere between 40 and 90 per cent). Just the experience of sharing the hopes and tribulations of basic training and coming through together tends to make soldiers connect with one another in a way that cannot be understood by many civilians. During Royal Marine training in Norway, all soldiers (except those over 30, who have the option of not participating) have to undergo a test in which they jump fully clothed through an ice hole into freezing water. Without any assistance, they must use their skis to clamber out of the hole. Yet once they are out, their fellow recruits will then set to work stripping them, drying them and putting them into dry clothing before hypothermia has the chance to take hold. Such is typical of the trust and intimacy that training builds up between the men. Furthermore, the process of training in elite forces is designed to weed out those individuals who have anti-social tendencies. Training effectively acts as a screening process for those who will not contribute to the team mentality.

Surviving Combat

As many war veterans have noted, sharing the experience of actual fighting can bring even the most ardent enemies together in a bond of friendship. Soldiers often report a sense in which the frustrations that tire most of us in civilian life suddenly seem totally irrelevant. Enmities and suspicions can be quickly forgotten and the soldiers have a common understanding which in itself breeds loyalty and a shared awareness of tactical performance. The writer Philip Caputo, a former combat officer with the US Marine Corps in Vietnam, recounts in his book *A Rumour of War* how two Marine soldiers were killed attempting to retrieve the bodies of fallen comrades despite their action almost guaranteeing their deaths. Such actions illustrate how combat and the esprit de corps can make the bonds between combatants extend even to those who are no longer living (it is part of the Marine code of honour not to leave the unit's dead behind on the battlefield).

Rituals

A final but far from unimportant element of team mentality is that of military rituals. The two most visible of these are ceremonies dealing with induction – particularly when a recruit passes training and becomes a full-fledged elite soldier – and ceremonies dealing with the burial of the dead. To take the latter as an example, prior to the American Civil War, the bodies of soldiers tended to be dispensed with little ritual and formality. More often than not, they were simply buried in ditches on the battleground, left where they were to rot or given over to looters. However, from the later 19th century, the dead started to attract greater memorialisation. Monuments sprung up on battlegrounds – such as the monument on the Somme listing the names of 73,412 missing men – and, by World War II, cemeteries were created not only for the fallen of a particular nation, but also those of particular regiments and units. Most elite units today have some form of official cemetery and the often ornate rituals of burial give the regiments an intense feeling of pride in their abilities and sacrifice.

The factors which bring combatants together as a team in a military unit are many and are difficult to quantify. We have already noted four elements – belonging to an elite, surviving training, surviving combat and rituals – which help produce the correct commitment to the greater unit. So what type of qualities should the archetypal squad member demonstrate? After answering this question, we shall proceed by looking at how team-centred attitudes actually express themselves in the tactics and methods of combat. For, in the final analysis, military teams are created for fighting.

THE ELITE TEAM MEMBER

Returning to the Korean War again, research was conducted into the personalities typically found within those fighting squads which had consistently demonstrated success in combat. As we would expect, there were certain types of attitude or outlook which did not fit into an efficient squad. Men who were fearful of combat tended to demotivate combat squads and place a drain on their morale; fear, like anger, can be contagious within a squad. Also, men who were paranoid or overly imaginative could introduce an unwelcome friction into already overstretched frontline units. The final type of personality to have a detrimental effect on combat teams was that with poor social skills. Antisocial or unwelcoming personalities tend to repel people and, in a combat squad, this meant that the lines of communication had a weak link, as other squad members were reluctant to associate with the difficult person.

Yet, when looking at what was the right type of personality, what tended to come to the fore was that the individual members of the squad had to share a significant amount in common to be most successful in combat. The good team member usually displayed an open, personable character underlined with a mental strength which was not easily disturbed by adverse circumstances. People tend to learn much of their behaviour from those around them, so a strong-minded individual produces the beneficial effect of inspiring others around him to emulate his qualities. Interestingly, squads also seemed to benefit from being composed of men who were of a similar social standing in life, presumably because they shared a common language about life and experiences. A third factor in the competent fighting squad was that, if the individuals tended to display more barracks-type discipline – such as keeping their quarters clean and organised, responding quickly to orders, maintaining high levels of personal hygiene – then this seemed to express itself in a good fighting attitude.

An overall conclusion to emerge out of all studies into group behaviour in military units is that one bad apple can spoil the batch. During the Korean studies, good fighters were shifted together with other good fighters and these specially composed units were visibly effective in combat roles. Yet the more people the squad contained that were poor fighters, the more the efficiency of all the fighters was pulled down.

No Bad Apples

Here we are getting to perhaps the primary reason why elite forces are capable of such exceptional performance. Because training and standards are so high, there are in effect no bad apples. All elite soldiers are the best in their fields and thus the teams are consistently motivated to fight without reserve. Furthermore, studies since Korea have shown that, if a soldier feels himself a member of a prestigious team, he is capable of pushing himself to limits he would not achieve otherwise. A soldier who belongs to a team he is proud of is scientifically proven to be prepared to suffer more pain, more indignity and more suffering to maintain the welfare of the group than someone who is less committed to group thinking. Thus it is that all recruits to elite regiments are screened during training for their ability to

SAS 'Buddy-Buddy' system

The SAS 'buddy-buddy' system involves separating the men into pairs; each man in the pair looks out for the other, taking team trust to very high levels.

contribute to groups, rather than just their personal endurance or mental fitness. Essentially it is an issue of maturity. The soldier who keeps thrusting himself to the fore and taking charge may be eager to demonstrate confidence to his instructors, but the instructors may be more interested in the individual who is mature enough to step in and out of leadership roles according to the talents of the group.

By now, it will have become evident that being an elite soldier is about much more than just a tough attitude. Soldiers in units such as the SAS can be extremely individualistic, a tendency necessitated by the types of covert operation which are often pursued in isolation of human contact. Individualism, however, must not express itself as a lack of co-operative spirit, especially when it comes to the responsibilities of team operations.

THE FIGHTING SQUAD

Whether in the four-man teams of the US Marine Corps Force Recon or the 20-man patrol groups of the Italian Folgore brigade,

elite soldiers in combat formation rely on the team mind to form and apply effective tactical groupings. Perhaps the most obvious scenario for this is found in the work of the combat patrol.

Combat patrols come in many different shapes and varieties, but in terms of team co-operation, each patrol must have a similar set of priorities. First, the formation must allow quick and easy movement across the particular terrain. Secondly, the formation must present the squad's weaponry in its most advantageous configuration for both repelling attack and forming itself into a rapid attack. Thirdly, each member of the patrol must take responsibility for monitoring a certain sector of the patrol's aspect, each soldier adding to a 360-degree patrol observation effort.

One of the simplest formations is the six-man single-file patrol. This is ideally suited to covert operations in difficult terrains such as jungle, where the patrol may have to follow narrow tracks. The soldiers in this formation simply walk in line with about 3–10m (10–32ft) between each man. Although it seems a simple pattern, the teamwork to make this formation a strong one is considerable. The man at the front of the patrol – known in US circles as the point man – focuses his efforts in a 180-degree arc facing the direction of travel. His purpose is to pick up on any signs of enemy activity, watch out for booby traps or ambushes, and set the pace for negotiating the terrain. Behind him is the team leader. His role is not only to navigate the patrol (leaving the point man free to concentrate on his immediate environment), but also

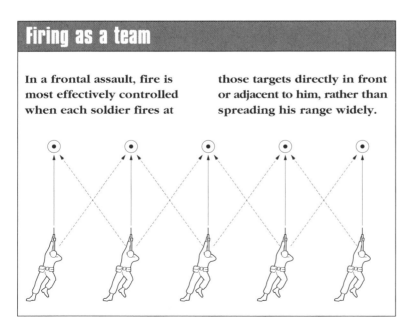

Firing as a team

In a frontal assault, fire is most effectively controlled when each soldier fires at those targets directly in front or adjacent to him, rather than spreading his range widely.

Team tactics in a river crossing

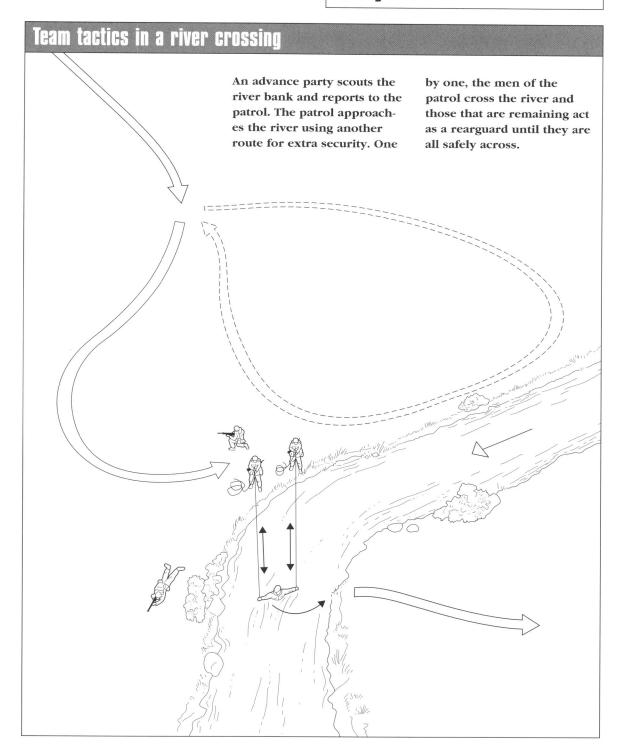

An advance party scouts the river bank and reports to the patrol. The patrol approaches the river using another route for extra security. One by one, the men of the patrol cross the river and those that are remaining act as a rearguard until they are all safely across.

Milling

Used in the British Parachute Regiment, this tests recruits' resolve and builds team empathy. The soldiers box for two minutes, being scored on spirit rather than on blows landed.

to provide covering fire to the point man if necessary and take responsibility for monitoring one flank of the patrol.

The man behind him – the first flank scout – acts as a checker on the navigation and also tends to be the radio operator. He monitors the opposite flank to the team leader (the remaining members of the patrol alternate their flank observations, with the last member monitoring the rear so that the whole patrol is covered). Next comes the second flank scout, responsible for support weapons deployment and also acting as

someone who can keep the group together at the midpoint in night or low-visibility conditions. Finally, there are the assistant team leader and the rear scout, the former providing yet another check on navigation and also simultaneouly supervising the countertracking efforts of the scout positioned at the rear.

When analysed, what appears to be a simple single-file line of men actually turns out to be a highly organised formation with strict roles for each man. Mentally, the soldiers who make up this patrol must demonstrate several key qualities without which the patrol will be in a weak and vulnerable position.

Observation

Each soldier must take responsibility for his field of vision. This is an act of both discipline and trust. Discipline is required to keep the eyes working on your defined sector of vision, and trust is needed in order to be able to rely on the other members to do the same. Different methods have been tested and evaluated for heightening observation. At night, soldiers are trained to look at silhouettes, rather than stare into shapes, and they combine this with the use of the other senses to glean as much information from around them as possible. In jungle surroundings, the soldiers are taught not to focus on isolated features, but open what is known as 'eagle vision', where the peripheral vision is also engaged fully to make the soldier aware of movements or changes from any direction.

Reaction

In combat, a team relies on fast reactions from its members. All members of the patrol must hone their receptivity so that, should they spot a potential threat, they can convey the information to the rest of the team quickly and appropriately. For example, if ambushed, the team members of a four-man unit will have to react by establishing a surpressing fire from the middle two of the patrol, while the outer members advance and take the battle back to the ambushers. Unless this response is instinctive, it will be a weak one.

Communication

Although the physical act of talking or signing a message may not actually seem like a combat skill, it is paramount to the success of a squad in the field. Most elite training courses feature programmes in which the soldiers have to present formal lectures or presentations on a wide variety of military subjects. The purpose of this is to build up the soldiers' conversance with language, in order that they will be able to explain situations to others rapidly and accurately with a minimum of confusion on either side.

Weapons skills

Elite soldiers must be able to bring their weapons quickly into focus upon the enemy and deliver accurate fire. This is in itself a mental discipline. Calculations during the Vietnam War placed the average ammunition expenditure of US units for each kill scored at an astonishing 200,000–400,000 rounds. An elite squad must not waste a single round, for if one member of the squad expends his ammunition supply, then his place in the formation will subsequently become structurally weak.

On a typical mission, a special forces soldier will usually carry about 12 magazines for a weapon such as the M16. This is a maximum total of about 360 rounds, although extra loose ammunition will often be carried to replenish magazines. A 30-round magazine can be emptied from an M16 in about 3–4 seconds on full automatic, so elite soldiers rarely take their personal weapons off semi-automatic mode except for surpressing fire (full-automatic mode also has the tendency to result in muzzle climb and much-reduced accuracy). This restraint with ammunition is compensated for by exceptional marksmanship and targeting skills, and the elites' ammunition-to-kill ratio tends to be very low indeed. During contact between SAS soldiers and Iraqi troops in the Gulf War, even the SAS's belt-fed Minimi machine guns were only fired in three- to five-round bursts, although to stunning effect.

The file formation is only one example of a patrol organisation; others formations such as the spearhead and box formations are also used. Yet, regardless of the formation or of the purpose – whether they be ambush techniques, insertion patterns or open-battlefield units – the above principles of team support apply to all military groupings. Team co-operation enables elite units to form united firing positions at an instant and thus it gives them a force which often outweighs their numbers. During the Gulf War, for instance, a three-man group of US Special Forces soldiers around the village of Oawan al Hamzah was assaulted by Iraqi troops in large numbers. The situation was made even more acute by the fact that the US soldiers had only 300 rounds of ammunition between them. The group immediately fell into sensible and mutually protective positions and began a huge firefight. Unlike their adversaries, who had large supplies of ammunition and were pouring down fire on the US positions, the US soldiers settled into their positions and used single shots to pick off Iraqi troops, one by one. Through this tactic, plus the very brief use of automatic fire when their positions were immediately threatened, they succeeded in holding the superior forces at bay for a period of two hours. Eventually, US attack helicopters appeared and proceeded to lift them to safety.

The battle at Oawan al Hamzah illustrates that even a small group can have a great military effect on the course of a battle if its members think and act together as one. Indeed, it could be argued that team unity and motivation are perhaps the single biggest factors in the success of military operations.

When units lock together in combat, their primary purpose (alongside that of killing as many of the enemy as possible) is to impose such chaos on the enemy that its team structure disintegrates. There are many methods of doing this in battle. Using snipers to kill the enemy's officers is an excellent method of depriving an enemy team of its tactical direction (hence soldiers of special forces do not salute officers when

they are on operations in order to avoid identifying their rank). Straightforward tactical outmanoeuvring is another method. This aims to turn the enemy team into a confused and disorientated outfit as they try to respond to a constantly changing battlefield. More broadly, enemy unity can also be assaulted through using various techniques of psychological warfare.

PSYCHOLOGICAL WARFARE

An example of this last form of warfare was conducted by Algerian insurgents during the war against the French which took place between 1954 and 1962.

The French efforts at suppressing the insurgents were fairly crude and definitely controversial. The use of torture and casual execution of Algerians became commonplace in the conflict. It was noted that although 15,000 French troops died during the conflict, as many as 300,000–400,000 Muslims were killed before independence was granted to the state.

In many ways, objectively speaking, the Algerian insurgents had a more sophisticated programme of military action than simply producing numbers of fatalities, like the French. Their programme aimed to undermine French unity and morale, and it was caried out by a group within the insurgents who were known as the Service Psychologique du FLN. This group launched a three-pronged programme of mental warfare directed against the French armed forces.

Firstly, they targeted efforts into bringing the civilian population onto their side, either through propaganda or through tricking them into participating in terrorist meetings or acts, after which the civilians were then obliged to continue working in the terrorists' pay.

Secondly, but related to the first point, the Service Psychologique du FLN directed their ambushes and bombings exclusively against

Areas of fire

Each of the patrol members in this team has responsibility for an angle of fire, adding up to a complete protective circle thrown around the entire group.

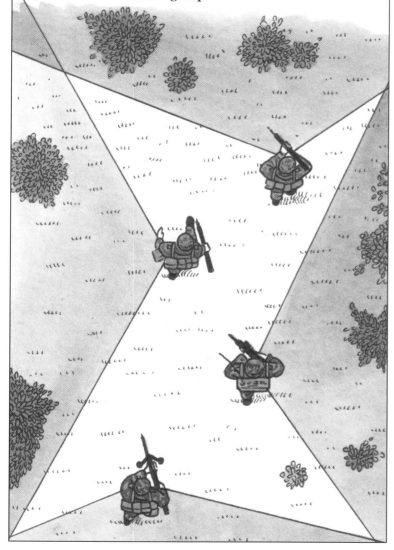

Thirdly, the group promoted their cause abroad, representing their efforts to foreign governments and pressure groups. In this way, they were to make the French actions of torture and execution seem all the more excessive to the outside world. (Ho Chi Minh in the Vietnam War applied similar strategies). This last form of action made many frontline French soldiers feel devalued and was effective both in sapping their morale and leading to several tactical and disciplinary problems.

The tactics used by the Algerian insurgents to attack the unity of the French cause can be equally applied by special forces soldiers as they conduct their operations against a wide variety of enemies. The key point to bear in mind is that once team unity has been destroyed, the enemy can then be dominated with much greater ease than they could have been previously.

The challenge for elite forces is to maintain not only a level of skills much advanced over that of regular forces, but also to create units which are capable of operating as a single fighting body in combat situations. In these units, every member understands his role and capabilities. To be a member of such a team requires character, humour and a certain willingness to contribute to something larger than you as an individual.

the military. This had the effect of chipping away at French morale, while simultaneously managing not to alienate civilian groups.

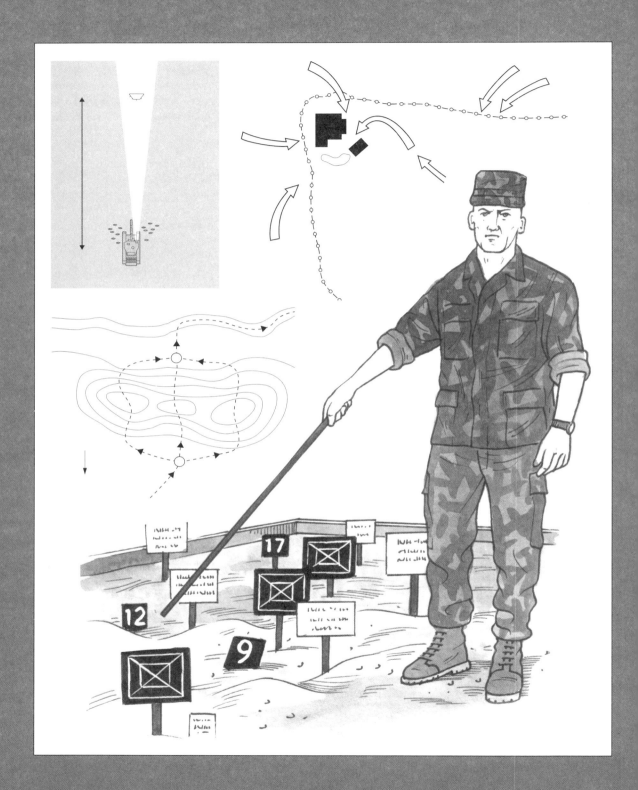

CHAPTER SIX

Leadership

Leadership is a vital component of a fighting unit's success. In the early hours of 19 July 1972, residents of the port of Mirbat in Dhofar province, southern Oman, awoke to the sound of gunfire. Underway was an attack by 250 Adoo insurgents against an SAS-led group which numbered only some nine men commanded by Captain Mike Kealy.

What followed was an astonishing defensive victory on the part of the SAS and an astonishing act of leadership by Captain Kealy. Captain Kealy's actions in the battle included instantly bringing mortar fire to bear on the attackers, racing through machine-gun and shellfire to keep a 25-pounder (11.3kg) artillery weapon in action, co-ordinating aerial bombing, holding an ammunition pit and killing Adoo attackers in the process.

Further SAS reinforcements eventually arrived and Mirbat was held against the odds. Every SAS soldier there acted with astonishing bravery, but Captain Kealy illustrated some of the fundamental qualities of leadership that we will explore in this chapter. He responded quickly and intelligently to the attack. He had a full knowledge of weapons deployment, which he brought to bear against the Adoo. Communications were controlled so that the forces outside Mirbat had clear mission directions. He showed evident concern for the welfare of his men while demonstrating enormous bravery. For his actions, he was awarded the Distinguished Service Order.

Captain Kealy demonstrated the best of elite military leadership and it is these qualities of mind and body which military recruiting stations around the world attempt to spot in their hunt for successful officer candidates. Not everyone is fit to be a leader or commander of soldiers. Indeed, those leaders who are held up as examples to the rest seem to be as much a product of their natural character as their military training. A successful leader is a mixture of character and

Handling patrol formations

A military leader must be able to visualise manoeuvres in the abstract – such as this **patrol route – but then transfer them through practical skills into a working tactic.**

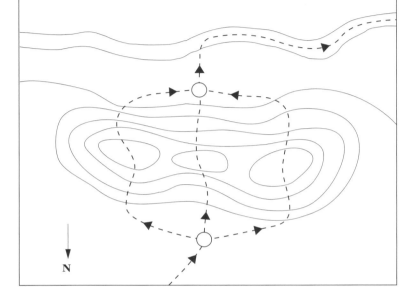

N

Leadership. As the title implies, the manual is intended for army officer instruction, but its principles are common to all services, including those of the elite forces (although differences will also be noted). It defines leadership essentially as 'influencing people – by providing purpose, direction and motivation – while operating to accomplish the mission and improving the organisation'. This, in turn, is boiled down to three key-words which must stand as the foundations of any military leader's success. These are 'be', 'know' and 'do'.

● **Be** – 'Be' refers to personality, having the character of a leader and exemplifying qualities such courage, loyalty and integrity. 'Be' also refers to having the necessary mental, physical and emotional skills to be able to command effectively.
● **Know** – 'Know' simply refers to knowledge, understanding the tools, tactics and organisation of a fighting unit so that they can be used intelligently.
● **Do** – 'Do' is the final part of the leader's initiative, when he takes his skills and character into battle and has to accomplish his objectives.

Regardless of the military formation, we can see that these three elements must all be present for the leader to be a strong example to his men and a powerful force of guidance in action. First, we will look at the 'be' part of this equation, the character which the leader has which should separate him from those not suited to the nature of command.

training, and, while the military establishment can provide the latter, the former is a much more elusive property.

LEADERSHIP AND CHARACTER

When talking about military leaders, it is usual to distinguish between being a 'leader' and being a 'commander'. Whereas a leader is someone who has the personality skills to make men and women follow him, a commander is someone who has the actual skills of directing people and machines in combat or another military situation. Only when personal and technical skills come together can the person be classified as an effective leader in a fuller sense.

This fact is recognised by one of the key publications on leadership, the US Army's Field Manual 22-100, entitled *Army*

Arguably, character is the most important element a leader brings to any elite force. An indication why this is so is to be found in the various mottoes which act as the moral standard for elite regiments. Such mottoes include (given here in English):

- **SAS** Who Dares Wins
- **US Marine Corps** Always Faithful
- **US Army Special Forces** Free from Oppression
- **Delta Force** Surprise, Speed and Aggression
- **Canadian Paratroopers** We Dare
- **Royal Netherlands Marine Corps** Wherever the World Extends

These mottoes vary in their emphasis, but what does not change is that each implies an exemplary standard of moral character to do the motto justice and to keep it respected. It falls to the officers to demonstrate the unit ethos to its fullest extent, so elite recruiters have a keen eye on who passes through their doors to see that they have the right character to stand as an example to the rest.

Each leader's character varies and, in a sense, there is no such thing as the archetypal leader. However, there are certain qualities which must be present for the soldier to function as a leader and offer the guidance and example required of his position.

Loyalty

A leader must show loyalty to his men, his branch of arms and his mission. If he does not give himself wholeheartedly to his unit, and remain unswerving from that commitment, the men under his command will not return that loyalty and so the efficiency of the chain of command will suffer and morale will weaken. Conversations with US Marines revealed that one of the greatest motivations behind soldiers' efforts was to justify their leader's trust, so in return the leader must show himself worthy of that position.

Personality characteristics in leaders

COMBAT LEADERS	GARRISON LEADERS
Mental composure	Sociable
Bravery	Meticulous
Aggressive action	Organised
Social tact	Highly motivated
Puts group before self	Self-restraint
Able to make rapid decisions	Disciplined
Confident	Intelligent
Able to inspire confidence	Versatile
Adaptable to circumstances	Able to discipline others with tact
Rapid thought processes	Strong communicator
Strong sense of humour	Understands people
Disciplined	Maintains high standards
Strong communicator	Able to juggle multiple tasks

Courage

Company grade officers – those who actually lead men into combat – have to possess the courage not only to deal with personal danger, but also demonstrate courage to their whole unit in order to inspire confidence. Courage should not be a blind force of will that overlooks the needs of the men. Indeed, modern military officers are taught to be very open to the welfare of the men under their charge. Instead, courage should simply be the resolve to hold to the mission's objective or the value of the regiment or unit in the face of adversity, without giving in.

Integrity

Respect for an officer must be earned – it is not something given automatically to the position. This respect is generally earned by consistently demonstrating the values of the unit and regiment, which in turn gives rise to an aura of integrity. The high value placed on integrity is suggested by the oath of office taken by commissioned officers in the US forces:

I [full name], *having been appointed a* [rank] *in the United States Army, do solemnly swear (or affirm) that I will support and defend the Constitution of the United States against all enemies, foreign and domestic; that I will bear true faith and allegiance to the same; that I take this obligation freely, without any mental reservation or purpose of evasion, and that I will well and faithfully discharge the duties of the office upon which I am about to enter. So help me God.*

The pledge which the US officers give is based on personal integrity, in which the soldier 'freely' commits himself to defending the values of his country and accepts

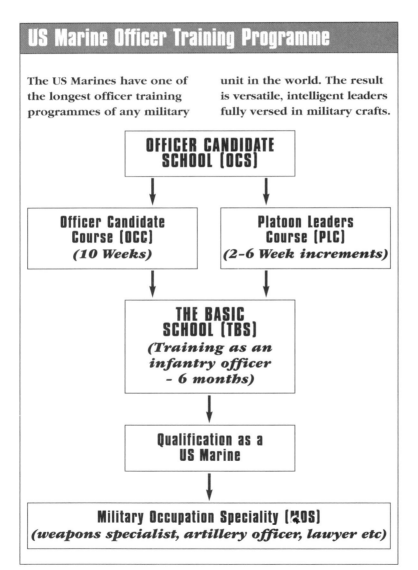

US Marine Officer Training Programme

The US Marines have one of the longest officer training programmes of any military unit in the world. The result is versatile, intelligent leaders fully versed in military crafts.

OFFICER CANDIDATE SCHOOL (OCS)

Officer Candidate Course (OCC) (10 Weeks)

Platoon Leaders Course (PLC) (2-6 Week increments)

THE BASIC SCHOOL (TBS) (Training as an infantry officer - 6 months)

Qualification as a US Marine

Military Occupation Speciality (MOS) (weapons specialist, artillery officer, lawyer etc)

the responsibilities of his position 'faithfully' and without duplicity. Military officers the world over take similar pledges to defend their own governments and nations.

Respect

General-Major Kurt Student, the founder of the elite German parachute regiments – the Fallschirmjäger – demonstrated the principle of respect as well as any other great military leader. During the early days of the parachute units, he used to give heavily of his time and energy talking to the men and discovering their concerns. 'During my frequent visits I made to the parachute units, I tried to set an example by talking to individual paratroopers, discussing their personal problems and eliciting their opinions. I was pleased with the way this approach was received, and there is no doubt that the parachute *esprit de corps* grew from strength to strength as the parachute corps expanded.' Although far higher in rank than the enlisted men, Student's evident respect for the opinions of those beneath him enhanced morale and also served to bond the paras to their leadership.

Student's approach to leadership is one endorsed by modern leadership training. Arrogance and dismissiveness are soon detected in would-be officers and, in most armies, these qualities tend to preclude the man from an officer position. This is not only a moral choice. The opposite of respect is disrespect and, if an officer displays this towards his men, their willingness to perform for him will be based on fear, a weak motivator. Consequently, respect is essential to secure the best unit performance.

Self-Denial

Although of a higher position than the men below him, the officer is there to serve others, not himself. In combat and in the garrison, he must put the welfare of his men, his regiment and his country before that of his own. During the Falklands War, for example, officers of units such as the Parachute Regiment and Royal Marine Commandos had to ignore their own exhaustion at the end of punishing marches to make inspections. They also had to ensure that the men were properly fed and that adequate foot care was being pursued to stop the onset of trench foot, a condition which afflicted many during the conflict. By serving others first, not only did respect for their position and natural authority build, but the chain-of-command was also able to operate at its full efficiency.

Apart from loyalty, courage, respect, integrity and self-denial, there is a whole range of other qualities that the officer must bring to his position. These qualities include self-motivation, enthusiasm, a sense of humour and a mind for detail. Yet there is no

Respect

It is possible to impart instruction and to give commands in such manner and such a tone of voice to inspire in the soldier no feeling but an intense desire to obey, while the opposite manner and tone of voice cannot fail to excite strong resentment and a desire to disobey. The one mode or the other of dealing with subordinates springs from a corresponding spirit in the breast of the commander. He who feels the respect which is due to others cannot fail to inspire in them regard for himself, while he who feels, and hence manifests, disrespect toward others, especially his inferiors, cannot fail to inspire hatred against himself.

Major General
John M. Schofield
Address to the
United States Corps of Cadets
11 August 1879

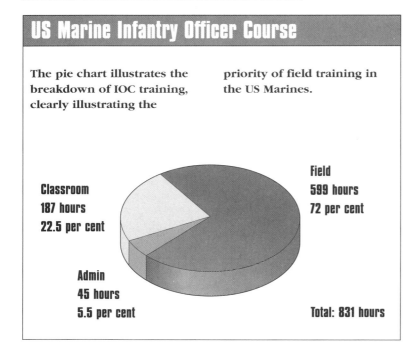

US Marine Infantry Officer Course

The pie chart illustrates the breakdown of IOC training, clearly illustrating the priority of field training in the US Marines.

Classroom
187 hours
22.5 per cent

Field
599 hours
72 per cent

Admin
45 hours
5.5 per cent

Total: 831 hours

rule book, athletic, possessed of a passion for detail, had a good physical bearing and personal tact. None of these [qualities] was found to be relevant for an officer to be effective as a leader in wartime.'

So what are the marks of a strong and capable combat leader? Leadership in any walk of life is demanding, but there are surely no greater tests of command skills than those to be found in the chaos and horror of a violent military action.

THE COMBAT LEADER

The extent of a military leader's authority is exceptionally broad. Within the barracks alone, an officer will have responsibility for the organisation of his unit, the receipt, distribution and maintenance of equipment, unit accounting, and administration for food, clothing, accommodation, transport, health and welfare, discipline, pay, promotions and leave. As if this were not enough in itself, the officer also has to prepare himself for the experience of leading men into combat.

Under fire, a leader has to cope with enormous levels of distraction. Modern theory of warfare recognises that chaos is the primary ingredient of battle, with the situation shifting from one second to the next according the manoeuvres and casualties. A combat officer has not only to cope with the violence of the battle around him, but also to try to make tactical decisions in the midst of explosions and the dead and injured.

Producing the chaos-proof leader is never easy and training must be hard, realistic, pressurised and stressful to test who has the mettle. In the US Marine Corps, the officer

set formula for how each individual officer should actually behave, because that alters with different roles and different services. Officers in the SAS, for example, require fewer disciplinarian skills because the soldiers under their command are almost always highly motivated and self-disciplined. Thus it is that SAS soldiers and NCOs tend to call their officers 'boss' instead of 'sir'. Discipline is assumed, and being in such a close working relationship with individual men means that SAS officers have to have excellent interpersonal skills to gain the respect of some of the world's best fighting men.

Peter Watson, in his seminal book *War on the Mind* (London: Hutchinson; 1978), also investigated the difference between garrison and combat officers. Looking at studies done on company grade officers in the 1950s, Watson found that, while good garrison leaders 'were found to be aggressive, as were combat leaders [they] were also found to do better if they were sticklers for the graduate is meant to emerge with a clearly described set of skills and aptitudes, these being applicable to most elite units throughout the world. The officer has to be a:

- leader/commander
- decision-maker
- communicator
- warfighter/executor
- lifelong student of the art of war

Similar skills are also set out by the US Army's manual of leadership, in which four main sets of skills are set down:

- interpersonal
- conceptual
- technical
- tactical

Major Qamar Hasmain's advice for giving orders

- Use a clear and firm tone that is easily heard and understood.
- Address the order to a very specific person or group of people.
- Be precise about what it is you expect the soldiers to achieve.
- Give few orders to avoid confusion and make sure that each is intelligible.
- Only give realistic orders in order that the soldiers can be reasonably confident about their achievability.
- Orders should be justifiable in the context of the situation or battle.
- Set down a proper timeline for the accomplishment of the order.

Although the two lists use very different language, they actually share the same principles. Foremost among these is the act of communication. This is not just about the act of giving orders. Orders are a primary part of the officer's communications, but in addition to that is the two-way communication that sees the officer actually listening to what soldiers are saying. Good listening skills are required to absorb all the relevant information, respond to it and make the men feel that their contributions are valuable. Listening skills have been described as 'staring with the ears' and should place the emphasis on letting the person talk without interruption and without the listener constantly thinking up the next point of speech.

When an officer does speak, the voice should be clear, the language plain and easily understood, and the message should communicate the officer's high standards.

Furthermore, as some 70 per cent of the total message a person receives from another comes from non-verbal communication – body language, in other words – it is especially important that the officer projects physical strength and stature. A strong voice and strong body posture are taught on the parade ground, but their application is equally vital on the battlefield. In addition, the officer should also be able to change the mood of his voice so as to be able to deal with civilian presences on the battlefield, including those of children and old people.

While this accounts for the 'interpersonal' aspects of leadership skills, of equal importance is obviously the officer's knowledge of the tools of war: technical skills. In a modern military unit, the officer has tremendous resources of firepower on which to draw. A field officer in the 82nd Airborne Division, for example, may have at his disposal in a major action a company of troops armed with their personal M16A2 assault rifles, M60 and SAW machine guns, TOW, LAW and Dragon anti-tank rockets, mortars, Stinger anti-aircraft missiles, close-air support consisting of Cobra, Apache and Black Hawk attack helicopters, and howitzer artillery support. Co-ordinating such immense destructive potential on the battlefield is only possible if the officer understands the limits and applications of each weapon, and is also capable of orchestrating the communications technology that will bring all this firepower together. Added to this is the fact that vehicles such as tanks, jeeps and logistic trucks must also be harmonised behind the combat effort.

If the officer has a true grip on the equipment at his disposal, and also keeps himself up to date with new technology introduced into his unit, only then is he able to exercise possibly the most important element of a combat leader's ability: tactical skills. All tactical thinking comes from what is referred to in the US Marine Corps as 'decision-making' and what the US Army calls 'conceptual skills'. During officer training in most armies, officer candidates are put through a series of decision-making and tactical exercises which develop the individual's skills in responding rapidly to fluctuating situations or seemingly insoluble problems. In the British Army, for example, officer trainees are often given a piece of rope, a couple of oil drums and some board, and have to use these tools to cross a fast-flowing river – all done, of course, against a fast-ticking clock. The aim of the exercise is to see how these potential leaders can handle the realities of decision-making when the pressure is on.

Of course, the pressures of actual fighting are far greater than those encountered in the exercise just described. To attempt to simulate the reality of tactical decision-making, officers are tested in major field exercises during which they become accustomed to live-firing co-ordination. The exercises are valuable because, with powerful ordnance being used, the consequences of incorrect thinking could result in a loss of life as real as on the battlefield itself.

Barrel challenge

British Army officer candidates have often been tested by this: get yourself and your colleagues across a fast-flowing river using a barrel, some planks and a length of rope.

Once the officer candidate emerges from his training, he should possess the correct technical knowledge, decision-making skills and mental composure to be able to make tactical choices on the battlefield. The US Army defines tactics as 'the art and science of employing available means to win battles and engagements'. Yet here one of the key differences between elite and regular units emerges. The officer of a regular army unit may have his tactical focus set on the use of long-range weaponry, such as that commonly used in the Gulf War. During that conflict, tank commanders in US Abrams tanks would often engage the enemy vehicles at some 2700m (9000ft), in many cases out of range of the naked eye. For artillery and aircraft assaults, the ranges would be much greater. Without sight of the enemy, the tactical deployment of such weapons could be dispassionate and clean. Yet for elite units such as counterterrorist groups, the tactics revolve around the immediacy of human-to-human contact. Prior to the assault by troops

Map of a typical tank commander test

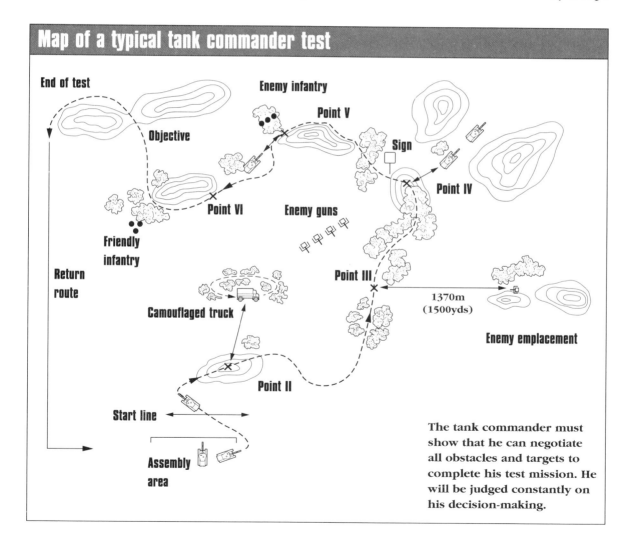

The tank commander must show that he can negotiate all obstacles and targets to complete his test mission. He will be judged constantly on his decision-making.

US Marine decision-making

All US Marine soldiers are taught an effective method of decision-making which helps them to cope with the chaos of war and the constantly changing circumstances. It is called the 'Rule of Three'. When faced by any situation, the Marine soldier should define the problem as clearly as possible and then produce three possible courses of action. Any less than three and there are too few genuine options; any more than three and the soldier can become paralysed by indecision. From these three options, the soldier must choose one and then execute it vigorously. The overall result of the 'Rule of Three' is to give each soldier a decision-making method that avoids confusion and muddied thinking.

Unit allegiance

Special Forces take a unique pride in their regimental badges. It is up to the officer to act as an exemplary model of unit values and discipline while being an effective and humane leader of men.

of the German anti-terrorist squad, GSG 9, against the hijacked Lufthansa airliner set down at Mogadishu (the capital of Somalia) in 1977, the leaders were faced with tactical decisions of the most pressing kind. They would be attacking an aircraft isolated on a runway, containing four terrorists, 86 passengers and five aircrew. The terrorists' threat of blowing up the aircraft hung over every move. Somehow the GSG 9 operatives (and two SAS soldiers lent by the British Government) had to board the plane, take

out the terrorists and protect the hostages, all within the confines of an aircraft fuselage.

The plan was eventually put into action at 0205 hours on the morning of 18 October. A small fire was lit just ahead of the plane. This acted as a distraction to the terrorists, who had not noticed the elite troops mount the wings of the aircraft and move into position. At 0207 hours, the GSG 9 soldiers blew off the aircraft's emergency doors with explosives and stormed inside while throwing stun grenades and killing three of the terrorists

SAS battle – Mirbat

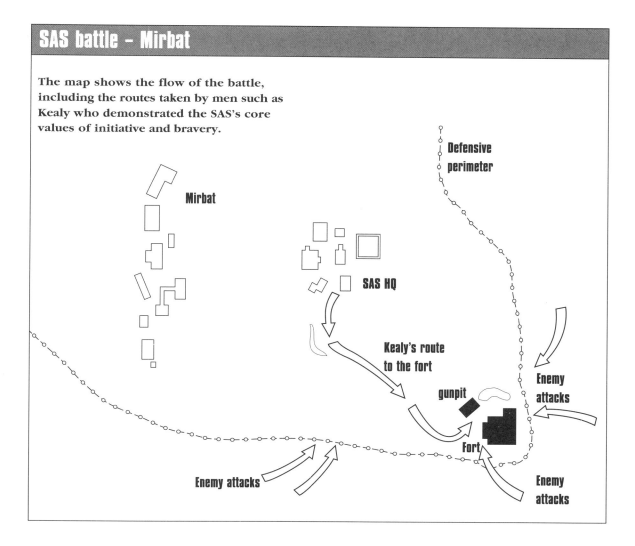

The map shows the flow of the battle, including the routes taken by men such as Kealy who demonstrated the SAS's core values of initiative and bravery.

Mirbat

Defensive perimeter

SAS HQ

Kealy's route to the fort

gunpit

Fort

Enemy attacks

Enemy attacks

Enemy attacks

Academic learning

Officers must posses a high degree of technical, historical and military knowledge to be competent leaders. Classroom learning adds a vital complement to their field skills.

and wounding the fourth. The operation was a stunning success (only three hostages were wounded, none killed) and GSG 9 achieved the same notoriety in Germany as the British SAS would achieve in the United Kingdom after the Iranian embassy siege.

The Mogadishu rescue shows the tactical pressures faced by the officers of the elite forces. Their operations are often judged in a matter of seconds, rather than the week-long schedules of major warfare, and so they must show two primary qualities. The first of these is an intense attention to preparation, making sure that everything and everyone is in place before an operation begins. The second is that they are so well trained that they respond instinctively to the second-by-second developments of the action

itself, as conscious thought processes are just too slow. Elite officers do spend time doing rigorous and slow tactical planning, often using the 'sand table' technique of old (effectively a sand-covered war games table on which the tactical elements of the forthcoming battle are plotted). Yet equal, if not more, amounts of time are spent honing their skills under conditions of chaos and change, which is what they will actually face in the heat of battle.

PRACTICAL LEADERSHIP

Under the 'do' principle outlined in the US Army leadership manual, there are three categories of action listed which the leader should attempt to fulfil in his actual performance. These are:

- influencing
- operating
- improving

Influencing means that everything the leader does in action imparts a positive influence over the men under his command. During his training, the officer himself will have learnt much from wanting to emulate the officers above him and earn approval. Part of every officer training the world over is time spent listening to the stories of seasoned field officers. By giving accounts of their experiences in battle, experienced officers not only give valuable tactical lessons to the junior officers, but also act as examples which can inspire and motivate the junior officers during training. In the same way, the junior officers will then go out to their first command hoping to inspire confidence and determination. By influencing the men through example, and also through positive leadership skills such as communication and tactical awareness, the leader will aim to instil the motivation that leads to exceptional performance in the field.

When it comes to actually operating in combat missions, the true leader must control the process of battle deployment from beginning to end. Once he has received his mission, he must first begin the process of operational planning. Planning and preparation for battle involves several key actions which must be directed towards the central goal of using, in Clausewitz's words, 'physical force in order to compel the other to do his will'. Planning is a massive topic in its own right and could occupy an entire book (it is covered in more detail in the next chapter). However, a common way in which officers are trained in planning and preparation is to use what is known in military language 'reverse planning'. As its name suggests, this is based on defining the end result you are looking for from the action and then working backwards in time and

filling in all the stages required to meet that objective. Once you have worked back to your starting point, you have a complete plan for the mission.

Ceremonial duties

An officer must oversee ceremonial events and combat and garrison duties which are central to building up a strong esprit de corps within regiments and squads.

Any officer must also be aware at this stage of all the minor logistical needs that could upset his actual combat action. During some of the early campaigns in the Pacific during World War II, the US Marine Corps found that soldiers landing on the ferociously defended beaches of Japanese-held islands were running out of ammunition and had no adequate resupply. The problem, it emerged, was that ammunition was all too often stacked behind other supplies on the logistics ships waiting out in the bay. Thus the planning had to be readjusted so that officers consciously made sure that ammunition was placed at the front of the landing craft during the boat-loading phase of the operation.

As this example demonstrates, a good combat officer does not just focus his attention at the battle itself, but also on all the pre-battle factors that will exert their influence once battle has begun. An ideal way of ensuring that everything has been thought of, if there is time to do so, is to rehearse the action mentally from opening shots to completion. By doing this as realistically as possible, and building in some contrived disasters, the officer will reveal errors and problems without the life-or-death consequences of real battle.

Once the officer is actually in battle, the sum of his training, experience, planning and character will come into effect. The actual tactics of combat are covered in more detail later in this book. However, in summary, the officer in charge of a unit at the front during a battle must try to retain a close grip on the facts of the unit situation as it shifts and changes with the context of the fighting. If a machine gun jams, the officer must be aware that this is the case and alter his immediate battle plan accordingly. If he is wounded, he must have already made plain the mission's intentions to his subordinates. If the enemy suddenly capitulates, he must respond to the need for controlling prisoners and processing intelligence gained from the battlefield. Yet, while the status of the battlefield will shift from minute to minute, the officer must make sure that he keeps his attention firmly locked on the final objective. He may well be the only guiding force for his men, so, if he loses his sense of direction or purpose, then so will his unit.

Problem-handling

Leaders develop their subordinates by requiring those subordinates to plan. A lieutenant, new to the battalion staff, ran into a problem getting all the resources the unit was going to need for an upcoming deployment. The officer studied the problem, talked to the people involved, checked his facts, and generally did a thorough analysis – of which he was very proud. Then he marched into the battalion executive officer's (XO's) office and laid it all out in a masterly fashion. The XO looked up from his desk and said, 'Great. What are you going to do about it?' The lieutenant was back in a half-hour with three possible solutions he had worked out with his NCOs. From that day on, the officer never presented a problem to any boss without offering some solutions as well. The lieutenant learned a useful technique from the XO. He learned it so well he began using it with his soldiers and became a better coach and mentor because of it.

An example from the
US Army Leadership Manual

Sand-table exercises

The sand-table is an age-old method for officers to hone their tactical skills and decision-making. It provides more three-dimensional awareness than flat paper.

Even when fighting is actually finished, the combat officer's job goes on in improving the efficiency of his unit for when they next go into combat. Tactics, people, weaponry and the enemy must be rigorously and honestly analysed after the battle. The results of this assessment will then be shaped into a programme of improvement that systematically drives out the weakening factors present in the unit or its individuals. It is often in this time of reconstruction that the true qualities of leadership are needed.

Physical posture

A strong physical posture is emphasised in military forces because it actually leads to greater confidence of mind and a feeling of self-worth.

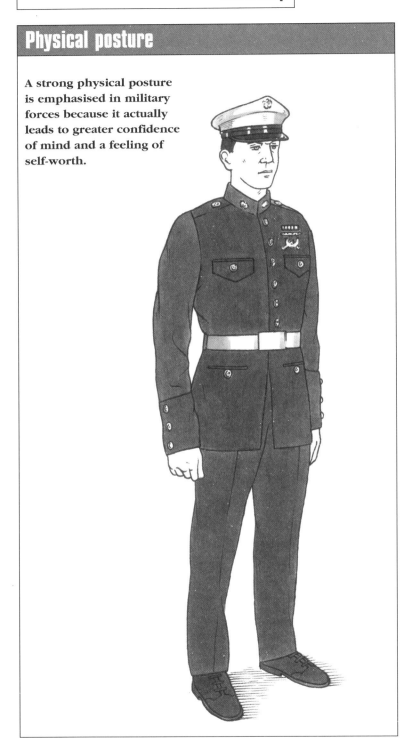

Many studies of effective military leaders have found that praise motivates soldiers more than criticism, so the officer must be diligent in giving sincere commendations to any personnel who have demonstrated good performance. For those who have not, punishment may be appropriate. This must not be overdone, however, and should fit into a clearly established scheme of punishment that is understood by all and is seen as fair. However, in many cases constructive criticism may be all that is required, especially if the officer makes the third party feel that he has let himself, his unit and his officer down by his performance.

At the beginning of this chapter, I commented that officers were mostly born and not made. Training and leadership development can produce fine leaders, but they tend to build on the fact that the candidates have strong personal characteristics. Good officers are vital. The consequences of poor military leadership can be truly awful for those on the front line (as history has testified), so military selection now weeds out the most unsuitable before training even begins. Of course, leadership is not just confined to the officers and ranked leaders. During World War II, it was actually discovered that in many cases it was the NCOs

Technical awareness

Officers should possess above-average awareness of the tools at their command. For instance, a searchlight should be gradually angled away from an enemy position during an advance to hide the troops behind the light beam.

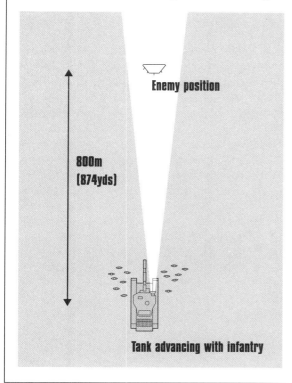

**800m
(874yds)**

Enemy position

Tank advancing with infantry

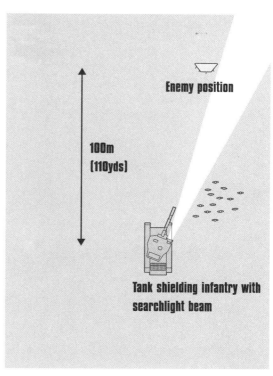

**100m
(110yds)**

Enemy position

Tank shielding infantry with searchlight beam

(non-commissioned officers such as corporals and sergeants) and even strong-minded privates which made up perhaps the most important layer of leadership. NCOs act as the intermediaries between the officers and the rest of the men. As such, they play a vital role in sustaining the emotional and physical welfare of the men. The NCOs also have to bear the brunt of training new recruits in the art of war.

Whatever the position within the unit, leaders must essentially exhibit the self-belief and confidence that enables them to make sound decisions and make others take

up those decisions as their own. Leadership is a constant learning experience and decision-making ability does not grow overnight. This is recognised in the Marine Corps axiom that all Marines should be 'Lifelong students of the Art of War'. Marines are required to read incessantly on military issues and study accounts of battles ancient and modern. In this way, their understanding of war grows and thus so does their potential for being good leaders. Whether they have achieved such a status can only be tested in the front line.

CHAPTER SEVEN

Battle Tactics 1
Handling Major Manoeuvres

Once all the training is done, the elite soldier is left with the final test of combat itself. This is the defining examination of the soldier's mental stamina, personal courage and military expertise. Psychologically, his training will stand him in good stead, yet there are many things which he will only discover about himself once he actually begins to both face and deliver death.

This chapter is about how the mind applies itself to tactical combat, particularly on major missions where the fighting can be heavy (more covert operations are dealt with in the next chapter). As we shall see, the pressures of battle are intense because they draw heavily on both intellect and emotions, often in situations where the two are pulling against one another. The US soldiers who walked into the storm of fire at Omaha beach during the D-Day landings had to face a situation where to stay where they were would result in almost certain death, yet to leave their cover positions seemed to imply the same. Theirs was the challenge of battle, which is possibly the toughest psychological situation that any human being can face. Here, we will look more closely at this challenge and see how the elite soldier puts his mind to tactical situations to make him a truly formidable fighting force.

WARFIGHTING

There are few better interpretations of the nature of modern warfare than that found in the US Marine Corps' doctrinal manual, *Warfighting*. This was written in 1989 by the Marine General A. M. Gray as an attempt to define the principles of marine warfare in the context of modern fighting conditions. The manual defines the way a soldier should think about combat and how he should respond to it. Although it was written specifically for the US Marine Corps, its lessons have spread around the world to many military units and it will influence thinking about combat for many years to come.

Warfighting begins with a definition of war itself. In short, war is a chaotic and changeable situation characterised by traits such as 'uncertainty', 'fluidity', 'disorder' and 'complexity'. A military unit may hold clear objectives and focused targets, but General Gray states that once the enemy is actually engaged, unpredictable human factors come

Combat intelligence

In this illustration, a soldier places a pole charge. His application of this weapon means that he is enabled to employ a large destructive force with the minimum risk to his own safety, as he remains behind stable and solid cover.

into play and the situation becomes muddied and constantly shifting. Psychologically, therefore, the challenge for the elite soldier is not necessarily to impose order upon this nervous state of affairs (General Gray states that this is an impossibility), but to perform well, despite the chaos and the friction. This is an amazing burden and one which needs incredible qualities of character to handle it.

PREPARATION

Some battles are lost in the mind even before the first shot is fired. This is usually because either the soldier's morale is weak or the preparation for battle has been inadequate. Actually, these two factors feed off one another; weak preparation tends to result in a lack of confidence. Planning a battle or special action is an incredibly difficult and demanding process which requires every ounce of a soldier's mental skills. Preparation is the first stage in overcoming the chaos of war and as such it is vital.

The penalties of poor preparation for military encounters are written in blood throughout history. For example, on 5 September 1972, eight Arabic terrorists of the Black September gang burst into the Olympic village in Munich, killing an Israeli wrestler and his coach, and taking nine other Israeli athletes hostage. German police units were put into action to retrieve the hostages, despite the fact that they were not properly trained for the role. They also turned down assistance from Israel's elite Sayeret Mat'kal counterterrorist unit. The police group decided that the best plan was for police

General Gray on war

War is characterised by the interaction of physical, moral and mental forces. The physical characteristics of war are generally easily seen, understood, and measured: equipment capabilities, supplies, physical objectives seized, force ratios, losses of matériel or life, terrain lost or gained, prisoners or matériel captured. The moral characteristics are less tangible. (The term 'moral' here is not restricted to ethics, although ethics are certainly included, but pertains to those forces of a psychological rather than a tangible nature.) Moral forces are difficult to grasp and impossible to quantify. We cannot easily gauge forces like national and military resolve, national or individual conscience, emotion, fear, courage, moral, leadership, or esprit. War also involves a significant mental, or intellectual, component. Mental forces provide the ability to grasp complex battlefield situations; to make effective estimates, calculations, and decisions; to devise tactics and strategies; and to develop plans.

Although material forces are more easily quantified, the moral and mental forces exert a greater influence on the nature and outcome of war. This is not to lessen the importance of physical forces, for the physical forces in war can have a significant impact on the others. For example, the greatest effect of fires is generally not the amount of physical destruction they cause, but the effect of that physical destruction on the enemy's moral strength.

Because it is difficult to come to grips with moral and mental forces, it is tempting to exclude them from our study of war. However, any doctrine or theory of war that neglects these factors ignores the greater part of the nature of war.

USMC, *Warfighting*, pp.15-16
(US Government, 1997)

Weapon control

A soldier should be so familiar with his firearm that it is an extension of his own body. Such familiarity will pay off in increased first-round kills on the battlefield.

sharpshooters to kill the terrorists as they crossed the tarmac at Fürstenfeldbruck Airport to a waiting Lufthansa Boeing 707 which was provided seemingly in compliance with the terrorists' escape plans.

Everything about the preparation was wrong. The snipers had single-shot bolt-action rifles unsuited to the demands of the mission; there was not enough illumination at the site; lines of fire were not judged correctly; there was no back-up force; and faulty intelligence had put the number of terrorists at four when there were actually eight. The

tragic consequence of this inadequate preparation was that the first volley of sniper fire only killed one terrorist. There ensued a four-hour battle in which the Israeli hostages were slaughtered and aircraft were destroyed by terrorist hand grenades. Only when the army was deployed was the situation brought under control, by which point the Israeli military leaders were openly crying with frustration and anger. Germany did learn from its mistakes; the truly elite GSG 9 antiterrorist squad was formed in the wake of Munich. However, the example does serve to show how, for military-style operations, those in charge of preparation must have the skills of mind and experience to judge what is needed and what may go wrong.

There are many mental ingredients to planning a military operation. Perhaps the primary of these is the skill of organisation. For a military force to be effective, its actions and its logistics must be organised properly from top to bottom. At the top level, there is the problem of co-ordinating supplies, transport, weapon supplies, fire support, delivery and extraction methods, food, relief and tactics. This requires a mind that can work from the smallest detail to the biggest picture and see how the two relate to the final objective. At the other end of the scale, each individual soldier must be able to accept responsibility for organising his own preparations for battle. For example, when looking at the Spetsnaz soldier and his equipment, the

diligence required in putting together such a kit is exceptional. Even straightforward items such as the AKM assault rifle require proper pre-operation maintenance, correct ammunition supplies and a full cleaning kit to be a sustainable field weapon. Add all the other bits of kit – including highly technical ones such as the anti-tank missile launcher – and the elite soldier has to have very good concentration and an established packing routine to ensure that he goes into action with everything he needs to be able to use his weapons.

Of course, organisational planning is shaped by tactical planning, and it is here that the mental abilities of the officers and NCOs really come into play. Returning to *Warfighting,* the manual gives us a soldier's perspective on the psychological traits required for designing tactics and effective combat plans:

Observation in urban combat

Placing himself low to the ground, the soldier can look round the corner with less risk of quick returning fire; the enemy expects a head to show at a higher level.

The Marine Corps' style of warfare requires intelligent leaders with a penchant for boldness and initiative down to the lowest levels. Boldness is an essential moral trait in a leader for it generates combat power beyond the physical means at hand. Initiative, the willingness to act on one's own judgment, is a prerequisite for boldness.

USMC, Warfighting, p. 57

The 'boldness' to which General Gray subscribes is something which enables a leader to design tactics that are shocking to the enemy. This is the hallmark of elite forces' thinking. If you go against an enemy with conventional tactics, the enemy will quickly grasp your intentions and react accordingly. Thus what you must do is design a method of combat that overwhelms the enemy's expectations and puts him in a continuous state of disadvantage.

Like the act of organisation, tactical planning requires the mental ability to juggle many considerations. Take as an example a theoretical raid on an enemy border post. The list of

Field targeting

By using a simple 180 degree clock system, the soldier can roughly identify positions to his colleagues. The point straight ahead is called 'axis of arc' and 45 degree to either side is called respectively, 'quarter left' and 'quarter right'.

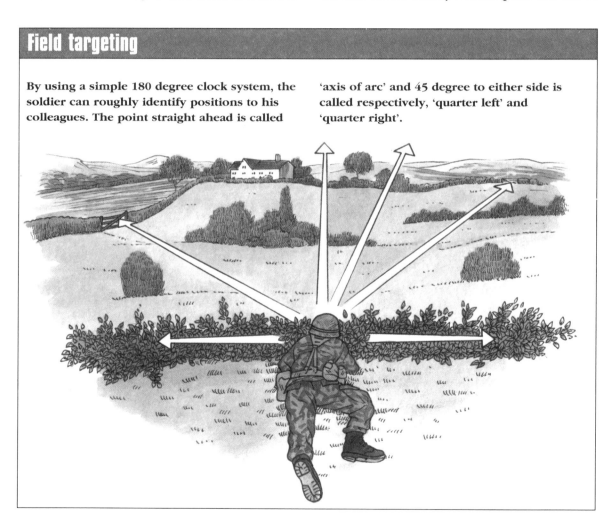

Urban combat firing positions

A soldier should select his firing position according to the following criteria: a) to reduce his silhouette to the barest possible minimum; b) to provide solid physical protection; and c) to allow the maximum arc of fire for his weapon.

considerations for such a mission is truly enormous and would fill a book of its own. Just a few of the issues at stake would be:

- How is it best to insert the attacking unit bearing in mind that the approach ground is scanned continually by thermal imagining cameras, motion-sensor equipment and dog patrols, and the approach air corridors have advanced radar surveillance?
- What is the strength of the enemy at the site? This includes manpower, experience of troops, weapons available, state of readiness and proximity of reinforcements.
- How is the border zone structured to generate maximum confusion once the attack occurs? How will the enemy troops respond once the firing starts and what are their positions of strength?
- Who are the best people for the mission within the units available? What is the status of their training, availability and experience?
- How will climatic factors affect the nature of the deployment, either to advantage or disadvantage?

The list of questions could go on and on, and it is imperative that the tactical designer comes up with satisfactory answers to each before the mission can go ahead. However, the tactical designer will also have to build in contingency plans should the mission not go as expected. In constructing the final plan, there are several criteria the planner must follows. The missions tactics must be:

Coherent

A tactical operation must be understandable by all involved and not be confused as to the objective or procedure. By ensuring this, the

Special forces ambush tactics

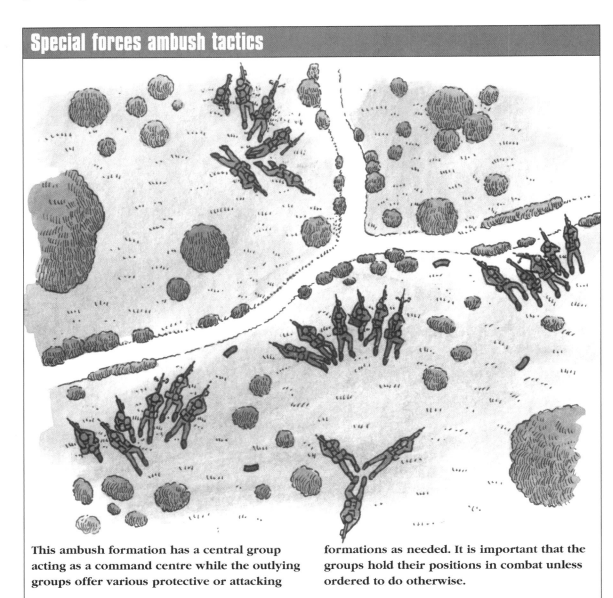

This ambush formation has a central group acting as a command centre while the outlying groups offer various protective or attacking formations as needed. It is important that the groups hold their positions in combat unless ordered to do otherwise.

leader knows that every man will be clear about his role in the operation and thus be able to give his maximum contribution.

Achievable

All military plans involve an aspect of daring and, in the case of special forces operations, this is especially so. Yet, however risky a manoeuvre, all soldiers must set out on their mission knowing that it is achievable, if only at the extreme. If a mission appears almost suicidal in nature, the motivation of the unit will tend to be low, as the individual skills each soldier possesses will feel largely irrelevant. Instead, the operational plan must have a definite programme of deployment, objective and withdrawal that emphasises survivability as much as boldness.

Daring

In balance with the last point, elite forces' missions must have a dash of daring about

The V-shaped ambush

By adopting two arcs of soldiers in mirror image, these soldiers are able to ambush an enemy whose direction of travel is not known.

Because of their formation in these arcs, the soldiers are able to spread their fire across a wide area of attrition.

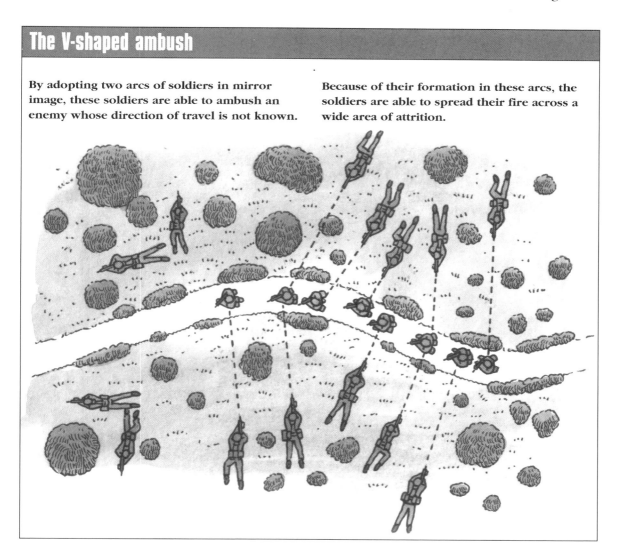

them. This is not simply for the pride of the unit, though doubtless that is important, but innovative and daring plans also tend to disrupt the enemy's defence by giving them a less predictable enemy to fight. A good example would be the SAS's raid on Pebble Island airfield during the Falklands War. Pebble Island acted as an air base for Pucara ground-attack aircraft; the aircraft had to be destroyed if the subsequent assault on the Falklands was not to be hampered. The SAS did this with great vigour, moving in under an offshore barrage from HMS *Glamorgan* before hitting the Argentine garrison hard with M203 grenade launchers, 66mm LAW rockets and 81mm mortars. Under this cover, an SAS assault team physically planted explosives on each aircraft to ensure destruction. By the time the raid was over, the entire Argentine garrison had been defeated and six Pucaras, four Turbo-Mentors and a Skyvan transport aircraft lay wrecked on the airfield. The mission illustrated how an attack of unexpected daring threw the enemy into total disarray and gave the elite forces a mental edge over their rivals. No SAS soldiers were lost in the mission.

Violent

If the mission is a destructive one by nature, the planning should result in a destructive force of great power being unleashed in a controlled manner. This principle can be applied defensively, as well as offensively. When Vietcong and NVA forces attacked US Special Forces camps in the Vietnamese highlands at places such as Plei Mrong and Nam Dong, they often found themselves slaughtered by US firepower despite being numerically superior. The Green Berets had set up interlocking defensive networks of machine guns, mortars, Claymore mines and assault rifles. During attacks such as that which occurred on 3 January 1963 at Plei Mrong, large numbers of attackers were hewn down by bullets, mortar rounds and ball-bearings (from the Claymore mines) with appalling injuries. The successful defence of the camp proved the fact that firepower can be decisive when applied with maximum violence. The problems arise (as in the case of the Munich massacre) when weaponry is not intelligently used. Elite forces tend to be so familiar with weaponry that they do not overestimate the potential of firearms and thus plan weapon defences much more coherently.

Tactical planning is a difficult skill and it needs a great deal of confidence and vision to be done effectively. Not everyone is capable of assuming the responsibility, especially in life-or-death military situations, and some find it hard to live with the distinction between the clean ideas of the planning table and the bloody horror that results once their plan is put into life. However, what has emerged is that having someone detached from the nitty-gritty of the fighting is essential to the success of a mission. This is the role of the officer who is not actively present at the site of combat.

Information coming back from the battlefield tends to be very partial – soldiers see individual events before them and magnify them in their importance (although elite soldiers are trained in dispassionate observation). Thus, in World War II, it was common for infantry who had been attacked by tanks to report many tens of enemy vehicles when there were only a few. What a behind-the-lines tactician must do is interpret all the information coming to him from the battlefield and make cold decisions on a bloodless basis so that his judgment is not clouded by emotion (although he must remain sensitive to his men's welfare). Diagrammatic representation of the battlefield – such as the representation of the raid on a railway bridge – helps give the clarity of thought required when deciding on tactical advantage. It is this clarity of thought that should steer the action once the firing begins.

Anti-ambush measures

By nature, an ambush cannot be planned for; however, it can be controlled. This is done through utilising the correct formation. Here an ambushed party (top) make optimum use of a rearguard in order to perform a flanking retaliation.

THE MIND TO FIGHT

Those who have had to fight in actual combat missions describe a unique psychological experience. Many have described it as a sensation of 'hyper-reality' in which the experience of living under the incredible proximity of death and witnessing cataclysmic events makes the senses work unbelievably fast and ironically produces an incredible rush-like sensation of being alive and powerful. Such was described by SAS Captain Derrick Harrison during combat in France in 1944. Having driven into the French village of Les Ormes accompanied by a small unit of SAS troopers, he found himself faced by a truckload of SS soldiers. The firefight that broke out left him isolated under a hail of bullets:

I had grabbed my carbine and was now standing in the middle of the road firing at everything that moved; Germans seemed to be firing from every doorway. I felt my reactions speed up to an

Tactical challenges

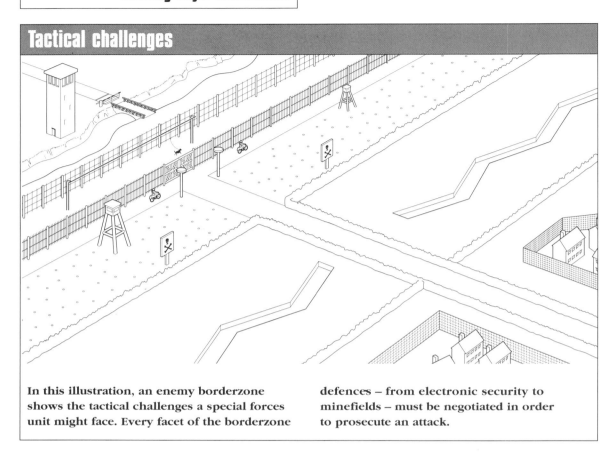

In this illustration, an enemy borderzone shows the tactical challenges a special forces unit might face. Every facet of the borderzone **defences – from electronic security to minefields – must be negotiated in order to prosecute an attack.**

incredible level. It was almost as if I could see individual bullets coming towards me as I ducked and weaved to avoid them. All the time I was shooting from the hip, and shooting accurately.

Harrison's sensation of 'speeded-up' reactions is a typical description of the way many soldiers feel in the height of combat. Modern psychology is indeed starting to reveal some of the basis of this response, often through the study of international athletes and disaster survivors. During extreme situations, the mind tends to adopt a tunnel-vision principle which focuses every effort on the act of survival or, in a military situation, on the act of either killing or avoiding death. This state of

mind produces tremendous energy and mental acuity, and can often be the factor that decides whether a soldier lives or dies.

However, this is not all. Even in the fog of war, an elite soldier must draw on his training and mental discipline to think as clearly as possible in the circumstances. This is tactical thinking 'on the ground', the focus of the rest of this chapter. In making a shift from the tactical planner to the people who actually execute the tactics, we shall see how the elite forces training described earlier comes alive in practical decision-making on the battlefield.

INTO THE FIELD

Deployment is one of those times when nerves can be almost unmanageable. Sat in a helicopter or an APC, being rushed to a future that may be very short, the soldier can experience an overload of emotional demands at the very point where he should be thinking clearly. As we have already seen, however, there are steps that the soldier can take to control the anxiety. The first of these is mission focus – directing the attention entirely towards the mission at hand and mentally rehearsing the training and planning that has gone before. This has the effect of making the soldier more outward-looking and avoiding the introversion that leaves the soldier vulnerable to his imagination. Physically, deep, slow breaths will also help blood pressure and anxiety to fall to balanced levels. However, anxiety has a purpose in that it provides adrenaline for the demands of combat and so it is important not to push relaxation exercises to an extreme. As an old saying goes: 'It's OK to have butterflies as long as they are all flying in the same direction.'

If the soldiers are being deployed by helicopter into an isolated and uncontested area – such as British and US special forces were in the deserts of Kuwait and Iraq in the Gulf War –immediately after they are dropped at the landing zone, they tend to spend up to five minutes completely still and without talking to one another (if the situation allows). This serves several important psychological functions. First, it enables the men to adjust to their new environment and switch their minds from a training mode to a combat mode. Secondly, it helps their senses adjust to the sights and sounds around

them, especially after being in the noise and clatter of a military helicopter. This is particularly important if they are being deployed at night, as it gives them time for their eyes and ears to adjust to and process night-time sensory information.

Once this period is over, they can move out into their mission. At this point, the principles of co-operation and communication which were discussed earlier come into play. Each soldier must take charge of his role and communicate what he is doing to others, while making sure that he understands the function of each other member. Elite training is designed to make communication simple and practical in the field and thus remove the possibilities for misunderstanding. For example, when pinpointing targets or objectives to other soldiers, each man expresses the world in front of him as a semicircle divided into five axis points – left, quarter left, ahead, quarter right and right (see illustration). This can be indicated by hand signals if silence is nec-

Principles of tactical movement

Move at night; behind cover; parallel to roads and tracks; use recessed ground (streams, gullies); cross hills at three-quarter height; clearings at their narrowest point.

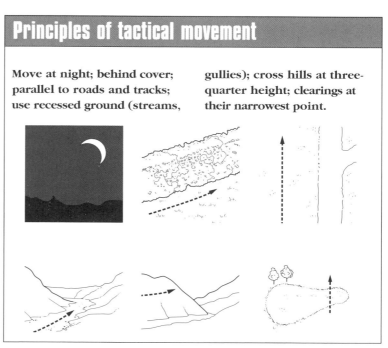

essary and gives the soldiers the ability to target features with limited room for confusion. That way the group stays working with a shared understanding of both where they are and where they are going.

Raiding a railway bridge 1

A good example of tactical intelligence in action. The raiding party attack the bridge itself while two other groups deploy as protective elements either side of the bridge.

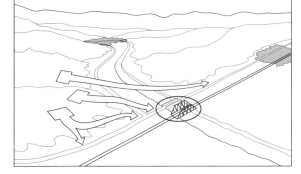

Raiding a railway bridge 2

Once the demolition charges are placed, the groups withdraw in two different directions in order to confound the tracking enemy forces.

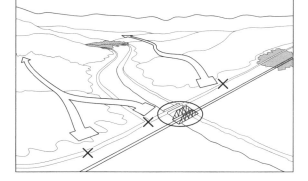

By communicating effectively, the team will have a clear understanding of where they stand in relation to one another and that builds confidence in the competence of the team. When moving into position, each team member must adopt a coherent position in relation to everyone else so that the group functions as a single entity. This is well demonstrated by ambush technique. The diagram nearby shows a typical special forces ambush in readiness to receive enemy soldiers down a rural track. The main attack and command element is set close to the track and will basically control the pace and tempo of the ambush, but these soldiers will also act as the guiding point of communication for the four security elements surrounding them as back-up. The virtue of this configuration is that the assault party can draw in reinforcements from any direction around them. Furthermore, the security troopers can also catch any escaping enemy soldiers in a vicious net of firepower, as well as protect the withdrawing assault party and fight off any enemy reinforcements who come to the scene. The important issue for when the ambush is sprung is that each soldier holds his position unless guided to do otherwise. The security troopers may be positioned some distance from where the main attack is taking place, but, despite their eagerness to enter the fight, they must not do so unless it becomes part of the group strategy as a whole. This example shows how self-discipline and team-mindedness are essential ingredients of any special forces squad, as each man has a dependency on the man next to him.

The example of an ambush also leads us to another factor of tactical and psychological performance that is crucial to the success of a special forces operation: fire control. Fire control covers the spectrum from the way a soldier uses his rifle in personal combat to the manner in which he brings in air strikes. The quality which should distin-

SAS tactics – Iranian Embassy siege

Note how the SAS team took command of the building from the top down. When attacking buildings, descent is always faster than ascent.

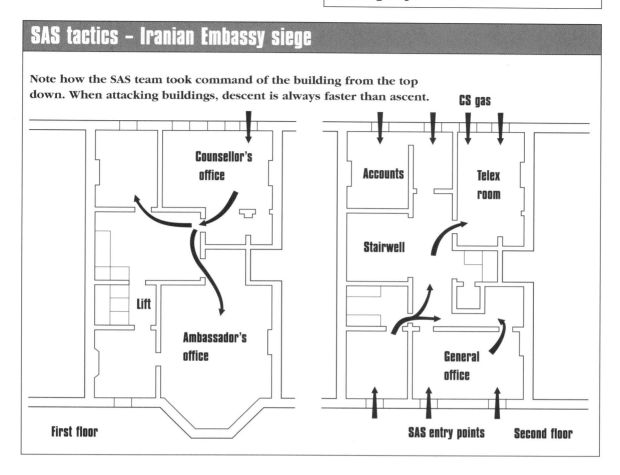

CS gas

Counsellor's office

Accounts

Telex room

Stairwell

Lift

Ambassador's office

General office

First floor

SAS entry points

Second floor

guish a special forces soldier from the rest is that his application of firepower is controlled and deliberate. We have already seen how ordered semi-automatic fire is often much more effective than heavy automatic fire at medium to long ranges. Special forces soldiers are trained to handle their rifles in a very conscious and aware manner. If faced by a large group of enemy soldiers, by far the most effective fire is delivered when a single individual is picked out at a time, aimed at and fired at until he goes down. Each victim is consciously selected, targeted and killed, this fire discipline resulting in a much higher percentage of kills than random, erratic 'spraying' and also conserving

more ammunition. It was such a style of weaponcraft that confused Iraqi soldiers over SAS unit strength in the Gulf War – they could not quite believe that so few men could injure the large numbers of their soldiers dropping from gunshot wounds. Elite soldiers also tend to pick their targets more intelligently. Killing an officer or a radio operator creates greater confusion in the enemy camp than simply shooting a regular foot solider; putting an LAW rocket into a truck's engine or communication equipment starts to impact on the enemy's logistical capabilities.

Controlled firing requires a disciplined mind in the furore of combat and an in-depth

1) Why would you avoid a skyline when acting as a scout?
2) What sort of background would you choose if exposed to view in sight of the enemy?
3) What is the reason for track discipline? What is revealed by aerial photography?
4) Why is the time factor so important in war? Can you give an example of its value?
5) When is the best time to attack parachute troops? How are they armed?
6) What is the distinction between parachute troops and airborne troops?
7) How are parachute troops trained?
8) What is the spearhead of a German panzer division?
9) Why cannot chemical fire extinguishers be used to put out incendiary bombs?
10) Give some examples of good camouflage.
11) What is the purpose of Axis propaganda?
12) What is the meaning of total war as practised by Germany?
13) Do you know any rules of war as recognised by civilised nations?
14) When is it particularly advantageous to use hand grenades, bayonets?
15) What equipment is used for crossing water obstacles?
16) What preparations would you make before starting a long march?
17) What action should be taken if a gas shell has made a crater in the road?
18) In which part of the sky would you expect to find the 'Great Bear'?
19) How could you conceal a loophole?
20) How might the concealment of a weapon pit be endangered?
21) What is the modern method of designing a fire trench?

knowledge of firearm usage and effects. The same discipline is also required in the art of tactical movement. Every act of relocation changes how much a soldier can see and be seen. The soldier's objective is to present as little of himself to enemy view while maximising his tactical advantage, meaning that the special forces soldier must be expert in reading terrain and position, and deciding on a course of movement before taking it.

The nature of tactical movement varies with the type of terrain. We will look at two types here. The first, urban environment, is perhaps the most psychologically cruel of all the warfare scenarios. It is apt to produce tremendous confusion, as attacks lose coherent lines and opposing forces mingle together. Fire can come from any direction and the effect of explosions is compounded by the enclosed spaces. Yet even in this environment, the special forces soldier can control his tactical movement by doing the following:

● Present as small a silhouette as possible. Urban landscapes consist of right angles; the human form stands out clearly when framed by the side of a wall edge or door. Thus, adopt firing positions at small apertures such as a hole in a wall and, when moving, try to stay parallel with a flat surface to confuse the enemy's eye (such as rolling over a wall).

● As the enemy will probably be at close quarters, know your next position of movement. A fixed firing position in urban combat is dangerous because of the risk of being outmanoeuvred from many angles. Grenades or rocket launchers may get a bead on you – the enemy can pinpoint your position to a certain window or doorway – thus, move intelligently to positions which minimise your danger, but put the enemy at a disadvantage.

● Hide behind structures capable of stopping heavy-calibre weapons. This is not as obvious as it sounds – .50 calibre machine-gun bullets can punching through concrete pillars and brick walls. Go for multiple-layer structures and angled features such as the corners of buildings.

● When crossing between points of cover, make the crossing as quick as possible.

● When looking around a wall, peer around it at a level close to the ground; an enemy watcher will not expect to see a head at foot height and this will delay spotting time.

- Take a building from the top; moving down through it enables the attacking force to achieve greater speed and momentum. It helps with fire deployment, as grenades can be thrown down stairs; throwing them up stairs risks the grenade rolling back towards you.

- Select firing positions which present little of you to the outside world, but enable you to traverse a wide arc of fire. This principle has been applied for centuries. Archery holes on castles are often no more than a few inches wide, but have angled side facets to allow the archer to fire over a 90-degree radius.

Combat in a rural setting has different challenges. Principles of movement are based on presenting the slightest and briefest target possible to your enemy:

- When moving around a hill, loop around it two-thirds of the way up the slope; this allows you the quickest passage around it without exposing yourself as a silhouette at its crest.

- Avoid open ground, especially if framed by woodland or hedgerows. Use vegetation features as natural tracks for covered movement. Cross open ground quickly at its narrowest point.

- Do not use roads or tracks, as they are strong fields of fire and ambush. If you have to move up along a road, do so at either side of the road, where you are less visible (termed 'handrailing').

- If you are trained in countryside night fighting, use it; it will compound confusion in your enemy. .Principles of camouflage can be exploited in a countryside setting, but changing seasons require different colours (snow is an obvious example).

Whether operating in a city or in the countryside, such principles of manoeuvre will be second nature to a special forces

soldier by the time he has completed his training. In combat, the mental blueprint of these tactical considerations should allow him to respond appropriately as a reflex action. Psychologically speaking, tactical combat skills enable the soldier to operate amid confusion and chaos with some degree of clarity. The principles of his training impose shape on a fairly shapeless scenario. Also, being conversant with tactically controlling chaos allows the pursuit of what the *Warfighting* manual terms 'maneuver warfare':

... a warfighting philosophy that seeks to shatter the enemy's cohesion through a variety of rapid, focused, and unexpected actions which create a turbulent and rapidly deteriorating situation with which the enemy cannot cope.

**USMC, Warfighting
(US Government; 1997), p. 73**

Not only is the special forces soldier intended to increase the level of control over the battlefield, but also at every level to inflict snowballing degrees of chaos on the enemy. The aim is to attack the parts of the enemy's psychology and physical strength that result in that enemy's collapse as a coherent force for fighting.

The manual goes on to highlight the main areas in which this can be achieved: focus, the aggressive focus from when the point of attack is decided and the full force of arms is brought against it; surprise and deception, highlighting the importance of doing what your enemy does not expect; and shaping the action, encompassing a range of tactical actions such as judging the enemy's overall composition and understanding his surfaces (points of strength) and gaps (points of weakness). By understanding both of these, you are able to control the action by directing your efforts against the enemy's gaps, and in this way destabilising his entire system.

CHAPTER EIGHT

Battle Tactics 2
Counter-insurgency

Counterinsurgency forms perhaps the most significant operational profile of most elite regiments. Termed variously 'low-intensity conflict', 'guerrilla war' and 'terrorism', this half-war of violent struggle is not an engagement of major armies using instruments of mass destruction (although conflicts such as Vietnam show us that can be its outcome).

Nor is counterinsurgency predominantly fought by conventional soldiers with regular soldiering skills. Instead, the new way of war is the conflict which sits awkwardly somewhere between civilian and military struggle. It features sporadic acts of violence – the car bomb, assassination or ambush –

often propagated by an unseen enemy who shrinks invisibly back into the populace after each attack.

The new war requires a new breed of soldier. Insurgency has to be fought by soldiers who can actually insert themselves into a foreign society – either as combatants or as

Watch navigation

In the northern hemisphere bisect the angle between the hour hand pointing at the sun and the 12 mark to give a north-south line. In the southern hemisphere point 12 at the sun.

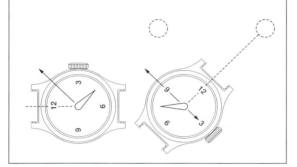

undercover operators – and use all their skills to unearth this enemy from within. The skills of counterinsurgency are the focus of this chapter. Yet, rather than exploring the minutiae of counterinsurgency applications, we will reveal the exceptional personal qualities a man or woman should possess to make the ideal antiterrorist fighter or agent. Counterinsurgency, as we shall see, demands possibly the greatest level of intelligence, creative thinking and self-control of all military roles. Those who execute its undercover missions are some of the world's most talented military minds.

THE ENEMY WITHIN

The postwar military situation is unique in that the war against terrorism has taken an equal priority to the conduct of major military operations by regular armies on the battlefield. Yet this is not to say that guerrilla warfare – fighting conducted by irregular forces outside of standard acts of engagement – is a new phenomena. Indeed, the opposite is the case. Small-scale terrorist attacks go back to ancient times, when individual Roman soldiers died as a result of furtive stabbings when on guard duties in the Empire's far-flung Middle Eastern and southern European colonies. Still, many military analysts have defined the true birth period of guerrilla war as the late 18th and early 19th centuries. What changed was that insurgency became an actual way of war, rather than something incidental to a larger conflict. At this turning point, we see 'guerrilla' actions such as the Vendée uprising in France (a revolt by people in western France and Brittany against the revolutionary government) and the attacks by Spanish insurgents made against Napoleonic French troops in Spain from 1807. In fact, this latter conflict spawned the term 'guerrilla' itself, the translation 'little war' indicating the difference from the usual conflicts of massed armies and open battlefields.

It was exactly the massed armies' inflexibility and massive inertia in movement which the insurgents sought to exploit. More and more nationalist and politically motivated groups were finding that an apparently smaller, weaker force could take on a far greater military unit if it did not fight on conventional terms. From the early 18th century, guerrilla-style warfare spread across the world to become more of a deliberate tactical choice. France would endure many more periods of violent insurrection following the Franco-Prussian war. Italy spawned guerrilla heroes such as Guiseppe Garibaldi, who fought against Austrian power in Italy. In the US Civil War, bands of Confederate insurgents attacked Union troops in the Shenandoah Valley. At the end of the 19th century, British troops clashed in the African Transvaal and Orange Free State for almost two years with the unpredictable and fast-moving horse-mounted Boer irregulars.

The 20th century if anything increased the pace of guerrilla conflict, especially as movements became increasingly tied to new political philosophies of Marxism and revolutionary theology. From 1916, the British struggled with Irish independence movements, a bloody beginning to a terrorist war which has lasted to this day. Arab insurgents conducted campaigns against the Turks between 1916 and 1918, a conflict which involved the famous participation of Captain T.E. Lawrence ('Lawrence of Arabia'), who later wrote on guerrilla warfare and declared that 'granted mobility, security, time and doctrine, victory will rest with the insurgents'.

Lawrence's comments are evidence that, by the early decades of the 20th century, guerrilla warfare was entering a kind of tactical respectability and, indeed, the 20th century saw perhaps the fullest flowering of guerrilla warfare. This was particularly so with the end of World War II, as many nations such as the United Kingdom, Portugal and France struggled to hang onto their crumbling colonial power in the postwar era. Colonial conflicts led to the greatest proliferation of guerrilla warfare, particularly in the Far East and Africa.

However, conflicts such as those in French Indochina between 1946 and 1954 and the Congo in the 1960s were also shadowed against the international backdrop of the Cold War. The Soviet and NATO superpowers may not have clashed directly during the tense period following World War II, but they expressed their political wills in small proxy wars around the world's battlezones. Their military sponsorship of various affiliated groups allowed guerrilla wars to grow into major outright conflicts – Vietnam being the classic example. Escalating from small guerrilla war to full-blown war, Vietnam showed the military world that counterinsurgency was perhaps the most difficult yet imperative role for its forces to assume. A nation like the United States found that, despite its unsurpassed might, the daily political and human consequences of sporadic shootings and ambushes added up to a wearing tactical quagmire.

Day/night vision

Light is projected onto the cones at the back of the eye; the peripheral rods become more sensitive at night, when the soldier looks to the sides of objects and the rods do the work.

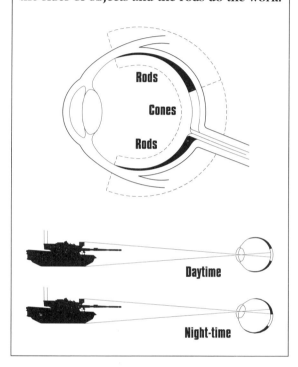

That lesson stays with us. Although the Cold War is now over, insurgency flourishes all over the world, expanding with a variety of new themes and intentions. Although the communist and capitalist ideologies which fuelled actions in the past may have been replaced by religious and sectarian motivation, however, the horrendous effects of murder and bombing are still the same and governments are still destabilised by the slow and unpredictable grind of violence. It is little wonder, therefore, that counterinsurgency can perhaps be said to have become the dominant role for elit forces worldwide.

TERRORISM VERSUS COUNTERINSURGENCY

On many occasions, forming an effective military response to guerrilla activity has actually been the catalyst for the development of many of the world's elite units – for example, the re-establishment of the SAS during the Malayan Emergency of 1948–60.

The reasons why counterinsurgency so often falls to small, elite squads are many. Chief amongst these is the fact that counterinsurgency operations require a level of tactical sophistication and practical skills which would be impossible to transfer to large squads. A singular illustration of this was the

Walking at night

Walking silently at night requires that the soldier ensures that the foot is picked up high and placed down slowly. This is done by leading with the toe. True mental stamina is required to keep this up hour after hour and resist rushing.

Testing the ground

At night, a soldier must remain aware of possible booby traps. A soldier tests for trip wires with a wooden stick to avoid completing an electrical current.

role of the SAS in Malaya. Britain's efforts to quench the violence of the Malayan Communist Party (MCP) guerrillas not only included major regular army operations, but also sophisticated SAS missions in which the elite troops conducted social actions, as well as military ones. In 1952, the Military High Commissioner in Malaya, General Sir Gerald Templer, channelled more military energy into winning over the support of the common Malayans than was spent in trying forcibly to defeat the communists. This became known as the 'Hearts and Minds' campaign, a term which has grown in currency ever since. The SAS soldiers involved in the campaign had to mingle with the Malayans, learn their language and culture, and offer them friendship and support, as well as occasionally act ruthlessly against the terrorists. By helping the locals, the British hacked away at the communists' social support base and left them more isolated and easier to target. Thus, when the SAS emerged from the jungles at the end of the emergency, many had acquired skills such as dentistry, building and midwifery, as well as veterinarian care.

The example of Malaya illustrates how counterinsurgency is a job requiring an above-average intelligence and a sophisticated approach to conducting campaigns without necessarily using violence. Yet violence is also required and counterinsurgency soldiers must also be trained to deliver that with brutal focus. Counterinsurgency is often the province of elite squads because terrorism is an innovative form of warfare and one which demands the constant upgrading of tactical skills. In Malaya and Vietnam, jungle-based counterinsurgency combat had to be perfected. From the moment Palestinian terrorists hijacked an El Al Boeing 707 from Rome to Algiers, counterterrorist forces had to develop tactics for dealing with the hijack of civil passenger aircraft. Embassy-based terrorism pushed the development of rapid building assaults such as those used by the SAS against the Iranian embassy in the 1980s. The use of bombs in urban settings – the most visible in recent years being incidents such as the bombing of the World Trade Centre in New York – necessitate against-the-clock reactions and also the ability to defuse ordnance. The list of counterinsurgency threats and countermeasures goes on and on, but what is evident is that the men and women given the task of working against terrorism in either aggressive missions or undercover work have to be the most highly trained in the world.

So what type of person do you need to be to fulfil this role? To answer that effectively, we need to see what the counterinsurgency soldier faces, and we can do this by stepping inside the mind of the terrorist.

TERRORIST PERSONALITIES

In recent years, the traditional profiles of the insurgent have dissolved. Whereas, in the 1960s, terrorists tended to be motivated by hardened political ideals, today's 'insurgents' can be anything from extreme Islamic guerrillas to isolated individuals who commit violence for reasons known only to them. Yet when the target is more military in nature – as in defined terrorist groups such as the IRA in Northern Ireland or the Basque separatist ETA in Spain, or the Vietcong in Vietnam – there does seem to be a typical group of characteristics or definitions.

Insurgents are recruited to the cause through a variety of routes: threats, bribes, promises of social improvements, or political ideals. In Indochina in the 1950s, the Viet

Minh would organise political rallies at which trained observers would monitor the crowd for those individuals who reacted positively to the message. These would then be approached after the meeting with a view to joining the ranks. Other recruitment strategies were less subtle. A common tactic used in Vietnam was for the insurgents to commit an action against US or ARVN forces, which in turn provoked retaliation against a certain village or district. The populace that suffered under this retaliation thus came to associate the US soldiers with aggression and violence, and expressed their animosity by becoming members of the Vietcong.

All recruits to an insurgent organisation tend to be 'loyalty tested' – made to perform some task which establishes their loyalty to the cause or puts them in an incriminating position. This testing will start simply and build up slowly, working from, say, the delivery of an apparently important letter to the receipt of illegal arms. Needless to say, the penalties for betrayal can be appalling. The Vietcong used tactics such as cutting open the 'traitor' and letting wild pigs eat him. Naturally, such horrific treatment brought in more totally faithful recruits through abject fear.

Recruitment of insurgents also tends to be focused on those individuals who are discreet. Like their elite opponents, insurgent organisations cannot work with those who will brag about their role in the struggle and thus reveal the operational workings. Recruits, therefore, might be tested by first being given a piece of seemingly vital but actually spurious information. They are then given the opportunity to reveal it (perhaps using an attractive member of the opposite sex to increase the desire to impress). Should the person reveal their information, they are ejected from the organisation, or worse.

Interestingly, when studies were conducted into what motivated terrorists in the Indochina and Vietnam conflicts, in the majority of cases, the simple desire to improve material wealth seemed to be dominant. Less than 40 per cent of Viet Minh captured in French Indochina actually proclaimed an acceptance of the communist cause. The rest were more inspired by the pursuit of greater wealth, which tends to explain why so many recruits to terrorist organisations come from disadvantaged backgrounds, particularly the rural working class. In the Korean War, 70 per cent of insurgents were labourers, farmers or peasants. Once inside the terrorist organisation, the individual is indoctrinated as to its values and beliefs, and they are also placed into its structure. Studies have tended to show that insurgents generally work in 'cells' of five to eight people – any less than five and individ-

ual personalities tend to become too dominant and any more than eight and the group tends to split into factions. Of course, there are exceptions to this. Mao Tse Tung constructed his guerrilla forces into squads of 9 to 11 men and these in turn into companies of 120. Yet, regardless of size, each squad tends to be assigned a distinct role. Thus, in organisations such as the IRA, some squads would work in an intelligence-gathering capacity, whereas others would function as assassination groups.

Becoming a full member of the organisation tends to involve initiation rituals of many types. These are important in that they give the individual a sense of belonging to his new group and also make him feel that he has achieved a special status within his

Undercover operator

A counter-insurgency soldier must consciously select the most inconspicuous routes possible to move around. Here a soldier uses a culvert to cross a road.

Watchtower attack

Guards are particularly vulnerable to fatigue and boredom, especially at night, when most special forces units will choose to conduct their attack.

The leader is usually the most publicly visible element of the group, but especially in the earlier stages of a campaign, terrorists tend to be almost invisible within their society. This is their source of ultimate strength. The advantages that insurgents have over their conventional opponents are extensive, but the key factors which make them so problematic to deal with can be listed as follows:

●**Freedom of movement**. Terrorists are not constrained by conventional patterns of strategic movement. During the Vietnam War, the threat from the Vietcong could emerge from almost any quarter, ranging from a bomb attack in central Saigon to an ambush in the mountainous Vietnamese jungles. Because insurgents rarely fight open battles, counterinsurgency forces face a difficult challenge in knowing exactly where they are and what are their tactical intentions.

society. Often the rituals will be in some way inspired by the words of the movement's overall leader – a very important figure for the insurgent. The list of leaders is extensive: Che Guevara for the Cuban revolutionaries, Mao Tse Tung during the Chinese Civil War, Ho Chi Minh for the Viet Minh, Osama Bin Laden for Islamic fundamentalists. Such figures give their groups a psychological cohesion and a figure who resolves disputes, gives direction and doctrine, and inspires.

● **Anonymity.** Insurgents rarely wear uniforms and tend to be fully integrated into their national society. This means that, unless they are caught in an act of terrorism or intelligence reveals them, their identity will be almost entirely unknown. Such anonymity gives terrorists the advantage of being able to select and observe prominent targets at leisure, and also to lull the enemy troops into a false sense of security by apparently offering them friendship and various services.

- **Social support.** Few terrorist organisations operate in isolation from significant levels of social support. Insurgents are not simply comprised of fighters, but also of an entire network of support from a willing sector of the populace who provide logistical, financial and operational assistance. During the war in French Indochina between 1945 and 1954, some 340,000 Vietnamese were members of the Village Militia, a grass-roots organisation of men and women aged 18–45 who rarely fought, but gave the logistics and intelligence for the Viet Minh to function as a truly effective fighting force. Breaking the link between the terrorists and their social support is a primary task of counterinsurgency forces.

- **Unpredictability.** Terrorism can be run with military efficiency, but more commonly it is a loose and unpredictable expression of violence. Sometimes terrorist organisations appear out of nowhere and commit horrific acts before melting back into obscurity. Terrorist leaders can often be psychologically unstable characters whose operations are conducted on the basis of whim and mood. Also, terrorist organisations tend to change shape rapidly, forming alliances and renaming themselves according to new goals. Such makes the movements of insurgents incredibly difficult to predict and pre-empt. Italy, for example, has an estimated 150 terrorist organisations living and operating within its borders, a presence which has resulted in a disturbing trend of murder and bombings over the past 30 years. Looking at the situation worldwide, whereas almost 80 per cent of terrorist violence before 1970 was expressed against property, since the 1980s that

percentage has now been taken by attacks directly against people. Diverse organisations and shifting trends make it hard to pin the terrorists down to any single pattern of operational focus.

Against this backdrop of terrorist strengths, what can the elite counterinsurgency troops offer to control insurgency? The scale of the problem is massive – a study conducted in Tel Aviv found that only one in 10 terrorists is ever actually caught – and there are doubtless too few elite soldiers to combat such a worldwide phenomenon. Thus, police and security forces conduct most antiterrorist work. However, in certain instances, a more superior military presence is required and this is when the acute mental skills of the counterinsurgency fighter come into play.

THE COUNTERINSURGENCY FIGHTER

Elite troops tend to be employed for counterinsurgency in two distinct roles. One is in the scenario of urban terrorism, in which they are applied to hostage and building assault situations. The other is the deep-insertion mission, often in the context of serious rural terrorism. Here, the elite soldier is placed deep within the environment of the insurgent, acting either as a hidden combat presence, working undercover within the terrorist organisation itself, or taking an active role in building civilian resistance against the presence of insurgents. It is this second role that is our focus here, as it demonstrates more fully than most other circumstances the mental agility of the special forces soldier.

To look at the mental profile of the counterinsurgency soldier, we must examine the general skills of undercover operations used by elite soldiers and the mental intelligence that goes with them. Undercover operations range from reconnaissance within enemy territory to impersonating enemy personnel, and they are an extraordinarily demanding element of special forces work. First, we shall look at the essential combat skills of counterinsurgency and undercover operations, and secondly at the equally important and fascinating social skills required.

Combat Skills

The psychological challenge of undercover operations begins from the moment of deployment. For covert operations, night insertion is typical, often by parachute or helicopter. This presents its own set of mental challenges. If entering the contested territory by parachute, special forces often do so by one of two challenging methods of parachute technique which bring their own psychological problems.

The first of these techniques is High-Altitude High-Opening (HAHO). With this technique, the parachutist is dropped some miles from his destination at an altitude of up to 7620m (25,000ft). The canopy is quickly deployed and thereafter the parachutist 'flies' silently to the destination in a shallow-angle drop which can last more than an hour and requires nimble steering.

By contrast, High-Altitude Low-Opening (HALO) parachuting sees the soldier dropped at a similar altitude or higher, though this time he freefalls for several minutes and only deploys the parachute in

HAHO parachuting

The parachutist is deployed from a high altitude, deploying his parachute quickly and fliying to his target many miles away. Mental problems: severe cold and oxygen deprivation.

HALO parachuting

The parachutist is deployed from high altitude, but freefalls and opens his parachute in the last 609m (2000ft). Mental problems: timing must be perfect despite freefall disorientation.

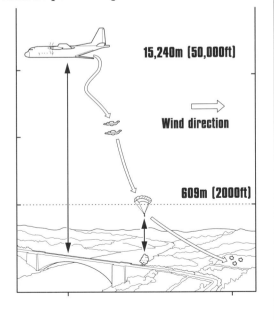

15,240m (50,000ft)

Wind direction

609m (2000ft)

the last 609m (2000ft) of the jump. This gives an extremely rapid deployment method.

Both techniques pose psychological problems. The oxygen levels at 25,000ft and over are very low indeed, and temperatures can be –50°F (–45°C). Lack of oxygen and severe cold can induce feelings of sluggishness, disconnection from reality, unconsciousness, confusion and blurred vision. All these are anathema to the sharp mind required at this dangerous moment of the operation, so enough oxygen should be carried on both types of jump in order to supply the soldier to beneath 3048m (10,000ft). Clothing should also be extremely insulated.

Landing in the operational area by parachute, or by the much noisier helicopter deployment, requires a switch of mind. Unless the situation demands it, the soldier should spend a few minutes still and silent in his new environment, adjusting to sights and sounds, and becoming familiar with his operational world. At night in particular, the soldier's senses are placed under acute strain. The human eye takes about 30 minutes to adjust fully from normal daylight to night vision, even longer if the soldier has been exposed to bright sunlight in the daytime (which explains why special forces soldiers in bright conditions tend to stay indoors or wear very dark sunglasses). This is

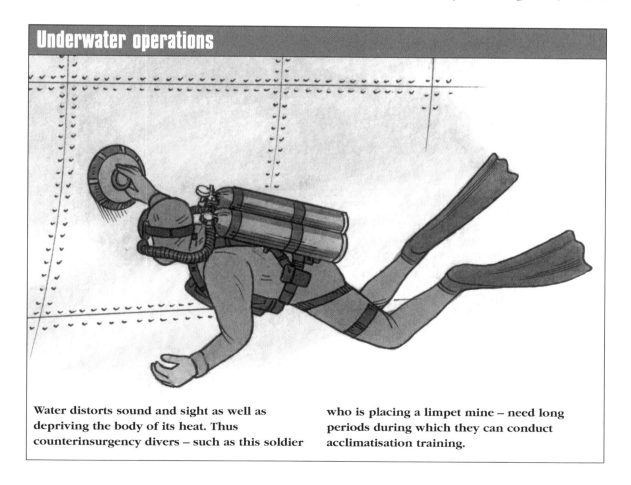

Underwater operations

Water distorts sound and sight as well as depriving the body of its heat. Thus counterinsurgency divers – such as this soldier who is placing a limpet mine – need long periods during which they can conduct acclimatisation training.

Reading the ground

Undercover soldiers must become expert in 'reading' for signs of enemy presence. Footprints and litter can offer vital clues to enemy numbers and force.

because at the back of the human eye are two types of cell: rods, which pick out the general shape of objects; and cones, which give more precise colour definition. Rods are positioned more peripherally around the eye, whereas the cone cells sit directly behind the retina. At night, however, the rods become more receptive to light. The effect for the soldier is that staring directly at the silhouette of a human figure at night results in the shape fading from vision, whereas looking to the side or above the shape allows the peripheral vision of the rods to work better and define the shape more clearly. In training for night combat, therefore, the elite soldier must practise shooting using peripheral vision, as looking directly at the target will usually result in the soldier shooting high. Instead, the gun should be pointed at the base of the target, trusting to the fact that the gun is actually on target. This is a difficult

mental skill to master and must be reinforced by continual night-firing exercises.

Once on the move at night, the soldier must bring all his other senses into play. Smell can give vital indicators of an enemy presence. Elite soldiers are taught to angle their noses 45 degrees to the wind and breathe slowly, but punctuate this with short, sharp sniffs to maximise their scent detection. When detecting noises, the head should be shifted from side to side to try to locate the exact position of the sound. Sounds directly to the front or to the rear can be misinterpreted for the opposite positions if there is no other sensory information. For this reason, head-turning is vital in order to gain a correct bearing.

When on the track of an insurgent or regular enemy, observation and memory are perhaps the two key mental qualities that a soldier must bring to bear. These two mental qualities feed off one another: observation builds clues as to the nature of the enemy presence and the memory enables the soldier to sort these into a meaningful pattern of behaviour of which he can take advantage. Observation is more of a skill than is first imagined. Every scrap of information must be taken in – colours, shapes, textures, movements, intuitive responses – and then assembled so that anything out of the ordinary is received and understood. In this way, the soldier is able to pick up on the signs of enemy presence.

Any indicators of enemy presence are known as 'sign' and are divided into four categories: ground sign (below knee height), top sign (above knee height), permanent sign (sign that does not degrade with the

elements) and temporary sign (sign that does degrade with the elements). If his training is good enough, a simple sign such as a set of footprints should tell the soldier how many enemy passed that point, roughly how long ago, the direction of travel, whether any of the men had an injury and even whether the soldiers were carrying heavy equipment. Combine this with all the other available sign – such as disturbed foliage, human waste, discarded equipment – and the soldier is able to build up a strong profile of whom he is facing and also be aware of ambushes and booby traps.

Of course, the undercover soldier must conduct all his operations without being detected. This in itself requires great self-control and patience. For example, walking at

Footprints

Footprints provide the soldier with clues about the enemy. A moist, well-defined footprint is recent; the state of others can tell soldiers when the enemy passed.

night requires that the soldier raise his knee high, place his toe down slowly onto the ground, then gradually roll the rest of his foot onto the ground to take the pressure. This movement is easy to sustain for a couple of minutes, but to do this hour after hour requires enormous self-discipline to resist the impulse to walk as usual and make greater speed. Similarly, covert surveillance positions are often cramped, damp and uncomfortable and, once occupied, physical strain and mental boredom must be dealt with. During training for the British Parachute Regiment, recruits are often given an exercise where they have to sit cross-legged facing a stone wall, all located on the summit of a bleak Welsh mountain. The instructors monitor the men for those who are unable to cope with the prolonged still-ness and mental inactivity. Those who become agitated and restless would make

poor counterinsurgency, undercover or sniper soldiers, as such roles demand men-talities which can cope with little stimulus for hours or days on end, but then sudden-ly become alert and focused when the situation changes.

It will now be apparent that the under-cover operative is a truly special individual who must display a formidable breadth of mental skills. During the 1960s, US Special Forces devised tests for the entry of its counterinsurgency soldiers. Psychologists at the US Army Personnel Research Office (USAPRO) conducted a varied and punishing range of tests which produced a list of eight psychological characteristics for counterin-surgency soldiers:

● resistance to mental and physical fatigue;
● ability to make decisions in fluid and unstructured circumstances;

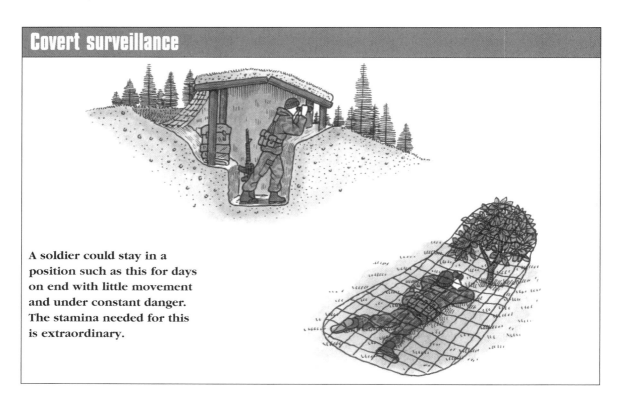

Covert surveillance

A soldier could stay in a position such as this for days on end with little movement and under constant danger. The stamina needed for this is extraordinary.

Remaining invisible

The undercover soldier must know how to detect the enemy but how to remain undetected. A trooper steals food, making sure he leaves no footprints.

- ability to operate as part of a team;
- ability to face combat situations with resolution, courage and tactical skills;
- ability to absorb and retain military information;
- the right frame of mind to treat training as real;
- ability to cope with missions in which the level of progress or the course of action is not known;
- acceptance of the training course as something which cannot be left voluntarily.

If the recruiters could find people with this distinctive mind-set, they could then produce efficient and dependable counterinsurgency teams to be left in the field for long periods without the weakening of morale or resolve. Of course, genuine and extensive combat skills were also required to cover all missions' outcomes, from pure reconnaissance to a major engagement with the enemy. In the early 1970s, the Human Resources Research Office (HRRO) conducted research at Fort Benning in the US and produced a list of areas of skill needed for counterinsurgency units (in this case labelled 'small independent action force', or SIAF):

- individual weapons
- explosives and demolitions
- hand grenades
- machine guns
- physical and mental strength
- using aerial reconnaissance pictures
- maintaining physical wellbeing
- tracking
- communications
- navigation

- using techniques of covert movement
- delivering artillery fire and air strikes
- setting and detecting mines and booby traps
- mountaineering
- survival, evasion and escape
- leadership
- tactical organisation
- first aid
- intelligence
- liaising and using air mobility
- using image intensification equipment
- applications for boats and techniques for river crossings
- applying sensors
- social missions, including the training of foreign troops

(For more details see Peter Watson, War on the Mind, *London: Hutchinson; 1977.)*

Hearts and Minds

A 'hearts and minds' campaign builds up the local civilian or military population to fight its own battle against the insurgents, either by direct military action or by depriving the enemy of popular support. The US 5th Special Forces Group (5SPG) in Vietnam created 42,000 Civilian Irregular Defense Groups (CIDGs), made up of Vietnamese soldiers who were persuaded to fight for the South Vietnamese cause against the Vietcong and NVA, capably adding to the South Vietnamese war effort. Living for long periods amongst the Vietnamese populace, the US soldiers picked up their language and customs, using them against the communists. Such talented influence has led elite soldiers worldwide since the Vietnam War to be trained extensively in these kind of techniques. Cultures can differ in extraordinary ways. Some cultures place a lower value on human life than Western cultures. Oriental cultures often give greater credence to unchanging nature, rather than human progress. In the Middle East, it is regarded as

rude to talk about an important issue straight away. A social minefield awaits the elite soldier on a hearts and minds operation, compunded by the fact that he is usually trying to get a community or group to commit to patterns of behaviour which could place them under threat of violence. Training involves lengthy studies of the target culture and acquisition of the language. The soldier must develop:

Language skills

The soldier should be able to speak without preparation on almost any given topic without undue pausing or lack of vocabulary, switch between formal and informal forms of address and demonstrate competence in language-based intelligence tests.

Negotiation and Argument

The soldier should be able to reason and argue using the different conventions of the society for which he is destined. In any negotiation, the soldier must take into account religious standards, moral codes, styles of argument and whether decisions are made by groups or individuals. The soldier should be an adviser in the foreign group's midst, letting the decision-making proceed naturally.

Modesty

Recruiters have long avoided what they call the 'James Bond type', an individual who is attracted by the role of the undercover operator due to its status. Those who can carry out impressive deeds without confiding details to anyone are favoured. In the British Intelligence Corps, on a scale of 1 to 5, 1 is someone modest and stable enough to keep secrets without tension, and 5 someone who will talk too readily. Only people who score 1 or 2 enter the intelligence corps.

Impersonation

Soldiers working closely with a foreign culture must also be able to impersonate its

Observation

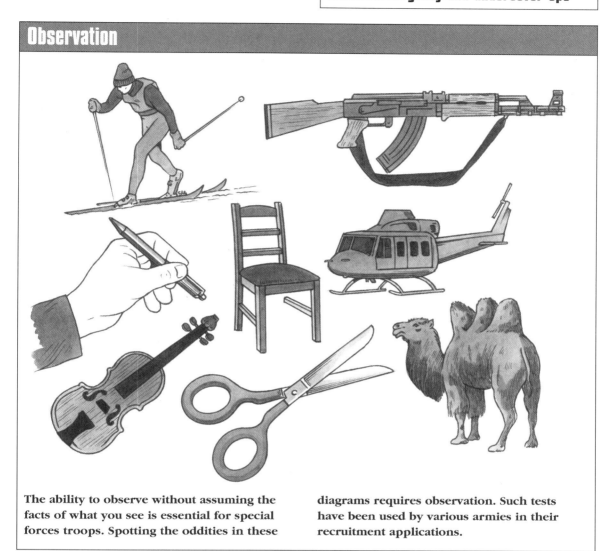

The ability to observe without assuming the facts of what you see is essential for special forces troops. Spotting the oddities in these **diagrams requires observation. Such tests have been used by various armies in their recruitment applications.**

physical mannerisms. For example, Middle Eastern peoples stand close to each other, using constant expressive body gestures to back up their speech.

These are just a few of the qualities that the counterinsurgency soldier must display during operations. If he can combine his combat and social skills with an understanding of his enemy, he will make an effective force against insurgency. He can create an environment of hostility which will control the possibilities of what the enemy can do. The intelligence and mental versatility of individual agents and soldiers, rather than large-scale manoeuvres, is essential. As terrorism and guerrilla war are increasing worldwide, elite soldiers will continue to receive training in the varied skills of this exacting form of warfare.

CHAPTER NINE

Detention, Escape, Survival

Elite soldiers are valuable assets worth preserving, and governments are keen to avoid their special forces falling into the enemy's hands. In terms of cash expenditure alone, each soldier of an elite regiment such as the SAS or US Marines, or specialists such as aircrew, has more money invested in their training than perhaps an entire squad of regular soldiers.

Add to this equation the fact that they are usually privy to some of the world's best-kept military secrets and it becomes apparent how desirable it is for the enemy to capture one of these personnel.

This is obviously easier said than done. Part of the training which elite soldiers receive is in the very tactics of evading detection and capture. They are also often formidable warriors in their own right and, should the enemy try to capture them by force, it can expect to have to work very hard to secure its prize. Yet special forces soldiers and airmen are captured and do have to endure the discomforts, boredom and sometimes horrors of detention. Ironically, it is their elite status which puts them in acute danger of this fate because their ability means that they are chosen for missions often deep within enemy territory and far from the safety net of back-up forces. Furthermore, their missions can be of such secrecy that, in some cases, they will not be acknowledged officially, a situation that all too often puts the soldier outside the protection of the fair-treatment guidelines of the Geneva Convention.

Since the development of the special forces during World War II, and the expansion in airforce personnel following World War I, more and more elite units have been recognising the seriousness of the threat of capture for its soldiers. Thus it is that most elite units in modern military nations actively train their soldiers in the techniques of escape, evasion and detention survival. All fighter or bomber pilots are trained in how to survive for several weeks in hostile territory while waiting for a rescue attempt. Organisations such as the British Joint Services Intelligence Unit (JSIU) specialise in teaching British soldiers how to survive the psychological and physical challenges of torture and forced isolation. US Special Forces troops undergo the SERE course, which gives them the ability to survive should they be cut off deep behind enemy lines, or captured and placed in violent detention.

Such programmes of training are much needed. During the Vietnam War alone, some 586 US pilots were either captured or went missing over North Vietnam during attack raids there. More recent conflicts such as the Gulf War saw SAS personnel taken prisoner by the Iraqi forces and subsequently having to survive the most appalling attempts to extract information. Those that return from such imprisonment often recount the most dreadful depredations and conditions, and tortures which would break the most iron will. So it is that the modern training in the psychology of detention, escape and evasion produces some of the toughest courses in the world. Their aim is to make men and women who are capable of withstanding cruelty and psychological violence from their captors without giving up their vital knowledge and lethal skills. Cruelty and

suffering are actually built into the training to give the elite as real a taste as possible of the life of a captive without actually risking their lives (although, as we shall see, death in training is a precarious possibility). This chapter is about this training.

DETENTION

For a special forces soldier, capture by the enemy is sometimes held as the worst possible outcome of an engagement, with some holding it as even worse than death. If the enemy understands the nature of the operative it now holds – and usually they will because of the circumstances and place of the capture – their total priority will be to extract as much valuable information out of that person as possible. Many regimes around the world pay scant attention to human rights and so torture will often feature as a tool for extracting information should the soldier be unwilling to share his knowledge (and, with elite soldiers, that is almost always the case). Thus a terrible battle begins, the captor using all the means at his disposal to pull information forcibly from the captive's lips and the captive relying on his training, but more importantly his strength of will and intelligence, to resist divulging vital facts.

Whatever the mental strength of the captive, in the hands of an intelligent interrogator, the odds are stacked against him. Many countries invest as much time and science into investigating how to make people talk as others do in resisting interrogation. Furthermore, expert interrogators will usually know exactly what type of training the individual has had for this situation and so can modify their techniques accordingly.

Ultimately, being an elite captive is about participating in a cruel and lonely mental game in which personal resilience is the vital factor in holding out against interrogation. We shall look at how this resilience is fostered by elite units in a moment, but first we should examine the circumstances of deten-

Evasion mentality

Evasion is a claustrophobic, frightening experience, needing the patience to be concealed and make small movements towards one's goal of escape when safe to do so.

tion for elite soldiers in order to gain a true picture of what they face.

The Enemy Against
When we think of the horrors of detention, we tend to give priority to the experience of torture. Yet this is only one possible element of detention and far from the most common. From the point of view of psychological resistance, everything about military detention is usually geared to sap morale and motivation at every level, and leave the captive

bored, lonely, uncomfortable and confused. Once the captive is in this condition, it is easier for the captors to apply a bit of extra pressure to break the captive's will.

There are several general elements in particular which threaten the mental stability of a captive in a prison situation where rules of humanity do not apply. We shall examine the main ones here.

Loneliness and Boredom

Soldiers tend to be people who, up until the point of capture, have enjoyed full and dynamic lives in a social group of strong personalities and constant interest. Captors often realise this and so tend to place elite soldiers in places where they are isolated from human contact, the only people they

see usually being their captors. The place of their confinement is frequently very small, offering little free movement and, without human contact, several unfortunate mental problems can start to develop. First, the soldier can start to withdraw into himself so that the outside world becomes less real. This allows the captors to begin drawing information from the prisoner because somehow the information handed over seems of diminished importance.

A further problem is that of prisoner dependency. Because the only human contact the prisoner receives is that of the guards, the ironic result is that the prisoner actually comes to look forward to the guards' visits, especially if the captors deliberately send friendly faces who talk with the

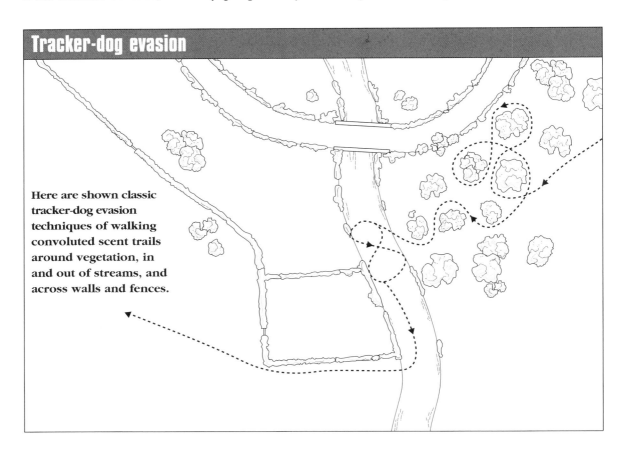

Tracker-dog evasion

Here are shown classic tracker-dog evasion techniques of walking convoluted scent trails around vegetation, in and out of streams, and across walls and fences.

Reading the liar

With an expert interrogator, the soldier must avoid the physical clues to lying. Touching the face or focusing eyes upwards can indicate the stress of lying.

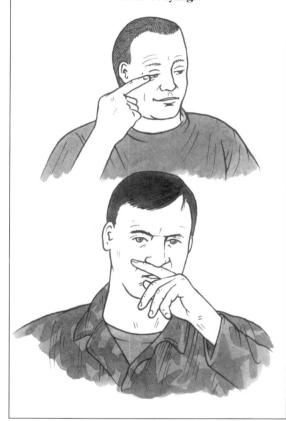

prisoner. This again may make the prisoner more willing to divulge information, if only to prolong the contact with the enemy visitor. The longer the prisoner spends in detention, the further removed he can feel from his family and friends, and the more despairing of his situation. Thus any degree of warm human contact is likely to become desirable and the enemy interrogators may cleverly fill this gap.

Of course, detention is such that the soldier can even be in a communal cell and still feel lonely. During severe imprisonment, individuals tend to start looking after themselves more than others (although there are many examples to the contrary). Reports from inmates of the Nazi concentration camps often spoke of a ghost-like quality of detachment from one another, as fear and anxiety took hold and made people withdraw within themselves. Boredom is a problem which compounds this situation. Often the captive will not have access to anything remotely mentally stimulating and this in itself will cause time to draw by crushingly slowly. Boredom causes physical discomfort as the mind makes the body fidget in an attempt to relieve the monotony. This is turn leads to a build-up of anxiety which, given some months to run, can easily crush the will to carry on.

Fatigue

There are two essential causes of fatigue in a detention centre or prison camp. One is work. Prisoners of war are often put to work as a source of free labour, doing everything from constructing roads to making ammunition for the enemy war effort. A grim example from history is the Burma–Thailand railroad network which was constructed by Allied POWs and native labourers during World War II, in which the level of labour forced by the Japanese resulted in the deaths of some 102,000 prisoners. Although not all places of detention force such levels of labour, many do work the prisoners hard. The hard work is usually not supported by proper nutrition or adequate rest, so the prisoners start to suffer from intense fatigue that can soon tip into illness or mental despair. At the other extreme, enforced inactivity will have a similar result. The human mind tends to follow the actions of the body. Try sitting very still for a few hours with limited options for movement or entertainment. Your mind will

Effects of boredom

Boredom can be a great enemy in captivity. If the soldier can't find a way to cope, after only four days he will be fearful and apathetic in equal measures.

start to feel very tired in spite of no physical energy being expended.

Illness and Poor Nutrition

Military prison camps tend to produce weak, undernourished individuals who are prone to the inevitable illnesses that occur when many men are stuck in cramped, unsanitary conditions for long periods of time. A poor diet results in a suppressed immune system, so the prisoner is much more likely to contract illnesses – and they tend to be serious should he do so. The presence of serial illness is primarily a physical problem, but it has major psychological impact by lowering the prisoner's sense of self-esteem as his appearance and strength lose their vitality.

These factors are just a few of the general elements that assault the mind of an inmate under the detention of the enemy. Such conditions are faced by almost all those captured by an enemy and they can, for the unfortunate, be the thin end of the wedge which leads up to starvation, active cruelty and torture. Elite soldiers are more likely than, say, an army cook to attract the attention of the special interrogator. His (or her) purpose is to use physical or psychological methods to induce the captive to talk. As we shall see, the interrogator's 'skills' and tools can be very powerful indeed.

TORTURE AND INTERROGATION

One of the first methods of the interrogator relates to the room in which the prisoner is kept. US prisoners in Vietnam's infamous 'Hanoi Hilton' found themselves in squalid, tiny cells, often almost pitch black, with no toilet facilities and full of rats, cockroaches and huge spiders. The prisoner thus becomes soiled by his own waste and has to constantly fight off the often aggressive wildlife. Also, the rats and other creatures enjoy a freedom of movement which he cannot, placing his status, in effect, below that of vermin. Although the cell may seem a place utterly forgotten by human hands, it is important to the interrogator as somewhere which the prisoner will long to escape from, hopefully by divulging information. The prisoner will also be 'softened up' by having to listen to the cries of torture victims from other cells. Sometimes these are real, sometimes not, as many states have made use of recordings supposedly of the prisoner's fellow inmates being tortured during interrogation, though these are actually impersonations.

The interrogator, however, may choose a different environment for the prisoner, one which focuses more on sensory deprivation. This is usually a featureless cell without natural light (thus the prisoner loses track of time and date), without noise and where there is absolutely nothing to do. Clothing is also selected to be very soft so as to create little sensation on the skin. Research has shown that sensory deprivation is actually one of the cruellest tortures of all. Subjects undergoing sensory deprivation experiments started to show symptoms of behaviour abnormality after only 16 hours. After several days, the subjects were repeatedly hallucinating, disorientated, alternating between deep lethargy and hyperactivity, and suffering from extreme symptoms of fear and worthlessness. They particularly fell prey to any pre-detention mental fears.

Both the filthy cell and the sensory-deprivation environment help the interrogator to demonstrate his absolute power over the captive's life. He can then progress to ask-ing the prisoner direct questions backed up by various methods of coercion – torture, in short. Before we look at torture, it is worth reminding ourselves of the non-violent method of 'brainwashing'. This was often used to extract a renunciation of the soldier's war aims for propaganda and was effectively practised by the North Koreans and Chinese during the 1948–50 Korean War, and by the North Vietnamese during the Vietnam War.

During brainwashing, the captive will usually be placed in civilised but uncomfortable surroundings (such as sat on an armless, hard chair which is too small for him and facing a window with direct sunlight coming through). There he will meet a smart interrogator who will begin lengthy discussions about the conflict in which the soldier is involved. The interrogator will generally excuse the soldier's participation in the war and put the blame on the government of his home nation. The interrogator will then proceed to back up his case not by waving Marx under the prisoner's nose (this is far too unsubtle), but by showing anti-war literature produced in the prisoner's home country itself (Time magazine was often used during the Vietnam War). Other material such as information about tax rises in the prisoner's home state or country is also used to make the prisoner feel less affectionate about home government.

By these methods, and through keeping the conversations going for many hours, the interrogator can hopefully whittle away the prisoner's belief in his initial war aims and make a conversion. He is also trained to pick up on the physical traits someone displays when he or she is lying. These include evasive eyes (particularly if they look upwards, often indicating that the person is accessing their imagination, rather than their memory) and a nervous wiping of the mouth or nose while the lie is being told. However, if the mental interrogation is not successful (it is often not attempted for it is a time-consuming and skilled job), the interrogators will resort to more physical means such as those outlined below.

Torture

Torture comes in a whole spectrum of shapes and forms, too many to document here. However, there are several principles a 'skilled' torturer will apply. First, the level of torture is usually built up in gradual increments, thus keeping the prisoner in a state of constant terror about the next session. Secondly, the torture is backed by descriptions of what is happening to the prisoner's

Deprivation

Many prison cells are deliberately constructed to break the prisoner's will and make the interrogator's job easier. Sources of light are small and inadequate. The prisoner will often have no toilet facilities and so is forced to live in his own waste. Vermin and insects are often introduced to emphasise their freedom over the prisoner's confinement. Finally, the guards will degrade the cell even further in order to illustrate that they have complete control over the destiny of the prisoner.

body and what will happen in the future. Thus the torturer may say that he is going to cut off the prisoner's thumbs and proceeds to tell the prisoner what life will be like without opposable grip if he does not talk. Thirdly, the torture will mix the infliction of pain with the infliction of panic. A common example of the latter is to pull a towel over the victim's head and keep it soaked with water. Breathing under the towel slowly becomes impossible and the sensation of slow asphyxiation induces tremendous panic and fear which cannot be controlled. Using these three techniques, the torturer will keep his prisoner in terrible pain and fear, but keep emphasising how easy it would be for him to stop the treatment by simply opening his mouth. Any snippet of information given results in an instant diminution of the pain. Thus, like a dog being trained, the captive comes to associate talking with reward and, if the pain is severe enough, the temptation to divulge information is enormous.

Mental torture comes in as many different forms as physical torture and is just as destructive. Returning to communist brainwashing, one technique to emerge from the Korean conflict was the classic 'good cop/bad cop' routine', in which one quietly spoken and unthreatening interrogator would be replaced by a manic screamer who would bellow abuse in the prisoner's face. These two would then keep rotating their routines, disorientating the prisoner and naturally leading him to talk to the 'good cop' to keep him there longer, instead of the frightening opposite number. Humiliation is also an important factor in mental torture. Prisoners are usually kept stark naked and cold for each session, and female personnel are often invited in to make filthy disparaging remarks about the soldier's physique. This worthlessness gives the prisoner – if he does not mentally resist – an acute sense of

his vulnerability and an awareness of the power of his captors.

Set against this are some even more extreme forms of mental torture. Blasting the prisoner with indecipherable noise at a deafening pitch for hour after hour before plunging him into total silence causes intense mental pain and confusion. The same effect is achieved by setting the prisoner within an environment of startling flashing lights. In both cases, intense head pain, nausea and disorientation result, and the prisoner will start to become desperate to get out of these unreal and hallucinatory environments.

Other Methods

An imprisoned elite forces soldier has to be on his constant guard for the stool pigeon – someone inserted into the cell or camp by the enemy to look like a neutral party (such as a fellow prisoner), but who reports back to the interrogators about his conversations. The 'double agent', as it were, will be made to look as realistic as possible to the situation and will often have a very detailed knowledge of the soldier's home culture and a perfect command of the language.

As an alternative to trying to break the soldier's will, some interrogators will attempt to bend the soldier's mind artificially with substances. Drug interrogation is something for which the elite soldier can do little to prepare. The list of drugs used is extensive and what they tend to do is not make the soldier tell the truth, but predispose him to talking more easily. This can be done through making him drowsy and less in command of his own voice, through making him hyperactive and garrulous, or through inducing feelings of anxiety or unreality which make him less committed to defending his information.

As we have seen, the array of methods and devices arraigned against the captured soldier is formidable in the hands of those prepared to use them. So what can the soldier do against such fearsome odds? How do you prepare the mind for detention and interrogation by the enemy?

DETENTION TRAINING

Training a special forces soldier for surviving detention and interrogation follows the primary rule for any type of military training: the training must be realistic enough to replicate the real experience, but without putting the soldier in any actual physical danger. One of the best examples of interrogation training is that conducted for the SAS by the Joint Services Interrogation Unit (JSIU). Based in Ashford, Kent, in the United Kingdom, the JSIU is manned by SAS soldiers and other personnel. It provides interrogation training for all the major UK forces, focusing mainly on elite units at risk from capture such as Royal Air Force pilots, special forces and units such as the Royal Marine Commandos and the Parachute Regiment.

During SAS training, the JSIU step in towards the end of the escape and evasion part of the training programme. Their mission is to put the SAS candidate through a punishing series of psychological and non-damaging physical tortures to see if the soldier has the mental resilience to withstand capture – if he has not, he will have failed to enter the SAS regiment. Much of the actual detail of what goes on during this part of training is protected by the Official Secrets Act, but insights have started to emerge from personnel who have been through the course. The staff of the JSIU make the scenario as realistic as possible, often dressing in the uniforms of possible captors and speaking in foreign languages. Treatments recounted by former candidates include:

- A towel is placed over the head and soaked with water (as described above), the towel only being removed when the 'prisoner' is on the verge of losing consciousness.

- A 24-hour period of interrogation is carried out in which the prisoner is subject to bright flashing lights and blaring white noise for long periods, resulting in a high degree of disorientation and fear.

- The JSIU staff conduct a beating in the next cell to the prisoner, with horrible sounds of impact, pain and vomiting. The object of the beating is actually a mattress and the JSIU personnel make the sounds of terror.

- The prisoner is stripped naked and verbally abused by a large panel of 'captors', including female personnel. Often the prisoner is left naked in cold conditions for hours before the interrogation, shrinking his penis, which then becomes the object of much derision.

- One scenario recounted involved a prisoner being shackled to a railway line in a siding. Then the interrogators pretend that they have made a mistake and there is actually a train coming (this is true, although the carriage is actually on another line). Despite seemingly frantic efforts on the part of the interrogators to unshackle the soldier, at the last second, they call off the attempts and pretend to run away. The prisoner's reactions are then judged as to the clarity of his thinking and reaction.

- The prisoner is tied to a board and dunked under water for periods of about 20 seconds before being brought up for air.

The brutal training of the JSIU has attracted some controversy (in one instance, an SAS soldier had his arm broken after being thrown from a moving lorry), but it doubtless has taught a generation of soldiers valuable lessons about themselves and about surviving detention. Similar courses are run throughout the world for special forces troops and, combined with the analysis from returning POWs, there is a growing general body of knowledge about the best way to stay sane and true in detention.

Much of this comes down to a simple issue of will and determination. To survive such terrible experiences as torture and isolation, the soldier must have a strong character to keep a sense of himself and also maintain hope for release. Character cannot be taught, but some principles can. Examples are:

● **Control what can be controlled.** Set up as much of a routine as possible, perhaps holding discussion groups with colleagues at certain times or simply

cleaning one corner of the cell. Use any unsupervised periods to remind yourself of who you are and what you are capable of, so take charge of any aspects of your life in detention that are not controlled by your captors.

● **Keep fit.** Keeping fit in detention is not always easy, especially if you are held in cramped conditions and the food is poor. Fitness helps the mind to stay stronger, so try to maintain some form of exercise programme. However, be cautious about burning up more calories than you can afford and rest if injured. If you are in very cramped conditions, simple stretching exercises and basic arm and leg strengthening exercises will

Non-violent interrogation

The prisoner sits, dirty and worn out, on a low stool, while the interrogator is smartly dressed on a tall seat. Lighting is arranged so that it is in the prisoner's face. Questioning is relentless and nimble, usually backed by the threat of return to torture.

Survival shelter

Constructing a survival
shelter provides a break
from the act of evasion.
However, the soldier must
not start to prefer its false
sense of security over
active escape.

stop muscles from wasting and help the
mind stay healthier.

- **Keep the mind alert.** Mental alertness
  is extremely difficult to maintain when
  isolated and bored. Try to develop
  mental projects for yourself – such as
  writing a novel in your head (doing, say,
  a chapter each day) or planning a
  business idea – anything to keep the
  brain processes animated. Doing such
  mental tasks will also make you feel
  that your own personality and
  intelligence are not lost in the
  experience of captivity.
- **Do not encourage beatings.** Being
  aggressively defiant towards the captors
  is generally inadvisable as, if you attract
  further physical abuse, that will impair

your fitness and hence your survivability.
Be as cunning as possible with your
captors. Strike up conversations with
ones who are in any way friendly – this
personalises you in the captors' eyes and
may make them less willing to harm
you and it may even bring about
better treatment.

- **Develop support networks.** If you
  are in the company of other prisoners,
  try to maintain the formalities of rank
  and military structure (although beware
  of giving away rank information to your
  captors). Rely on each other as support
  during times of interrogation and, if
  possible, design co-operative tasks
  between you to keep a sense of
  social interaction.

- **Plan to escape.** Even if escape might be verging on the impossible, it is still valuable to plan such an attempt. This is not only because it may well come to fruition, but also because it gives you a certain sense of strength over your captors and keeps the mind alert and lively as well.

By following these principles and mental activities, a period in detention can be made, if not exactly bearable, certainly slightly less harsh. A lot of these activities require good self-discipline to pursue and this is again where character comes in. The main point is not to become dependent upon the prison environment and to keep enough dignity to assure yourself that this is not where you belong.

ESCAPE AND SURVIVAL

There are no hard and fast rules about escaping from imprisonment. Indeed, it is not always productive in itself and may have severe repercussions for those left behind. Yet the prospect of escape can provide a psychological tingle that is a tremendous motivator to survive detention. A successful escape plan thrives on luck as much as judgement, but the thought processes should dwell on some of the following factors. Watch out for any patterns in the prison which you can use to your advantage, such as times when there are less guards on duty or when vehicles make deliveries. Remember these patterns and build up a profile in your mind of how the prison operates and when or where there are security lapses. This also involves utilising acute observation skills. Keep eyes and ears open at all times to gather more and more information to add to your stock of knowledge and try to get friendly guards inadvertently to reveal crucial information.

You must also have a plan. Escape can be about a moment of seized opportunity, but

even if this does occur, you should have planned in detail what your course of action will be. Planning helps the mind to stay in focus and effectively acts as training for the escape event. Rehearse the escape in your mind time and time again, introducing various disasters to test out the efficiency of your plan. This basic mental preparation can help give drive and motivation during an escape attempt, but even if such an attempt should be initially successful, there is still the problem of how to survive during the flight to safety and how to evade capture.

EVASION AND SURVIVAL

Evasion is a skill taught to most troops as it applies not only to those who have escaped, but also to those who have yet to be caught. The practicalities of actually how to evade capture are covered in other books, but less is said about the mental requirements for evasion. Surviving in the wild while trying to evade capture is an extremely demanding mental situation. The body will quickly become tired and dirty, which itself can impair the thought processes and lead to depression and demotivation. Fear may also prey on the mind – the fear of what will happen to you if you are captured or recaptured. Importantly, your training should have made you aware of how the environment will attack the thought processes and what mental indicators of impending illness you should be looking for. The psychological essentials of evasion are:

- Have a clear idea of where you are going. Uncertainty can lead to despair, so the soldier must have some idea of what his objectives are. These should be broken down into hourly, daily and weekly objectives so that time is tightly controlled.
- During the initial escape or evasion period, the soldier should try to put as much distance from his starting point as

Effects of heat, wet, cold etc

When evading the enemy, soldiers must avoid unnecessary exposure to the elements and dehydration, all of which can increase his tiredness and his chances of making a mistake.

more fluidity in his planning. Also, every kilometre walked can increase motivation to continue. Studies have shown that the nearer to the objective, the greater the motivation, so achieving distance is a positive factor for mental endurance.

● Use your intelligence and training to avoid the pursuers. If moving through a civilian area, try to look as natural as possible; carrying a spade or similar civilian item can help you to blend in as to others this gives you a status that makes you less unfamiliar. Try to stay away from children and dogs, these often being the first to pick up on strangers. If in the countryside, create convoluted tracks through woodland and in and out of streams so that tracker dogs will become confused and turn back on themselves. In ways such as these, you are using the psychological processes of the pursuers, civilians and animals against them and thus giving openings to develop your escape.

● Do not be so committed to putting distance between you and the pursuers (unless it is absolutely necessary) that you overlook the necessity to eat and rest. Both sleep deprivation and malnutrition will cause apathy, clouded thought processes and insecurity, all of which can lead to making mistakes and errors in judgement. So sleep when necessary for short periods and do not

possible. If only 8km (5 miles) are travelled from the starting point, that will give a possible 200 square km (78 square mile) area for the searchers to deal with (assuming that they are aware of the starting point and that all directions of travel are equally valid). Psychologically, the greater the distance from the beginning, the greater sense of options the soldier will have and the exert yourself trying to remedy minor discomforts if the energy could be better used elsewhere. Steal food if possible to maintain your energy supplies, but be careful not to leave any tracks or be detected.

Torture

Torture makes the soldier physically weak; reality then seems unimportant and thus confession feels detached from consequences in the world outside of the prison.

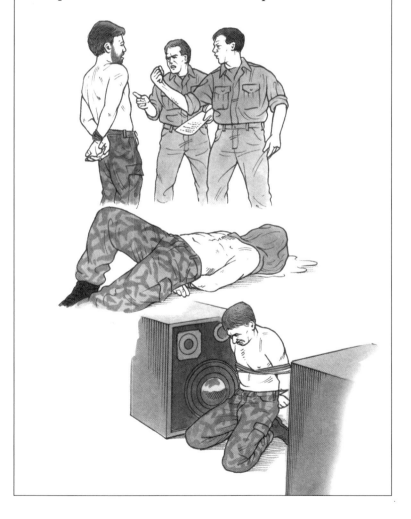

By looking after the body as much as possible, by having a plan and by fully entering into mind games with the pursuers, chances are the soldier will stay focused and committed to an escape attempt. Of course, this assumes that the soldier has a generally firm will. Regardless of training, the soldier attempting to escape must apply himself with a blind focus on the end result and learn to tolerate discomfort, pain and fear along the way. Thankfully for elite soldiers, their initial training period should have provided these skills anyway.

SURVIVAL

The final element of this chapter is that of survival. Being in a wilderness without food, shelter or water presents probably more of a danger to life and health than to those in pursuit. The actual techniques of survival are not really our focus here. Rather, what should be understood is how the environment affects mental processes and the will to survive.

The need for rest and food has already been discussed. Shelter is an equal priority. This applies even in warm countries because the two central enemies of anyone exposed are cold and heat. Exposure to extreme cold and extreme heat can lead, respectively, to hypothermia and hyperthermia. Hypothermia is a drop in body temperature

Skin heating techniques

The efficiency of this is best tested on your hands. If they are particularly cold, first touch them against a warm part of your body to gauge their temperature, then practise the following technique:

● First, imagine that the blood vessels in your hands have become wide open and that hot blood is pumping right through the hands and into the fingertips.

● While you are doing this, also imagine that you are immersing your hands in a thick, very warm orange liquid.

● Finally, while doing the above, actually look at your hands and believe that you have total control over all of your bodily processes.

If you follow the stages above, after one or two minutes the temperature of your hands should be warm, even hot if done successfully. Oriental practitioners of martial arts such as aikido and chi gong have long demonstrated the power of temperature change, a practice which is just starting to become accepted in the West.

below its safe core temperature range of 36–38°C (97.8–100.4°F), while hyperthermia is the opposite. Both can be fatal if not treated immediately and mental symptoms for both include deterioration in coherence, massive mood swings, withdrawal and inability to make decisions or absorb information. Yet even before this severe stage, cold and heat affect the mentally abilities of those in a survival situation.

The Effects of Cold

Studies were conducted as far back as World War I into the effects of cold on military skills. The loss of skin sensitivity and flexibility of the digits meant that marksmanship was severely disrupted. Further effects of cold later discovered were dips in attention, a reduction in the versatility of thought processes and the problems of having to balance the need to keep moving with the need to conserve energy. One fascinating product of studies conducted by the US Advanced Research Projects Agency in the 1970s was that psychologists found that skin temperature could actually be improved by up to 9°C (16°F) just by training soldiers to imagine heat

deflecting to the area in question. Personal testing of this training has showed me how achievable this is (see box for details of technique).

Extreme heat proves just as much of a challenge as extreme cold. The soldier will become tired and apathetic, and must follow common sense precautions such as staying out of the sun and drinking as much as possible. Psychologically, both heat and cold present the survival problem of generating fear, in that the soldier will start to think in terms of 'freezing to death' or 'dying of thirst'. This can actually speed the progress of these fates for, through mechanisms we still do not quite fully understand, the loss of willpower often results in a deterioration in health. Doctors have long noted that cancer patients become ill with greater rapidity once the diagnosis has been made and the term 'cancer' introduced.

Training can compensate for this effect by giving the soldier exact physical descriptions of the symptoms of cold and heat exposure and specific remedies. This enables the soldier to feel some degree of control over his illness. However, details of

Blending in

While in populated areas, the escaped soldier blends in by carrying an item, preferably trade-related, and avoiding children or animals (they can often spot strangers).

the advanced stages of the illness are often withheld from the soldier to avoid panicking should the symptoms be monitored.

The Desire to Live

In any survival situation, be it in a prison camp or on the run from pursuers, having clear goals and a strong desire to survive are possibly the most important tools the soldier has to come out of the situation alive. Training does impart essential skills of survival, but the lesson seems to be that character can be the determiner of whether someone lives or dies in a survival situation, and that may also be true of the fighting man as a whole.

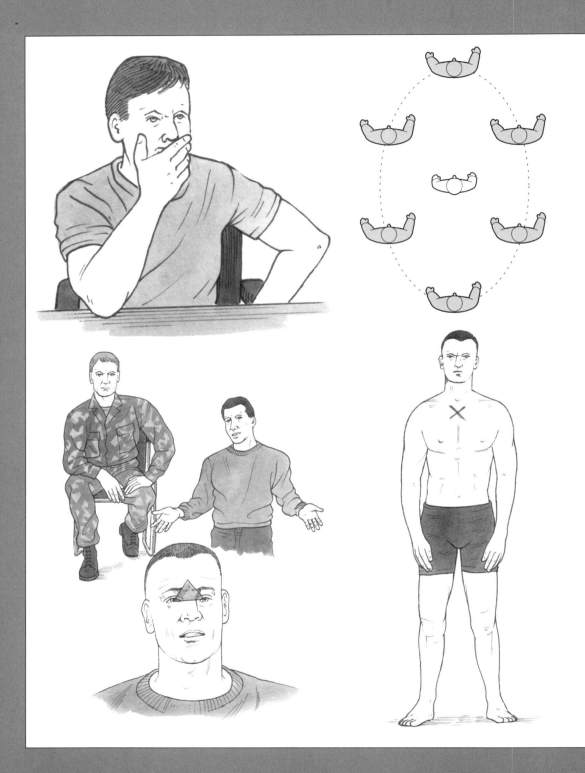

CHAPTER TEN

Peacekeeping and Diplomacy

Of all operational functions, peacekeeping and humanitarian work have become perhaps the likeliest destinations for the modern soldier. Although actual combat is unlikely, it is an ever-present threat, and soldiers have a vast array of other mental challenges to face in what is usually a confused and emotionally-charged environment and an alien culture.

The reasons for the growth in peacekeeping operations are politically and historically complex, and to a large extent revolve around the adoption of the role of the 'world's policeman' by the United States in particular and international organisations such as NATO and the United Nations. The fact now remains that few of the world's developed nations politically can afford to ignore world events in which images of suffering and helpless civilians are broadcast daily into the televisions of homes around the world.

For many soldiers, elite and regular, this has meant adjusting to a new environment of operations often situated somewhere between war and peace. Recent peacekeeping duties in places such as Sierra Leone, Bosnia, Kosovo and Somalia have placed soldiers in situations where they must perform a bewildering array of roles. These roles include separating warring factions, disarming those factions, providing food and medical relief, dispersing aggressive crowds and negotiating with local warlords. The list of duties is vast and so the mental qualities required of peacekeeping operations are similarly extensive. Combat skills alone are not enough, although they are essential. In addition, negotiating skills, knowledge of crowd psychology, ability to handle legal restraints, and the tact to care for traumatised civilians are just some of the extra skills a soldier must show in the peacekeeping and humanitarian role.

THE 'THREE-BLOCK' WAR

Peacekeeping has proved what the US Marine Corps calls the principle of the 'three-block war'. In the domain of low-intensity conflict, where violently opposed groups' factions can also see the peacekeepers as an unwelcome intrusion, soldiers can go from outright combat to humanitarian relief in the space of three blocks of a city centre. Thus peacekeeping soldiers must still possess the spirit of combat readiness at all times. A tragic illustration of this took place on 3 October 1993. The United States was at that time heavily involved in peacekeeping duties in war-ravaged Somalia. In an attempt to control the country's spiralling violence, a team of elite US Rangers and members of Delta Force were sent into the Somali capital, Mogadishu, to apprehend Mohammed Farah Aidid, a local warlord. What was meant to be a 90-minute apprehension operation descended into a 17-hour bloodbath. Following the downing of a US Blackhawk helicopter, the US team found itself trapped in a nightmarish maze of intricate, claustrophobic streets while hundreds of armed Somali civilians and soldiers opened up on them with automatic weapons. In the utter chaos which followed, 18 Americans and more than 350 Somalis were killed, and 84 US servicemen were injured.

The incident in Somalia showed how the peacekeeping environment can escalate into violence within minutes. In this chapter, we will look at how elite and regular forces are now preparing their soldiers mentally for this alternative world of war.

THE DUTIES OF PEACEKEEPING

The list of duties that fall under the remit of peacekeeping operations is bewilderingly large. This is primarily because peacekeeping demands roles which are traditionally not those of the soldier. The US Army's Field Manual 100-23, *Peace Operations*, opens with a quotation from former UN Secretary-General Dag Hammerskold: 'Peacekeeping is not a job for soldiers, but only a soldier can do it.' Hammerskold's observation is insightful because, however orientated towards humanitarian relief, combat skills are still required to deal with the unpredictabilities of explosive civilian and military situations. What is needed by the military for these roles are men and women who are able to take the discipline of their combat training, but mix it with incredible flexibility both in thinking and the handling of people.

The manual goes on to list the multitude of occupations in which the soldier may find himself during a peacekeeping operation. The list includes some surprising tasks:

- diplomatic support
- preventing violence
- monitoring ceasefires and truces
- maintaining essential services such as water, electricity etc.
- investigating allegations of war crimes
- supervising the exchange of prisoners of war
- relocating refugees
- acting as mediators between belligerent parties
- building bridges and roads
- establishing protected zones
- apprehension of war crimes suspects

As we can see from this very partial list alone, the skills required by peacekeeping units are extremely broad. Furthermore, it is not just regular army units who are involved in these situations. Special forces are also widely utilised in peacekeeping operations. Elite troops bring with them specialist intelligence and combat skills which have a valuable place within missions aimed at restoring civil order. FM 100-23 states:

Special Forces (SF) assets deployed rapidly in denied or hostile areas can collect intelligence through area surveillance and reconnaissance. They can provide initial assessments in the areas of engineering, medical, security, and intelligence. With their language and area orientation, they can provide liaison with the local population, multinational forces, non-military agencies, and other military organizations. SF may assist in training and organizing local security forces. They may also enhance multinational interoperability by cross training with these forces. In humanitarian assistance operations, they can assist in providing and securing relief supplies. In peace operations, SF may execute precision strikes to destroy certain facilities and military capabilities by employing terminal guidance techniques for precision-guided munitions. SF may also be used to preclude or preempt terrorist activities and to conduct liaison with local militias.

As we can see, the talents of special forces in languages, counterinsurgency, surveillance and close protection all come to life within peacekeeping operations, as well as more conventional military roles.

The exhaustive scope of peacekeeping has drawn most elite units at one time or another into civil functions. Although some military observers have seen this as a dilution of traditional combat skills, most accept peacekeeping as adding a valuable new dimension into military thinking. The US Marine Corps has an alternative motto to their standard 'Semper fidelis' (Always faithful). This is 'Semper Gumby', Gumby being a flexible, bendy children's TV character popular with whole generations of US schoolchildren. The implication is obvious. The Marine Corps will bend and adapt to all manner of problems, military and civil, and peacekeeping is an ideal milieu in which to prove that capacity.

So what mental characteristics are required for a soldier to act as a successful peacekeeper? The US Army has defined a list of characteristics for the conduct of what it calls 'Operations Other Than War' (OOTW). These characteristics are:

- the objective
- unity of effort
- legitimacy
- perseverance
- restraint
- security

The Objective
Any soldier engaged in peacekeeping is generally faced with a situation that is confusing – mentally, morally and militarily. Thus it is imperative that the soldier forms a clear objective as to his actions and the actions of the group to give him direction and also stop the wasting of time and energy through diversions.

Unity of Effort
This is the team-mindedness spoken of in an earlier chapter. Peacekeeping requires a serious use of resources. In the Kosovo conflict, it was estimated that some three million Kosovan Albanians were displaced into neighbouring countries. To handle such an enormous influx of traumatised and

destitute people, military units had to have clear and strong group interaction to make sure that relief efforts were coherent.

Legitimacy

Skills of tact, diplomacy and friendliness must be used to make the indigenous people accept the peacekeeping force as a legitimate one and accept its authority. This is easy to define, but difficult to achieve. Many Kosovan Albanians heralded the NATO troops who returned them to their villages initially as saviours, yet, once the troops prevented them from exacting revenge on Serbian homes, the Kosovans' attitude grew increasingly hostile. This is why combat skills are required – legitimacy sometimes has to be enforced.

Perseverance

Because peacekeeping operations have to deal with protracted problems, perseverance is an essential unit and individual attitude. Peacekeeping troops are still based in heavy numbers in the former Yugoslavia, many years after official hostilities ceased. The job of rebuilding trust between communities and preventing the flare-up of fighting requires a steady application of military presence and diplomatic pressure which cannot be rushed.

Restraint

Peacekeeping can be mentally cruel on the soldiers who participate in it. Many times their rules of engagement will specify that they cannot open fire during their missions, unless they are specifically targeted and fired upon, to avoid escalating the situation and adopting sides. In Yugoslavia, this meant that soldiers had to bury the innocent victims of massacres (including women and children) without being able to retaliate against the perpetrators of the war crimes. Such situations require personalities who can exercise considerable restraint and clearly follow the

ROE (Rules of Engagement) laid down in their missions parameters.

Security

Security is defined by FM 100-15 as '[n]ever permit hostile factions to gain an unexpected advantage'. This is the active part of peacekeeping thinking – staying one step ahead of possible attacks and security infringements using conventional patrolling and combat techniques.

Added to these principles of OOTW are a host of other, more intimate psychological qualities which are needed for peacekeeping operations, all of which go to support the above. Chief amongst these as recommended by the US Army is the distinctive characteristic of being 'inquisitive'. Soldiers on peacekeeping operations are encouraged to find out as much as they can about the local culture with which they are dealing. This is not just to make them more broad-minded or better adjusted to handling the local population. It also serves to make soldiers more aware of any anomalies in their environment which might signify a possible terrorist threat (such as vehicular movement not consistent with the standard pattern of traffic, which could indicate a possible car-bomb attack).

Tact and Impartiality

Another pair of key qualities to advance is 'tact' and 'impartiality'. In the context of volatile civil relations, these attributes are essential. During the peacekeeping operations in Kosovo immediately after the repatriation of the Kosovan Albanian refugees, there were two major headaches for the peacekeepers. These were disarming the KLA fighters who had been fighting the Serbians and stopping the Albanian portion of the population exacting revenge on those Serbs who had stayed in Kosovo and not fled to Serbia itself. Justifying the protection of Serbs after the horrific war crimes perpetrated against many Kosovan Albanians was far

Reading aggression

The peacekeeping soldier should recognise signs of aggression. People stand up straight, place the hands on the hips and maintain a more direct eye contact.

Finger-poking, pushing and single-syllable threats are signs of impending violence. If these precede a sharp intake of breath, the soldier uses restraint techniques.

from easy and it required a firm, reasonable manner which demonstrated that the soldiers were not there to be partisan, but actually to maintain the peace.

Finally, the US Army (FM 100-23) advocates that soldiers practice 'imagination' and 'flexibility' during peacekeeping duties. Imagination, in particular, seems to be a curious recommendation, but both it and flexibility are concerned with a soldier's capacity for putting himself in another person's shoes and then deriving plans of action which are not set in stone, but which can adapt to the human elements of the problem.

As already stated, special forces soldiers are not withheld from becoming involved in peacekeeping missions. One of their main tactical remits is what are called Civil Affairs (CA) operations. CA units are not small – usually they operate at brigade strength to cope with the scale of humanitarian disasters – but they are expertly trained. A typical CA unit consists of language specialists, tactical squads and peacekeeping specialists, and their primary role is gathering information about the situation which is then relayed to the wider military and also to the various civil aid organisations present on the ground.

Unarmed combat point of focus

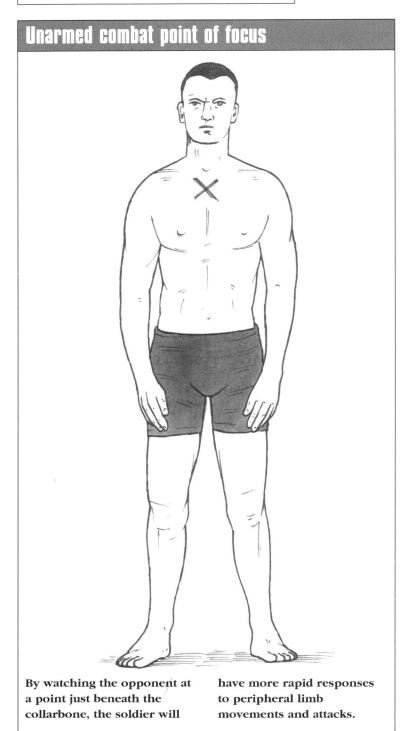

By watching the opponent at a point just beneath the collarbone, the soldier will have more rapid responses to peripheral limb movements and attacks.

Yet the case of the Rangers in Mogadishu shows that elite forces may also be called in in a more aggressive, combat-orientated role. The US Marines, for example (a good one, as they are heavily used in peacekeeping operations), are frequently applied as an advance body which enters a war zone or disaster area and uses bold military tactics to prepare the ground for the arrival of the conventional forces and civil organisations.

Each of the Marine Expeditionary Units (MEU) that enter a peacekeeping area will have already received realistic simulation training in coping with civil disorder and conflict. Members of the US Marine Corps are trained in 23 standard missions and one of these is an authentic training exercise in which actors play distressed crowds and the landscape is modelled accurately around a war-torn city. The training is so realistic that, in the words of Captain Lando Hutchens, on officer who has participated in several peacekeeping operations in Africa and Europe, the conditions they encounter for real 'don't surprise us'.

So far we have looked at the overall spectrum of mental qualities required for a peacekeeping soldier, but now we will turn our attention to two of the more demanding specific scenarios which a soldier may face on the ground during these delicate and exacting operations – crowd control and negotiation.

CROWD CONTROL

Crowds can be one of the most disorderly and unpredictable phenomena to face. This is not to say that a crowd of people may not be motivated by a clear and well-voiced idea. Yet, many soldiers will tell you that legitimate protest may all too easily turn into outright violence. Although rioting crowds may seem utterly without order, studies since World War II (especially those conducted in countries such as Northern Ireland, where civil disorder has been unfortunately commonplace) have shown that there are some patterns to how riots start, develop, are fought and are best controlled. The clash between soldiers and civilians is one which hangs on mental warfare, as more often than not the use of killing weapons is not an option or leads to political disaster.

Well before a crowd actually gathers, something has to bring them together. This is usually the role of the media, whether state-controlled or in the hands of the general populace. The ill-fated student pro-democracy protesters in Tiananmen Square in China did not have any access at all to the state television or radio, so they used hand-operated printing presses to publicise their intentions and also give instructions about the general direction of the movement. This is what is described as a 'planned' crowd, a group of people with a specific idea about what they are doing. The other reason for crowd gatherings is in the aftermath or expectation of a dramatic event (an accident or a football match being obvious examples). These are 'unplanned' gatherings and can be just as volatile as the more controlled version.

The problem in both cases is that, once a crowd is gathered, it starts to attain a life of its own. This is best put by the US Army's own document on crowd control, *Civil Disturbance* (FM 19-15):

Simply being a part of a crowd affects a person. Each person in a crowd is, to some degree, open to actions different from his usual behavior. Crowds provide a sense of anonymity because they are large and often temporary congregations. Crowd members often feel that their moral responsibility has shifted from themselves to the crowd as a whole. Large numbers of people discourage individual behavior; the urge to imitate is strong in humans. People look to others for cues and disregard their own background and training. Only well-disciplined persons or persons with strong convictions can resist conforming to a crowd's behavior. Crowd behavior influences the actions of both the disorderly participants and the authorities tasked to control them.

The task facing a group of peacekeeping soldiers when confronted by a large crowd gathering on a street is to stop the crowd behaviour gathering in aggression and emotion such that it suddenly starts to express itself in violence. The catalysts for this ugly turn are many:

- Specific individuals may encourage the crowd to turn to violence by using inflammatory speeches.
- The crowd may redirect what it feels is a legitimate anger against a third party towards those controlling the crowd, these then becoming the object of their hatred.
- The crowd may simply be taken to greater and greater heights of emotion

until it can no longer control itself and bursts into violence.

● Two or more crowds with opposing views may confront one another. Ironically, if the parties try to fight one another, both will turn their violence on those who try to stop the fighting (that is, the peacekeepers).

Once a riot gets out of control of the soldiers, the results can be frightening. On 30 January 1972 in Derry, Northern Ireland, some 20,000 civilians took part in a mass protest against the British policy of internment without trial. The march began in what was described by some afterwards as a 'carnival atmosphere', but when the march moved into William Street, stone-throwing began. The targets for the missiles were soldiers from the British Parachute Regiment. The soldiers were embarking on an arrest mission in the Bogside area of Derry when the incipient riot became more and more vitriolic. Thirty minutes later, and for reasons that are being legally debated to this day, the soldiers had shot dead 13 men and injured 13 others with their high-powered 7.62mm SLR rifles. What had begun as a legitimate protest, authorised by law, had ended in what would become forever known as 'Bloody Sunday'.

The experience in Derry all those years ago was precipitated by many different factors: the anger of the crowds; the context of violence that hung over Northern Ireland's daily life; fatigue and lack of proper riot-control training in the soldiers. Nor is it an isolated incident. During the Vietnam War, the United States saw student anti-war protestors being shot dead by soldiers from the National Guard at Kent State University. So, with the benefit of hindsight, how should a soldier think and behave during a crowd disturbance?

Studies conducted for the US Army have shown that soldiers who face riots are susceptible to several mental dangers. The first is that they will also get caught up in the excessive emotion of the crowd and start to be led by their feelings, rather than their judgement. This can lead to a soldier jettisoning his sense of restraint and acting impulsively, something very dangerous when he has weaponry. The key point is that riot-control soldiers and especially their leaders must have an iron grip on their emotions, remain self-aware and not allow themselves to be carried with a flow of emotions. One particular responsibility of the leader is to make sure that he moves amongst his men addressing them by their names repeatedly. This clarification of names stops the soldiers losing their own personalities in that of the crowd and therefore keeps them thinking about their commitments.

Verbal Abuse

The soldiers who confront a riot also need to be mentally prepared for some of the psychologically disturbing tactics that the crowd may use against them. Verbal abuse is likely to be very personal and ferocious, and will often focus on criticising the soldier's moral position in relation to the rioters. The soldier must adopt a distance from any comments made and only judge the rioter's abuse in the context of tactical developments (there will be plenty of time for reflection once the riot has been controlled). This can be extraordinarily difficult. One soldier from Northern Ireland recounts how, after two of his friends had just been shot down in the street, he had to endure the chants of children only yards away giving the football score chant 'Two – nil'. Resisting a violent response to such provocation is incredibly hard, but vital.

As a further challenge to the soldiers, women and children may be placed in the front ranks of the crowd to intimidate them into non-resistance. Again, self-control must be used to avoid sympathising with a

Gestures to recognise in negotiation

When people feel defensive towards what you are saying, they will often make physical barriers across their body and face with their arms and legs. Here are three classic defensive gestures.

Negotiating gestures

Leaning forward invites closure of a meeting, exposing the palms implies honesty, **and focusing on the triangle between eyes and forehead implies concentration.**

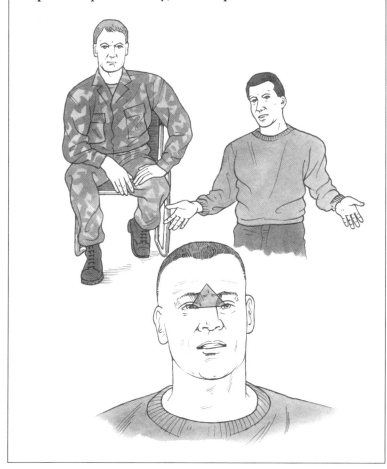

● Fireworks are dipped in glue and covered with nails or BB shotgun pellets to act as grenades.

● Nail-firing guns used in the construction industry are fired through thin pieces of plywood – the nail guns are designed to fire nails into solid concrete, so the nail simply cuts straight through the plywood and flies onwards towards the soldiers.

More serious is when the riots are conducted in tandem with terrorist attacks. A classic tactic used by Republican terrorists in Northern Ireland was to position themselves ready with their weapons in a van behind the crowd. When the time was right, they would blow a whistle and the crowd would part before them. At this point, they would open fire on the British troops for a few seconds, before blowing the whistle once more, and allowing the crowd to close in front of them as a protective shield.

Naturally, the best way to defend against this type of attack, and against the dangers of the riot in general, is to get the rioters to disperse. Here some strong psychological tactics are needed to break the crowd's emotional momentum. Any officer in charge of riot-control troops has a sliding scale of options for dispersing the crowd, ranging from withdrawal at one end of the scale to the use of deadly force at the other.

particular face, gender or age. Finally, the soldiers should be prepared for all manner of weapons. Petrol bombs, stones and sticks are the most expected, but other inventive weapons have been created in riots:

● Balloons are filled with paint to use against vehicle windscreens.

However, the key principle is that the minimum force should be used to diffuse the situation. Indeed, studies have shown that the use of killing weapons generally leads to the precipitation of violence.

Colonel Rex Applegate, one of the United States' most robust military thinkers and an expert in both riot control and unarmed combat, came up with several psychological principles of crowd handling which are used to this day. Applegate's principles boiled down to several key tactics:

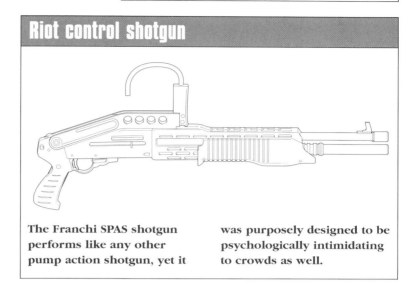

Riot control shotgun

The Franchi SPAS shotgun performs like any other pump action shotgun, yet it was purposely designed to be psychologically intimidating to crowds as well.

- Display force at the earliest possible juncture. Note that the force is not actually used, but many crowds in the early stages of development will actually disperse if they suddenly find themselves confronted by large groups of well-organised and powerfully armed soldiers. Certain weapons can encourage dispersion. The SPAS shotgun (see illustration), for instance, is no more powerful than any normal shotgun technology, but its intended 'Mad Max' appearance can have a great deterrent effect upon would-be rioters.
- Use crowd control formations. Many different configurations are possible, but generally a solid wall of men, charging with riot-shields presented, can disrupt the confidence of even the most courageous crowd. The important principle appears to be that the soldiers should act as one, thus giving the crowd the impression that they are dealing with one solid force, rather than a collection of individuals.

- Rotate the soldiers regularly. If engaged for long periods of time in riot control, the soldiers will become mentally and physically exhausted. Once this occurs, the emotions are more able to take control during riot conditions. Taking soldiers regularly out of the 'front line' enables them to regain perspective and energy.
- Target the weakest members of the crowd. These tend to be located at the back, so applications of tear gas or other weaponry aimed at this point can cause the crowd to disintegrate from the 'tail to the teeth'.
- Give strong commands. Leaders must stand before the crowd with absolute confidence and give clear orders for dispersal. Many people instinctively succumb to authority figures and someone standing in front of them and refusing to back down may sap their momentum.

Applegate's views are much respected and are still taught today in military training. However, the modern soldier now also has an

179

incredible array of non-lethal weapons at his disposal which also assault the mental force of a crowd. Some of these weapons have been around for decades. The water cannon, for example, remains effective not for blasting rioters out of the picture, but for the fact that people become less ardent and motivated once they are soaked and cold (self-interest kicks in again and this causes the crowd

mentality to break up). Yet other weapons seem to come from the ranks of science fiction. A sound system is currently being developed which can send out deep vibrating musical notes beneath the audible range of the human ear. The powerful vibrations pulse through the rioter's bowels and cause involuntary defecation – few people would maintain rioting after this had occurred.

Deafening blasts of sound are also used to break up the rhythmic chants crowds often use to mobilise themselves and this sound has a double effect in that it often induces nausea, vomiting and severe head pains.

Whatever the weapons options available, nothing will replace a confident and resolute soldier as a riot deterrent. In this crucial peacekeeping role, personal courage and the resilience to stop oneself being immersed in group hysteria are enough to survive riot conditions, if not control them.

NEGOTIATION

From the very physical duty of riot control, we turn now to the equally vital peacekeeping responsibility of negotiation. This skill usually falls to officers when it comes to, say, acting as a mediator between two warring factions, but each soldier will usually encounter a situation where verbal intelligence alone will be vital in defusing a potentially violent situation. Most soldiers will be taught some level of negotiating

VIP protection 1 – analysing threats

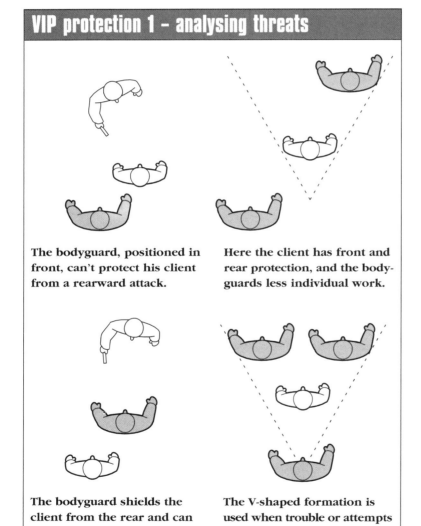

The bodyguard, positioned in front, can't protect his client from a rearward attack.

Here the client has front and rear protection, and the bodyguards less individual work.

The bodyguard shields the client from the rear and can respond to frontal attacks.

The V-shaped formation is used when trouble or attempts on the client's life are likely.

VIP protection 2 – giving protection

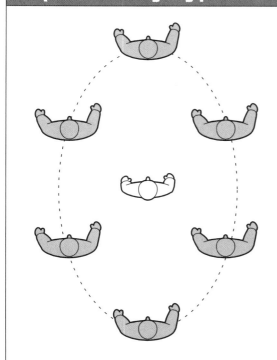

A double V for the very important. As a part of soldier's peacekeeping tasks, protection duties need an understanding of assassination countermeasures and crowd psychology.

skills when destined for a peacekeeping zone – elite soldiers may well be trained in these techniques to an advanced degree, as we saw in the case of counterinsurgency operations in the last chapter. Negotiating tactics are a very broad subject, but we can deal with some of the essentials here.

The key point that most soldiers are taught is that the first rule of negotiation is to genuinely listen to the grievances of all parties before starting to formulate proposals. This is where the maxim of 'impartiality' comes in. FM 100-23 defines why impartiality should be adhered to:

A force must guard against unequal treatment and avoid controversial, off-the-record remarks that may reach unintended audiences. These comments may lead to a demand for the offender's removal and, if reflecting a prejudice believed to be widely held in a national contingent, to pressure for the withdrawal of the entire national contingent.

Rushing to judgement tends to leave one party feeling that their reasoning has not been heard and consequently they are less likely to stick with the fine points of any agreement. True listening – or 'staring with ears', as it has been called – will also tend to bring down the aggression of an argument because the speaker will feel obliged to make his argument as coherent as possible.

Once the soldier has heard all sides of the argument, he must make up his mind as to whether it is within his jurisdiction to make a decision; if it is, he must stick to the principle of impartiality. Take the following imagined scenario:

A refugee family (husband, wife, two children under the age of four) has been resettled in their old village after a period of some six months of being dispersed during a civil war. Their neighbour (a 62-year-old man, widowed), though he did not actively participate in any action against the family, belongs to the ethnic group that committed most of the atrocities and ethnic cleansing against the family's people. The husband of the family claims that the man should therefore give up his land to them as a penalty for what his people did. If this is not done, then the husband (backed by a group of sympathetic relatives and friends) threatens to burn the neighbour's house to the ground. The old man, for his part, says he wishes

nobody any ill, that he never partici-
pated in the war and that, as he has
lived in the house all his natural life, he
could never leave.

This scenario is based upon actual cases encountered in Kosovo after the war there. Presented to the negotiator, this situation calls for the qualities of flexibility and imagination asserted by the US Army Field Manual. What is important is that the negotiator reflects on all the implications of any possible course of action. If he relocates the old man, will he be safe in his new destination and, being widowed, will he be able to look after himself outside of familiar surroundings? Can the army or relief agencies offer any financial assistance to the family in return for their tolerance of their neighbour? How soon will violence occur if no action is taken? If the family's request is granted, will it lead to other similar requests in the village? Only the soldier's intimate understanding of the local culture and the people involved will lead him to a decision. Yet, during the process of negotiation itself, there are several techniques he can apply that will make the negotiations more amicable.

Principle amongst these is a basic understanding of how body language works. Studying body language is no longer the preserve of the business world. A recent television recruitment advertisement for the British Army featured a squad of British soldiers confronting a group of armed African civilians around a well and asking for a drink of water. For some reason, we cannot tell because of the language barrier, the African men become agitated and start getting to their feet and menacingly toy with their weapons. The officer of the British troops then takes off his sunglasses, allowing the leader of the other group to see his eyes. The situation calms itself and the British soldiers are allowed to drink.

The advertisement was meant to show that to be an officer requires a good understanding of negotiating skills and body language techniques – people tend not to trust someone whose eyes they cannot see. As psychological understanding expands, more soldiers are receiving training in aspects of reading others' thoughts through the mannerisms of the human body and we can see how this might be valuable in negotiations.

For example, there is a sequence of body language gestures which is useful to watch out for in the other person. Although a person's words might be coming out steady and strong, their body may well give away the fact that they are lying. Typical signs are:

● Rubbing the mouth or nose when talking – If this is done only lightly, this is most likely a nervous action, rather than an itch. The person is in effect using the gesture to distract them and you away from the lie.
● Casting the eyes upwards when talking – People often look upwards when they are accessing their imagination, hence, if the person is not actually looking at something, he could be inventing what he is saying.
● Inability to maintain eye contact – This literally stems from the fact that the person subconsciously fears you will pick up on the lie as it is being told or that the person is too embarrassed to make eye contact.

Many of these signals we pick up automatically, but, in the situation of peacekeeping negotiations, the soldier must look out for them consciously to make sure that he is getting the truth from his interlocutor. By contrast, the soldier should adopt body postures which convey trust and reliability at every stage. When making a frank point, turning the palms upwards is a gesture of sincerity which travels well in most cultures.

Riot control

A psychological method of riot control used in places such as Northern Ireland involved placing a line in the path of the rioters, and announcing that anyone crossing the line would be shot.

Eye contact should be maintained, but not be intimidating – studies have shown that, for serious discussions, people make a triangular point of focus which has its base with the two eyes and its apex in the centre of the forehead. Generally, the overall body language in negotiations should be open and broad to convey trust and enthusiasm. If the soldier notices the person across from him has his arms and legs crossed, and that he is avoiding eye contact, this most likely means that the person is not happy with the way the conversation is proceeding. (People tend to cross parts of their bodies in front of themselves to form protective barriers when they are feeling threatened or tense, although they also do this when they are cold!) Through building up a profile of body language, the soldier in negotiations is able to at least read some of the emotional content behind what a person is saying, which is actually a better indicator of what they will do.

Whether in negotiation or standing behind a shield facing a riot, the peacekeeping soldier faces an environment neither civilian nor military, but which demands the best skills of both worlds. Peacekeeping and diplomacy are not traditional military tasks, but they are increasingly becoming the dominant form of operation for many of the world's soldiers, particularly those members of NATO and the United Nations. The volatility of world politics and the hints of wars to come suggest that armies will continue to need men who are capable of adapting their minds to the 'three-block war' and the need to use wits as much as weaponry.

CHAPTER ELEVEN

Future Wars

As we left the twentieth century, our understanding of military psychology seemed almost complete. Research conducted since 1945 means we now know most things about human behaviour in combat – from the effects of sleep deprivation to the psychological effect of artillery fire and ways of creating discipline. The question now is whether there is anything left to be discovered.

As we inch into the 21st century and look to the future of combat psychology, there is one area of development that will perhaps challenge notions of the warrior personality to a greater extent than any other has done so far. It is, in a sense, not a new area at all, but it is reaching such futuristic achievements that the 21st century will probably see the most significant overhaul of fighting technique and military mental skills since World War I.

This area is that of technology. It is doubtless that the 20th century changed the face of war through technological advance. In one century, this advance proceeded at a pace faster than in the previous four or five centuries put together. With each new weapon introduced, with each new piece of communications equipment utilised, the sol-dier's role on the battlefield expanded and became more complex, and the speed of reactions required became faster. Whereas in World War I an artillery officer' firing patterns were based on observation and calculation, today's soldier can use satellite reconnaissance to pinpoint targets to within a few metres and destroy them with advanced ordnance at a range of 40-50km (25-30 miles). A good expression of the new demands of technology came from a US fighter pilot who had served in both World War II and Vietnam. 'In World War II, if you saw the enemy at a distance you had about ten minutes to start planning your evasive manoeuvres. In Vietnam, in the jets that we were using, you had about five seconds.' This fighter pilot was expressing what most modern soldiers now know: each advance in technology pushes up the demand for skills and reactions. It is into this arena that governments have poured huge sums of money in order to discover ways in which they can maximise the effective human use of such complex combat technology.

LONG RANGE COMBAT

One result of advancing military technology for the common soldier is that, in many ways, he is becoming more distant from the enemy he confronts. Artillery, missile and air ordnance delivery have become so sophisticated that the only contact some soldiers will have with their enemy will be a blip on a computer screen prior to pressing the launch button. Attack-helicopter pilots who served in the Gulf War often remarked on how much the convoys they were destroying looked like figures in a computer game as they peered at them through their thermal imaging cameras and head-up display units (the latter projects combat and cockpit information onto the inside of the pilot's visor). And yet, there were still soldiers on the ground and tanks in action, engaging the enemy, taking prisoners, burying the dead. Some conflicts, such as that in Kosovo, have shown up the limits of current technology in taking on an enemy consisting of individual men attacking small villages with assault rifles and machine guns. As such, the lesson of the 20th century seems to be one of caution about presuming that traditional combat skills are no longer needed. There will always be situations in which there is no substitute for a highly trained individual on the ground to make decisions at a human level.

However, technology has a habit of surprising us. New types of weaponry and communications are appearing all the time and many scientists are chasing

Humanitarian work

Soldiers are increasingly called upon to act in humanitarian roles, needing mental and social skills perhaps not required of many earlier generations of soldiers.

after new methods of conducting war that theoretically could dispense with a human battlefield presence altogether. An example of this is the Boeing X-45A. This is an experimental ground-attack aircraft which is intended to deliver anti-radar missiles and high-explosive ordnance with exceptional manoeuvrability and high speed, and all without a pilot. That is not strictly true: the 'pilot' will be sat in front of a computer screen potentially thousands of miles away, controlling the aircraft remotely.

Unmanned aircraft are nothing new. Unmanned reconnaissance planes were developed after the U-2 spy jet piloted by Gary Powers was shot down over the Soviet Union in 1960. Since then, they have performed usefully in conflicts such as the Gulf War and Kosovo. The difference with the X-45A is that, in carrying weapons, it heralds the automation of a job previously regarded as the sole preserve of human beings. This will be controversial, but the arguments for the X-45A and its type (Unmanned Combat Aerial Vehicle – UCAV) are robust. UCAVs are predicted to be 75 per cent cheaper to operate and they can manoeuvre in patterns that would kill a human pilot with G-force. Also, training the terminal operator would be considerably cheaper than the $2 million currently spent on training pilots in the United States ($1 billion a year is spent in the United States purely on maintaining the skills of F16 pilots).

The fact is, however, that, if the X-45A reaches production stage and exceeds human pilot ability, military recruiters and psychologists will have to start looking for a new type of 'virtual warrior'. The operator of the X-45A would be using two flat-screen monitors, one showing cockpit information, and the other a digital 3D image of the battlespace. Thus, what the military would require is not a person who can endure great physical stress and still

The technological soldier

Uniforms are no longer items of clothing, but have become kit which enhances the soldier's mental and physical performance, including eyesight, temperature-control and hearing.

function, but someone who can operate a computer terminal under great mental pressure, without actual threat to his life, and still remain focused, attentive and aggressive in action.

VIRTUAL WAR

This is what some commentators have called 'virtual war' and it is also spreading to land combat. Military technicians are already seeing unmanned tanks and mobile artillery pieces as distinct possibilities. Yet, even for those soldiering roles that require a man to physically be present on the battlefield, times are changing. In the United States at present, the army is experimenting with head-up visual display units which, like more advanced thermal-imaging goggles, allow a soldier to operate in zero-visibility conditions while receiving combat information projected onto the screen before his eyes. The soldier thus equipped would have knowledge beyond that of his senses – he could 'see' behind buildings and receive satellite data on the units facing him. Furthermore, advances are being made in thought-weaponry. Brain-scanning techniques have been developed over the past 20 years which enable a person to control simple mechanical processes just by thinking the action. The process is extremely complex and at present its potential is rudimentary. Yet, in the future, we can imagine a soldier who goes into combat without a trigger and with just his mind to control and fire weapons with lightning-fast response times.

Perhaps the extreme of the 'virtual war' scenario is those soldiers who will be trained purely to 'fight' in the cyberspace of computer terrorism. Almost every level of advanced world society runs upon computerised systems and one talented hacker could effectively destroy the infrastructure of a nation, if competent enough. In light of this bloodless threat, more and more military personnel are being shocked into action and have started training personnel to deal with this new threat. The shock to the system is great. Men who have traditionally considered an enemy to be fixed within a time, place and boundary are now facing an utterly nameless and faceless threat. This threat could be one individual with enough computer power to bring down an entire system of military logistics (recent international computer virus infections have shown us that this is perfectly possible).

FUTURE ROLE?

So where does the virtual war leave the elite soldier? Most authorities admit that there will always be a place for highly trained, highly motivated soldiers to do

Remote warfare

An unmanned reconnaissance vehicle in development by the US. More and more battlefield duties will be executed by machines over the coming decades.

The future warrior?

Today's soldier must adjust to the very different psychological pressures of delivering devastation from a computer screen. However, recent conflicts have shown that there is always the need for a real human presence at the actual place of battle.

some of a nation's less palatable jobs. Despite technological advances, there is no computer in existence to touch the human mind's ability to decipher chaos and deal with it in innovative ways. Yet what will occur is that a new breed of warrior, one who perhaps never even holds a gun, will have to be trained in the skills of computerised warfare such as never before. Such an individual will create new mental issues for world military forces. When sitting thousands of miles behind the front line, is an individual capable of maintaining the aggression which is needed for combat ? What are the psychological implications when war cannot be distinguished from a game in a computer? Does such a soldier need to be trained in traditional forms of combat at all?

The questions go on. However, what is certain is that the role of the soldier is changing and his mental skills must change adapt with it. In today's high-technology, ultra-fast war zones, individuals are required who can shift from a muddy battlezone to computer-terminal warfare in minutes and still retain their sense of the overall battle raging around them. This scene-shifting will require a mind of extraordinary flexibility and intelligence. We wait to see how the next generation of soldiers will look and behave.

index